Mao

A Life

Philip Short

Hodder & Stoughton

Copyright © 1999 by Philip Short
First published in Great Britain in 1999
by Hodder and Stoughton
A division of Hodder Headline

The right of Philip Short to be identified as the Author of
the Work has been asserted by him in accordance with the
Copyright, Designs and Patents Act 1988.

10 9 8 7 6 5 4 3 2

British Library Cataloguing in Publication Data
A CIP catalogue record for this title is available from the British Library

ISBN 0 340 75198 3

Printed and bound in Great Britain by
Clays Ltd, St Ives plc

Hodder and Stoughton
A division of Hodder Headline
338 Euston Road
London NW1 3BH

For Marion

CONTENTS

Acknowledgements

A book of this kind is the cumulation of many people's goodwill. Some I am able to thank publicly here, including Zhang Yufeng, the companion of Mao's last years; Li Rui, Mao's former secretary; and Wang Ruoshui, courageous former deputy editor of the *People's Daily*.

Many others I cannot name. China is a far more tolerant and liberal country today than when I made my home there twenty years ago, and its people now take for granted freedoms which were unthinkable when Mao was alive. But it has yet to reach the stage where its citizens can be quoted on-the-record on sensitive political topics without fearing the wrath of their superiors or inquiries from the police.

No one has a monopoly of wisdom about Mao. CCP officials, Party historians, Chinese academics and former members of the Chairman's household who shared with me their private insights disagreed on many key points. Sometimes I found all their views unpersuasive (as they did mine). But, together, they helped to illuminate areas of Mao's life that, until now, have remained artfully obscured, in the process demolishing much conventional mythology. To all of them I express my gratitude.

The writing of this book was greatly aided by Karen Chappell and Judy Polumbaum, who enabled me to spend a blissful year in scholarly retreat in Iowa; by Yelena Osinsky; and by Dozpoly Ivan, of Sophia University in Tokyo. Special thanks are due to my friend and colleague, Mary Price, whose blue pencil sought valiantly (if sometimes unavailingly) to impose on my drafts a corset of brevity and intellectual rigour. My editors, Roland Philipps in London and Jack Macrae in New York, deserve credit for sustaining a project to which, at times, neither they nor I could see an end. Jacqueline Korn, who never lost faith, provided life-saving resuscitation.

My wife, Renquan, has not only lived with this book for seven years – which was hard enough – but spent much of that time poring over the Chinese texts of Mao's speeches and Central Committee documents, helping me unravel their ambiguities. To her, more than anyone, and to our six-year-old son, Benedict, who forwent days on the beach and bedtime stories to allow me to wrestle with 'blank sheets of paper', my deep appreciation.

Beijing – La Garde-Freinet, June 1999

List of Maps

List of Illustrations

Photographs courtesy of Xinhua (New China News Agency) unless listed below.

Section 1
Queue cutting – *Harlingue-Viollet*, Paris
Slow Execution – Joshua B. Powers Collection, Hoover Institution, Stanford University
Mao's family home – Marc Riboud, *Magnum Photo Agency*
He Zizhen, Mao's third wife – Courtesy of Maoping Revolutionary Museum, Jiangxi
Generalissimo Chiang Kai-shek – *Sygma*, Paris
Mao and Zhou Enlai – Peabody Museum of Archeology and Ethnology, Harvard University (Owen Lattimore Foundation)

Section 2
Yan'an – Edgar Snow's China, by Lois Wheeler Snow, reprinted by permission of Random House
Wang Shiwei – Courtesy of China Youth Press
Mao and Khrushchev – Courtesy of Du Xiuxian, Beijing
Zhang Guotao – *United Press International Photos*, New York

Section 3
Magic Talisman – Paolo Koch, *Rapho Agency*

Note on Spelling and Pronunciation

Chinese names drive all who are unfamiliar with them to despair. Yet it is impossible to write about China and its leaders without identifying the protagonists. This book employs the *pinyin* transcription, which was officially adopted by Beijing in 1979 and has the merit of being simpler and more accessible than the older Wade-Giles romanisation. Nevertheless, a few basic rules need to be observed.

The consonants *C*, *Q* and *X* are used to represent Chinese sounds which have no precise English equivalent. *C* is pronounced similarly to *Ts* [in Tsar]; *Q* like *Ch*; *X* like *Sh* [*Hs* in the Wade-Giles system].

Vowels are trickier. Terminal *–a* rhymes with car; *–ai* with buy. *–an* [as in *tan, fan*, etc.] rhymes with man, except after *–i* and *y* [*lian, xian, yan*, etc.], when it rhymes with men; and after *w* [*wan*], when it is sounded as in 'want'. *–ang* rhymes with sang, except after *–u* and *w* [*huang, wang*, etc.], when it rhymes with song. *–ao* rhymes with cow.

Terminal *–e* [as in *He* Zizhen, Li *De*, Li *Xue*feng, etc.] rhymes with her, except after *–i* and *y* [as in Ran *Tie*, *Ye* Jianying], when it rhymes with the American yeah. *-ei* rhymes with say. *–en* [as in Li *Wen*lin, Tianan*men*] rhymes with sun, except after *ch* and *y* [*Chen, Yen*] when it rhymes with men. *–eng* [as in *Deng, Meng*, etc.] rhymes with bung.

Terminal *–i* [as in *li, qi, di*, etc.] rhymes with see, except after *c-*, *ch-*, *r-*, *s-*, *z-* and *zh-* [*ci, chi, ri, si, zi, zhi*] when it rhymes with sir; *–iu* rhymes with stew.

Terminal *–o* [as in *wo*] and *–uo* [as in *Luo*] rhymes with war. *-ong* [*dong, long*] is similar to the *–u* in 'full'. *–ou* rhymes with toe.

Terminal *–u* rhymes with moo; *–ui* with sway; *–un* [*dun, lun*] with soon.

In a very few cases, where the *pinyin* transliteration is so unfamiliar as to be unrecognisable, traditional forms have been retained. These are (with *pinyin* in parenthesis): Amoy [Xiamen]; Canton [Guangzhou]; Chiang Kai-shek [Jiang Jieshi]; Hong Kong [Xianggang]; Shensi [Shaanxi]; Sun Yat-sen [Sun Zhongshan]; Soong Ching-ling [Song Qingling]; her sister Mei-ling and her brother, T. V. Soong; Tibet [Xizang]; Whampoa [Huangpu]; Yangtse [Yangzi].

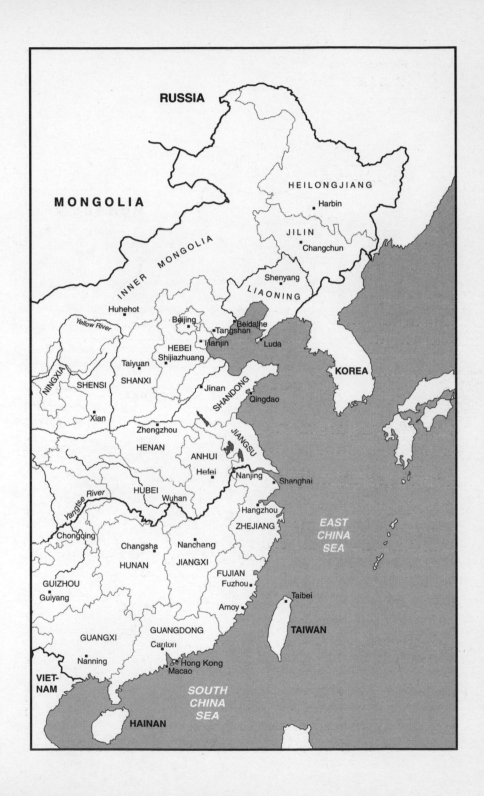

Prologue

Few people today, even in China, have heard of the little market town of Tongdao. It extends for about a mile along the left bank of the Shuangjiang, squeezed into a narrow strip of land between the wide, brown river and a range of terraced hills. Tongdao is the centre of a small non-Han minority area where the three provinces of Guangxi, Guizhou and Hunan meet. It is a scruffy, run-down place, with one long, muddy main street, few shops and fewer modern buildings, where even the locals say resignedly that nothing of interest ever happens. Yet once something did happen there. On December 12, 1934, the Red Army leadership gathered in Tongdao for a meeting which was to mark the beginning of Mao Zedong's rise to supreme power.

It was one of the most obscure events in the history of the Chinese Communist Party. The only written trace of the Red Army's passage is an old photograph of a faded slogan, chalked up by the troops on a wall: 'Everyone should take up arms and fight the Japanese!' All the participants are now dead. No one knows exactly who was present, or even where the meeting took place. Premier Zhou Enlai, years later, recalled that it had been in a farmhouse, somewhere outside the town, where a wedding party was in progress. Mao was two weeks short of his forty-first birthday, a thin, lanky man, hollow-cheeked from lack of food and sleep, whose oversize grey cotton jacket seemed perpetually about to slide from his shoulders. He was still recovering from a severe bout of malaria, and at times had to be carried in a litter. Taller than most of the other leaders, his face was smooth and unmarked, with a shock of unruly black hair, parted in the middle.

The left-wing American writer, Agnes Smedley, who met Mao not long afterwards, found him a forbidding figure, with a high-pitched voice and long, sensitive woman's hands:

> His dark, inscrutable face was long, the forehead broad and high, the mouth feminine. Whatever else he might be, he was an aesthete . . . [But] despite that feminine quality in him he was as stubborn as a mule, and a steel rod of pride and determination ran through his nature. I had the impression that he would wait and watch for years, but eventually have his way . . . His humour was often sardonic and grim, as though it sprang from deep caverns of spiritual seclusion. I had the impression that there was a door to his being that had never been opened to anyone.

Even to his closest comrades, Mao was hard to fathom. His spirit, in Smedley's words, 'dwelt within itself, isolating him'. His personality inspired loyalty, not affection. He combined a fierce temper and infinite patience; vision, and an almost pedantic attention to detail; an inflexible will, and extreme subtlety; public charisma, and private intrigue.

The nationalists, who had put a price on his head, executed his wife and vandalised his parents' tomb, viewed Mao throughout the early 1930s as the dominant Red Army political chief. As so often, they were wrong.

Power was in the hands of what was known as the 'three-man group' or 'troika'. Bo Gu, the 27-year-old acting Party leader (or, as he was formally known, 'the comrade with overall responsibility for the work of the Party Centre') had graduated from the University of the Toilers of the East in Moscow. He had the face of a precocious schoolboy, with bulging eyes and black-rimmed spectacles, which a British diplomat said, unkindly but accurately, reminded him of a golliwog. The Comintern* had parachuted him into the leadership to ensure loyalty to the Soviet line. The second member, Zhou Enlai, General Political Commissar of the Red Army and the

---

* The Communist International (Comintern) was established by Lenin, in March 1919, as an instrument whereby Moscow could control the activities of foreign communist parties. These were treated as Comintern branches under the orders of a Russian-dominated Executive Committee.

real power behind Bo Gu's throne, also had Moscow's trust. The
third, Otto Braun, a tall, thin German with a prominent nose and
horsey teeth, set off by a pair of round spectacles, was Comintern
military adviser.

Over the previous twelve months, these three men had presided
over a shattering series of communist military reverses. The nationalist leader, Chiang Kai-shek, had consolidated his hold over most
of the rest of China and was determined to extirpate what he rightly
saw as a potentially fatal long-term challenge to his rule. With the
help of German military advisers, he began building lines of fortified blockhouses around the region the communists controlled.
With excruciating slowness, the lines were pushed forward, the vice
around the base area tightened, the communist forces hemmed in.
Very gradually, the Red Army was being strangled. It was a strategy
to which the troika could find no adequate response.

Mao might have been no more successful. But Bo Gu had sidelined him more than two years before. Mao was not in power.

In October 1934, after months of agonised debates among the
Party leadership, the Reds abandoned their base area in a last
despairing gamble to ward off total defeat as Chiang's forces closed
in for the kill. Their 6,000-mile trek across China would later be
celebrated as the Long March, an epic symbol of courage in adver-
sity, selfless discipline and indomitable will. At the time it was
called, more prosaically, the 'strategic transfer', and a little later, the
March to the West. The plan, in so far as there was one, was to make
for north-west Hunan, where the local warlords were wary of
Chiang's ambitions and reluctant to make common cause with him,
and there to link up with other communist forces to create a new
central Red base area to replace the one they had just lost.

It started well enough. The Red Army slipped through the first
line of blockhouses, meeting little resistance. The next two lines also
fell. More than three weeks passed before nationalist intelligence
realised that its prey had escaped. But Chiang's fourth line, on the
Xiang River, was different.

The battle lasted more than a week, from November 25 to
December 3. When it ended, the Red Army had lost between
15,000 and 20,000 combat troops. Up to 40,000 reserves and
bearers had deserted. Of the 86,000 men and women who had set
out in October, not many more than 30,000 were left. The baggage
train, which had stretched for fifty miles, a serpentine leviathan

which, Mao said later, resembled a house-moving operation more than an army on the march, had its back broken at the Xiang River. Scattered in the mud and littering the hillsides were the office furniture, the printing presses, the Party archives, the generators – all the paraphernalia that the communists had amassed in three years' rule of a region bigger than Belgium – which had been lugged painfully on the backs of porters over mountain paths and paddy fields for hundreds of wearisome miles. Artillery pieces, heavy machine-guns, the one X-ray machine the communists possessed, all were jettisoned. But not before they had so slowed the army's progress that, bloated and weak, it had dragged itself into the trap which Chiang Kai-shek had set.

It was a worse disaster than even the most phlegmatic Red Army leaders were prepared for. In October, the base they had spent years building had been abandoned; now two-thirds of their army had been lost as well.

A week later, having thrown off their pursuers, the remnants of the communist forces crossed into southern Hunan. They had regrouped and were in good order. But among the senior leadership, mutiny was in the air. The time was fast approaching when the troika would be called to account.

But not quite yet. The eight or nine weary men who met that afternoon at Tongdao faced a much more pressing question: where to head next? Bo Gu and Otto Braun insisted they keep to the original plan and make for north-west Hunan. The military commanders refused. Chiang Kai-shek had 300,000 troops blocking the route north. To try to force a passage was to court annihilation. A decision had to be made fast. Word came that Hunan warlord troops were closing in from the east.

After a tense, hurried debate, it was agreed as an interim measure that the army would go west, into the mountain fastness of Guizhou. There a full meeting of the Politburo would be called to discuss future strategy. The compromise proposal came from Mao. It was the first time since his dismissal from the military command in 1932 that his views had been heard and accepted in the inner circle of power. His presence was due only to the gravity of the Xiang River defeat. But a journey of 10,000 li, say the Chinese, starts with a single step. For Mao, Tongdao was that step.

*

Guizhou is, and has been for centuries, one of the poorest of China's provinces. In the 1930s, the villages were opium-sodden, the people illiterate and so impoverished that whole families possessed only a single pair of trousers. Girls were frequently killed at birth; boys were sold to slave-merchants for resale in richer areas near the coast. But it was a place of exquisite natural grandeur: the countryside that unrolled before the Red Army, as it marched west, was drawn from the fantastic landscapes of a Ming scroll.

Beyond Tongdao the hills grow steeper, the mountains wider and more contorted: great conical limestone mounds, thousands of feet high; mountains like camels' humps, like giant anthills; plum-pudding mountains like ancestral tumuli. Miao villages perch on the bluffs – clusters of thatched roofs and ochre walls, with overhanging eaves and latticed paper windows, standing out dark against a yellowish-green carpet of dead winter grasses and early shoots of spring. Hawks circle above; frost lies white on the rice stubble below. Guizhou people say: 'No three days without rain; no three li without a mountain.' In this part of the province there are only mountains and, in December and January, perpetual drizzle and fog. The higher slopes, wrapped in mist, are thick with pine forests, golden bamboo and dark green firs, while far below, the valley bottoms are filled with bright lakes of white cloud. Chain bridges are slung across the rivers, and alongside the torrents that cascade down from the heights are pocket-handkerchief sized patches of cultivated land, where a peasant works on a fifty-degree slope to coax a few poor vegetables from the dark red soil.

The soldiers remembered only the rigours of the journey. 'We went up a mountain so steep that I could see the soles of the man ahead of me,' one army man recalled. 'News came down the line that our advance columns were facing a sheer cliff, and . . . to sleep where we were and continue climbing at daybreak . . . The stars looked like jade stones on a black curtain. The dark peaks towered around us like menacing giants. We seemed to be at the bottom of a well.' The cliff, known locally as the Thunder God Rock, had stone steps a foot wide carved into its face. It was too steep for stretcher-bearers: the wounded had to be carried up on men's backs. Many horses fell to their deaths on the rocks below.

The Red Army Commander, Zhu De, remembered the poverty. 'The peasants call themselves "dry men",' he noted. 'They are sucked dry of everything . . . People dig rotten rice from the ground

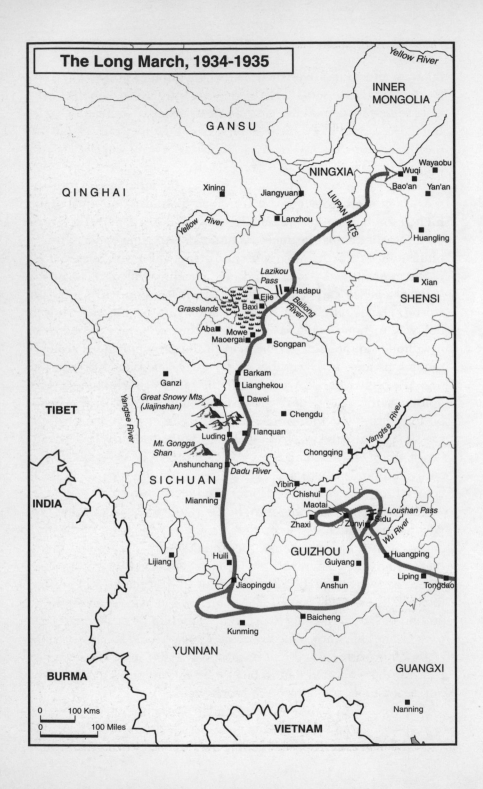

The Long March, 1934-1935

Yellow River

INNER MONGOLIA

GANSU

QINGHAI

NINGXIA

Xining
Jiangyuan
Lanzhou

Wayaobu
Wuqi
Bao'an
Yan'an

Huangling

Yellow River

LIUPAN MTS

Lazikou Pass
Hadapu
Ejie
Grasslands
Baxi
Bailong River

Xian

SHENSI

Aba
Mowe
Maoergai
Songpan

Barkam
Lianghekou
Ganzi
Dawei
Great Snowy Mts.
(Jiajinshan)
Chengdu

Yangtse River

TIBET

Luding
Tianquan

Mt. Gongga Shan
Chongqing

Yangtse River

INDIA
Anshunchang
Dadu River

SICHUAN
Yibin
Chishui
Maotai
Loushan Pass
Mianning
Zhaxi
Zunyi
Sidu
Wu River

Lijiang
Huili
Guiyang
Huangping

GUIZHOU
Liping
Jiaopingdu
Anshun
Tongdao

Baicheng

Kunming

YUNNAN

GUANGXI

BURMA

Nanning

VIETNAM

0   100 Kms
0   100 Miles

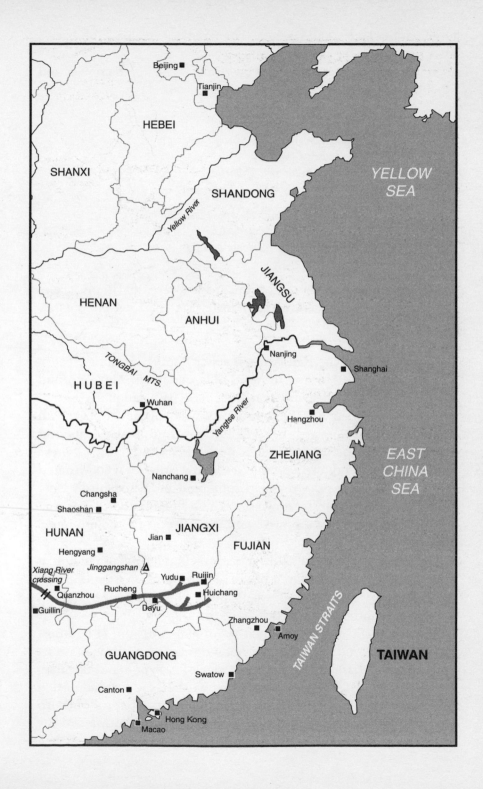

under a landlord's old granary. The monks call this "holy rice",
Heaven's gift to the poor.'

Mao saw these things too. But he wrote instead of the power and
beauty of the country through which they were passing:

> *Mountains!*
> *Surging waves in a tumultuous sea,*
> *Ten thousand stallions*
> *Galloping in the heat of battle.*
>
> *Mountains!*
> *Blade-sharp, piercing the blue of heaven.*
> *But for your strength upholding*
> *The skies would break loose and fall.*

These short poems, composed in the saddle, were not simply a celebration of the elemental forces of nature. Mao had reason to exult.

On December 15, the Red Army reached Liping, a county seat in
a valley surrounded by low, terraced hills, and the first level ground
they had seen since leaving Tongdao. Military headquarters were
set up in a merchant's house, a spacious, well-appointed place with
a small inner courtyard, ornamented by Buddhist motifs and
emblems of prosperity. It had four-poster beds and a tiny Chinese
garden behind, and opened on to a narrow street of wood-fronted
shops and houses with grey-tiled roofs and upturned bird's-wing
eaves. A few doors further down stood a German Lutheran mission.
The missionaries, like the merchant, had fled at the communists'
approach.

It was here that the Politburo met for its first formal discussion of
policy since the Long March began. There were two main issues:
the Red Army's destination, which the earlier discussion had left
unresolved; and military tactics.

Braun and Bo Gu still wanted to join up with the communist
forces in northern Hunan. Mao proposed heading north-west, to set
up a new Red base area near the border of Guizhou and Sichuan,
where, he argued, resistance would be weaker. He was supported
by Zhang Wentian, one of the four members of the Politburo
Standing Committee, and Wang Jiaxiang, Vice-Chairman of the
Military Commission, who had been gravely wounded in battle a

year earlier and spent the whole of the Long March in a litter with a rubber tube sticking out of his stomach. Both were Moscow-trained. Both had initially backed Braun and Bo Gu, but had grown disillusioned. Mao had been cultivating them ever since the march began. Now they swung the balance in his favour. Sensing the mood of the meeting, Zhou Enlai added his voice and most of the rest of the Politburo fell in behind. Bo Gu's proposal was rejected. Instead they resolved to set up a new base area with its centre at Zunyi, Guizhou's second city, or, if that proved too difficult, further to the north-west.

But Mao did not have it all his own way. On tactics, the resolution was more even-handed. It warned against 'underestimating possible losses to our own side, leading to pessimism and defeatism' – an implicit reference to the rout on the Xiang River and thus a criticism of the military line of the three-man group of Zhou, Bo Gu and Braun; in the same vein, it ordered the army to refrain from large-scale engagements until the new base area had been secured. But it also spoke of the danger of 'guerrillaism', a codeword for the 'flexible guerrilla strategy' associated with Mao. Zhou Enlai evidently was not prepared to yield to Mao without a fight.

Next day, December 20, the Red Army resumed its march. Bo Gu and Otto Braun were fatally weakened. The real conflict shaping up was now between Mao and Zhou.

They had so little in common, these two men: Zhou, a mandarin's son, a rebel against his class, supple, subtle, the quintessential survivor, who had learned the cheapness of life as a communist working underground in Shanghai, where death was never more than a whisper of betrayal away; Mao, a peasant to his roots, earthy and coarse, his speech laced with picaresque aphorisms, contemptuous of city-dwellers. One was urbane and refined, the indefatigable executor of other men's ideas; the other, an unpredictable visionary. For most of the next forty years they would form one of the world's most enduring political partnerships. But as 1934 drew to a close, that was far from both their minds.

On December 31, the army command halted at a small trading centre called Houchang (Monkey Town), 25 miles south of the River Wu, the last natural barrier before they reached Zunyi. That night the Politburo met again. Otto Braun proposed that the army make a stand against three warlord divisions which were reported to be closing in on them. The military commanders reminded him

that they had agreed at Liping to avoid large-scale set-piece battles
and give priority to securing the new base area. After a furious argument lasting late into the night, Braun was suspended as military
adviser. To underline the importance of the change, the Politburo
resolution approving it included a ringing endorsement of one of
Mao's cardinal principles, which had been ignored for the previous
two years. 'No opportunity should be missed,' it declared, 'to use
mobile warfare to break up and destroy the enemy one by one.
Then we shall certainly gain victory.'

The tide had turned. The old chain of command under the troika
had broken down. As a temporary measure, it was agreed that all
major decisions would be referred to the leadership as a whole. The
old strategy had been abandoned. A new one had to be worked out
to replace it. In the early hours of New Year's Day, the Politburo
agreed to convene an enlarged conference at Zunyi. It was to have
three tasks: to review the past, determine what had gone wrong, and
chart a course for the future. The stage was set for a showdown.

Deng Xiaoping was thirty years old, a stocky man, very short, with
a close-shaven bullet head. As a teenager in Paris he had learned
how to produce a news-sheet for the local branch of the Chinese
Communist Youth League, scratching characters on to a waxed
sheet with a stylus and rolling off copies in black Chinese ink, made
from soot and tung oil. His reputation as a journalist had stuck. Now
he was editor of the Red Army newspaper, an equally crude mimeographed one-page broadsheet called *Hongxing* (Red Star).

The issue of January 15, 1935, related how the people of Zunyi
had welcomed the communist forces after they had taken the city
without a shot being fired: the advance guard had persuaded the
defenders to open the city gates by pretending to be part of a local
warlord force. Other articles described in glowing terms 'the Red
Army's image in the hearts of the masses', and recorded the establishment of a Revolutionary Committee to administer the city.

Nowhere did it give the slightest hint that the Politburo was about
to hold the most important meeting in its history, which Deng
himself would attend as note-taker – a meeting so sensitive that, for
almost a month after, senior Party officials were kept in ignorance
of its decisions, until the leaders had met again to decide how the
news should be broken to them.

Twenty men gathered that night on the upper floor of a handsome, rectangular, two-storey building of dark-grey brick,
surrounded by a colonnaded veranda. It had been the home of one
of the city's minor warlords until Zhou and the military commanders took it for their headquarters. Bo Gu and Otto Braun were
billeted close by, along a lane leading to the Roman Catholic
Cathedral, an ornate, imposing structure with a fanciful three-tiered
roof, more chinoiserie than Chinese, set amid flower gardens where
the Red Army detachment escorting the leadership was encamped.
Mao and his two allies, Zhang Wentian and Wang Jiaxiang, with
six bodyguards, were in another warlord's house, with art-deco
woodwork and stained-glass windows, on the other side of town.
Ever since they had arrived, a week earlier, Mao had been
canvassing support. Now the preparations were over. The two sides
were ready to do battle. In Otto Braun's words:

> It was obvious that [Mao] wanted revenge . . . In 1932 . . . his mili-
> tary and political [power] had been broken . . . Now there emerged
> the possibility – years of partisan struggle had been directed at
> bringing it about – that by demagogic exploitation of isolated organi-
> sational and tactical mistakes, but especially through concocted
> claims and slanderous imputations, he could discredit the Party
> leadership and isolate . . . Bo Gu. He would rehabilitate himself
> completely [and] take the Army firmly into his grasp, thereby sub-
> ordinating the Party itself to his will.

The small, crowded room where the meeting was held overlooked
an inner courtyard. In the centre, a brazier full of glowing charcoal
threw its puny heat at the damp, raw cold of the Zunyi winter. Wang
Jiaxiang and another wounded general lay stretched out on bamboo
chaise-longues. Braun and his interpreter sat away from the main
group, near the door.

Bo Gu, as acting Party leader, presented the main report. He
argued that the loss of the central Red base area and the military
disasters that had followed were due not to faulty policies, but to the
enemy's overwhelming strength and the support the nationalists
had received from the imperialist Powers.

Zhou Enlai spoke next. He acknowledged having made errors.
But he, too, refused to concede that the strategy itself had been
wrong. Zhou still had hopes of saving something from the ruins.

Then Mao opened the attack. Braun remembered, forty years

later, that he spoke not extempore, as he usually did, but from a manuscript, 'painstakingly prepared'. The fundamental problem, Mao said, was not the strength of the enemy: it was that the Party had deviated from the 'basic strategic and tactical principles with which the Red Army [had in the past] won victories', in other words, the 'flexible guerrilla strategy' which he and Zhu De had developed. But for that, he claimed, the nationalist encirclement would probably have been defeated. Instead, the Red Army had been ordered to fight a defensive, positional war, building blockhouses to counter the enemy's blockhouses, dispersing its forces in a vain attempt to preserve 'every inch of soviet territory' and abandoning mobile warfare. Temporarily surrendering territory could be justified, Mao said. Jeopardising the Red Army's strength could not, because it was through the army – and the army alone – that territory could be regained.

Mao laid the blame for these errors squarely on Otto Braun. The Comintern adviser had imposed wrong tactics on the army, he said, and his 'rude method of leadership' had led to 'extremely abnormal phenomena' within the Military Council, a reference to Braun's hectoring, dictatorial style, which was widely resented. Bo Gu, Mao declared, had failed to exert adequate political leadership, allowing errors in military line to go unchecked.

When Mao sat down, Wang Jiaxiang launched his own tirade against Braun's methods. Zhang Wentian followed. Another Moscow-trained leader, He Kaifeng, sprang to Bo's defence. Some of those present, like Chen Yun, a former print-worker who had been close to Zhou in Shanghai, found Mao's attack one-sided. Although Chen had no military role, he was a Standing Committee member and his opinions carried weight. But the ground commanders, whose armies had had to pay the price of the troika's mistakes, showed no hesitation. Peng Dehuai, a gruff, outspoken general who cared for only two things in life, the victory of the communist cause and the welfare of his men, likened Braun to 'a prodigal son, who had squandered his father's goods' – a reference to the loss of the base area for which Peng, with Mao and Zhu, had expended so much time and blood.

Braun himself sat immobile in his corner near the door, smoking furiously, as his interpreter, growing increasingly agitated and confused, tried to translate what was said. When he finally spoke, it was to reject the accusations en bloc. He was merely an adviser, he said; the Chinese leadership, not he, was responsible for the policies it followed.

This was disingenuous. Under Stalin in the 1930s a Comintern representative, even an adviser, had extraordinary powers. Yet there was some truth in what he said. Braun had not had the last word on military affairs. That had rested with Zhou Enlai.

Mao had no illusions that Zhou was his real adversary. He had known it since Zhou had arrived in the Red base area at the end of 1931 and unceremoniously elbowed him aside. Neither the amiable Zhang Wentian nor, still less, Bo Gu was a serious contender for ultimate power. Zhou Enlai was. But to have attacked Zhou head-on at Zunyi would have been to tear the leadership apart in a battle which Mao could not win. So, in a move characteristic of his political and military style, he concentrated his attack on the weakest points of Zhou's armoury, Braun and Bo Gu, while leaving his chief opponent a face-saving way out.

Zhou took it. On the second day of the conference he spoke again. This time he acknowledged that the military line had been 'fundamentally incorrect', and made a lengthy self-criticism. It was the kind of manoeuvre at which Zhou excelled. From being Mao's opponent, he transformed himself into an ally. Mao, of course, knew better. So did Zhou. But for the moment there was a truce.

The resolution drawn up afterwards excoriated Zhou's two colleagues in the troika for their 'extremely bad leadership'. Braun was accused of 'treating war as a game', 'monopolising the work of the Military Council' and using punishment rather than reason to suppress 'by all available means' views which differed from his own. Bo Gu was held to have committed 'serious political mistakes'. But Zhou escaped unscathed, even managing, on paper at least, to achieve a short-lived promotion: when the troika was officially dissolved, he took over its powers with the cumbersome title of 'final decision-maker on behalf of the Central Committee in dealing with military affairs'. His role in the débâcle that had preceded the Zunyi conference was passed over in silence. The resolution condemned the 'elephantine' supply columns which had slowed the advance, but omitted to say that it was Zhou who had organised them. It referred to 'the leaders of the policy of pure defence', and on one occasion, to 'Otto Braun and the others', but did not say who those 'others' were. Zhou was mentioned explicitly only once, as having given the 'supplementary report' following Bo Gu's. Even then, in all copies of the resolution except those distributed to the highest-ranking cadres, the three characters of his name were left blank.

Mao was named to the Politburo Standing Committee, and became Zhou's chief military adviser. Small recompense, it might seem, for two years in the wilderness. But, as so often in China, the spirit of these decisions counted far more than the letter. Even Braun acknowledged that 'most of those at the meeting' ended up in agreement with Mao. In spirit, Mao's cause had triumphed. Zhou, notwithstanding his new title, was identified with the discredited leadership whose policies had been condemned.

Over the next few months the spirit was given flesh. Early in February, Bo Gu was replaced as acting Party leader by Mao's ally, Zhang Wentian. A month later a Front Headquarters was established, with Zhu De as Commander and Mao as Political Commissar, which effectively removed a large measure of Zhou's operational control. Soon afterwards, his power was further eroded when a new troika was established, consisting of Zhou, Mao, and Wang Jiaxiang. By early summer, when the Red Army succeeded in crossing the River of Golden Sand into Sichuan, Mao had established himself as its uncontested leader.

Other battles lay ahead. It would be eight more years before Mao was formally installed as Chairman, the title he would keep until his death. But Zhou's challenge was over. He would pay dearly for it. In 1943, his position was so precarious that the former head of the Comintern, Georgy Dimitrov, pleaded with Mao not to have him expelled from the Party. Mao kept him. Not because of Dimitrov but because Zhou was too useful to waste. The future Premier was instead humiliated. In the new Party Central Committee, formed two years later, he ranked twenty-third.

Twenty-five years after Zunyi, in the spring of 1961, Mao was aboard his private train, travelling through his home province of Hunan in southern China.

The years seemed to have been good to him. Adulated and glorified as China's Great Helmsman, the ageing, corpulent figure whose moon face gazed out serenely from the Gate of Heavenly Peace appeared to the rest of the world as undisputed ruler of the most populous nation on earth and standard-bearer of a puritanical global revolution which the fleshpots of Khrushchevite revisionism had abandoned.

Yet Mao was not as the rest of the world imagined.

He was accompanied on this journey, as on all such trips, by a number of attractive young women with whom he shared, severally or together, the pleasures of an oversized bed, which was specially installed wherever he went, not so much for carnal reasons as to accommodate the piles of books he insisted on keeping at his side. Like Stalin, who, after his wife's suicide, was provided with attractive 'housekeepers' by his security chief, Lavrentii Beria, Mao in late middle age had given up on family life. He found in his relations with girls a third his own age a normality which was denied him elsewhere.

By the 1960s Mao was totally cut off from the country that he ruled, so isolated by his eminence that bodyguards and advance parties choreographed his every move. Sex was his one freedom, the one moment in his day when he could treat other human beings as equals and be treated as such in return. A century earlier the boy Emperor, Tongzhi, used to slip out of the palace incognito, accompanied by one of his courtiers, to visit the brothels of Beijing. For Mao that was impossible. Women came to him. They revelled in his power. He revelled in their bodies. 'I wash my prick in their cunts,' he told his personal physician, a strait-laced man whom he took a perverse delight in shocking. 'I was nauseated,' the good doctor wrote afterwards.

Mao's peccadilloes, like the private lives of all the leaders, were hidden behind an impenetrable curtain of revolutionary purity. But on the train one afternoon that February, the veil was suddenly pierced.

He had spent the night with a young woman teacher and, as was his custom, had risen late and then left to attend a meeting. Afterwards she was talking with other members of Mao's suite when a technician joined them. Mao's doctor takes up the story:

'I heard you talking today,' the young technician suddenly said to the teacher, interrupting our idle chatter.

'What do you mean you heard me talking?' she responded. 'Talking about what?'

'When the Chairman was getting ready to meet [Hunan First Secretary] Zhang Pinghua, you told him to hurry up and put on his clothes.'

The young woman blanched. 'What else did you hear?' she asked quietly.

'I heard everything,' he answered, teasing.

Thus did Mao discover that, on the orders of his senior colleagues, for the previous eighteen months all his conversations, not to mention his lovemaking, had been bugged and secretly tape-recorded. At the time, the only heads to roll, and those not literally, were of three low-level officials, among them the hapless technician. But four years later, when the first political tremors announcing the Cultural Revolution began to roil the surface calm of Party unity, Mao's fellow leaders would have done well to have reflected more deeply on what had led them to approve those secret tape-recordings.

In one sense their motives had been innocent enough. The six men who, with Mao, made up the Politburo Standing Committee, at the summit of a Party which now counted 20 million members, were all Zunyi veterans, part of the minuscule elite which had accompanied him throughout the long odyssey to win power. By the early 1960s, they found the Chairman increasingly difficult to read. They wanted advance warning of what he was thinking, so as not to be caught off-guard by a sudden change in political line or an off-the-cuff remark to a foreign visitor. Yang Shangkun, another Zunyi survivor, who headed the Central Committee's General Office, decided that modern technology, in the shape of recording machines, was the obvious answer. From that standpoint it was almost a compliment. Mao had achieved such Olympian status that his every word must be preserved. But it also reflected an uneasy awareness within the Politburo of the mental gulf that had developed between the Chairman and his subordinates – which was all that the other leaders now were.

From this mental chasm sprang an ideological and political divide which, before the decade was out, would convulse all China in an iconoclastic spasm of terror, destroying both the Zunyi fellowship and the ideas that it had espoused.

The struggle in the 1960s was more subtle, more complex, and ultimately far bloodier and more ruthless than that of thirty years before. Small wonder: all that had been at stake at Zunyi was the leadership of a ragtag army of 30,000 men playing an apparently dwindling role on the periphery of Chinese politics. In Beijing the battle was for control of a nation which would soon number more than a billion people. But the ground rules were the same. On that earlier occasion, Mao himself had spelt them out:

> Under unfavourable conditions, we should refuse . . . battle, withdraw our main forces back to a suitable distance, transfer them to the rear or flanks of the enemy and concentrate them in secret, induce the enemy to commit mistakes and expose weaknesses by tiring and wearing him out and confusing him, and thus enable ourselves to gain victory in a decisive battle.

'War is politics,' he wrote later. 'Politics is war by other means.'

CHAPTER ONE

A Confucian Childhood

In winter, in Hunan, the wind howls bone-cold across bare fields of dry yellow earth, kicking up the dust so that it stings the eyes of the horses and makes men squint as they lean into the frozen air, their faces like leather masks. This is the dead season of the year. The peasants, in unheated mud-brick huts, bundle themselves up in layers of dirty, quilted cotton, drawing their hands up into their sleeves so that only their heads protrude warily from the folds of blue cloth, tortoise-like, waiting for better days.

Mao was born into a Hunanese peasant household in the village of Shaoshan, a few days after the winter solstice, the great mid-winter festival when the Emperor Guangxu in far-off Beijing was borne in solemn procession to the Temple of Heaven to perform the sacrificial rites and give thanks for another year safely passed. It was the nineteenth day of the eleventh month of the Year of the Snake by the old calendar, December 26 1893 by the new.

By tradition, which was strictly adhered to in the case of a first-born son, the baby was not bathed until three days after the birth. A fortune-teller was then called in and a horoscope drawn up, which in Mao's case evidently showed that the family was lacking in the water element. His father therefore named him Zedong, because the character *ze*, which means 'to anoint', is held in Hunanese geomantic lore to remedy such a deficiency.* That

---

* Attempts to translate Chinese names are misguided. The name Mao Zedong means literally 'Anoint the East' Hair, for that is what the characters *ze, dong* and *mao*

marked the start of a year of the Buddhist and Daoist folk-rituals with which Chinese peasants through the ages have tempered the harshness of their existence, adding a touch of colour and excitement to the severe Confucian teachings around which their lives were fashioned and society revolved. After four weeks, the baby's head was shaved, apart from a small tuft left on the crown by which 'to hold him to life'. A few copper cash, or sometimes a small silver padlock, attached to a red cord, were placed around his neck for the same purpose. In some families, the hair that had been cut was mixed with the hairs of a dog and sewn into the child's clothing so that evil spirits would see him as an animal and leave him alone. Others made a boy-child wear an earring so that the spirits would think he was a girl and not worth bothering with.

By the standards of the time, Mao's family was comfortably off. His father, Rensheng, had enlisted at the age of sixteen in the army of the Viceroy of Hunan and Hubei, and within five or six years had accumulated a small capital, with which he bought land. By the time Mao was born, the family owned two-and-a-half-acres of rice paddy, a substantial holding in a county renowned as being among the wealthiest and most fertile in one of the richest rice-growing provinces in China. His father, a thrifty man who counted every copper cash, later bought another acre and took on two farm labourers. He gave them a daily ration of rice and, as a special concession once a month, a dish of rice cooked with eggs – but never meat.

His penny-pinching coloured Mao's image of his father from an early age. 'To me,' he later recalled pointedly, 'he gave neither eggs nor meat.' Although there was always enough to go round, the family ate frugally. To Mao as a small boy, this stinginess was

---

individually signify. Used together in a name, however, they no more have that connection to a Chinese than Philip signifies 'Lover of Horses' in English or the name, Pierre, suggests 'stone' to a Frenchman. There are exceptions, both in antiquity and in recent times (during the Cultural Revolution, for example, many Chinese changed their names to make them more revolutionary), but even where a name does have an unambiguous meaning, it is often not understood as such. Shaoshan, for instance, has the literal meaning, 'Music Mountain', but to its inhabitants it is simply the name of the village.

compounded by a lack of paternal affection, a deficiency made all the more glaring by the warmth and gentleness of his mother. It blinded him to his father's good points, the single-mindedness, drive and determination which Mao would later demonstrate in such abundance in his own life. While still a child he came to view the family as split into two camps: his mother and himself on one side, his father on the other.

A combination of parsimony and unrelenting grind soon made Mao's father one of the most prosperous men in Shaoshan, which then had a population of about three hundred families, most of them also surnamed Mao, theirs being the dominant clan.

In those days, a peasant family in Hunan was thought to be doing well if it had an acre-and-a-half of land and a three-roomed house. Mao's parents had more than twice that much, and built a large, rambling farmhouse, with a grey-tiled roof and upturned eaves, beside a cascade of terraced rice-fields tumbling down a narrow valley. Pine woods stood behind and there was a lotus pond in front. Mao had a bedroom to himself, an almost unheard-of luxury, and when he was older would sit up late at night reading, hiding his oil-lamp behind a blue cloth so that his father would not see. Later, after his brothers were born, they too had rooms of their own. His father's capital amounted to two or three thousand Chinese silver dollars, 'a great fortune in that small village', as Mao himself acknowledged. Rather than extend his own land-holdings, he bought mortgages on other peasants' land, thus indirectly becoming a landlord. He also purchased grain from poor farmers in the village and sent it for resale in the county seat, Xiangtan, thirty miles away. A sprawling agglomeration of several hundred thousand people, Xiangtan was then the hub of the provincial tea trade and an important entrepot and financial centre because of its position on the Xiang River, Hunan's largest navigable waterway and the main artery of trade in the province. From Shaoshan, it was two days' journey by oxcart along a rutted earthen track, although porters could do it in one, carrying 80 kilograms of merchandise on their backs.

Much as he might complain about his father's meanness, Mao inherited his sense of thrift. Throughout his adult life, at least where his own person was concerned, he was famously unwilling to buy anything new if the old one could be patched up and made to serve a little longer.

The earthiness of his childhood proved equally tenacious. Hygiene was rudimentary, and washing as much a rarity as in medieval Europe. 'A total apathy in regard to matter in the wrong place pervades all classes from the highest to the lowest,' wrote a contemporary observer. 'Gorgeous silks conceal an unwashed skin, and from under the rich sable cuffs of the official protrude finger-nails innocent of soap or penknife.' To the end of his days, Mao preferred a rub with a steaming towel to washing with soap and water. Nor did he ever get the hang of using a toothbrush. Instead, like most rural southerners, he rinsed his mouth with tea.

The other constants of peasant life were bedbugs, lice and itch-sores. When Mao itched, he scratched: at Bao'an, in the 1930s, he had no compunction about lowering his trousers, while receiving a foreign visitor, to search for an uninvited guest in his underwear. In part, he disdained convention; in part, it was ingrained peasant habit. Nowhere was that more viscerally evident than in his attitude to the workings of his own body. The Chinese as a nation have always been unfazed by natural processes which send Anglo-Saxons in particular into contortions of squeamishness. Small children were, and in most parts of the country still are, brought up wearing split trousers so that they can squat and relieve themselves wherever the urge takes them. Adults use communal latrines, where defecation is a social event. Mao was never reconciled to Western-style lavatories with a seat and flushing water. Even at Zhongnanhai in the early 1950s, when he was already Head of State, it was one of the duties of his personal bodyguards to follow him out into the garden with a shovel, and dig a hole in the ground for Mao to perform his bowel movement. The practice ended only after Zhou Enlai arranged for a specially built latrine which met with Mao's approval to be installed next to his bedroom. He was equally ill at ease with Western-style beds, insisting all his life on having hard wooden boards to sleep on.

When Mao was six he started helping in the fields like other children of his age, carrying out the small tasks which Chinese families always leave to the old and the very young: watching over the cattle and tending the ducks. Two years later, his father sent him to the village school – an important decision for it cost four or five silver dollars a year, nearly six months of a labourer's wages.

Among all except the very wealthy, every family's dream in nine-teenth-century China was to have a son whose brilliance in expounding the classical Confucian texts would win him a place of honour in the imperial examinations, opening the way to an official career with all the prestige, and opportunities for 'squeeze', which that entailed. In the words of one of the most sympathetic Western observers of Chinese life at that time:

> Education is the royal road to the honours and emoluments that the state has to bestow, and it is by means of it that the wildest ambition that ever ran riot through a young man's brain can ultimately be satis-fied. In the West there are many ways by which a man may rise to eminence, and finally occupy a prominent position as a member of Parliament, or as holding some office under Government that will bring him before the notice of the public. In China they are all narrowed down to one, and it is the one that leads from the school-house . . . It may be confidently asserted that every schoolboy carries in his satchel a possible viceroyship when . . . untrammelled by parliaments, he may rule over twenty or thirty millions of people.

Yet the dream was for the few. Most of the population was too poor to take even the first step: learning to read and write.

Mao's mother, Wen Qimei, literally 'Seventh Sister', the peasant custom then being not to name girls, but simply to number them in order of their birth, may have had dreams for him. Three years older than her husband, she was a devout Buddhist. She introduced her son to the mysteries of the village temple with its fantastic images of arhats and bodhisattvas, blackened by grime and smoke, the air heavy with the smell of incense; and later she grieved when, as an adolescent, his faith began to falter.

Mao's father did not dream. His ambitions, typical of the small landlord he had become, were much more down-to-earth. He himself was barely literate, having had but two years' schooling. He wanted his son to do better, but for strictly practical ends: to keep the farm accounts, and then later, after an apprenticeship with a rice merchant in Xiangtan, to take over the family business and support his parents in their old age.

Royal road it might be, but a village school in the last days of the Chinese Empire was a grim place, calculated to dampen the boldest spirit. It consisted of a single room with bare mud-brick walls and a floor of beaten earth, unheated in winter, sweltering in summer, with a central door and two small apertures at each end allowing in air and a little light to pierce the gloom. The school year began in February, on the 17th of the First Moon, two days after the Lantern Festival, which brought to an end the festivities marking the Chinese New Year. Each boy waited at the school gate, carrying a small desk and stool which he had brought from home. Usually there were about twenty of them, the youngest, like Mao, seven or eight years old, the oldest seventeen or eighteen. They all wore identical loose jackets, cross-tied at the front, of homespun blue cotton, and loose, baggy trousers made from the same material. The teacher sat at a table, with an ink-stone and water-dropper, a small earthenware teapot and cup, bamboo tallies to record the presence of each pupil, and a stout bamboo rod before him. Tradition held that he should show no sign of interest in, or sympathy for, his students lest it endanger his authority, which was absolute.

Mao's teacher was in that mould. He belonged to the 'stern-treatment school . . . harsh and severe', Mao remembered. They learned to fear his bamboo rod, which he used frequently, and his 'incense board' – a slatted wooden washboard on which a pupil would be made to kneel for the time it took an incense-stick to burn down.

If the material conditions were depressing, the method of teaching was more so. There were no picture books to excite the imaginations of Mao and his classmates, no simple stories to capture the attention of their young minds. Instead, they were subjected to a system of rote-learning, which had been handed down almost unchanged for two thousand years and whose guiding principle was to keep knowledge the preserve of the elite by making it as difficult as possible to acquire.

The first schoolbook with which the children of Mao's generation were presented was the *Three Character Classic*, so-called because each of its 356 lines contains three Chinese characters. Written in the eleventh century to introduce young people to Confucian ideas, it opens with the lines:

> Men at their birth are by nature radically good,
> In this, all approximate, but in practice widely diverge.

To which a fifteenth-century commentator adds:

> This is the commencement of a course of education and explains first
> principles . . . That which heaven produces is called 'man'; that which

it confers is called 'nature'; the possession of correct moral principle
is called 'goodness' . . . This refers to man at his birth. The wise
and the simple, the upright and the vicious, all agree in their nature,
radically resembling each other, without any difference. But when
their knowledge has expanded, their dispositions and endowments
all vary . . . thus perverting the correct principles of their virtuous
nature . . . The superior man alone has the merit of supporting rectitude. He does not allow the youthful buddings of his natural
character to become vitiated.

That is heavy going for eight-year-olds in any circumstances. But to
the strain of mastering such abstruse metaphysical notions was
added another, more fundamental obstacle.

The textbooks were printed on flimsy paper in large characters,
five pairs of lines to a page. First the teacher would summon the
pupil to his table and make the child repeat after him the lines he
was to learn, until he had them off by heart. Then the next child
would come up, until the whole class had been seen, and each boy
had returned to his desk to practice what he had learned while
tracing, on thin slips of paper, the shapes of the corresponding
characters. But not in silence:

After [being] informed what sounds to utter, each [pupil] spends his
time in bawling out the characters at the top of his voice to make sure
he is not idle, as well as to let the teacher hear whether the sounds
have been correctly caught. When the lesson has been 'learned', that
is when the scholar is able to howl it off exactly as the master
pronounced it, he stands with his back to the teacher and repeats (or
'backs') the lesson in a loud sing-song voice until he reaches the end
of his task, or the end of what he remembers, when his voice suddenly
drops from its high pitch like a June beetle that has struck a dead wall.

As each one practised in his own time, the result was an incomprehensible cacophony. Incomprehensible, not merely to others but
also to themselves. For the meanings of Chinese characters are, in
most cases, not immediately apparent from their form. The teacher
did not explain what any of the lines meant: he merely required his
pupils to be able to reproduce, singly or as blocks of text, the characters they had learned and the sounds they represented.

Altogether six books had to be memorised in this way. After the
Three Character Classic came the *Book of Names*, which lists in an arbitrary and unbroken sequence the 454 permitted Chinese surnames;

the *Thousand Character Classic*, written in the sixth century, composed of a thousand characters, no two of which are the same; the *Odes for Children*, on the importance of study and literary pursuits; the *Xiaoqing*, or *Filial Classic*, which is ascribed to Confucius himself and dates back at least to the fourth century; and the *Xiaoxue*, or *Filial Learning*, which sets out in exhaustive detail the duties of each member of the Confucian family and state.

It was like asking a child in Britain or America, speaking only English, to learn by heart a sizeable part of the Old Testament in Greek. The result was that many Chinese completed their schooling without ever learning to read or knowing the meanings of more than a handful of characters.

For two years, until Mao was about ten, he spent his days from sunrise to dusk memorising, copying and reciting moralistic phrases like, 'Diligence has merit; play yields no profit', having no idea what they meant. The only respite was on festival days, which came round on average once a month, and in the three weeks' holiday when the school closed over the Chinese New Year.

Then, finally, the teacher began to work through the texts again, this time explaining their meaning.

For Mao, as for all Chinese of his generation, the importance of these texts and their commentaries, together with the Four Books – the Confucian *Analects*, the *Great Learning*, the *Doctrine of the Mean* and the works of Mencius – which he studied next, cannot be overstated. The ideas they contained, the way those ideas were formulated and the values and concepts that underpinned them, fixed the underlying pattern of Mao's thought for the rest of his life, just as surely as, in Western countries, the parameters of thought for atheists, no less than believers, are defined by Judæo-Christian values and ideas.

Learning the Classics may have been drudgery, but Mao realised early on that they were extremely useful. Confucian thought was the common currency of Chinese intellectual life, and quotations from the Master an essential weapon in argument and debate – as even Mao's father recognised after the family had been defeated in a lawsuit because of an apt Classical quotation used by their opponent.

Moreover, there were passages which, as a boy of eleven or twelve, Mao must have found exhilarating, prefiguring his lifelong exaltation of the power of the human will:

> *Men must rely on their own efforts . . .*
> *In all the world there is nothing that is impossible,*
> *It is the heart of man alone that is wanting resolution.*

The textbooks stressed, too, the importance of studying the past, another Confucian pursuit which was to stay with Mao all his life. His fascination with history may have come initially from novels like *The Romance of the Three Kingdoms* and *The Journey to the West*, whose hero, the Monkey King, had captivated thousands of generations of Chinese, but his approach to it was that set out in the *Three Character Classic*:

> *Records of rule and misrule, of the rise and fall of dynasties,*
> *Let he who studies history examine these faithful chronicles,*
> *Till he understands ancient and modern things as if before his eyes.*

More broadly, Mao drew from Confucianism three key ideas which were to prove fundamental to the whole of his later thought. These were, first, the notion that every human being, and every society, must have a moral compass; if not Confucianism, then something else which fulfils that role. The second was the primacy of right-thinking, which Confucius called 'virtue': only if a person's thoughts were right – not merely correct, but morally right – would his actions be right. Third was the importance of self-cultivation.

Mao claimed to dislike the Classics, but his fondness for quoting them belies that. His speeches in later life were packed with allusions to Confucius, to the Daoist thinker, Zhuangzi, to the Mohists and other early philosophical schools, far outnumbering those to Lenin and Marx. Theirs were the ideas with which he grew up, and which he knew better than any other. The Confucian legacy would prove at least as important to him as Marxism, and in the last years of his life it became once more ascendant.

While he was at the village school, Mao continued to help out with odd jobs on the farm and, at his father's insistence, learned how to use an abacus so that in the evenings, when he got home, he could do the daily accounts.

The family had grown. When he was two-and-a-half years old, Mao's mother had given birth to a second son, Zemin. Four other children, two boys and two girls, died at birth, but in 1903 a third brother, Zetan, survived, and soon afterwards Mao's parents adopted a baby girl, Zejian, the child of one of his paternal uncles. By 1906 there were six mouths to feed as well as the hired labour. So, shortly after Mao's thirteenth birthday, his father decided that he must work full-time.

Mao's relations with his father were difficult, though perhaps not more so than for most Chinese boys of his time. Filial piety was a fine concept, and Mao, like all his classmates, was brought up on exemplary tales, supposed to have come down from the deepest antiquity, of sons who performed extraordinary feats to show their devotion to their parents: Dong Yong of the Han, who sold himself into slavery to raise the money to give his father a proper burial; Yu Qianlu, who ate his dying father's excrement in the hope that the old man's life might be saved; and many others still more far-fetched. In theory, a father had the right to put to death an unfilial son. But in practice, all this was honoured in the breach.

'The term "filial" is misleading, and we should not be deceived by it,' wrote an American missionary towards the end of the nine-teenth-century. 'Of all the people of whom we have any knowledge, the sons of the Chinese are the most unfilial, disobedient to parents and pertinacious in having their own way from the time they are able to make known their wants.'

That was certainly so in Mao's case. While he accused his father of being hot-tempered, miserly and excessively strict, frequently beating himself and his brothers, even his own account makes clear that the blame was not all on one side:

> My father invited many guests to his home, and while they were present a dispute arose between the two of us. My father denounced me before the whole group, calling me lazy and useless. This infuri-ated me. I cursed him and left the house. My mother ran after me and tried to persuade me to return. My father also pursued me, cursing at the same time that he commanded me to come back. I reached the edge of a pond and threatened to jump in if he came any nearer . . . My father insisted that I apologise and kow-tow as a sign of submission. I agreed to give a one-knee kow-tow if he would promise not to beat me.

Mao neglected to mention that it was against every rule of pro-priety for a thirteen-year-old to argue with his father before guests, and the family must have lost much face as a result.

Years afterwards, Mao portrayed such experiences as teaching him the value of rebellion against authority: 'I learned that when I defended my rights by open rebellion my father relented, but when I remained weak and submissive he only beat me more.'

Yet what comes across most strongly is the essential ordinariness of it all. Mao's mother, whom he loved deeply – a kind woman, generous and sympathetic and ever ready to share what she had – trying to make peace. His father, angry and hurt, but wanting somehow to retrieve the situation. And Mao himself, recalcitrant but also wanting a way out. Hardly an untypical relationship between parents and a teenage child.

As Mao grew older, however, the atmosphere at home soured. His father perpetually nagged and found fault with him, and he became increasingly alienated. Then came the fiasco of his marriage. At the age of fourteen, his parents betrothed him, in keeping with custom, to a girl six years older than himself, the daughter of another peasant. She would be an extra pair of hands to work in the fields and, in time, would assure the family's posterity. Gifts were exchanged, the bride-price paid – no small matter in those days, when a marriage portion could amount to a family's annual income – and the young woman, Miss Luo, moved into the family home. But Mao refused to go along with the arrangement. By his own account, he never slept with her, he 'gave little thought to her' and did not consider her to be his wife. Shortly afterwards, he compounded his offence by leaving home and going to live with a friend, an unemployed law student.

Mao is oddly reticent about this episode. His father should have been furious, not only because of the money wasted but because of the shame brought on the family by such egregious flouting of social convention. Yet he says nothing of the arguments and bitter recriminations that might have been expected to follow. Nor is it known what happened to Miss Luo. One account suggests that she remained in Mao's father's household, perhaps to become the older man's concubine. Whether for this or other reasons, Mao's mother eventually left the family home in Shaoshan to live instead with her brother's people in her native village in Xiangxiang.

When she died, ten years later, after a long illness, Mao gave vent to his bitterness over these events in an emotional oration at her funeral, in which the sole reference to his father was the cryptic line: '[Mother's] hatred for lack of rectitude resided in the last of the three bonds.' The last of the 'three bonds' is that between husband and wife. That Mao should have made this charge at the funeral ceremony, before his father and all their relatives, testified to extraordinary depths of hostility and unwillingness to forgive. Interviewed in the 1930's in Bao'an by the American journalist, Edgar Snow, he said of his father, 'I learned to hate him', a statement of such enormity that when Snow's book was published in Chinese, that phrase was edited out.

Mao's opposition to the marriage his parents had arranged may have been due partly to suspicion that his father wanted to tie him to the land, and to a life of rural drudgery which he had come to loathe. From then on he showed a growing determination to strike out on his own. He started studying again, this time at a private school in the village run by an elderly scholar who was a clansman, and shortly after his fifteenth birthday, told his father he no longer wished to be apprenticed at Xiangtan. He wanted to enrol at junior middle school instead.

In this, as in much else, he eventually had his way. What followed showed a side of his father for which, in later life, Mao gave him little credit.

Where the older man consistently underestimated his son's strength of character and stubbornness, so Mao failed to recognise that behind the skinflint exterior there dwelt a parent's pride. Implicit in Confucian thought is the notion of a continuum between the generations. A man counts his life a success if his children succeed; their success in turn brings glory to himself and to his ancestors. Mao's father may have been uneducated, but he recognised that Mao was, in his own words, 'the family scholar', and alone had a chance to succeed beyond the narrow confines of their native village.

For most of the next ten years, the father whom Mao portrayed as an avaricious, tight-fisted tyrant, blinkered by the narrow prejudices of his class, paid his school fees and living expenses, and continued to do so even when it became clear that his son had no intention of returning home permanently and would therefore bring him no practical advantage.

A generation earlier, such repeated challenges to parental

authority would not have been tolerated. But China was changing. Even in remote Shaoshan, the old immutable ways were crumbling.

Change was wrought by internal decay and by foreign pressure. In the century-and-a-half since the Emperor Qianlong had dismissed King George III's request for trade facilities with the contemptuous words, 'China has . . . no need of the manufactures of outside barbarians', the balance of power in the world had altered. China had stagnated, its wealth haemorrhaging away in bloody rebellions and civil unrest. Europe, through the Industrial Revolution, developed undreamed-of power and irresistible pressures for expansion. Conflict between the two was inevitable. In 1842 came the First Opium War, in which Britain acquired Hong Kong, and foreign settlement was permitted for the first time in Shanghai and four other Treaty ports. In the Second Opium War, in 1860, British and French troops marched on Beijing and burned to the ground the Emperor's Summer Palace. Foreign privileges expanded to include the right of residence in the capital itself.

But not in Hunan. Of all the Emperor's subjects, the Hunanese were the most conservative and the most virulently hostile to outsiders. '[They] seem to be a distinct type of the Chinese race [and] . . . appear to trust no other provincial in the Empire', one early traveller related, 'and from all I can see and hear, this feeling is thoroughly reciprocated.' The Prince Regent, Prince Gong, called them 'turbulent and pugnacious'. Hunan's people boasted openly that 'no Manchu ever conquered *them*'. To foreigners, it was 'the closed province'. When the English missionary, Griffith John, arrived outside the walls of the capital, Changsha, in 1891, he was stoned by the mob. 'Like the Forbidden City at Beijing and the kingdom of Tibet,' he wrote afterwards, 'it is one of the few places left in the whole world which no foreigner may presume to enter. It is perhaps the most intensely anti-foreign city in the whole of China, a feeling kept up by the literati with the full sympathy of the officials.' Yet the early travellers were also struck by 'the keenness of the people' and their 'stubborn disposition', in contrast to the 'disheartening apathy' found in other parts of China.

Already in the eighteenth century the Jesuits regarded Hunan as the most impenetrable part of China, a place 'where persecution is most to be feared'. More recently, in Mao's grandfather's time, Hunan had held firm against the Taiping Rebellion, which devastated eight provinces and claimed 20 million lives. Changsha withstood a siege lasting eighty days, and afterwards called itself 'the City of the Iron Gates'. The resistance was not out of loyalty to the throne, but rather because Changsha's elite saw the Taipings' Christian-inspired teachings as heretical to Confucianism. A Hunanese viceroy, Zeng Guofan, who became one of Mao's childhood heroes, defeated the Taiping forces. Another Hunanese, Hong Tachuan, was one of the two main Taiping leaders.

'Independence and aloofness have long been characteristic of the Hunanese,' one writer noted at the turn of the century. 'Certain intellectual qualities have tended to make them marked men.' The province produced a disproportionate number of high imperial officials and an equally large number of reformers and revolutionaries.

The Chinese Empire's reaction to the foreigners at its gates was initially to do nothing. But then, in the 1870s, the so-called self-strengthening movement began. Under the slogan, 'Western function, Chinese essence', reformers argued that if the country had access to modern weapons, it could repel the invaders and preserve unchanged its Confucian way of life. That was seen to have failed when China was again humiliatingly defeated in 1895 and, to add insult to injury, not by a Western power but by fellow Asians, the Japanese, who until then had been regarded contemptuously as dwarves. Three years later an attempt to reform the imperial system, initiated by the young Emperor Guangxu, was crushed by conservatives led by the Empress Dowager. It was assumed abroad that China would be partitioned by the Powers. The issue was debated in London in the House of Commons, and in 1898 Hunan, along with the rest of the Yangtse Valley, was declared part of the British sphere of influence. Then came the Boxer Rebellion, last spasm of a moribund regime. To Chinese progressives and foreigners alike, the old order was dead. It only remained to be cut down.

Little of this reached Shaoshan. News was exchanged in the teahouses, and there was a noticeboard, surmounted by an awning, where official proclamations were posted. Traders came and went through the nearby port of Xiangtan from Canton, Chongqing in Sichuan and Wuhan on the Yangtse, bringing with them, as in medieval Europe, the gossip of the roads. Yet the peasants heard only vague rumours of the Boxers, and nothing at all of the menace weighing down on China from without. Even the death of the Emperor in 1908 did not become known in the village until nearly two years after it occurred.

Mao first became aware of his country's predicament when he was about fourteen through a book he borrowed from one of his cousins, called *Words of Warning to an Affluent Age*, written shortly before the Sino-Japanese War by a Shanghai comprador named Zheng Guanying. It urged the introduction of Western technology to China. Its descriptions of telephones, steamships and railways, things beyond the understanding of a village which knew nothing of electricity and where the only power came from draught animals and human brawn, fired Mao's imagination. He was then working full-time on the farm. The book, he said later, was instrumental in deciding him to stop farm work and start studying again.

Zheng Guanying denounced the treatment of Chinese by foreigners in the treaty ports. He advocated parliamentary democracy, a constitutional monarchy, Western methods of education and economic reforms.

But these ideas made less impression on Mao than a pamphlet he came across a few months later, which described China's dismemberment by the Powers. Nearly thirty years on, he still remembered the opening sentence: 'Alas, China will be subjugated!' It told how Japan had occupied Korea and the Chinese island of Taiwan, and of China's loss of suzerainty in Indochina and Burma. Mao's reaction was that of millions of patriotic young Chinese. 'After I read this,' he recalled, 'I felt depressed about the future of my country and began to realise it was the duty of all the people to help save it.'

The other major influence on Mao at this time was the growth of banditry and internal unrest as the Qing Empire decayed.

Tales of rebels, like the 108 heroes of Liangshanpo, in the novel, *Water Margin*, and of secret societies and sworn brotherhoods, pledged to right wrongs and protect the poor, had entranced him since he was first able to read. Most of his classmates at Shaoshan devoured the stories too, hiding them under copies of the Classics when their teacher walked by, discussing them with the old men of the village and reading and rereading them until they knew them by heart. Mao recalled being 'much influenced by such books, read at an impressionable age', and he never lost his love of them.

Much more important in shaping his ideas, however, were the food riots that broke out in Changsha in the spring of 1910, an event which Mao said later, 'influenced my whole life'. The previous year, the Yangtse had burst its banks twice, flooding much of the riceland of northern Hunan and Hubei, on the second occasion so suddenly that 'people were obliged to flee, being unable to rescue even their clothes'. The British consul in Changsha, citing treaty rights, opposed the provincial Governor's proposal to limit rice exports to other provinces. So did some of the leading gentry, who saw the famine as an opportunity to make fat profits by cornering the market. By early April the price of rice reached 80 copper cash a pint, three times the normal level. Reports from the interior of the province spoke of 'people eating bark and selling children, of corpses piling up along the sides of the road, and of cannibalism'.

On April 11, a water-carrier and his wife who lived near the city's South Gate committed suicide. In the words of one contemporary account:

> The man carried water all day and his wife and children begged, and still they could not get enough to keep the children from being hungry, for the price of rice was so high. One day the woman and children came back after begging all day, and there was not rice enough for the children's supper. She built a fire and got some mud and made some mudcakes and told the children to cook them for their supper. Then she killed herself. When the man came home he found his wife dead and the little children trying to cook their mud cakes for supper. It was more than he could stand and so he killed himself too.

The suicide triggered an uprising which the Japanese consul at the time described as 'no different from a war'. A mob gathered by the South Gate, seized the Police Commissioner, and then, instigated, it later transpired, by arch-conservative xenophobes among the Changsha gentry, began a wild night and day of burning and looting directed mainly at foreign-owned targets – among them, foreign steamship companies, blamed for sending rice downriver and aggravating the grain shortage; the foreign operated customs service; foreign missions; and Western-style schools which disseminated foreign learning. Not until next morning did the rioters, now numbering some 30,000, remember their grievance against the Chinese authorities and turn their attention to the Governor's yamen, which they burned to the ground. Another seventeen buildings, most of them either occupied by or having connections with foreigners, were totally destroyed, and many more vandalised.

The Powers reacted swiftly. Although no foreigner was harmed, Britain sent gunboats up the Xiang River to bring out its citizens, and the United States alerted its Asiatic Fleet, based in Amoy. Later a large indemnity was imposed.

But it was the Qing government's response that was most revealing. The Governor and other officials were dismissed. Several of the gentry, including two Hanlin scholars, holders of imperial China's highest literary distinction, were impeached for fomenting the unrest and subjected to what was termed 'the extreme penalty', which turned out to mean little more than being degraded in rank. But two of the poor of the city, 'unfortunate wretches' as one foreign resident called them, a barber and a boatman, alleged to have been among the leaders of the riot, were taken through the streets in wicker cages to the city wall, where they were decapitated and their heads exposed on lamp-posts.

For days, Mao and his friends talked of nothing else:

> It made a deep impression on me. Most of the other students sympathised with the 'insurrectionists', but only from an observer's point of view. They did not understand that it had any relation to their own lives. They were merely interested in it as an exciting incident. I never forgot it. I felt that there with the rebels were ordinary people like my own family, and I deeply resented the injustice of the treatment given to them.

A few weeks later, another incident occurred at a small town called Huashi, about twenty-five miles south of Xiangtan. A dispute broke out between a local landlord and members of the Gelaohui (the Elder Brother Society), a secret brotherhood with branches throughout Hunan and the neighbouring provinces. The landlord took his case to court and, in Mao's words, 'as he was powerful . . . easily bought a decision favourable to himself'. But instead of submitting, the members of the brotherhood withdrew to a mountain fastness called Liushan and built a stronghold there.

They wore yellow head-dresses and carried three-cornered yellow flags. The provincial government sent troops against them, and the redoubt was destroyed. Three men were captured, including their leader, known as Pang the Millstone Maker. Under torture they confessed that they had been instructed in the methods and incantations used by the Boxers, which they had believed would make them invulnerable. Pang was beheaded. But in the eyes of the students, Mao wrote, 'he was a hero, for all sympathised with the revolt'.

Mao's views, however, were not yet as clear-cut as these statements make it appear. Early the following year another rice shortage arose, this time in Shaoshan itself. Mao's father continued to buy grain and send it for sale in the city, aggravating the shortage. Eventually one of the consignments was seized by hungry villagers. His father was furious. Mao did not sympathise with him but 'thought the villagers' method was wrong too'.

By this time Mao was enrolled at the junior middle school which he had bullied and cajoled his father into letting him attend. It was in the neighbouring county of Xiangxiang, where his mother's family lived, and was a 'modern' establishment with Western-inspired teaching methods, opened a few years earlier as part of the Qing court's belated endeavours to come to terms with foreign learning after the defeat of the Boxers. Mao, on his first journey outside his native Shaoshan, was overwhelmed:

> I had never before seen so many children together. Most of them were sons of landlords, wearing expensive clothes; very few peasants could afford to send their children to such a school. I was more poorly dressed than the others. I owned only one decent coat-and-trousers suit. Gowns were not worn by students, but only by the teachers, and none but 'foreign devils' wore foreign clothes.

Dongshan Upper Primary School, as the place was officially named, had in earlier times been a literary academy. It was surrounded by a high stone wall with thick black-laquered double doors, reached by a balustraded white stone bridge across a moat. On a hillside nearby stood a seven-storeyed white pagoda.

Mao paid 1,400 copper cash (equivalent to about one silver dollar, or five English shillings) for five months' board, lodging, books and tuition fees. To attend such a school was an exceptional privilege: not one child in two hundred at that time had access to education of this level. In these elite surroundings, the unmannered, gangling youth from Shaoshan, older and taller than most of his classmates and with an accent different from theirs, was given a hard time. 'Many of the richer students despised me because usually I was wearing my ragged coat and trousers,' Mao remembered. 'I was also disliked because I was not a native of Xiangxiang . . . I felt spiritually very depressed.'

It took all the fortitude acquired in his clashes with his father to overcome this hostility, which Mao himself frequently made worse by the arrogance, mulishness, and sheer childish pig-headedness with which he stuck to his guns when he thought he was right. But eventually he made friends, among them Xiao San, who later became a writer under the name Emi Siao. He was also close to a cousin, one of his maternal uncles' children, who had started at the school a year before him.

Despite his problems, Mao made good progress and his teachers liked him. It quickly became clear that his inclinations were literary rather than scientific. History was his favourite subject, and he read every book he could about the two great founding dynasties of modern China, the Qin and the Han, which flourished around the time of Christ. He learned to write Classical essays, and developed a love of poetry which was to become one of the lasting pleasures of his life. A quarter of a century later, he could still quote the words of a Japanese song, celebrating victory in the Russo-Japanese War, which the music teacher, who had studied there, used to sing to them:

> *The sparrow sings, the nightingale dances,*
> *And the green fields are lovely in the spring.*
> *The pomegranate flowers crimson, the willows green-leafed,*
> *And there is a new picture.*

Japan had become the inspiration for all those who made up what the newspapers called 'Young China', the reformers and intellectuals who saw their country's salvation in a modernisation movement on the lines of Japan's espousal of foreign ideas after the Meiji restoration. By its defeat of China in 1895, Japan had forced them to face the reality of their country's weakness. By its defeat of Russia ten years later, Japan had shown that an Asian army could defeat a European one. For China, the latter victory would prove a mixed blessing, since Japan replaced Russia as the dominant power in Manchuria. But to young men of Mao's generation, what mattered was that the yellow race had proved it could defeat the white.

'At that time,' he said, 'I knew and felt the beauty of Japan, and felt something of her pride and might in this song of her victory over Russia.'

Starting in the 1890s, thousands of Chinese had made their way to Tokyo to soak up the new Western learning. Among the most influential were Kang Youwei and Liang Qichao, the architects of the Emperor Guangxu's abortive reform movement, who had fled into exile there after the reforms were crushed. Kang's great contribution to the modernisation debate had been to redefine Confucianism to make it forward-looking and therefore compatible with reform, instead of perpetually harking back to a supposed golden age in the remote past. Liang, a Hunanese, took Charles Darwin's thesis, 'the survival of the fittest', and applied it to China's national struggle against the encircling Powers. He argued that China had to modernise in order to survive.

Kang Youwei and Liang Qichao were Young China's idols. Mao's cousin gave him two books about the reform movement, one by Liang himself. 'I read and reread those books until I knew them by heart,' he wrote. 'I worshipped Kang Youwei and Liang Qichao.'

As he turned seventeen, Mao still supported the imperial system: 'I considered the Emperor as well as most officials to be honest, good and clever men,' he declared. 'They only needed the help of Kang Youwei's reforms.'

That was about to change.

CHAPTER TWO

Revolution

At around noon on October 9, 1911, a partly-completed bomb exploded in a house owned by a Chinese army officer in the Russian concession at Hankou, the main commercial city of central China, two days downriver from Changsha. The man who had been making it, Sun Wu, was the youthful leader of the Forward Together Society, a splinter group of the Tongmenghui, the secret Revolutionary Alliance led by the Cantonese anti-monarchist, Sun Yat-sen.

Sun Wu's friends succeeded in getting him to the safety of a Japanese hospital. But the concession police searched the house, and found revolutionary flags and proclamations and a list of activists. The Qing authorities sprang into action. Thirty-two people were arrested and, next day at dawn, three of the leaders were executed. The Manchu Viceroy, Ruizheng, telegraphed Beijing: 'Now all . . . is peaceful and quiet. This case was broken so early that the area was not harmed.'

The executions proved a fatal mistake. Rumours spread among the Han troops garrisoned across the river at Wuchang that the Viceroy was planning wholesale reprisals against all who were not of Manchu blood. That evening an engineering battalion mutinied. Officers who resisted were shot. Two infantry regiments joined them; then an artillery regiment. The heaviest fighting, which took several hundred lives, was around the Viceroy's yamen, which was defended by a machine-gun emplacement. In the early hours of the morning, Ruizheng fled aboard a Chinese gunboat, leaving

Wuchang in the insurgents' hands. Years of revolutionary agitation had finally paid off. Yet victory, when it came, was fiercer and bloodier than its architects had planned. The white flags of the rebels, edged with red, bore the legend, '*Xin Han, Mie Man*' – 'Long Live the Han, Exterminate the Manchu'. The Manchu 30th Regiment was virtually wiped out in a racial massacre. A civilian pogrom followed. Three days afterwards, a local missionary counted eight hundred Manchu corpses lying in the streets, 'fifty being heaped together outside one gate alone'.

Revolutionary proclamations appeared, inflaming feelings further. The 'descendants of Holy Han', one asserted, were 'sleeping on brushwood and eating gall' under the yoke of a northern, nomadic tribe. Another diatribe warned:

> The Manchu government has been tyrannical, cruel, insane and unconscious, inflicting heavy taxations and stripping the people of their marrow . . . Recollect that when the Manchus first entered the Chinese domain, cities full of men and women were put to the sword without exception . . . To leave the wrongs of our forefathers unavenged would shame us who are gentlemen. Therefore all our brothers should . . . help the revolutionary army in the extirpation of such barbarous aliens . . . Today's opportunity is bestowed on us by Great Heaven. If we do not seize and make use of it, until what time shall we wait then?

The outside world reserved judgement. In London, *The Times* reported that most educated Chinese unreservedly supported the revolution, adding snootily: 'Little sympathy is expressed for the corrupt and effete Manchu dynasty with its Eunuchs and other barbaric surroundings.'

But there was little sense that history was in the making, that the obscure events unfolding in Wuchang were the harbingers of millennial change for the oldest and most populous of the world's nations. No one predicted the imminent collapse of a system of rule that had endured without interruption since pre-Christian times, longer than any other in history. Indeed the prevailing view then, and for several weeks after, was that the imperial house would rally, and as had happened so often in the past, the rebellion would eventually be put down.

Chinese bonds weakened slightly, but financial markets took the view that the movement would probably be beneficial to foreign commerce with China. Even in the English-language newspapers in Shanghai, first reports of the revolution had to compete for space with the Italian bombardment of Tripoli; the assassination of Prince Troubetzkoy by a student in Novocherkassk; the illness of Prince Luitpold, the ninety-year-old Regent of Bavaria, who had caught a chill while out stag-hunting; and 'the most brilliant wedding of the year, at St Peter's, Eaton Square, between Earl Percy and Lady Gordon Lennox'.

Only in Beijing itself was the true gravity of the situation recognised. Guards were doubled outside the palaces of the Prince Regent and other dignitaries; imperial cavalry patrolled the streets; and as reports came in of Manchu families in the provinces being hunted down and killed by revolutionary mobs, Manchu women in the capital abandoned their elaborate hair ornaments and characteristic high-soled shoes and started wearing Chinese dress.

Mao was in Changsha when these events occurred. Six months earlier he had come by riverboat from Xiangtan, carrying with him a letter of recommendation from one of his teachers, who had helped him convince his father that he should enrol at a secondary school in the capital for students from Xiangxiang county.

He had heard before setting out, he said later, that it was 'a magnificent place', with 'many people, numerous schools and the yamen of the Governor', but his first sight of the city as the little steamer came slowly downstream must have exceeded all his imaginings. A 'perpendicular wall, of noble grey-stone blocks' reared up from the water's edge, fifty feet thick at its base and more than two miles long, with a forest of junks before it. Inland it continued for eight miles more, with ramparts 40 feet high, wide enough at the top for three carriages to ride abreast, encircling the city like a medieval fortress, which indeed it was. On each quarter, the wall was pierced by two massive gates, guarded by militiamen wearing dark blue turbans, short military cloaks with red cloud-pattern collars and brightly-coloured facings, wide, loose sleeves, and cotton trousers tied at the calf. They were armed with a motley collection of spears, halberds, tridents, two-handed swords, muskets, flintlock and even matchlock guns.

Within lay a warren of grey-tiled roofs and 'dark tunnel-like streets, burrowing away into the city's heart', paved with granite slabs, often no more than six feet wide, and reeking with squalour and bad smells, 'all the encumbrances and filth of too much living like spawn', as one Western resident put it. But, hidden from view behind windowless street-walls, were also splendid mansions, where the great officials lived among 'flower-decked courtyards, gracious reception halls with stately blackwood furniture and wall paintings on silk scrolls', and two immense Confucian temples, with curved yellow-tiled roofs and vast teak columns, surrounded by ancient cypress trees.

In the commercial district, during business hours, the wooden shopfronts were removed, so that the shops opened directly on to the street, and bamboo matting was stretched over poles between the roofs, turning parts of the city into an immense covered arcade. Long hanging wooden shop-signs, written in gold characters on a black lacquer ground, greeted prospective customers and advertised what was on sale.

There were no bicycles, no motor-cars, no rickshaws. The wealthy used sedan chairs. For everyone else the main form of transport, whether for people or goods, was the humble wheel-barrow. All day long the city resounded with the deafening squeals of ungreased axles, as labourers hauled loads of coal, salt, antimony and opium; firecrackers, calico and linen; and medicinal supplies of foxglove, monkswood, and rhubarb, to the junks along the river. Water was carried in on men's backs, in buckets slung from bamboo poles, from the 'Sand Spring' by the South Gate. Pedlars cried their wares, or made their presence known by shaking wooden rattles and bells. The sweetmeat-seller had a tiny gong and chanted, in a thick Hunanese accent:

> *They cure the deaf and heal the lame,*
> *Preserve the teeth of the aged dame!*

Daoist monks, in dark blue robes, and Buddhists, wearing saffron, walked in procession, chanting prayers for the sick. Beggars, blind or hideously disfigured, sat at the roadside asking for alms, and each year extorted 'squeeze' from the householders, promising in return to stay a respectable distance from their homes.

At dusk, the wooden boards were replaced on the shopfronts. The pious bowed three times, to heaven, earth and man, and placed glowing sticks of incense over their doors to protect them from evil during the night. The city gates were closed, each secured by a huge beam which took three men to lift. There was electricity at the Governor's yamen and in the Western-style houses on an island in the river where the foreign consuls lived. But in the rest of the city, the only light was from the sputtering wicks of small oil-lamps provided by the street guilds. Later, the district gates were locked too, isolating the different wards of the city. After that, the only sound was the sharp crack of the constable's stick striking a long bamboo gong as he beat out the watches of the night.

Mao had at first been doubtful whether he would be able to stay in the city: 'I [was] exceedingly excited, half fearing that I would be refused entrance, hardly daring to hope that I would actually become a student in this great school.' To his surprise, he was accepted without difficulty. In the event, however, the six months he spent at the middle school did more for his political education than for his academic progress.

Changsha had been seething with anti-Manchu feeling since the rice riots the year before. Secret societies put up placards, calling in cryptic language for the Han to rise: 'All should bind their heads with a white kerchief and each should carry a sword . . . The eighteen provinces of China will be returned to the descendants of [the legendary Chinese emperor] Shen Nong.' The slogan 'Revolt and drive out the Manchus' was chalked up on walls.

That spring, soon after Mao's arrival, came news of an anti-Manchu uprising in Canton under the leadership of a Hunanese revolutionary named Huang Xing, in which seventy-two radicals had been killed. Mao read about it in the *Minli Bao* (People's Strength), which supported the revolutionary cause. It was the first newspaper he had seen, and he remembered afterwards how impressed he had been that it was so 'full of stimulating material'. Here, too, he first encountered the name of Sun Yat-sen and the Tongmenghui, then based in Japan. It inspired him to write a poster, which he put up on the school wall, calling for a new government with Sun as President, Kang Youwei as Premier and Liang Qichao, Minister of Foreign Affairs. It was, he admitted later, a 'somewhat muddled' effort: Kang and Liang were both constitutional monarchists, opposed to republican government. But Mao's new willingness to renounce the Empire, and the fact that he had been moved for the first time to try to give public expression to his political ideas, showed how a few weeks in the city had already changed his thinking.

This was demonstrated most dramatically by his attitude to the queue. At Dongshan he and the other schoolboys had ridiculed one of the teachers who had had his queue cut off while studying in Japan, and now wore a false one in its place. The 'false foreign devil', they called him. Now, Mao and one of his friends clipped off their own pigtails in a show of anti-Manchu defiance, and when others who had promised to do likewise failed to keep their word, 'my friend and I . . . assaulted them in secret and forcibly removed their queues, a total of more than ten falling victim to our shears'. Similar scenes had been taking place in schools in Changsha and Wuchang since the beginning of the year, horrifying traditionalists – who held that hair was a gift from one's parents and destroying it a violation of filial piety – no less than, for quite different reasons, the Manchu authorities.

Two other events occurred in April which helped to bring the Hunan gentry on to the revolutionaries' side. The Court announced the appointment of a cabinet, which the elite had long been demanding as a step towards constitutional government. But, to the fury of reformists, it was dominated by Manchu princes. It also became known that the government intended to nationalise the railway companies as a preliminary to accepting foreign loans to finance railroad construction, which was widely regarded as a sell-out to the Powers. These issues, Mao recalled, made the students in his school 'more and more agitated', and when in May the foreign loans were confirmed, most of the schools went on strike. With other boys of his age, he went to listen to older students making revolutionary speeches at open-air meetings out-side the city walls. 'I still remember', he wrote later, 'how one student, while making a speech, ripped off his long gown and said, "Let's hurry to get some military training and be ready to fight."' Inflammatory handbills were posted, and the situation appeared so threatening that Britain and Japan sent gunboats. By summer, a precarious calm was restored, but anti-Manchu rallies continued at the site of the former imperial examination halls. The reformist gentry gathered under the guise of holding meetings of the Wenxue Hui, the Association for Literary Studies, to discuss the dynasty's impending collapse. In neighbouring Sichuan, a full-scale rebellion broke out.

*

On Friday, October 13, a Chinese steamer arrived in Changsha, bringing the first confused reports of the rising in Wuchang. The passengers spoke of fighting between army units, of the sound of firing from the military camps, and of reports of soldiers tearing off the red facings and insignia from their black winter uniforms and putting on white armbands instead. But nobody seemed certain who was fighting whom or what the outcome was. In 1911, the Hunanese capital was linked to the outside world by a single telegraph line to Hankou and that weekend it was down. Even the officials at the governor's yamen had no way to discover what was going on.

The following Monday, the 16th, there was a run on the provincial banks, which ended only when the Governor sent fully-armed militia detachments to stand guard outside. Most schools suspended classes. The British consul, Bertram Giles, warned his legation in Beijing: 'News is scarce, wild rumours are current and great excitement prevails.' That evening, a Japanese steamer arrived from Hankou with a thousand passengers aboard, who provided detailed accounts of the revolutionaries' success. Next day, Mr Giles noted, 'a distinct change in the situation was perceptible'.

The new arrivals included emissaries from the Wuchang revolutionaries, who had come to urge fellow radicals in the Hunan garrison to speed up plans for their own mutiny. One of them visited Mao's school:

> [He] made a stirring speech, with the permission of the principal. Seven or eight students arose in the assembly and supported him with vigorous denunciation of the Manchus, and calls for action to establish the Republic. Everyone listened with complete attention. Not a sound was heard as the orator of the revolution . . . spoke before the excited students.

A few days later, Mao and a group of classmates, fired by what they had heard, decided to go to Hankou to join the revolutionary army. Their friends collected money to pay their steamer tickets. But events moved ahead of them before they could set out.

While the revolutionaries plotted, the Governor took countermeasures. The regular garrison troops, the 49th and 50th regiments, which were known to have been infiltrated by the radicals, were redeployed to other districts away from the provincial capital. The six hundred men who remained, in a barracks outside the East Gate, were ordered to surrender their ammunition. The militia, who were judged more reliable, were substantially reinforced.

The first attempt by the revolutionaries to take the city by strat-agem, on Wednesday night, failed. The men at the East Gate barracks set fire to some straw in the stables, and then demanded that the city gates be opened to allow fire-engines to pass. The militia, pleading neutrality, refused. But in the confusion, the garrison men recovered most of their ammunition, which had been locked in a nearby arsenal. As a result their next foray, on Sunday morning, turned out very differently. Mao gave his own account of what he saw that day:

> I went to borrow some [oilskin boots] from a friend in the army who was quartered outside the city. I was stopped by the garrison guards. The place had become very active, the soldiers . . . were pouring into the streets. Rebels were approaching the city . . . and fighting had begun. A big battle occurred outside the city walls . . . There was at the same time an insurrection within the city, and the gates were stormed and taken by Chinese labourers. Through one of the gates I re-entered the city. Then I stood on a high place and watched the battle, until I saw the Han flag raised over the yamen.

Even now, it makes dramatic reading. Unfortunately, so little of it is true that one might be forgiven for wondering whether Mao was there at all. There were no rebels, no battle, no insurrection and the gates were not stormed. Mr Giles, the British consul, reported drily:

> At 9.30 a.m. [I was informed] . . . that a number of the regular troops had entered the city, where they had been joined by certain repre-sentative revolutionaries and had proceeded to the Governor's yamen . . . The militia, adhering to their policy of neutrality, had refused to close the city gates [which were already open for the day]; and the Governor's bodyguard, already won over, offered no resis-tance. By 2 p.m. the whole city was in the hands of the revolutionaries without a shot having been fired, the white [rebel] flag was flying everywhere, guards with white badges on their sleeves were patrolling the streets to keep order, and the excitement of the morning subsided as quickly as it had arisen.

The discrepancies are a salutary reminder of the dangers of eyewit-ness testimony, decades after the event. Yet Mao's overblown description is hardly to be wondered at. As an excited teenager, he had been present at one of the defining moments of modern

Chinese history. As a communist leader years later, his memories were of what the day should have been, rather than what it was.

The Governor and most of his senior aides escaped. But the militia commander, whom the soldiers blamed for confiscating their ammunition, was led off to the East Gate and beheaded. Several other officials were executed near the yamen, their 'gory heads and trunks' left lying in the street.

Both in Wuchang, where the civilian revolutionary leaders were thrown into disarray by the raid on Sun Wu's bomb factory, and in Changsha, where their plans had been delayed by the Governor's countermeasures, the driving force behind the uprisings consisted of radical non-commissioned officers and rank-and-file troops. Once victory had been achieved, there was considerable confusion over who should head the new revolutionary order.

In Hubei, a brigade commander, Li Yuanhong, who had initially opposed the mutiny, agreed reluctantly to be sworn in as Military Governor. The same day he issued a proclamation renaming the country the Republic of China, little guessing that less than six months later, he would become Vice-President in Beijing and, eventually, Head of State.

The situation in Changsha was more complicated. Within hours of the uprising, the flamboyant young leader of the Hunan branch of the Forward Together Society, Jiao Dafeng, was proclaimed Military Governor, with a leading member of the city's reformist elite, Tan Yankai, as his civil counterpart. A dashing figure, who rode through the streets on horseback to wild acclamations from the populace, Jiao had close ties with Hunan's secret societies. Their leaders flocked to the provincial capital to help him consolidate his power (and to share the spoils of victory), turning the Governor's yamen, in the words of one contemporary source, into 'a sort of bandits' lair'.

This was not what Changsha's reformist gentry had anticipated. Four days after the uprising, Consul Giles reported that tensions within the ruling group had reached such a pitch that 'revolvers were drawn and bayonets fixed'. Then Jiao made the fatal error of sending his own loyal units to help the revolutionaries at Wuchang. On October 31, Jiao's deputy was ambushed outside the North Gate and decapitated, whereupon, in the consul's words, 'the soldiers rushed into the city with his head and killed Jiao in his yamen'. Jiao Dafeng was twenty-five years old. He had been Governor for just nine days.

Mao saw the two men's bodies lying in the street. Years later, he would remember their deaths as an object lesson in the perils of revolutionary enterprise. 'They were not bad men,' he said, 'and [they] had some revolutionary intentions.' They were killed, he added, because 'they were poor and represented the interests of the oppressed. The landlords and merchants were dissatisfied with them.' It was not quite that simple. Jiao's regime was too short-lived for anyone to have known what his policies might have been. But certainly the provincial elite saw him as a threat. His successor, the reformist Tan Yankai, who was sworn in as Governor later the same day, was one of their own, a Hanlin scholar from an eminent gentry family.

The situation in Changsha, and in the Yangtse Valley as a whole, remained extremely volatile. A pathetic edict, issued in the name of the six-year-old Emperor, declared:

> The whole Empire is seething. The minds of the people are perturbed ... All these things are my own fault. Hereby I announce to the world that I swear to reform . . . [In] Hubei and Hunan . . . the soldiers and people are innocent. If they return to their allegiance, I will excuse the past. Being a very small person standing at the head of my subjects, I see that my heritage is nearly falling to the ground. I regret my fault and repent greatly.

Early in November, rumours swept Hong Kong that Beijing had fallen and the imperial family been taken prisoner, provoking 'extraordinary scenes of enthusiasm'. It proved to be untrue, but residents in the capital reported that they were in 'a state of siege' and cannon were being mounted on the walls of the Forbidden City. Then came news, immediately denied, that the Emperor had fled to Manchuria. Yet at the same time there were signs that the Empire was fighting back. Only four provincial capitals were firmly in revolutionary hands. Troops loyal to the Throne counter-attacked at Hankou using German-made incendiary shells, and most of the Chinese city was burned to the ground. Soon afterwards, imperial forces seized Nanjing. Any Chinese found without a queue was summarily executed. Students who, like Mao, had sheared them off earlier in the year, now hid in terror.

With the outcome apparently hanging in the balance, Mao revived his earlier plan to join the revolutionary forces. A student army had been organised but, considering that its role was unclear, he decided to enlist instead in a unit of regular troops. Many others were doing the same. Recruitment in Hunan in the first weeks of the revolution exceeded 50,000. None the less, given the prevailing uncertainty and the violence being meted out to the losers, it was an act of no little courage. Many of the new recruits were being sent to Hankou, where the revolutionaries were under fierce attack from imperial army units. One foreign resident described the fighting there as 'possibly the bloodiest . . . that has yet taken place. Day and night now for four days the battle has been raging . . . The slaughter on both sides is terrific.' Even for those, like Mao, who remained in Changsha, life under martial law was brutal and often perilously short. Consul Giles reported: 'Brawls are continually taking place, either among the soldiers themselves or between them and the civilians . . . One man alleged to be a Manchu spy was hacked to pieces in the street by the soldiery. His head was then cut off and borne to the Governor's yamen. Another man was triced up on to a sort of triangle . . . and riddled with bullets.'

There were attempts at mutiny, and on one occasion Mao's regiment was called out to prevent several thousand rebellious troops from entering the city. A senior Chinese commander complained that the men were totally without discipline: 'They regard destruction as meritorious action and disorder as correct conduct. Insolence is equated with equality and coercion with freedom.' As anarchy loomed, the American Legation in Beijing ordered its citizens to leave Hunan until stability was restored.

The company to which Mao belonged was quartered at the Court of Justice, which had been set up in the former provincial assembly building. The new recruits spent much of their time doing chores for the officers and fetching water from the Sand Spring by the South Gate. Many were illiterate, 'chair-bearers, ruffians and beggars', whose idea of soldiering was to assume the poses of military figures in traditional Chinese opera, as one contemporary source witheringly put it. Mao made himself popular by writing letters for them. 'I knew something about books,' he said later, 'and they respected my "great learning".' For the first time in his life he came into contact with workers, two of whom, a miner and an ironsmith, he particularly liked.

But there were limits to his revolutionary zeal. 'Being a student,' he explained, '[I] could not condescend to carrying [water]', as the other soldiers did. Instead, he paid pedlars to carry it for him, demonstrating precisely the same scholarly elitism that he would spend his later years condemning. And while some of the men in his regiment vowed to take a reduced monthly food allowance of two dollars until the revolution triumphed, Mao took the full seven dollars. After paying for food and water-carrying, he spent whatever was left on newspapers, of which he became an avid reader, a habit that he retained all his life.

In early December, two events occurred which signalled the end of Manchu resistance. Imperial troops abandoned Nanjing, their last major southern stronghold. And Yuan Shikai, former Viceroy of Zhili and the leading military power-broker in north China, whom the Court had summoned to act as interim Premier, approved a ceasefire at Wuchang.

In Changsha, the news provoked another orgy of forcible queue-cutting, this time carried out by troops. The British consul, Bertram Giles, was outraged:

I protested strongly [to] . . . the authorities, [telling them] that one of the first duties of a government was to preserve the public peace, and that if they allowed the soldiery to commit assault wholesale with impunity, then they could no longer lay claim to the title of Government but were merely an anarchical faction.

Others, with a better sense of humour, saw the farcical side:

Farmers and peasants . . . came in from the countryside to the city gates, carrying their huge loads of rice or vegetables, or trundling their heavy wheelbarrows. The guards rushed out, seized every man's queue, and hacked it off with a sword or clipped it off with huge scissors. For many a man it was like parting with a limb to lose the queue which he had brushed and braided so painstakingly since early boyhood. We saw some of them on their knees, kowtowing to the guards as they pled for respite. Others actually fought the soldiers and many tried to run away . . . But before the week was out, all the city-dwellers and many of the villagers of central China were largely rid of this mark of Manchu control.

Ever wary of the winds of political change, many at first kept a false queue coiled under their turbans, ready to let down should the Manchus return. But that was not to be. On New Year's Day, 1912, the veteran revolutionary, Sun Yat-sen, was sworn in at Nanjing as China's first President. To mark the occasion, the authorities in Changsha held a military parade: 'Bugles were blown, flags were waved, bands played and the soldiers sang lustily . . . Every shop displayed a coloured flag. Two border strips of red with a central strip of yellow.' There was talk of sending an expeditionary force to Beijing to make Yuan Shikai and the northern military accept Sun's leadership, and mass meetings were held to oppose Yuan's nomination as Head of State. But, as Mao remembered it, 'just as the Hunanese were preparing to move into action, Sun Yat-sen and Yuan Shikai came to an agreement, the scheduled war was called off.' On February 12, the Emperor abdicated, and two days later Sun stepped down in Yuan's favour.

Mao remained in the army until the spring. Then the cost of maintaining the swollen ranks of the revolutionary forces imposed wholesale demobilisation. 'Thinking the revolution was over,' Mao said later, 'I . . . decided to return to my books. I had been a soldier for half a year.'

CHAPTER THREE

Lords of Misrule

For a few glorious months, China abandoned itself to a turbulent confusion of new fashions, new ideas, new enthusiasms and new hopes, as the dead hand of dynastic orthodoxy was suddenly thrown off. Hunan's new Governor, Tan Yankai, was by his own lights a liberal, opposed equally to imperialism and to centralised control by Beijing. Under his regime, opium-growing was stopped and importation of the drug prohibited. New, independent courts were established in every district. For a time, a free press was permitted, to the dismay of the British consul, who protested vehemently at its outbursts against the Powers. The provincial administration encouraged the development of local industry to try to check the outflow of funds abroad, and the education budget tripled, financed partly by punitive land taxes imposed on conservative gentry families regarded as pro-Manchu. 'Modern schools sprang up like bamboo shoots after the spring rain,' Mao remembered. So did wine-shops, theatres and brothels. Even foreigners in Changsha caught the spirit of the times. 'The new men really do want to be good rulers,' one wrote, '[and] they have on the whole done very well.'

As always in periods of revolutionary flux, the first changes were symbolic. Teenage girls started to bob their hair, and to appear in public unchaperoned. Their mothers timidly approached foreign doctors to ask whether anything could be done for their crippled lily feet. The demise of the queue opened an exotic new world for shaven Chinese heads. 'People are wearing billycocks, bishop's hats, blue velveteen jockey caps, anything they can lay their hands on,' commented one bemused correspondent. 'The old red turban with its round button [has been] . . . forbidden by revolutionary law, for the button was the mark of honour under the Manchu rule . . . Felt hats, cotton hats, abound, but the funniest sight of all is to see a company drilled by a captain wearing a silk top hat.'

Bizarre and confused it may have been, but it spoke of a sea change in the public mood. Large numbers of Chinese for the first time began to question traditional values and behaviour. The slow accretion of foreign influences, kept at bay by the conservative gentry who took their cue from the Court, abruptly became a flood, which in the course of the next decade would provoke an intellectual ferment unmatched in Chinese history.

To Mao, eighteen years old and newly demobilised, it was a time of muddle, uncertainty and endless possibilities, which he seized with all the naive optimism of youth:

> I did not know exactly what I wanted to do. An advertisement for a police school caught my eye and I registered for entrance to it. Before I was examined, however, I read an advertisement of a soap-making 'school'. No tuition was required, board was furnished and a small salary was promised. It was an attractive and inspiring advertisement. It told of the great social benefits of soap-making, how it would enrich the country and enrich the people. I changed my mind about the police school and decided to become a soap-maker. I paid my dollar registration fee here also.
>
> Meanwhile a friend of mine had become a law student and he urged me to enter his school. I also read an alluring advertisement of this law school, which promised many wonderful things. It promised to teach students all about law in three years and guaranteed that at the end of this time they would instantly become mandarins . . . I wrote to my family, repeated all the promises of the advertisement and asked them to send me tuition money . . .
>
> Another friend counselled me that the country was in economic war and what was most needed were economists who could build up the nation's economy. His argument prevailed and I spent another dollar to register in [a] commercial middle school . . . I actually enrolled there and was accepted . . . [But then] I read [an advertisement] describing the charms of a higher commercial public school . . . I decided it would be better to become a commercial expert there, paid my dollar and registered.

The higher commercial school turned out to be a disaster. Although his father, pleased that he had finally seen sense and was embarking on a potentially profitable business career, provided his tuition fees readily enough, Mao discovered that most of the courses were taught in English, of which he knew little more than the alphabet. After a month, he left in disgust.

The next of what he would later call these 'scholastic adventures' took him to the First Provincial Middle School, a large, well-respected establishment which specialised in Chinese literature and history. He came top in the entrance exam, and for a while it seemed he had found what he was looking for. But after a few months he left this school, too, citing its 'limited curriculum' and 'objectionable regulations', and instead spent the autumn and winter of 1912 studying on his own in the city's newly opened public library. By his own account he was 'very regular and conscientious', arriving each morning as it opened, pausing just long enough to buy two rice-cakes for lunch, and staying until the reading room closed for the night. In later life, he described the time he spent there as 'extremely valuable'. But his father thought otherwise and after six months cut off his allowance.

Having no money concentrates the mind. Like generations of students before and since, Mao was forced, as he put it, to begin 'thinking seriously of a "career"'. He thought of becoming a teacher, and in the spring of 1913 saw an advertisement for a training college, the Hunan Fourth Provincial Normal School:

> I read with interest of its advantages: no tuition [fees] required, and cheap board and cheap lodging. Two of my friends were also urging me to enter. They wanted my help in preparing entrance essays. I wrote of my intention to my family and I received their consent. I composed essays for my two friends and wrote one of my own. All were accepted – in reality, therefore, I was accepted three times . . . [After this] I . . . managed to resist the appeals of all future advertising.

The years Mao spent in Changsha, from his arrival during the final months of Manchu rule until his graduation in 1918, were tumultuous for China and for the world. The nations of Europe devoured each other in war. In Russia, 30 million peasants starved while the Tsar's government exported wheat. The Bolshevik Revolution created the world's first communist state. The Panama Canal opened;

the *Titanic* sank; the dancer, Mata Hari, was executed as a spy.

This was the decade in which Mao laid the foundations of his intellectual development.

Already at Dongshan, his horizons had begun to widen. There, for the first time, he learned something of foreign history and geography. A schoolfriend lent him a book entitled *Great Heroes of the World*, in which he read about George Washington and the American Revolution; the Napoleonic War in Europe; Abraham Lincoln and the fight against slavery; Rousseau and Montesquieu; the British Prime Minister, William Gladstone; and Catherine and Peter the Great of Russia. Later, in the provincial library, he found translations of Rousseau's *Du contrat social* and Montesquieu's *De l'esprit des lois*, expounding Western notions of popular sovereignty, the social contract between ruler and ruled, and individual freedom and equality. He read Adam Smith's *The Wealth of Nations*, and works by other prominent nineteenth-century liberals, including Darwin, Thomas Huxley, John Stuart Mill and Herbert Spencer. The half-year he spent in this way, 'studying capitalism' as he later put it, also introduced him to foreign poetry and novels, and to the legends of ancient Greece. In the library, too, for the first time, he saw a map of the world.

A teacher at the First Provincial Middle School encouraged him to read the *Comprehensive Mirror for the Aid of Those Who Govern* (*Zizhi tongjian*), the great Song dynasty text by Si-Ma Guang, regarded as a masterpiece by generations of Chinese scholars and in Mao's day, nearly a millennium later, still the pre-eminent model for the study of political history. The book is a panoramic chronicle of the rise and fall of dynasties, on a scale never attempted in China again, covering some 1,400 years starting from the fifth century BC. Its guiding principle is that described in the opening lines of one of Mao's favourite novels, *The Romance of the Three Kingdoms*: 'Empires wax and wane, states cleave asunder and coalesce.' An eighteenth-century French Jesuit wrote of its author: 'He paints for us the personages whom he places on history's stage, characterised by their actions and coloured by their brilliance, their interests, their views, their faults and their virtues . . . He lays before the reader the chain of events, illuminating first this aspect and then that, until their most distant and astounding consequences are made plain. His genius . . . shows us history in all its majesty . . . giving to it a voice of such philosophical eloquence that even the most indolent souls are subdued and forced to reflect.' Si-Ma Guang's depiction of a world in ceaseless flux, where history is a continuum and the past provides the key to managing the present, made the *Mirror* one of the most influential books in Mao's life, which he continued to read and reread up to his death.

Changsha also brought him into contact with contemporary ideas. In the *Xiang River Daily* (*Xiangjiang ribao*), in 1912, he first encountered the term, socialism. Soon afterwards he came across some pamphlets by Jiang Kanghu, an advocate of progressive causes who had been influenced by a Chinese anarchist group based in Paris. Shortly after the revolution, Jiang had founded the Chinese Socialist Party, whose doctrines were expressed by the slogan: 'No government, no family, no religion: from each according to his ability, to each according to his need.' This was strong stuff, and Mao wrote enthusiastically about it to several of his classmates. Only one, he remembered, sent a positive response.

More important still were the five years he spent training to be a teacher. It was the closest Mao came to a university education, and he spoke of it later as the period when his political ideas began to take shape. He started preparatory classes at the Fourth Normal School in the spring of 1913, a few months after his nineteenth birthday. A year later, it merged with First Normal, which had been built on the site of a twelfth-century literary academy outside the South Gate, and boasted a spacious, well-equipped campus with the newest Western-style buildings in Changsha.

Two professors, in particular, helped to shape his ideas: Yuan Jiliu, nicknamed 'Yuan the Big Beard', who taught Chinese language and literature; and Yang Changji, the head of the philosophy department, known irreverently to his students as 'Confucius', who had recently returned to Changsha after spending ten years abroad, studying at Aberdeen, Berlin and Tokyo. In the 1930s, when Mao reminisced about his schooldays to Edgar Snow, it was to them that his thoughts immediately turned:

> Yuan the Big Beard ridiculed my writing and called it the work of a journalist . . . I was obliged to alter my style. I studied the writings of Han Yu, and mastered the old Classical phraseology. Thanks to Yuan the Big Beard, therefore, I can today still turn out a passable Classical essay if required. [But] the teacher who made the strongest impression on me was Yang Changji . . . He was an idealist and a

man of high moral character. He believed in his ethics very strongly
and tried to imbue his students with the desire to become just, moral,
virtuous men, useful in society. Under his influence I read a book on
ethics [by the neo-Kantian philosopher, Friedrich Paulsen] . . . and
was inspired to write an essay entitled 'The Power of the Mind'. I was
then an idealist, and my essay was highly praised by Professor Yang
Changji . . . He gave me a mark of 100 for it.

The essay has been lost, but Mao's marginal notes on a Chinese
translation of part of Paulsen's *System der Ethik*, totalling more than
12,000 words in a microscopic and often almost illegible hand, have
been preserved. They contain three core ideas, which would pre-
occupy Mao throughout his political career: the need for a strong
state, with centralised political power; the overriding importance of
individual will; and the sometimes conflictual, sometimes complementary relationship between the Chinese and Western intellectual
traditions.

The notion of a strong state, with a wise, paternalistic ruler, was
rooted in the Confucian texts Mao had learned as a child. It formed
the centrepiece of an essay he had written while still at middle
school about Shang Yang, Chief Minister of the State of Qin in the
fourth century BC, who was one of the founders of the Legalist
school of thought. Law, Mao declared, was 'an instrument for
procuring happiness'. Yet the law-making of wise rulers was often
frustrated by 'the stupidity . . . ignorance and darkness' of the
people, whose resistance to change had 'brought China to the brink
of destruction'. It was enough to make more 'civilised peoples laugh
[until] they have to hold their stomachs'. Mao's teacher thought so
highly of this effort that he circulated it to the rest of the class.

The theme of Chinese backwardness, and the need to overcome
it, recurred constantly in his writings at this time. The country's
future difficulties, he told a friend, would be 'a hundredfold those of
the past', and extraordinary talents would be needed to overcome
them. The Chinese people were 'slavish in character and narrow-
minded'. Over five thousand years of history, they had accumulated
'many undesirable customs, their mentality is too antiquated and
their morality is extremely bad . . . [These] cannot be removed
and purged without enormous force.'

His pessimism was reinforced as, year by year, China yielded
ever more abjectly to pressure from the Great Powers. On May 7,

1915, Yuan Shikai was handed a Japanese ultimatum, the so-called
'Twenty-one Demands', claiming for the Mikado's government a
virtual protectorate over China, including exclusive rights in the
former German sphere of influence in Shandong, and a shared
presence with the Tsarist Empire in Manchuria. It was, Mao wrote,
a day of 'extraordinary shame'. He urged his fellow students to remonstrate with the government, and gave vent to his own feelings in a
poem, written a few days later to mark the death of a schoolfriend:

> *Repeatedly the barbarians have engaged in trickery,*
> *From a thousand li they come again across Dragon Mountain . . .*
> *Why should we be concerned about life and death?*
> *This century will see a war . . .*
> *The eastern sea holds island savages,*
> *In the northern mountains hate-filled enemies abound.*

The 'island savages' were the Japanese; the 'hate-filled enemies', the
Russians. Of the two, the Japanese were the more formidable.
'Without a war,' Mao wrote a year later, 'we will cease to exist within
twenty years. But our countrymen still sleep on without noticing,
and pay little attention to the East. In my view, no more important
task confronts our generation . . . We must sharpen our resolve to
resist Japan.'

Mao's first attempt to help remedy what he perceived as China's
failings was eminently practical. Early in 1917, he submitted an
article on physical education to *New Youth* (*Xin qingnian*), then the
country's leading progressive magazine, edited by the radical
scholar, Chen Duxiu. It opened with the words:

> Our nation is wanting in strength; the military spirit has not been
> encouraged. The physical condition of our people deteriorates daily
> . . . If our bodies are not strong, we will tremble at the sight of [enemy]
> soldiers. How then can we attain our goals, or exercise far-reaching
> influence?

This was not, in itself, original. His philosophy teacher, Professor
Yang Changji, had lectured Mao's class in very similar terms three
years before. Attempts to introduce sports and other forms of physical exercise into Chinese schools had been under way since the
Qing reforms introduced after the Boxer Revolt.

The problem, Mao wrote, was that these efforts had been half-hearted. Tradition stressed literary accomplishment and rejected the idea of physical exertion, which led students and instructors to look down on it:

> Students feel that exercise is shameful . . . Flowing garments, a slow gait, a grave, calm gaze – these constitute a fine deportment, respected by society. Why should one suddenly extend an arm or expose a leg, stretch and bend down? . . .
>
> The superior man's deportment is cultivated and agreeable, but one cannot say this about exercise. Exercise should be savage and rude. To charge on horseback amidst the clash of arms and to be ever-victorious; to shake the mountains by one's cries and the colours of the sky by one's roars of anger . . . All this is savage and rude and has nothing to do with delicacy. In order to progress in exercise one must be savage . . . [Then] one will have great vigour and strong muscles and bones.

As a parting shot at his compatriots' effcte ways, he proposed that exercises be done in the nude.

The *New Youth* article, published in April 1917, was significant, not only as Mao's first modest contribution to the national debate over China's future, but because it contained in embryo the second of the core themes that emerged in his thinking at this time: the supreme importance of individual will.

'If we do not have the will to act,' he wrote, 'then even though the exterior and the objective [conditions] are perfect, they still cannot benefit us. Hencc . . . we should begin with individual initiative . . . The will is the antecedent of a man's career.' That autumn he attempted to refine this definition. 'Will is the truth which we perceive in the universe,' he suggested. '[But] truly to establish one's will is not so simple.' Each person must find his own truth, and 'act in accordance with [it], instead of blindly following other people's definitions of right and wrong'. A few months later he told friends, in terms reminiscent of the *Three Character Classic*: 'If man's mental and physical powers are concentrated together . . . no task will be difficult to accomplish.'

To these traditional Chinese notions, Mao joined the Western concept of individual self-interest:

> Ultimately, the individual comes first . . . Society is created by individuals, not individuals by society . . . and the basis of mutual

assistance is fulfilment of the individual . . . Self-interest is indeed
primary for human beings . . . There is no higher value than that
of the individual . . . Thus there is no greater crime than to suppress
the individual . . . Every act in life is for the purpose of fulfilling the
individual, and all morality serves [that end].

This emphasis on 'the power of the will [and] the power of the mind',
coupled with Mao's view of history, and his enduring attachment to
the legendary heroes of novels like *The Romance of the Three Kingdoms*,
led him to the view that 'great and powerful men are representatives
of an era, and . . . the whole era is but an accessory to these representative people':

The truly great person develops . . . and expands upon the best, the
greatest of the capacities of his original nature . . . [All] restraints and
restrictions [are] cast aside by the great motive power that is
contained in his original nature . . . The great actions of the hero are
his own, are the expression of his motive power, lofty and cleansing,
relying on no precedent. His force is like that of a powerful wind
arising from a deep gorge, like the irresistible sexual desire for one's
lover, a force that will not stop, that cannot be stopped. All obstacles
dissolve before him. I have observed from ancient times the fierce
power of courageous generals on the battle line, facing undaunted
ten thousand enemies. It is said that one man who scorns death will
prevail over one hundred . . . Because he cannot be stopped or eliminated, he is the strongest and most powerful. This is true also of the
spirit of the great man and the spirit of the sage.

The hero had to contend, in Mao's scheme of things, with a world
in which order continually degenerated into chaos, from which new
order was born. 'There is only movement in heaven and on earth,'
he wrote. 'Throughout the ages there have been struggles between
different schools of thought.' In a striking passage, he went on to
argue that while men yearn for peace, they were also bored by it:

A long period of peace, pure peace without any disorder of any kind,
would be unbearable . . . and it would be inevitable that peace would
give birth to waves . . . I am sure that once we entered [an age] of
Great Harmony, waves of competition and friction would inevitably
break forth that would disrupt [it] . . . Human beings always hate
chaos and hope for order, not realising that chaos too is part of the
process of historical life, that it too has value . . . It is the times when
things are constantly changing and numerous men of talent are

emerging that people like to read about. When they come to periods of peace, they . . . put the book aside . . .

Mao's reflections on these 'scholarly issues [and] weighty affairs of state', as he put it to a friend, took place against a backdrop of growing awareness of the tension between the Chinese traditions he had absorbed as a child and the new Western ideas to which he was being exposed.

At first he consciously emulated the views of Kang Youwei and other nineteenth-century reformers. 'I have come to the conclusion that the path to scholarship must first be . . . Chinese and later Western, first general and later specialised,' he had written in June 1915. Three months later he expanded on this idea:

> One ought to concentrate on the comparison of China and the West and choose from abroad what is useful at home . . . [A friend] introduced me to . . . [Herbert Spencer's] *Principles of Sociology*, and I took this book and read it through. Afterward, I closed the book and exclaimed to myself, 'Here lies the path to scholarship' . . . [This book] is most pertinent . . . [and contains much] to be prized . . . However, something even more important . . . is Chinese studies . . . Chinese studies are both broad and deeply significant . . . General knowledge of Chinese studies is most crucial for our people.

In almost all Mao's writings, throughout his life, Chinese rather than Western experience was given pride of place. Even when the topic was physical education, an alien, Western practice that had been transplanted into China, a list of Chinese exemplars came first, starting with a group of late Ming dynasty scholars. Only afterwards did he mention such 'eminent [foreign] advocates of physical education' as Theodore Roosevelt and the Japanese, Jigoro Kano, the inventor of judo. Grounding foreign ideas in Chinese reality to establish their relevance became a cardinal principle that he never afterwards relinquished.

In 1917, however, he began for the first time to question whether traditional Chinese thought really was superior. The country's ancient learning was 'disorganised and unsystematic', he complained that summer. 'This is why we have not made any progress, even in several millennia . . . Western studies . . . are quite different . . . The classifications are so clear that they sound like a waterfall dashing against the rocks beneath a cliff.' But a few weeks later he was not so sure. 'In my opinion Western thought is not necessarily all correct either,' he wrote. 'Very many parts of it should be transformed at the same time as Eastern thought.'

He found a provisional answer in one of Paulsen's theses. 'All nations inevitably go through the stage of old age and decline', the German had written. 'With time, tradition acts as an obstacle to the forces of renewal and the past oppresses the present.' This was China's position, Mao decided. 'All the anthologies of prose and poetry published since the Tang and Song dynasties [should] be burned,' he told a friend. 'Revolution does not mean using troops and arms, but replacing the old with the new.'

He did not propose, however, that the Classics should be destroyed. The foundations of Chinese culture were inviolate. Only the tangled superstructure needed to be cleared away, so that China's originality and greatness could flourish anew.

As the decade unfolded, the prospects for national renewal had begun to look increasingly bleak. The Xinhai Revolution of 1911, so-called because it took place in the year of the Iron Pig in the traditional sixty-year cycle, lived up to none of its ambitions. Its one achievement had been destructive: the overthrow of the Manchu Court.

The Hunanese reformists had suspected from the start that Yuan Shikai's administration would be a replica of the Qing autocracy he had previously served, and tried to keep him at arm's length. The provincial government, led by Tan Yankai, supported instead the newly formed Guomindang (Nationalist Party) of Sun Yat-sen, which won an overwhelming victory in the parliamentary elections held in the winter of 1912. Yuan proved every bit as unscrupulous as they had feared. The following spring, Sun Yat-sen belatedly launched the expedition to curb Yuan's power from which he had shrunk the year before. Jiangxi and five other southern provinces declared their support. But the Second Revolution, as it was called, failed to ignite. By the end of August 1913, the southern armies had been soundly defeated, and their leaders fled into exile. The southern military governors, loosely aligned with Sun's forces, retained control over their fiefdoms in Guangdong, Guangxi, Guizhou and Yunnan. But in Hunan, Yuan was able to reimpose the Beijing government's rule, appointing Tang Xiangming, a conservative loyalist, to replace the liberal Tan. Soon afterwards the Guomindang was banned throughout China by presidential decree, accused of 'fomenting political troubles.'

Such remote, elite manoeuvrings, as they must have seemed to a nineteen-year-old student who not long before had watched a dynasty collapse, evidently left Mao cold. The one incident from this time that stuck in his mind was the explosion that summer of the Changsha arsenal – and that for the spectacle it created rather than for political reasons. 'There was a huge fire, and we students found it very interesting,' he recalled. 'Tons of bullets and shells exploded, and gunpowder made an intense blaze. It was better than fire-crackers.' The fact that it had been blown up by two of Yuan's supporters to deprive the Hunanese of weapons, he passed over in silence.

For most of the next five years, Mao's studies came first; republican politics a distant second – and then only if they became a major issue for the nation's youth. That happened in the spring of 1915, when Yuan capitulated to Japan's 'Twenty-one Demands'; and again the following winter, when he began manoeuvring to restore the monarchy. That year, Mao became a member of the Wang Fuzhi Society, named after a Hunanese Ming patriot who had fought against the Manchus, the weekly meetings of which served as a cover for reformist scholars to foment opposition to Yuan's imperial ambitions. He also helped to organise the publication of a collection of anti-restoration writings by Liang Qichao and Kang Youwei, entitled *Painful Words on Current Affairs*, a move which so angered the authorities that police were sent to the college to investigate.

At the end of December 1915, Yuan proclaimed himself Emperor, taking the reign name Hongxian. Yunnan's Military Governor promptly revolted, followed by Guangdong, Zhejiang and Jiangxi. The following spring, the new Emperor began having second thoughts, and offered to become President again. But he had left it too late. The southern armies were on the march; the smell of blood was in the air. In Hunan, secret society members rose in rebellion, triggering a mutiny led by one of Governor Tang's commanders. It failed. But it was the signal for Tang, who had helped to orchestrate Yuan's imperial ambitions, to scramble frantically to distance himself from his erstwhile patron. At the end of May, he declared Hunan independent of both the northern and southern forces. Then, on June 4, as all-out civil war loomed, Yuan died of a brain haemorrhage, and the northern generals and their troops beat a hasty retreat to Beijing to argue over the succession. Their departure brought the collapse of the delicate military balance that had been keeping Tang in power. A month later, disguised as a peasant, the Governor slipped out of the back door of his yamen, accompanied by a few trusted servants, and boarded a British steamer bound for Hankou. With them went 700,000 dollars from the provincial treasury.

Tang's overthrow triggered two weeks of blood-letting in Changsha and the surrounding area, in which at least 1,000 people died, followed by prolonged political chaos, as rival factions disputed his position.

Mao made his way back on foot to Shaoshan. In a letter to his classmate, Xiao Yu, the younger brother of Emi Siao, he related how the southern troops – 'a rough crowd . . . from the mountain wilds, [who] talk like birds and look like animals' – swaggered about, looking for trouble, ate at restaurants without paying, and held gambling parties on street corners. 'The atmosphere is white-hot with debauchery,' he lamented. 'The disorder is extreme . . . Alas, it is like the Reign of Terror in France!'

Yet, far more striking than Mao's contempt for the soldiery was his defence of the ex-Governor, who had been almost universally hated.

If anyone had carried out a reign of terror in the province, it was 'Butcher' Tang, as he was soon known. He had come to power with a mandate to root out Guomindang influence, and he went to work with a will from the first day he took office. An American missionary doctor in Changsha remembered having invited him to lunch, with several of his cabinet officers, to celebrate his appointment:

The following day we had bad news about three of our luncheon guests. That noon, in a public square near the yamen, the treasurer of the province was publicly shot, while the other two senior cabinet members . . . were thrown into a common prison, sentenced to be executed within two days. The atmosphere was tense. The leading gentry and the students in all the city schools were stirred as seldom before . . . Guards were . . . placed at the front gates to prevent pupils from leaving for student-union meetings. 'Any principal', the Governor's proclamation read, 'permitting students to hold political assemblies on school grounds will be dismissed . . .' We went down,

every couple of hours, to the central public square to make inquiries
. . . Bystanders told us that executions had been going on there
steadily ever since daybreak.

Sixteen other former members of Tan Yankai's government were
arrested and shot in an amphitheatre used for athletics events. In the
three years that Tang held power, at least 5,000 people were
executed for political offences, together with an unknown number
of common criminals. Independent accounts, by Chinese and
foreigners alike, described him as 'ruling with an iron hand', and in
China, in the first decades of the twentieth century, that phrase was
not a metaphor. A missionary reported the treatment of three
thieves, one only seventeen years old:

> As they would not name their accomplices, the [magistrate] made
> them kneel on broken tiles, with a pole on the upper side of their legs,
> on which two men jumped in order to bring pressure. He [took] thick
> incense sticks – as thick as one's finger and as hard as wood – and
> thrust the red-hot ends into their eyes and up their nostrils. He then
> used these burning incense sticks to draw characters and figures on
> their naked bodies. Finally, with hands and feet fully extended on the
> ground and firmly secured to stakes, smouldering incense sticks were
> left to burn out upon their flesh, after having had their bodies severely
> ironed with red hot irons. All three men succumbed, and when
> removed from before the seat of justice were scarcely recognisable
> as human bodies.

Even by such standards, the methods of 'Butcher' Tang were
extreme. The head of the Hunan Office of Military Law acquired
the nickname, 'The Living King of Hell', so barbarous were the
tortures conducted there. Special police units were set up to search
out Guomindang supporters. Many schools were closed, as the
educational budget was sharply reduced, and those that remained
open were kept under surveillance. Newspapers which questioned
Tang's policies were banned, and in 1916, when press censorship
was introduced, those which were left appeared with blank spaces.
'Detectives are everywhere and the people as silent as cicadas in
winter,' one Chinese journalist wrote. 'On guard against each other,
they dare not speak about current affairs.'

Mao knew all this. His own school had been forced to close during
the wave of executions that had ushered in Tang's rule. Yet, in his

letter to Xiao Yu, he stubbornly defended the disgraced Governor's conduct:

> I still maintain that Military Governor Tang should not have been sent away. Driving him out was an injustice, and the situation now is growing more and more chaotic. Why do I say it was an injustice? Tang was here for three years, and he ruled by the severe enforcement of strict laws. He . . . [created] a tranquil and amicable environment. Order was restored, and the peaceful times of the past were practically regained. He controlled the army strictly and with discipline . . . The city of Changsha became so honest that lost belongings were left on the street for their owners. Even chickens and dogs were unafraid . . . Tang can proclaim his innocence before the whole world . . . [Now] the gangsters [of the old Hunanese military and political elite] . . . are everywhere, investigating and arresting people, and executing those they arrest . . . There is talk from every sector of government officials robbed and [county] magistrates defied . . . How strange and crazy, the doings of Hunan!

The letter provides an intriguing insight into Mao's cast of mind as a 22-year-old. When, in 1911, he had enlisted in the revolutionary army, he had merely done the same as thousands of other young men of his age. This time he was defying the views of the majority to defend a deeply unpopular, politically dangerous cause. 'I'm afraid I'll get myself into trouble,' he told Xiao Yu. 'Don't let anyone else see this. It would be best if you burn it when you have finished reading it.'

His view of 'Butcher' Tang would later change. But his method of analysis – focusing on what he considered the principal aspect of the problem (in this case, the maintenance of law and order), and disregarding what was secondary (Tang's cruelty) – would form the basis of his approach to politics all his life. And his defence of authoritarianism offered a chilling hint of future ruthlessness:

> The fact that [Tang] killed well over 10,000 people was the inescapable outcome of policy. Did he kill any more than [the northern military commander] Feng [Guozhang] in Nanjing? . . . One can say that he manufactured public opinion, pandered to Yuan [Shikai], and slandered good men. But did not this kind of behaviour also occur [elsewhere]? . . . Without such behaviour, the goal of protecting the nation would be unattainable. Those who consider these things to be crimes do not comprehend the overall plan.

Such ideas had been foreshadowed in Mao's essay, four years earlier, praising the Legalist statesman, Shang Yang, for 'promulgating laws to punish the wicked and rebellious'. But now he went much further, arguing that the killing of political opponents was not merely justified, it was inevitable.

Mao's support of Tang's rule as exemplifying strong leadership, and his disparagement of Hunan's progressive elite, reflected his disgust at the squabbling of local politicians. Similar reasoning led him to find merit in Yuan Shikai. While others castigated the would-be Emperor as a turncoat who had betrayed the republic and kowtowed to the hated Japanese, Mao continued to regard him as one of the three pre-eminent figures of the time, together with Sun Yat-sen and Kang Youwei. Not until eighteen months later, in the winter of 1917, when Hunan was once again in the throes of civil conflict and all over China military governors were degenerating into warlords, did he recognise that Yuan and Tang had been, after all, no more than tyrants, bent on their own power.

Mao's years at the Normal School were formative in other ways. The headstrong youngster who had been admitted in 1913, hiding his fears and self-doubt behind a show of bravado, developed into a well-liked, apparently well-adjusted young man, regarded by his professors and his friends as an exceptional student who would one day make a first-rate teacher.

It was a slow transition. As at Dongshan, it took him a year or more to find his feet. Xiao Yu, who became one of his earliest and closest friends, described Mao's first, hesitant approach to him in the summer of 1914:

At that time, since I was a senior student, he did not dare speak first to me . . . [But] from reading [each other's] essays [which were posted up in class], we learned of each other's ideas and opinions, and thus a bond of sympathy formed between us . . . [After] several months . . . we met one morning in one of the corridors . . . Mao stopped in front of me with a smile. 'Mr Xiao' [he said]. At that time everyone in the school addressed his fellow students in English. 'Mr Mao,' I replied . . . wondering vaguely what he was about to say . . . 'What is the number of your study?' [he asked] . . . Naturally he knew this quite well and the question was merely an excuse to start conversation. 'This afternoon, after class, I'd like to come to your study to look at your essays, if you don't mind . . .'

Classes finished for the day at four o'clock and Mao arrived at my study within the hour . . . [We] enjoyed our first talk. Finally he said, 'Tomorrow I would like to come and ask your guidance.' He took two of my essays, made a formal bow, and departed. He was very polite. Each time he came to see me he made a bow.

Mao went to some lengths to seek out those he regarded as kindred spirits. 'Except for the sages, man cannot be successful in isolation,' he wrote in 1915. 'Choosing one's friends is of primary importance.' That year he circulated a notice to be posted up in the city's schools, inviting 'young people interested in patriotic work' to contact him. He specified that they must be 'hardened and determined, and . . . ready to make sacrifices for their country', and signed it with a pseudonym, 'Twenty-eight Stroke Student', which derived from the twenty-eight brush strokes required to write his name.

At the Provincial Women's Normal School, it was suspected of being a covert appeal for female companionship, and an investigation was launched. But that was far from Mao's thoughts. He was merely, he explained to Xiao Yu, 'imitating the birds who call to seek friendly voices'.* 'These days,' he added, 'if one's friends are few, one's views cannot be broad.'

Twenty years later, he told Edgar Snow that he received 'three and one half replies' – three from young men who later became 'traitors' or 'ultra-reactionaries', the 'half reply' from 'a non-committal youth named Li Lisan', later to become a leader of the Communist Party and Mao's bitter opponent. In fact, half-a-dozen young people responded, and gradually a loose-knit study circle formed:

> It was a serious-minded little group of men [Mao recalled], and they had no time to discuss trivialities. Everything they did or said must have a purpose. They had no time for love or 'romance' and considered the times too critical and the need for knowledge too urgent to discuss women or personal matters . . . Quite aside from the discussions of feminine charm, which usually play an important role in the discussions of young men of this age, my companions even rejected talk of ordinary matters of daily life . . . [We] preferred to talk only of large matters – the nature of men, of human society, of China, the world, and the universe!

* This is a quotation from the *Shi jing*, the Book of Poetry.

Influenced by Professor Yang Changji, who had become a fitness
fanatic while in Japan, and by the principles Mao set out in his *New
Youth* article in 1917, the group also followed a spartan physical
regime. Every morning, they went to the well, took off their clothes
and doused each other with a bucketful of cold water. In the
holidays, they went on long hikes:

> We tramped through the fields, up and down mountains, along
> city walls, and across the streams and rivers. If it rained, we took off
> our shirts and called it a rain bath. When the sun was hot, we also
> doffed shirts and called it a sun bath. In the spring winds we shouted
> that this was a new sport called 'wind bathing'. We slept in the open
> when frost was already falling and even in November swam in the
> cold rivers.

Mao's admiration for Professor Yang was unbounded. 'When I
think of [his] greatness, I feel I will never be his equal,' he confided
to a friend. The feeling was mutual. 'It is truly difficult', Yang
wrote in his diary, 'to find someone as intelligent and handsome
[as Mao].' He was among a small group of students who went
regularly to Yang's home in the evenings to discuss current events,
and the professor's voluntarist, subjective approach to life – stressing the cultivation of personal virtue, will-power, steadfastness
and endurance – was to have an abiding influence on him. When
Yang died some years later, allegedly as a result of too many
cold baths in the icy winters of Beijing, the student newspaper
recalled that Mao and his friend, Cai Hesen, had been his favourite
students.

Yet Mao, in his early twenties, must also have been a cross to bear
for everyone around him. The frustrated, rebellious teenager from
Shaoshan was still a troubled young man, brilliant but difficult,
racked by bouts of self-questioning and depression.

One moment he was complaining: 'Throughout my life, I have
never had good teachers or friends.' Next minute he wrote intimately to Xiao Yu: 'Many heavy thoughts . . . multiply and weigh
down on me . . . Will you allow me to release them by talking to
you?' His obstinacy was legendary, even towards those he liked and
respected, such as Yuan the Big Beard, with whom he had a furious
row over the title-sheet for an essay which he refused to change.
After another dispute, this time with the principal, it took the
combined intervention of Yuan, Yang Changji and several other

professors to prevent him being expelled. In the privacy of his journal he flagellated himself:

> You do not have the capacity for tranquillity. You are fickle and excitable. Like a woman preening herself, you know no shame. Your outside looks strong but your inside is truly empty. Your ambitions for fame and fortune are not suppressed, and your sensual desires grow daily. You enjoy all hearsay and rumour, perturbing the spirit and misusing time, and generally delight in yourself. You always emulate what the peony does, [producing green calyxes and vermillion blossoms] without any end product, but deceive yourself by saying, 'I emulate the [humble] gourd [which has no flower but produces fruit]'. Is this not dishonesty?

Mao lived frugally. Xiao Yu remembered him at their first meeting as a 'tall, clumsy, dirtily dressed young man whose [cotton] shoes badly needed repairing'. While others of his age were busy experimenting with the new Western fashions, he possessed only a blue school uniform, a grey scholar's gown with a padded underjacket and a pair of baggy white trousers. He was equally careless of what he ate. This was partly from necessity: the allowance he received from his father amounted only to some 25 dollars a year. But he was also influenced by one of his teachers, Xu Teli, a nonconformist renowned for the simplicity of his lifestyle, who always walked to school, rather than use a rickshaw or sedan chair as the other professors did.

Mao's budget was further strained by the amount he spent on newspapers and magazines, which took up, by his own estimate, almost half his income. His classmates remembered him sitting in the college library, making minuscule notes on long strips of paper, clipped from the sides of the pages, as an aide-memoire about foreign countries and their leaders.

He was equally diligent at his studies, but only in subjects he liked. His mood alternated wildly between fascination with what he learned and despair at his own failings. He railed against the college regulations for forcing him to take courses he found boring. 'Natural sciences did not especially interest me and I did not study them, so I got poor marks,' he recalled. 'Most of all I hated a compulsory course in still-life drawing. I thought it extremely stupid. I used to think of the simplest subjects possible to draw, finish up quickly and leave the class.' Once he drew a straight line with a semicircle above it, claiming that it was a scene from Li Bai's poem, 'A Dream of Wandering on Mount Tianmu', which describes the sun rising out of the sea. In the year-end exam, he drew an oval and said it was an egg. The teacher failed him.

Periodically he would try to take himself in hand. 'In the past, I had some mistaken ideas,' he acknowledged in 1915. 'Now I . . . [have] grown up a bit . . . Today I make a new start.' A few months later he was in despair again. 'This is no place to study,' he wrote angrily to a former teacher. 'There is no freedom of will, the standards are too low, and the companions too evil. It is truly distressing to see my serviceable body and precious time dwindle away in pining and waiting . . . Schools like this are certainly the darkest of dark valleys.' Soon afterwards, he was enthusing once more over a new study plan:

> In the early morning I study English; from eight in the morning to three in the afternoon I attend class; from four in the afternoon until dinner, I study Chinese literature; from the time the lights are lit until they are extinguished, I do homework for all classes; and after the lights are extinguished, I exercise for one hour.

Half a year on, he was yet again 'starting afresh . . . studying from morning to night without rest', only to suffer another relapse. 'Who does not want to seek advancement?' he wrote unhappily. 'But when one's ambitions are continuously frustrated and when one gets lost in a maze of twists and turns, one's bitterness is too much to describe. For a very young man, all this represents a world of bitterness.'

As Mao's confidence developed, such outbursts became less frequent. In the late spring of 1917, when he was twenty-three, his schoolmates elected him 'Student of the Year'. His article in *New Youth*, a few weeks earlier, had been the first the magazine had accepted from a student in Hunan. In other ways, too, he grew more self-assured. The deference of his early letters to Xiao Yu gave way to a more equal relationship, in which Mao, Xiao's junior, frequently appeared the dominant voice. That summer he criticised a teaching manual Xiao had written, urging him to rewrite it, 'retaining the gems and discarding the dross'. Soon after this, to the dismay of their teachers, the two of them defied convention by spending their summer vacation on a month-long walking tour, begging food and lodging from Buddhist temples and from sympathetic gentry in the counties through which they passed.

In a poem written that year, Mao likened himself to a *peng*, a mythical bird like the roc, which 'thrashed a wake three thousand miles long' as it journeyed from the Southern sea. Of his boyhood heroes, only the Qing Viceroy, Zeng Guofan, still commanded his admiration. Liang Qichao and Kang Youwei he both now found wanting.

The publication of the *New Youth* article encouraged Mao to cast about for other ways to contribute to the building of the new China he and his friends so ardently desired. The elite, he argued, had a moral duty to help those less fortunate than themselves.

> Superior men already possess lofty wisdom and morality . . . But the little people are pitiable. If the superior men care only for themselves, they may leave the crowd and live like hermits. There were some who did so in ancient times . . . [But] if they have compassionate hearts, then they [recognise] the little people as . . . part of the same universe. If we go off by ourselves, they will sink lower and lower. It is better for us to lend a helping hand, so that their minds may be opened up and their virtue increased.

The opportunity to put these ideas into practice came in October 1917, when Mao was elected head of the Students' Society, which organised extracurricular activities at the college. One of its first decisions was to revive an evening school for local workers which had been started six months earlier but then abandoned. At a time when the great majority of China's people had no education, such initiatives were 'extremely critical', Mao wrote. 'Plants and trees, birds and animals, all nurture and care for their own kind. Must not human beings do the same?' The 'little people' were not 'evil by nature' or 'originally inferior', they were simply unlucky, which was why 'the humane person should show [them] sympathy'. Even advanced countries in Europe and America, he added, regarded evening schools as useful. Furthermore, they enabled students to acquire teaching experience and, most important of all, they helped build a sense of solidarity between the mass of the people and the country's educated elite:

> School and society constitute two poles, two things separated by a huge gulf. Upon entering a school, the students look down on society

as if they had climbed into the heavens. Society, too, looks on the schools as something sacred and untouchable. This mutual alienation and suspicion causes three evils. One is that the students cannot find jobs in society . . . Another evil is that society does not send its children to school . . . The third evil is . . . [public resentment leading to] the burning of schools and the blocking of funds. If these three evils can be removed . . . people in society will look on the students as their eyes and ears and will rely on their guidance to reap the benefits of prosperity and development. The students will look on the people in society as their hands and feet, whose help will make it possible for them to accomplish their goals. [In the end] all the people . . . will have graduated from [one kind of] school [or another]. One part of schooling will be the big school one attends for a while, and the whole of society will be the big school that one attends for ever.

To this notion of an anti-elitist, open system of education, Mao joined an abhorrence of book-worship. 'Of the little progress I have made over these last few years,' he had written in 1915, 'only the smaller part was achieved through books. The larger part of my gains was the result of questioning and seeking solutions to [practical] difficulties.' He commented approvingly on Kant's insistence that 'our understanding must come from the facts of experience', and castigated the formalism of traditional Chinese teaching methods:

In the educational system of our country, required courses are as thick as the hairs on a cow. Even an adult with a tough, strong body could not stand it, let alone those who have not reached adulthood . . . Speculating on the intentions of the educators, one is led to wonder whether they did not design such an unwieldy curriculum in order to exhaust the students, to trample on their bodies and ruin their lives . . . And if someone has an above-average intelligence, they give him all sorts of supplementary readings . . . How stupid!

The ideas Mao expressed here with such passion informed his attitude to education all his life. Yet, at the same time, his views were less radical than they might sound today. Chinese pedagogy was then so dominated by rote-learning, and the curricular overload so extreme, that in 1917, seven of Mao's fellow students died, having fallen ill – so their classmates and some of their teachers believed – as a result of excessively long hours studying without proper breaks.

For the sixty or so Changsha workers who enrolled at the evening

school that November, these principles were reflected in the use of
vernacular, rather than classical Chinese; a simplified curriculum,
geared to everyday life, 'writing letters and adding up accounts,
things which all you gentlemen have need of all the time', as Mao
put it in the school prospectus; and an effort to instil 'patriotic spirit',
by encouraging, among other things, the buying of Chinese-made
products rather than foreign goods.

But even before the school had properly opened, conflicts among
the military power-brokers in Beijing plunged Hunan once again
into civil war, bringing destruction to the province on a scale far
greater than anything Mao had witnessed before.

When Tang Xiangming had fled Changsha, in July 1916, he had
been replaced, after a period of confusion, by his predecessor, the
gentry leader Tan Yankai.

For a time all had gone well. Tan proceeded to install a Hunanese
administration, enjoying considerable autonomy and supported by
the provincial elite, similar to that which he had headed during his
previous governorship, from 1911 to 1913. The new Premier in
Beijing, Duan Qirui, who had been one of Yuan Shikai's principal
subordinates, was too busy trying to consolidate his position against
the manoeuvres of his northern rivals to be able to give much
thought to bringing the province to heel.

The following summer, however, the situation changed. The
power struggle in the capital achieved a farcical denouement
when a conservative military leader decided to restore the Manchu
Emperor to the throne, immediately if temporarily uniting all the
other northern generals against him. The resulting realignment
culminated in the establishment of two distinct northern militarist
cliques – one, the so-called Anhui (or Anfu) group, headed by Duan
Qirui; the other, the Zhili clique, led by the new President, Feng
Guozhang, whose occupation of Nanjing Mao had cited a year
earlier as a precedent for Tang Xiangming's harshness in Hunan.
Their rivalry, in turn, would soon unleash a bloody warlord conflict
that raged intermittently over central and eastern China for most of
the next decade. But for the moment a truce was observed, and
Duan was able to turn his attention to the unruly Hunanese.

In August 1917, he named Fu Liangzou, a relative by marriage
and former Vice-Minister of War, to replace Tan as Provincial

Governor. Like Tan, Fu was Hunan-born. But he had spent most of his life in the north and was regarded in his native province as a foreigner. Three days after taking up his appointment, he tried to remove two senior military officers whose loyalty he regarded as suspect. Their units mutinied, triggering a chain reaction which, by early October, had caused nearly half the troops in the province to come out in open rebellion. Two divisions of northern soldiers were despatched to suppress the revolt. But that merely convinced the independent military governors in neighbouring Guangxi and Guangdong that they, too, should intervene, to prevent the northern forces from threatening their own borders. Thousands of green-coated Guangxi infantrymen, accompanied by artillery units armed with maxim and mountain guns, poured into Hunan, under orders to block the northern advance before it penetrated the southern part of the province.

Having twice narrowly avoided becoming a battleground between the northern and southern armies – in 1913, when the Second Revolution fizzled out, and in 1916, when Yuan Shikai's death ended the anti-Monarchical war – it looked as though, this time, Hunan's luck had run out. In Changsha, martial law was proclaimed, while the two armies skirmished inconclusively along a narrow front near the southern city of Hengzhou. But the combatants had reckoned without the intrigues of the politicians in Beijing. One day in mid-November, Duan Qirui was forced to resign, Governor Fu fled, the northern units withdrew, and 'at nine o'clock [next morning], as if by electricity, the whole city was beflagged', awaiting with trepidation the arrival of the triumphant southerners. When they arrived, 'armed wherever bullets could be carried on the body', as one observer put it, women and children took refuge in Red Cross shelters. But, in the event, there was little looting, and the city congratulated itself on getting off remarkably lightly.

During these stirring times, Mao and other members of the First Normal Students' Society organised a volunteer force, which patrolled with wooden rifles to deter malefactors. Mao's contribution, one of his classmates recalled, had been to teach them to cut bamboo stakes with sharpened points, to be used to put out the eyes of any soldier rash enough to try to climb over the school wall. He and his closest friends, Xiao Yu and Cai Hesen, called themselves 'the three heroes' and cultivated physical toughness and a martial spirit. But while Mao had matured a great deal since the days when, as a frightened teenager, he had once hidden in a latrine to escape from brawling troops, there were still prudent limits to the young heroes' bravado. The *First Normal School Record* claimed proudly that Mao's volunteers had been 'exceptionally efficient'. But the following March, when real trouble resumed, they were conspicuously absent. That month, Duan Qirui and his rivals agreed to make a fresh attempt to bring Hunan to heel. Now it was the turn of the Guangxi men to withdraw without a fight.

> With nightfall, (a foreign resident reported) the deepest silence fell on the city. From about [8 p.m.] onwards, a succession of shots, the crash of glass and the smashing of shutters was heard from the busy South and West Streets right on to dawn . . . I [went] to see for myself what was happening . . . There was a more or less continuous stream of soldiers tracking off south. But there were also groups of a dozen . . . looting. They commenced with the silver ornament shops . . . Some eight or nine men gathered round the door and windows . . . The butt end of the rifles soon opened a way through the woodwork . . . The percentage of looted shops is great.

By morning, there was 'no one in charge and a very scared city'. The northern troops marched in twenty-four hours later. Duan Qirui, now back as Premier, appointed a trusted follower, Zhang Jingyao, to take over the governorship, which had been vacant since the flight of Fu Liangzou, four months earlier.

Hunan would pay dearly for that decision. 'Zhang the Venomous', as he was known, was a 'cruel, sadistic dictator', whose methods resembled those of 'Butcher' Tang, but on a larger scale. In the poorer suburbs of Changsha, foreign missionaries reported, 'the honour of women and the possession of anything that can be turned into money is at an end'. One district on the outskirts of the city drew up a detailed list of the crimes committed by Zhang's men in the first few days of April:

> Mrs S— , 20 years of age, [was] attacked by three soldiers at 11 a.m. and so badly abused by each of them as to be still unable to walk . . . L— was strung up in his own house and then pricked with bayonets. After that, a lighted candle was applied to the wounds . . . H— ran out to protect his daughter, a girl of eight years, who had been shot. He was also shot . . . A girl of 14 was violated by two men; [she] died from the injuries . . . A father-in-law, attempting in vain to protect his daughter-in-law, who was six months with child, by running off to

the hills, was followed by the soldiers who wounded the man and abused the woman . . . The sickening tales run on from every other quarter.

Along the main highway from Changsha to Pingjiang, in the north-east, 'all the cattle have been killed; all the seed rice taken; all the inhabitants scared away'. Liling, sixty miles to the south, fared even worse. When an American missionary reached the town in May, he found only three people left alive, amid a wasteland of rubble in which, here and there, part of a wall was still standing. In Liling county, out of a population of 580,000, more than 21,000 people had been killed and 48,000 homes had been razed.

From the safety of the foreign concessions in Shanghai, newspapers published angry editorials accusing 'selfish, greedy generals' of 'making one of the fairest provinces in China a scene of daily ruin and lamentation'. Ironically, south Hunan, where the rebellion had begun, seven months before, suffered least. General Wu Peifu, whose forces had spearheaded the northern advance, halted after capturing Hengzhou and negotiated a ceasefire, ignoring Duan Qirui's demands to press on to Guangdong and leaving the southernmost part of the province under southern army control. Once again, Beijing politics were at work. Wu was a member of the Zhili clique, and saw no factional advantage, once a northern governor had been installed, in continuing to aid a cause championed by Duan and his Anfu rivals.

From April onwards, Mao's college played reluctant host to a regiment of Zhang's troops, who were billeted in the classrooms. The new Governor, taking his cue from 'Butcher' Tang, five years earlier, halted the disbursement of the education budget. Teachers at First Normal went unpaid; most of the students fled; and the Principal had to find the money for the meals of those who stayed out of his own pocket. Like Tang, too, 'Zhang the Venomous' set up a network of informers and special agents to cow the population. For each alleged 'spy' captured, a substantial reward was paid. One man was arrested simply for wearing shoes of different colours. 'Gruesome corpses are lying about in all sorts of uncanny places,' one report stated, 'some right in the heart of the city, some on the military road. There is no publicity in any part of the trial of suspects. It is only with great difficulty that [even] members of the family get to hear of the whereabouts of anyone who has disappeared.' The result was 'much secret terror and very little open talk'.

At the beginning of June 1918, Mao received his teaching diploma. He still had no clear idea of what he wanted to do with his life. 'I find it all extremely confusing,' he wrote to a former professor, 'and what has its source in confusion will certainly result in confusion.' One possibility that he considered was to start a private school, to teach 'the essentials of Chinese studies, [after which] the students would go abroad to study . . . the essentials of Western thought'. But the times could hardly be less propitious, and such a venture would have required money, which Mao did not have.

He spent the next few weeks living with a group of friends in an abandoned classical academy on a mountain on the far side of the Xiang River, where they gathered their own firewood and drew water from a spring. All were members of the informal study group he had set up three years before, now renamed the *Xinmin xuehui*, or New People's Study Society. Personal connections in China are the indispensable springboard for any major endeavour, and Mao set great store by this network. The society had been formally inaugurated in April, with Xiao Yu as its secretary and Mao his deputy. Among the thirteen founder members, some, including Xiao himself, eventually went their separate ways. But the majority were to remain at Mao's side in the years of bloodshed and turbulence that followed, many at the cost of their own lives.

The society was one of the first of many progressive student associations formed in China at that time – among them the *Fu she* (Renaissance Society), in Beijing; and the *Juewu shi* (Awakening Society), founded by Zhou Enlai in Tianjin – as patriotic young people sought a response to the depredations of the warlords and the pressures of the imperialist Powers. One of Mao's classmates, Luo Xuezan, explained in a letter to his family that summer:

> You should know that the foreigners want to take China's land, they want to take China's money and they want to harm China's people . . . I can't live with that prospect and do nothing about it. So now . . . [we are] trying to set up an association . . . [which will work] to make China strong, so that the Chinese people can find a new way. Our aim is to look forward to the day of China's resurrection.

The very name, New People's Study Society, reflected the transition through which the country was passing. *Xinmin* has a dual meaning – 'new people', or 'renovate the people' – which gives it a radical, almost revolutionary consonance. Liang Qichao had used it in the title of his reformist journal, *Xinmin congbao* (New People's Magazine), fifteen years before. But it was also a classical term, found in the Confucian texts. To 'renovate the people' was the Confucian scholar's duty.

Ambivalence towards China's classical heritage was a hallmark of the time.

At the evening school which Mao had helped to organise, the pupils bowed each night three times before a portrait of the Sage. Yet he, and others of his generation, were increasingly critical of orthodox Confucian virtues. 'Our country's three bonds must go,' he wrote in the summer of 1917, referring to the three relations which were at the core of Confucian morality, between prince and minister, father and son, and husband and wife. He denounced 'the churches, the capitalists, monarchy and the state' as 'the four evil demons of the world', and urged 'a fundamental change' in national attitudes.

But where others simply rejected the past, Mao sought a synthesis that would reconcile the traditional dialectic of the country's ancient ways of thought with Western radicalism. The vision that resulted was astonishingly modern:

All phenomena in the world are simply a state of constant change . . . The birth of this is necessarily the death of that, and the death of that in necessarily the birth of this, so birth is not birth and death is not destruction . . .

I used to worry that our China would be destroyed, but now I know that this is not so. Through the establishment of a new political system, and a change in the national character, the German states became the German Reich . . . The only question is how the changes should be carried out. I believe that there must be a complete transformation, like matter that takes form after destruction, or like the infant born out of its mother's womb . . . In every century, various nationalities have launched various kinds of great revolutions, periodically cleansing the old and infusing it with the new, all of which are great changes involving life and death, formation and demise. The demise of the universe is similar . . . I very much look forward to its destruction, because from the demise of the old universe will come a new universe, and will it not be better than the old universe? . . .

I say: the concept is reality, the finite is the infinite, the temporal senses are the super-temporal senses, imagination is thought, form is substance, I am the universe, life is death and death is life, the present is the past and the future, the past and the future are the present, small is big, the yang is the yin, up is down, dirty is clean, male is female, and thick is thin. In essence, the many are one, and change is permanence.

I am the most exalted person, and also the most unworthy person.

Those words, written at the age of twenty-four, eerily foreshadowed events half a century later, when Mao, at the apex of his power, would unleash a continuous revolution of wrenching, convulsive change to bend the thinking of a quarter of humanity to conform to his will, when instability would indeed become permanent and harmony, struggle.

Achieving the 'complete transformation' of China and maintaining the momentum of the dialectic which was destined to bring it about were to be the overriding goals of Mao's political life. He knew already that it could not be done piecemeal. A guiding ideology would be required:

Those who wish to move the world must move the world's hearts and minds, [and] . . . to move people's hearts one must have great ultimate principles. Today's reforms all begin with minor details such as the parliament, the constitution, the presidency, the cabinet, military affairs, business and education – these are all side issues . . . Without ultimate principles, such details are merely superfluous . . . For the ultimate principles are the truths of the universe . . . Today, if we appeal to the hearts of all under heaven on the basis of great ultimate principles, can any of them fail to be moved? And if all the hearts in the realm are moved, is there anything that cannot be achieved?

What such principles might be was another matter. But to Mao and his idealistic little group of graduates, contemplating the benighted rule of Zhang Jingyao, it must have been clear they would not be found in Changsha. Early in May, Luo Zhanglong, one of the six founder members of Mao's original study circle, set out for Japan. Mao's old teacher, Professor Yang, who was now in Beijing, wrote with news of a programme to help Chinese students to go to France. In June, the members of the New People's Study

Society decided to send Cai Hesen to the capital to find out more. Two months later, Mao followed with a group of twenty others. Before leaving, he visited his mother in Xiangxiang and reassured her, disingenuously: 'Sightseeing is the only aim of our trip, nothing else.'

CHAPTER FOUR

A Ferment of 'Isms'

'**B**eijing is like a crucible', Mao wrote, 'in which one cannot but be transformed.' As the train drew slowly past its massive grey-brick walls, beside the crenellated battlements of the Tartar City, antique symbol of China's departed power and glory, to come to a halt in the new Western-style railway station, symbol of its need for foreign techniques and ideas, the young provincial student from the south entered a world in political and intellectual ferment. He would emerge from it, seven months later, with very different notions of how China should be saved.

Even before he left Changsha, Mao had serious doubts as to whether he wanted to go with the others to France. One difficulty was money. Although he could raise the 200 yuan for the boat fare, he told a friend, he could not get the additional hundred yuan he would need for language training. Language, in fact, seems to have been the nub of the problem: Mao struggled to master English all his life, and though eventually he learned to read with the help of a dictionary, speaking it was completely beyond him. French, he evidently concluded, was bound to be still worse. His ear for language was so poor that even mandarin lessons were a trial, and to the end of his days he conserved a thick Hunanese brogue which fellow provincials immediately identified as the speech of a Xiangtan man. There were other considerations, too. Mao still saw his future as a teacher. 'Of course, going [for language training] is one thing to do,' he conceded, 'but it is not as beneficial as engaging in education ... Education is inherently superior.' He also persuaded himself that it was important that not all the leaders of the New People's Study Society leave China at the same time. If Cai Hesen and Xiao Yu went to France, he reasoned, he should stay behind to ensure that the society continued to promote reform. Yet had language not been such an insurmountable obstacle, the other factors might not have loomed as large.

Talking later to Edgar Snow, he put a different gloss on it. 'I felt that I did not know enough about my own country, and that my time could be more profitably spent in China,' he said. 'I had other plans.'

Professor Yang, in whose house Mao and Xiao Yu stayed for a time after their arrival in Beijing, provided a letter of introduction to the university librarian, Li Dazhao, who found him a job as an assistant. Li was only five years older than Mao, but his intellectual status and national prominence set him a generation apart. A well-built, dignified man, with piercing eyes and a bristling black moustache, whose small wire-rimmed spectacles made him look like a Chinese Bakunin, Li had recently joined Chen Duxiu, the head of the Department of Letters, as co-editor of Mao's favourite magazine, *New Youth*. Working in such surroundings, in a room beside Li's office in the south-east tower of the old university library, not far from the Forbidden City, should have been everything Mao could have wished for. He had obtained, he told his family proudly, 'a position . . . as a staff member of Beijing University'. It sounded wonderful. But the reality was a crushing disappointment:

> My office was so low that people avoided me. One of my tasks was to register the names of people who came to read newspapers, but to most of them I didn't exist as a human being. Among those who came to read, I recognised the names of famous leaders of the [Chinese] 'renaissance' movement, men . . . in whom I was intensely interested. I tried to begin conversations with them on political and cultural subjects, but they were very busy men. They had no time to listen to an assistant librarian speaking southern dialect.

Mao was once again a small fish in a very big pond. In his reminiscences, nearly twenty years later, one can still sense a lingering resentment. When he tried to ask a question after a lecture by Hu Shi, who had pioneered the use of the vernacular in literature and was then completing his seminal *Outline of the History of Chinese Philosophy*, the great man, two years Mao's senior, discovering that his questioner was not a student but a mere library assistant, brushed him aside. Younger student leaders like Fu Sinian, soon to found the *Xin chao* (New Tide) Society, the most influential of the Beijing University reform groups, were equally distant.

To compound his problems, life in the capital was expensive and the eight dollars a month he was paid – half the wage of a rickshaw coolie – covered only the barest necessities. With Xiao Yu and six other Hunanese students, he rented a room in a traditional grey-tiled Beijing house, a single-storey dwelling built around the four sides of a small courtyard, about two miles from the university, in the Sanyanjing (Three Eyes Well) area near Xidan, a bustling commercial street west of the Forbidden City. It had no running water and no electric light. The eight young men possessed between them only one warm coat, which meant that in the coldest weather, when the temperature fell to 10 degrees below freezing, they had to take turns to go out. There was a small pot-bellied Chinese stove for cooking, but they had no money to buy the compacted blocks of coal dust and clay which were used to heat the kang – the traditional northern brick bed, covered with felt, with a brazier underneath – and at night they huddled together for warmth. 'When we were all packed fast on the kang, there was scarcely room enough for any of us to breathe,' Mao recollected. 'I used to have to warn people on either side of me whenever I wanted to turn over.'

Gradually, however, he began to find his way in the city. One of those who encouraged him was Shao Piaoping, a writer who headed the Journalism Research Society, whom Mao remembered, years afterwards, as 'a liberal, and a man of fervent idealism and fine character'. He also met Chen Duxiu, whose insistence on the total transformation of traditional Chinese culture as a prerequisite to modernisation influenced him, he said later, 'perhaps more than anyone else'. He attended meetings of the Philosophy Society, and he and his companions immersed themselves in the 'latest new theories' being aired in the discussion groups and magazines that sprang up all over the campus that winter and the following spring.

Like other educated young Chinese, Mao was still 'looking for a road', bewildered yet fascinated by a cornucopia of Chinese and Western ideas which alternately reinforced and contradicted each other: 'My mind was a curious mixture of ideas of liberalism, democratic reformism, and utopian socialism,' he recalled. 'I had somewhat vague passions about "nineteenth-century democracy", utopianism and old-fashioned liberalism, and I was definitely anti-imperialist and anti-militarist.'

The utopianism came from Jiang Kanghu, the anarchist-influenced leader of the Chinese Socialist Party, whose writings Mao had first encountered as a soldier during the 1911 revolution in Changsha; and from Kang Youwei, who had tried to unite the materialist universality of Euclidian mathematics with traditional Chinese idealism, picturing a realm of Great Harmony in which the family and the nation would wither away and the citizens of the world would live in self-governing economic communities without distinction of race or sex. At one point, carried away by such notions, Mao himself imagined a time when 'all under heaven will become sages . . . We may destroy all secular laws, breathe the air of harmony and drink the waves of a crystal clear sea.' A few months later, he pulled himself up: 'I am sure that once we entered [such a world],' he wrote, 'competition and friction would inevitably break forth.' Yet the visionary in Mao never quite let go of Kang's romantic, utopian dreaming. There would always be a part of him that longed to be a sage-king, free, as he put it, to roam 'a heaven-made world, wishing to share his celestial transformation with all living beings.'

From Liang Qichao he drew the conviction that no new order could be built unless the old were destroyed. Adam Smith, Huxley and Spencer furnished what he termed his 'old-fashioned liberalism', while the Ming philosopher and strategist, Wang Yangming, inspired him to link man to society, theory to practice, knowledge to will, and thought to action. From the Hunanese Ming patriot, Wang Fuzhi, came the image of a world in constant flux, in which the mutability of things, driven by the dialectical contradictions inherent in the material world, was the basic principle moving history forward.

Mao's assimilation of these men's ideas was not uncritical. He tried to weigh each proposition before approving or rejecting it, and often embraced a concept only to discard it a few months later. In the process, he strove for an approach to politics which, in his own words, combined 'the clarity that comes from introspection and . . . the knowledge that come from observing the outside world'.

The goal was to find a unifying doctrine that would weld these disparate elements into a coherent whole.

Marxism was not his first choice. In 1918, none of Marx's works, or Lenin's, was available in Chinese translation. That spring, an account of the Bolshevik Revolution had appeared in a small Shanghai anarchist magazine. But its circulation was limited, and in November, when Li Dazhao published in *New Youth* the first substantial article on the subject in Chinese, the topic was so unfamiliar that the printer at one point transliterated 'Bolshevism' as 'Hohenzollern'. Even Li, despite his enthusiastic assertion that 'the world of tomorrow . . . will assuredly belong to the Red flag', did not seem very sure what the new Bolshevik Party really represented. 'What kind of ideology is it?' he asked. 'It is very difficult to explain it clearly in one sentence.' None the less, he told his readers, it was clear that the Bolsheviks were revolutionary socialists who followed the doctrines of 'the German economist, Marx', and aimed to destroy national boundaries and the capitalist system of production.

Mao must have read this article, but it does not seem to have made much impression on him and he never referred to it subsequently. Instead, he was drawn to anarchism, which at that time was being vigorously promoted by Chinese exile groups in Paris and Tokyo. Its attraction lay in its rejection of authority, which resonated with Young China's attempts to break free from the stifling conventions of the Confucian family system, and its vision of social change engendering a new era of peace and harmony. The work-study programme to send young Chinese to France, in which Mao and his New People's Study Society were participating, had been established by Chinese anarchists. When educated Chinese talked of 'social revolution', it was usually anarchism, not Marxism, that they had in mind. Even Li Dazhao's chiliastic description of Bolshevism as an 'irresistible tide', ushering in the dawn of freedom, was couched in anarchist terms. 'There will be no congress, no parliament, no prime minster, no cabinet, no legislature and no ruler,' he had written. 'There will be only the joint soviets of labour, which . . . will unite the proletariat of the world and create global freedom . . . This is the new doctrine of the twentieth-century revolution.' Right up to the early 1920s, Chinese Marxists and anarchists continued to view each other as siblings in the same socialist family, fighting the same battle by different means.

Under the influence of its radical chancellor, Cai Yuanpei, Beijing University became a major centre of anarchist activity. Classes were offered in Esperanto, the anarchists' chosen language for their new frontier-free world. Students secretly circulated copies of the *Fuhuzhi* (Collected Essays on Tiger Taming) by Liu Shifu, founder of the quaintly named *Huiming xueshe*, the Society of Cocks Crowing in the Dark, which advocated 'communism, anti-militarism, syndicalism, anti-religion, anti-family, vegetarianism, and international language and universal harmony'.

To Mao, anarchism was a revelation. Years later he acknowledged that he had 'favoured many of its proposals' and had spent long hours discussing its possible application in China. His views emerged graphically in an article written in the summer of 1919:

There is one extremely violent party, which uses the method, 'Do unto others as they do unto you', to struggle desperately to the end with the aristocrats and capitalists. The leader of this party is a man named Marx who was born in Germany. There is another party more moderate than that of Marx. It does not expect rapid results, but begins by understanding the common people. Men should all have a morality of mutual aid and work voluntarily. As for the aristocrats and capitalists, it suffices that they repent and turn toward the good, and that they be able to work and to help people rather than harming them; it is not necessary to kill them. The ideas of this party are broader and more far-reaching. They want to unite the whole globe into a single country, unite the human race in a single family, and attain together in peace, happiness and friendship . . . an age of prosperity. The leader of this party is a man named Kropotkin, who was born in Russia.

The passage is revealing both for Mao's ignorance of Marxism and its Russian apostles – Lenin does not even get a mention – and for his explicit rejection of revolutionary violence. His ideas had matured since his passionate defence, three years earlier, of the brutal rule of 'Butcher' Tang, whose harsh dictatorship, he had held, had been justified because it produced tranquillity and order. As he turned twenty-five, Mao was beginning to think more deeply about means as well as ends, and the type of society that such means implied. Anarchism, with its stress on education, individual will and the cultivation of the self, accorded better than Marxism with the one-world utopianism Mao had absorbed from Kang Youwei, and with his traditional, Chinese scholar's belief in the power of virtue and example. He may not have been a full-fledged anarchist when he left Beijing, but for the next twelve months, anarchism, in the broad-church sense in which it was then

understood in China, provided the frame of reference for all his
political action.

The winter Mao spent in Beijing influenced him in other ways.
China's capital in 1918 was a metaphor for the country's transformation, by turns painful and exhilarating, glorious and mundane.
Behind the faded, red walls of the Forbidden City, the deposed
young Emperor still lived, surrounded by more than a thousand
Court eunuchs. Manchu bannermen, their families and retainers,
accounted for a third of the capital's one million people. Camel
trains came down from the north, from the land beyond the Great
Wall. Dignitaries in richly-embroidered brocade robes travelled in
antiquated glass-windowed carriages, with outriders on shaggy
Mongolian ponies who went ahead to clear the way.

Yet the wide, Ming-dynasty avenues, which the north wind filled
each spring with choking grey, desert dust, had been macadamised,
and motor-cars now careered about the city, carrying warlord
generals and venal politicians, their mistresses and their bodyguards, scattering the blue-hooded Beijing carts in which lesser
mortals rode. Jinrickshas, still a rarity in Changsha, jammed
Beijing's streets, 20,000 of them in 1918, twice that number three
years later. Foreign soldiers drilled on the glacis in front of the
Legation Quarter.

Wealthy families amused themselves with sleigh-rides on the ice
of the imperial lakes, pulled by coolies with iron crampons attached
to their cloth shoes, while in the narrow, unpaved lanes, the children of the poor were 'sickly and stunted, their little arms and legs
like sticks', barely surviving amid appalling deprivation. 'Most have
ulcerous sores or scars left by sores', a Chinese resident wrote.
'Many exhibit oversized heads, blindness, crooked mouths, missing
noses and other signs of having been maimed or crippled.'

Yet Mao's memories in later years were not of the clash of
old and new, ancient grandeur and Western modernity, or the
squalor and clamour of Beijing – 'a cacophony, a pandemonium,
that had no counterpart in Europe', as one Western resident put it
– but of its timeless beauty:

In the parks and the old palace grounds I saw the early northern
spring. I saw the white plum blossoms flower while the ice still

held solid over Beihai [lake]. I saw the willows over Beihai with the ice crystals hanging from them, and remembered the description of the scene by the Tang poet, Zhen Zhang, who wrote about Beihai's winter-jewelled trees looking like 'ten thousand peach trees blossoming'. The innumerable trees of Beijing aroused my wonder and admiration.

Here was the same romantic young student who, three years earlier, fleeing Changsha to escape the depredations of the Guangxi army, had stopped to describe to Xiao Yu the emerald-green of the paddy fields, luxuriant with new rice-shoots. 'Smoke hangs in the sky,' Mao wrote then, 'the mountain mists unfold; the gorgeous clouds inter-mingle; and as far as one can see, everywhere it is like a painting.' At First Normal, he had copied into his notebook the *Lisao*, the Song of Sorrow, by Qu Yuan, an ill-fated statesman of the third century BC, whom Chinese remember each spring at the Dragon Boat Festival as a paragon of princely virtue. Mao's love of poetry, kindled as an adolescent at Dongshan Upper Primary School, would remain with him through all the tumultuous years that followed, offering a soaring counterpoint to the brutishness of war and release from the arid logic of revolutionary struggle.

In March 1919, Mao received word that his mother's illness had grown worse. He was about to leave for Shanghai with the first group from the New People's Study Society which was setting out for France, and decided to go ahead with the trip anyway. When finally he did reach Changsha, having spent three weeks in Shanghai seeing off his friends, he found that his mother had already arrived in the city, accompanied by his younger brothers, to seek medical treatment. It was unsuccessful, and in October she died from what today would be an easily treatable case of lymph gland inflammation. His father, who fell ill with typhoid, followed her a few months later.

Mao felt deep guilt, not only for having been away, but because the previous autumn he had promised himself to take her to Changsha for treatment, but had done nothing about it. In a letter to his uncles, he sought to justify himself: 'When I heard [her] illness had become serious,' he wrote, '[I] rushed back home to look after her.' As he well knew, this was untrue. After her death, he wrote, more candidly, to a close friend who had also recently lost his mother: 'For people like us, who are always away from home and therefore unable to take care of our parents, such an occurrence especially causes sorrow.' Years later, his dereliction of filial duty still nagged at his conscience. In Bao'an, he pretended to Edgar Snow that his mother had died when he was a student, in what can only have been a deliberate attempt to camouflage his absence.

To support himself, Mao took a part-time job teaching history at a local primary school. Almost immediately, however, Hunan, and the rest of China, were engulfed in a new political storm.

Ever since the start of the Great War, Japan had been angling to take over the former German concession in Shandong. At the peace conference in Versailles, the Chinese government's position was that, since China had sided with the Allies, it should be permitted to recover the territory under the principle of national self-determination, championed by the American President, Woodrow Wilson. But in April it emerged that, as the price of a new Japanese loan, Premier Duan Qirui had made a secret agreement the previous autumn – which the government was now seeking to repudiate – signing away Shandong to Japanese control. Wilson, who had been supporting China, now gave up in disgust, and on April 30, 1919, he, Lloyd-George and Clemenceau – the 'Holy Trinity', as they were known – ratified Japan's take-over of German treaty rights.

When the news reached Beijing on Saturday, May 3, it provoked an unparalleled outpouring of rage, frustration and shame. This time anger was directed not at Japan alone, but at all the imperialist Powers, America first among them, and above all at China's own government, which had sold out the country's interests before the peace conference had even begun. A group of students in Shanghai wrote bitterly: 'Throughout the world, like the voice of a prophet, has gone the word of Woodrow Wilson strengthening the weak and giving courage to the struggling. And the Chinese have listened . . . They have been told that secret covenants and forced agreements would not be recognised. They looked for the dawn of this new era; but no sun rose for China. Even the cradle of the nation was stolen.'

On Sunday afternoon, 3,000 young people gathered outside Tiananmen, the Gate of Heavenly Peace, refusing appeals from the Education Minister and the Police Chief to disperse. A manifesto was approved, drafted by Lo Jialun, a student leader from Beijing University's New Tide Society. China was facing annihilation, he wrote. 'Today we swear two solemn oaths with all our fellow country-men: (1) China's territory may be conquered but it cannot be given away; (2) The Chinese people may be massacred, but they will not surrender.' The crowd, whipped up to fever pitch, called for the heads of the Communications Minister, Cao Rulin, the *éminence grise* of the warlord cabinet; and his two principal supporters, Zhang Zong-xiang, Minister at the Chinese Legation in Tokyo, and Lu Zongyou, who were blamed collectively for arranging the fatal loan. In a solemn declaration, the leaders of the protest urged the nation to resist:

> We now approach a crisis in which our country is threatened with subjugation . . . If her people cannot unite in indignation in a last-minute effort to save her, they are indeed a worthless race of the twentieth century and should not be regarded as human beings . . . As for those who willingly and traitorously sell out our country to the enemy, as a last resort we shall have to rely on pistols and bombs to deal with them. Our country is in imminent peril – its fate hangs by a thread! We appeal to you to join our struggle.

The meeting over, they marched to the Legation Quarter. The students, including many children, carried white banners on which they had written, 'Down with the nation-selling clique!' and, 'Protect our country's earth!'. Before them went two huge five-coloured national flags and a pair of scrolls with a mock funeral inscription:

> Cao Rulin, Lu Zongyou and Zhang Zongxiang
> will stink for a thousand years.
> The students of Beijing mourn them with bitter tears.

A delegation handed in petitions at the American, British, French and Italian missions. Then the cry went up: 'On to the house of the traitor!' The crowd surged forward to the home of Cao Rulin, in a side-street near the Foreign Ministry, which they found well-guarded by militia and police. When the police tried to move them on, five young diehards, led by a student anarchist, Kuang Husheng, leapt over the wall and broke a window to get inside. The imposing double doors were thrown open, and the students stormed in after them. An eyewitness reported:

> The change which came over this procession of apparently innocent schoolboys was astounding . . . The 3,000 bunched up in the narrow

street . . . went through police, gates and all in a fine indifferent frenzy
and set about making a ruin of Cao's residence in the most systematic manner. They did not find the man they were looking for,
however. With rare agility he went through a back window, over the
back wall, and landed with a badly injured leg in another street,
where he was picked up and taken to the sanctuary of a foreign hotel.
Instead, the infuriated students found an unhappy victim in Zhang
Zongxiang [who had been hiding with another Chinese official and
a Japanese journalist] . . . The mob fell upon Zhang with all their fury.
Everyone insisted upon hitting him at least once. He was dragged
into the street and then mauled in the dust until past recognition.

Kuang and his group of anarchists then set the building on fire. In the
confusion the Japanese journalist, with the help of some of the police,
managed to get Zhang away to the safety of a nearby store. There
another group of students found him and beat him unconscious again.
Eventually reinforcements arrived, and in the ensuing mêlée, a
number of students were injured, one of whom died later, and thirty-
two were arrested. As they were marched off to prison, they were
'heartily cheered by all foreigners and Chinese en route', reflecting
general contempt for the warlord government's cravenness.

Cao's elderly father, his son and young concubine, whom the
students had allowed to leave, were then driven with a military
escort to the Legation Quarter, where, in a final indignity, the legation police arrested their driver for speeding.

The May Fourth Incident, as these events were afterwards called,
spawned a nationwide movement for national renewal that spread
to every corner of China, triggering a tidal wave of cultural, political and social change that has been regarded ever since as one of
the defining periods of modern Chinese history.

In Hunan, Zhang the Venomous issued a proclamation, forbidding agitation. A handful of students distributed tracts urging people
to protest. But they were pitifully few compared with the thousands
who gathered in other provincial capitals, and Zhang's troops made
short work of dispersing them. The Governor was less successful in
preventing an economic boycott. There was a run on Japanese-
owned banks, as Chinese refused paper notes and withdrew their
savings in silver; Chinese newspapers rejected Japanese advertise-
ments; merchants refused to sell Japanese goods. The city was
plastered with crudely drawn posters, depicting China's humiliation
at the hands of the 'Eastern dwarves', and consignments of Japanese

silk, smuggled in by profiteers, were publicly burned. But even here, Hunan was merely following the lead of other provinces, which had acted sooner and more forcefully. Zhang's condemnation of the boycott as 'a national disgrace' had its effect. In Changsha, there was no merchants' strike and no Japanese shops were looted. Zhang himself noted with satisfaction that the province had been 'quite a model [compared] to other places'.

Mao played little part in these early stages of the campaign. At the end of May, he had helped set up the Hunan United Students' Association, which sent out inspection teams, working jointly with the trade guilds, to ensure that the boycott was complied with; and he reportedly wrote a 'fiery appeal', urging national resistance.

Very quickly he realised, however, that such efforts were peripheral to the main task at hand. To Mao, as to Chen Duxiu and Li Dazhao in Beijing, the boycott and the issue of Shandong were merely symptoms of China's national malaise, of which the cause, and the cure, lay far deeper. They were invaluable as a vehicle to mobilise public feeling. But if lasting change were to be achieved, the sense of national outrage would need to be channelled so as to bring about fundamental political reform. The May Fourth Incident was merely a catalyst. The energy it had released had to be made to trigger China's hoped-for renaissance, rather than being dissipated by sops, like the dismissal of Cao Rulin and his two cohorts, announced with much fanfare by the Beijing government at the beginning of June, or China's symbolic refusal, later that month, to sign the Paris peace treaty.

With this aim in mind, and with the support of the Students' Association's Chairman, Peng Huang, a fellow member of the New People's Study Society, Mao decided to produce a weekly newspaper, *Xiangjiang pinglun* (Xiang River Review), whose purpose was to agitate for thoroughgoing reform. In a front-page editorial in the first issue, published on July 14, he nailed his colours to the mast:

> Today we must change our old attitudes . . . Question the unquestionable. Dare to do the unthinkable . . . Religious oppression, literary oppression, political oppression, social oppression, educational oppression, economic oppression, intellectual oppression and international oppression no longer have the slightest place in this world. All must be overthrown under the great cry of democracy . . .
>
> The time has come . . . The floodgates . . . have opened! The vast and furious tide of the new thought is already rushing, surging along

both banks of the Xiang River! Those who ride with the current will live; those who go against it will die. How shall we greet it? How will we propagate it? How will we study it? How will we carry it out? This is the most urgent, most pressing task, for all of us Hunanese . . .

He attempted to answer that question in a long essay entitled 'The Great Union of the Popular Masses', published in three consecutive issues in late July and early August. In it, he argued that the chances of reform were brightest when 'the decadence of the state, the sufferings of humanity and the darkness of society have all reached an extreme'. To seize the opportunity so presented, what was needed was a 'great union' of all progressive forces in society – formed from 'a multitude of small unions' representing workers and peasants; students; teachers; and such disadvantaged groups as women and jinricksha-pullers, often regarded in the May Fourth period as a symbol of the country's exploitation. If only they would struggle together, Mao wrote, no force would be able to withstand them.

Could such an enterprise really succeed? 'Some doubts may well be expressed,' Mao conceded. 'Hitherto . . . organised undertakings on a large scale were something of which the people of our country were quite simply incapable.' But now, he insisted, it was different. The consciousness of the Chinese masses had been raised, the Empire had been overthrown, and democracy, 'the great rebel', was waiting in the wings:

We are awakened! The world is ours, the state is ours, society is ours! If we do not speak, who will speak? If we do not act, who will act? . . . Ideological liberation, political liberation, economic liberation, liberation between men and women and educational liberation are all going to burst from the deep inferno where they have been confined and demand to look at the blue sky. Our Chinese people possess great inherent capacities! The more profound the oppression, the more powerful its reaction, and since this has been accumulating for a long time, it will surely burst forth quickly. I venture to make a singular assertion: one day the reform of the Chinese people will be more profound than that of any other people, and the society of the Chinese people will be more radiant than that of any other people . . . [and] it will be achieved earlier than that of any other place or people. Gentlemen! Gentlemen! We must all exert ourselves! We must all advance with the utmost strength! Our golden age, our age of glory and splendour, lies before us!

The essay was remarkable not only for its clarity and force, its unabashed confidence in the future and its implicit exaltation of youth as the primary motor of change, but because it offered a coherent, practical programme for achieving it. That made it stand out from the flood of material being published in the four hundred or more student news-sheets that sprang up in China at that time, fifteen of them in Changsha alone, and overnight it won Mao, and the *Xiang River Review*, a national reputation. The liberal philosopher, Hu Shi, who had snubbed Mao nine months earlier, described it as 'one of the [truly] important articles' of the time, and praised its author's 'exceedingly far-reaching vision and effective and well-chosen arguments'. Li Dazhao reprinted it in the *Meizhou pinglun* (Weekly Review), which he edited in Beijing. The New Tide leader, Lo Jialun, another of those who had spurned Mao's overtures when he was a library assistant, said it conveyed the essence of the student movement's aims.

More important in the long-term for Mao's development was the new emphasis he placed on organisation, which eventually would lead him to Marxism. For the moment, however, he continued to view the world revolution, which he maintained was moving inexorably eastward from Leningrad to Asia, in essentially anarchist terms. His articles dealt with educational policy, the struggle for women's rights, and such well-worn anarchist themes as 'whether or not to retain the nation, or the family, or marriage, [and] whether property should be private or public'. The Marxist concept of class struggle, to the extent that he understood it at all, he found entirely alien: '[If] we use oppression to overthrow oppression,' he wrote, 'the result [will be] that we still have oppression. This would be not only self-contradictory, but also totally ineffectual.' Rather than waging a 'revolution of bombs [and] . . . of blood', oppressors should be shown the error of their ways. Indeed, he used the word 'class' very rarely, and then usually in such un-Marxist categories as 'the classes of the wise and of the ignorant', or 'the strong and the weak'.

Writing for a wider audience gave Mao for the first time an opportunity to apply to contemporary politics the analytical tools he had developed as a student. In 'The Great Union of the Popular Masses', he asserted a dialectical relationship between oppression and the reaction against it, which was straight out of Paulsen's *System der Ethik*. The same sense of historical flux informed his assessment of Germany's defeat: 'When we look at history in the light of cause

and effect, joy and suffering are often closely interrelated, inseparable. When the joy of one side reaches an extreme, the suffering of
the other side will inevitably also reach an extreme.' Thus the invasion of France by the Holy Alliance in 1790 contained within it the
seeds of Napoleon's rise; Napoleon's subjugation of Prussia in 1815
created the conditions for the French defeat of 1870, which in turn
paved the way for Germany's defeat in 1918. Nor would it end
there: the harshness of the conditions imposed by the Allies at
Versailles made another cycle of conflict inevitable. 'I guarantee',
Mao wrote, 'that in ten or twenty years, you Frenchmen will yet
again have a splitting headache. Mark my words!'

  Mao's sympathy for Germany, shared by many educated
Chinese, reflected admiration for its 'towering strength' and 'spirit
of greatness', which had enabled it to become the most powerful
nation in Europe. Yet here, too, his sense of history gave him a
prescience which few others at that time shared.

> We must realise [he wrote at the end of July] that Japan and Germany
> are a couple of dogs, male and female, that have tried to mate on a
> number of occasions, and although they haven't made it up to now,
> their lusting after each other will never go away. If the militarist
> adventurers of the authoritarian Japanese government are not ex-
> terminated, if the German . . . government is not overthrown by
> revolution, and if this lustful stud and lascivious bitch are still not
> separated, the danger will be truly great.

When those lines were written, he was still only twenty-five years old.

By the beginning of August 1919, an uneasy calm had returned to
China. The government in Beijing had made symbolic amends. The
strikes and demonstrations were over.

  Only in Hunan did friction continue. At a meeting with student
representatives, Governor Zhang, fanned by four bodyguards,
yelled furiously: 'You are not permitted to march in the streets, you
are not permitted to hold meetings . . . You should work hard at
studying and teaching. If you don't listen, I'll cut off your heads!'
Soon afterwards the Students' Association was banned and Peng
Huang, its chairman, fled to Shanghai.

  Mao was unimpressed. On August 4, the *Xiang River Review*
published a wickedly mischievous petition, which he himself had

written, begging the Governor to allow the reopening of Changsha's leading newspaper, the *Dagongbao*:

> We, the students, have long been worried about the Honourable Governor . . . We did not in the least expect that the paper would be banned, and its editor arrested, just because it published a manifesto . . . expressing opposition to [an] illegal election [rigged by Zhang's supporters] . . . We sincerely hope that Your Honour, for the sake of both interest and profit, will reach a correct decision [and release him]. In that case, the people of Hunan will forever remember your virtuous action. Otherwise . . . ill-informed outsiders may proclaim that this government is abolishing the right to free speech. We should guard against evil tongues more than a flooding river . . . Your Honour is enlightened and farsighted, and it is impossible that you do not agree with us.

The Governor's response was predictable. Despite Mao's claim that the *Review* dealt solely with social and academic affairs, the next issue was confiscated and the journal ordered closed. A few days later, a group of soldiers, led by Zhang's adopted son, bayoneted to death two young radicals from Shanghai who were helping the students to organise the anti-Japanese boycott. The following month, Mao took over as editor of another student journal, *Xin Hunan* (New Hunan). In the first issue, he proclaimed defiantly: 'Naturally we will not be concerned whether things go smoothly or not. Still less will we pay attention to any authority whatsoever.' After four weeks, it, too, was banned.

At this point, Mao's mother died. When he resumed writing, more than a month later, for the *Dagongbao*, which Zhang had permitted to reopen, the plight of China's women and the strait-jacket of the Confucian family were uppermost in his mind.

During the summer, in 'The Great Union of the Popular Masses', he had already taken on the role of spokesperson for women's equality:

> Gentlemen, we are women! . . . We are also human beings . . . [yet] we are not even allowed to go outside the front gate. The shameless men, the villainous men, make us into their playthings . . . But so-called 'chastity' is confined to us women! The 'temples to virtuous women' are scattered all over the place, but where are the 'pagodas to chaste men'? . . . All day long they talk about something called being 'a worthy mother and a good wife'. What is this but teaching

us to prostitute ourselves indefinitely to the same man? . . . Oh, bitterness! Bitterness! Spirit of freedom! Where are you? . . . We want to
sweep away all those devils who rape us and destroy the liberty of
our minds and our bodies!

In 1919, such views were widely shared among progressive young
Chinese, revolted by the extremes of suffering which many Chinese
women were routinely expected to endure.

That autumn, a particularly ghastly case occurred in Changsha,
involving a young woman who had been affianced by her parents
as the second wife of an elderly merchant. Twenty-three-year-old
Zhao Wuzhen was borne in procession in her bridal sedan chair,
decked out in red silk, to her future husband's home. But when the
door was opened, it was discovered that, on the way, she had cut
her throat with a razor.

Mao, with bitter memories of his own arranged marriage, and
still in mourning for his mother, whom he saw as having been
trapped in a similarly loveless union, threw himself into the debate,
publishing no fewer than ten articles in the *Dagongbao* in the space
of a fortnight. Her family, he acknowledged, were partly to blame,
by forcing her to marry an old man she did not love. But the root
cause of the tragedy was 'the darkness of the social system', which
had left her no alternative but to take her own life. Citing one of his
favourite proverbs – 'Better a shattered piece of jade than an
unbroken pot of clay' – he argued that what she had done was 'an
act of true courage', and disagreed with those, like Peng Huang, who
suggested that she could have found other ways of struggling against
her fate:

Mr Peng wonders why Miss Zhao didn't just run away . . . First let
me raise a few questions, after which I shall present my view.

1)   Within the city of Changsha, there are more than forty pedlars
[who go from house to house, selling linen goods to women in the
inner quarters] . . . Why is this?
2)   Why is it that all the lavatories in the city of Changsha are for
men only, and none for women?
3)   Why is it you never see women entering a barber shop?
4)   Why is it single women are never seen staying in hotels?
5)   Why is it you never see women going into tea-houses to
drink tea?

6) Why is it that the customers in [the big shops] . . . are always men, never women?

7) Why is it that of all the carters in the city, not one is a woman? . . . Anyone who knows the answers to these questions will understand why it was that Miss Zhao could not run away . . . Even if [she] had wanted to, where could she have run to?

Mao's new emphasis on social factors, and on first-hand observation, made him re-examine his political goals. To change China, he concluded, it was first necessary to change society. To change society, one must first change the system. To change the system, one must begin by changing those in power.

Some of his colleagues in the New People's Study Society demurred, holding that it was the role of scholars to set forth great ideas, not to 'concern ourselves with small problems and petty affairs'. True up to a point, Mao replied, but so long as the larger aim was not forgotten, promoting practical, political change was the 'most economical and most effective means' to influence the current situation and bring about fundamental reform.

Under his influence, this pragmatic, nuts-and-bolts approach was adopted by Changsha's students that winter when renewed efforts to enforce the anti-Japanese boycott provoked a showdown with Zhang Jingyao.

On December 2, some 5,000 students and others including representatives of the Chamber of Commerce, members of the Society for Promoting National Goods, factory workers and clerks, marched to the former imperial examination hall, for a rally at which they planned to burn fourteen boxes of smuggled Japanese cloth. As the proceedings neared their climax, several hundred soldiers, led by the Governor's youngest brother, Zhang Jingtang, debouched from the surrounding streets, and encircled the demonstrators, rifles at the ready. 'What kind of people are you, making this disturbance?' he shouted at the crowd. 'You should realise that we Zhang brothers are the ones who give you money for your studies.' Spurring his horse forward, he went on angrily: 'I know how to set fire to things as well as you . . . I am also a military man and know how to put people to death. I'll have some of you put to death for certain if this sort of thing goes on.' When a student protested that the rally was patriotic, he laid about him with the flat of his sword and the troops began to advance. 'You Hunanese are bandits,' he

cried, 'and your women are bandits too.' The leaders of the protest
were forced to kneel on the ground, while Zhang boxed their ears,
and a number of arrests were made.

The incident, trivial in itself, was the final straw for the Hunanese.
Those whom Zhang had insulted were the sons and daughters of the
elite. Already, that autumn, a leading Changsha banker had told a
foreign acquaintance: 'This time the trouble is [among] the gowned
classes, not the short-coated masses . . . Better for this city to be
looted and get rid of Zhang Jingyao than to have to continue longer
under the present conditions.' After eighteen months of northern
rule, the economy had collapsed. In many areas even the troops
were no longer being paid, prompting Zhang, like other local
warlords, to issue secret orders to farmers to resume opium cultivation, which, though banned by treaties with the Powers (and by
a new presidential decree, issued in Beijing), generated large
amounts of tax revenue. Now the local gentry decided the Governor
would have to go.

Two weeks after the confrontation in Changsha, a delegation left
secretly for Beijing to plead for Zhang's removal. Mao was among
its members, charged with setting up a 'People's News Agency' to
distribute information about the anti-Zhang campaign to Chinese-
language newspapers. On December 24, the 'news agency' scored
a notable scoop when students at Wuhan discovered forty-five sacks
of opium poppy seeds, each weighing 200 lbs, in a railway freight
shed, awaiting shipment to Changsha, addressed to Governor
Zhang. For the next two months, the delegation produced a hail of
petitions denouncing Zhang's 'insatiable greed' and 'tyrannical
rule'. They held a meeting, which Mao attended, with an official at
the Prime Minister's Office, and Hunanese members of the National
Assembly pledged to resign their seats unless Zhang was dismissed.
But the Governor remained firmly in place, and at the end of
February, the frustrated delegates decided they could do nothing
more.

In the end, when Zhang fell, four months later, it was not because
of popular protests but warlord politics. In May 1920, Wu Peifu,
sensing that the simmering conflict between his Zhili clique and
the rival Anfu government was coming to a head, decided to aid
Tan Yankai's southern forces to recover Hunan, while he himself
headed north to Beijing to do battle with Duan Qirui. On June 11,
the Governor fled, signalling his departure by blowing up a

munitions dump. In a characteristic final gesture, he extorted one last million dollars from local merchants by threatening to burn down the city and execute their leaders. The arrival of the southern forces the following afternoon provoked, one resident wrote, 'the greatest day of rejoicing I have ever seen in Changsha', as joyful crowds marched through the streets and innumerable firecrackers exploded late into the night. Little more than a month later, Duan Qirui's armies were defeated by Wu and other Zhili generals, and the Anfu clique, which had ruled northern China for three years, was formally dissolved.

If Mao's trip to Beijing was a failure as an exercise in practical politics, it turned out to be instrumental in his eventual conversion to Marxism. Already the previous autumn, when Zhang's crack-down on the students was at its height and the *Xiang River Review* had been banned, he had established a 'Problem Study Society', one of the aims of which was to see how the 'union of the popular masses' could be advanced. The society was eclectic in scope, and the list of more than a hundred issues with which it proposed to deal, ranging from 'whether or not socialism can be established' to such esoteric matters as 'the problem of drilling traffic tunnels under the Bering Sea, the English Channel and the Straits of Gibraltar', illustrated the sense of limitless possibility that the May Fourth movement unleashed.

The society had been inspired by a celebrated debate that year between Hu Shi and Li Dazhao. Hu had argued that China needed 'More Study of Problems; Less Talk about Isms'. Li contended that without 'isms' (or theories), problems could not be understood. Mao, in September, 1919, had tried to straddle the two.

As the months passed, however, the 'isms' loomed larger. A major influence was an article by Li Dazhao, entitled 'My Marxist Views', published in *New Youth*, the second part of which, dealing with Marx's economic theories, appeared in November 1919. Almost overnight, Mao's vocabulary changed. For the first time he started to realise that the system which he wanted to transform was essentially economic in nature. The 'core relationship' of traditional marriage, he announced, was 'economic, and thus controlled by capitalism'. If the marriage system was to change, women must obtain economic independence. If society was to change, the old economic relationships would have to go, and a new economic system must be put in their place. A month later, Mao began referring to his colleagues in the New People's Study Society as 'comrades', and to working people as 'toilers'.

In the spring of 1920, Russia's decision to repudiate the 'unequal treaties', under which, like the other Powers, it had enjoyed extra-territorial rights in China, provoked a surge of popular gratitude towards the Bolshevik regime, and immense interest among Chinese radicals in the principles by which it ruled.

Mao was deeply impressed, and tried to learn all he could about the new government in Moscow. Russia, he told a friend, was 'the number-one civilised country in the world'. He became desperate to go there, to see communism for himself, and talked to Li Dazhao about the possibility of setting up a work-study programme to send young people to Moscow, similar to the scheme under which Chinese were travelling to France. At one point he even announced that he was going to learn Russian. Yet at heart Mao remained deeply ambivalent about the benefits of foreign travel. 'Too many people are infatuated with the two words, "going abroad",' he grumbled – only to add wistfully, a few lines later: 'I think the only correct solution is for each of us to go abroad once, just to satisfy our craving for it.' In the end, he resolved his dilemma by postponing a decision, remaining in China to study 'for the time being'.

Even in Beijing, however, this was easier said than done.

Very little Marxist literature was available in Chinese. The first complete translation of the *Communist Manifesto* did not appear until April 1920, when Mao was about to leave for Shanghai, and none of Lenin's writings was translated until the end of the year. What there was, he eagerly sought out. The *Manifesto*, in particular, influenced him profoundly. So did Kautsky's *Class Struggle*, which advocated non-violent revolution. Li Dazhao, who had just founded a Marxism Study Society at Beijing University, also gave him encouragement, as did Chen Duxiu, whose faith in communism, Mao said later, 'deeply impressed me at what was probably a critical period of my life'.

But Mao was still a long way from embracing Marxism as a doctrine. While Chen was already on the point of setting up a Socialist Youth League branch and a 'communist group' in Shanghai, Mao was enthusiastically promoting the Japanese 'New Village' movement, which envisaged the establishment of communes based on Kropotkin-style mutual aid, shared resources, and work and study, as a first step towards the peaceful creation of a classless, anarchist society. Manual labour was compulsory, and to reduce the gap between town and country, and between students and society, members were required to go out among the peasantry to spread modern ideas, much as students in Russia were sent to the villages to spread Bolshevism.

That summer, after several such schemes had collapsed, in Beijing and elsewhere, Mao conceded that the communes were impractical. But he did not abandon the 'New Village' concept altogether. A year later he founded a 'Self-study University' in Changsha, based on the principles of communal living, whose members were pledged to teach, study, and 'practice communism'. He also set up a Cultural Book Society to disseminate in the province the new literature which the May Fourth movement had spawned. Once again, Marxism was not a major influence. The society sold more books by Kropotkin, Hu Shi and John Dewey, than by Kautsky or Marx. Mao at that time considered Dewey, who taught that 'education is life, school is society', to be one of the 'three great contemporary philosophers', along with Bertrand Russell and the French thinker, Henri Bergson.

Years later, in Bao'an, Mao told Edgar Snow that by the summer of 1920, he considered himself a Marxist. Nothing could have been further from the truth. He admitted to a friend at the time that he still did not know what to believe. Indeed, far from being a source of enlightenment, Mao's Marxism that summer was just another element of confusion. He castigated himself for not being better organised: 'I am too emotional and have the weakness of being vehement,' he confessed to one of his former teachers. 'I cannot calm my mind down, and I have difficulty in persevering. It is also very hard for me to change. This is truly a most regrettable circumstance!' He wished he had X-ray eyes, he went on, so that he could read more widely. 'I would like very much to study philology, linguistics and Buddhism, but I have neither the books nor the leisure to study them, so I slack off and procrastinate . . . It is hard for me to live a disciplined life.'

The desire to study Buddhism may sound strange in a man of strong radical beliefs. But to Mao, in 1920, Chinese culture was still the foundation on which everything else had to be built – and would remain so for the rest of his life.

He never repudiated the ideas of his youth. Instead, his thinking developed by accretion. The idealism he absorbed from Paulsen and Kant was overlain with the pragmatism of Dewey; the liberalism of John Stuart Mill with social Darwinism; Adam Smith with T. H. Huxley. Liang Qichao's constitutionalism gave place to the socialism of Jiang Kanghu and Sun Yat-sen. The utopianism of Kang Youwei prepared the way for anarchism and Marxism. All this 'modern knowledge' was buttressed by a classical inheritance – from Wang Yangming of the Ming to the Song neo-Confucian, Zhu Xi; from the great Tang essayist, Han Yu, to Qu Yuan of the Warring States – which itself was anchored in the bedrock of the traditional Chinese amalgam of Buddhism, Confucianism and Daoism which Mao had absorbed in his childhood in the village schools of Shaoshan. Each layer subsumed the others. Nothing was ever lost.

One result was a remarkable capacity, which grew more pronounced as Mao aged, for metaphor and lateral thinking. But more crucially, his approach to Marxism, when finally he embraced it, was coloured by other, very different intellectual traditions.

The Cultural Book Society stocked, alongside anarchist texts, such determinedly traditional offerings as a repunctuated edition of *Water Margin* in the classical literary language. And in the spring of 1920, when Mao was finally able to do some of the sightseeing he had spoken of two years before, it was to the classical sites of antiquity that his footsteps first turned:

> I stopped at Qufu, and visited Confucius' grave. I saw the small stream where Confucius' disciples bathed their feet, and the little town where the sage lived as a child. He is supposed to have planted a famous tree near the historic temple dedicated to him, and I saw that. I also stopped by the river where Yan Hui, one of Confucius' famous disciples, had once lived, and I saw the birthplace of Mencius. On this trip I climbed Taishan, the sacred mountain of Shandong, where General Feng Yuxiang retired and wrote his patriotic scrolls . . . I walked around Dongting lake, and I circled the wall of Baodingfu. I walked on the ice of the Gulf of Beihai. I walked around the wall of Xuzhou, famous in [the novel, *The Romance of*] *the Three Kingdoms*, and around Nanjing's wall, also famous in history . . . These seemed to me then achievements worth adding to my adventures . . .

As that account, sixteen years later, to Edgar Snow, made clear, to Mao the journey back through China's past was in its way as much an accomplishment as his journey into the new, foreign world of the 'isms' which held the key to China's future.

Well before Zhang Jingyao was forced to abandon the governorship of Hunan, a lively debate developed over how the province should be ruled once he went. The Republic of China, which Sun Yat-sen had founded, was now widely viewed as a failure. Since 1913, Hunan had been ruled by three northern warlords – 'Butcher Tang, Fu the Tyrant and Zhang the Venomous' – each worse than the one before. Tens of thousands of Hunanese had died in a futile civil war; hundreds of thousands had lost their homes. Among the provincial elite, the barbarism of the last two years had convinced conservatives and progressives alike that Hunan would be far better off under Hunanese control. From there it was but a small step to proposing that the province declare its independence – not just in words, but in fact – first from the government in Beijing and then from the rest of China. In 1920, the new watchwords were self-rule and self-government. The slogan, 'Hunan for the Hunanese!', resonated anew, and the old 'independent kingdom' mentality, on which nineteenth-century travellers had remarked, underwent a dramatic revival.

Mao was initially sceptical. 'I do not really understand just how we should [do this],' he wrote in March of that year. 'Since it is a province within China, it would not be easy for Hunan to establish its independence, unless the whole situation changes in future and our status becomes like that of an American or German state.'

But less than three weeks later he was won over, and joined Peng Huang in founding an 'Association for Promoting Reform in Hunan', based in Shanghai and subsidised by a group of wealthy Hunanese businessmen. The overthrow of Governor Zhang, he warned, risked being a 'tiger's head with a snake's tail' – a brave beginning not followed through. The 'evil system' itself had to be changed, or another warlord would take Zhang's place. But to change the system throughout China was not possible. The best approach, therefore, was to start in one local area, in this case, Hunan, applying the principle of self-determination, in the hope that it would become a model for other provinces to follow. Then, eventually, all would 'join together in providing a general solution to the problems of the whole country.'

In June 1920, ten days after Zhang fell, Mao took these arguments a step further in a letter published in the Shanghai newspaper, *Shenbao*:

> From now on the essential things for us to do are . . . to abolish the military governorship, cut back the military forces, and . . . to build the people's rule . . . There is no hope of fully establishing people's rule in China within the next twenty years. [So] during this period, Hunan had best protect its own boundaries and implement its own self-rule . . . without bothering about the other provinces or the central government. Thus it can [become like] one of the [American] states . . . a hundred years ago . . . By bringing into full play the spirit of the people of Hunan, we can create a Hunanese civilisation within the territory of Hunan . . . For the past four thousand years, Chinese politics has always opted for grand outlines of large-scale projects with big methods. The result has been a country outwardly strong but inwardly weak; solid at the top but hollow at the bottom; high-sounding on the surface but senseless and corrupt underneath. Since the founding of the Republic, famous people and great men have talked loudly about the constitution, the parliament, the presidential system and the cabinet system. But the more noisily they talk, the bigger the mess they make. Why? Because they try to build on sand, and the edifice collapses even before it is completed. We want to narrow the scope and talk about self-rule and self-government in Hunan

For the next two months, Hunanese of all social strata, from the peasantry in their burnt-out villages to the great merchants in the cities, were too busy trying to repair their shattered livelihoods after the destruction wrought by Zhang's army to give much thought to politics. Mao spent several weeks with his brothers in Shaoshan, looking after the affairs of the family which, as the eldest son, he now headed. In Changsha, Tan Yankai began, for the third time in his career, to piece together what had survived of the provincial administration. But he refused the now hated title of *dujun*, or Military Governor, preferring instead to be called 'Commander-in-Chief' of the forces which had liberated the city.

Hunan was thus in name, and in fact, independent of Beijing's control, but the form of its future government was undecided. In late August, this issue was addressed by Xiong Xiling, a Hunanese scholar who had been Prime Minister in the early years of the Republic. He proposed that the new Governor be elected by a college composed of local assembly-men and members of educational and business associations. Counter-proposals followed, and when Mao returned to Changsha at the beginning of September, he found the debate once more in full swing. He immediately contributed an essay of his own, published in the *Dagongbao*. 'A storm of change is rising throughout the entire world,' he proclaimed; 'the call for national self-determination echoes to the heavens.' Hunan should become the first of 'twenty-seven small Chinas' which would break free from 'foundationless big China', inaugurating a process of change that would lead to a 'thoroughgoing general revolution' of new progressive forces.

Tan Yankai hesitated. Self-government would confer a broad-based legitimacy that would make his position less vulnerable to the ambitions of local military commanders. But he wanted to ensure that the deliberations remained firmly under his own control.

In mid-September, therefore, Tan summoned a convention of gentry and officials to begin drafting a new constitution. When this was criticised as too narrow, he suggested giving the provincial assembly the task. To Mao, Peng Huang, and their ally, the *Dagongbao* editor, Long Jiangong, that was unacceptable, too. 'If we want self-government,' Long wrote, 'we cannot rely on this small number of people from a special class . . . We must find salvation for ourselves! . . . We must throw off the snare of top-down rule!' They proposed a constitutional convention, elected through universal suffrage by all the people of Hunan over the age of eighteen (or in one of Mao's early proposals, over fifteen).

A petition to this effect was approved at a public meeting Mao chaired on October 8, at which he urged his fellow townspeople not to let slip the chance the self-government movement was offering:

Citizens of Changsha! . . . If you succeed, [the] 30 million people [of Hunan] will benefit. If you fail, 30 million people will suffer. You must know that your responsibility is not light. The political and social reforms of the Western countries all started with movements of the citizens. Not only did the great transformations in Russia . . . and other countries which have shocked the world recently originate with the citizens, but even in the Middle Ages it was the citizens alone who wrested the status of 'freemen' from the autocrats . . . Citizens! Arise! The creation of Hunan's future golden age is being decided now.

Two days later, on the Chinese Republic's National Day, a huge demonstration wound its way in pouring rain through the narrow

streets of the old inner city, banners flying and bands playing, to
the Governor's yamen, where a copy was presented to Tan.
The *North China Herald* reported at length on the event under the
headline, 'Provincial Home Rule in China: Every Province its Own
Master':

> The document was the work of three gentlemen: Mr Long
> [Jiangong], the editor of the *Dagongbao*; Mr Mao [Zedong] of the First
> Normal School; and Mr Peng [Huang], a bookseller . . . Of the 430
> [signatories] . . . about 30 [were said to] be connected with the press
> of the city; perhaps 200 were teachers or men of the scholar class;
> about 150 [were] merchants, and, say, 50 [were] working men. It is
> interesting that not only were working men invited to sign but that
> representatives of their class stood side by side with some of the most
> cultured men in the city as members of the deputation of 15 which
> took the document to the governor . . . There can be no doubt that
> the eyes of China are fixed on Hunan at this juncture. Hunan has a
> chance that [other provinces] have not . . . If Hunan does act, its
> example will spread.

But even as the petition was delivered, Tan was having second
thoughts. As the campaign had gathered pace, it had grown more
radical. The petitioners wanted a political system based on 'democracy and socialism', and had hinted that if they did not get it 'a
bloody revolution' might ensue. In his articles in the *Dagongbao*,
Mao had stated explicitly that their object was not to have 'one
Hunanese' – in other words, Tan – rule Hunan, '[for then] the ruler
is made master and those he rules are made slaves'; the aim was
'rule by the people'.

In fact, this was largely rhetoric. Mao himself conceded that, in
a country where 90 per cent of the population was illiterate, a mass-
based Leninist-style revolution to 'make a clean sweep of the
reactionary parties and wash away the upper and middle classes'
was not possible. The best that could be hoped for was to create a
movement of the educated elite, to 'push things forward' from the
outside.

But even with those caveats, conservatives were alarmed. 'Hunanese civilisation' was one thing; 'people's rule' was quite another.

During the National Day march, a group of demonstrators, disregarding the organisers' warnings against disorderly conduct, had
climbed on to the roof of the provincial assembly building – symbol

of elitist rule – and, amid cheers and ribaldry from below, ripped down the Assembly's flag. The following day, Tan seized on this incident as proof that the kind of popular self-government the radicals were advocating was unworkable, and announced that he was withdrawing his support.

The movement then collapsed. On November 1, John Dewey and Bertrand Russell, both of whom were then visiting China, addressed a conference in Changsha on constitutional issues, in which Mao also took part. But no conclusion was reached. A few weeks later, Tan was repaid for his timidity when a local army commander, Zhao Hengti, overthrew him in just the kind of military power-play he had been hoping a popular mandate would prevent.

Zhao ordered the drafting of a provincial constitution of his own, which was published the following April and promulgated in January 1922. But it was only a pale shadow of the 'total self-rule' that Mao and his friends had been fighting for. For a time Zhao maintained friendly relations with the southern government in Canton, and became known as a leading proponent of federalism in China. In reality, however, one warlord had replaced another, as Mao had warned might happen. Zhao continued as Governor until 1926, when he was overthrown in his turn by another rebellious military officer.

To Mao, the failure of the independence movement was a grievous disappointment. All his efforts over the past year, he told friends, had been 'to no avail'. The Hunanese had shown themselves to be 'muddle-headed, with neither ideals nor long-term plans. In political circles, they are lethargic and extremely corrupt, and we can say that there is absolutely no hope for political reform.' It was time to start afresh, he wrote, to 'carve out a new path'.

Characteristically, this provoked a feverish bout of soul-searching, as he reproached himself for everything from emotional shortcomings to lack of progress in his studies. But instinctively he felt the way ahead lay through the New People's Study Society, which had languished during the campaign against Zhang, and whose future role and activities were now the subject of intense debate.

What was needed, Mao believed, was a 'dedicated group of

comrades', sharing common goals, who would combine their intellectual resources to work out a joint strategy for thoroughgoing
reform. They should work quietly behind the scenes, without
'seeking for vain glory or trying to cut a figure', and should
'absolutely not jump on the political stage to [try to] grasp control'.
Secondly, in order to 'overthrow and sweep away the old order', it
was necessary to mobilise 'the people of the whole country, not [just]
a few bureaucrats, politicians and military men'. An 'ism' – any 'ism'
– required a movement to put it into effect, and the movement, in
turn, required a broad popular base. As Mao put it in a letter to his
friend Luo Zhanglong in November 1920:

> We really must create a powerful new atmosphere . . . To [do this]
> naturally requires a group of hard-working and resolute people, but
> even more than that it requires an ism that everyone holds in
> common. Without an ism, the atmosphere cannot be created. I
> think our study society should not merely be a gathering of people
> bound by sentiment; it must become a group of people bound
> together by an ism. An ism is like a banner; only when it is raised
> will the people have something to hope for and know in which
> direction to go.

But the question remained: which 'ism'? Already, that July, sharp
differences had emerged among the sixteen members of the group
in France. At a meeting in Montargis, sixty miles south of Paris,
where they had gone for language studies, Cai Hesen had argued
that China needed a Russian-style revolution. Xiao Yu disagreed,
proposing instead a moderate anarchist-inspired reform
programme, similar to that which Mao had championed in the *Xiang
River Review* a year earlier, based on education and mutual aid. The
differences were papered over with a compromise that the society's
guiding principle would be 'to reform China and the world'. But
afterwards Xiao and Cai wrote separately to Mao, setting out their
rival positions. The main mission of socialism, Cai argued, was to
destroy the capitalist economic system, using the dictatorship of the
proletarist as its weapon:

> I don't think anarchism will work in the world today, because obvi-
> ously there exist two antagonistic classes in this world. In
> overthrowing the dictatorship of the bourgeoisie, there is no way the
> reactionary classes can be suppressed save by the dictatorship of

the proletariat. Russia is a clear illustration. Therefore I think that
in the future reform of China . . . we must first organise a Communist
Party, because it is the initiator, propagandist vanguard and operational headquarters of the revolutionary movement.

Cai was not alone in drawing this conclusion. In August, Chen
Duxiu had founded China's first 'communist group' in Shanghai. In
an article in *New Youth*, shortly afterwards, he called for 'revolutionary means [to] be used to establish a state of the working class'.

In Changsha, Mao and Peng Huang, with the backing of
a wealthy sympathiser in the provincial administration, set up a
Russian Studies Society, which, over the next three months,
recruited more than a dozen young Hunanese, including such future
communist luminaries as Ren Bishi and Peng Shuzhi, to go to
Moscow to attend the newly established University of the Toilers of
the East.

In October, at Chen Duxiu's suggestion, a Marxist Study Circle
was set up in Hunan by the Principal of the Wang Fuzhi Academy,
He Minfan, an old-fashioned literary scholar with a flowing white
beard falling on to his formal silk gown, who had developed, somewhat improbably, a keen interest in socialism. Mao and a fellow
teacher, He Shuheng, were among its five founding members, and
together began discussing the establishment of a Socialist Youth
League branch.

Yet Mao was a reluctant convert. Where Cai Hesen understood
at once that Bolshevism was the answer to China's problems, and
embraced it enthusiastically, Mao came to it despite himself. 'Cai is
the theorist, Mao the realist', their friends used to say. In the end, it
was realism that led Mao to endorse what he called Russian 'terrorist
tactics'. It was, he told Cai, 'a last resort' after 'other, better means'
– a reference to the self-government movement and the anarchist
'new village' experiment – had failed. 'Russian-style revolution'
looked like being the only one that would work:

The Russian method represents a road newly discovered after all
the other roads have turned out to be dead ends. This method alone
has more potential than other methods of transformation . . . Social
policy is no method at all, because all it does is patch up some
leaks. Social democracy resorts to a parliament as its tool for trans-
forming things, but in reality the laws passed by a parliament always
protect the propertied class. Anarchism rejects all authority, and I

fear that such a doctrine can never be realised. The moderate type of communism, such as the extreme freedom advocated by [Bertrand Russell], lets the capitalists run wild, and therefore it will never work either. The radical type of communism, or the ideology of the workers and the peasants, which employs the method of class dictatorship, can be expected to achieve results. Hence it is the best method to use.

The alternative, advocated by Xiao Yu, was to use 'the method of education', to persuade the bourgeoisie of the error of their ways, so that 'it would not be necessary to limit freedom or to have recourse to war and bloody revolution'. In theory, Mao wrote in December, this would of course be best. But in practice it was not possible. 'Historically no despot, imperialist or militarist, has ever stepped down of his own free will without waiting for people to overthrow him':

Education requires: (1) money, (2) people, and (3) institutions. In today's world, money is entirely in the hands of the capitalists. Those in charge of education are all either capitalists or the slaves of capitalists . . . If you teach capitalism to children, these children, when they grow up, will in turn teach capitalism to a second generation of children. If education has thus fallen into the hands of the capitalists, it is because they have 'parliaments' to pass laws protecting the capitalists and handicapping the proletariat. They have 'governments' to execute these laws and to enforce actively the advantages and prohibitions they contain. They have 'armies' and 'police' to provide passive guarantees for the safety and happiness of the capitalists and to repress the demands of the proletariat. They have 'banks' as their treasury to ensure the circulation of their wealth. They have factories, which are the instruments by which they monopolise the commodities produced. Consequently, unless the Communists seize political power . . . how could they take charge of education? . . . That is why I believe the method of education is not feasible . . .

He concluded that Xiao Yu's view was untenable, and expressed 'profound approbation for the views of [Cai] Hesen'. On New Year's Day, 1921, eighteen members of the New People's Study Society made their way through a snowstorm to a meeting at the Cultural Bookstore in Changsha, where, after two days' discussion, they voted by a margin of twelve to three, with three members undecided, in favour of Bolshevism as the society's common goal.

By now the Marxist Study Circle had been transformed into a 'communist group', with Mao, He Minfan, Peng Huang, He Shuheng and another teacher as its first members. On January 13, the Hunan branch of the Socialist Youth League, composed mainly of students and New People's Study Society members, held its inaugural meeting. From Shanghai, Mao received copies of the underground journal, *Gongchandang* (Communist), which Chen Duxiu's group had started in November, and of a draft Party Manifesto, issued at about the same time. It called for common ownership of the means of production, the abolition of the state and the creation of a classless society, and declared:

> The instrument to defeat capitalism is class struggle . . . [The] task is to organise and concentrate the power of this class struggle and to make the force opposing capitalism stronger . . . The objective is to organise some large industrial associations . . . and also to organise a revolutionary, proletarian political party – the Communist Party. The Communist Party is to guide the revolutionary proletariat to fight against capitalists and to seize political power from them . . . Power will be placed in the hands of workers and peasants, just as the Russian Communist Party did in 1917.

Soon after this, Mao wrote to Cai Hesen, explicitly rejecting anarchism as a practical political doctrine, and endorsing Marx's 'materialist conception of history' as the philosophical basis for the new party they were planning to create. His conversion was complete.

Mao's Marxism would always retain an anarchist tincture. But the long search for an 'ism' was over.

Becoming a Marxist was not the only change in Mao's life in 1920. His personal circumstances altered markedly too. As a student, he had been proverbially penniless, and remained so after he graduated. Much of the time he borrowed to get by, relying on the Confucian tradition of mutual aid, whereby friends who have money help those who have not (in the knowledge that one day the roles may be reversed, and they will be helped in turn). None the less, it was a precarious existence. He recounted, years later, how his much-vaunted sightseeing trip that spring had almost ended in disaster when he ran out of money soon after leaving Beijing:

I did not know how I was to get any further. But as the Chinese proverb says, 'Heaven will not delay a traveller', and a fortunate loan of 10 yuan from a fellow student . . . enabled me to buy a ticket as far as Pukou [not far from Shanghai] . . . On the way [I visited the classical sites] . . . But when I reached Pukou I was again without a copper . . . Nobody had any money to lend me; I did not know how I was to get out of town. But the worst of the tragedy happened when a thief stole my only pair of shoes! Ai-ya! What was I to do? But again, 'Heaven will not delay a traveller', and I had a very good piece of luck. Outside the railway station I met an old friend from Hunan, and he proved to be my 'good angel'. He lent me money for a pair of shoes, and enough to buy a ticket to Shanghai.

In Shanghai, Mao was reduced to taking in washing to help pay for the room he shared with three Hunanese students. Doing washing was not so bad, he told friends, but he had to spend most of his earnings on tramcar fares in order to collect and deliver it.

Once back in Changsha, however, his fortunes improved dramatically. In September he was appointed Principal of the primary school attached to First Normal, which gave him for the first time a regular, well-paid job, and a status that accorded with his increasingly influential role in provincial politics. It also made possible the second big change in Mao's life. That winter he married Yang Kaihui, the twenty-year-old daughter of his ethics professor at First Normal, Yang Changji, who had died in Beijing the previous January.

In the liberal circles in which Mao moved, relations between the sexes in China in the early part of the century were not that different from those in contemporary Europe or America. Like all Chinese cities, Changsha had its entertainment district, known as the 'willow lane quarter', where singing girls entertained the wealthy, and common prostitutes, the poor. As in Edwardian Britain or *belle époque* France, brothel-going attracted no social stigma. Indeed, so universal was the practice that every new radical group which claimed to have China's future at heart, from the anarchist 'Six Noes Society', founded by Cai Yuanpei in 1912, to Mao's New People's Study Society, laid down as a condition of membership that those who joined must abstain from visiting prostitutes to show their moral commitment to the reformist cause.

There is an early hint of Mao's own attitude in a memorial poem for a schoolfriend, which he wrote in 1915 at the age of twenty-one: 'Together we denounced the licentious, but how shall we purge the evil in ourselves?' Two years later, he likened the heroic drive of great men to 'the irresistible sexual desire for one's lover, a force that will not stop, that cannot be stopped'. Sex and food, he wrote then, were the two basic human instincts.

By his own account, Mao fell in love with Yang Kaihui during the winter of 1918, when he was working as an assistant librarian at Beijing University. Whether he had an opportunity to declare his feelings is unclear. Meals at the professor's home, according to Xiao Yu, always took place in complete silence, and even in a liberal household it was not considered proper for young people of opposite sexes to be alone together. But from this time on, Mao's writings began to sound a more romantic note. 'The power of the human need for love is greater than that of any other need,' he proclaimed. 'Unless people have yielded to the irresistible natural force of love, they either . . . start big rows [after marriage], turning the bedroom into a battlefield of deadly mutual hostility, or find themselves a world of secret amours "amid the mulberry fields of the Pu River." '*

The course of love, however, did not run smooth. After his return to Changsha he was smitten by another young woman, Tao Yi, who became his first serious girlfriend. She was an early member of the New People's Study Society, and their romance evidently lasted through most of the spring and summer of 1920, when they worked together in the Hunan self-government movement and on setting up the Cultural Book Society. Then they drifted apart, and in the autumn Mao was back courting Kaihui.

Cai Hesen and his girlfriend, Xiang Jingyu, had written in the meantime from Paris to say they had decided to flout convention, and instead of getting married, had concluded 'a union based on love'. Mao was lost in admiration:

> I think we should regard Xiang and Cai as our leaders and organise an 'Alliance for the Rejection of Marriage' [he wrote]. Those who have marriage contracts should break them (I am opposed to humanism!). Those who do not have marriage contracts should not enter into them . . . I think that all those men and women who live under the marriage system are nothing but a 'rape brigade'. I have long since proclaimed that I would not join this rape brigade.

* This has been a synonym for illicit love-affairs since ancient times. The phrase derives from a line in the *Liji*, or Book of Rites, which links debauchery on the banks of the Pu River with the ruin of the State of Wei.

Yet less than three months later, he did marry. Yang Kaihui's family no doubt insisted on it. For a professor's daughter to marry a peasant's son, even one who had become as prominent as Mao, was enough of a social gamble, without adding to it the opprobrium that in Changsha, far more than in France, would attach to an irregular union. In any case, the kind of marriage Mao railed against was the traditional one arranged by a matchmaker. To him, the criterion of marriage was that 'the man and the woman both know in their hearts that they have a deep and mutual affection for each other'. The key to happiness was free choice.

In the autumn of 1921, they moved into a small house in an area called Clearwater Pond, just outside Changsha's Small East Gate. For the next few years, perhaps for the only time in Mao's life, he had a truly happy family to come home to. His first son, Anying, was born in October 1922; the second, Anqing, in November 1923; the youngest, Anlong, in 1927. It was a surprisingly traditional Chinese household: Kaihui stayed at home with the children, while Mao roamed far and wide, working for the cause to which they were both now committed. As the years passed, the cause took over, and the family was left behind.

CHAPTER FIVE

The Comintern Takes Charge

On Friday, 3 June, 1921, the Lloyd Triestino steamer, the *Acquila*, docked at Shanghai after a six weeks' voyage from Venice. Among the passengers who disembarked was a Dutchman. Powerfully built, in his late thirties, with close-cropped dark hair and a swarthy moustache, he reminded those who met him of a Prussian army officer. He had had a trying journey. Even before he took ship, he had been arrested in Vienna, where he had gone to obtain a Chinese visa. A week later the Austrian police released him, but not before notifying the governments of all the countries for which he had entry permits in his passport. At Colombo, Penang, Singapore and Hong Kong, the British posted police guards at the docks to prevent him going ashore. The Dutch Legation in Beijing asked the Chinese government to deny him entry too, but received no reply. Shanghai was a law unto itself, where Beijing's writ did not run. It was the soft, wet maw of China, which, with each new tide, sucked in the dispossessed, the ambitious and the criminal – ruined White Russian families, Red adventurers, Japanese spies, stateless intellectuals, scoundrels of every stripe – and sent out in return idealistic youths, seeking foreign learning in Tokyo and Paris. The Chinese called the city a 'hot din of the senses'. To foreigners, it was 'the Whore of the East'. The aesthete, Sir Harold Acton, remembered it as a place where 'people had no idea how extraordinary they were; the extraordinary had become ordinary; the freakish commonplace'. Wallis Simpson was rumoured to have posed nude, with only a lifebelt round her, for a local photographer.

Eugene O'Neill, accompanied by a Swedish masseuse, had a
nervous breakdown in Shanghai. Aldous Huxley wrote of its 'dense,
rank, richly clotted life . . . nothing more intensely living can be
imagined.' The journalist, Xia Yan, saw 'a city of 48-storey
skyscrapers, built upon 24 layers of hell'.

Mr Andresen, as the Dutchman called himself, proceeded along
the bund, past the towering, granite-built citadels of British capitalism – the Hong Kong and Shanghai Bank, the Customs House with
its mosaic ceiling of Yangtse river junks, Jardine & Matheson, and
the East Asiatic Company – past the park with its apocryphal sign,
'Chinese and dogs not allowed', past the Seamen's Hostel and
Suzhou Creek, to take a room at the Oriental Hotel.

As he looked around him, at the pavements crowded with
Chinese men, wearing long gowns and Panama hats; immaculately
dressed taipans in chauffeur-driven sedans; nightclubs full of Eur-
asian taxi-dancers, where young expatriates caroused through the
night; ragged coolies, glistening with sweat, straining at huge loads;
the textile mills, in which women and children worked fourteen-
hour shifts; and the filthy slums across the river, where this emerging
new proletariat lived, he might have been forgiven for feeling a
surge of missionary zeal. For Hendricus Sneevliet, to give him his
real name, also known as Martin Ivanovich Bergman, Comrade
Philipp, Monsieur Sentot, Joh van Son and Maring, amid a host of
other aliases, was a missionary of a kind. He had been sent to
China by Lenin as the first representative of the Comintern, the
Communist International, to help the Chinese comrades organise a
party which would give fraternal support to the Bolshevik leadership in 'Mekka', as he referred to Moscow, and help spread the
worldwide revolution in which they all fervently believed.

Sneevliet was not the first Russian emissary to China. Initial
contact had been made in January 1920. Three months later,
Grigory Voitinsky had been sent on a fact-finding visit, with the
Comintern's approval, by the Bolshevik Party's Far Eastern
Bureau, based in Vladivostok. In the summer, two more Russians
had been despatched to Canton, under cover of being news agency
correspondents.

Voitinsky's arrival had been skilfully timed to coincide with the
upsurge of enthusiasm for the Soviet Union triggered by Moscow's
announcement that it would renounce its extraterritorial rights. He
was a man of great tact and charm, and the Chinese with whom he

had dealings saw him as the perfect example of everything a revolutionary comrade should be. During the nine months he spent in China, he helped Chen Duxiu organise the 'communist group' in Shanghai, the Socialist Youth League and the communist journal, *Gongchandang*, and drafted the Party Manifesto, which Mao and others received that winter, as a preliminary to the holding of a founding Congress to bring the provincial groups together to form a full-fledged Communist Party.

Hendricus Sneevliet was a man of a very different stamp. He was a member of the Comintern Executive, and had already spent five years in Asia as an adviser to the Communist Party of Dutch-ruled Indonesia. He exuded a mixture of obstinacy and arrogance which signalled not only that he knew better than any of the Chinese comrades, but that it was his bounden duty to bring them into line. Zhang Guotao, a Beijing graduate who had helped Li Dazhao set up the North China 'communist group', recalled their first meeting, shortly after the Dutchman's arrival:

> This foreign devil was aggressive and hard to deal with; his manner was very different indeed from that of Voitinsky . . . He left the impression with some people that he had acquired the habits and attitudes of the Dutchmen that lived as colonial masters in the East Indies. He was, he believed, the foremost authority on the East in the Comintern, and this was a great source of pride to him . . . He saw himself coming as an angel of liberation to the Asian people. But in the eyes of those of us who maintained our self-respect and who were seeking our own liberation, he seemed endowed with the social superiority complex of the white man.

At the end of June 1921, Mao and He Shuheng left Changsha by steamer, amid great secrecy, to join eleven other delegates, from communist groups in Beijing, Canton, Jinan, Shanghai, Tokyo and Wuhan, to attend the founding Congress which Voitinsky had initiated. It began on July 23, in a classroom at a girls' school in the French concession, which had closed for the summer holidays. Neither Chen Duxiu nor Li Dazhao attended. In their absence the proceedings were chaired by Zhang Guotao, whom Mao had met in Beijing two-and-a-half years earlier when he had worked as a library assistant there. Sneevliet and an aide, Nikolsky, from the newly established Comintern bureau in Irkutsk, were present for the first two days, but then withdrew to let the Chinese argue among themselves.

The discussion turned on three points: what kind of party they should create; what stance it should adopt towards bourgeois institutions, specifically the National Parliament and the Beijing and Canton governments; and its relationship with the Comintern.

Sneevliet, in his opening address, noting that all those present were students or teachers, had stressed the importance of forging strong links with the working class. The Marxist scholar, Li Hanjun, who represented the Shanghai group, immediately disagreed. Chinese workers, he retorted, understood nothing of Marxism. It would take a long period of education and propaganda work before they could be organised. In the meantime, Chinese Marxists needed to decide whether their cause would best be served by an organisation propagating Russian Bolshevism or German-style Social Democracy. To rush headlong into building a working-class party, dedicated to proletarian dictatorship, would be a serious mistake. Sneevliet was scandalised. But on this issue, at least, the Dutchman carried the day, and in its first formal statement, the new Chinese Communist Party (CCP) declared in true Bolshevik fashion:

> The programme of our party is as follows: With the revolutionary army of the proletariat, to overthrow the capitalistic classes and to reconstruct the nation from the working class until class distinctions are eliminated . . . To adopt the dictatorship of the proletariat . . . To overthrow the private ownership of capital, to confiscate all the means of production, such as machines, land, buildings . . . and so on, and to entrust them to social ownership . . . Our party, with the adoption of the soviet form, organises the industrial and agricultural labourers and soldiers, propagates communism, and recognises the social revolution as our chief policy; it absolutely cuts off all relations with the yellow intellectual class and other such groups.

On the other two points in dispute, the outcome was less satisfactory to Moscow. This was partly because of the way the Congress ended. On July 29, when it became clear that serious disagreements remained, Sneevliet said he wished to put forward some new ideas and asked that the next session take place not at the school but at Li Hanjun's house, which was also in the French concession. Next evening, soon after the meeting began, a man looked through the door, muttered something about having come to the wrong house and hurriedly departed. On Sneevliet's instruction, the delegates immediately dispersed. A group of Chinese detectives, led by a French officer, arrived a few minutes later, but despite a four-hour search, found nothing. After that, it was thought too dangerous to hold further meetings in Shanghai, and the final session was held on a pleasure boat on the reed-fringed South Lake at Jiaxing, a small town on the way to Hangzhou, forty miles to the south. There, too, Sneevliet was unable to speak: it was felt that the presence of foreigners would make the group too conspicuous, so he and Nikolsky did not take part. As a result, when the boat trip ended at dusk, and the delegates shouted in unison, 'Long live the [Chinese] Communist Party, long live the Comintern, long live Communism – the Emancipator of Humankind', they had taken what one of them called 'many furious and radical decisions', but not all of them were to the Comintern's liking.

They had resolved, for instance, to adopt 'an attitude of independence, aggression and exclusion' towards other political parties, and to require Communist Party members to cut all ties with non-communist political organisations. This sectarian stance was at odds not only with Sneevliet's hopes for a tactical alliance with Sun Yat-sen's Guomindang, which he rightly saw as the strongest revolutionary force in China at that time, but also with Lenin's thesis, approved by the Second Comintern Congress in Moscow a year earlier, that communist parties in 'backward countries', in so far as they were able to exist at all, would have to work closely with national-revolutionary bourgeois democratic movements.

No agreement was reached at all on the respective merits of the Beijing and Canton governments. In Sneevliet's eyes, as in Chen Duxiu's, the southern regime was much more progressive.

Still worse, from the Dutchman's perspective, the delegates refused to acknowledge Moscow's supremacy. Although the Party programme spoke of 'uniting with the Comintern', it made clear that this was as an equal, not a subordinate.

Tension over relations with 'Mekka' continued after the Congress ended.

When, in September, Chen Duxiu took up his responsibilities as Secretary of the provisional Central Executive Committee, he found that Sneevliet, as Comintern representative, was not only issuing orders to Party members on his own authority, but expected him to submit a weekly work report.

For several weeks, Chen refused to have anything to do with the

Dutchman. The Chinese Party was in its infancy, he told members of the Shanghai group. China's revolution had its own characteris-tics, and did not need Comintern help. Eventually a modus vivendi was realised, mainly because, Chen's disclaimers notwithstanding, the Comintern provided the money, some 5,000 US dollars a year, which the Party needed to survive. But bad blood remained, and not only because of Sneevliet's authoritarian style. He was to be the first in a long line of Soviet advisers to offend Chinese sensibilities, reflecting a cultural and racial divergence which the internation-alism of the communist movement initially papered over, but which forty years later would exact its own revenge.

Mao played a minor role in the First Congress. He made a report (which has been lost) on the work of the Hunan group, which by July accounted for ten of the fifty-three members of the communist movement in China; and he and Zhou Fuhai, a Hunanese student representing the Tokyo group, which boasted all of two members, were appointed official note-takers. Zhang Guotao remembered him as a 'pale-faced youth of rather lively temperament, who in his long gown of native cloth looked rather like a Daoist priest out of some village'. Mao's 'rough, Hunanese ways', Zhang wrote, were matched by a fund of general knowledge but only a limited under-standing of Marxism. None of the participants recall him having contributed much to the debates. He evidently felt intimidated by his more sophisticated companions, most of whom, he told his friend Xiao Yu, who was visiting him in Shanghai at the time, 'are very well-educated, and . . . can read either Japanese or English'. That brought back all his old feelings of inadequacy about languages, and as soon as he returned to Changsha, he plunged into his English lessons again. Two months later, the Hunan branch of the CCP was established, with Mao as its Secretary, on the symbolic date of October 10, the anniversary of the Xinhai Revolution launched ten years before.

For the next few months, Mao devoted himself to building up the Party's tiny following. In November, the provisional Party Centre issued a directive, requiring each provincial branch to have at least thirty members by the summer of 1922. Mao's branch was one of three to meet the target, the others being Canton and Shanghai. The same month he organised a parade to celebrate the Bolshevik

Revolution. This became an annual event, drawing coverage from the Republican daily, *Minguo ribao*, in Shanghai:

> An immense red flag fluttered from the flagpole on the esplanade in front of the Education Association building, with on each side two smaller white banners, bearing the slogan: 'Proletarians of the World, Arise!' Other small white flags were inscribed, 'Long live Russia! Long live China!' Then came a multitude of small red flags, on which were written: 'Recognise Soviet Russia!' . . . 'Long live socialism!' and 'Bread for the workers!' Tracts were handed out to the crowd. Just as the speech-making was about to begin, a detachment of police appeared, and the officer in charge announced that, by order of the Governor, the meeting must disperse. The crowd protested, invoking Article 12 of the Constitution, which gave citizens the right of free assembly . . . But the officer refused to discuss it, and said the Governor's order must be obeyed. The crowd grew angry and shouted: 'Down with the Governor!' At that, the police set about their business. All the flags were torn down and the demonstrators forcibly dispersed. It was 3 o'clock in the afternoon, and torrential rain began to fall, preventing any further resistance.

Such tensions with Governor Zhao notwithstanding, Mao was able to win enough support from his allies in the provincial elite to establish the 'Self-study University' of which he had written a year earlier, financed by an annual local government grant of some 2,000 US dollars, a substantial sum for the time.

The school's stated objectives were 'to prepare for reforming society' and 'to bring together the intellectual class and the working class'. In practice it served as a training ground for future Party activists, numbering at its peak some two dozen full-time students. At first, the fact that it was sponsored by the Wang Fuzhi Society, and was housed in the former Wang Fuzhi Academy, obscured this political purpose, but with time it came closer to Mao's original concept of an academic commune, where teachers and students 'practised communist living'. Mao gave up his job at the primary school to serve as the university's director, while also teaching Chinese at First Normal. He Shuheng was academic dean. He Minfan acted as Principal, until Mao's unconventional ideas about health and fitness caused them to fall out. In the sweltering heat of the Changsha summer, Mao encouraged the students to attend classes in what by the standards of the time was considered a scandalous state of undress. He Minfan, who was of an earlier, more conservative generation,

was deeply offended, and after other disagreements they parted on
bad terms.

The main thrust of Mao's activities over the next two years,
however, was as a labour organiser. Bolshevik orthodoxy held that
the revolution must be built by the proletariat, and the First Congress
had laid down that the 'chief aim' of the Party was to establish industrial unions. There were then about one-and-a-half million
industrial workers in China, as against 250 million peasant farmers.
Conditions in the factories were Dickensian. The noted American
labour campaigner, Dr Sherwood Eddy, reported after an investigation in China on behalf of the YMCA:

> At the Beijing match factory, there are 1,100 workers, many of them
> boys between 9 and 15 years old. Work starts at 4 a.m. and stops at
> 6.30 p.m. with a few minutes rest at midday . . . seven days a week . . .
> The ventilation is inadequate, and the vapour from the low-grade
> phosphorus damages the lungs. After thirty minutes, my throat was
> burning. The workers breathe it all day long . . . On average, 80 fall
> ill each day. [I also visited] a Beijing textile plant. It employs 15,000
> young people. The workers are paid nine dollars a month for an
> 18-hour workday, seven days a week. Half are apprentices, who
> receive no training and are paid no wages, but are simply given
> food . . . Their families are too poor to feed them, and are glad to give
> them to the factory . . .
>
> In a lodging house I visited, each room, no more than seven feet
> square, was occupied by 10 workers, half of whom worked by day
> and half by night. In the whole of that house there was no stove, not
> a stick of furniture, no fireplace and no lavatory . . . Nearby,
> belonging to the same owner, is a sort of windowless cavern with a
> single door. A group of girls, aged between 10 and 15, sleep there
> during the day. At night they work in the factory, earning 30 cents a
> shift. They sleep on a wooden board under a pile of rags. Their
> biggest worry is that they won't hear the factory siren, and if they
> arrive late they'll lose their jobs. These people do not live. They exist.

In Hunan, female and child labour was less common than in the
coastal settlements, but otherwise conditions were little different.
Until 1920, workers and artisans were organised, as they had been
since medieval times, by the traditional trade guilds. But in
November of that year two young anarchist students, Huang Ai and

Pang Renquan, had established an independent body, the Hunan Workingmen's Association. By the following August, when the Party, at Sneevliet's suggestion, set up a Labour Secretariat under Zhang Guotao, with Mao as head of its Changsha branch, the association had some 2,000 members and had already led a successful strike at the city's Huashi cotton mill.

Pang was a Xiangtan man, from a village about ten miles from Shaoshan. In September 1921, Mao accompanied him on a visit to the Anyuan coal-mines, part of a big Chinese-owned industrial complex on the border of Hunan and Jiangxi, to see what possibilities might exist for organising the workers there.

The trip itself was inconclusive, but two months later the relationship had progressed sufficiently for Mao to contribute an article to the association's newspaper, the *Laogong zhoukan* (Workingmen's Weekly). 'The purpose of a labour organisation', he wrote, 'is not merely to rally the labourers to get better pay and shorter working hours by means of strikes. It should also nurture class consciousness so as to unite the whole class and seek the basic interests of the class. I hope that every member of the Workingmen's Association will pay special attention to this very basic goal.' Soon afterwards, Huang and Pang secretly joined the Socialist Youth League, and in December helped to organise a mass rally, which drew 10,000 people, in protest against manoeuvres by the Powers to extend their economic privileges in China. Mao's strategy of co-opting the anarchists, and gradually shifting their focus towards a more Marxist agenda, seemed to be succeeding.

But then, in January 1922, disaster struck. After the New Year holiday, 2,000 workers at the Huashi mill downed tools when the management announced that it was withholding their annual bonus. Equipment and furniture were smashed, and fights broke out with the company police in which three workers were killed. On January 14, Zhao Hengti, who was a major shareholder in the company, declared the strike to be 'an anti-government act' and sent in a battalion of troops. After handing out random beatings, they forced the men to resume work by training machine-guns on them. Next day, the 15th, a plea for help was smuggled out. The Workingmen's Association sprang into action. A message came from Governor Zhao asking the two young organisers to come to the mill to negotiate. When they arrived, at nightfall on January 16, they were detained and taken to the Governor's yamen, where Zhao questioned them at length. The workers were granted their bonus. But Huang and Pang were brought to the execution ground by the Liuyang Gate and beheaded, and the Workingmen's Association was banned.

Their deaths, coming less than three weeks after Zhao had promulgated an ostensibly liberal provincial constitution, enshrining the principle of Hunanese autonomy, sent shock waves across China. Sun Yat-sen urged that Zhao be punished. Cai Yuanpei, at Beijing University, and other eminent Chinese intellectuals, sent telegrams of protest. Mao spent most of March and part of April in Shanghai, fanning a virulent campaign against Zhao in the Chinese-language press. Even the *North China Herald* declared the Governor's methods to be 'inexcusable'.

On April 1, Zhao issued a long, extremely defensive statement, justifying his conduct:

> Unfortunately the general public does not seem to know the correct reasons for the executions, and has mixed them up with matters of the Workingmen's Association in such a way as to bring a charge against me of injuring the association . . . The two criminals Huang and Pang . . . [colluded with] certain brigands . . . in a plot to get arms and ammunition . . . Their plan was to overturn the government and spread their revolutionary ideas by causing trouble at the time of the Lunar New Year . . . On me rests the burden of the government of the 30,000,000 people of Hunan. I dare not allow myself to be so confused as to exhibit kindness to merely two men at the peril of the province. Had I not acted as I did, disaster could not have been averted . . . From the first I have always protected the interests of the workers . . . I look for Hunan labour to flourish and prosper.

No one believed these assertions. But, by denying that the executions were linked to the activities of the Workingmen's Association, and explicitly affirming that the pursuit of the workers' interests was legitimate, Zhao opened the way for the labour movement to resume.

Mao's next move was to develop a network of workers' night schools. In this, he received unwitting assistance from the YMCA, which, with the backing of the provincial government, had just launched a mass education campaign of its own. Party members were organised to volunteer as teachers, and Mao had a simple textbook written, which, under cover of being a literacy aid, propagated socialist ideas.

The most successful of these ventures was at Anyuan, where Mao despatched Li Lisan to act as full-time organiser. Li, the same callow youth who, six years earlier, had sent 'half a reply' to Mao's appeal for members for the New People's Study Society, had joined the Party in France. Mao liked him no better than before, but he proved a first-rate union man; in May, he persuaded the Anyuan magistrate to authorise the establishment of a 'Miners' and Railwaymen's Club', which boasted its own library, schoolroom and recreation centre. Four months later, it had 7,000 members.

Meanwhile Mao, sometimes accompanied by Yang Kaihui, now pregnant with their first child, travelled to factories and railway depots all over the province, to assess the prospects for opening new clubs elsewhere. The Party Centre in Shanghai had given instructions that labour agitation among railway workers must have top priority. A Railwaymen's Club was established in Changsha, followed in August by one in Yuezhou, on the main line north to Hankou.

It was at Yuezhou that the trouble began.

On September 9, a Saturday, groups of workers blocked the line by sitting on the rails, demanding higher wages and modest welfare improvements. Troops were sent to disperse them, killing six workers and seriously injuring many more, along with women and children who had come to support their menfolk. When the news reached Changsha, Mao sent an incendiary telegram to other workers' groups, seeking their support:

Fellow workers of all the labour groups! Such dark, tyrannical and cruel oppression is visited only on our labouring class. How angry should we be? How bitterly must we hate? How forcefully should we rise up? Take revenge! Fellow workers of the whole country, arise and struggle against the enemy!

Governor Zhao let it be known that he would stay neutral. Yuezhou was garrisoned by northern troops loyal to Wu Peifu, the head of the Zhili warlord clique in Beijing, whom at this point Zhao viewed as an adversary; any disruption of the rail link to the north could only be to his advantage.

Word of these events reached Anyuan late on Monday night. For some time, trouble had been brewing there over the mining company's refusal to pay back-wages. Now, Mao urged, the moment had come for the Anyuan men to strike too. Li Lisan drew up a list of demands, and forty-eight hours later, at midnight on September 13, the electricity supply to the mineshafts was cut; the mine entrance barricaded with timbers, and a three-cornered flag planted in front of it, bearing the defiant legend: 'Before we were beasts. Now we are men!'

The miners left two generators running, to prevent the mine flooding. But the following weekend, with negotiations going nowhere, there were calls for them to be switched off. At that, the mine directors capitulated, approving an across-the-board payrise of 50 per cent; union recognition; improved holidays and bonus conditions; the payment of back-wages; and an end to the traditional labour contract system, under which middlemen creamed off for themselves half the annual wage bill. A few days later, more than a thousand delegates from the country's four main rail systems met in Hankou, and threatened a national rail strike unless immediate wage increases were granted. Their demands, too, were met.

In both the railwaymen's and the miners' strike, Mao's role was indirect. As CCP Secretary in Hunan, he had guided the strike movement and acted as its political spokesman, but he played no active part in the conflict. A dispute among masons and carpenters, which began a week later in the provincial capital itself, involved him much more closely.

All through the summer, a row had been simmering in the ancient trade guild of the Temple of Lu Ban, the patron saint of journeymen builders. Their earnings had been eroded by inflation of the paper currency, and in July they asked the Temple Board to persuade the District Magistrate to approve a wage increase. But the pressures of the market economy had eroded guild solidarity, too, and contrary to custom, the board insisted that the guild members subscribe 3,000 silver dollars to finance the negotiation.

'They went off to all the fancy restaurants, like the Cavern Palace Spring, the Great Hunan and the Meandering Gardens, and held sumptuous banquets,' one guild member recalled. 'These bloodsuckers managed to fill their bellies with food and wine, but they didn't come up with a penny for us.'

The stalemate was broken by a man named Ren Shude. The orphaned son of a poor peasant-farmer, he had joined the guild twenty years before as a thirteen-year-old carpenter's apprentice. The previous autumn he had done some work for the Wang Fuzhi Society, helping to get its premises ready for the new Self-Study University. Mao had befriended him, and at the beginning of 1922 he had become one of the first Changsha workers to join the Communist Party.

Ren now proposed that the men go to the Temple and demand an explanation. About eight hundred did so, but the board's negotiators fled to an inner sanctum, known as the Hall of Five Harmonies, where the workers dared not follow. At his suggestion, a small group then met Mao, whom Ren introduced as a schoolteacher involved in the workers' night-school movement. He advised them to create an independent organisation, with a system of '10-man groups', or cells, like that used by the railwaymen's and miners' unions. Three weeks later, on September 5, Ren presided over the founding congress of the Changsha Masons' and Carpenters' Union, with an initial membership of nearly 1,100 men. Mao himself drafted its charter, and appointed another Party member to act as union secretary.

For the next month, as the mine and rail strikes unrolled at Anyuan and Yuezhou, Ren and his colleagues carefully laid their plans. Activists surreptitiously handed out pamphlets and, late at night, went to the barracks where, after the officers had retired, they fired arrows with tracts tied to them over the walls, to get the workers' case across to the soldiers. Mao mobilised the sympathies of liberals within the provincial elite, former associates of Tan Yankai and members of the Hunan autonomy movement. The editor of the *Dagongbao*, Long Jiangong, inveighed against the very principle of the government regulating wages, noting that there was no comparable restriction on landlords raising rents. 'In the provincial constitution,' he wrote, 'free enterprise is guaranteed. If employers object that [workers'] wages are too high, they should just refuse to hire them. Why do you want to restrict their demands and stop them raising the price of their labour?'

On October 4, the magistrate announced that the wage increase had been rejected. Next day, which was a local holiday, the union

leaders met at Mao's home at Clearwater Pond, outside the Small
East Gate, and resolved to launch a strike for more money, and for
the right to free, collective bargaining. This was underlined in the
strike declaration that Mao wrote, which was pasted up on walls in
the city:

> We, the masons and carpenters, wish to inform you that for the sake
> of earning our livelihood, we demand a modest pay increase . . .
> Workers like us, engaged in painful toil, exchange a day of our lives
> and of our energy for only a few coppers to feed our families. We are
> not like those idlers who expect to live without working. Look at the
> merchants! Hardly a day goes by without them raising their prices.
> Why does no one object to that? Why is it that only we workers, who
> toil and sweat all day long for a pittance, have to go through such an
> ordeal of being trampled on? . . . Even if we cannot enjoy our other
> rights, we should at least have the freedom to work and to carry out
> our business. On this point we will make our stand, and go to our
> deaths if need be. This right we will not surrender.

The following day, all construction work in the city ceased. The
magistrate, supported by the guildmasters, hoped to sit out the
dispute. But winter was approaching. The authorities encountered
growing public pressure for a rapid end to the strike, so that people
could get repairs done to their homes before the cold weather
arrived. On October 17, the magistrate appointed a mediation
committee, and ordered the strikers to settle quickly: 'If you refuse
to listen, you will be bringing bitterness on yourselves,' he warned.
'You should all think long and hard. Do not wait till it's too late and
you regret it!' But the committee's offer, though more generous
than earlier proposals, would have ended the traditional craft distinction between older and younger workers' wages. It, too, was
rejected, and the union announced that the workers would march
en masse to the magistrate's yamen on Monday, October 23, to
deliver a petition. The march was promptly banned, and doubts
began to surface among the union leaders. The banning order
described them as 'fomenters of violence', a term which had last
been used to justify the executions of Huang Ai and Pang Renquan
in January. By the weekend, the future of the strike was in the
balance.

Mao spent much of Sunday night talking to Ren Shude and other
members of the union committee. The situation, he argued, was

totally different from that of January. Strikes were now occurring in many parts of China, and in this particular dispute, the masons and carpenters had widespread public support. Zhao Hengti had no direct interest in the outcome, as he had had at the Huashi cotton mill, of which he had been a shareholder. Moreover he was now politically isolated, having close relations neither with Sun Yat-sen in the south nor Wu Peifu in the north.

Next morning, almost all the 4,000 masons and carpenters in the city assembled in the square outside the former imperial examination hall, and marched in good order to the District Magistrate's yamen. There they found the main gate blocked by a table. On top of the table were two benches, on which stood a broad arrow, symbol of the military's right to carry out summary executions. Next to it was a board setting out the mediation committee's last offer.

Mao had marched in the ranks with them, wearing workman's clothes. A union delegation went inside, but emerged some hours later saying that the magistrate refused any concessions. Then a second delegation was admitted. Mao remained outside. At dusk, when extra troops appeared to reinforce the yamen guards, he led the workers in chanting slogans to keep their spirits up. Darkness fell with still no agreement. Supporters brought lanterns, and they prepared to settle in for the night.

The prospect of several thousand angry men on the loose in the centre of Changsha overnight did not please Governor Zhao, who sent a staff officer to try to persuade them to leave. A missionary, who acted as an occasional correspondent for the *North China Herald*, happened to be on hand:

> About 10 p.m. I wandered across to the precincts of the yamen, and found myself just in time to witness a most interesting interview . . . The staff official . . . was well-matched in the 10 representatives of the workmen . . . On both sides there was perfect courtesy. The staff official 'mistered' each of the representatives, and used not only the ordinary terms of respect but maintained the bearing of ordinary intercourse among gentlemen. The workmen, while speaking with complete ease and fluency, made no slips in etiquette . . .
>
> The staff officer mounted a table . . . After [he had exhorted] the men to return to their homes . . . one of the 'ten', not the acknowledged leader, asked permission to put the officer's suggestion to a vote. 'Will you go home? Those who are willing to do so, hold up their hand.' Not a hand was held up. 'Those who intend to stay hold

up their hands.' Not a hand was wanting. 'You have your answer,' was all that the representative commented . . .

The staff officer . . . openly admitted not only that the District Magistrate, but that even the Governor, had no right to fix the rate of wages by proclamation without the agreement of both sides . . . Now and again things became lively; but the workmen paid pretty good attention to the commands for order and silence from their own delegates. After an hour's enjoyment of as well-conducted debate as I have ever listened to, I left the disputants at it. It was 2 a.m. before, tired out and hungry (the soldiers prevented anyone from carrying in either food or clothing), the workmen agreed to go back to their headquarters.

The 'acknowledged leader' whose debating skills so impressed the worthy prelate was Mao. The union representative who called the vote was probably Ren Shude. Before the workers left, they had extracted a promise that talks would resume at the Governor's yamen next morning. For two days more, Mao and the union leaders negotiated with Governor Zhao's deputy, Wu Jinghong. If a businessman could stop selling goods because it was no longer profitable, Mao argued, why could a worker not stop work? If a merchant could raise the price of a product, why could a worker not raise the price of his labour? The right to petition, he noted, was laid down in the provincial constitution. 'What law, then, are we breaking? Please inform us, honourable Director, sir!' In the end, the Governor's decision not to use force, and the administration's concern lest the strike trigger civil disorder, left it no way to resist. Director Wu, Mao, Ren Shude and a dozen other union delegates signed an accord, to which the official seal was solemnly affixed, acknowledging that 'all wage increases are a matter of free contractual relations between labourers and employers'.

With that, the power of the guilds, which had lasted almost unchanged since the Ming dynasty, five hundred years earlier, was effectively destroyed in Changsha. The daily rate for the masons and carpenters was raised from 20 to 34 silver cents. It was still 'not much more than the barest living wage, [on which] no man could support a family of two adults and two children', the missionary noted. But for Mao, for the Party, and for all the city's workers it was a resounding success, and next day some 20,000 of them marched through a cannonade of firecrackers to the yamen to celebrate. 'Organised Labour's Victory', the *Herald*'s headline proclaimed:

> The government capitulated completely to the express wish of the strikers' delegates . . . It is the first encounter of the new form of Workmen's Union with the officials . . . They gained all they asked; the officials gained nothing in their attempts to compromise. In as much as the workmen's demands were moderate, that is all to the good, but the precedent gives the workmen an enormous power of leverage.

It was not Mao's only triumph that week. While he was negotiating with Director Wu at the Governor's yamen on October 24, Yang Kaihui, who had gone for her confinement to her mother's home in the suburbs, gave birth to a son.

The strike epidemic spread quickly to other trades. Garment-makers struck twice in September. They were followed by barbers, rickshaw-pullers, dyers and weavers, cobblers, typesetters and writing-brush makers. By the beginning of November, when the All-Hunan Federation of Labour Organisations was established, with Mao as its general secretary, fifteen unions had been formed, including the country's first inter-provincial association, the Canton-Hankou General Rail Union, with headquarters at Changsha's main railway station. At one time or another, Mao himself served as nominal leader of about half of them.

In December, as head of the new Federation, he took a joint delegation of union representatives to meet Governor Zhao, the Changsha police chief and other top provincial officials, to discuss the government's intentions in view of the workers' growing demands. According to Mao's minutes, published afterwards by the *Dagongbao*, Zhao assured them that constitutional guarantees protecting the right to strike would be maintained, and that his government 'had no intention of oppressing them'. In reply, Mao explained that what the unions really wanted was socialism, but 'because this was difficult to achieve in China at present', their demands would be limited to improvements in wages and working conditions. The Governor agreed that 'while socialism might be realised in the future, it would be hard to put it into practice today'.

The delegation did not get all it wanted. The administration refused to give an undertaking never to intervene in labour conflicts; nor would it register the Federation as a legally constituted body. But the two sides did agree to have regular contact to 'avoid mis-understandings'.

December 1922 marked the peak of the labour movement in
Hunan, and a highpoint in Mao's own life. He was Secretary of the
provincial Party committee; a highly successful trade union organiser, whom even Governor Zhao had to listen to; and the father of
a two-month-old baby boy. On his twenty-ninth birthday, the last
of the great wave of strikes he had orchestrated in the province that
year, at the Shuikoushan lead and zinc mines near Hengyang, came
to a successful conclusion.

Yet amid the movement's triumphs, there were warning signs as
well. Shanghai, the biggest industrial centre of all, was so tightly
controlled by an alliance of Western and Chinese capitalists, foreign
police and triad labour recruiters, that the Party's Labour Secretariat
found it impossible to operate there and in the autumn moved to
Beijing. Even in Hunan, where the movement was strongest, some
prominent sympathisers within the provincial elite were beginning
to ask themselves whether the agitation was not going too far.

In the end it was from Beijing that the fatal blow descended. The
Labour Secretariat had gone there partly because the dominant
northern leader, Wu Peifu, who early in 1922 had strengthened his
position by defeating the Manchurian warlord, Zhang Zuolin, was
seen as a relatively liberal figure. Wu liked to play up the contrast
between his new government and that of the hated pro-Japanese
Anfu clique that had preceded it, and proclaimed that the protection of labour was one of his priorities. The communists took note,
and that summer the Secretariat and its provincial heads, Mao
among them, petitioned the Beijing parliament to enact a labour law
providing for an eight-hour workday, paid holidays and maternity
leave, and an end to child labour. In a separate move, Li Dazhao
reached agreement with Wu's officials for six Party members to
act as 'secret inspectors' on the Beijing–Hankou railway, the
main north–south artery for troop movements. Wu's interest was to
eliminate Zhang Zuolin's supporters from the railwaymen's labour
associations. But the result was that, by the end of the year, most of
the railway workforce had been reorganised into communist-led
workers' clubs.

Meanwhile Soviet Russia sent a new emissary, Adolf Joffe, for
fresh talks on the thorny problem of diplomatic recognition.
Russian diplomats began to dream of an alliance between Wu and
Sun Yat-sen, which would combine northern power with southern
revolutionary credentials. But Joffe could not give Beijing what it

wanted – the restitution of the Russian-administered Chinese Eastern Railway in Manchuria, and an acknowledgement of Chinese interests in Mongolia – and Wu's interest in the Russians and their local protégés waned.

Against this background, the communist-led railway workers' clubs on the Beijing–Hankou line called a founding congress, to be held in Zhengzhou on February 1, to establish a General Rail Union, similar to the one Mao had founded in Hunan the previous autumn. A few days before the meeting was to open, Wu Peifu ordered it banned. When the delegates went ahead anyway, troops occupied the union headquarters and a national rail strike was declared. On February 7, 1923, Wu and other warlords cracked down simultaneously in Beijing, Zhengzhou and Hankou. At least forty men were killed, including the branch secretary in Hankou, who was beheaded in front of his comrades on the station platform. More than two hundred others were wounded.

The 'February Seventh Massacre', as it became known, punched a huge hole in the communists' ambitions to use the labour movement as the motor of political change. Work stoppages fell by half, and those that did take place were brutally suppressed. Labour activism was further reduced by rising unemployment as Chinese manufacturers cut back in the face of increased foreign competition.

In Hunan, where Zhao Hengti was continuing his efforts to keep north and south at arms' length, the clampdown was initially muted. Mao's Labour Federation sent off angry telegrams, denouncing the 'unspeakably evil warlords', led by Wu and his nominal ally, Cao Kun, and warning graphically: 'Every compatriot who has seen these traitors . . . regrets that he cannot devour their flesh and make a bed of their skins.' The registration of new unions continued, and Mao sent his brothers, Zemin and Zetan, to Anyuan and Shuikoushan to help run the workers' clubs there. In April, he helped to organise a gigantic demonstration, which brought 60,000 people on to the streets of Changsha, as part of a nationwide campaign to demand that Japan return Port Arthur (Lushun) and Dairen (Dalian). But that was the last hurrah. Two months later, during a general strike to protest the deaths of two demonstrators killed by marines from a Japanese gunboat, Zhao declared martial law, filled the streets with his troops and issued arrest warrants for union leaders.

By then, however, Mao had already left Hunan. In January 1923,

Chen Duxiu had invited him to come to Shanghai to work for the
Party Central Committee. Li Weihan, three years Mao's junior, a
former First Normal student and an early member of the New
People's Study Society, was named to succeed him as provincial
Party Secretary. The communist rail union leader, Guo Liang,
became head of the Labour Federation; and another former New
People's Study Society member, twenty-year-old Xia Xi, became
secretary of the provincial Youth League. For Mao, it was a substantial promotion. But he was evidently in no hurry to depart, and
delayed until mid-April before bidding farewell to Yang Kaihui
and his baby son, and boarding the Yangtse steamer which was to
take him to the coast.

The row between Chen Duxiu and Hendricus Sneevliet, over the
Party's relations with Moscow, had been more or less papered over.
But a second, much more serious, dispute had arisen over the
relationship between the CCP and Sun Yat-sen's Guomindang
(GMD). It dated from the winter of 1921, when Sneevliet had met
Sun in Guilin. The old revolutionary flummoxed him by declaring
that there was 'nothing new in Marxism. It had all been said 2,000
years ago in the Chinese Classics.' None the less, Sun's revolutionary
credentials, and the Guomindang's effectiveness in supporting
the seamen's strike in Hong Kong, which Sneevliet witnessed
for himself in Canton, convinced him that a Communist–
Guomindang alliance was highly desirable.

   The Chinese comrades strongly disagreed. To them, the Guomindang was a patriarchal, pre-modern party, with its roots in the secret
societies, the dynastic struggle against the Manchus, and the diffuse,
shadowy world of literary and intellectual cliques mobilised by the
cultured elite. Sun, who was known simply as 'the Leader', ran it as
a personal fiefdom, requiring his followers to swear an oath of allegiance. It was profoundly corrupt. Its core support was limited to
Guangdong and the other southern provinces. It was not, and had
no ambition to be, a mass party, capable of mobilising China's
workers and peasants, its merchants and industrialists, to struggle
against the warlords and imperialists. In Sun's scheme of things, the
warlords were not so much enemies as potential partners in future
deal-making.

   At the beginning of April 1922, Chen Duxiu called together Mao,

Zhang Guotao, and members of three other provincial Party branches who happened to be in Shanghai, to 'pass unanimously a resolution expressing total disapproval' of any alliance. He then fired off an angry note to Voitinsky, who had become head of the Comintern's Far Eastern Bureau, informing him of this decision, and declaring that the Guomindang's policies were 'totally incompatible with communism'; that, outside Guangdong, it was regarded as 'a political party scrambling for power and profit'; and that whatever Sun Yat-sen might say, in practice his movement would not tolerate communist ideas. These factors, Chen concluded, made any accommodation impossible.

The signatories, Mao included, returned to their home provinces, assuming that that was an end to the matter. However, Sneevliet was not so easily discouraged. Over the next few months, the Party leaders in Shanghai found themselves under conflicting pressures from the Comintern, the Russian government, Guomindang leftists and sympathisers within the Party's own ranks, and from the complex interplay of warlord rivalries. By early summer, when Sun was expelled from Canton in a palace coup by his erstwhile military supporters – and became notably more receptive to the idea of co-operation with Moscow and its allies – the CCP was ready to signal grudging acceptance of the idea of a common front, so long as the GMD changed its 'vacillating policy' and took 'the path of revolutionary struggle'.

The Second CCP Congress, in July, confirmed the change in policy. A resolution was passed, acknowledging the need for 'a temporary alliance with the democratic elements to overthrow . . . our common enemies'.

But the Guomindang was not mentioned by name, and the resolution insisted that 'under no circumstances' should the proletariat be placed in a subordinate position. If the communists joined a united front, it was to be for their own benefit, not anyone else's. That message was reinforced by the Party's new constitution, which proclaimed its adherence to the Comintern and warned that CCP members could not join any other political party without express authorisation from the Central Committee itself. This was slightly less harsh than the policy of 'exclusion and aggression' that the First Congress had laid down, but it was hardly extending a welcome to the Guomindang's 50,000 members to join the common cause. Coming from a minuscule political grouping, which at that time, in all of China, had a paid-up membership of 195, it showed astonishing gall.

Mao did not attend the Second Congress. He claimed later that when he arrived in Shanghai, he 'forgot the name of the place where it was to be held, could not find any comrades and missed it'. But it seems more likely that he stayed away because he disagreed with the compromise being fashioned. If so, he was not alone: the representatives of the Canton Party committee, who were likewise hostile to an alliance with Sun, also failed to attend.

In August, Sneevliet returned from Moscow, armed with a directive from the Comintern that the Guomindang was to be viewed as a revolutionary party. Two weeks later, at a Central Committee meeting at Hangzhou, he invoked Comintern discipline to ram through, against the vigorous opposition of all the Chinese who attended, a new strategy known as the 'bloc within', under which CCP members would join the Guomindang as individuals, and the Party would use the resulting alliance as a vehicle to advance the proletarian cause. Shortly afterwards, a small group of CCP officials, including Chen Duxiu and Li Dazhao, were inducted into the Guomindang at a ceremony presided over by Sun Yat-sen himself. A new Party weekly, *Xiangdao zhoubao* (The Guide Weekly), edited by Mao's old friend, Cai Hesen, was set up to promote the alliance, and to try to nudge the Guomindang towards a more revolutionary course. Then, in January 1923, Sun met Adolf Joffe in Shanghai, signalling the start of a closer relationship with Moscow, and the first steps were taken towards reorganising the Guomindang on what would eventually be Leninist lines.

To many communists, however, the 'bloc within' strategy remained anathema, and vigorous opposition continued.

There were other reasons, too, that spring, for the Party leadership to be demoralised. Their one great success, the labour movement, had been smashed. The Party had no legal existence, and was forced to operate underground. Internal divisions had become so acute that, at one point, Chen Duxiu had threatened to resign. Sneevliet himself acknowledged that the CCP was an artificial creation, which had been 'born, or more correctly, fabricated' before its time, while Joffe had stated publicly that 'the Soviet system cannot actually be introduced into China, because there do not exist here the conditions for the successful establishment of communism'.

Even Mao, whose work in Hunan had been singled out for special praise, was, according to Sneevliet, 'at the end of his Latin with labour organisation, and so pessimistic that he saw the only salvation for China in intervention by Russia'. China's future, Mao told him gloomily, would be decided by military power, not by mass organisations, nationalist or communist.

In this depressed mood, forty delegates, representing 420 Party members, twice as many as the previous year, gathered in Canton for the CCP's Third Congress, where once again the relationship with the Guomindang became the dominant issue. The crux of the dispute this time was over Sneevliet's insistence that all Party members should join the Guomindang automatically. Mao, Cai Hesen and the other Hunanese delegates, who voted as a bloc, opposed him.

Unlike Zhang Guotao, who held that the very principle of collaboration with the Guomindang was wrong, Mao's assessment was pragmatic. After the February incident in Zhengzhou, his thinking about a tactical alliance had changed. The Guomindang, he concluded, represented 'the main body of the revolutionary democratic faction', and communists should not be afraid to join it. But the proletariat would grow stronger as China's economy developed, and it was essential that the Party guard its independence so that, when the moment came, it could resume its leading role. The bourgeoisie, Mao argued, was incapable of leading a national revolution; the Comintern's optimism was misplaced:

The Communist Party has temporarily abandoned its most radical views in order to co-operate with the relatively radical Guomindang . . . in order to overthrow their common enemies . . . [In the end] the outcome . . . will be [our] victory . . . In the immediate future, however, and for a certain period, China will necessarily continue to be the realm of the warlords. Politics will become even darker, the financial situation will become even more chaotic, the armies will further proliferate . . . [and] the methods for the oppression of the people will become even more terrible . . . This kind of situation may last for eight to ten years . . . But if politics becomes more reactionary and more confused, the result will necessarily be to call forth revolutionary ideas among the citizenry of the whole country, and the organisational capacity of the citizens will likewise increase day by day . . . This situation is . . . the mother of revolution, it is the magic potion of democracy and independence. Everyone must keep this in mind.

The prospect of another decade of warlord rule, even leavened by Mao's insistence on the unity of opposites, was too grim for most of his colleagues, and Sneevliet was moved to remark that he did not share his pessimism.

When the vote was taken, the Comintern line was narrowly approved. But the Congress documents could not conceal the latent conflicts enshrined in the new policy. The Guomindang, the delegates declared, was to be 'the central force of the national revolution and assume its leadership'. Yet, at the same time, the Communist Party, which was assigned the 'special task' of mobilising the workers and peasants, was to expand its own ranks at its ally's expense by absorbing 'truly class-conscious, revolutionary elements' from the GMD's left wing; while in policy terms its goal was to 'force the Guomindang' to move closer to Soviet Russia.

If the communists were determined to act as a ginger group, however, the Guomindang was no less determined not to let the tail wag the dog. And so the stage was set for a bruising struggle of wills, and ultimately of arms, which would dominate communist strategy for the rest of the decade and beyond.

When the Third Congress ended, Mao was elected one of nine members of the Central Committee (CC) and, more significantly, Secretary of the newly established Central Bureau,* which was responsible for day-to-day Party affairs, and comprised himself, the General Secretary, Chen Duxiu, and three others: Mao's fellow Hunanese (and fellow founder members of the New People's Study Society), Cai Hesen and Luo Zhanglong; and the head of the Canton Party committee, Tan Pingshan (soon to be replaced by Wang Hebo, a Shanghainese railwayman and union organiser).

The Party had emerged from its tribulations stronger, more centralised, and more Leninist, at least in the organisational sense, than in its first two years. The struggle to overcome the divisions

* The First and Second Central Committees had consisted of three and five members respectively, with no Central Bureau. The Second Congress, which urged 'centralisation and iron-like discipline' to prevent individualism and anarcho-communism, laid down detailed organisational rules, but for the most part these remained a dead letter until the Third Congress, which expanded the CC to nine full members and five alternates.

which had driven Chen Duxiu to threaten resignation the previous
autumn had tempered the leadership. Being forced to accept
Comintern instructions and to submit to the will of the majority had
confronted them for the first time with the principles of democratic
centralism on which all Bolshevik parties had to operate. Some,
like the Marxist scholar, Li Hanjun, who had argued at the First
Congress for a loose-knit, decentralised Party, resigned in disgust.
But the outline of an orthodox Party structure was now in place, and
Chen Duxiu could no longer complain that 'the Central Committee
internally is not organised . . . [Its] knowledge is also insufficient . . .
[and its] political viewpoint is not sufficiently clear'. Even though
the new leadership had no more real grasp of Marxist theory than
the old, the basis of a common ideology, guiding and uniting its
action, was at last discernible.

For Mao, these few months in the late spring and summer of 1923
marked a turning-point. At the provincial level, in Hunan, he had
been able to influence events as a labour leader and a progressive
intellectual with close links to the liberal establishment. Except to a
small circle of initiates, his role in the Party had been secret. Now
he became a full-time cadre, still operating clandestinely, but with
a commanding position in the Party's national leadership. His ties
to labour, and to the liberal elite, were abandoned.

Intellectually, too, it was a time for exploring new possibilities.
The lesson of the 'February Seventh Massacre', that the working
class alone could not open the road to power, led him for the first
time to consider other options: the military route, which he had
discussed with Sneevliet in July and mentioned again, a few weeks
later, in a letter to Sun Yat-sen, in which he called for the creation
of a 'centralised national-revolutionary army'; and the peasant
route, which involved mobilising the most numerous and oppressed
sections of China's vast population.

For the time being, however, such thoughts were mere speculation, for the route that the Party had chosen was the 'united front'.
Shortly after the Third Congress, Mao joined the Guomindang. He
would spend the next eighteen months trying to make the front
succeed.

In the first weeks, the learning curve was steep for both sides. Sun
rejected virtually every proposal the communists made. At a
meeting in mid-July, Chen, Mao and the other members of the
Central Bureau complained: 'Nothing can be expected [in terms of]

the modernisation of the Guomindang . . . so long as Sun keeps [to] his [present] notion of [what] a political party [should be], and so long as he does not want to make use of the communist elements [to carry out] the work.' Sneevliet, as the architect of the front, was especially frustrated. Supporting Sun, he grumbled to Joffe, was simply 'throwing away money'.

At the same time, having finally accepted the Comintern's thesis that the way to the future lay through a GMD-led national revolution, the CCP leaders seized on every twitch and whimper that seemed to comfort this strategy. Even Mao, who, a few weeks earlier, had derided the very notion that the bourgeoisie would play a leading role, now lauded the Shanghai business community for supporting the anti-militarist cause:

> This revolution is the task of all the people . . . But . . . the task that the merchants should shoulder in the national revolution is more urgent and more important than the work that the rest of the Chinese people should take upon themselves . . . The Shanghai merchants have risen and begun to act . . . The broader the unity of the merchants, the greater will be their influence, the greater their strength to lead the people of the entire nation, and the more rapid the success of the revolution!

To some extent this must have been tongue-in-cheek. Mao did not really believe, as he claimed, that of all the Chinese people the merchants suffered 'most keenly, most urgently' from warlord and imperialist oppression. Nor did he have much confidence that their new-found revolutionary spirit would last. On the other hand, so long as the warlords were the main enemy, the bourgeoisie had to be an ally. For the moment Mao was ready, like the rest of the Party leadership, to give them the benefit of the doubt.

The key issue remained, however, how to force the Guomindang to change its traditional, elitist ways and become a modern party with a genuine mass base.

At the end of July, after the Central Bureau returned to Shanghai, it was decided to employ a Trojan Horse strategy: Party activists would build up from scratch networks of GMD organisations in northern and central China (where none currently existed), so that these new, communist-dominated regional branches could serve as pressure groups to swing the whole party to the left. Li Dazhao was charged with carrying out this mission in north China, and in

September Mao went secretly to Changsha to do the same in the central provinces.

Hunan was once again in the throes of civil war. That summer, one of Zhao Hengti's commanders had mutinied. The former Governor, Tan Yankai, who had been biding his time in the south, where he had established links with Sun Yat-sen, seized the opportunity to invade at the head of a 'bandit-suppressing army' bent upon Zhao's overthrow. At the end of August, Tan's allies seized Changsha and Governor Zhao was forced to flee for his life. It was this that persuaded Chen Duxiu to grant Mao leave of absence from his new responsibilities as Secretary, naming Luo Zhanglong to act for him while he was away. Mao was evidently delighted. He did not relish the dry, administrative work which was the Secretary's daily fare. Shanghai, a city created by imperialists and capitalists, would always be foreign to him; and back home in Changsha, Yang Kaihui, whom he had not seen since April, was pregnant with their second child. But even as he travelled up on the steamer, the tide of warfare turned and when he arrived at Changsha he found it once more in Zhao's hands.

For the next month, the city was under siege and intermittent bombardment. Tan's allies held the west bank of the Xiang River, Zhao's forces the east. To the foreigners, safe in their consular residences, it seemed 'an *opéra-bouffe* war', with the odd, jagged moment of danger to relieve the tedium. For the Chinese it was very different:

> In the city the big shops never took down their night shutters, rich men fled or lay in hiding. All feared the officers who walked or rode through the streets carrying the red paddles [the 'broad arrows'] of life or death, under the power of which they commandeered rice and money. None dared say nay . . . [for] those who did . . . were in danger of being marched to the open space near the Customs House where the executioner stood with a long knife to behead them.

In the countryside, the villages were subjected to an orgy of rape, plunder and arson reminiscent of the worst days of Zhang Jingyao. Mao still thought Tan would win, and wrote to the Guomindang's General Affairs Department in Canton that Zhao would be unable to hold his ground. Then, one sunlit morning, came the sound of distant gunfire. Wu Peifu had sent troops to shore up Zhao's support, and Tan's men had been routed. The foreigners watched through binoculars as the victorious force returned, 'carrying-coolies, machine-guns borne in chairs like invalids, soldiers swinging lanterns and straw shoes, officers shielding themselves from the sun with paper parasols'.

Zhao's victory came at a price. Hunan's role as a buffer between north and south was at an end. Changsha once more felt the heel of northern soldiers' boots. The liberal elite allied with Tan, on whose protection Mao had relied, were deprived of power and scattered. On Zhao's orders, the Self-Study University was closed, the Labour Federation and the Students' Union banned. Mao himself, who two months earlier had published a long inventory of Zhao's crimes, describing him as 'an outrageously and unpardonably wicked creature', lived under an assumed name, Mao Shishan ('Mao the Stone Mountain').

There could hardly have been a worse moment to try to launch a nationalist party linked to Zhao's defeated adversary. Mao and the Socialist Youth League leader, Xia Xi, who, on his recommendation had been named the Guomindang's preparatory director in Hunan, were able to establish a provisional Party headquarters for the province, with clandestine branches in Changsha, in Ningxiang (through He Shuheng) and at the Anyuan coal-mines (where, a year earlier, he had left a serious young man, newly returned from Moscow, named Liu Shaoqi, in charge). But they were little more than empty shells, operating in total secrecy. Mao remained in Hunan until late December, and celebrated his thirtieth birthday with Yang Kaihui, Anying and their second son, Anqing, born six weeks before. That his staying on had more to do with his family than any political commitments is clear from a love-poem he wrote for her soon after his departure, which was evidently marred by a quarrel:

> *A wave of the hand, and the moment of parting has come.*
> *Harder to bear is facing each other dolefully,*
> *Bitter feelings voiced once more.*
> *Wrath looks out from your eyes and brows,*
> *On the verge of tears, you hold them back.*
> *We know our misunderstandings sprang from that last letter.* *
> *Let it roll away like clouds and mist,*

* Nothing more is known about this letter, or the nature of the quarrel it evoked, but given Mao's references to misunderstandings in the plural and 'bitter feelings once more', it was plainly not something his wife easily forgave.

For who in this world is as close as you and I?
Can Heaven fathom our human maladies?
  I wonder.
This morning frost lies heavy on the road to East Gate,
The waning moon lights up the pool and half the sky –
How cold, how desolate!
One wail of the steam whistle has shattered my heart,
Now I shall roam alone to the furthest ends of the earth.
Let us strive to sever those threads of grief and anger,
Let it be as though the sheer cliffs of Mount Kunlun collapsed,
As though a typhoon swept through the universe.
Let us once again be two birds flying side by side,
  Soaring high as the clouds

While Mao had been in Hunan in the autumn and early winter of 1923, the relationship between the Guomindang and the Russians had undergone a transformation. The Soviet leadership had decided that, given Moscow's international isolation, a progressive Chinese regime, even led by a bourgeois party, would be a valuable ally. Mikhail Borodin, a highly regarded revolutionary who had worked with Lenin and Stalin, was named special envoy to Sun Yat-sen. The Guomindang Chief of Staff, Chiang Kai-shek, a slim, slightly cadaverous man in his mid-thirties, went to Moscow to learn about the Red Army, and was treated royally. Although Sun's quixotic proposal for a Russian-led force to attack Beijing from the north – 'an adventure doomed in advance to failure', as the Soviet Revolutionary Military Council put it – was firmly rejected, the Russians agreed to finance a military training school and, at a meeting in November, Trotsky himself promised 'positive assistance in the form of weapons and economic aid'.

Meanwhile in Canton, Counsellor Bao, as Borodin was called, was deftly working his way around the sensitivities of the two Chinese parties over the triangular alliance Moscow was determined to build.

A thoughtful, patient man, nearly forty years old, Borodin was in many respects the opposite of the domineering Sneevliet. He managed to win Sun's trust while persuading both the Guomindang and the Communists that each had most to gain from the new relationship that was being put in place. In October, while Borodin was preparing to help Sun fight off yet another attempt by local warlords to unseat him, the old conspirator cabled Chiang in

Moscow: 'It has now been made entirely clear who are our friends and who are our enemies.'

On that note, the Guomindang convened its first National Congress in Canton on January 20, 1924. Mao had arrived via Shanghai two weeks earlier with a six-member delegation representing the still largely notional Hunan GMD organisation, including Xia Xi and the provincial CCP leader, Li Weihan.

The congress approved a new constitution, drawn up by Borodin on Leninist lines, emphasising discipline, centralisation and the need to train revolutionary cadres to mobilise mass support; it adopted a more radical political programme, denouncing imperialism as the root cause of China's sufferings; and it called, for the first time, for the development of workers' and peasants' movements to promote the revolution. The communists, mostly younger, livelier spirits than the nationalist party veterans, made a strong impression. At one session, Mao and Li Lisan reportedly so dominated the proceedings that the older men 'looked askance, as if to ask, "Where did those two young unknowns come from?"' The radical leader, Wang Jingwei, one of Sun's companions from the early days of the Tongmenghui, the Revolutionary Alliance, commented afterwards: 'The young people of the May Fourth movement are something to be reckoned with, after all. Look at the enthusiasm with which they speak, and their energetic attitude.'

The new GMD Central Executive Committee (CEC), elected by acclamation on Sun Yat-sen's proposal, included three communists among its twenty-four full members: Li Dazhao; Yu Shude from Beijing; and the Canton CCP leader, Tan Pingshan, who was also named Director of the Organisation Department, one of the most powerful positions in the party, and in that capacity became one of the three members of the CEC's Standing Committee, together with the party Treasurer, Liao Zhongkai, representing the left wing of the Guomindang, and Dai Jitao, representing the right. Mao was appointed one of sixteen alternate (or non-voting) CEC members, seven of whom were communists, including Lin Boqu, a fellow Hunanese who became Director of the GMD Peasant Department; a young literary lion named Qu Qiubai, who had worked in Moscow as correspondent of the progressive Beijing newspaper, *Chenbao*, and was now Borodin's assistant in Canton; and Zhang Guotao, who had apparently put aside his reservations about the two parties' unnatural alliance.*

In mid-February Mao moved back to Shanghai, where he shared a house in Zhabei, not far from Bubbling Well Road, in the northern part of the International Settlement, with Luo Zhanglong, Cai Hesen and Cai's girlfriend, Xiang Jingyu. For the rest of the year he had a double workload, serving as Secretary for the CCP Central Bureau, which operated from the same address under cover of being a Customs Declaration Office, providing secretarial services for Chinese businesses which had to deal with the foreign-controlled Customs Administration; and carrying out similar duties for the Guomindang's Shanghai Executive Committee, with an office in the French concession. The latter was responsible for the work of GMD branches in the four provinces of Anhui, Jiangxi, Jiangsu and Zhejiang, as well as in the city itself.

This was not the easiest of roles. Despite the best efforts of Borodin in Canton, and Grigory Voitinsky in Shanghai (who had come as Comintern representative to replace Hendricus Sneevliet), friction between the two parties intensified. GMD conservatives, not without reason, saw the CCP as a fifth column. In late April or early May 1924, they obtained a copy of a Central Committee instruction, ordering communists within the Guomindang to establish a system of tight-knit 'party fractions', to transmit and implement Party directives and maintain their communist identity. The right-wing GMD Control Commission began moves to impeach the communist leadership for creating 'a party within the party'. Mao, Cai Hesen and Chen Duxiu argued that the alliance with the GMD had failed and the united front should be broken, but were told by Voitinsky that this was unacceptable to Moscow. Sun Yat-sen eventually ruled in favour of maintaining the status quo, but even Borodin grew concerned that an anti-communist coalition was forming which was only deterred from taking action by the fear of losing Russian aid.

* The communists, holding 10 of the 40 CEC positions, were disproportionately well-represented, given that the Guomindang had more than 100,000 members where the CCP had only about 500. However, Sun saw it as part of the bargain to obtain Russian aid. Only the full communist CEC members had voting rights, and several of them were his former associates: Tan Pingshan was an old Tongmenghui man, and Lin Boqu, initially an alternate but subsequently promoted a full member, had belonged to Sun's Revolutionary Party, the predecessor of the Guomindang.

In July, Chen and Mao issued a secret Central Committee
circular, reaffirming the 'bloc within' strategy laid down by the
Third Congress a year earlier, but noting that it was proving
'extremely difficult' to carry out:

> Overt and covert attacks on us and attempts to push us out have been
> mounting daily on the part of a majority of Guomindang members . . .
> Only a very few Guomindang leaders, such as Sun Yat-sen and Liao
> Zhongkai, have not yet made up their minds to break with us, but
> they, too, certainly do not wish to offend the right-wing elements . . .
> For the sake of uniting the revolutionary forces, we must absolutely
> not allow any separatist words or actions to emerge on our side, and
> we must try our best to be tolerant and co-operate with them. [At the
> same time] . . . we cannot tolerate non-revolutionary rightist policies
> without correcting them.

That set the tone for communist tactics throughout the next three
years. So long as the united front held, the CCP would not be
permitted to reject it. Rather, at the Comintern's behest, it would
increasingly bend over backwards to accommodate its nationalist
partners. But not all of them. The most important decision to
emerge during the summer of 1924 was that the Guomindang must
be treated as a divided party, having a left wing, with which the
communists could ally themselves, and a right wing, which could
not be won over and must be fought by all means at their disposal.

The problem with this approach was summed up by Mao in a
pithy Chinese folk-saying, '*Chongshuang diehu*', meaning literally,
'duplicate bed, duplicate household'. In other words, if the front
were simply a means for the Party to associate itself with a pro-
communist Guomindang Left which shared the same ideas and
goals, one or the other was redundant. The question was, which
one?

The CCP seemed to be going nowhere. Recruitment was painfully slow. The labour movement was at a standstill. Despite all the
Comintern's propaganda depicting the proletariat as thirsting after
communist policies, Chinese workers had little interest in politics
and communist energies were being dissipated in sterile turf battles
for survival. Some prominent communists that summer decided
their own Party was the one bed too many and resigned to pursue
Guomindang careers. Mao never quite took that step. But as the
year wore on he became increasingly despondent. A young

Hunanese communist named Peng Shuzhi, visiting Shanghai after three years spent studying in Moscow, found him morose and apathetic:

> He looked in a pretty bad way. His thinness seemed to make his body even longer than it actually was. He was pale, and his complexion had an unhealthy, greenish tinge. I was afraid that he had contracted tuberculosis, as so many of our comrades had done, or would do, at one time or another in their lives.

During the autumn, from Mao's point of view, the situation went from bad to worse. Money stopped arriving from GMD headquarters, and work at the Shanghai committee ground to a halt. He began to suffer from neurasthenia – a form of depression, marked by chronic insomnia, headaches, dizziness and high blood pressure – which would plague him for the rest of his life. His relations with the rest of the CCP leadership, which had rarely been easy, deteriorated further. The Fourth Congress, which he was organising, was postponed until the following January because Voitinsky was away in Moscow. Finally, in October, there was yet another political shift in Beijing, which brought to power Feng Yuxiang, an independent warlord known as the Christian General because he had baptised his troops with a fire hose. Feng appointed the hated Anfu leader, Duan Qirui, as head of government, and invited Sun Yat-sen to Beijing for talks on national reconciliation.

To Mao, Sun's acceptance of this invitation was the last straw. Over the previous two years, he had seen the labour movement collapse; the liberal, progressive elite, silenced; and the CCP locked into policies which appeared to have no chance of success. Now the Guomindang was reverting, in the Central Committee's words, to 'the same old game of militarist politics' that had failed so often in the past.

Towards the end of December, barely three weeks before the CCP's Fourth Congress was to open, Mao set out for Changsha, accompanied by Yang Kaihui, her mother and their two children, who had joined him in Shanghai in the summer. Officially, he had been granted leave of absence due to ill-health. But, as his doctor, Li Zhisui, would note many years later, Mao's neurasthenia was always political in nature: 'The symptoms became much more severe at the beginning of a major political struggle.' Only this time it was a different kind of struggle: Mao was undergoing a crisis of faith.

As 1925 began, and his erstwhile comrades met to chart the future of a Party which now boasted 994 members, Mao celebrated the Chinese New Year at the Yangs' old family home where, ten years earlier, as a student at First Normal, he had come to sit at the feet of his beloved ethics teacher, Kaihui's father. The wheel seemed to have turned full circle. He had no contact with his old friends in Changsha, or with the provincial CCP or Guomindang committees there. To all intents and purposes, his withdrawal from politics was complete. In February he set out with the family for Shaoshan, taking with him several crates full of books. He was sick, Kaihui told their neighbours. For three months, from winter until late spring, Mao saw no one except members of his family and fellow villagers. It was a return to the beginning, to the peasant roots from which, as an ambitious young intellectual, he had tried to free himself. Yet it was there, among the companions of his childhood, that he discerned the first glimmerings of a new, and more hopeful, way forward.

To the Chinese Communists, in the first half of the 1920s, the peasants barely existed. They were, as they had been for centuries, part of the background of Chinese life, an unvarying yellow wash against which great events, and great men, were depicted, larger than life, on the endless scroll of Chinese history.

When Lenin, at the Second Comintern Congress in 1920, derided as utopian the idea that a proletarian party could win power in a backward country without forging a strong relationship with the peasantry, the founders of the Chinese Party, Mao among them, responded with stony silence. Two years later, under the prodding of the Comintern, the Second CCP Congress acknowledged that China's 300 million peasants were 'the most important factor in the revolutionary movement', but made clear that the CCP had no intention of leading them. Its task was to organise the workers; the peasants must liberate themselves. Chen Duxiu, the Party's General Secretary, was persuaded during a visit to Moscow in November 1922 that the peasants were potentially 'a friendly army . . . which the CCP cannot afford to ignore', and at the Third CCP Congress, the following summer, the Party's thinking had evolved sufficiently for 'workers and peasants' to be bracketed together as the two classes whose interests the CCP must at all times support.

By then, a young man named Peng Pai, the scion of a wealthy landlord family, had led the peasants in a successful seizure of power in Hailufeng, in eastern Guangdong, which would defy all the authorities' attempts to suppress it for the next five years. But Peng was not yet a Party member; and had carried out his activities entirely alone. His movement, in full spate only 150 miles from where the Congress was meeting, did not even get a mention.

Mao, too, was belatedly beginning to show interest in the role the peasantry might play. That spring he had sent two communists from the Shuikoushan lead-mine back to their home villages to investigate the prospects for peasant associations in Hunan.* Zhang Guotao remembered him telling the Congress that in Hunan there were 'few workers and even fewer GMD and CCP members, whereas the peasants there filled the mountains and fields'. With their long history of revolt and insurrection, Mao argued, the peasants could become a powerful ally in the national revolution. Chen Duxiu agreed, and a decision was taken to try to unite 'tenant-peasants and rural labourers to . . . oppose the warlords and strike down corrupt officials and local tyrants'. But no attempt was made to put it into practice.

The Comintern's frustration at the obtuseness of the Chinese comrades where the peasants were concerned was shown vividly in a directive which reached Shanghai shortly after the Congress ended:

> The National Revolution in China . . . will necessarily be accompanied by an agrarian revolution among the peasantry . . . This

---

* As a result of their efforts, the Yuebei Peasants' and Workers' Association, the first of its kind in Hunan, was inaugurated in September 1923, just as the former Provincial Governor, Tan Yankai, was mounting an invasion from the south. At its peak the association had more than a thousand members. It campaigned for lower grain prices, rent reductions, and an end to the usurious rates of interest which local landlords extorted for peasant debts. Tan's presence gave the peasants some protection against the landlords' initial reprisals. But the area was part of the home district of Governor Zhao Hengti, and when at the end of November Tan's men were defeated, Zhao's troops set fire to the peasant association headquarters and the homes of many of its supporters. At least four peasants were killed and dozens more arrested, and the movement collapsed.

revolution can only be successful if the basic masses of the Chinese population, the small peasants, can be attracted to take part. Thus, the central point of all policy is precisely *the peasant question*. To ignore this fundamental point for any reason whatsoever means to fail to understand the whole importance of the socio-economic basis upon which alone a successful struggle . . . can be carried out.

This too fell on deaf ears, as did subsequent appeals.

There were reasons for the CCP's obstinacy. To the young, mostly bourgeois intellectuals who made up the Party leadership, industry, however primitive, was by definition modern. The new working class in the cities, exploited and downtrodden though it might be, was the proper standard-bearer for the bright new society this modern world would engender. The peasants, in contrast, represented all that was most backward and benighted in China. Mao himself, despite his rural origins, confessed that as a young man he regarded them as 'stupid and detestable people'. Their revolts, even when successful, as at the end of the Yuan and the Ming dynasties, were capable of producing a new emperor but never a new system. Party workers, one report noted in 1923, 'do not like the rural areas. They would rather starve than return to the villages.' Far from being the wave of the future, the peasantry were the amorphous core of the dark legacy of Confucian empire that the revolution had to sweep away.

In Shaoshan, this began to change.

At first, Mao was so lacking in energy that he did little except read books and receive social calls from neighbours, who discussed 'family matters and local events'. But a few weeks later, through the intermediary of a young clansman named Mao Fuxuan, he began discreetly encouraging some of the poorer peasants to form an association. Yang Kaihui set up a peasant night school, a pared-down version of the workers' school Mao had organised as a student at First Normal, to teach reading, arithmetic, politics and current events.

These small-scale, grass-roots experiments might have continued indefinitely, and probably inconclusively, had it not been for the actions of a unit of British-officered settlement police, 600 miles down the Yangtse in Shanghai.

There, on May 30 1925, an incident occurred that set off an explosion of nationalist fervour not seen since the May Fourth movement six years before. The fuse had been lit two weeks earlier when Japanese guards fired on a group of Chinese workers during a strike at a textile plant, killing a communist organiser. In the protests which followed, six students were arrested, triggering more marches and rallies urging their release. The British Police Commissioner ordered that the demonstrations be stopped before the authorities lost control. Further arrests were made. Each day the crowds grew angrier, and the atmosphere more menacing. Shortly after half past three on a warm, muggy Saturday afternoon, in the city's main shopping street, Nanking Road, the officer-in-charge at the central police station, a British inspector, fearing that his men were about to be overrun, ordered Chinese and Sikh constables to open fire. The volley left four demonstrators dead and upwards of fifty wounded, of whom eight later succumbed to their wounds. Rioting followed, in which ten more Chinese died, and a general strike was declared.

Anti-British and anti-Japanese demonstrations broke out all over China. In Canton, troops in the foreign concession opened fire on the protesters with machine-guns, killing more than fifty, winding still tighter the spiral of anger and hatred, and provoking a sixteen-month-long strike against the British authorities in Hong Kong, which by the time it ended had crippled the colony's trade.

When the news reached Changsha that weekend, workers and students poured on to the streets and began chanting anti-foreign slogans. The *Dagongbao* rushed out a special edition. On Tuesday, 20,000 people attended a rally at which an All-Hunan 'Avenge the Shame' Association was founded and a boycott of British and Japanese goods declared. Three days later, a reported 100,000 people marched through the city, plastering every wall with posters calling for the expulsion of the imperialists, the abrogation of the unequal treaties and, most disturbing of all for the provincial authorities, an end to warlord rule. It was the biggest demonstration Changsha had ever seen. Governor Zhao Hengti responded as he usually did, sending troops with loaded weapons to quarantine the schools, imposing a 24-hour curfew and putting up notices warning that 'disturbers of the peace' would be shot. But the 'Avenge the Shame' Association was able to maintain its activities, and when the students left for the summer holidays, they continued the campaign in their home districts.

The effect on Mao was electric, and he plunged back into the political fray.

In mid-June, he founded a CCP branch in Shaoshan, with Mao Fuxuan as Secretary. Socialist Youth League and Guomindang branches followed. The peasant night-school movement spread rapidly. Peasant 'Avenge the Shame' branches were formed. A young GMD provincial committee staff member named He Erkang (an ex-student of the preparatory school attached to Mao's old Self-Study University and, like many Hunanese GMD activists, also a CCP member) came down from Changsha to help, and on July 10, the inaugural meeting of the grandly named 'Xiangtan County West Second District "Avenge the Shame" Association' was held in Shaoshan. Mao made a speech denouncing British and Japanese imperialism, and afterwards the meeting resolved to boycott all foreign goods. Officially sixty-seven delegates attended, but virtually the entire adult population of Shaoshan and of several neighbouring hamlets, some four hundred people in all, came along to watch.

Finally, in early August, all this patient spadework began to pay off. A drought had set in, and, as always, the local landlords were hoarding rice in order to create a shortage. After a meeting at Mao's house, the Shaoshan peasant association sent two of its members to petition for the granaries to be opened. Not only was their plea rejected, but they were told that the grain was to be shipped to the city where it would command higher prices, just as Mao remembered his own father doing. On his instructions, Mao Fuxuan and another local CCP member led several hundred peasants, armed with hoes and bamboo carrying-poles, who forced the landlords to sell the grain locally, and at a fair price.

In the epic scale of the Chinese revolution, it was a minimal event, seemingly of no consequence whatever in the greater scheme of things. But it was the first such movement in Hunan since the smashing of the Yuebei association two years earlier. Within days similar conflicts broke out in other villages. Before the month was out more than twenty peasant associations had been formed in Xiangtan county and the surrounding area. At that point, word of Mao's activities reached Zhao Hengti, who sent a terse secret telegram to the Xiangtan County Defence Bureau: 'Arrest Mao Zedong immediately. Execute him on the spot.' The order was seen by a clerk who knew Mao's family, and a messenger was sent post-haste to warn him. With that, Mao's days as a peasant organiser came to an abrupt end. He set out the same afternoon for Changsha, disguised as a doctor, travelling in a closed sedan chair.

With him went the conviction that the Comintern had been right: China's peasants were a force the nationalist movement would neglect at its peril. The revolution would succeed, Mao concluded, once it was able to mobilise the huge, untapped reservoir of peasant discontent against the classes which oppressed them.

In a poem written while in hiding in Changsha at the beginning of September, he reflected sombrely on the magnitude of the task that lay ahead:

> *A hundred boats battle the current.*
> *Eagles strike at the endless void,*
> *Fish hover in the shallow bottoms,*
> *All creatures strive for freedom under the frosty sky.*
> *Baffled by this immensity,*
> *I ask the vast expanse of earth,*
> *Who, then, controls the rise and fall of fortunes?*

In a strikingly nostalgic passage, he went on to lament the passing of those 'glorious years' when he and his student companions, 'with the scholar's idealistic fervour, upright and fearless, spoke out unrestrainedly' and 'counted as dung and dust the high and mighty of the day'. Then they had been convinced they had the answers to all of China's problems. Now, at the age of thirty-one, the blithe certitudes of youth were gone.

In the seven months Mao spent at Shaoshan, the complexion of Chinese politics changed dramatically. Sun Yat-sen had died in March 1925, leaving behind a testament urging his followers to uphold the decisions of the First Guomindang Congress, which had underwritten the united front, and to support the alliance with Russia. The leftist, Wang Jingwei, emerged as Sun's likely successor, triggering a conservative backlash which before the year was out would see the right-wing rump, known as the 'Western Hills Group', mount a failed leadership challenge. Wang's support surged with the great wave of anti-imperialist fervour provoked by the May 30 Incident, which sent young radicals flocking to join both the Guomindang and the Communist Party. Soon afterwards his rival,

Hu Hanmin, was banished to Moscow, allegedly suspected of complicity in the assassination that summer of the veteran GMD radical, Liao Zhongkai; while Chiang Kai-shek, now Canton garrison commander, began to build a base of support in the newly created National Revolutionary Army. The result was a party that was not only much more powerful than it had been when the year began, but which had also moved sharply leftward.

That alone would have been enough to commend the GMD to Mao, living underground in Changsha, as he conferred with Xia Xi and other former protégés, and pondered what to do next. But other factors were pushing him the same way. At Shaoshan, Mao had become convinced that his political instincts a year earlier had been correct. Ultimately China's salvation would come through class struggle, waged by the Communist Party leading the country's workers and peasants in the violent overthrow of their oppressors. But until that day dawned, the Guomindang, which could operate legally where the communists could not, which had its own army, trained and paid for by the Russians, and a secure territorial base in Guangdong, was far better placed than the CCP to carry the revolution forward. Accordingly, Mao's peasant night schools did not try to teach Marxism, they taught Sun Yat-sen's 'Three Principles of the People' – nationalism, democracy and socialism. Mao's efforts at party-building, after he resumed political activity in June, were geared more to helping the Guomindang than the CCP or the Youth League. His new political creed was set out in a resumé he wrote later that year.

I believe in Communism and advocate the social revolution of the proletariat. The present domestic and foreign oppression cannot, however, be overthrown by the forces of one class alone. I advocate making use of the national revolution in which the proletariat, the petty bourgeoisie [the peasantry] and the left-wing of the middle bourgeoisie co-operate to carry out the Three People's Principles of the Chinese Guomindang in order to overthrow imperialism, overthrow the warlords, and overthrow the comprador and landlord classes [allied with them] . . . and to realise the joint rule . . . [of these three revolutionary classes], that is, the rule of the revolutionary popular masses.

Personal considerations must have played a part too. Mao was still an alternate member of the Guomindang Central Executive

Committee; in the CCP, he held no post. Moreover, the GMD, with its roots in the secret societies and the anti-dynastic struggle, had from the start shown more interest in the peasantry than the urban-based Communist Party. By the autumn of 1925, it had set up a Peasant Department and a Peasant Movement Training Institute for rural organisers. The CCP at that time had done nothing.

In short, Canton, rather than Shanghai, had become the fulcrum of the revolutionary struggle. So when Mao slipped out of Changsha at the end of the first week in September, it was to travel south. He was evidently uncertain how he would be received. One of his companions on the journey remembered that he was suddenly seized by panic, burning all his notes for fear that they run into a patrol of Zhao Hengti's troops. His neurasthenia returned, and on arrival he spent several days in hospital.

Yet he had been right to go to Canton. He recalled years later that 'an air of great optimism pervaded the city'. At Guomindang headquarters, he secured an appointment with Wang Jingwei, the Chairman of the newly formed national government, who was then consolidating his position as the most powerful man in the party. It was Wang who had been so impressed with Mao's youthful enthusiasm at the First GMD Congress in January 1924. Now he proposed that, to lessen his own workload, Mao stand in for him as acting head of the GMD Propaganda Department. Two weeks later, the appointment was formally confirmed.

As a senior official, Mao was a man of substance. Yang Kaihui, her mother and the two children came from Changsha to join him. They rented a house in the pleasant tree-lined suburb of Dongshan, where the Russian military advisers and many of the Guomindang leaders, including Chiang Kai-shek, had their homes.

For the next eighteen months, Mao devoted himself to the two issues he now regarded as crucial to the revolution's success: the consolidation of the Guomindang Left and the mobilisation of the peasantry. His first action, that winter, was to start a new party journal, *Zhengzhi zhoubao* (Political Weekly), to counter the challenge to the united front being mounted by the right-wing Western Hills Group and to stiffen the resolve of those 'whose revolutionary convictions are wavering'. The first issue proclaimed:

> Uniting with Russia and accepting communists are important tactics
> of our party in pursuing the goal of victory in the revolution. The late

> Director-General [Sun Yat-sen] was the first to decide on them, and . . . they were adopted at the First National Congress . . . Today's revolution is an episode in the final decisive struggle between the two great forces of revolution and counter-revolution in the world . . . If our party's revolutionary strategy does not take as its starting point union with Soviet Russia; [and] . . . if it does not accept the communists, who advocate the interests of the peasants and workers; then the revolutionary forces will sink into isolation and the revolution will not be able to succeed . . . He who is not for the revolution is for counter-revolution. There is absolutely no neutral ground.

The choice, Mao argued, was between a 'Western-style, middle-class revolution', urged by the GMD right; and the formation of a broad left-wing alliance, leading to the joint rule of 'all revolutionary forces'. Those who tried to wear 'the grey mask of neutrality' would soon be forced to decide on which side they would stand.

Exactly which forces could be counted as revolutionary was the subject of a long article entitled 'An Analysis of All the Classes in Chinese Society', which Mao published on December 1, 1925, in *Geming* (Revolution), the magazine of the new National Revolutionary Army. It set out in magisterial fashion the results of the long months of reflection he had spent in Shaoshan:

> Who are our enemies? Who are our friends? He who cannot distin-guish between enemies and friends is certainly not a revolutionary, yet to distinguish between them is not easy. If the Chinese revol-ution . . . has achieved so little, [the] . . . strategic error has consisted precisely in the failure to unite with real friends in order to attack real enemies.

Mao went on to enumerate no fewer than twenty different social strata in China, divided into five main classes. They ranged from the big bourgeoisie, which was 'a deadly enemy', and its allies on the right; to the left-wing of the middle bourgeoisie, which 'absolutely refuses to follow imperialism' but 'is often seized with terror when faced with "Red" tendencies'; and the three categories of petty bourgeoisie (comprising rich peasants, merchants, craftsmen and professional people), whose degree of revolutionary awareness was in direct proportion to their poverty. In addition, there were six categories of semi-proletariat (mainly poor and middle peasants, shopkeepers and street vendors), and four categories of urban, rural and lumpen- proletariat. Of these, the urban workers and coolies were described as the revolution's 'main force'; the agricultural proletariat, the poor peasants and street vendors were 'extremely receptive to revolutionary propaganda' and would 'struggle bravely'; and the lumpenproletariat, made up of bandits, soldiers, robbers, thieves and prostitutes, would 'fight very bravely . . . if we can find a way to lead them'.

Accordingly, Mao concluded, out of China's 400 million people, one million were irredeemably hostile; four million were basically hostile but might be won over; and 395 million were revolutionary or at least benevolently neutral.

All the objective conditions for revolution were therefore present, Mao wrote; the only thing missing was a way to mobilise the masses. Through all the years that followed, he never wavered in this belief. It would sustain him in the darkest moments, when all hope seemed to be lost. But it offered scant comfort to the Guomindang centrists, the representatives in the party of the 'vacillating middle bourgeoisie', to whom Mao's homilies that winter were constantly addressed. The choice that was bearing down on them would come sooner than anyone imagined.

By the end of 1925, Chiang Kai-shek had become the most powerful leader of the Guomindang after Wang Jingwei. As commander of the First Corps of the National Revolutionary Army, he had directed a series of successful military campaigns that autumn which effectively secured Guangdong for the GMD government against attacks by local warlords. He controlled the Canton garrison, and headed the Whampoa Military Academy, which became his headquarters. His loyalty seemed beyond question: when the Western Hills Group had challenged Wang Jingwei's leadership the previous November, he had immediately issued a statement of support. But during the Second GMD Congress in January 1926, Chiang grew restive. The meeting saw a further sharp lurch to the left, both in the make-up of the CEC Standing Committee – where Chiang was one of only three moderates, sharing power with three members of the GMD-Left and three communists – and in its policy pronouncements, which were far more radical than anything the Party had approved before. The 'Resolution on Propaganda', which Mao drafted, warned ominously: 'Only those who endorse the liberation movement of the Chinese peasants are faithful revolutionary members of the party; if not, they are counter-revolutionaries.' The notion that the peasant movement was central to the revolution was widely accepted by GMD moderates. But the use of the term, 'liberation', signifying social revolution in the countryside, was not. The Guomindang was still a bourgeois party, and much of its support came, directly or indirectly, from members of landowning families. Such people favoured reform, but the violent overthrow of the existing rural order was not part of their agenda.

To Chiang, like many others, the new radicalism was unnerving. It came, moreover, at a time when his own position was suddenly under pressure. The new head of the Soviet military adviser group, General N. V. Kuibyshev, who had arrived two months before and used the improbable codename, Kisanka (Pussycat), was an arrogant, inflexible man, whose contempt for the Chinese generals, and Chiang in particular, was matched only by his determination to bring the National Revolutionary Army firmly under Soviet control. Chiang soon came to hate him and, on January 15, resigned in disgust as First Corps commander. The main area of disagreement was the timing of the long-awaited Northern Expedition, which was to carry out Sun Yat-sen's dream of unifying the whole of China under a GMD government, crushing the warlords and humbling their imperialist allies. Kuibyshev argued that much more preparation was needed (a view shared by the CCP leaders in Shanghai). Chiang wanted to press ahead. When Wang Jingwei appeared to support Kuibyshev, the battle lines were drawn. The situation was neatly summed up by Vera Vishnyakova-Akimova, one of the Russian mission's interpreters. 'Everyone knew', she wrote, 'that a hidden struggle for power was going on between Chiang Kai-shek and Wang Jingwei. On one side was political prestige; on the other, military force.'

Yet when Chiang struck, in the early hours of March 20, it came in a way no one had expected. He declared martial law; ordered the arrests of all communist officers and political workers in the Canton garrison, and of the commander of a gunboat, the *Zhongshan*, which he said was acting suspiciously; and sent troops to surround the residences of the Soviet military advisers and to disarm their guards. Chiang claimed afterwards to have evidence that Wang Jingwei, with Kuibyshev's backing, was planning to have him kidnapped by a communist-led naval unit and banished to Moscow. This may well have been true. But even if it were not, a confrontation was by then inevitable.

Chiang's 'coup', as it was afterwards called, was over almost as soon as it began. No one was injured, much less killed. Next day he was already apologising that his subordinates had exceeded their orders. But by then his point had been made. He did not oppose Russia, or the CCP, he explained, but 'certain individuals' had overstepped their powers. Seventy-two hours later, Kuibyshev and two other senior Soviet advisers boarded a ship for Vladivostok. Wang Jingwei was given 'sick leave' and departed quietly for Europe. The Russians tried to smooth things over and the Party leadership in Shanghai decided, apparently without Comintern prodding, that it had no choice but to do the same.

As so often, Mao disagreed. The most senior communists in the GMD army were Zhou Enlai, then aged twenty-eight, and a young Hunanese named Li Fuchun, a former New People's Study Society member married to Cai Hesen's sister, Cai Chang. Both men had come to Canton in 1924 after studying in France. Zhou was Director of the Political Department at the Whampoa Academy, and Deputy Commissar of Chiang Kai-shek's First Corps; Li held the same post in the Second Corps under the command of Tan Yankai. A few hours after the coup, Mao met Zhou at Li Fuchun's home. According to Zhou, Mao argued that Chiang was isolated; four of the other five Corps commanders were hostile to him; and in both the First Corps and the Academy, communists held most of the key posts. If the Left-GMD acted decisively, he asserted, Chiang's support would crumble. Other Canton CCP leaders reportedly reached similar conclusions. But when Zhou put this to Kuibyshev, the Russian vetoed the idea, apparently on the grounds that Chiang's forces were too strong.

That led to further recriminations, with Mao and others complaining that Zhou, who was responsible for military affairs under the Canton CCP committee, had spent too much time infiltrating Chiang's First Corps and the Whampoa Academy, while neglecting to place communist cadres in other sections of the Revolutionary Army. But by then such questions were academic. What mattered was that Chiang had won hands down and was well on the way to establishing himself as the indispensable Guomindang leader, a role he would continue to play, in and out of office, for the next forty-nine years.

Mao was now in a delicate position. Wang Jingwei had been his
principal patron. Thanks to him he had been reappointed as acting
head of the Propaganda Department after the Second Congress, and
in February and early March had acquired several other key posts.
But his relations with the CCP remained problematic. There is no
record of the Party leaders' reaction when they learned in October
1925 that Mao had secured this plum assignment, which the CCP
had been angling for ever since the spring of 1924. Of all possible
communist candidates, he was certainly the last person they would
have chosen. He was unruly; heterodox in his ideas; held no CCP
office; and had had no contact with the Party Centre for the best
part of a year.

Mao's determination to think for himself had been shown by his
call that winter for 'an ideology that has been produced in Chinese
conditions', and by his emphasis on the primacy of the masses:

> Academic thought . . . is worthless dross unless it is in the service of
> the demands of the masses for social and economic liberation . . . The
> slogan for the intelligentsia should be, 'Go among the masses.'
> China's liberation can be found only among the masses . . . Anyone
> who divorces himself from the masses has lost his social basis.

To the Party Central Committee, imprisoned in a straitjacket of
Comintern orthodoxy, the notion of an ideology 'produced in
Chinese conditions' was utterly heretical. China's salvation, they
held, would come not from 'the masses', amorphous and undefined,
but from the urban proletariat which led them.

These differences came to a head when Mao submitted to the
Party journal, *Xiangdao*, his 'Analysis of All the Classes in Chinese
Society', summarising the lessons he had drawn from his sojourn in
Hunan. Chen Duxiu refused to allow its publication on the grounds
that it laid too much stress on the role of the peasantry.

Mao's estrangement from the Shanghai leadership was less
damaging than it might have been had the Party Centre been united.
But by the beginning of 1926 the CCP was riven by internecine
squabbles, in which policy and personalities were inextricably
mixed. Peng Shuzhi and Chen Duxiu were on one side, and Qu
Qiubai on the other. Cai Hesen hated Peng, who had recently
seduced his wife, while Zhang Guotao hovered in the middle. If that
were not enough, the Centre and the Canton Party committee

followed such different policies that, as Borodin later acknowledged, at times they seemed two different parties. One more dispute, with Mao, not even a member of the Central Committee, was simply not that important. Indeed, to the Party leaders, Mao's only real significance was that he had managed to amass a number of powerful GMD jobs.

In April 1926, as the communists waited uneasily for Chiang Kai-shek to make his next move, Mao deliberately kept in the background. Zhang Guotao, who had been sent to Canton as the Central Committee's plenipotentiary, remembered how 'from beginning to end, [Mao] stayed away from the dispute and remained a bystander', adding perceptively: 'He seemed to have gained considerable experience from it.'

After a month of acrimonious bargaining between Chiang (who held in reserve the possibility of a complete break with the Russians) and Borodin (who controlled the flow of Russian arms Chiang needed) a compromise was reached, heavily weighted in Chiang's favour. The Guomindang Central Executive Committee met in plenary session on May 15 and passed a series of resolutions, barring communists from heading GMD departments or from holding more than a third of the posts in high-level GMD committees; banning communist fractions in GMD organisations; prohibiting GMD members in future from joining the Communist Party; and requiring the CCP to provide a complete list of existing GMD members with dual-party allegiance. In return, Chiang agreed to a crackdown on the GMD-rightists, many of whose leaders were arrested or sent into exile (a move which was in his own, as much as the CCP's, interests), and to preserve the *status quo ante* of GMD–CCP relations. The Russians, for their part, undertook to give full backing to the Northern Expedition.

This time the CCP leadership was, for once, unanimous in its disapproval. Chen Duxiu proposed (yet again) an end to the 'bloc within' strategy and the reassertion of the Party's independence. But Stalin insisted that the deal with Chiang must go through. From then on, in Borodin's sardonic phrase, the CCP was 'fated to play the role of coolie in the Chinese revolution'. Though not seen as such at the time, the nationalist coup had marked a turning-point in the Chinese communists' relations with Moscow. Until March 1926, the Comintern's advice to the Chinese Party was on the whole well-intentioned and well-informed, and frequently more realistic than the views of the inexperienced CCP leaders in Shanghai. After the coup, Moscow's China policy became the plaything of Kremlin politics, an extension of Stalin's conflicts with Trotsky and his other main rival, Nikolai Bukharin, the representative of the Soviet Party's moderate wing.

In the end, Mao came out of it far better than he could have expected. Along with other communist GMD officials, on May 28 he resigned as head of the Propaganda Department. But he retained his other key posts, as Principal of the Peasant Movement Training Institute, which was then growing rapidly in size and importance, and as a member of the GMD Peasant Movement Committee, which dealt with policy matters.

These decisions reflected Chiang's recognition of the role the peasantry could play during the Northern Expedition. In 1926, Mao was one of the few real authorities on peasant matters the Guomindang possessed. He had given lectures on the subject at the officers' training school of the Second (Hunanese) Corps of the National Revolutionary Army; at the GMD's provincial Youth Training Institute; and at a middle school attached to Guangdong University; as well as at the Peasant Movement Institute itself. Moreover, his expertise was in the central provinces of China through which the Northern Expedition would pass. Chiang's Russian advisers were adamant that the expedition could succeed only if the peasantry along the way were mobilised to support it. Mao shared that view. Since March he had been urging the GMD Peasant Movement Committee to 'pay the utmost attention to the areas the revolutionary armies will traverse'.

Less than two months after the May plenum, on July 9, 1926, the Revolutionary Army, numbering about 75,000 men, set out on the long-awaited campaign which was to crush the warlords and finally reunify China under the Guomindang flag.

It had been launched hurriedly to take advantage of events in Hunan, where the local army commander, Tang Shengzhi, who had staged a successful rebellion and declared in favour of the south, was facing attack from Wu Peifu's northern troops. The decision to back Tang proved well-founded (at least in the short term), for by the end of the month Hunan was in southern hands, and Chiang, as Commander-in-Chief, resplendent in a light grey military cloak and a panoply of new titles and powers, installed himself in Changsha.

With him went the Soviet advisers, now led by General Vasily Blyukher, the original head of the Soviet military mission, who had returned to replace Kuibyshev. He and Chiang got on well, and the 'Generalissimo', as he would later be known, whose military skills were limited, was wise enough to leave questions of tactics in Blyukher's experienced hands.

Mao, along with other Central Executive Committee members, went to the parade ground to see the troops depart, but otherwise he stayed aloof from GMD politics.

Instead, he immersed himself in his work with the peasantry, who, as he had anticipated, soon began playing a significant part in the southern forces' advance. After the Revolutionary Army passed through Xiangtan, he sent fifty students from the Training Institute to Shaoshan, to see the peasant associations in action. A month later, he published an article in the GMD Peasant Department journal, *Nongmin yundong* (Peasant Movement), where for the first time he explicitly identified the landlords as the principal obstacle to revolutionary change, and the peasants as the principal instrument by which they would be overthrown:

> Right down to the present day, there are still a number of people, even within the revolutionary party, who do not understand . . . that the greatest adversary of revolution in an economically backward semi-colony is the feudal-patriarchal class (the landlord class) in the villages . . . [This] class constitutes the only solid basis for the ruling class at home and for imperialism abroad. Unless this basis is shaken, it will be absolutely impossible to shake the superstructure built upon it. The Chinese warlords are merely the chieftains of this rural feudal class. To say that you want to overthrow the warlords but do not want to overthrow the feudal class in the countryside is quite simply to be unable to distinguish between the trivial and the important, the essential and the secondary.

For the revolution to succeed, Mao argued, the peasants had to be liberated and the power of the landlords smashed.

The implication was that all else, including the proletariat, was secondary. Far from trying to disguise this, Mao offered a robust defence. The class struggle of the peasantry, he wrote, was 'different in nature from the workers' movement in the cities'. The latter was at that stage directed not at destroying the political position of the bourgeoisie but merely at obtaining trade union rights. The peasants, on the other hand, were locked in an elemental battle for survival:

> Hence, although we are all aware that the workers, students and middle and small merchants in the cities should rise and strike fiercely at the comprador class and directly resist imperialism, and although we know that the progressive working class in particular is the leader of all revolutionary classes, yet if the peasants do not rise and fight in the villages to overthrow the privileges of the feudal-patriarchal landlord class, the power of the warlords and of imperialism can never be hurled down root and branch.

Mao had developed this analysis gradually over a period of many months. The notion that the peasantry were, as he now put it, 'the central problem of the national revolution', dated back to the previous December. In January he had described the big landlords as 'the real foundation of imperialism and the warlords, the only secure bulwark of feudal and patriarchal society, the ultimate cause for the emergence of all counter-revolutionary forces' – a phrase which Borodin had seized on and used in a report to a high-ranking Soviet mission a month later.

But if Mao was not alone in concluding that the feudalism of the Chinese countryside was the chief obstacle to change, no one else had tried, as he now did, to explore the implications of this thesis and take it to its logical conclusion – which was as unacceptable ideologically to the CCP as it was, on practical grounds, to the Guomindang.

The *Nongmin yundong* article was omitted from the official canon of Mao's works, when compilations began to appear in the 1940s and '50s; it was simply too unorthodox. Yet beneath the subsequent veneer of ideological rectitude, the communist triumph, more than twenty years later, did come, as he had described, through mobilising the peasantry, not the urban proletariat.

While Mao was thus engaged in fashioning the intellectual underpinnings of his future strategy, the peasant organisers which his institute had trained – most of them CCP members using the Guomindang's name as a cover – fanned out into the countryside to foment rural revolts. First in Hunan, then in Hubei and Jiangxi, they prepared the ground for the nationalist armies, staying on after the troops had passed in order to consolidate the new peasant associations, which from then on were able to operate openly.

Events moved swiftly, too, on the battlefield. On August 12, Chiang Kai-shek convened a military conference in Changsha at which it was decided that Tang Shengzhi, now installed as Hunan's GMD Governor, should lead a mixed force of his own and Chiang's units against the expedition's next target, Wuhan. Wu Peifu himself took command of the northern forces, but his men were no match for the southerners and Tang captured Hankou and Hanyang on September 6 and 7. The third of Wuhan's three cities, Wuchang, held out against the besiegers until October 10, when Chiang's men suborned one of the defending commanders. Then, for two nerve-racking weeks, the southern offensive stalled, until finally, in November, the city of Nanchang fell, giving the southern armies and their allies a clean sweep of Hunan, Hubei and Jiangxi. Guangxi was already part of the nationalist camp and Guizhou had switched sides in July. Of all the provinces contiguous to Guangdong, only the northern half of Fujian was still in hostile hands, and that fell in December.

Throughout this period, the CCP leadership had been well and truly marginalised. In September, the Canton committee, which saw the success of the Northern Expedition as showing where the real power in the Guomindang lay, called for a reappraisal of the Centre's policy of uniting with the GMD-Left, arguing (correctly, as events turned out) that its leaders were an unprincipled congeries, without ideological unity, banding together to defend their own interests only because they 'could not co-operate with the [GMD-]Centre and Right'. Chen Duxiu found himself yet again in the invidious position of having to defend a united front which privately he detested, but which the Comintern insisted must continue.

Mao's sympathies were with the Canton group. Like them, he had learned at first-hand how supine and self-interested the GMD leftists really were. Like them, too, he saw the Northern Expedition as a huge step forward for the revolutionary cause. At a GMD conference in October, called to approve the move of the nationalist capital from Canton to Hankou, he despaired at the hypocrisy of men who in one breath solemnly promised an end to the extortion of land taxes years in advance, and in the next confessed apologetically that this year, exceptionally, because the party had run out of funds, it would have to continue after all. By then, he already knew that Canton held no future for him. His stint at the Training Institute had ended, and he was effectively out of a job.

Once again, the peasants were to prove Mao Zedong's salvation.

The explosion of peasant activism that followed the Northern Expedition had finally made the CCP leaders realise that the peasant movement was important, and that it was being led entirely under the Guomindang banner. On November 4, Chen Duxiu proposed that the Central Bureau draw up a rural work programme that would meet peasant demands without creating 'too great a distance' over the issue between the CCP and the Left-GMD and risking 'a premature split'. The question was, as it had been for Chiang Kai-shek, six months earlier, who should be put in charge? In September, Mao's article in *Nongmin yundong,* calling for class war against the landlords, had caught the eye of Qu Qiubai who, despite its departures from Leninist orthodoxy, read it with approval. Qu was close to Voitinsky, and counted as one of the most influential members of the Shanghai leadership. He evidently concluded that Mao would be a useful ally.

A few days later, Mao took ship for Shanghai, while Yang Kaihui, now pregnant with their third child, returned with the family to Hunan. On November 15, 1926, the Central Bureau announced that he had been appointed Secretary of the CCP CC's Peasant Movement Committee.

So ended twenty-three months of political self-exile. It had been a fruitful period. Mao had acquired an undying belief in the revolutionary power of the peasantry, as well as vital skills in operating within the top leadership of a big, complex party machine, learning how to manipulate committees and to haggle over the fine print of party resolutions. Yet after his long dalliance with the effete charms of the Left-GMD, it must have been a relief to discover that he could still find himself a niche, albeit a narrow one, within the Party fold. From now on his primary loyalty would be not just to 'communism', in the abstract, as he had written in 1925, but to the growing body of Chinese men and women who, despite hesitations and setbacks, were attempting to bring it about.

Ten days after his appointment, Mao set out for Wuhan, shortly to become the nationalist capital, where the Party had decided the new Peasant Committee should be based. He travelled via Nanchang, which Chiang Kai-shek had made his headquarters, and there witnessed the first storm-clouds gathering in the protracted struggle that was to develop between Chiang and the GMD-Left for control of the party and its strategy.

During the autumn, Chiang's position as Commander-in-Chief had come under pressure from Tang Shengzhi, whose stature had been bolstered by his successes in Hunan and at Hankou and Hanyang. By the time the nationalist government's Finance and Foreign Ministers, T. V. Soong and Eugene Chen, accompanied by Borodin, Sun Yat-sen's widow, Soong Ching-ling, and other senior GMD leftists, reached Nanchang at the beginning of December, Tang's challenge had receded. None the less, Chiang felt obliged to agree to a new *modus vivendi* with the Left, whereby his military leadership would be confirmed, but his political role would be restricted and Wang Jingwei would be invited to return as head of government. This episode convinced him that, once the move to Hankou was complete, he would face further attempts to curb his powers, and that it would be more prudent for him to remain in Nanchang, where he would be better placed to resist whatever challenges his adversaries might throw at him.

The result was the creation of two rival capitals. On December 13, the GMD leaders in Wuhan, advised by Borodin, formed a 'Provisional Joint Council', which promptly passed a resolution basing the government and party headquarters there. Three weeks later, after Tan Yankai joined Chiang at the head of a second group of GMD dignitaries, they resolved that, 'for the time being', the nationalist party and government should remain in Nanchang.

The Communist Party leaders saw the split as justifying their support for the GMD-Left. At a CC plenum in Hankou in mid-December, Chen Duxiu warned that the nationalist party's left wing was an essential buffer, preventing direct conflict breaking out between the communists and the GMD-Right. The Left, he acknowledged, was often 'weak, vacillating and inconsistent'. But negating it in the hope that something better would providentially appear was like 'refusing to eat bean curd and vegetables because next week there might be meat and fish'. The Party's strategy, Chen argued, was correct. Communists must work discreetly in the background, bolstering the GMD-Left's support against what was now termed the 'new Right' (the former GMD-Centre), led by Chiang Kai-shek; and they must avoid controversial measures – such as the forced redistribution of land to the peasantry – which might impair the alliance. 'The Left's existence', the plenum declared in its final resolution, 'is the key to our co-operation with the Guomindang.'

This cautious optimism stemmed in part from the phenomenal growth in the CCP's membership over the previous two years. From fewer than a thousand at the time of the Fourth Congress in January 1925, this had jumped to 7,500 a year later (in the wake of the May 30 Incident); and to 30,000 by December 1926, thanks largely to the Northern Expedition. Equally important, about 1,000 unit commanders, political workers and staff officers in the National Revolutionary Army were Communist Party members, whom Zhou Enlai's Military Committee was now beginning to organise into regimental 'nuclei', or secret Party cells.

The trouble with the strategy which Chen Duxiu, and behind him, the Comintern, stood for – 'playing the coolie', in Borodin's phrase; 'Right-capitulationism', as Chen's critics would call it – was that it assumed that the GMD-Left, with no army of its own and, at best, notional support from Tang Shengzhi, could somehow compel Chiang Kai-shek to submit to its control. Mao put his finger on it during the plenum debate, in which he participated as a non-voting member in his capacity as head of the Peasant Committee. 'The Right has troops,' he said, 'the Left has none; even with a single platoon, the Right would be stronger than the Left.' That observation earned him a stinging rebuke from Chen, who said the remark was 'absurd' but offered no substantive rebuttal.

As the weeks passed and the nature of the split became clearer, the Party Centre acknowledged that its hopes of a left-wing resurgence were not being realised, and that instead the GMD-Right was becoming 'more and more powerful'. But the only answer it could suggest was for the Party to make even greater efforts to reassure the Guomindang, and especially the GMD-Left, that the CCP was a loyal and harmless ally.

Mao, too, in public, hewed closely to this ultra-cautious, conciliatory line. Soon after the December plenum, he left Hankou for Changsha to attend the first Congress of the Hunan Provincial Peasants' Association. There he assured his audience that 'the time for us to overthrow the landlords has not yet come'. Rent reductions, a cap on interest rates and higher wages for rural labourers were legitimate demands, he said. But beyond that the national revolution must take priority, and the landlords should be allowed some concessions.

Within two months, Mao would reject those views totally.

Then he would proclaim, in messianic tones, that the peasant movement was a 'colossal event', which would alter the face of China, and that the Party must change its policy completely – or become irrelevant:

> In a very short time, several hundred million peasants in China's central, southern and northern provinces will rise like a fierce wind or tempest, a force so swift and violent that no power, however great, will be able to suppress it. They will break through all the trammels that bind them and rush forward along the road to liberation. They will, in the end, send all the imperialists, warlords, corrupt officials, local bullies and bad gentry to their graves. All revolutionary parties and all revolutionary comrades will stand before them to be tested, to be accepted or rejected as they decide. To march at their head and lead them? To stand behind them, gesticulating and criticising them? Or to stand opposite them and oppose them? Every Chinese is free to choose . . . [but] you are fated to make the choice quickly.

The extraordinary change in Mao's views – even allowing for hyperbole, the picture he painted was utterly different from anything any Party official had written before – was the result of a month-long journey he made through Xiangtan and four other rural counties in January and early February 1927.

It was a revelation. The reality of the peasant movement, he told the Central Committee on his return, was 'almost totally different from what we have seen and heard in Hankou and in Changsha'. He set out his conclusions in a document which was to become famous as the 'Report on the Peasant Movement in Hunan'. It was a brilliant intellectual *tour de force*, nearly 20,000 words in length and, like Mao's subsequent rural investigations, in Jiangxi in the early 1930s, based on meticulous field research. 'I called together fact-finding conferences in villages and county towns, which were attended by experienced peasants and by comrades in the peasant movement,' he reported. 'I listened attentively . . . and collected a great deal of material.'

The peasant movement, he was told, had developed in two phases. From January to September 1926, peasant associations had been organised, first in secret, then, after the Northern Expedition, openly. From October to December, the countryside rose in revolt.

The associations' membership, which stood at 400,000 in late summer, shot up to two million. All over central Hunan, the old feudal order collapsed:

> The main targets of their attack are the local bullies, the bad gentry and the lawless landlords, but in passing they also hit out against patriarchal ideas and institutions of all kinds . . . The attack is quite simply tempestuous; those who submit to it survive, and those who resist, perish. As a result, the privileges the feudal landlords have enjoyed for thousands of years are being shattered to pieces . . . The peasant associations have now become the sole organs of authority . . . Even trifling matters, such as quarrels between husband and wife, must be brought before [them] for settlement . . . If a member of a peasant association so much as farts, it is [regarded as] sacred. The association actually dictates everything in the countryside . . . Quite literally: 'Whatever it says, goes'.

Mao defended the movement against those in the Left-GMD, and even in the Communist Party, who argued that it had become too extreme and too 'terrible', and ought to be reined in:

> The fact is that the broad peasant masses have risen to fulfil their historical mission . . . It is fine. It is not terrible at all. It is anything but 'terrible' . . . To give credit where credit is due, if we allot 10 points to the accomplishments of the democratic revolution, then the achievements of the city dwellers and the military rate three points, and [those of] the peasants the remaining seven . . . True, the peasants are in a sense 'unruly' in the countryside . . . They fine the local bullies and bad gentry, they demand contributions from them and they smash their sedan chairs. Should [such individuals] oppose the peasant association, a mass of people swarm into their houses, slaughtering their pigs and consuming their grain. They may even loll on the ivory-inlaid beds belonging to the young ladies in the households of the local bullies and evil gentry. At the slightest provocation they make arrests, crown the arrested with tall paper hats and parade them through the villages . . . They have even created a kind of terror in the countryside.
>
> This is what ordinary people call 'going too far', or 'going beyond the proper limits in righting a wrong', or 'really too much'. Such talk may seem plausible, but in fact it is wrong . . .
>
> A revolution is not like inviting people to dinner, or writing an essay, or painting a picture, or doing embroidery; it cannot be so refined, so leisurely and gentle, so 'benign, upright, courteous, temperate and complaisant'. A revolution is an uprising, an act of

violence whereby one class overthrows the power of another . . . If the peasants do not use extremely great force, they cannot possibly overthrow the deeply rooted power of the landlords, which has lasted for thousands of years . . . All the [peasants'] excessive actions were extremely necessary . . . To put it bluntly, it is necessary to bring about a brief reign of terror in every rural area . . . To right a wrong, it is necessary to exceed the proper limits; the wrong cannot be righted without doing so.

What this 'terror' should consist of, Mao discussed in the last section of his report. Declaring the smashing of the landlords' power and prestige to be the central task of the peasants' struggle, he listed nine different methods they could use, ranging from public denunciation and fines to imprisonment and death: 'The execution of one . . . big member of the local gentry or one big local bully reverberates through a whole county and is very effective in eradicating the remaining evils of feudalism,' he asserted. 'The only effective way of suppressing the reactionaries is to execute at least one or two in each county . . . When [they] were at the height of their power, they killed peasants without batting an eyelid . . . How [then] can one say that the peasants should not now rise and shoot one or two?'

The aims of the revolt were multiple: to reduce land rents and interest rates on debt; to end hoarding so as to bring down grain prices; to disband the landlord militias and replace them with peasant spear corps, equipped with 'pointed double-edged blades mounted on long shafts . . . the mere sight of which makes the local tyrants and evil gentry shiver'; and to create a new rural administration, based on village assemblies, which Mao and the provincial party leaders hoped would become the building blocks of a rural front between the peasant associations and the Guomindang. Beyond these economic and political goals, there was also a social agenda. The associations, Mao noted approvingly, opposed opium-smoking and gambling – and also clan and religious authorities:

A man in China is usually subjected to the domination of three systems of authorities: (1) the state system (political authority) . . . (2) the clan system (clan authority) . . . and (3) the supernatural system (religious authority) . . . As for women, in addition to being dominated by these three, they are also dominated by men (the authority of the husband). These four authorities – political, clan, religious and male – are the embodiment of the whole feudal-patriarchal ideological system, and are the four thick ropes binding the Chinese people, particularly the peasants . . . The political authority of the landlords is the backbone of all the other systems of authority. [Once it is] overturned, the clan authority, the religious authority and the authority of the husband all begin to totter . . . [The collapse of] the clan system, superstitious ideas and one-sided concepts of chastity will follow as a natural consequence . . . It is the peasants who made the idols with their own hands, and when the time comes they will cast the idols aside with their own hands; there is no need for anyone else to do it for them prematurely.

The intensity of Mao's experiences during those few weeks in Hunan was such that the lessons he drew from them would stay with him all his life. Revolution, he now understood, could not be micromanaged. In any revolutionary venture, there would always be excesses, just as there would always be those who lagged behind. He quoted Mencius: 'Our policy in such matters is, "Draw the bow, but do not release the arrow, having seemed to leap."' The leadership could point the direction, but then it was up to the people to carry the revolution forward. Only when disaster threatened (as, in the end, it almost always did) would the leaders have to slam on the brakes.

No less important, and outwardly more dramatic, was Mao's open espousal of violence. A year earlier, in January 1926, he had conceded that 'in special circumstances, when we encounter the most reactionary and vicious local bullies and evil gentry . . . they must be overthrown completely', but without specifying what that meant. In a lecture at the Peasant Movement Training Institute six months later, he spoke for the first time of using 'brutal methods' against counter-revolutionaries, if there were no other way to deal with them. Now, the ambiguities were lifted. If the landlords were the chief obstacle to the revolution and the peasantry the chief instrument for removing them, the appropriate method was revolutionary violence – the same violence that, seven years earlier, a younger, more idealistic Mao had rejected when choosing between Marx and Kropotkin. Revolutionary violence was qualitatively different from the violence of war, which was fought over territory and power. It was aimed at men who were enemies not because of what they did, but because of who they were. It came from the same deep well of class hatred that the Bolsheviks had drawn from to overthrow the Russian bourgeoisie, and would have similar results.

Mao's report was incendiary, and when it was received at Party headquarters in the last week of February 1927, there was sharp disagreement over whether it should be made public. Qu Qiubai was strongly in favour. Chen Duxiu and Peng Shuzhi had reservations. Mao himself had admitted that the peasant associations, and all other forms of local authority, had been overwhelmed by the force of the movement, and that the countryside was, in his own words, 'in a state of anarchy'. The Guomindang, Left and Right, was appalled by the reports of blind Red Terror, spiralling out of control, and held the communists responsible. Moreover, it quickly became clear that the killings were not as isolated and exemplary as Mao had claimed: the elderly landlord father of Li Lisan, now a CCP Central Committee member, returned to his home village with a letter from his son to the local peasant association. The letter was ignored; the old man was summarily executed.

Meanwhile, unexpected new instructions arrived from Moscow. Until then the Comintern line, laid down by Stalin himself, had been to hold back the peasant movement, for fear it would undermine the united front with the GMD. Now the Russian leader declared that this had been 'a profound mistake'. The theses of the Comintern's Seventh Plenum, approved in Moscow in mid-December, which were received in Shanghai shortly before Mao's report, insisted on the contrary: 'The fear that the aggravation of the class struggle in the countryside will weaken the anti-imperialist front is baseless . . . The refusal [to promote] the agrarian revolution . . . for fear of alienating the dubious and indecisive co-operation of a section of the capitalist class, is wrong.' Although the theses also made clear that the united front was to be maintained (Stalin, as ever, wanted to have his cake and eat it), the thrust was now much more aggressive, and the Chinese leaders were unsure how to respond.

In the end, a bastard compromise was reached. The first two parts of Mao's report were published in *Xiangdao* in March (and reprinted widely by the Comintern, which shared none of the Chinese comrades' inhibitions about revolutionary violence). But the final section – in which Mao referred to execution rallies and peasants beating landlords to death, and mocked the GMD-Left for 'talking of arousing the masses day in and day out, and then being scared out of their wits when the masses do arise' – was omitted. Later Mao was able to arrange for the full text to be published as a pamphlet in Wuhan, to which Qu Qiubai contributed an enthusiastic preface.

The incident solidified his political alliance with Qu, while his relations with Chen became increasingly embittered. 'If the peasant movement had been more thoroughly organised and armed for a class struggle against the landlords,' he told Edgar Snow ten years later, 'the [communist base areas] would have had an earlier and far more powerful development throughout the whole country. But Chen Duxiu violently disagreed. He did not understand the role of the peasantry in the revolution, and greatly underestimated its possibilities.'

Part of the problem was that Chen and the Central Bureau had more pressing problems to contend with. On February 17, nationalist troops had seized Hangzhou, the capital of Zhejiang. Next day their advance units were at Songjiang, only twenty-five miles from Shanghai. Believing the city's fall to be imminent, the communist-backed labour unions declared a general strike. But the nationalist advance never came. The Shanghai garrison commander, Li Baozhang, sent execution squads on to the streets to hunt down activists. An American correspondent watched them at work, only a few minutes' walk from the city's fashionable thoroughfares:

> The executioners, bearing broadswords and accompanied by a squad of soldiers, marched their victims to a prominent corner where the strike leaders were forced to bend over while their heads were cut off. Thousands fled in horror when the heads were stuck on sharp-pointed bamboo poles and were hoisted aloft, and carried to the scene of the next execution.

By this time the Central Bureau and the Soviet advisers had concluded, apparently independently, that compromise with Chiang Kai-shek was impossible, and that the CCP and the GMD-Left, backed by Tang Shengzhi's forces in the army – which the Russians now supported – would have to find a way to ease him out of power. Such an outcome, moreover, appeared feasible. Chiang's own supporters were wavering. His vanity and personal ambition, his 'Napoleon complex', as his critics called it, his obsession with removing Borodin and, most damning of all, reports, which were widely believed, that he was preventing Wang Jingwei's return, cost him crucial moderate support. There was a sense abroad that the focus of the revolution was shifting from Nanchang to Wuhan, and that there was nothing Chiang could do to stop it.

The earliest known portrait of Mao,
as a teenager around the time of the 1911 revolution.

Left A soldier preparing to shear off a peasant's queue after the overthrow of the Manchus.

Below One of the many forms of death by slow execution common in Mao's youth. These prisoners are being slowly asphyxiated as the weight of their bodies stretches their necks.

Opposite above The Mao family home at Shaoshan.

Opposite below left [from right] Mao at the age of 25, with his mother, Wen Qimei, and his brothers, Zemin, 22, and Zetan, 15, in Changsha in 1919.

Opposite below right Mao's father, Rensheng, the same year.

Left Mao's close friend, Cai Hesen, who converted him to Marxism.

Below Mao and other members of the Hunanese delegation in Beijing, petitioning for the removal of Governor Zhang Jingyao in January 1920.

Right China's first president, Sun Yat-sen.

Below The spiritual fathers of the Chinese Communist Party. *(left)* Li Dazhao, of Beijing University, whose writings popularised Bolshevism in China, and *(right)* Chen Duxiu, editor of *New Youth* and the CCP's first General Secretary.

Opposite far left Mao's second wife, Yang Kaihui, with their sons, Anying, 3, and Anqing, 2, in 1925.

Opposite left Mao's third wife, He Zizhen.

Below [from left] Ren Bishi; Red Army Commander-in-Chief, Zhu De; Political Security director, Deng Fa; Xiang Ying; Mao; and Wang Jiaxiang, on the eve of the proclamation of the Chinese Soviet Republic at Ruijin in November 1931.

Generalissimo Chiang Kai-shek.

Zhou Enlai with Mao in north Shensi in 1937.

The balance tipped irrevocably on March 6, 1927, when five of the eight GMD CEC members in Nanchang boarded a steamer for Wuhan. Four days later, when the GMD's long-awaited Third Plenum opened in Hankou, it was dominated by the GMD-Left and the communists.

Chiang himself and the Standing Committee Chairman, Zhang Jingjiang, refused to attend. In their absence, a new leftist-dominated GMD Political Council was established as the supreme organ of party power, and further steps were taken to subordinate the military to civilian control. The Left-Guomindang–CCP alliance started to look like a genuine coalition. Two communists, Tan Pingshan and Su Zhaozheng, a seamen's leader who had helped organise the Hong Kong–Canton strike, were given ministerial portfolios in the new nationalist government, a step which Borodin (and Moscow) had been urging since the beginning of the year. The Northern Expedition resumed. Shanghai surrendered with hardly a shot being fired, and Chiang moved his headquarters there from Nanchang on March 26. Wang Jingwei made his way back from Europe. There were widespread hopes that the two men would resume the military–civilian duumvirate that had been shattered by Chiang's coup a year earlier.

Mao spoke at length at the GMD's Third Plenum, which approved (more readily than his own party) many of the ideas he had brought back from his rural investigation in Hunan, including the establishment of village governments, protected by peasant defence forces; the death penalty or life imprisonment for tyrannical landlords; and, for the first time, the confiscation and redistribution of land belonging to 'corrupt officials, local bullies, bad gentry and counter-revolutionaries'.

Land, the plenum declared, was 'the core issue' for the poor peasants who were the motive force of the revolution, and the party would support their struggle 'until the land problem has been completely solved'. This sounded more radical than it was. The crucial question – *how* the land issue was to be dealt with – was not addressed. But at least it was now on the agenda, and afterwards Mao threw himself into preparations for launching an All-China Federation of Peasant Associations, a GMD Land Committee, and other bodies which were to be charged with putting the new policies into effect.

By now Yang Kaihui and the children had joined him. They

rented a house in Wuchang, where the Peasant Training Institute had reopened with Mao, once again, as Principal. At the beginning of April, their third child, another boy, was born. Mao gave him the name Anlong. Life, it seemed, was finally returning to normal.

The same day, April 4, 1927, Wang Jingwei and Chen Duxiu issued a joint statement in Shanghai, affirming their common cause. The declaration, Zhang Guotao wrote later, had a 'slightly hypnotic effect', producing a warm glow of nostalgia for CCP–GMD amity. True, the air was thick with rumour. The foreign newspapers in the treaty ports bubbled with speculation about a communist coup against Chiang, or a coup by Chiang against the communists. Wang and Chen, in their joint statement, dismissed the rumours as fabrications. Bukharin wrote in *Pravda* that while differences were inevitable, there was 'no place for pessimism', and Stalin told a closed meeting in Moscow that Chiang Kai-shek had no choice but to support the revolution. Once he had played his role, he would be 'squeezed out like a lemon and then flung away'. Until that day, communists in both countries would give him the benefit of the doubt. 'The peasant keeps his old worn-out jade as long as she is necessary,' Stalin said laconically. 'He does not drive her away. So it is with us.'

CHAPTER SIX

Events Leading to the
Horse Day Incident and its
Bloody Aftermath

Shortly after 4 a.m. on Tuesday, April 12, 1927, the doleful sound of a river steamer's foghorn echoed across the western districts of Shanghai. It was the signal for nationalist troops, supported by a thousand 'armed labourers', wearing identical blue denim uniforms with white armbands, on which was inscribed the character *gong* (labour), to begin moving silently into position around communist strongholds in the working-class Nandao and Zhabei quarters of the city. To facilitate their task, the municipal council had granted the nationalist commander, Bai Chongxi, free passage for his men through the foreign concessions.

As dawn was breaking, a concerted attack began. The 'labourers' were actually members of the Green Gang, the dominant Shanghai underworld organisation. The communists, caught unprepared, were outgunned and outfought. Only at the General Labour Union headquarters, and the offices of the Commercial Press, where arms had been stockpiled and communist-led workers were able to barricade themselves in, was serious resistance offered. By late morning, after the army brought up machine-guns and field artillery, that, too, had been crushed. 'It is too much, perhaps, to say that the Communist power is broken,' the correspondent of *The Times* reported, 'but certainly the Communists have had a heavy setback.' The British-officered municipal police estimated that

400 people had been killed, and many more wounded and arrested.

The following day, Zhou Enlai, who was the top-ranking communist then in Shanghai, ordered a general strike, which brought much of the city to a standstill. About a thousand workers, including women and children who worked in the textile mills, then marched to the Military Headquarters to hand in a petition. What happened next was conveyed succinctly by the *North China Herald*'s headline: 'Horrible Fight in Zhabei: Communists' Women and Children Placed in Front Line . . . Soldiers Fire Nonetheless'. The demonstrators, the newspaper noted, had been unarmed; the troops had fired a single volley at a few yards' range. About twenty people died instantly. Up to two hundred others were shot as they fled. Witnesses reported lorry-loads of corpses being taken for burial in mass graves. After that, there were no further demonstrations. Chiang Kai-shek and his allies were firmly back in control.

It is almost impossible to understand why the CCP and the Left-Guomindang did not anticipate Chiang's putsch. Part of the problem was Stalin's insistence that the united front be maintained at all costs. Stalin believed that the Guomindang had a far better chance than the communists of unifying China and weakening Moscow's enemies, the Powers, and that therefore the Soviet–GMD alliance must be preserved. His strategy for China was *realpolitik*, rather than revolution. In the process he blinkered the Comintern, which in turn blinkered the CCP.

Yet that was not the whole story. Even allowing for Comintern discipline, the Chinese Party leaders permitted themselves to be lulled in a quite extraordinary manner. For an entire month before the Shanghai coup, they deliberately closed their eyes to mounting evidence that Chiang had turned decisively against them. Starting in mid-March, when the GMD's Third Plenum reaffirmed the Left-Guomindang–CCP alliance (signalling an attempt to marginalise Chiang and the GMD-Right within the party apparatus), a systematic pattern of violence, directed against the Left, developed throughout the areas that Chiang's forces controlled. From Chongqing, in far-off Sichuan, to Amoy (Xiamen), on the China Sea coast, the procedure was everywhere the same. Thugs recruited from secret societies (usually linked to the Green Gang), backed up when necessary by troops, smashed the mass organisations of the

Left, and new 'moderate' groups were hastily set up to replace them.

Other forces also came into play. Hankou, under Left-GMD rule, had been an economic disaster. Labour militancy forced dozens of Chinese banks to close. Trade was at a standstill. To the wealthy Chinese financiers and industrialists watching nervously from Shanghai, the 'Red capital', as it was called, exemplified everything they wanted to avoid. If that were not enough, a workers' insurrection in Shanghai in March, ruthlessly controlled by communist enforcers – 'black-gowned gunmen', the London *Times* called them – and frighteningly effective, offered an alarming foretaste of what communist government might portend.

In the foreign community, too, pressure was building for action by the Powers to stop the 'Bolshevik menace'. Lurid accounts of depravity were seized on eagerly. One story, widely reprinted, described how the Communists, already well-known for 'communising wives', had staged a 'naked body procession' of selected women 'having snow-white bodies and perfect breasts' through the streets of Hankou. One senses wishful thinking. An American missionary trembled at the consequences 'if the mad dog of Bolshevism is not checked . . . but is allowed to jump across the seas to our own beloved America'. Another resident remembered: 'A fear psychology possessed us. We were all to be murdered by our own servants. And the truth was that the first real warnings came from boys and coolies and amahs, who kept repeating: "Plenty trouble – more better go Japan side."'

On March 24, an event occurred which raised these fears to fever pitch. When the nationalist armies occupied Nanjing, soldiers looted the American, British and Japanese consulates, and fired on a group of foreigners awaiting evacuation. The British consul was wounded, and two Britons, an American, a French and an Italian priest and a Japanese marine were killed. The 'Nanking Outrage', as it was called, convinced Western capitals that the time had come to act.

Thus by the beginning of April, the Powers and the Shanghai capitalists were both looking for a means to halt the slide into anarchy and chaos. The question on every foreigner's lips was whether Chiang Kai-shek, GMD Commander-in-Chief, but also apparently a man with reservations about the communist cause, would answer to that purpose. 'Chiang Kai-shek stands at the dividing of the ways,' wrote the *North China Daily News*. 'He . . . [is]

now the only protection of China south of the Yangtse from being submerged by the Communist Party . . . But if General Chiang is to save his fellow countrymen from the Reds, he must act swiftly and relentlessly. Will he prove himself the man of action and decision? . . . Or will he, too, go down with China in the Red flood?'

The answer came in stages, artfully obscured. The Shanghai Chinese business community secretly paid over three million dollars, the first instalment of a 'loan', variously estimated at $10 to $25 million, made on the explicit understanding that the communists would be curbed. On April 6, the representatives of the Powers in Beijing authorised the northern government, then controlled by the fiercely anti-communist Manchurian warlord, Zhang Zuolin, to send Chinese police into the Legation quarter to search parts of the Soviet Embassy compound, where many local CCP leaders, including Li Dazhao, had taken refuge. Soviet premises in Tianjin were also searched. In Shanghai, guards were posted at the Soviet consulate, with orders to deny access to all but Russian officials. The Green Gang's leader, Du Yuesheng, whose mentor, 'Pockmarked Huang' (Huang Jinrong), had befriended Chiang when he had been a young officer in Shanghai a decade earlier, established a 'Common Progress Association', to furnish the so-called 'armed labourers' for the coming confrontation. And all the while in neighbouring cities, from Fuzhou to Nanjing, the steady drumbeat of anti-communist repression continued.

Yet even after all this, when the axe finally fell, 'the defenders of the revolution', in one contemporary observer's words, 'were taken unaware'. Not only was no defence prepared, but Wang Shouhua, the young head of the CCP CC Labour Committee and Chairman of the Shanghai General Labour Union – arguably the most important communist leader in the city – accepted, unsuspecting, a dinner invitation on the night of April 11 from Du Yuesheng himself. When he arrived, he was strangled and his body dumped in a shallow grave in wasteland in the suburbs.

The problem was not a failure of analysis. As early as January, the CC's Central Bureau had warned that an 'extremely dangerous situation' would arise in the event of 'an alliance of foreign imperialists with the right or moderate wing of the Guomindang'. But the Generalissimo had disguised his moves with such consummate skill that no one outside his own inner circle had guessed his true intentions. Foreigners and communists alike were bewildered. In early

April, while the *North China Daily News* was lamenting Chiang's refusal to take a 'frankly anti-communist' stand, the Central Bureau remained convinced that the attacks on communist-led organisations in the provinces were piecemeal efforts, not the prelude to a full-scale confrontation. The bottom line was that, in 1927, the CCP was so wedded to the alliance with the bourgeoisie that it could not conceive of a revolution without it.

In Hankou, on April 12, Mao spent the morning attending a meeting of the new GMD Land Committee, which was trying to devise a land redistribution policy that would satisfy peasant demands without alienating the GMD's landlord supporters. He was still brimming with optimism after his experiences in Hunan, and urged a radical approach: Let the peasants themselves take action, by refusing to pay rent – legal recognition could come later. He and Qu Qiubai were drawing up similar recommendations for the CCP's Fifth Congress, which was to take place later that month. The new Comintern delegate, Mahendranath (M. N.) Roy, who had just arrived from Moscow, was far more sympathetic to the agrarian revolution than Borodin had ever been. Wang Jingwei was in Hankou, and Chen Duxiu was on his way.

That afternoon, as the first urgent radio messages began coming in from Shanghai, all these carefully contrived hopes came crashing to the ground.

For the next six days, the CCP Central Bureau met in almost continuous session, while Moscow's two counsellors gave radically differing advice. Borodin, supported by Chen Duxiu, proposed a 'strategic retreat', involving severe restraints on the peasant and labour movement in the territories controlled by the Wuhan government, and an immediate resumption of the Northern Expedition under the command of Tang Shengzhi. He proposed that Tang link up with the Christian General, Feng Yuxiang, in Henan, who was receiving substantial Soviet aid, and mount a joint campaign against the northern forces of Zhang Zuolin. Once Zhang's troops had been defeated, there would be time enough to deal with Chiang Kai-shek and to revive the revolutionary movement that was being temporarily shelved. Roy held that this was 'a betrayal of the peasantry, of the proletariat . . . and the masses'. The Chinese revolution, he declared, 'will either win as an agrarian revolution or it will not win at all'. Going north meant 'collaborating with the very forces of reaction that are betraying the revolution at every step'. Borodin's advice, he concluded, was 'very dangerous', and the Party must reject it.

The dispute brought into the open the fundamental contradiction inherent in Stalin's policy in China. Should the workers and peasants take precedence? Or the alliance with the bourgeoisie?

As the argument raged on, a telegram arrived from Zhou Enlai and the other leaders in Shanghai, urging a third option. Chiang Kai-shek's military position, they said, was far weaker than it seemed. If Tang Shengzhi marched on Nanjing and took 'resolute punitive action', Chiang's forces could be defeated. If, on the other hand, indecision continued, he would consolidate his position. Qu Qiubai supported the Shanghai group. Chen Duxiu revived the idea, originally proposed by Sun Yat-sen, of making for the north-west, where the imperialist forces were weakest. Tan Pingshan and Zhang Guotao wanted to march south and reconquer the GMD's old base in Guangdong.

The futility of all these discussions, and the CCP's impotence, were shown graphically the following weekend, when the Bureau eventually endorsed Roy's position and issued a resolution declaring that, at this stage, to continue the Northern Expedition would be 'harmful to the revolution' – only to find that, next day, Wang Jingwei, urged on by Borodin, announced the expedition's imminent resumption.

Mao did not attend these meetings. His rank was too lowly (he was not even a Central Committee member); and since the row over his report from Hunan, Chen Duxiu had refused to have anything to do with him. But his sympathies were with Roy.

He spent that month labouring in the GMD Land Committee with a mixed group of young leftists and older, more conservative Guomindang officials, trying to come up with a formula for land redistribution which would satisfy all the different interests in play. The key issue was how extensive land redistribution should be. Should all private land be confiscated, as Mao proposed? Or only holdings in excess of 30 mu (5 acres), a little more than Mao's father had possessed? Or more than 50 or 100 mu, as the older delegates wanted? In the end, this, too, proved a pointless exercise, for even the restrictive version that Mao's drafting committee finally recommended was set aside by the GMD Political Council on the grounds that it might upset the army, many of whose officers were from landowning families.

Mao's efforts in his own party fared no better. At the Fifth Congress his draft resolution, calling for all land to be confiscated, was shelved without discussion. Lip service was paid to the principle of 'land nationalisation', but it was made meaningless because the Communists, like the GMD, forbade confiscation from 'small land-lords', a term which was left prudently undefined.

By this stage Mao was once again 'very dissatisfied with Party policy'. The feeling was mutual. When the new Central Committee was elected, he scraped in as an alternate member, ranking thirtieth in the Party hierarchy. A week later, when the CC Peasant Committee was 'reorganised', his position as Secretary was taken by Qu Qiubai, who had been promoted to the Standing Committee of the new Politburo (as the Central Bureau was now called). He retained his committee membership, and continued to work for the All-China Peasants' Association. But his chances of building throughout China a peasant movement 'so swift and violent that no power . . . will be able to suppress it', as he had written on his return from Hunan, looked increasingly remote.

Meanwhile, the torrent of bad news from other provinces grew into a flood.

In Canton, the right-wing GMD Governor proclaimed martial law. Two thousand communist suspects were rounded up, and scores executed. In the areas Chiang controlled directly, a 'Party Purification Campaign' was launched to root out communists. In Beijing, Li Dazhao, and nineteen of those detained with him during the raid on the Soviet Embassy, were strangled on the orders of Zhang Zuolin.

By early May, only Hubei, Hunan and Jiangxi, whose Governor, Zhu Peide, was a long-time ally of Wang Jingwei, were still under Wuhan's control.

Even more serious was the economic crisis. The militancy of the labour movement had brought the cities to a state of anarchy. Hankou, Hanyang and Wuchang had 300,000 unemployed. The foreign population had dropped from 4,500 to 1,300, and the plight of those that remained was described in *The Times* under the head-line, 'Red Terror at Hankou':

> The Government is now completely Communist, business is impos-
> sible, the labour unions and pickets dominate the city, while the

soldiers display an ugly temper and it is unsafe for British [subjects] to appear in the streets. The heads of firms are now the special object of the mob's violence, some having been chased from the streets with bayonets.

Matters were made still worse when the Chinese banks in Canton and Shanghai, on Chiang Kai-shek's orders, suspended dealing with Wuhan. Tax collection ceased; the government printed money without revenue to support it; daily necessities disappeared from the shops. By late April there were even fears of a rice shortage, because the revolutionary authorities in Hunan halted grain exports to try to hold down prices.

At Borodin's insistence, the GMD Political Council announced a ban on wildcat strikes, and measures to impose 'revolutionary discipline' on the labour movement, stabilise the currency, regulate prices and provide relief for the unemployed.

At that point, the military balance began to tip again. Tang Shengzhi's forces had moved north to link up with Feng Yuxiang's New People's Army in Henan. Only a skeleton garrison had remained behind in Hubei, which gave Chiang Kai-shek an opportunity to probe Wuhan's defences. In mid-May, General Xia Douyin, the nationalist commander at Yichang, two hundred miles upriver, rallied to Chiang's banner and marched on Hankou at the head of a force of 2,000 men. With Chiang's encouragement, other generals nominally loyal to Wuhan deployed their troops behind him. On May 18, Xia's advance guard was reported a few miles from Wuchang. Shopkeepers put up their shutters, and the ferry service across the river was halted. Ye Ting, a communist who had been named acting garrison commander, gathered a few hundred military cadets and men from a training division, and prepared as best he could to give battle. Mao was asked to mobilise the 400 students at the Peasant Movement Institute, each of whom had been given an old-fashioned rifle and rudimentary military training, to patrol the city streets.

Next morning, Ye Ting's improvised force marched out, and Xia's men were routed. But the fire which he had lit would not easily be extinguished.

In Changsha, wild rumours began circulating that Wuhan had fallen, Wang Jingwei had fled and Borodin had been executed. Already that spring, factional conflict between leftists and moderate elements had spiralled out of control. In April, several prominent citizens with right-wing or foreign connections, including Ye Dehui, the old, arch-conservative scholar who had helped instigate the 1910 rice riots which had so impressed Mao as a child, had been arrested and shot. Now, clashes broke out between soldiers and peasant association activists. On May 19, the father-in-law of He Jian, Tang Shengzhi's deputy commander, was beaten by communist demonstrators.

Two days later, on May 21, 1927, the Day of the Horse in the old calendar, the Changsha garrison commander, Xu Kexiang, decided he had had enough.

The Hunan CCP leaders, unlike their colleagues in Shanghai, six weeks earlier, got wind of what was planned. But the 3,000 workers' pickets they commanded were armed only with wooden sticks and spears, and no contingency plans had been made for resistance. That afternoon, emergency funds were distributed among the Party leaders, and women and children sent to places of safety. The shooting began at 11 p.m., and continued until dawn. 'Flames lighted the heavens', one leader's wife wrote later. 'I heard shots coming from the [peasant association headquarters], machine-guns and rifles . . . Everyone in our house got up and sat quietly in the altar-room, all afraid. Our six-month-old boy lay on my lap sucking at my breast, but the milk would not come. He cried and cried.'

Xu Kexiang boasted later: 'By dawn the Red fog of terrorism that had shrouded the city for so long was blown away by one puff of mine.'

In the course of the next three weeks, an estimated 10,000 people were killed in Changsha and its immediate vicinity. Groups of suspected communists were taken each day, at sunrise and at dusk, to the old execution ground outside the West Gate. Others died in an abortive uprising by members of the peasant self-defence forces, which the Hunan Party committee ordered to take place on May 31. At the last minute, instructions arrived from Hankou to cancel it. Two groups, attacking Changsha and Xiangtan, were not told of the change of plan and were annihilated.

From Hunan, the wave of conservative repression spread into Hubei, where Xia Douyin's defeated troops went on the rampage, slaughtering thousand of villagers. In Jiangxi, the peasant associations were dissolved, triggering a storm of gentry-sponsored revenge. All over central China, Red terror gave way to White, as the *mintuan*, the landlord militias, visited horrific reprisals on the peasants who had dared to rise against them. In an account prepared in mid-June for the All-China Peasants' Association, Mao reported:

> In Hunan . . . they beheaded the chief of the Xiangtan general labour union and kicked his head about with their feet, then filled his belly with kerosene and burned his body . . . In Hubei . . . the brutal punishments inflicted on the revolutionary peasants by the despotic gentry include such things as gouging out eyes and ripping out tongues, disembowelling and decapitation, slashing with knives and grinding with sand, burning with kerosene and branding with red-hot irons. In the case of women, they pierce their breasts [with iron wire, with which they tie them together], and parade them around naked in public, or simply hack them to pieces . . .

In Liling in Hunan, 80,000 people were dead by the time the killing stopped. In the four counties of Chaling, Leiyang, Liuyang and Pingjiang, nearly 300,000 perished. The slaughter far exceeded anything that even Zhang the Venomous had done, when his troops had devastated Hunan, a decade earlier. There had been nothing like it in China since the blood bath the Taipings had created in the 1850s.

The 'Horse Day Incident' and its horrific aftermath were a turning-point for the Communist Party. 'From this bloody lesson,' Zhang Guotao wrote later, 'the CCP learned that "only armed force can deal with armed force".'

But that was with the benefit of hindsight. The Party's response at the time was dilatory and confused. First reports of the massacre in Changsha reached Wuhan as the communists were still digesting Xia Douyin's failed rebellion, and concluding for the umpteenth time that the peasant movement would have to be damped down to prevent such things happening in future. Indeed, the Politburo's initial reaction, on May 25, was that the peasants, by their excesses, had brought it on themselves. Next day, with Wang Jingwei's approval, Borodin set out for Changsha at the head of a joint CCP–GMD Commission to try to establish what had really happened. As they left, Mao, on behalf of the All-China Peasants' Association, sent a message to the Hunan leaders, urging them 'to be patient and wait for the government officials in order to avoid further friction'. The commission never arrived. It was turned back at the Hunan border (according to some accounts, with a warning from Xu Kexiang that if it went on, its members would be killed). Only then did the Central Committee appeal to the GMD leadership to dissolve Xu Kexiang's 'insurrectional committee'; to send a punitive expedition to Changsha, led by Tang Shengzhi, then regarded by the communists as an ally; and to supply arms to enable the peasantry to defend themselves. None of these demands was met.

At the end of May, Mao asked the Politburo to send him to Hunan to help rebuild the Party organisation there. Ten days later, he was instructed to go to Xiangtan, to organise a new provincial committee with himself as Secretary. The decision was rescinded almost at once. But from early June, Mao had substantial day-to-day responsibility for dealing with Hunan affairs, and for the next few weeks attempted with some success, in statements and directives, to conciliate the Party's demands that the peasantry be brought back into line with a robust defence of what he insisted were their legitimate 'violent means of resistance'.

In the meantime, another blow descended on the beleaguered Chinese communists from a most unexpected quarter.

Ever since Chiang's coup in April, Stalin had been locked in conflict with Trotsky over his responsibility for the Chinese débâcle. As a result, the Chinese Party had been left to get on with things on its own. But on June 1, 1927, after an extended and unusually secretive Comintern plenum in the Kremlin, a telegram arrived in Hankou. In it Stalin instructed the Central Committee to start taking a much tougher line. They must promote the agrarian revolution 'in every possible way'. Excesses were to be dealt with by the peasant associations themselves. The GMD must organise a revolutionary tribunal, which would mete out severe punishment to officers who maintained links with Chiang Kai-shek or used their troops to curb the masses. 'Persuasion is not enough: it is time to act,' Stalin declared. 'The scoundrels must be punished'. A dependable new army should be formed 'before it is too late', by mobilising 'about 20,000 Communists and 50,000 revolutionary workers and peasants from Hunan and Hubei', so as 'to liquidate the dependence on unreliable generals immediately'. The GMD Central Executive Committee also needed an infusion of new blood. Bold new leaders must be brought in from the peasantry and the working class to stiffen the resolve of 'certain of the old leaders', who were now 'vacillating and compromising', or to drive them out altogether.

When this missive was read out, members of the Politburo, according to Zhang Guotao, 'did not know whether to cry or laugh'. Chen Duxiu wrote later that it was 'like taking a bath in shit'. Even Borodin and Voitinsky agreed that there was no way of implementing it.

It was not that Stalin's ideas were wrong. A year earlier the CCP leaders had begged Moscow for 5,000 rifles to arm an independent peasant force in Guangdong, but had been turned down on the grounds that it might create mistrust among the GMD army. Mao and Cai Hesen had long argued for peasant excesses to be handled within the peasant associations, not by outside forces. The problem lay elsewhere. Not only were the new orders too late. But Stalin's assessment of the balance of forces in the revolutionary movement might as well have come from another planet. Neither the Left-GMD, nor, still less, the CCP, had any power to discipline 'unreliable generals'. Nor could the communists reorganise the GMD Central Executive Committee, which was shifting so rapidly to the right that it took all the CCP's energy just to keep the alliance intact.

At this juncture, Roy, who had hoped the telegram would galvanise the Party into supporting the peasant movement more strongly, took matters into his own hands.

Without consulting Borodin or any of the Chinese leaders, he showed the telegram to Wang Jingwei. His motives have never been adequately explained, but it appears that, like Stalin, he misjudged the balance of forces, believing that communist support was still so important to Wang that proof of Moscow's disillusionment with the Guomindang would shock him into adopting more radical policies. As it turned out, the effect was precisely the reverse. Wang concluded that the CCP–GMD alliance was finished. Next day, June 6, he led a Left-GMD delegation to Zhengzhou in Henan, which had just fallen to Feng Yuxiang, ostensibly to discuss their alliance against Chiang Kai-shek, but actually to start putting out peace feelers for an eventual reconciliation with the right wing of the party in Nanjing.

Roy's blunder hastened the inevitable. The two madly galloping steeds the CCP was trying to ride – peasant revolt and bourgeois revolution – had been pulling apart for months. Even without his action, the Horse Day Incident had signalled the final parting of the ways.

On June 15, Chen Duxiu sent Stalin the Politburo's response, which was as remarkable for its unconcealed exasperation at the Soviet leader's handling of affairs as for its sense of impending doom. Chen explained, as if to a child:

> The peasant movement showed a particularly rapid development in Hunan. Ninety per cent of the national army comes from Hunan. The whole army is hostile toward the excesses of the peasant movement . . . In such a situation, not only the Guomindang but the Communist Party, too, must decide on a policy of concessions . . . Otherwise . . . a split with the Guomindang will occur . . . [Indeed,] it is probable that it will be impossible [to prevent this] in the nearest future . . . Your instructions are correct and important. We express our full agreement . . . but it is impossible to achieve this in a short time . . . Until we find ourselves in a position to fulfil these tasks, it is necessary to maintain good relations [with the leaders of the Left-GMD and the national army].

The only one of the Russian leader's instructions to which Chen did not make a direct reply was the order to create 'your own reliable army'. This was no accident. As late as May 26, less than a week before Stalin's telegram was received, the Politburo had still been insisting that armed conflict was to be avoided, indeed, this was why the planned May 31 attack on Changsha was called off. Now that was to change. However belatedly, the issue of an independent communist force was at last being seriously discussed.

The enduring significance of Stalin's telegram, long after the immediate controversy which it provoked had been forgotten, was that it sowed the seed from which, in the months that followed, the Chinese Red Army would grow.

By the time Chen sent off the Politburo's response, a secret Central Committee commission had been established, headed by Zhou Enlai, then Secretary of the CC's Military Committee, which drew up a detailed plan to infiltrate into Hunan more than a hundred communist agents to organise armed peasant uprisings against Xu Kexiang's forces. At a meeting in Wuhan, shortly before they were to set out, Mao told them that their mission was to return to their home areas and 'maintain the revolutionary struggle by armed force'. The calculation, apparently, was that if the insurrections succeeded, the communist-led peasant units would form the nucleus of the 'reliable army' that Stalin was calling for.

On June 24, Mao was appointed Hunan Party Secretary, and left immediately for Changsha to see what might be salvaged amid the continuing repression. A few days later, he told a group of surviving Party and Youth League officials in Hengshan that the time for hesitation was over. From now on, they must 'counter guns with guns'.

But even as Mao spoke, the ground was being cut from beneath the communists' feet.

An open breach was imminent between Wang Jingwei and the Russians. The Soviet advisers themselves could see the writing on the wall and began quietly packing to leave. Not only was Wang wavering, but Moscow's other protégé, Feng Yuxiang, had switched sides, and was now supporting Chiang Kai-shek, in return for a subsidy of $2 million a month.

A mood of black pessimism settled on the Politburo. Cai Hesen remembered how '[we all] wandered aimlessly, looking depressed . . . and were unable . . . to agree upon a firm and definite stand on anything'.

Signs of desperation appeared. On June 23 the Central Committee Secretariat issued a melodramatic warning that 'an immediate break with the Guomindang will mean the immediate liquidation of our Party', and proposed creating a new 'May 30 Incident', like that which had set China on fire in 1925, to 'lead us out of this dangerous crisis'. It was left to Roy to scotch such a lunatic venture. 'The idea of collaboration with the Guomindang', he told the leadership sternly, 'is being converted into a real fetish to which everything must be sacrificed.' The warning was ignored. On June 30, in a last desperate effort to stave off final collapse, the Politburo approved a craven resolution, reaffirming the Guomindang's 'leading position in the national revolution', placing workers' and peasants' organisations – including peasant self-defence forces – under GMD supervision, restricting the role of workers' pickets, and limiting strike demands.

At about the same time, Mao received an urgent summons to abandon the planned Hunan uprisings and return to Wuhan. Borodin had evidently concluded that the risk to what remained of the alliance with the Left-GMD outweighed any possible gains.

On Monday, July 4, Mao and Liu Zhixun, the head of the

now-banned peasant association in Hunan, attended an enlarged meeting of the Politburo Standing Committee in Wuchang to try to decide what to do next. The surviving minutes show a leadership grasping at straws. Much of the discussion concerned the relationship between Tang Shengzhi and his subordinate, General He Jian, who was Xu Kexiang's commanding officer. He Jian was openly anti-communist, and Tang was now moving rapidly to the right. But the meeting still wanted to believe that, in Mao's words, it might be possible to 'promote dissension . . . between Tang and He [and] draw Tang to our side'. This was sheer wishful thinking. By July 1927, the communist leaders had lost the capacity to exert any political influence at all, and in their hearts they all knew it.

The key question they faced was what to do with the local peasant self-defence units that had already been assembled before the uprisings were called off. Cai Hesen suggested they should 'go up the mountains' and launch the rebellion that way. Li Weihan objected that they might turn to banditry. He proposed that they should become an officially-sanctioned local peace-keeping force. If that was not possible, he added, they should hide their weapons and wait. Chen Duxiu maintained that the peasants could form an effective armed force only after they had been trained by the (GMD-led) national army. Mao summed up:

> Apart from [a peace-keeping force, which in practice will be too difficult to establish legally], there are two lines: (a) to go up the mountains; or (b) to join the army. By going up the mountains, we can create a foundation for a real military force . . . If we do not maintain [such a] force, then in future, as soon as an emergency arises, we will be helpless.

The discussion dragged on, and no decision was taken. But clearly in Mao's mind, and in that of Cai Hesen, the germ of a future strategy was beginning to form.

Even as they talked, however, events were moving to a conclusion.

Stalin had not been pleased by Chen Duxiu's message of June 15. By the first week of July, if not sooner, he had decided that Chen must go. Roy and Voitinsky were both recalled to Moscow, and on July 10, Bukharin, writing in *Pravda*, denounced the CCP leadership for rejecting Soviet advice as 'impractical'. Two days later, Chen submitted his resignation and a five-member CC 'Provisional Standing Committee' – comprising Zhang Guotao, Li Weihan, Zhou Enlai, Li Lisan and Zhang Tailei – was established to oversee day-to-day affairs while Borodin and Qu Qiubai, who was to be designated Chen's successor, withdrew to the mountain resort of Lushan to consider the Party's options.

Next day, July 13, the new Party Centre approved, but did not immediately announce, a manifesto accusing the Left-GMD leadership of 'betraying the toiling masses'. On July 14 and 15, the Left-GMD leaders, also meeting in closed session, passed measures further restricting the communists' role, a step tantamount to exclusion. Finally, on July 16, both manifesto and resolutions were made public.

The pretence was not quite over. On Moscow's instructions, the CCP maintained the fiction that a united front with 'progressive Left-GMD elements' continued to exist. In reality, however, the alliance was at an end. Within hours, General He Jian's troops occupied the Labour Union and began rounding up communist suspects. Mao and the rest of the Party leadership went into hiding. Chen Duxiu, wearing a disguise, boarded a steamer for Shanghai. The remaining Soviet advisers departed. Borodin, who was among the last to leave, was given a ceremonial send-off by an assembly of Guomindang luminaries, headed by Wang Jingwei himself, at Hankou railway station. He eventually reached Siberia, after an exhausting motor journey across the Gobi, early in October. Moscow's influence in China, on which Stalin had spent millions of gold roubles, had been reduced to nothing.

By the end of the year, the Left-GMD, too, would collapse, and Wang Jingwei would flee for Europe. By the end of the decade, Chiang Kai-shek would take Beijing and become China's new ruler.

But all that still lay in the future. In the leaden heat of late July 1927, Yang Kaihui and her three small children made their way back for the last time to Changsha. The united front was over. The communist revolution was about to begin.

CHAPTER SEVEN

Out of the Barrel of a Gun

Besso Lominadze did not hit it off with his Chinese charges. He was young, inexperienced, knew little about the world beyond the Soviet Union's borders and appeared to care less. Zhang Guotao remembered meeting him the day he arrived in Wuhan, July 23. It was, he wrote later, 'the worst conversation in my memory . . . His character seemed to be that of a spiv after the October Revolution, while his attitude was that of an inspector-general of the Czar . . . [treating] the intellectuals of the CCP . . . as serfs.'

Besso Lominadze was Stalin's man. At the age of twenty-eight, he had been sent to ram down the throats of the Chinese leaders the Comintern's new line, and to ensure that they, not Stalin, were blamed for the egregious failures of the recent past. To Lominadze, Moscow was the fount of all possible wisdom. He came, in Zhang's words, bearing 'an imperial edict': all that the vacillating, petty-bourgeois leaders of the Chinese Party had to do was to apply Soviet experience and Comintern directives correctly and the Chinese revolution would triumph, to the greater glory of Russia and those who ruled it. Unlike Borodin, who had spent a lifetime subtly fomenting revolution abroad, or Roy, who had debated agrarian policy with Lenin, Lominadze and the small group of arrogant and insecure young men who came to China with him were simply cogs in Stalin's personal power machine. In the second half of 1927, the master of the Kremlin was far less concerned with the future of the Chinese revolution than with being able to show that Trotsky's views were wrong and his own, correct.

The Chinese communists were by this time just starting to pull themselves together after Chen Duxiu's enforced resignation and the united front's collapse. The massacre of Party cadres that had begun in Jiangxi in March, accelerated in Shanghai in April and reached its zenith in Hunan in May, was now seen clearly for what it was: the fate of a parasite party which, when its host organism turns against it, has neither the means nor the will for self-defence. Very quickly, therefore, after the July 15 break with the Guomindang, the CCP's new provisional leadership, basing itself on Stalin's order to build a communist-led peasant army, began to sketch out guidelines for an independent strategy.

On July 20, a secret directive on peasant movement tactics, which Mao almost certainly helped to draft, asserted that 'only if there is a revolutionary armed force can victory be assured in the struggle of the peasants' associations for political power', and called on association cadres to give '120 per cent of [their] attention to this issue'. It went on to discuss in detail the different means the Party could use to assemble such a force. These included seizing weapons from landlord militias; sending 'brave and trained members of the peasants' associations' to act as a fifth column inside the warlord armies; forming alliances with secret society members; the clandestine training of peasant self-defence forces; and, if all else failed, then, as Mao and Cai Hesen had urged two weeks earlier, 'going up the mountains'.

At the same time, the Central Standing Committee began preparing for a wave of peasant insurrections in Hunan, Hubei, Jiangxi and Guangdong, to be staged during the Autumn Harvest Festival in mid-September, when land rents fell due and seasonal tensions between peasants and landlords would be greatest; and for a military uprising in Nanchang, the capital of Jiangxi, where several communist-officered units in the Guomindang's National Revolutionary Army were based.

Moscow knew nothing of these plans, and when consulted by an anxious Lominadze, who had no desire to be crucified for yet another débâcle, responded with a delphic double negative: 'If the uprising has no hope of victory, it would be better not to start it.' But by then the Chinese leaders had had enough of the Comintern's studied ambiguities. After the long months of humiliating retreat under Borodin and Chen Duxiu, they were determined to act at almost any price. Ignoring Moscow's reservations, Zhou Enlai, at the head of a specially constituted Front Committee,* ordered the insurrection to commence in the early hours of August 1. Nanchang fell with hardly a shot fired and remained in communist hands for four days – delighting Stalin, for whom it provided a victory to flaunt before the Trotskyist opposition.

The list of participants read like the *Almanac de Gotha* of the Communist revolution.[†] Zhu De, afterwards the Red Army's Commander-in-Chief, was Chief of Public Security in Nanchang. He Long, a moustachioed Sichuanese with a colourful history of secret society allegiance, later a communist marshal, commanded the main insurrectionary force. Ye Ting, then a divisional commander, would go on to head the communist New Fourth Army during the war with Japan. Ye's Political Commissar, Nie Rongzhen, and Chief of Staff, Ye Jianying, were also future marshals. So was one of the youngest officers to take part, a slim, rather shy graduate of the Whampoa Military Academy named Lin Biao. He had just turned twenty.

The communist force, some 20,000 strong, left Nanchang on August 5, heading south, where they hoped, as a communist-inspired proclamation put it, to establish 'a new base area . . . outside the spheres of the old and new warlords', in Guangdong.

While these events were unfolding, Mao remained in Wuhan, where, on the Comintern's instructions, Qu Qiubai and Lominadze, helped by a young member of the Secretariat named Deng Xixian, subsequently better known by his *nom de guerre*, Deng Xiaoping, were preparing an emergency Party conference. Its declared purpose was to 'reorganise [the Party's] forces, correct the serious mistakes of the past, and find a new path'.

---

* A CCP Front Committee was the supreme Party organ providing overall guidance to the military units under its control. It had authority over the Military Committee, responsible for military strategy and tactics, and over the local Party committee (at county or special district level) in its area of operations. It was, itself, however, subordinate to the provincial committee in the province where it operated. Thus in Nanchang, Zhou's Front Committee was (theoretically, at least) under the authority of the Jiangxi Party committee. In Guangdong, it had to answer to the Canton Party committee.

† Seven of the ten marshals of the People's Liberation Army named in 1955 were veterans of the insurrectionary force at Nanchang. The anniversary of the uprising is now celebrated in China as marking the PLA's foundation.

Two days later, twenty-two CCP members, all men, gathered in a large Western-style house belonging to a Russian economic adviser in the Japanese concession in Hankou. They were told not to leave while the conference was in progress, for fear of attracting unwelcome attention, and to say, should anyone come to the door, that they were holding a shareholders' meeting. Qu was dressed incongruously in a loud flannel shirt. He was ravaged by tuberculosis, and the swollen veins on his face stood out in the suffocating August heat. Because of the haste with which the conference had been organised, the need for secrecy and the absence of many leaders in Nanchang, fewer than a third of the Central Committee attended, which, under Party rules, fell short of a quorum. But Lominadze insisted that, in the emergency the Party was now facing, the meeting could take interim decisions, which would be ratified by a congress to be held within the next six months.

The new strategy which the August 7 Conference endorsed reflected Stalin's instructions of the previous winter and spring, in which he had laid down that there was no contradiction between class struggle against the landlords and national revolution against the warlord regime. The revolution's centre of gravity, Lominadze argued, should shift to the labour unions and the peasant associations; peasants and workers should play a greater role in the Party's leading organs; and a co-ordinated strategy should be developed of armed workers' and peasants' insurrections. In this respect, he said, the Nanchang uprising marked 'a clear turning-point'. The old, irresolute policy of compromise and concessions, followed by the outgoing leadership of Chen Duxiu, had been abandoned.

Lominadze hammered home two other lessons from Moscow. The Comintern's instructions must always be obeyed: by rejecting its guidance in June, the Party leadership had committed not just a breach of discipline but 'a criminal act'. And since the Party could no longer function openly, even in GMD-ruled areas, it must be refashioned into a militant, clandestine organisation with 'solid, combative secret organs'.

Ostensibly to unify thinking, but equally to save Stalin's face, the conference issued a 'Circular Letter to All Party Members', containing a lengthy self-criticism which left few of the former leaders unscathed. Chen Duxiu, whom Lominadze (like Roy) charged with Menshevism,* was denounced by name for 'standing the revolution on its head', restraining the peasant and labour movements, kowtowing to the Guomindang and abandoning the Party's independence. Tan Pingshan was castigated for his conduct as GMD Minister for Peasant Affairs, when he allegedly 'abandoned the struggle' and 'shamefully . . . refused to support the rural revolution'. Li Weihan, though not named, was blamed for countermanding the peasants' attack on Changsha in late May, and Zhou Enlai was reproached for having approved the disarming of workers' pickets in Wuhan in June. Even Mao was implicitly criticised for having omitted to protest against the GMD's failure to implement land redistribution, and for not having taken a radical enough line in the directives he had drafted for the All-China Peasants' Association.

None the less, he found the new team of Lominadze and Qu Qiubai much more to his liking than the Borodin–Chen Duxiu leadership it had replaced. Their explicit stress on class struggle, on the primacy of the peasants and workers as the main engine of revolt, and on the use of armed force, was music to his ears. He also approved of the connection which Lominadze drew between imperialism abroad and feudalism at home.

Lominadze, in turn, found Mao 'a capable comrade', and when the new provisional leadership was announced, he was rewarded by being made a Politburo alternate (returning to that body for the first time since his withdrawal to Shaoshan in January 1925). Of the nine full members of the Politburo, four were new appointees with working-class backgrounds, one of whom, Su Zhaozheng, was named to the three-man Standing Committee, together with Qu Qiubai and Li Weihan, in line with Lominadze's insistence that workers play a larger role. Peng Pai, who was with the Nanchang rebels, represented the peasant movement, and Ren Bishi, the Youth League. Zhang Guotao and Cai Hesen, both regarded as moderates, were demoted. Zhang hung on for a few months as an alternate member, while Cai, who had been part of the top

* The Mensheviks (literally, 'minority faction') split from the Bolshevik majority of the Russian communist movement in 1902 over the issue of class violence. Since then, Soviet communists have used the term 'Menshevism' to denote any form of right-wing opposition or advocacy of class reconciliation.

leadership since 1922, left to become Secretary of the CCP Northern Bureau.

Why was Peng Pai, rather than Mao, chosen for full Politburo membership as peasant movement representative? One factor may have been the leadership's hopes of re-establishing a strong base in Guangdong, Peng Pai's home territory. But there was also the problem of Mao's character. He was unconformable. Immediately after Chen Duxiu's fall, Zhou Enlai had tried unsuccessfully to re-assign him to Sichuan, partly, it seems, to detach him from his Hunan power base. Qu, who had worked with him on the Peasant Committee earlier in the year, had had plenty of opportunity to observe how headstrong and stubborn he could be: a good man to have as an ally – but not as a rival, or a subordinate to try to control.*

Shortly before Lominadze's arrival, Mao had been given responsibility for planning the Autumn Harvest Uprising in Hunan. His first proposal, approved by the Standing Committee on August 1, envisaged the creation of a peasant army, comprising a regiment of regular soldiers from Nanchang, and two regiments, each of about a thousand peasant self-defence force troops, from eastern and southern Hunan. They were to occupy five or six counties in the south of the province, promote agrarian revolution and set up a revolutionary district government. The aim was to destabilise the rule of Tang Shengzhi and create 'centres of revolutionary force' from which a province-wide peasant uprising would be launched to overthrow him.

On August 3, the Standing Committee incorporated this plan into its outline for the full four-province Autumn Harvest Uprising, now defined as an 'anti-rent and anti-tax' revolt, which it hoped would ultimately lead to the formation of a new revolutionary government covering both Hunan and Guangdong.

The success of the Nanchang uprising, however, persuaded Qu and Lominadze that the action in Hunan should not be limited to the south but should cover the entire province. Two days later, a revised plan was sought from the Hunan Party committee.

---

* After the August 7 Conference, Qu thought of assigning Mao to work for the Centre in Shanghai. But Mao demurred, claiming whimsically that he did not like tall buildings and preferred a life in the countryside among 'the heroes of the green-wood'. The idea was quickly dropped.

Apparently it was unsatisfactory, for on August 9, Lominadze, acting on advice from the new Soviet consul (and Comintern agent) in Changsha, a Russian known only as 'Comrade Meyer', declared that the committee – headed by Yi Lirong, Mao's old friend and a former New People's Study Society colleague – was incompetent and needed to be reorganised. To Mao's credit, when this issue was raised before the Politburo, he defended Yi and his team, arguing that they had been trying courageously 'to pick up the pieces in the tragic situation after the [Horse Day Incident]'. But to no avail. Lominadze named Peng Gongda, a Hunanese Politburo alternate, as the new provincial Party Secretary.

On August 12 Mao was appointed Central Committee Special Commissioner for Hunan, and set out for Changsha to begin preparing to get the uprising under way. A week later the new, 're-organised' Hunan Party committee, which included, as Lominadze had instructed, 'a majority of comrades with worker-peasant back-grounds', held its first meeting, in the presence of the Comintern agent, Meyer, at a country house near Changsha, to discuss its plan of campaign.

At this point, three problems emerged. The first was relatively minor. Meyer briefed the meeting on the latest messages from Hankou, transmitted while Mao was en route, and either he or Mao, or both, concluded – mistakenly, as it turned out – that Stalin had at last authorised the setting-up of worker-peasant soviets on the Russian model as organs of local power. Mao was ecstatic, and wrote to the Central Committee at once:

> On hearing this, I jumped for joy. Objectively speaking, the situation in China has long since reached 1917, but formerly everyone held that we were in 1905. This has been an extremely great error. Soviets of workers, peasants and soldiers are wholly adapted to the objective situation . . . As soon as [their power] is established [in Hunan, Hubei, Jiangxi and Guangdong], [it] should rapidly achieve victory in the whole country.

It followed, he argued, that the time had come for the Party to act in its own name, rather than maintaining the pretence of being in a revolutionary alliance with progressive elements of the discredited GMD. 'The Guomindang banner has become the banner of the warlords,' Mao wrote. '[It] is already nothing but a black flag, and we must immediately and resolutely raise the Red flag.'

In a province where the peasantry associated the Guomindang emblem, a white sun on a blue ground, with the terrible massacres perpetrated by Xu Kexiang, this was no more than common sense. But the issue was politically sensitive because it had become enmeshed in the ongoing dispute between Stalin and Trotsky. In the event, Mao was four weeks ahead of the game. The setting-up of soviets, and the abandonment of the Guomindang flag, were finally approved a month later. In Stalin's Russian paradigm, it was indeed 1917, as Mao claimed, but April, not October.

The second problem had to do with the perennial question of land confiscation. The August 7 Conference had skirted round this issue. Mao had spent several days, after his return to Changsha, canvassing peasant views. He now put forward a far-reaching proposal, which sought to reconcile the Party's policy of 'land nationalisation' and the land hunger of the poor. 'All the land,' he told the provincial committee, 'including that of small landlords and owner-peasants . . . [should be taken] into public ownership' and redistributed 'fairly' (a demand for which, afterwards, endless ink and blood would be spilled) on the basis of each family's labour power and the number of mouths it had to feed. Small landlords and their dependents (but not big landlords) should be included in the share-out, he added, 'for only thus can the people's minds be set at ease'.

The question of definitions was of more than passing interest. It was to be the anvil on which argument about land reform, the very core of the Chinese communist revolution, would be hammered out ceaselessly right up to the eve of victory in 1949.

In August 1927, however, Mao's proposals were more radical then even Qu Qiubai's Politburo was ready to accept. In a detailed reply sent off on August 23, the Party Centre told him that, while not wrong in principle, on this issue – as on the question of forming soviets, and not using the GMD flag – he was, at the least, premature. Confiscating small landlord holdings was bound to occur at some point, it declared; but to raise it as a slogan immediately was tactically unwise.

The third problem to emerge from the debates in Changsha was still more fundamental, and far less easily disposed of, for it went to the heart of the entire strategy of armed insurrection on which Qu Qiubai and his colleagues were counting to revive the communist cause. Since Stalin's telegram in June, a broad consensus had developed that to carry forward the revolution the Party would have to use armed force. But that was as far as the analysis went. Such questions as the form this force would take; the role it should play; how it might be combined with the peasant and worker mass movements and how it should be harnessed to promote the Party's political power, had not been addressed at all. Mao had set out the issue succinctly on August 7 in Hankou:

> We used to censure [Sun] Yatsen for engaging only in a military movement, and we did just the opposite, not undertaking a military movement, but exclusively a mass movement. Both Chiang [Kaishek] and Tang {Shengzhi] rose by grasping the gun; we alone did not concern ourselves with this. At present though we have paid some attention to it, we still have no firm concept about it. The Autumn Harvest Uprising, for example, is simply impossible without military force . . . From now on we should pay the greatest attention to military affairs. We must know that political power is obtained out of the barrel of a gun.

At the time, nobody objected to this memorable formulation. Lominadze himself acknowledged that the Nanchang insurrection had put army units at the Party's disposal which would help 'assure the success' of the Autumn Harvest Uprising. Very quickly, however, that judgement was revised. The Hunanese leaders were warned against 'putting the cart before the horse'. Popular insurrection must come first, the Politburo ruled; military force, second. Mao's dictum about political power – 'gun-barrel-ism', as it would later be called – was viewed more sceptically. It 'did not quite accord' with the opinion of the Centre, the Standing Committee decided ten days later. The masses were the core of the revolution; the armed forces, at most, auxiliary.

For young Chinese radicals in the 1920s, this was no idle debate. Throughout the last decade, China had been devastated by men for whom political and every other kind of power grew from the barrel of a gun: the warlords. How a political force could control a military one was a burning issue, made fiercer by the communists' recent experience with the Guomindang, whose civilian leadership had signally failed to master its own generals. Added to that was the insurrectionary myth of 1917, which held that popular uprisings were somehow more 'revolutionary' than military conquest; that military power could be used to defend revolutionary gains, but the initial spark must come from the peasants and workers themselves throwing off their chains. Moreover, Qu Qiubai maintained, this was precisely what the peasants were waiting for: all the Party had to do was 'light the fuse', and unquenchable rural revolution would explode across southern China.

The provincial leaders charged with carrying out the insurrection knew better. Local Party officials in Hubei sent in a steady stream of discouraging reports about peasant demoralisation. In Hunan, one committee member said bluntly that the peasants had no stomach for a fight; all they wanted was good government, whatever its political complexion. Mao agreed. Had the communists acted in the spring, the situation would have been different. But after three months in which their rural networks had been driven underground or dismantled, and the peasants had been bludgeoned into submission through a general blood-letting of appalling ferocity, to stage uprisings without military support was to court disaster. 'With the help of one or two regiments, the uprising can take place,' Mao warned. 'Otherwise it will inevitably fail . . . To [think otherwise] is sheer self-deception.'

Unsurprisingly, given this divergence of views, Mao's revised plan, which was presented to the Standing Committee in Wuhan on August 22, fell far short of the Centre's expectations.

In his written proposals, he tried to disguise his intentions, assuring his Politburo colleagues that although the uprising would need to be 'kindled' by two regiments of regular troops, the workers and peasants would be 'the main force'; that while it would 'start' in Changsha, 'southern and western Hunan would rise up simultaneously'; and that 'if by any chance it should prove impossible to take [all of] southern Hunan at present', a fall-back plan was in place for an uprising in just three southern counties. But either they saw through him, or the young provincial committee member who had brought the Hunan documents to Wuhan, along with a verbal proposal that the uprising begin on August 30 – ten days earlier than planned – spilled the beans. In any event, the plan was rejected. Changsha was a legitimate starting-point, the Standing Committee acknowledged, but:

First, both your written report and the verbal report . . . reveal that your preparations for a peasant uprising in the [surrounding] counties are extremely feeble, and that you are relying on outside military force to seize Changsha. This sort of one-sided emphasis on military strength makes it appear that you have no faith in the revolutionary strength of the masses. This can only lead to military adventurism. Secondly, in your preoccupation with Changsha work, you have neglected the Autumn Harvest Uprising in other areas – for example, your abandonment of the plan for south Hunan . . . Furthermore, as events have turned out, you will not have two regiments [of regular troops] at your disposal [because they will not be available].

The Politburo's reading of Mao's intentions was absolutely correct. He had indeed abandoned the idea of a province-wide uprising, being convinced that the whole venture would fail unless all available forces were concentrated on Changsha. The news that regular troops would not after all be available for the attack on the provincial capital merely strengthened that conviction. In Hubei, the provincial leadership, faced with a similar dilemma, bent reluctantly to the Centre's will. Mao, who had seen the Chen Duxiu leadership wrongly reject his views on the peasant movement in the spring, was not about to yield in the autumn to what he saw as the wrong views of Qu Qiubai. After a week spent bolstering the courage of the provincial committee, including a reluctant Peng Gongda, he penned a robust reply – stating in effect that Hunan would do as it saw fit – and despatched the unfortunate Peng to deliver it:

> With regard to the two mistakes pointed out in [your] letter, neither facts nor theory are at all compatible with what you say . . . The purpose in deploying two regiments in the attack on Changsha is to compensate for the insufficiency of the worker-peasant forces. They are not the main force. They will serve to shield the development of the uprising . . . When you say that we are engaging in military adventurism . . . this truly reflects a lack of understanding of the situation here, and constitutes a contradictory policy which pays no attention to military affairs while at the same time calling for an armed uprising of the popular masses.
>
> You say that we pay attention only to the work in Changsha and neglect other places. This is absolutely untrue . . . [The point is that] our force is sufficient only for an uprising in central Hunan. If we launched an uprising in every county, our force would be dispersed and [then] even the [Changsha] uprising could not be carried out.

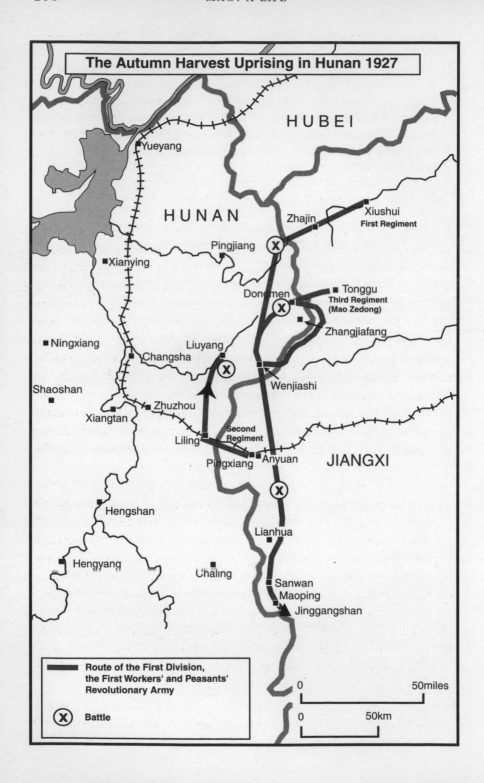

The Autumn Harvest Uprising in Hunan 1927

No record has survived of the Standing Committee discussion when Peng arrived with this message of defiance. But on September 5, the Party Centre gave vent to its frustration in an angry counterblast:

> The Hunan Provincial Committee . . . has missed a number of opportunities for furthering insurrection among the peasantry. It must [now] at once act resolutely in accordance with the Central plan, and build the main force of the uprising on the peasants themselves. No wavering will be permitted . . . In the midst of this critical struggle the Centre instructs the Hunan Provincial Committee to implement Central resolutions absolutely. No wavering will be permitted.

By then, however, as the Standing Committee well knew, this was too late to have the slightest effect. The 'Central plan' it spoke of, which had been sent to Changsha a few days earlier, had laid out an even more elaborate programme, drawn up by Qu Qiubai, for a general insurrection in which co-ordinated popular uprisings, carried out in the name of a so-called 'Hunan and Hubei Sub-Committee of the Revolutionary Committee of China', would lead to the capture, first of county towns, then of provincial capitals, and finally the whole of China. To Mao, it bore no relation to the available resources, and he simply ignored it.

While Peng was in Wuhan, he left for Anyuan, where he established a Front Committee and began gathering his forces for the assault on Changsha, the centre-piece of the limited action the provincial Party committee had approved.

These comprised a regiment of about a thousand regular troops, formerly part of the GMD's National Revolutionary Army (renamed by Mao the 1st Regiment), which had defected to the communists and was now based at Xiushui, near the Jiangxi–Hubei border, 120 miles north-east of Changsha; a poorly armed peasant force (the 3rd Regiment), at Tonggu, a small town in the mountains on the Jiangxi–Hunan border; and, at Anyuan itself, a mixed unit of unemployed miners (thrown out of work when the coal-mines closed in 1925), and members of the local West Jiangxi Peasant Self-defence Force (the 2nd Regiment). Together they made up the 1st Division of what the Politburo had agreed should be called the 1st Workers' and Peasants' Revolutionary Army.

By September 8, the timetable for the insurrection had reached the different units (and had also, unknown to Mao, been betrayed to the Changsha authorities). At his orders, the Guomindang banner was discarded. Local tailors in Xiushui worked through the night making what the troops called 'axe and sickle' flags, the first ever carried by a Chinese communist army. Next day, the railway lines to Changsha were sabotaged and the 1st Regiment set out for Pingjiang, fifty miles north-east of the capital.

At that point an event occurred which might have changed not just the course of the uprising but the future of China. As Mao and a companion were travelling from Anyuan to Tonggu, they were captured by Guomindang militiamen near the mountain village of Zhangjiafang:

> The Guomindang terror was then at its height and hundreds of suspected Reds were being shot [Mao recalled years later]. I was ordered to be taken to the militia headquarters, where I was to be killed. Borrowing several tens of dollars from [my] comrade, however, I attempted to bribe the escort to free me. The ordinary soldiers were mercenaries, with no special interest in seeing me killed, and they agreed to release me. But the subaltern in charge refused to permit it. I therefore decided to attempt to escape, but I had no opportunity to do so until I was within about 200 yards of the militia headquarters. At that point I broke loose and ran into the fields.
>
> I reached a high place, above a pond, with some tall grass surrounding it, and there I hid until sunset. The soldiers pursued me, and forced some peasants to help them search. Many times they came very near, once or twice so close that I could almost have touched them, but somehow I escaped discovery, although half-a-dozen times I gave up hope, feeling certain I would be recaptured. At last, when it was dusk, they abandoned the search. At once I set off across the mountains, travelling all night. I had no shoes and my feet were badly bruised. On the road I met a peasant who befriended me, gave me shelter and later guided me to the next district. I had seven dollars with me, and used this to buy some shoes, an umbrella and food. When at last I reached [Tonggu] safely, I had only two copper [cash] in my pocket.

This episode seemed to exhaust whatever good luck Mao had left. The 1st Regiment marched into an ambush set by a local force which coveted its superior weapons, and two of its three battalions were wiped out. The following day, September 12, Mao's 3rd Regiment occupied the small town of Dongmen, ten miles inside the Hunan border. But there the advance stalled. Provincial government troops counter-attacked, and the insurgents were driven back into Jiangxi where, two days later, Mao learned of the disaster that had befallen the 1st Regiment. That night he sent a message to the provincial committee, recommending that the workers' insurrection which was to have been launched in Changsha on the morning of September 16 be called off.

Next day, Peng Gongda endorsed his proposal, and to all intents and purposes the uprising was over. There was still one last piece of bad news to come. The 2nd (Anyuan) Regiment, after seizing Liling, a small county seat on the railway line, just inside the provincial border, proceeded as planned to Liuyang to await Mao's forces. When they failed to appear, it attacked alone on September 16 but was repulsed. The following day the regiment was surrounded and wiped out to the last man.

The failure could hardly have been more complete.

Of the 3,000 men who had started out eight days earlier, only half remained, the rest lost through desertion, treachery or combat. Mao himself had been captured and barely escaped with his life. The insurgents had managed to occupy two or three small towns along the provincial border, but none for more than twenty-four hours. Changsha itself had never been remotely threatened.

For three days, they argued over what to do next. Yu Sadu, the 1st Regiment's deputy commander, wanted to regroup and make a fresh attempt to seize Liuyang. But Mao and Lu Deming, the most experienced military officer in the force, disagreed. Early in August, when Qu Qiubai's newly elected Politburo had met for the first time in Wuhan, Mao had told Lominadze that if the insurrection in Hunan were defeated, the surviving forces 'should go up the mountains'. On September 19, the Front Committee, after an all-night meeting in the border village of Wenjiashi, approved this course. Next day, Mao called a meeting of the whole army outside the local school, where he announced that the attack on Changsha was being abandoned. The struggle, he told them, was not over. But at this stage their place was not in the city. They needed to find a new rural base where the enemy was weaker. On September 21, they set out, heading south.

In Hubei and elsewhere, the uprisings were equally unsuccessful. The insurrectionary army that left Nanchang lost 13,000 of its

21,000 men in two weeks, mostly through desertion. By the time the survivors reached the coast, their spirit had been broken. At the beginning of October, most of the leaders, including He Long, Ye Ting, Zhang Guotao and Zhou Enlai (who by then had to be carried on a stretcher), made their way to a fishing village, 'hired boats and simply fled to Hong Kong' – even in those days a refuge for rebellious Chinese. The expedition, Zhang acknowledged later, was 'politically and militarily very juvenile' and had pitiful results. Only two small military units survived more or less intact: one linked up with Peng Pai's forces in Hailufeng; the other, under Zhu De and his young deputy, Chen Yi, reached an accommodation with a local warlord and based itself in northern Guangdong.

In November, the Politburo met in Shanghai to take stock. The Party's 'general line' and insurrectionary strategy, it declared, had been 'entirely correct'. The uprisings had failed only because they had been carried out from 'a purely military viewpoint' and insufficient attention had been paid to mobilising the masses.

Punishments were then announced. The Hunan leaders were held to have relied excessively on 'local bandits and a handful of motley troops'. At Lominadze's insistence, Mao was dismissed from the Politburo, although he was apparently allowed to retain his membership of the Central Committee. Peng, whom the Comintern's Changsha agent, Meyer, accused of 'cowardice and deception', lost all his posts. Blame for the collapse of the Nanchang forces was attributed to Zhang Guotao, who was also removed from the Politburo, and to Tan Pingshan, the Chairman of the Nanchang Revolutionary Committee, who was expelled from the Party. Zhou Enlai and Li Lisan were let off with reprimands.

It was the Chinese leaders' first experience of Bolshevik discipline, Stalinist-style.

Because the basic policy was held to be correct, these decisions paved the way for another round of doomed uprisings, which reached its climax in Canton in December. There the insurrectionist forces, backed by 1,200 cadets from a Guomindang officers' training unit, commanded by Ye Jianying, held out for nearly three days. But in the massacre that followed, thousands of Party members and sympathisers were killed. To save bullets, groups of them were roped together, taken out to sea on barges and thrown overboard. Five Soviet officials at the consulate were put up against a wall and shot. Soon afterwards, all Soviet missions in China were ordered to close.

Yet even this was not enough to deter the Politburo. In a year which had seen Party membership collapse from 57,000 in May to 10,000 by December, each new setback became cause to stoke still higher the fires of militancy and revolutionary ardour. Stalinists like Lominadze, Meyer in Changsha and Heinz Neumann in Canton, added fuel to the flames. But the underlying reason was frustration with the failed alliance with the Guomindang, which caught up the Party's leaders and rank and file alike in a furious spiral of ever-increasing radicalisation.

The following spring, all that remained from this explosion of pent-up revolutionary fervour were a few isolated communist hold-outs in the poorest and most inaccessible regions, many of them situated along the fault-lines where two or more provinces met and the authorities' writ did not run: in northern Guangdong; on the Hunan-Jiangxi border; in north-eastern Jiangxi; on the Hunan–Hubei border; in the Hubei–Henan–Anhui border triangle; and on Hainan Island in the far south.

For the next three years, the politics of the Chinese Communist Party would be forged through a quadrilateral struggle between Moscow, the Politburo in Shanghai, the provincial Party commit-tees, and the communist military leaders in the field, over two key issues: the relationship between rural and urban revolution; and between insurrection and armed struggle.

Mao would play a key role in these crucial debates. But in the autumn of 1927, his immediate concern was survival.

On September 25, four days after setting out from Wenjiashi, his little army was attacked in the hill country south of Pingxiang. The divisional commander, Lu Deming, was killed. The 3rd Regiment was scattered, and two or three hundred peasant troops and a quantity of equipment were lost. The remainder regrouped in the mountain village of Sanwan, 25 miles north of the massif of Jinggangshan.

There Mao reorganised his forces, consolidating the remnants of the division into a single regiment – the '1st Regiment, 1st Division, of the First Workers' and Peasants' Revolutionary Army' – and appointing political commissars, modelled on the system which General Blyukher's Soviet military advisers had developed for the GMD army, based on Russian practice. Each squad had its Party group; each company, a Party branch; and each battalion, a Party committee. All were under the leadership of the Front Committee, of which Mao remained Secretary.

But the originality of the changes made at Sanwan lay elsewhere. Most of Mao's previous experience had been as a political theorist. His only direct exposure to mass struggle had been as a labour organiser in Changsha, and as an observer of the Hunan peasant movement. Now, for the first time in his life, he found himself having to motivate and lead a ragged, undisciplined band of Guomindang mutineers, armed workers and peasants, vagabonds and bandits, which somehow had to be transformed into a coherent revolutionary force capable of resisting a vastly superior enemy.

To that end, he announced two policies which laid the basis for a very different army from any other existing in China at that time. In the first place, it was to be an all-volunteer force. Any man who wished to leave, Mao told them, was free to do so and would be given money for the journey. Those who stayed were promised that officers would no longer be permitted to beat them, and that soldiers' committees would be formed in each unit to ventilate grievances and ensure that democratic practices were followed. Secondly, Mao said, the soldiers would be required to treat civilians correctly. They must speak politely; pay a fair price for what they bought; and never take so much as 'a solitary sweet potato' belonging to the masses.

In a country which lived by the aphorism, 'Do not waste good iron making nails, nor good men as soldiers', where a 'good' army merely took what it wanted and a 'bad' army marauded, looted, burned, raped and killed, and where officers routinely employed barbaric methods of discipline, this was a genuinely revolutionary concept.

The question remained, however, where Mao's forces should go next.

A week after arriving at Sanwan, he made contact, through a former student at the Peasant Movement Training Institute, with a man named Yuan Wencai, in Ninggang county, fifteen miles to the south. Five years earlier, as a poor peasant in his early twenties, Yuan had joined a group of brigands who called themselves the Horseknife Society. In 1926, they had come under the influence of local communists. Yuan himself had become a Party member, and the men had been reorganised as a peasant self-defence force. They possessed sixty antiquated guns, not all in working order, and had close ties with a similar movement, led by a former tailor named Wang Zuo, on Jinggangshan.

With Yuan's agreement, Mao brought his men to the small town of Gucheng in Ninggang, and, at their first meeting on October 6, offered him the gift of a hundred rifles as a token of good faith. It was a shrewd move. Yuan responded with provisions for Mao's forces, and next day proposed that they set up their headquarters at Maoping, a small market town in a river valley, encircled by low hills, from which the main western route into Jinggangshan, a narrow, sandy track, no wider than a footpath, wound its way up through the forest to the heights, 1,500 feet above.

For a week or so, Mao hesitated. The alternative was to go further south, to the Hunan–Guangdong border, and to try to link up with Zhu De and He Long, who should have arrived there from Nanchang. But in mid-October, he learned from a newspaper that He's forces had been defeated and scattered, and the die was cast.

Militarily, Jinggangshan, if properly defended, was all but impregnable. It lies at the junction of four counties – Ninggang, Yongxin, Suichuan and Lingxian – in the heart of the Luoxiao range, which follows the Hunan–Jiangxi border southward as far as Guangdong. The massif itself consists of a swathe of louring black mountains, wreathed in cloud, with blade-sharp ridges, thickly forested with Chinese larch, pine and bamboo, where waterfalls cascade down sheer gorges to lose themselves in thin, blue torrents, far below, and tall pinnacles of bare rock jut from unseen cliffs behind an impenetrable weft of subtropical vegetation. It is a poet's landscape, majestic but desperately poor.

On the heights there was barely enough farmland, carved from the hillsides and small areas of plateau, to support the population of just under 2,000, who lived in ramshackle wooden houses and small, almost windowless stone huts, scattered between the main settlement, Ciping, where half-a-dozen merchants had built shops and a weekly market was held, and the five villages – Big Well, Little Well, Middle Well, Lower Well and Upper Well – from which Jinggangshan (Well Ridge Mountain) took its name. The villagers ate a local variety of red-coloured wild rice, and trapped squirrels and badgers for food. Grain for the troops had to be brought up the mountain on men's backs from the more fertile counties in the plains.

Maoping became Mao's main forward base. For the next twelve months, whenever the military situation stabilised, the army made its headquarters there. He set the troops three main tasks. In battle, Mao said, they must fight to win. In victory, they must expropriate the landlords, both to provide land for the peasantry and to collect funds for the army's own needs. And in peacetime they must strive to win over 'the masses', the peasants, workers and petty bourgeoisie. In November, the army occupied Chaling, thirty miles to the west, and proclaimed the setting-up of a 'Workers', Peasants' and Soldiers' Soviet Government', the first in the border area. It was overthrown a month later, when GMD forces returned, but other border soviets soon followed, in Suichuan in January 1928, and in Ninggang in February.

When the pressure of Guomindang attacks became too great, Maoping was abandoned and they withdrew up the mountain to Wang Zuo's stronghold at Dajing (Big Well), about twelve miles to the south, from which they could control the passes. Wang lived in a former landlord's house which his men had commandeered, a palatial residence for that poor place, with whitewashed walls and gables, delicately upturned eaves beneath roofs of slate-coloured tile, ornamented ridgework, and more than a dozen wood-panelled rooms, furnished with tables and four-poster beds, built around three large inner courtyards, each open to the sky with a sunken well in the middle to drain away rainwater. Mao had approached Wang Zuo, as he had Yuan Wencai, with a large gift of rifles and the offer of communist instructors to give his force military training. Wang was initially wary, but after the training group's leader, He Changgong, helped him defeat a landlord militia unit which had been harassing his men, he, too, was won over.

That winter gave Mao a breathing space to start learning his new military trade. He had grasped the importance of leading by example, compelling exhausted men to follow him by sheer force of will. Since most of the soldiers were illiterate, he started using folk-tales and graphic images to get his points across. 'The God of Thunder strikes the beancurd', he told them, explaining why they should concentrate their forces to attack the enemy's weak points. Chiang Kai-shek was like a huge water-pot, while the revolutionary army was just a small pebble. But the pebble was hard, and by dint of constant tapping, one day the pot would break.

The lull could not continue indefinitely. In mid-February, Yuan

Wencai's and Wang Zuo's forces were combined to form the army's 2nd Regiment, with He Changgong as Party representative and a leaven of communist cadres down to company level. Ten days later, news came that the GMD's Jiangxi Army had despatched a battalion to occupy Xincheng, about eight miles north of Maoping. During the night of February 17, Mao led three battalions of his own men to surround them. At dawn, as the enemy troops were at their morning exercises, he gave the order to attack.

The fighting lasted several hours. When it was over, the enemy commander and his deputy were both dead and more than a hundred prisoners had been taken. After they had been escorted back to Maoping, Mao told them, to their amazement – as he had his own men at Sanwan, five months earlier – that anyone who wished to leave would be given money and allowed to depart. Those who decided to stay would be enrolled in the revolutionary army. Many did stay. The technique proved so effective that some GMD commanders began setting free communist prisoners in an attempt to emulate it.

Mao's victory had its price. As the Hunan and Jiangxi commanders realised the nature of the enemy they were dealing with, they began assembling stronger forces to attack the Jinggangshan redoubt, and imposed an economic blockade. But his concerns on that score were soon to be overshadowed by problems of a very different kind.

Since October 1927, Mao had been trying to get in touch with the Hunan provincial committee, the hierarchical superior of the Front Committee he now headed. Some of his messages evidently got through, for in mid-December the Party Centre was sufficiently informed of his activities to write to Zhu De, who was then in northern Guangdong, suggesting that he link up with Mao. Unknown to the leaders in Shanghai, Zhu had already made contact with the Jinggangshan base some weeks earlier, sending as a messenger none other than Mao's youngest brother, Zetan, who had accompanied Zhu's forces from Nanchang. From then on the two armies were in sporadic communication. But the Politburo was divided in its appraisal of Mao's conduct. Qu Qiubai, who recognised and admired Mao's independent spirit, was ready, within limits, to let him act as he saw fit. Zhou Enlai, who remained in

charge of military affairs and had become one of Qu's most
powerful colleagues, strongly disapproved of Mao's tactics.* His
troops had 'a bandit character', Zhou argued, and were 'continually
flying from place to place'. In a CC circular on armed insurrection
issued in January 1928, he cited Mao's leadership of the Autumn
Harvest Uprising in Hunan as an example of how not to behave:

> [Such leaders] do not trust in the strength of the masses but lean
> towards military opportunism, they draft their plans in terms of mili-
> tary forces, planning how to move this or that army unit, this or that
> peasant army, this or that workers' and peasants' armed suppression
> group, how to link up with the forces of this or that bandit chieftain . . .
> and in this way how to unleash an 'armed uprising' by a plot
> masquerading as a plan. Such a so-called armed uprising has no
> relation whatever to the masses.

Zhou was almost certainly responsible for another CC directive,
which also reached Changsha in January 1928, accusing Mao of
'serious political errors' and authorising the Hunan provincial
committee to remove him as Party leader in the border area and to
draw up a new work plan for the army which would 'accord with
practical needs'.

The bearer of these tidings, Zhou Lu, a junior official in the South
Hunan Special Committee,† arrived at Maoping in the first week of
March. He went to work with a vengeance, not only telling Mao that
he had been dismissed from the Politburo and the Hunan provincial committee – which despite his rows with the Party Centre six

---

* As head of the CC's Military Committee, Zhou was responsible for enforcing the
Centre's military policy, and quickly developed a reputation as a stickler for Party
discipline. It is tempting to see Zhou's attacks on Mao in the winter of 1927 as an
early instance of his lifelong practice of seeking the winning side (in this case, the
Qu–Lominadze military line) and aligning himself behind it. But the fact that he
was still criticising Mao in June 1928, when the line had already changed, suggests
a deeper animus, perhaps reflecting earlier clashes, either in Canton at the time of
the March 20 Incident in 1926, or in Wuhan in June 1927, when they worked
together on the first, aborted Hunan uprising plan.
† In January 1928, the CCP Hunan provincial committee had been subjected to
such severe repression that it had virtually ceased to exist, so, *faute de mieux*, the
South Hunan Special Committee (even though its members were then under criticism for 'incorrect and unproletarian political tendencies') was acting in its place.

months earlier must have come as a bolt from the blue – but also informing him, falsely, that he had been expelled from the Party. Whether this was a simple mistake, or a deliberate manoeuvre to destroy Mao's authority, is unclear. But, coming as it did, after months of hardship, just as the army had won its first victory and the base area was at last beginning to take shape, it must have been a crushing blow. The injustice of the rebuke, Mao wrote later, had been intolerable.

In his new, 'non-Party' role, Mao became divisional commander (a post which had been left vacant when the 2nd Regiment was formed in February). The Front Committee was abolished, and Zhou Lu acted as Party representative.

At this point, local rivalries intervened. The prime concern of both the Hunan and Jiangxi provincial committees was to promote the revolution in their own areas. In December, Zhu De's force had left its base in Guangdong and marched north into south-eastern Hunan, where it sponsored peasant uprisings and founded 'Workers', Peasants' and Soldiers' Soviets' in the border town of Yizhang, and at Chenxian and Leiyang, further north. Zhou Lu's first action on taking charge at the beginning of March was to order Mao's division to Hunan to support Zhu's army. Mao complied, but hurried slowly. Two weeks later his forces were still only a few miles from the Jiangxi border. But when Zhu's troops were attacked by regular Hunan and Guangdong GMD units, Mao's 2nd Regiment had to rush to their aid. By the time they had extricated themselves,

---

The repeated physical liquidation of CCP committees in the provinces during this period, and the dearth of qualified senior officials to replace them, meant that Party veterans like Mao often worked under hierarchical superiors who were inexperienced, incompetent, or both. Zhou Lu, despite his grand title of 'Head of the Military Affairs Department of the South Hunan Special Committee', was a non-entity. 'Special committees' had been set up in all the southern provinces to guide Party work (especially the fomenting of insurrections) in their geographical areas. They were subordinate to the respective provincial committees (where these existed), but had a measure of operational autonomy as well. In theory, Hunan, early in 1928, had Southern and Eastern special committees; Jiangxi had South-Western, Eastern and Northern committees. Some existed only on paper and others operated sporadically.

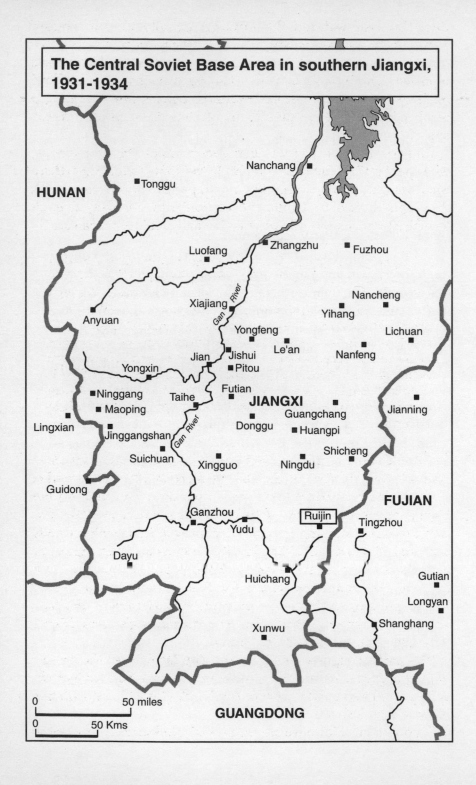

The Central Soviet Base Area in southern Jiangxi, 1931-1934

HUNAN

Tonggu

Nanchang

Luofang

Zhangzhu

Fuzhou

Xiajiang

Gan River

Nancheng

Anyuan

Yihang

Yongfeng

Lichuan

Jishui

Le'an

Nanfeng

Jian

Pitou

Yongxin

Futian

JIANGXI

Ninggang

Taihe

Guangchang

Jianning

Maoping

Donggu

Huangpi

Lingxian

Jinggangshan

Gan River

Shicheng

Suichuan

Xingguo

Ningdu

Guidong

Ganzhou

Ruijin

FUJIAN

Tingzhou

Yudu

Dayu

Gutian

Huichang

Longyan

Xunwu

Shanghang

0   50 miles

0   50 Kms

GUANGDONG

Zhou Lu had suffered the ultimate penalty for the Hunan committee's mischief-making: he had been captured and executed. Mao marched north to Lingxian, where the pursuing forces were repulsed. The base area, which had been overrun by landlord militia, was reconquered, and either in Lingxian or Ninggang – recollections differ – he and Zhu met for the first time towards the end of April.

Zhu was forty-one, seven years Mao's senior. Agnes Smedley, who spent several months with him in the 1930s, wrote that where Mao, with his 'strange, brooding mind, perpetually wrestling with the ... problems of the Chinese revolution', was essentially an intellectual, Zhu was 'more a man of action and a military organiser':

> In height he was perhaps five feet eight inches. He was neither ugly nor handsome, and there was nothing whatever heroic or fire-eating about him. His head was round and was covered with a short stubble of black hair touched with grey, his forehead was broad and rather high, his cheekbones prominent. A strong stubborn jaw and chin supported a wide mouth and a perfect set of white teeth which gleamed when he smiled his welcome ... He was such a commonplace man in appearance that had it not been for his uniform [which was worn and faded from much wear and long washing], he could have passed for almost any peasant in any village in China.

Yet Zhu's life encapsulated, even more than Mao's, the welter of contradiction and change that had swept across China at the end of the old century and the beginning of the new. Born into a poor Sichuanese peasant family, he had won a degree as a *xiucai*, the first step towards becoming a mandarin. Instead, he became a petty warlord and an opium addict. In 1922, after a cure in Shanghai, he took ship to Europe. There he met Zhou Enlai, who inducted him into the Communist Party. For four years he studied in Berlin, before returning to China to resume his military career – this time on the communists' behalf – in the Guomindang's crack Fourth Army, the proudly named 'Ironsides'.

The partnership between Mao and Zhu De marked the heyday of the Jinggangshan base area, which rapidly expanded to include, at its peak that summer, parts of seven counties with a population of more than 500,000.

Mao's political fortunes also improved. He learned from Zhu in

April that his expulsion from the Party had never happened. Then, in May, word came from the provincial Party leadership that the establishment of a Hunan–Jiangxi Border Area Special Committee, which Mao had been urging since December, had at last been authorised, with himself as Secretary. A border area Soviet Government, chaired by Yuan Wencai, was set up shortly afterwards.

The two armies merged to form the Fourth Workers' and Peasants' Revolutionary Army (so numbered after the GMD Fourth Army, from which Zhu and most of his officers had come), soon afterwards rechristened – with the Politburo's blessing – the Fourth 'Red Army', a name-change of no small importance for it signalled the beginning of the end of the long and sterile debate over the respective roles of the army and the insurrectionary masses. A 'Red Army' was by definition insurrectionary, so no such distinction could arise.

The Zhu–Mao Army, as it became known, comprised four regiments, totalling about 8,000 men: the 28th, which had, as its core, the 'Ironsides' troops Zhu had brought from Nanchang; the 29th, composed mainly of south Hunanese peasant self-defence units; the 31st, which was Mao's old 1st Regiment; and the 32nd (the former 2nd Regiment) under Yuan Wencai and Wang Zuo. In the interest of unity, the two divisional commands were abolished. Zhu became Army Commander; Mao, Party representative; and Chen Yi, formerly Zhu's deputy, Secretary of the Party's Military Committee.

On May 20, sixty delegates from the Red Army and from six county Party committees gathered in the Clan Hall of the Xie, the richest landlord family in Maoping, for the First Congress of Party Organisations of the Hunan–Jiangxi Border Area.

Despite the junction with Zhu De, it was a time of considerable pessimism. The defeat of Zhu's forces in Hunan, and the ease with which landlord forces had regained control of the base area as soon as the Red Army left, had raised doubts in many minds about the validity of the insurrectionary strategy. In his speech, therefore, Mao posed the question: 'How much longer can the Red flag be upheld?' It was a theme to which he would return repeatedly as the year wore on:

> The prolonged existence inside a country of one or more small areas under Red political power, surrounded on all sides by White political power, is something which has never occurred anywhere else in

the world. There are special reasons for the emergence of this curious
thing . . . It occurs solely in [semi-colonial] China, which is under
indirect imperialist rule . . . [and where there are] prolonged splits
and wars among the White political forces . . . [Our] independent
regime on the borders of Hunan and Jiangxi is one of many such
small areas. In difficult and critical times, some comrades often have
doubts as to the survival of such Red political power and manifest
negative tendencies . . . [But] if only we know that splits and wars
among the White forces will continue without interruption, we will
have no doubts about the emergence, survival and daily growth of
Red political power.

A number of other conditions were also necessary, he maintained.
Red areas could exist only in provinces like Hunan, Hubei, Jiangxi
and Guangdong, where strong mass movements had developed
during the Northern Expedition, and only if 'the revolutionary situation in the nation as a whole continues to move forward' (as Mao
insisted was the case in China). They required regular Red Army
forces to defend them, and a strong Communist Party to lead them.
Even then, he acknowledged, there would be times when it was difficult to hold out: 'Fighting among the warlords does not go on every
day without ceasing. Whenever the White political power in one
or more provinces enjoys temporary stability, the ruling class . . .
will surely exert every effort to destroy Red political power.' But,
Mao declared, among the White forces, 'all compromises can only
be temporary; a temporary compromise today prepares the ground
for a bigger war tomorrow.'

The correct course at this stage, therefore, Mao argued, was not
to career about the country, setting off uprisings which collapsed as
soon as the army left, but to concentrate on deepening the revolution in a single area.

When the two-day Congress ended, Mao's policy was approved.

At a time when Jinggangshan was under constant enemy pressure – in the three weeks since Zhu De's arrival, two more sizeable
enemy offensives had been thwarted – such a strategy required solid
nerves. But Mao was growing more confident in his new role as a
military tactician. During the winter he had heard the peasants
telling stories of a legendary bandit leader in the mountains named
Old Deaf Ju, who fought by the maxim: 'All you need to know about
warfare is circling around.' The moral, he told his troops, was to stay
clear of the enemy's main forces; lead them in circles; and when

they were confused and disoriented, strike where they were weakest.

This was summed up in a pithy folk-rhyme, which conveyed the essence of the Red Army's future strategy. In its final form, drawn up by Mao and Zhu, and popularised throughout the army in May, it contained sixteen characters:

Di jin, wo tui,	[When the] enemy advances, we withdraw,
Di jiu, wo rao,	[When the] enemy rests, we harass,
Di pi, wo da,	[When the] enemy tires, we attack,
Di tui, wo jui.	[When the] enemy withdraws, we pursue.

In the months following, two further principles were laid down:

Concentrate the Red Army to fight the enemy . . . and oppose the division of forces so as to avoid being destroyed one by one.
In expanding the area under [our control], adopt the policy of advancing in a series of waves and oppose the policy of rash advance.

Meanwhile the guidelines for the army's treatment of civilians, which Mao had first issued at Sanwan in September 1927, were expanded into what became known as the 'Six Main Points for Attention'. Soldiers were urged to replace straw bedding and wooden bed-boards after staying at peasant homes overnight; to return whatever they borrowed; to pay for anything they damaged; to be courteous; to be fair in business dealings; and to treat prisoners humanely. Later, two further 'Points for Attention' were added by Lin Biao: 'Don't molest women' (in early versions, 'Don't bathe in sight of women'); and, 'Dig latrines well away from homes and cover them before leaving.' At the same time, 'Three Main Rules of Discipline' were issued: 'Obey orders'; 'Don't take anything belonging to the masses' (the original phrase, 'not so much as a sweet potato', was amended to 'not even a needle or thread'); and, 'Turn in for public distribution all goods confiscated from landlords and local bullies.'

The thrust of Mao's revolutionary strategy was thus fundamentally different from the insurrectionary approach of Qu Qiubai. Where Qu believed the old system could be overthrown by the raw fervour of untrained peasants and workers, rising to seize power with their own hands, Mao saw the peasantry as a reservoir of sympathy and support – a 'sea', as he would later describe it, in which the 'fish' (the Red guerrillas) could swim. Even on Jinggangshan, he noted soberly, few local people volunteered for the Red Army. As soon as the landlords had been toppled and their fields had been divided up, all the peasants wanted was to be left in peace to farm. For the same reason he urged moderation towards the urban petty bourgeoisie, the stall-holders and traders in the small market towns, in order to avoid driving them to oppose the revolution. Excesses were often unavoidable, he acknowledged, and could be a useful means of radicalising public opinion. But, in practice, they were frequently counter-productive: 'In order to kill people and burn houses, there must be a mass basis . . . [not just] burning and killing by the army on its own.' Revolutionary violence was helpful, he argued, only when it had a clear purpose and was backed by a movement strong enough to resist the retribution which would inevitably follow.

When Zhou Lu had arrived in March, Mao had been severely criticised for these views. His work was 'too right-wing', he had been told. He was 'not killing and burning enough, [and] not carrying out the policy of "turning the petty bourgeois into proletarians and then forcing them to make revolution".' But by then, unknown to Zhou (let alone to Mao), the Politburo in Shanghai was also having second thoughts:

> The peasant movement throughout the country [Qu Qiubai wrote in April] seems to feel that, besides killing the gentry, it 'must' set houses on fire . . . Many villages in Hubei have been reduced to ashes. The leader of a certain locality in Hunan proposed burning down an entire county town, taking with him only the things the peasant insurgents needed (stencil machines and so forth), and to kill everyone unless they joined the revolution . . . This [is a] petty bourgeois tendency . . . The proletariat was not leading the peasants, but the peasants were leading the proletariat.

The moderate policies Mao put forward at the First Border Area Party Congress in May came, therefore, at an opportune time. Less than a week later, the new Hunan provincial committee,* apparently chastened by the fiasco of Zhu De's expedition that spring, agreed that the Zhu–Mao Army should remain based at

---

* The provincial committee was re-established in March, and thereafter reclaimed from the South Hunan Special Committee its authority over the border area. Unfortunately, as Mao soon discovered, his new masters were even younger and less experienced than the old.

Jinggangshan, and warned indignantly of the foolishness of 'burning whole cities', allowing Mao to reply, tongue firmly in cheek: 'The provincial committee points out that it is wrong to burn cities. We shall never commit this mistake again.'

Soon afterwards the Central Committee approved Mao's strategy too. At the beginning of June, a letter from the base area finally reached Shanghai – the first direct communication since its creation the previous October. Most of the leadership was away in Moscow, preparing for the Sixth Party Congress, which the Comintern had decided should be held not in China, where Chiang Kai-shek's 'White terror' was in full flood, but in the Soviet Union (where the Russians could also exert tighter control). It fell to Li Weihan, Mao's friend from New People's Study Society days, who had been left in charge, to draft the Central Committee's reply. He enthusiastically supported Mao's leadership; proposed that the Front Committee, which Zhou Lu had abolished, be restored; and endorsed Mao's decision to focus on building up the Jinggangshan base as a centre from which to propagate the revolution in both Hunan and Jiangxi – decisions in keeping with the new spirit of realism which would mark the Congress proceedings.

Two weeks later, the 118 delegates who gathered in a dilapidated old country house near Zvenigorod, forty miles north-west of Moscow, frankly acknowledged that there was no 'revolutionary high tide' in China, and no sign that one was imminent.

The Party, they declared, had overestimated the strength of the peasants and workers, and underestimated the forces of reaction. China was still engaged in a bourgeois-democratic revolution, and the main tasks were to unify the country against the imperialists; to abolish the landlord system; and to set up soviets of workers, peasants and soldiers, in order 'to induce the vast, toiling masses to participate in political rule'. Socialist revolution could come later.

These themes had already been sounded (and in Shanghai had been largely ignored) in a Comintern resolution the previous February, which had also stressed the importance of co-ordinating rural revolution with uprisings in the cities. But Bukharin, who was overseeing the proceedings on Stalin's behalf, now introduced an important qualification. '[We may] maintain [the slogan of] carrying out uprisings,' he said. '[But] this does not mean that in a country as

large as China . . . the innumerable masses will suddenly rise up
in an extremely short period of time . . . That cannot happen.'
The Chinese leaders needed to steel themselves for an uneven,
protracted struggle, in which victories in some areas would be offset
by defeats in others. Even then, a long period of preparation was
essential before province-wide uprisings could occur.

Accordingly, the Congress approved a strategy of guerrilla
warfare to weaken the Guomindang's hold on the rural areas, and
establish local soviets, even if initially only 'in one county or several
townships'. Military power, it declared, was 'highly significant' in
the Chinese revolution, and the development of the Red Army must
be the 'central issue' in the countryside. By contrast, the doomed
heroics of small groups of fanatics, acting with no mass base, were
sharply condemned, especially in urban areas. In Bukharin's words:

> If uprisings directed by the Party fail once, twice, three times, four
> times, or are crushed 10 or 15 times, then the working class will say:
> 'Hey, you! Listen! You are probably excellent people; nevertheless,
> please get out of here! You do not deserve to be our leaders.' . . .
> This [kind of] excessive showing off is of no use to a Party, however
> revolutionary.

Urban uprisings were not explicitly ruled out. But the whole thrust
of Bukharin's speech, and of the Congress resolutions, was that, at
this stage at least, the peasantry, *not the workers*, were the main revolutionary force – the only proviso being that the peasants should
be under proletarian leadership to restrain their anarchistic, petty-
bourgeois leanings.

These decisions, Mao wrote later, provided 'a correct theoretical
basis' for the base areas and the Red Army to develop.

Neither the Central Committee's letter of early June, nor the
Congress resolutions, reached Jinggangshan until many months
later. But there were enough straws in the wind to indicate that the
Party line had changed. Mao's life changed, too, that summer, but
in a different way: he acquired 'a revolutionary companion'.

She was eighteen years old, and her name was He Zizhen. A
lively, independent-minded girl, with a slender, boyish figure, the
fine features and winning smile of her Cantonese mother, and the

literary bent of her father, a local scholar, she had joined the Party secretly at the age of sixteen while a student at a local mission school, run by a Finnish nun.

Yuan Wencai, who had been a classmate of her elder brother, introduced her to Mao, and that spring she began working as his assistant. She wrote later that when she realised she was falling in love with him, she had tried to hide her feelings. But, one day, Mao caught her gazing at him longingly and realised what had happened. He pulled up a chair, asked her to sit down, and then talked to her of Yang Kaihui and the children whom he had left behind in Changsha. Shortly after that conversation, they started living together.

Yuan favoured the match, and cooked them a nuptial supper, apparently hoping that Mao's partnership with a local girl would commit him more strongly to the area's defence. Mao himself had long since declared his disdain for marriage conventions, and on the Jinggangshan there seemed even less reason to heed them. Wang Zuo had three wives. Zhu De, who had left his own wife and small son in Sichuan, six years earlier, was also living with a much younger woman.

None the less, Mao evidently felt a twinge of guilt at his disloyalty to Yang Kaihui. To justify himself, he told He Zizhen that he had had no news from her and thought she might have been executed. Yet there is no evidence that, either then or later, he tried to contact his family in Changsha. His decision to take the young woman as his partner seems to have been an almost conscious step in a gradual cutting of the ties that bound him to the world outside, the 'normal' world that had been his before the revolution claimed him.

When word reached Kaihui, a few months later, that Mao had acquired a new 'wife', she became deeply depressed.* In the first years of her marriage, she had been consumed with jealousy of his old flame, Tao Yi, with whom she suspected (apparently wrongly) that he was carrying on an affair. Now, she wrote bitterly, he had

---

* In 1972, a cache of documents was found at the former home in Changsha of one of Yang Kaihui's aunts. Among them was a letter, dating from 1928 or '29, in which Kaihui wrote of learning of Mao's infidelity. Parts of the letter, the original of which is held in Central Party Archives, have been damaged by damp and insects and are illegible. Its existence has never been officially disclosed.

abandoned her completely. She had contemplated suicide, she added, but had held back for the sake of their children.

The political respite was soon over. Once more, the cause lay in provincial rivalries. The Jiangxi Party committee had been badgering Mao to attack the city of Jian, seventy miles to the northeast. Now a succession of envoys arrived from Hunan, demanding, each more insistently than the last, that the Fourth Red Army send its main forces to the districts south of Hengyang, for a further attempt at insurrection in the same area where Zhu De had been defeated in March.

This was not as illogical as it might sound. Hengyang controlled the main corridor from central to southern Hunan. A successful uprising there would make it possible to link Hunan and Guangdong – traditionally the two 'most revolutionary' provinces – by establishing a new base area in the region where Tan Yankai had stationed his southern armies, a decade earlier, while waiting his chance to attack Changsha. But precisely for that reason, as Mao and Zhu well knew, it was far too well-defended for the Fourth Army to attack.

The Hunan Party committee plainly expected Mao to resist, for it informed him that the Provincial Secretary himself, 23-year-old Yang Kaiming, was on his way to Jinggangshan to take personal charge of the Border Area Special Committee, adding peremptorily: 'You must carry out [our instructions] immediately without any hesitation.' Shortly before he arrived, however, a joint meeting of the Special Committee and the Fourth Army's Military Committee, held under Mao's chairmanship on June 30, flatly rejected the Hengyang plan. In a letter to Changsha, Mao warned that, if they went ahead, the entire Fourth Army might be lost. Yang evidently did not feel himself strong enough to countermand this decision and for the next two weeks there was an uneasy stand-off.

Word then came that elements of the Hunan and Jiangxi armies were preparing another attack on Jinggangshan. It was decided that Zhu's 28th and 29th regiments should cross into Hunan, to attack the Hunan army's rear. Mao's troops, the 31st and 32nd, would block the Jiangxi units' advance until Zhu's men could return.

The first part of the battle plan went well enough. But as Zhu was about to march back to link up with Mao's troops, as arranged, Yang

Kaiming and his still younger colleague, twenty-year-old Du
Xiujing, who were accompanying Zhu's forces, invoked superior
Party authority to insist that the provincial committee's original
orders must now be carried out. Obediently, Zhu's two regiments
set off for Hengyang. The result was exactly as Mao had foreseen.
His own troops were beaten back by a superior Jiangxi force and
compelled to retreat to the hills. For the second time that year
Ninggang and two neighbouring counties in the plain were overrun.
Yet another young envoy then arrived from Changsha to press Mao
to take his remaining forces to join Zhu in south Hunan – at which
point a messenger burst into the room where they were meeting
with the news that Zhu's forces had suffered a crushing defeat. The
29th Regiment had been so badly mauled that it had ceased to exist
as a fighting unit. The 28th was making its way back as best it could
to Jinggangshan. At that, the discussion ended.

The Fourth Army's troubles were not over yet, however. Zhu's
forces were further weakened by desertions, and when Mao set out
to join him at Guidong, south-west of Jinggangshan, the local
Guomindang commanders took advantage of their disarray
to launch another attack. This time they came perilously close to
occupying the fastness itself.

On August 30, a young communist officer named He Tingying
led a single under-strength battalion to hold the narrow pass of
Huangyangjie, commanding the heights above Ninggang, against
three regiments of the Hunanese Eighth Army and one regiment
of Jiangxi troops. The nationalists suffered heavy casualties, and
when at nightfall the attack was abandoned, their morale had been
broken. Mao was moved to take up his writing brush to commemorate the event:

> *Our defence is like a stern fortress,*
> *Our wills, united, form a yet stronger wall.*
> *The roar of gunfire rises from Huangyangjie,*
> *Announcing the enemy has fled in the night.*

Mao's position by this time had become highly ambiguous. Yang
Kaiming had taken over in mid-July as acting Secretary of the
Border Area Special Committee. But at Guidong, Mao had engineered the creation of a rival 'Action Committee', representing the
army, with himself as Secretary.

Meanwhile, the south Hunan expedition had revived tensions between himself and Zhu De that had been papered over when their forces had come together in April. Zhu had evidently relished the opportunity to break free from Mao's tutelage and resume his old role as sole military commander. Having tasted freedom anew – even though it had ended in defeat – he was now reluctant to allow Mao to regain the dominant position he had occupied during the summer. Moreover, some of Zhu's followers, and perhaps Zhu himself, privately attributed the débâcle to Mao's refusal to let the 31st and 32nd regiments go with them, as the Hunan Committee had originally proposed.

The formal division of powers between Mao and Yang Kaiming was confirmed at the Second Border Area Party Congress at Maoping in October. Yang remained head of the Special Committee, although in practice, because he was in poor health, a neutral figure, Tan Zhenlin, a former worker in his mid-twenties who had been head of the first soviet government Mao had set up at Chaling, was appointed to stand in for him. Mao retained his 'Action Committee' post – which effectively made him the Army's Political Commissar. But, in the Committee ranking, which was based on a free vote of delegates, he finished near the bottom of the list. The explanation was provided by the Congress's political resolution. 'In the past', it stated, 'the Party organs were all individual dictatorships, autocracies of the Party secretary; there was no collective leadership or democratic spirit whatsoever.' Comrade Mao, it noted drily, was among the main offenders.

His policies were still respected: the political strategy the Congress approved, based on the Comintern resolution of the previous February, details of which had reached the mountains that autumn, closely reflected Mao's ideas. But, his colleagues told him, his leadership style left much to be desired.

This anomalous situation was brought to an end at the beginning of November, when, after a journey lasting nearly five months, the Central Committee directive which Li Weihan had drafted in June arrived on Jinggangshan.

Mao could hardly contain his delight. It was, he declared, 'an excellent letter . . . [which] has corrected many of our mistakes and resolved many controversial issues here'. A new Front Committee was organised as the 'supreme Party organ' in the border area, with Mao as Secretary. Its other leading members were Zhu De, who now replaced Chen Yi as head of the Military Committee, and Tan Zhenlin, who on Mao's proposal became substantive Special Committee Secretary, replacing Yang Kaiming. Not only did this re-establish the traditional hierarchy of powers, under which the Front Committee had jurisdiction over local Party organs wherever it happened to be, but it implied that the interest of the Fourth Army would have priority over those of the base area, which was to prove of crucial importance during the coming winter. For while Mao's personal position had been assured, the future of the base area had not.

In a report to the Central Committee three weeks later, Mao described in detail the difficulties he faced. One key problem, he wrote, was that the Party membership in the border area consisted almost entirely of peasants, whose 'petty-bourgeois consciousness' resulted in a lack of steadiness, causing them to swing violently between reckless courage and panic-stricken flight.

The long-term answer to that, Mao asserted, was to increase 'proletarian consciousness', by putting more workers and soldiers into the Party's leading bodies. This was not simply a genuflexion to Marxist orthodoxy, inserted to please the ideologues in Shanghai. Having watched one peasant regiment after another fall to pieces under pressure – among them, his own 3rd Regiment at Sanwan, in September 1927, and Zhu De's 29th Regiment near Hengyang, in July – he now realised that 'proletarian leadership' was indeed a prerequisite for success, not for reasons of Party dogma but to put spine into the peasants' revolt. In the short term, another remedy was available, which was likewise to have far-reaching implications for the Party's later development: the purge.

During the summer, when the border area had reached its maximum extent, the communists were in firm control and joining the Party seemed to many a wise thing to do, membership had ballooned to more than 10,000. Now landlord and gentry elements, and many rich peasants, were weeded out, along with those who engaged in 'card-playing, gambling, hooliganism and corrupt activities'. The result, Mao reported proudly, was a smaller Party but a much more combative one.

However, the core activity in the border area was not political but military. 'Fighting', Mao told the Central Committee, 'has come to constitute our daily life.' Professional soldiers who had come over to the communists at the time of the Nanchang and Autumn

Harvest uprisings were the backbone of the Red Army. But only a third of their original number remained: the rest had been lost through death, injury or desertion. To fill the gaps, prisoners of war and 'vagrants' (i.e., bandits, vagabonds and thieves) had been recruited. Despite their unfortunate background, the latter, Mao maintained, were 'particularly good fighters', and the Red Army could not get enough of them. Most of the soldiers, he added, had developed class feelings; they knew what they were fighting for and endured the harsh conditions without complaint.

None the less, as winter closed in, the mood was grim. Mao wrote later of 'an atmosphere of exhaustion and defeat'. Zhu De remembered that 'the troops began to starve'. An ounce of salt cost one silver dollar – a month's wages for a labourer; other daily necessities were not available at all. There was no cloth to make winter clothing, and no medicine for the sick.

Because of the shortage of money, wages were abolished and a supply system instituted instead. Even so, it took 5,000 dollars a month to buy food, and every copper cash had to come from expropriating landlords and merchants. An 'official fund-raising letter', signed by Mao and Zhu De, explained politely:

> The Red Army . . . makes every effort to protect the merchants . . . [However], because of the current shortage of food supplies, we are writing to you now to request that you kindly collect on our behalf 5,000 dollars, 7,000 pairs of straw sandals and 7,000 pairs of socks, [and] 300 bolts of white cloth . . . It is urgent that these be delivered . . . before eight o'clock this evening . . . If you ignore our requests, it will be proof that [you] merchants are collaborating with the reactionaries . . . In that case we will be obliged to burn down all the reactionary shops in [the town] . . . Do not say we have not forewarned you!

The shopkeepers complied. However, as Mao noted, 'you can only expropriate once in a given locality; afterwards there would be nothing to take.' The longer the troops stayed in the base area, the further afield they had to go to find 'evil gentry and local bullies' who had not already been squeezed dry. Even then, it often happened that a landlord's only crop was opium, and the soldiers had to seize and sell that.

That November, Mao raised for the first time the possibility that the base might have to be abandoned. A contingency plan was drawn up to move to southern Jiangxi, but only – he stressed – if 'our economic situation worsens to such a degree that southern Jiangxi becomes the only place where we can survive'.

A month later, two events occurred which suddenly brought that much closer. A force of about 800 ex-Guomindang troops, who had mutinied in Pingjiang, in northern Hunan, in July, arrived in the border area. Their commander, Peng Dehuai, a gruff, plain-spoken man just turned thirty, a soldier to his boots, was from Mao's home district of Xiangtan. His Fifth Red Army, as it called itself, was amalgamated with the Fourth Army and Peng became deputy to Zhu De. Meanwhile, reports began coming in that the Jiangxi and Hunan GMD armies were preparing yet another encirclement campaign, this time on a far bigger scale than any attempted before. Upwards of 25,000 men from fourteen regiments were to converge on Jinggangshan along five different routes.

The question of future strategy took on new urgency.

Peng's arrival evidently tipped the balance. It made it impossible to sit out the offensive, because there would not be enough provisions to last the new, enlarged force through the winter; and it opened up fresh possibilities for a co-ordinated riposte.

Just after the New Year, an enlarged meeting of the Front Committee, held in Ninggang, agreed that Peng's men and the 32nd Regiment of Wang Zuo and Yuan Wencai should stay behind to defend the fastness, while Mao and Zhu, leading the 28th and 31st regiments, broke out to attack the enemy's rear by besieging one of the prefectural cities in the east, Jian or Ganzhou.

At dawn on January 14, the main force slipped away by a seldom-used route that led along the jagged crest of a mountain spur from Jinggangshan down to the foothills in the south. Zhu De described it: 'There was no path, not even the trace of a trail . . . The stones and peaks were worn to slippery smoothness . . . Snow lay in pockets and an icy wind lashed the bodies of the column that inched forward, crawling over huge boulders and hanging on to one another to avoid slipping into the black chasms below.' That night, they disarmed a Jiangxi GMD battalion at Dafen, 25 miles to the south, and ate their fill from the enemy's field-kitchens. But next day, instead of swinging east to threaten Ganzhou, as they had agreed, they went on marching south until they reached the border town of Dayu. There they were heavily defeated by a Guomindang army brigade and retreated in disarray into Guangdong.

Did Mao ever really intend to stage the diversion he had promised to relieve the pressure on Peng's few hundred troops, outnumbered by a margin of thirty to one? Or was it just a cynical manoeuvre to get the main force safely away? Peng himself felt that Mao had betrayed him. Forty years later, the memory still rankled.

Peng held out, unaided, for about a week. By then three of the five passes had been overrun. He gathered together his three surviving companies and, amid a heavy snowstorm, began the impossible task of trying to break through the enemy blockade, escorting more than a thousand women and children, and sick and wounded soldiers, that Mao's forces had left behind. 'For a whole day and a whole night', he wrote later, 'we followed goats' trails and climbed sheer precipices in the lap of the highest peak of the Jinggangshan.' Somehow they slipped through the first ring of enemy encirclement. Then the second line gave way. It began to look as though they would achieve the impossible. But at Dafen, fate turned against them and they marched into an ambush. Peng's troops were able to break through, 'but the enemy quickly sealed the gap and surrounded the wounded, sick and disabled, trailing behind'. There was no way to rescue them. After another battle a few days later, Peng held a roll-call: of the 800 soldiers who had accompanied him from Pingjiang, 283 remained.

Mao's army fared somewhat better. In the first month, he and Zhu De lost 600 men out of the 3,500 who set out from Jinggangshan. Even so, it was a ghastly period, the worst, he wrote, since the Red Army's creation. For He Zizhen, who marched with Mao and the troops, it was still harder: she was five months' pregnant with their first child. To Zhu De, it was simply 'a terrible time'. They soon abandoned, at least temporarily, any hope of establishing a permanent new base area, and tried instead, wherever they went, to set up clandestine soviet governments and Party committees, capable of operating underground after the Red forces had moved on. A new kind of warfare began: no longer the defence of fixed positions, but flexible guerrilla war.

*

Communications with the Party Centre, problematic on Jing-gangshan, were now severed altogether. For the first three months of 1929, Mao's forces were out of contact not only with Shanghai but with the provincial Party authorities as well. Before leaving the mountains, he had sent four ounces of gold to Pingxiang to pay for the setting-up of a secret message centre; another, more ambitious effort later involved sending 5,000 dollars' worth of opium to Fujian to finance a communications base in Amoy. None of it did any good. Mao's letters that year teem with reproaches about the absence of Central guidance and the incompetence of the Jiangxi committee in passing on documents.

This was not without advantages. Mao and Zhu were left alone to devise their own solutions to the problems they encountered, without being forced to apply inappropriate tactics dreamed up elsewhere. Indeed, one of the lessons of the Jinggangshan period, Mao wrote to the Central Committee that winter, was that 'future directives from higher levels regarding military action must, above all, not be too rigid'. Otherwise, the leaders in the field were put in the 'truly difficult position' of having to choose between 'insubordination . . . [and] defeat'. Being out of contact removed that difficulty. But it also meant that for months on end, Mao, along with the leaders of other, smaller Red enclaves in southern and central China, struggled to survive in ignorance of each another, and of the policies of Moscow and Shanghai for which they were supposed to be fighting. Most of the time even news-papers were unobtainable.

Communications problems formed the backdrop to a dispute between Mao and the Central leadership which would have far more serious repercussions than any of his earlier differences with the Hunan Party committee.

At the beginning of January 1929, when the main theses of the Sixth Congress, held in Moscow six months earlier, finally reached the Jinggangshan, they were received enthusiastically. 'The resolutions . . . are extremely correct and we accept them with great joy,' Mao wrote to Shanghai. He was no doubt delighted, too, to learn of his own re-election to the Central Committee, where he was listed twelfth out of the twenty-three full members, reflecting the Red Army's new-found prominence. What he did not know – and could not have guessed – was that the new

General Secretary, Xiang Zhongfa, a former dock worker and labour union leader from Wuhan, was a figurehead, and that real power lay with Zhou Enlai and Li Lisan, both of whom were listed well after Mao in the official Central Committee ranking.* Indeed, he remained in ignorance of Li's elevation until almost the end of the year.

The Party Centre, for its part, was equally ignorant of Mao's situation. In February, when the first reports reached Shanghai that his forces had left the Jinggangshan, the Politburo had not had any word from him for almost nine months. In these circumstances, Zhou Enlai drafted a letter, urging Mao and Zhu De to take all possible measures to conserve their military strength. To that end, he proposed, they should scatter their forces in the villages, broken down into units of a few dozen, or at most a few hundred, men, in order to 'mobilise the daily struggle of the peasantry' and spread the Party's influence, while waiting for a more favourable revolutionary climate to emerge.

Mao disliked this approach on principle. In his report to the Central Committee the previous November (which the Centre had still not received), he had written that, 'in our experience, [it] has led almost every time to defeat'. This time it was made still more unacceptable by the sting in its tail: Mao and Zhu, the letter said, should both return to Shanghai.

Zhou Enlai, having tried, and failed, to detach Mao from his Hunan base in July 1927, was keenly aware of the difficulties this

---

* The elections at the Sixth Congress were decidedly eccentric. This was partly because the meeting was unrepresentative (held in Moscow in the absence of key Party figures, such as Mao, Peng Pai and Li Weihan; and packed with Chinese students from Soviet universities to make up the delegate count), and partly because there was no single Chinese leader capable of uniting the Party behind him. As a result, when the Comintern produced a slate of candidates for Central Committee membership, all were duly elected – but not in the intended order. Of the new Politburo, Xiang Zhongfa was listed 3rd in CC rank order; Su Zhaozheng, 9th; Mao, 12th; Zhou Enlai, 14th; Cai Hesen, 16th; Xiang Ying, 17th; and Zhang Guotao, 23rd. Li Lisan ranked 22nd in the CC and just scraped into the Politburo as a non-voting alternate member; he did not become a full member until November 1928. Russian stage-management evidently left a good deal to be desired.

decision would entail, and mustered all the tact at his command to try to make it more palatable:

> The two comrades might feel reluctant to leave the army since they have worked in it for over a year. However the CC believes that . . . Zhu's and Mao's departure will not cause the army any losses and will help it implement the plan to disperse its forces . . . When Zhu and Mao come to the CC, they can introduce to our comrades all over the country their precious experience in leading a ten-thousand-strong armed force in dealing with the enemy for over a year. This will make a [still] greater contribution to the whole revolutionary cause.

This was not illogical: if the Red Army were dispersed, there would be no purpose in Mao and Zhu remaining. Had the directive reached Mao at the time it was written, in early February, when the communist forces were on the run and, to all appearances, in imminent danger of being wiped out, there might well have been a majority of the Front Committee ready to accept it. But the letter took two months to travel the six hundred miles from Shanghai to eastern Jiangxi, and by the time Mao and Zhu received it the situation had altered dramatically.

After the disorderly retreat into Guangdong, at the end of January, they had made their way north, along the Fujian–Jiangxi border, pursued by a brigade of GMD Jiangxi troops. At Dabodi, in the mountains fifteen miles north of Ruijin, on February 11, the Fourth Army decided to make a stand. Thanks largely to Lin Biao's regiment, which made a forced march through the night behind enemy lines, the pursuers were decisively defeated. Two hundred rifles, six machine-guns and about a thousand soldiers were captured. It was their first victory since leaving Jinggangshan four weeks earlier, and Mao reported afterwards that 'the morale of our army was thereby greatly raised'. A month later they captured the prefectural city of Tingzhou, just across the border in Fujian. The local strongman, Guo Fengming, who commanded the Fujian Second Brigade, was killed, and his body exposed in the street for three days.

Elated by these successes, Mao sent off a long letter to Shanghai, announcing that the Fourth Army planned to conduct guerrilla warfare across an area of some twenty counties, centred on Tingzhou and Ruijin, and then, when the masses were sufficiently mobilised, to establish a new, permanent base area in western Fujian and southern Jiangxi.

Two weeks later, Zhou Enlai's directive arrived, ordering the army to disperse.

Mao's response, endorsed by the Front Committee and by Peng Dehuai, whose troops had now rejoined the main force, was remarkable both for the bluntness with which he rejected the new instructions, and for the standpoint of complete equality he assumed towards the Shanghai Centre. He replied, not as a dissident field commissar being summoned to headquarters, but as a ranking Party leader arguing a case before his peers:

> The Central Committee's letter makes too pessimistic an appraisal . . . the [January] campaign against Jinggangshan represented the high-water mark of the counter-revolutionary tide. But there it stopped, and since then [it] has gradually receded while the revolutionary tide has gradually risen . . . In the present chaotic situation, we can lead the masses only if we have positive slogans and a positive spirit.

Dispersing the army, Mao said, was 'an unreal view' and smacked of 'liquidationism', which was as grave an error as the adventurism of Qu Qiubai. He and Zhu De would of course accept new assignments, if needed, but in that case 'capable replacements' must be sent. In the meantime, they intended to press on with their plans for guerrilla warfare in Jiangxi and Fujian, for which the prospects, Mao declared, were so bright that there was even a realistic hope of 'closing in on [the Jiangxi capital] Nanchang'. The current rifts between the warlords, he argued, portended the disintegration of Guomindang rule, and the Red Army should aim to establish an independent soviet regime in Jiangxi and the adjacent regions of western Fujian and Zhejiang 'within a time-limit of one year'.

This proposal would soon provoke charges that Mao, too, harboured 'adventurist' tendencies, and he later acknowledged that setting a time-limit had been a mistake. But while he was over-optimistic, his analysis was not fundamentally wrong. An independent soviet regime far bigger than any other in China would indeed be set up in Jiangxi, although it would take more than a year to do it.

Mao's belief that he was a better judge of policy than the leadership in Shanghai was reflected in his rebuttal of another key point in Zhou Enlai's letter. 'The Party's major task at present', Zhou had

written, 'is to establish and develop the Party's proletarian foundations, chiefly among the . . . industrial workers.' This was true, Mao
replied, but

> the struggle in the countryside, the establishment of soviets in small
> areas and . . . the expansion of the Red Army are prerequisites for
> aiding the struggle in the cities and hastening the revolutionary
> upsurge. [While], therefore, it would be the greatest mistake to
> abandon the struggle in the cities and sink into rural guerrillaism, it
> would also, in our opinion, be a mistake – should any of our Party
> members hold such views – to fear the development of the power of
> the peasants lest it outstrip the workers' leadership . . . For the rev-
> olution in semi-colonial China will fail only if the peasant struggle is
> deprived of the leadership of the workers; it will never suffer just
> because the peasant struggle develops in such a way as to become
> more powerful than the workers. The Sixth Congress has pointed out
> the mistake of neglecting the peasant revolution.

A year later, the argument over rural versus urban revolution
would become another major source of discord between Mao and
the Party leadership. But, for now, Zhou let it pass. As reports of the
Red Army's new victories came in, the recall order was also
rescinded, and in June, when Mao's letter finally arrived, the
Politburo acknowledged that the dispersal plan had been a
mistake.*

However, there was a sequel.

Mao's personal belief in dialectics as the motive force of history,
in which the blackest part of the night always comes just before
dawn, had been strengthened in the traumatic months following the
abandonment of Jinggangshan, when the Red Army had appeared
on the verge of collapse, only to pull itself together and emerge from
the ordeal stronger, and in a more favourable position, than before.
But not everyone in the Fourth Army had rationalised the loss of
the border area so easily. Many shared the Centre's bleak assessment of the prospects for the revolution, and argued that the army
should continue to wage flexible guerrilla warfare, as it had since
the end of January, rather than try to set up a permanent base.

At Yudu, in mid-April, these issues were debated at an enlarged

---

* It claimed that the call to disperse the Red Army had initially been made 'in
ignorance of Chinese conditions' by Bukharin (who had since been disgraced and
could therefore be blamed with impunity).

leadership meeting. With support from Peng Dehuai, Mao's line carried the day. It was agreed that the Fourth Army would try to establish itself in west Fujian, while Peng's forces returned to west Jiangxi to reoccupy the Jinggangshan. The target of creating an independent soviet regime in Jiangxi within a year was overwhelmingly approved.

But the appearance of unity was deceptive. Over the course of the next month, a deep cleavage developed between Mao and his supporters, on the one hand, and the majority of army commanders, most of whom identified themselves with Zhu De, on the other.

The rift sprang in part from the different histories of the two forces which had come together to form the Red Army a year earlier. Mao's troops had learned their military skills building up the Jinggangshan base area. Zhu De's men had been constantly on the move, from Nanchang to Swatow; then in northern Guangdong; and finally in southern Hunan. Their origins predisposed them to different forms of warfare. But it also reflected Mao's firm belief, proclaimed in his very first political address on the Jinggangshan – when he posed the question, 'How much longer can the Red flag be upheld?' – that setting up Red base areas was the only realistic route to nationwide revolution.

The disagreement over strategy was fundamental. But other, more personal, quarrels also played the part. Mao was an autocrat, as even He Zizhen admitted. Now, as on Jinggangshan the previous autumn, complaints were heard about his 'patriarchal style of rule', 'the dictatorship of the Secretary' and 'excessive centralisation of power'. This time Mao's opponents were more circumspect. Rather than attacking him directly they focused on the role of the Party in military affairs, arguing that '[it] is running too many things', and that, with the growth of the Red Army since the fall of Tingzhou in March 1929, 'the Front Committee cannot keep track of everything'.

This was a problem of Mao's own making. At the beginning of February, in the darkest days after the flight from Jinggangshan, the Military Committee, which Zhu De had headed, had been abolished. Not long afterwards, at Mao's suggestion, the regiments had been replaced by columns. The result was to reduce very markedly the power of the military headquarters. Zhu and his colleagues had no wish to be reduced to ciphers in Mao's political machine, and began demanding loudly that the Military Committee be restored.

Into this political snakepit walked a naive, highly opinionated, young communist named Liu Angong, who had been sent by Zhou Enlai to act as liaison officer to the Fourth Army, with a request that he be given a suitably responsible post. Liu had just returned from the Soviet Union, where he had learned that Leninist theory held the answers to every possible Chinese problem.

Mao may at first have seen Liu as a potential ally, or at least as a potential tool. After a rancorous meeting near Yongding, in Fujian, at the end of May, he informed Zhou that the Military Committee was being re-established with Liu as Secretary and head of the army's Political Department. The advantage of this to Mao was that it prevented Zhu De from taking back the secretaryship. Increasingly, in Mao's eyes, the contest was becoming a power struggle between Zhu, whom he accused privately of harbouring 'long-suppressed ambitions', and himself.

But Mao's attempt to finesse the dispute backfired. Liu's first act, when the new committee was set up, was to enlarge its role at the expense of the Front Committee. By the time the leadership next met, at Baisha on June 8, Mao had concluded that a full-scale confrontation was inevitable. The Front Committee, he said bitterly, was 'neither living nor dead'; it was expected to take responsibility for the Fourth Army, but without the power to direct it. In these circumstances, Mao announced, they must find someone else to be Secretary. He intended to resign.

This was bluff – and, at first, it seemed it would succeed. The meeting resolved, by thirty-six votes to five, to abolish the Military Committee which had been re-established only a week before. However it decided that the broader issues of strategy and leadership should be left to a full-scale Fourth Army Party Congress, the first to have been convened for eight months. When this body met, two weeks later, in a local school, requisitioned for the purpose, it was chaired not by Mao but by Chen Yi.

Mao was accused of 'patriarchal tendencies' and his work style vigorously criticised. Zhu De's conduct was likewise censured. Mao's counter-charge that the army was lapsing into a 'roving bandit mentality', by persisting in guerrilla warfare without trying to consolidate fixed base areas, was dismissed as 'not a real issue'; and his proposal of two months earlier, to try to occupy the whole of Jiangxi 'within a year', was now held to be a mistake. When the new Front Committee was elected, Mao and Zhu both remained members, Mao as Party Representative and Zhu as Army Commander. But Chen Yi took the post of Secretary. For the third time since retreating to the mountains, twenty-one months before, Mao had gone into eclipse.

While the political row was coming to a head, He Zizhen, then nineteen, gave birth to a daughter. As they could not keep the baby with them, she did as other women in the Red Army had to, and half an hour after the infant was born, gave it to a peasant family to look after, with a packet containing fifteen silver dollars. She wrote later that she did not weep.

For the next five months, Mao stood aside from the work of the Fourth Army leadership. The pretext was ill-health, but it was more psychological than physical. As He Zizhen put it: 'he was sick – and he was upset, which made him sicker.' That did not stop him spending July with the West Fujian Special Committee, advising them how to build up their new base area, which he hoped to link with south Jiangxi to form the core of the province-wide soviet that he had spoken of at Yudu. But he refused to have anything to do with the Front Committee's plans for a renewed guerrilla campaign, provoking a spectacular row with Chen Yi, which ended with them both, pale with rage, screaming at each other.

Faced with Mao's intransigence, the Front Committee decided at the end of July that Chen should go to Shanghai to ask the Centre to arbitrate, leaving Zhu as acting Secretary in his place.

A few days later, Mao contracted malaria, and withdrew to a remote hamlet in the mountains. There he and He Zizhen lived in a small bamboo hut, which he arranged as a scholar's retreat, naming it the 'Hall of the Wealth of Books', written on a wooden board suspended over the door.

His decision to remove himself from the fray, a tactic he would use often in his career, quickly proved its value. Even before Chen Yi reached Shanghai, the Politburo had received copies of the Congress resolutions, together with a letter Mao had written setting out his view of the dispute – and had concluded that the delegates had acted wrongly. On August 21, a directive was sent to Zhu's headquarters, emphasising the importance of centralised Party leadership, implicitly approving Mao's efforts to expand the Party Secretary's role, which, it declared, was 'absolutely not a patriarchal system', and pointing out that 'the Red Army is not just a fighting organisation, but has propaganda and political responsibilities'.

The chief blame for the mess was attributed to the unfortunate Liu Angong, who was accused of stirring up factionalism and told to return to Shanghai, only to die in battle before the order could be carried out.

At the end of September, when Zhu received this missive, he called another Army Congress and sent word to Mao to attend. Mao refused, saying: 'I cannot just casually return.' The Congress then sent him a letter, formally requesting him to return as Front Committee Secretary. This time he came, but had himself carried in on a stretcher to show he was in no state to work – an incident which had unintended consequences, for garbled reports of his condition reached Moscow the following spring, prompting the Comintern to publish his obituary. Three weeks later, Chen Yi returned, with yet another Central Committee document, which he himself had drafted and Zhou Enlai and Li Lisan had approved. This condemned 'the narrow view of those military comrades who think that in the revolution the Red Army is all that matters', but held that Mao was wrong to want to build up fixed base areas imme-diately and criticised his plan to seize the whole of Jiangxi within a year. On the crucial question of his relationship with Zhu, the Central Committee refused to take sides, blaming them equally for their 'mistaken work methods'. These consisted, it said, of 'adopting positions opposite in form and debating with each other'; 'doubting each other, and assessing each other from a standpoint that is far from a political standpoint'; and 'not being open in what they do' – in plain language, squabbling like children. Mao, it said, should remain Front Committee Secretary; but he and Zhu must correct their errors and learn to work together sensibly.

This letter, together with a note from the Front Committee, asking him to return at once, reached Mao in West Fujian in the last week of October. He ignored it.

This had nothing to do with his malaria; by then the local county committee had managed to get him some quinine, and he was cured. He was making a political point. Three times in the past two years his colleagues – first the Central Committee; then, the Hunan provincial leadership; and now, the Front Committee – had cast him into political limbo. This time they would have to be sure that they wanted him before he would agree to come back. For the next month he spent his days discussing land reform with local peasants, and the evenings in another of his episodic attempts to learn English.

On November 18, after a disastrous campaign in Guangdong in which the army lost a third of its strength, Zhu De and Chen Yi wrote to him a second time. Again, he did not respond. A week later, the entire Front Committee formally requested him 'kindly to come back and take charge of our work', and sent a detachment of troops as an escort. This time, he relented. On November 26, he resumed work.

Although Mao had assured the Party Centre that there would be 'absolutely no problem' in unifying the Fourth Army's thinking 'under the Central Committee's correct guidance' (implying that he would work to reconcile differing points of view), he proceeded ruthlessly to consolidate his own position, hammering home his personal interpretation of the Central documents and omitting what he did not like.

The conference he called in December 1929 at Gutian, a village in western Fujian, would serve as a model for the 'rectification campaigns' which in later years were Mao's preferred method of fashioning the Party's collective mind in the image of his own. For ten days, the participants met in small groups, guided by branch secretaries and political commissars, to 'dig out the roots of different mistaken ideas, discuss the harm they had caused and decide how to correct them'. Mao, as Secretary, had the main role in deciding which ideas were 'mistaken', and which 'correct'. Unsurprisingly, those of Zhu De and his followers were mostly in the former category.

The opening section of Mao's political report, entitled 'The Problem of Correcting Erroneous and Non-Proletarian Ideological Tendencies in the Party', set the tone for all that followed. It castigated 'the purely military viewpoint'; the 'pernicious root of ultrademocracy', which showed up as 'an individualistic aversion to discipline'; and the need for 'military comrades' at all times to be guided by, and to report to, the Party. Nine years later, Mao would make the same point more succinctly: 'the Party commands the gun: the gun shall never be allowed to command the Party.'

Without mentioning Zhu by name, Mao flayed the army leaders

unmercifully for tolerating feudal practices, and for 'grossly deficient military skills'. Corporal punishment, he complained, was still rampant, especially among officers of the Second Column (formed from Zhu's old 28th Regiment), where brutality had reached such a point that there had been three suicides, and the men said bitterly: 'Officers do not beat soldiers; they beat them to death.' Prisoners were maltreated; deserters, shot; and sick and wounded Red Army men left to die – all in flagrant violation of Party principles.

The Central directive made Mao's leadership unassailable. But it did nothing to change his views on the issue which had triggered the dispute in the first place – whether to wage guerrilla warfare, or to secure fixed revolutionary bases – as he made clear a few days later in a private letter to Lin Biao. The Central Committee, he argued, was too pessimistic, just as it had been a year earlier when it had proposed that the Red Army be dispersed. The contradictions in Chinese society in general, and between the warlords in particular, were growing so acute that 'a single spark can start a prairie fire' – and this would happen 'very soon':

> Marxists are not fortune-tellers . . . But when I say there will soon be a high tide of revolution in China, I am emphatically not speaking of something which, in the words of some people 'is possibly coming', something illusory, unattainable, and devoid of significance for action. It is like a ship far out at sea, whose masthead can already be seen at the horizon from the shore; it is like the morning sun in the East whose shimmering rays are visible from a high mountain top; it is like a child about to be born, moving restlessly in its mother's womb.

In writing these lines, Mao was totally at odds with Party policy, which held that no new revolutionary upsurge was discernible. The same Central directive that had restored him to power had warned the Front Committee specifically against reading too much into contradictions between the warlords. But, unknown to him, in the intervening two months, Party policy had changed.

All through 1929, China and Russia had been at loggerheads over the status of the Chinese Eastern Railway in Manchuria, which was under joint Russian and Chinese administration. Chiang Kai-shek's nationalist government in Nanjing, backed by the new Manchurian leader, Zhang Xueliang, wanted this dual system ended. In May, Chinese police raided the Soviet consulates in Harbin, Tsitsihar and other Manchurian cities (which had continued operating after those in China itself were closed), and seized documents showing that Soviet officials were continuing to promote communist subversion. In July, a number were deported, and soon afterwards all remaining consular ties were broken.

After some hesitation, Moscow decided to teach the Chinese a lesson. In October, the Comintern wrote to the CCP, asking it to 'strengthen and expand guerrilla warfare', especially in Manchuria and in the areas where Mao Zedong and He Long* were active, to coincide with a punitive expedition by Russian army units across the Chinese border. By the time this message reached Shanghai, at the beginning of December, the Nanjing government had backed down and was earnestly suing for peace. But the political analysis the letter contained quickly took on a life of its own.

To justify the call for a guerrilla offensive, Moscow had proclaimed that China had 'entered a period of deep national crisis', characterised by 'a rising revolutionary tide' and 'an objective presupposition that the revolutionary high tide will surely arrive'. The language was deliberately ambiguous, but its tone was strikingly different from the caution of previous Comintern pronouncements, and it convinced Li Lisan, now emerging as the dominant figure in the Central leadership, that he could at last assert that the long-awaited revolutionary upsurge was at hand.

This he did in a Central Committee directive issued on December 8, which called for a rapid expansion of the Red Army through the incorporation of peasant self-defence units; improved co-ordination among different communist military forces, with concentration, rather than dispersion, as the guiding principle; and a unified strategy for rural and urban areas. It was in this last connection that the most startling policy reversal occurred:

> The previous tactics of avoiding the capture of major cities must be changed. So long as there is a possibility of victory, and so long as

---

* After the defeat of the Nanchang forces in September 1927, He Long had returned to his home in north-western Hunan, where, in January 1928, he established a base area and set up a Workers' and Peasants' Revolutionary Army (which, confusingly, he also designated the Fourth Red Army).

the masses can be aroused, attacks should be launched against them and they should be occupied. Rapidly taking possession of major cities would have the greatest political significance. This strategy, if co-ordinated with the workers', peasants' and soldiers' struggle throughout the entire country, will promote the great revolutionary tide.

When this document reached Jiangxi towards the end of January 1930, Mao had the agreeable surprise of learning that the Central Committee's estimate of revolutionary prospects was now much closer to his own. A few days later, at an enlarged Front Committee conference at Pitou, near Jian, he was able to savour the spectacle of his comrades, one after another, humbly acknowledging the correctness of his analysis of the previous summer and pledging themselves once more to 'liberate the whole of Jiangxi province', starting with Jian.

To that end, a General Front Committee was established, with Mao as Secretary, to act as the 'supreme leading organ' of his own Fourth Red Army; of Peng Dehuai's Fifth Army, now 3,000-strong and based in the area north of Jinggangshan; and of the newly formed Sixth Army, headed by Peng's colleague, Huang Gonglue, which was operating along the southern reaches of the Gan River; as well as of the base areas in south-west Jiangxi, west Fujian and northern Guangdong.

The meeting issued a final statement, which Mao drafted, brimming with revolutionary fervour:

> A high tide of world revolution will burst forth! The high tide of the Chinese revolution will arrive very soon, Chinese soviets will appear as successors to the Russian soviets and they will become a powerful branch of the world soviet [system]! Within China, a Jiangxi soviet will appear first, because the conditions . . . are more mature in Jiangxi than in other provinces . . . The [final outcome of our] struggle will inevitably be that . . . the revolutionary forces in the south will merge together with the revolutionary forces in the whole country to bury the ruling classes completely.

But rhetoric was one thing; reality, another. When it came to putting these plans into practice, Mao proceeded with great caution. Even the decision to attack Jian was not quite what it seemed. 'This call to action is entirely correct,' he wrote. 'The first step, however, is not to strike at the town itself, but rather to encircle it, with the object of making life even more difficult [for those] inside, and sowing panic . . . After that, we will go on to the [next stage].' In the event, even the first step was aborted when the Guomindang went on to the offensive, and in March the attack was called off altogether. A few days later, an attempt to take Ganzhou was likewise abandoned. Instead, the General Front Committee decided to spend the next three months developing and expanding the existing rural base area, on the grounds that expansion without consolidation was 'serious opportunism'.

This circumspection did not pass unnoticed in Shanghai, where Li Lisan quickly realised that there was a fundamental divergence over what a 'revolutionary high tide' entailed.

Li's 'high tide' was grounded in theory. It originated in a Comintern document, written in Moscow to suit the requirements of Soviet national interests, which Li then bent to his own purposes. Mao's was a matter of practical politics. For the past year he had argued that the only correct way forward was to build up the rural base areas. The Central Committee's directive of September had held that this required a 'rising revolutionary tide'. To Mao, Li Lisan's affirmation that that condition had now been met simply gave added legitimacy to the policies he would have carried out anyway.

If, as part of the deal, Mao had to pay lip-service to the idea of capturing cities, he was quite willing to do so, provided it did not expose the Red Army to unnecessary risk. Moreover even the lip-service, to start with, was minimal. The Pitou meeting stated explicitly that the Party's 'main task' was 'to expand the territory of the soviet [base] areas'. The taking of cities, as a generic policy (as distinct from the specific plan to take Jian), was not even mentioned. Indeed, only a few weeks earlier, at Gutian, Mao had derided those who wanted to 'march into big cities' as being only interested in pleasure-seeking, and 'eating and drinking to their hearts' content'.

To Li, on the other hand, urban revolution was primordial. Most of his career had been spent with organised labour, from his apprenticeship, under Mao, among the Anyuan miners, to the May 30 movement in 1925, where he had gained national prominence. Just as Mao believed fervently that rural revolution held the key to China's future, so Li was convinced that the proletariat would be its salvation.

To this deep political divide was added a strong personal antipathy between the two men. Li was six years younger than Mao. They had failed to strike up a rapport when, as an eighteen-year-old student, Li had been non-committal towards the New People's Study Society. Ten years later, Mao's indifference when Li's land-lord father was executed turned coolness into enmity. The rather awkward note that Mao addressed to 'Brother Li' in October 1929, when he finally learned of his promotion, asking him to 'write me a letter with your excellent guidance', made plain the misgivings which this news had inspired.

Even putting personal factors aside, Mao's political differences with the Centre over the 'revolutionary high tide' would not have stayed hidden for long. In late February 1930, Zhou Enlai drafted a much fuller and more detailed exposition of the leadership's new strategy, issued as CC Circular no. 70, which criticised Zhu and Mao by name for 'persisting in concealing and dispersing their forces'. The Party's objective, it declared, was to achieve 'preliminary victory in one or several provinces', and to that end the Red Army's entire strategy must be geared to seizing key cities on major trans-port routes, in co-ordination with local uprisings, political strikes by workers and mutinies by GMD garrisons. Two weeks later, on March 10, the Politburo again criticised Mao's forces for aimlessly 'circling around'. Another Central directive charged that he was acting 'counter to his Party duty and the national revolutionary situ-ation'. Zhou then departed for Moscow, not to return until August, leaving Li Lisan in sole charge of Central policy.

Throughout the spring and early summer of 1930 Mao resisted these instructions.

His forces refused to budge from the Jiangxi–Guangdong border, where they skirmished with small GMD units and built up their military strength. Mao himself ignored Li's demands that he come to Shanghai for a 'Conference of Representatives from Soviet Areas', which, as a result, in mid-May, was convened in the absence of the most important of them. Carrying out mistaken directives, he told the Front Committee airily, was actually 'a form of sabotage', and he would have no part in it.

Meanwhile Li's own thinking – 'the Li Lisan line', as it was later known – came increasingly to resemble the radical views espoused by Qu Qiubai, three years earlier. Like Qu, Li declared that it was wrong to rely on the Red Army alone to carry out the revolution;

army units must operate in tandem with workers' insurrections. Like Qu, he insisted that there must be 'only attack, not withdrawal'. Mao's tactics of flexible warfare were 'no longer suited to modern requirements . . . now that we need to take key cities', and he and Zhu must 'change their ways', and rid themselves of their guerrilla mentality. Mao's concept of 'using the countryside to encircle the city', which had appeared explicitly for the first time in his plan for the attack on Jian, was likewise 'highly erroneous'; and his notion that 'rural work comes first, and urban work, second' was an even more serious mistake.

Matters came to a head in June. After a series of blistering criticisms, in which Mao was accused of being 'terrified of imperialism'; exhibiting a peasant viewpoint and 'roving bandit ideology'; and persistently disobeying Central Committee instructions, the Politburo passed a resolution rejecting his proposal to set up a revolutionary regime in Jiangxi alone, and holding out instead a far more apocalyptic prospect:

> China is the weakest link in the ruling chain of world imperialism. It is the place where the volcano of the world revolution is most likely to erupt . . . The Chinese revolution may even possibly . . . set off the world revolution and the final, decisive class war worldwide . . . Therefore the immediate task of the Communist Party is to call on the broad masses . . . to prepare resolutely for the concerted general uprising of all revolutionary forces . . . [and] actively to prepare from now on for armed insurrection . . . For the present, while the new revolutionary high tide approaches day by day, our general tactical policy is to prepare ourselves for winning preliminary successes in one or more provinces and for setting up a national revolutionary regime.

The plan which Li Lisan drew up on the basis of this assessment envisaged an initial attack by Mao's units on Jiujiang and Nanchang, followed by a concerted Red Army offensive against Wuhan.

To bring the communist forces more firmly under his own control, Li ordered an extensive political and military reorganisation. A network of Action Committees was set up, to serve as emergency organs of political power in each province, answering directly to the Centre (which meant in practice to Li himself). In the army, a Central Revolutionary Military Commission was established, also answerable to Li, to direct the work of four new army groups which replaced the existing military structure. Ten days later, a Central Committee special envoy, Tu Zhennong, reached Mao at Tingzhou, and handed him and Zhu De a direct order to begin moving their forces north. To sweeten the pill, Mao was offered the chairmanship of the new Military Commission. Zhu was made Commander-in-Chief. There was no choice but to obey.

A poem Mao wrote soon afterwards betrayed his ambivalence towards the whole venture:

> *A million workers and peasants rise eagerly together,*
> *Rolling up Jiangxi like a mat, striking straight at Hunan and Hubei,*
> *Yet the 'Internationale' sounds a melancholy note,*
> *A raging tempest falls upon us from the heavens.*

As though to underline Mao's doubts, the army moved extremely slowly. It left Tingzhou on June 28. Ten days later it had still not reached Xingguo, less than a hundred miles to the west. Two more weeks would elapse before it first engaged enemy troops at Zhangzhu, seventy miles further north. Then Mao and Zhu decided that Nanchang was too well-defended to risk a frontal attack, and that a symbolic gesture would have to suffice. Accordingly, on August 1, a detachment was sent to the railway station on the river-bank opposite the city, where they fired shots into the air to mark the anniversary of the Nanchang Uprising three years earlier. 'Since we had fulfilled our task of holding an August 1 demonstration,' Mao explained to the Central Committee shortly afterwards, 'we scattered in the area around Fengxin [on the far side of the mountains, 50 miles to the west] to mobilise the masses, raise funds, make propaganda and so on.'

So much for Li Lisan's grand design of a quick, co-ordinated drive against Wuhan. But by then, in any case, Li had other problems. His insurrectionary zeal had set off alarm bells in Moscow. In May the Comintern had ordered a letter to be drafted, underlining that 'no nationwide revolutionary high tide has yet appeared'. The strength of the revolutionary movement, it went on, 'is not sufficient to over-throw the rule of the GMD and the imperialists . . . [But while] it cannot dominate China, it can take control of a number of major provinces.' This was quite different from the line which Li Lisan had evolved. He had consistently argued that independent provincial regimes, or, for that matter, permanent base areas of any kind, could survive only in the context of a national uprising, and that to assert, as Mao had done, that individual local regimes could precede the nationwide upsurge was 'extremely erroneous'. Yet that was precisely what Moscow now required him to believe.

The letter arrived in Shanghai on July 23. At that point, it must have been clear to Li that the offensive he was planning did not have Moscow's backing and ought to be called off. Instead, no doubt hoping that victory would provide its own justification, he concealed it from the rest of the Politburo.

Two days later, Peng Dehuai made a surprise advance on Changsha, defeating a GMD force under He Jian four times bigger than his own and taking the city on July 27. After holding out for nine days – and provoking alarmist headlines in newspapers all over Europe – he was compelled to withdraw. Nevertheless, Li Lisan was ecstatic, and Mao, too, was evidently persuaded that seizing power in Hunan might, after all, be a realistic proposition. The two forces linked up in mid-August, and at a meeting near Liuyang on August 23, it was agreed that they should combine to form the First Front Army, with Zhu as Commander-in-Chief and Mao as Political Commissar and Secretary of the General Front Committee.* A Workers' and Peasants' Revolutionary Committee, with Mao as Chairman, was also established, to act as the supreme organ of power in the battle zone, with authority over both the Front Committee and local and provincial Party authorities.

The same meeting decided, after considerable debate, to make another attempt to take Changsha, and, this time, to hold it.

Mao himself appears to have had mixed feelings. He Jian's units had been severely shaken, and the Red Army's morale was high. On the other hand, the element of surprise had been lost. His misgivings were reflected in a letter the following day, in which he underlined the 'extreme importance' of large numbers of reinforcements being sent from Jiangxi – '10,000 men within two

---

* Mao had been named General Front Committee Secretary of the Fourth, Fifth and Sixth Armies (commanded by Zhu De, Peng Dehuai and Huang Gonglue) at Pitou in February 1930. He continued to hold this post through the reorganisations of the summer, but in practice acquired real authority over the three forces only after the Liuyang meeting in August. Similarly, in April, the Politburo had named Zhu as Commander-in-Chief of the three armies, but that appointment, too, took on practical significance only after the First Front Army was formed.

weeks, and another 20,000 within a month' – adding prudently that while it '*should* be possible' to capture Changsha, 'an intense campaign' would be necessary.

Those caveats proved well-justified. The nationalists put up stubborn resistance, and the communist attack bogged down a few miles south-east of the city. On September 12, with fresh Guomindang forces closing in, Mao gave the order to withdraw.

Twenty-four hours later, the troops were told they were going back to Jiangxi. The rhetoric was maintained about 'winning initial victory in Wuhan and seizing political power in the whole country', but the next target was much more modest. After three weeks for rest and re-equipment an attack would be made on Jian. It was the third-ranking city in the province, with a population of 40,000. Local communist forces had tried to capture it eight times, but each time had been driven back.

On the night of October 4, however, the defenders slipped away without a fight, and Mao was able to announce the 'first seizure of a major city by the Red Army and the masses [in Jiangxi] in several years of fighting . . . [and] the beginning of victory in the whole of Jiangxi province'. That was laying it on a bit thick: the communists actually held Jian for just six weeks. But it reflected well enough the jubilation among the Party leadership and the rank and file. Hyperbolic proclamations were issued, calling for the strength of the Red Army to be increased to one million men; pledging eternal solidarity with the Soviet Union and the world proletariat; and predicting that, in the current 'global revolutionary situation', soviet power would 'undoubtedly burst forth' in China and throughout the world.

Mao set up his headquarters in a landlord's house, a comfortable stone-built dwelling in the middle of the city. He and He Zizhen lived behind the inner courtyard, amid the red-lacquered splendour of what had been the women's quarters, while Zhu De and his young partner, Kang Keqing, occupied the outer rooms. For all Mao's warnings at Gutian about the snares of city life, everyone, himself included, was glad of the respite it offered.

In Shanghai, meanwhile, Li Lisan was in deep trouble.

In July, a Soviet military adviser had installed a secret radio transmitter, for use by the Central Committee to communicate with Moscow. Li's freedom of manoeuvre, which had been based on the months it used to take for letters to go back and forth to the

Comintern, disappeared overnight. One of the first messages received, on July 28, forcefully restated Soviet opposition to his plans for urban uprisings. Once again, Li concealed it. But a month later, after Moscow had condemned his plans as 'adventurist' and told him bluntly there was 'no serious chance of capturing big cities', he was forced to countermand planned insurrections in Wuhan and Shanghai.

By then, Zhou Enlai and Qu Qiubai were both back, and Li was no longer able to dissimulate Moscow's views. Even so, he refused to cancel the order to retake Changsha, and when, in September, a Central Committee plenum was held, he insisted that, all along, he had merely been following the Comintern's lead.

For a while, Li's defiance paid off. The Third Plenum, as it was known, concluded that, despite 'ambiguities and mistakes', stemming from excessive optimism, 'the Politburo's [general] line is correct'. But the reprieve was short-lived. In October, Moscow received details of some of Li's wilder statements that autumn, when he had proposed, among other things, an uprising in Manchuria to set off a war between Russia and Japan, and had spoken disparagingly of the Russians' understanding of Chinese affairs.

Stalin's patience snapped.

In a stinging letter of denunciation, which reached Shanghai in mid-November, the Comintern accused Li Lisan of having implemented an anti-Marxist, anti-Comintern, un-Bolshevik, un-Leninist line. In Moscow, a few days later, he made an abject and well-publicised confession, not to be heard from again for another fifteen years.

Mao's own views during this period are not easy to fathom. He plainly did believe that the revolution was gaining ground, both at home and abroad. The newspapers that fell into the communists' hands spoke of the Great Depression in the United States, a surge of industrial unrest in Europe and anti-imperialist uprisings in Asia and Latin America. On the other hand, his public insistence that autumn that 'the revolutionary upsurge in the entire nation is rising higher every day' was belied by his prudence in action. After the capture of Jian, he repeatedly held back colleagues who were convinced that Li Lisan was right and that their first duty was to seize Nanchang and then press on to Wuhan. Their first task, Mao countered, was to seize power in one province, Jiangxi: the rest would follow later.

The debate over Li's dream of nationwide conquest was cut short when Chiang Kai-shek announced that he would crush the 'Red menace' in Jiangxi, once and for all, in the coming six months. He planned to use 100,000 men, a vastly greater force than the Guomindang had ever assembled for an anti-communist campaign before. However, he now faced a very different army from the war-weary contingent of half-starved guerrillas who had been driven in disarray from Jinggangshan in the winter of 1928. Then Mao's and Peng Dehuai's men together numbered fewer than 4,000, only half of whom had guns; the rest had carried spears, or fought with staves and cudgels. Now the First Front Army had 40,000 troops, most of whom were equipped with modern rifles.

From a conventional military standpoint, their quality left a good deal to be desired. Most were illiterate peasants. Orders had to be posted: 'Don't shit all over the place!' and 'Don't rifle the pockets of prisoners!' Yet, from this primitive material, in the year since the Gutian conference, Red Army political workers had forged a highly motivated and increasingly sophisticated fighting force.

Literacy campaigns were conducted. Discipline was strengthened. A system of appraisal and promotion was introduced for the officer corps. Recruits had to be 'between 16 and 30 years old; at least 4 feet 11 inches tall; and in good health with no serious diseases.' It was a measure of the difficulty of the task that Mao found it necessary to explain:

> The reason [for these requirements] is that those with eye ailments are unable to aim and shoot; those who are deaf are unable to distinguish orders; those with a collapsed nose mostly have hereditary syphilis and are susceptible to [other] contagious diseases; those who stutter are unable to carry out the communications tasks of a soldier. As for those with [other] ailments, not only does their weak physical condition make them unable to fight, but there is a danger that they will spread their diseases to others.

On the battlefield, first-aid stations were set up and auxiliary units charged with burying the dead. Supply and transport departments were formed, responsible for the baggage trains and field kitchens. Reconnaissance, map-making, intelligence and security sections were established.

From June 1930 onwards, detailed military orders were issued by Zhu De and Mao once or several times a day, setting out the order of battle; marching plans; instructions for posting sentries; arrangements for river crossings; and all the other paraphernalia needed to keep twenty regiments on the move. Senior officers were assigned aides-de-camp, and field telephones began to replace the couriers and flag-signallers that had been the only means of battlefield communication before.

Only in one respect was the Red Army still desperately inferior to its Guomindang adversaries: military technology. After the failed assault on Changsha, Mao issued standing instructions for the capture of enemy radio sets (and operators, to train Red Army signallers in how to use them); and machine-gun and mortar sections were set up with captured enemy weapons. But as the Comintern noted, it remained 'poorly armed; extremely feebly supplied with war *matériel*; and exceptionally badly off when it comes to ordnance and artillery'.

In 1930, thanks partly to 'the Li Lisan line', the Red Army's tactics had begun to shift from guerrilla to mobile warfare. But to meet the challenge posed by Chiang's proposed encirclement campaign, a new strategy was needed. On October 30, at an enlarged meeting of the Front Committee in a small village near Luofang, on the Yuan River, 75 miles south-west of Nanchang, Mao outlined for the first time the principle of 'luring the enemy in deep'. Like many profound ideas, it was in essence extremely simple – little more than an extension of the tactic Mao had devised on the Jinggangshan: 'When the enemy advances, we withdraw; when the enemy tires, we attack.' In its new form, this became: 'Lure the enemy deep into the Red Area, wait until they are exhausted and annihilate them!' The corollary, Mao explained later, was 'the tactic of protracted war':

> The enemy wants to fight a short war, but we just will not do it. The enemy has internal conflicts. He just wants to defeat us and then to return to his own internal battles . . . We will let him stew, and then, when his own internal problems become acute, we will smite him a mighty blow.

The new strategy did not lack critics. Some argued that it was a negation of the offensive policy advocated by Li Lisan (as, indeed, it was), incompatible with the idea of a 'rising revolutionary tide' – which Mao continued to proclaim – and with the directive to attack key cities. Others, with good reason, feared the havoc the nationalists would wreak in the areas they overran. However, Zhu De supported Mao, and, with some misgivings, the Front Committee approved the plan, which was conveyed to military commanders next day.

For six weeks, Chiang's armies, harassed by local Red Guards, trailed the communist forces as they withdrew across the rugged hill country of central Jiangxi, never giving battle, abandoning one after another the counties they had occupied during the summer – first Jishui and Jian, then Yongfeng, Le'an and Donggu – in a slow, zigzag retreat towards the south, where peasant support for the Red forces was strongest.

At the beginning of December, Chiang himself arrived in Nanchang. Two additional divisions were despatched to seal the Fujian border, while the main force, in four columns, formed a slowly tightening arc, 150 miles long, across the middle of Jiangxi, in the centre of which, near the village of Huangpi, less than ten miles from the nationalist front line, the communist forces silently waited.

Their first chance came on Christmas Eve, two days before Mao's thirty-seventh birthday. Peng Dehuai's forces (now the Third Army Group) were sent north to lie in wait for Chiang's 50th Division, commanded by Tan Daoyuan. But Tan's men, sensing a trap, halted their advance. After four days, the plan was abandoned.

The entire Front Army then wheeled left towards Longgang, a small town thirteen miles to the south-west, where the other nationalist vanguard unit, Zhang Huizan's 18th Division, had arrived on the 29th. The communist forces moved into position that night, and at 10 a.m. next morning, a general offensive began. Five hours later it was all over: Zhang himself and his two brigade commanders were captured, along with 9,000 other prisoners, 5,000 rifles and 30 machine-guns. When the news reached Tan Daoyuan, he ordered a hasty retreat. But on January 3, the Front Army caught up with him, and at Dongshao, thirty miles to the north-east, took another 3,000 prisoners and large quantities of arms and equipment, including, to Mao's delight, a complete signals unit, which two weeks later became the basis of the Red Army's first radio section. It relied on hand-cranked generators and cat's-whiskers, but it was the most advanced technology of the day.

Zhang Huizan was executed and his head placed on a wooden board, to be floated down the Gan River to Nanchang, to taunt Chiang Kai-shek.

Mao, more than anyone, had reason to be pleased. Not only had his new strategy of 'luring the enemy in deep' succeeded better than anyone had dared hope, but in December he had learned that the Third Plenum had restored him to alternate membership of the Politburo, a position he had last held at the time of the Autumn Harvest Uprising, three years before.

It was too good to last.

In the middle of January, 1931, a member of the Politburo Standing Committee, Xiang Ying, by far the most senior leader ever to visit the base area, arrived unannounced at Mao's headquarters at Xiaobu, in the mountains north of Huangpi, to inform him that a new Central Bureau, headed by Zhou Enlai, had been established, with supreme authority over the soviet base areas not just in Jiangxi but all over China. The good news was that Mao, who had known nothing of this decision, had been appointed acting Secretary of the Central Bureau two months earlier. The bad news was that Xiang was now going to replace him.

Xiang was a former labour organiser, four years older than Mao. He had been elected a Standing Committee member at the Sixth Congress as part of the drive to increase the number of workers in the leadership. His mission was simple: to bring the base area back under direct Central Committee control. On January 15, Xiang ordered the dissolution of the Front Committee, which was Mao's principal power base, and of the Revolutionary Committee, which Mao also headed, and removed or replaced him in his other main posts.

However, the changes were deceptive. Xiang had seniority on his side, Mao had the Front Army behind him. The result was a compromise. Xiang assumed the appearance of power but Mao retained a good part of its substance.

The situation was complicated further by developments in Shanghai, where Stalin had sent his China specialist, Pavel Mif, to convene another Central Committee plenum to expose and denounce the disgraced Li Lisan. Unknown to both Xiang and Mao, this Fourth Plenum had approved a resolution, which soon became required reading for all Party members, condemning Li's errors in extremely harsh terms. It had also made personnel changes. Mao was not affected. Nor was the Party's nominal leader, Xiang

Zhongfa, who remained General Secretary. Zhou Enlai, too, had
survived, not for the last time, by deftly switching sides. But Qu
Qiubai had been dismissed, and Xiang Ying, while remaining in the
Politburo, lost his post on the Standing Committee.

The key appointment, however, was of a stocky, rather jowly
young man named Wang Ming, who was catapulted to full
Politburo membership without having previously been even a
member of the Central Committee.

Wang, then aged twenty-six, was the leading figure among a
group of Chinese students who had graduated from Sun Yat-sen
University in Moscow, where Mif was Rector, and returned to
Shanghai the previous winter. Others in the group were appointed
to head key Central Committee departments. Variously known as
the '28 Bolsheviks', 'Stalin's China Section', or simply the 'Returned
Students', they were to become the main force in the leadership for
the next four years.

The first reports of Li Lisan's disgrace reached the base area in
March 1931, followed, three weeks later, by a Central delegation
led by Ren Bishi, whom Mao's Russian Studies Society had sent, a
decade earlier, as a sixteen-year-old student to Moscow. Ren, who
had joined the Politburo in January, brought with him the texts of
the Fourth Plenum resolutions and a directive from the new
Party Centre stating that the General Front Committee, with Mao
as Secretary, should remain the supreme Party organ in Jiangxi
pending a review of the Central Bureau's activities. The Revolutionary Committee was also reinstated, giving Mao, as Committee
Chairman, and Zhu De, as Commander-in-Chief, nominal
authority over soviet and military work not only in Jiangxi, but in
all the Red base areas. This was not because the new leadership in
Shanghai had any special regard for Mao; indeed, it would quickly
become clear that the reverse was true. But it distrusted Xiang Ying,
who was too closely associated with Li Lisan and the old Third
Plenum group. By elevating Mao, it sought to curb Xiang's powers.

At this juncture, Chiang Kai-shek launched his second encirclement campaign. This time he had assembled 200,000 troops,
twice as many as in the winter. The strategy was much the same as
before. The nationalists' main army, Chiang's 'hammer', advanced
towards the base area from the north-west, planning to crush the
Red Army against the 'anvil' of warlord forces, pre-positioned on
the Guangdong and Fujian borders to block escape routes to the

south and east. This time, however, the nationalist commanders moved more cautiously, reinforcing the areas they occupied before each new advance.

Mao and Zhu De had been observing these preparations since February. But there had been disagreement with Xiang Ying over whether the tactic of 'luring the enemy in deep' was feasible when the disparity in numbers was so great, and since neither side could prevail, no clear counter-strategy was defined. The arrival of the 'Fourth Plenum Delegation', as Ren Bishi's group was known, muddied the waters further. They proposed that the Red Army should abandon the base area altogether and withdraw into southern Hunan. Mao and Zhu De disagreed. The other leaders were divided, some resurrecting the old argument that the Red forces should be dispersed.

As the debate continued, Chiang's columns rolled inexorably south. Already, in late March, the Red Army had pulled back its main forces to Ningdu county, not far from the area where the decisive battles of the first encirclement had been fought. There, in the village of Qingtang, matters came to a head.

On April 17, 1931, an enlarged meeting of the Central Bureau passed a series of resolutions harshly criticising Xiang Ying's leadership, and praising Mao's efforts to oppose 'the Li Lisan line'. Next day, Mao got his way on military strategy, too. Withdrawal was ruled out, and the meeting resolved 'to make the Jiangxi base area the foundation of a national soviet area'. The Front Army began moving northward, to confront the enemy where Chiang's deployment was weakest, in the hill country near Donggu, while Mao began drawing up plans for an ambitious counter-offensive to punch through enemy lines and march north-east towards Fujian.

Almost exactly a month later, he watched from a white-walled Buddhist temple on the highest peak of the Baiyunshan, the White Cloud Mountains, ten miles west of Donggu, as units of Zhu De's First Army Group poured down the hillsides to attack two Guomindang divisions. After an hour, at a prearranged signal, Peng Dehuai's troops struck at their flanks. More than 4,000 prisoners were taken, along with 5,000 rifles, 50 machine-guns, 20 mortars, and an entire nationalist signals unit, complete with operators. Over the next two weeks, the Red Army fought four more large-scale engagements, culminating, at the end of May, in the capture of Jianning, in Fujian, a hundred miles to the east. By then altogether

30,000 nationalist troops had been put out of action and 20,000 rifles had been captured. The second encirclement had been torn to shreds, and Chiang's commanders ordered a general retreat.

After this, there was no more argument about the tactics the Red Army should follow. Mao and the military commanders were given a free hand.

However, the very scale of their success nearly proved their undoing. As long as 'the Reds' could be dismissed as just another group of bandits, Chiang was not too concerned if, for a while, they went unpunished. But a Red Army capable of defeating his best generals was a very different matter. While the nationalist high command in Nanchang continued to trumpet 'military successes', Chiang hastily brought in reinforcements. By the end of June, he had amassed 300,000 men, half as many again as in April, for a third 'communist suppression campaign'.

Mao and the rest of the leadership were now caught wrong-footed. He had known since the end of May, when the second campaign was defeated, that a third offensive would follow. But he grossly underestimated the speed with which Chiang would turn his men round. In late June, the Red Army was scattered all across western Fujian, where it had been sent to 'mobilise the masses and raise funds', a task that became ever more important as the communist forces expanded. On the 28th, Mao was still counting on having another two or three months for fund-raising and laying in provisions. On the 30th, this was cut to ten days, and before the week was out, an 'emergency circular' had been issued, warning that the third campaign was imminent, that it would be 'extremely cruel', and that everyone would have to work ten times harder than before if victory was to be achieved.

In the next two months, the Red Army came close to total destruction.

The nationalists, this time under Chiang Kai-shek's personal command, advanced very slowly southwards in a vast pincer movement, consolidating the areas they occupied with defensive fortifications and taking pains to ensure that no division became isolated and thereby vulnerable to communist attack.

For the first ten days, the Red Army command scrambled to get its forces together and into some kind of battle order. In mid-July, they began withdrawing southward, hoping to persuade Chiang's eastern column, which followed them down the Fujian border, that they were fleeing into Guangdong. Then at Rentian, just north of Ruijin, the main force doubled back and headed west into northern Yudu county, trying to stay out of sight of Chiang's reconnaissance planes by using village paths and barrow-tracks, far from the main highways. Mao's plan was to lie in ambush and hit the weakest of Chiang's western units near Donggu, forcing the eastern column to come to their aid while the Red Army headed for Fujian, attacking the enemy's rear. Given the lack of preparation, it was probably the best Mao could do. But it was too similar to his strategy during the second campaign. This time Chiang was not fooled so easily.

After occupying Ningdu and Ruijin, the nationalist eastern column halted its southward march and began moving west. As they moved deeper into the base area, they were harassed constantly by local Red Guards, who blew bugles and fired old-fashioned muskets to prevent them sleeping at night, set booby-traps along the mountain trails, sabotaged communications lines and ambushed the sick and wounded. The nationalist commanders responded in kind. Zhu De remembered 'finding villages burned to ashes, and the corpses of civilians lying where they had been shot, cut down or beheaded; even children and the aged. Women lay sprawled on the ground where they had been raped before or after being killed.'

In the last week of July, the communists, exhausted from 300 miles of forced marches through the sweltering heat of the southern summer, stopped to rest in northern Xingguo. There, on the 31st, the main force was ordered to circle round under cover of darkness, get behind the enemy's front-line and launch a night assault on the rearguard of Chiang's western column about fifty miles away. After two gruelling night marches, the men were moving into position when Mao learned that the nationalist commanders had summoned reinforcements and the attack had to be called off.

As the Red Army headed back to Xingguo, nine enemy divisions converged from the north, east and south, hemming them into a narrow salient along the Gan River.

On August 4, Mao and Zhu De decided there was no choice but to try to break out while they still could. One division, accompanied by local Red Guards and peasant militiamen, made a dash westward, as though trying to cross into Hunan, drawing off four nationalist divisions in pursuit. That night, the Red Army's main force squeezed through a gap about twelve miles wide in the ring of encircling forces that had opened up as a result. Two days later, in the first major engagement of the campaign, they defeated two pursuing enemy divisions, and soon afterwards at Longgang, the site of the great communist victory in December, wiped out another large force, taking more than 7,000 prisoners.

But Chiang was getting better at anticipating the Red Army's manoeuvres. Now he sent eight divisions to envelop the communists in a much tighter ring. This time there was no gap.

Again, Mao tried a feint. Part of the First Army Group, pretending to be the main force, made a sortie towards the north. But the ring stayed sealed. The one possible escape route was blocked by a 3,000-foot mountain rearing up between the encampments of two nationalist divisions. The mountain had been left unsecured because it was judged impassable.

That night, under cover of darkness, the entire Red Army, more than 20,000-strong, climbed its precipitous flanks, less than three miles from nationalist sentries, and then raced to find safety in the hill country north of Donggu.

It was an extraordinary feat. But their escape, by a hair's breadth, from complete annihilation, made Mao realise that he was dealing with a much more redoubtable foe than in either of the earlier campaigns. He gave orders for all the heavy baggage to be jettisoned, and for the number of horses to be sharply reduced. The enemy had developed 'highly mobile forces', he warned. The Red Army had to be ready for a long, hard struggle involving frequent night marches, where victory would depend on its own mobility surpassing the enemy's 'not just ten but a hundred times'.

Salvation, however, was at hand. During the summer Chiang Kai-shek's old rivals, Hu Hanmin and Wang Jingwei, had formed an alliance with the Guangdong and Guangxi warlords to set up a government in Canton in opposition to Chiang's regime in Nanjing. At the beginning of September, this new southern government sent troops into Hunan, as ever the pivotal province in any north-south conflict. The threat could not be ignored. The 'suppression campaign' in Jiangxi was abandoned to allow Chiang's forces to meet the new menace from the west.

On September 6, Mao and Zhu De watched as the nationalists began to pull out of Xingguo, heading north. In a parting gesture, Chiang announced that he was doubling the rewards on their heads from 50 to 100,000 dollars, dead or alive.

Mao could claim that, once again, his strategy had proved victorious. Seventeen nationalist regiments had been demolished, and 30,000 enemy troops wounded, killed or taken prisoner. The communists had been left in possession of parts of twenty-one counties in southern Jiangxi and west Fujian with a combined population of over two million people. But, unlike the first two campaigns, communist losses this time had also been heavy. Chiang's forces had not been defeated. The Red Army had won by default.

On September 18, 1931, Japan invaded Manchuria. For the next year Chiang's attention would be occupied elsewhere. But he had unfinished business in Jiangxi. He and the communists both knew that in due course he would return.

Four years had elapsed since the united front with the Guomindang had sundered and the Communist Party had embraced a policy of armed insurrection. The four main players in the communist revolution in that time – Qu Qiubai, Li Lisan, Zhou Enlai and Mao – had in common an unswerving belief that the revolution would succeed, and China would one day be a communist state.

Their differences had been over method and timing. But in a revolution, method and timing are all.

Qu, the consumptive young writer, lover of Tolstoy and Turgenev, and Li Lisan, whose whole life was communism, both believed in an imminent revolutionary firestorm. Qu, in a memorable letter from a Guomindang prison in 1935, shortly before his execution, wrote that had he remained Party leader, he would have committed the same errors as Li. 'The only difference', he declared, 'would be that I could not have been so reckless as he was; that is, I would not have had his courage.'

Li's misguided obsession with 'the revolutionary high tide' left the communists far stronger than they were before he took power. Zhou Enlai, already emerging as the indispensable executive, served with discrimination and skill whatever Moscow 'line' happened to prevail at the time. Mao, while not immune to romantic visions, as witness the 'prairie fire' he conjured up before the young Lin Biao, was the most down-to-earth of the four and it was his views which prevailed.

By 1931, the two major strategic issues they had argued over – the primacy of the Red Army in the revolutionary struggle, and the relationship between city and countryside – had both been resolved

in Mao's favour. The Fourth Plenum vindicated his opposition to Li
Lisan just as the Sixth Congress, two-and-a-half years earlier, had
vindicated his opposition to Qu Qiubai. Li's (and Zhou's) policies,
the plenum acknowledged, had 'totally overlooked the necessity
of consolidating the base areas'. They had 'considered guerrilla
warfare outdated', and 'issued premature, adventurist and dogmatic
orders to the Red Army to attack big cities'. Mao could not have put
it better himself.

In future, the Comintern decided that summer, the Red Army
would be the principal motor of the revolution, 'the core around
which the revolutionary forces of workers and peasants are . . .
consolidated and organised'. The Party's chief tasks, it added, were
to strengthen the army still further, to expand and consolidate the
Red base areas, to set up a Chinese soviet government, and to
organise the workers and peasants in the Guomindang-ruled 'white
areas'. Since the peasant movement had 'far outstripped' the revolutionary movement in the cities, urban work was to be geared to
supporting the soviet districts in the countryside.

Workers' uprisings no longer got even a mention.

CHAPTER EIGHT

Futian: Loss of Innocence

The reappraisal of strategy that was forced on the Chinese leadership after 1927 by the practical needs of the revolution and the imperatives of survival was accompanied by fundamental change in the nature of the Party itself.

They described this process, approvingly, as 'Bolshevisation', and to an extent, the label was apt: they did make a conscious attempt to emulate Bolshevik practices; to instil Leninist discipline; to create an effective, centralised, political machine. But other factors were at work, too. Stalin's campaigns against Trotsky and Bukharin offered a model of intra-party strife which the Chinese Party dutifully replicated, expelling Chen Duxiu and Peng Shuzhi as Trotskyists in late 1929; and He Mengxiong and Luo Zhanglong (Mao's close friend since their student days in Changsha), as rightists fifteen months later. These tendencies were reinforced by the peculiar brutality of the Chinese revolution: White terror in the cities (where, from mid-1927 on, communists were mercilessly hunted down and killed); White terror in the countryside (where warlord soldiers and landlord militias routinely torched villages suspected of harbouring communist sympathisers); and the constant threat, in the Red areas, of nationalist encirclement and destruction.

In the early years, the violence fostered by Guomindang reprisals and Party sectarianism was usually directed outwards. The 'black-gowned gunmen' who forced Shanghai workers to strike in 1927 were ostensibly acting against 'yellow union leaders', who advocated class compromise; the widespread 'burning and killing' which accompanied Qu Qiubai's armed uprisings was, in theory, designed to force waverers to come over to the communist side.

By the time of the Sixth Congress, in mid-1928, such coercive tactics were condemned as counter-productive. When Mao's forces took Tingzhou in April 1929, he reassured the Central Committee that news reports of the Red Army burning down 500 houses and killing more than a thousand townspeople were 'all nonsense and unworthy of credence', that in fact 'only five people were killed, all of them most reactionary' and five houses had been burned down. Terror, Mao argued (as he had in his report on Hunan in the winter of 1926), was indispensable to the communist cause, and Red execution squads must be formed 'to massacre the landlords and the despotic gentry as well as their running dogs without the slightest compunction'. But the use of terror should be directed exclusively against class enemies.

Notwithstanding such caveats, the distinction between enemy and friend gradually became blurred. Inevitably, sooner or later, the methods applied to the one would be used against the other.

The flashpoint was reached in February 1930, at the enlarged Front Committee conference at Pitou. It had been called by Mao primarily to discuss Li Lisan's decision to launch attacks on cities, but a good part of the meeting was spent considering a much more parochial issue: the state of the Party in the adjacent districts of Donggu and Jian. A notice issued by Mao a week later, in the name of the Front Committee, explained:

> There is a severe crisis in the Party in western and southern Jiangxi. It consists in the fact that the local leading organs of the Party at all levels are filled with landlords and rich peasants, and the Party's policy is completely opportunist. If we do not thoroughly clean up this situation, not only will it be impossible to carry out the Party's great political tasks but the revolution will suffer a fundamental defeat. [We] call on all revolutionary comrades . . . to overthrow the opportunist political leadership, eliminate the landlords and rich peasants . . . and see to it that the Party is rapidly Bolshevised.

The problems concealed behind this jargon were twofold. The local leaders resented Mao's efforts to impose the centralised control of a Front Committee dominated by non-Jiangxi men, mainly Hunanese; they were also unenthusiastic about the harsh new land reform policies which these outsiders were promoting to the detriment of their own families and clans.

To Mao, they were 'mountaintop-ists', who put the interests of their small area ahead of those of the Party as a whole, and they had to be brought into line.

The meeting therefore decreed the dissolution of the existing Party hierarchy in the area, and the formation of a new South-west Jiangxi Special Committee, headed by Liu Shiqi, a young Hunanese communist who was married to He Zizhen's sister, He Yi (and was therefore, in effect, Mao's brother-in-law). A second, secret directive ordered the execution of four of the founders of the South-west Jiangxi Party, known locally as the 'Four Great Party officials', to serve as an example to others.

Why did Mao decide that the unwritten rule against killing Party comrades must be broken? There is a clue in the resolution he wrote at Gutian, six weeks earlier, when he warned that those in the Party and the Red Army who manifested an 'individualistic aversion to discipline' were acting in a manner that was 'objectively counter-revolutionary'. This was a pure Stalinist notion, which Mao would subsequently develop into a subtler, more flexible theory of 'contradictions between the enemy and ourselves' (antagonistic contradictions) and 'contradictions among the people' (which were non-antagonistic). But in 1930 it was already ample justification for considering that communists who obstructed the policies that the Party laid down, whatever their reason for doing so, had become part of 'the enemy' and should be treated as such. Since their guilt was political, the judicial process was irrelevant except as theatre, to educate the masses. In such cases Party leaders, Mao included, would proclaim that the accused should be 'openly tried and sentenced to death by execution' (no other verdict being possible since that was what had already been decided).

Judicial independence had never been a strong point in China, but whatever little there might have been Bolshevism now extinguished.

In this sense, Mao's espousal of revolutionary violence *within* the Party was just one more step on the road he had begun travelling a decade earlier, when he had concluded that Marxism – the same political philosophy that, as an idealistic young student, he had rejected as too extreme and too violent – could alone save China. The taboo against killing had been eroded in stages: first in theory, when Mao had defended the peasant jacqueries in Hunan; then in practice, a year later, when he had to lead troops into battle. Now, in 1930, the definition of 'enemy' became more diffuse and malleable.

That 'one more step' for Mao was to have extraordinary consequences for the Party and army organisations that he led.

Having been given a mandate to purge, Liu Shiqi worked with a will. Hundreds of cadres of landlord and rich peasant origin were expelled from the South-west Jiangxi Party over the next few months. In May, internal Party documents began referring for the first time to a mysterious 'AB-*tuan*' which had allegedly infiltrated local committees, especially in Jian and neighbouring Anfu, Yongfeng and Xingguo. This group, often referred to as the Anti-Bolshevik League (the letters A and B actually denoted the *tuan*'s senior and junior levels of membership), was a right-wing clique within the Guomindang. It had been established in Jian in 1926, and while moribund elsewhere in China, remained a significant presence in south-west Jiangxi, along with other reformist movements like the Reorganisationists (supporters of the former Left-GMD leader Wang Jingwei), the Third Party and the Social Democrats. In an area where communists, reformists and Guomindang supporters all came from the same social strata, often the same families and clans, and might well have divided loyalties, the idea of an AB-*tuan* fifth column was not inherently improbable. But the sheer number of agents claimed to have been found did strain credulity.

By October, when Mao's forces took Jian, more than a thousand South-west Jiangxi Party members – one in thirty of the total – had been executed as AB-*tuan* members.

The degree of Mao's personal involvement up to this point is uncertain. There is a prima-facie case that he must have been implicated to some extent. Even without his ties to Liu Shiqi, the Front Committee was ultimately responsible for the South-west Jiangxi Special Committee's work. Mao was informed of the alleged AB-*tuan* connection as soon as it was discovered, and he would have received a detailed briefing when the Red Army passed through the area in July on its way north to Nanchang. Yet at that stage, while large numbers had been arrested, relatively few people had been killed. The blood-purge began in earnest only after the Red Army had moved on.

The trigger was the return of one of the Jiangxi leaders who had been passed over when Liu Shiqi was appointed. Li Wenlin, a thirty-year-old intellectual who, like Mao, was of rich peasant origin, had been among the founders of the Donggu base area, and had impressed Mao by his leadership when the Red Army had sought refuge there in the spring of 1929. During the summer, he had gone to Shanghai to attend the Soviet Areas Conference, where he established good relations with Li Lisan. In August, while Mao was away in Hunan, he persuaded the Special Committee to call an enlarged plenum, which dismissed Liu Shiqi; endorsed Li Lisan's policy of using the Red Army to attack cities; and rescinded the radical land law which had been approved, at Mao's insistence, that spring. Li Wenlin himself was named Special Committee Secretary, and soon afterwards became head of the Provincial Action Committee established on Li Lisan's orders.

As one of its first acts, this new leadership ordered 'the most merciless torture' to ferret out AB-*tuan* members, warning that even 'those people who seem very positive and loyal, very left-wing and straightforward in what they say' must be doubted and questioned. The numbers being killed rose steeply, as each confession produced a new clutch of victims, and each victim a new confession. When Mao arrived in Jian in October, he therefore found himself confronted with a much bigger, more complex problem than he had imagined when the South-west Jiangxi purge had been launched. Then it had simply been a matter of local Party committees being filled with 'landlords and rich peasants'. Now, he told the Central Committee, they were 'filled with AB-*tuan* members', who were 'carrying out assassinations,* preparing to make contact with the [White] army, and plotting a revolt to eliminate the soviet base areas and the various revolutionary organisations'.

Mao's answer was to intensify the purge still further. On October 26, he and Li Wenlin issued a joint statement calling for the removal of 'rich peasant counter-revolutionaries' from local soviet governments; the 'execution of all AB-*tuan* activists'; and the

---

* The reference to 'assassinations' was not explained, but Mao may have had two incidents in mind: the deaths, that spring, of his old allies from the Jinggangshan, Yuan Wencai and Wang Zuo, who were shot in obscure circumstances, allegedly while trying to rebel; and the murder of another long-time supporter, Wan Xixian, some months earlier. In both cases, Jiangxi Party officials were alleged to have been implicated.

launching of a campaign against the AB-*tuan* in the Red Army.

Four days later, this appearance of unity was shattered by Mao's proposal to 'lure the enemy in deep', a strategy which the Jiangxi cadres adamantly opposed. To men whose villages were on the enemy's line of march, the new policy was a matter of life or death: it meant their womenfolk risked being raped and killed, their children and old people butchered, their homes burned down, and all that they possessed destroyed. As the Red Army retreated southward before Chiang Kai-shek's advancing armies, then beginning their first encirclement campaign, mutiny was in the air.

When the troops reached Huangpi, where they were to regroup and prepare for the coming battles, the Political Departments launched what was euphemistically called 'a consolidation campaign' to weed out doubtful elements. The first man to crack was a regimental cadre named Gan Lichen, who confessed after being severely beaten that he was a member of an AB-*tuan* network. That was all that it needed. Under extraordinary strain, facing an enemy many times stronger, the Red Army ignited.

The flames that had devoured the Party in south-west Jiangxi now began, with fine impartiality, to consume officers and men, as regiment after regiment turned inwards in a fury of self-destruction. Every unit, down to company level, established a 'committee for eliminating counter-revolutionaries'. Twenty-one-year-old Xiao Ke, already a division commander, later one of China's top generals, recalled in his memoirs:

> In that period, I spent all my time on the AB-*tuan* problem. Our division had killed 60 people . . . Then one night in our Divisional Party Committee, it was decided to kill 60 more. Next morning, I went to report . . . But at the Fourth Army Military Committee, [they] said: 'You're killing too many. If they are from worker and peasant backgrounds, you can just let them confess . . .' After that, I went back at once. The prisoners had already been taken to the execution ground. I said, 'Don't kill them. The Divisional Party Committee must discuss this again.' Afterwards, they decided to release more than 30 of them. But more than 20 were still killed. Altogether in the Fourth Army, 1,300 or 1,400 out of 7,000 men were struck down.

Political officers tried to outdo each other for fear of being thought weak. One ordered the execution of a fourteen-year-old 'little Red devil' for taking food to officers who, unknown to the child, were AB-*tuan* suspects. He was saved by the intervention of an army commissar. Elsewhere, an entire company was slaughtered after its commander questioned the need for the purge. In little more than a week, 4,400 officers and men of the First Front Army confessed to links with the AB-*tuan.* More than 2,000 were summarily shot.

What had begun nine months before as a simple dispute over land reform, fuelled by rivalry between Jiangxi natives and Hunanese, had taken on a monstrous life of its own.

The designations, 'rich peasant', 'AB-*tuan* member' and 'counter-revolutionary element', became inextricably confused. Local differences were coloured by national disputes as the South-west Jiangxi Party leaders, for their own purposes, championed Li Lisan's policies as a counterweight to Mao's. Amid deepening paranoia as the GMD encirclement tightened, the charge of AB-*tuan* membership became a bludgeon to strike down anyone who questioned Mao's strategy. The purge grew into a blood-bath in which his opponents perished. The stage was set for 'the Futian events'.

The small market town of Futian lies on the Fushui, a tributary of the Gan River, at the western edge of the White Cloud Mountains, which separate it from Donggu, ten miles to the east. Beside an old stone bridge, women squat, beating washing against flat stones. A few shops, a warren of crooked streets, and a jumble of grey-tiled houses with whitewashed antler-eaves, spread back, higgledy-piggledy, from the banks.

The landscape is Pyrenean. From the peaks, thickly covered with pine forest, fir and bamboo, and overgrown with creepers, the view extends across four counties. There are ferns underfoot, and rushing mountain torrents. In summer, the piercing green rice-paddies are worked by small, thin, bony men, with ragged blue jackets, baggy shorts, and wide-brimmed straw hats as big as dustbin lids to protect them against the blinding glare of the sun. In winter, the approaches turn to a sea of mud. The track from Donggu is impassable, and the only access is across the plain from the west, or at high water, by boat along the river.

After the Red Army abandoned Jian, in mid-November, Futian became the headquarters of the Jiangxi Provincial Action Committee.

On Sunday afternoon, December 7, 1930, shortly after lunch, a member of Mao's political staff named Li Shaojiu arrived from Huangpi at the head of a company of troops. With him he carried two letters from Mao's General Front Committee, addressed to the provincial government leader, Zeng Shan, and the head of the Action Committee's Propaganda Department, Chen Zhengren, both Mao loyalists. The letters ordered the arrests of Li Bofang (alleged to be the head of a secret AB-*tuan* headquarters inside the Action Committee); Duan Liangbi (an alleged AB-*tuan* section chief); and Xie Hanchang (Head of the Political Department of the 20th Army at Donggu, also allegedly an AB-*tuan* agent). Their names and supposed links to the AB-*tuan* had been revealed under torture by Red Army men who had confessed to being their accomplices.

Li Shaojiu took no chances. He ordered the Committee's offices surrounded by three rings of troops, before entering with an escort of ten soldiers, rifles at the ready. Li, Duan, Xie and five other Action Committee members were seized and bound hand and foot. Most of them were in their early to mid-twenties. When they asked for an explanation, Li merely took out his pistol and pointed it at their heads.

From the Committee's headquarters, the eight officials were taken to the former magistrate's yamen, an immense white-walled building, pierced by a massive central archway opening on to a spacious inner courtyard. Sweet-scented osmanthus trees grew from the raised stone terraces, and covered wooden walkways ran along each side. At the eastern end, a cantilevered grey-tiled roof, with delicately flaring eaves, formed an immense canopy, supported by four huge wooden pillars on carved stone pedestals, covering a raised dais where, in imperial times, the magistrate held court. A gilt signboard suspended from the ceiling proclaimed: 'The Hall of Sincerity and Respect'.

Behind the dais stood a large wood-panelled torture chamber, where for centuries yamen runners had applied the rigour of imperial law. There Li commenced his interrogation. Duan Liangbi was questioned first:

Li Shaojiu asked me [he wrote later]: 'Duan Liangbi, are you an AB-*tuan* member? Are you going to confess? If you do, you will avoid the torture.'

I replied sternly: 'Look at my history, and my work . . . Please go ahead and investigate. If I were an AB-*tuan* member, it would be a crime against the proletariat. Then I wouldn't need you to touch me. I'd take a gun and kill myself.'

But Li answered: 'As far as your history is concerned . . . I haven't the ability to debate theories with you. I have only seven kinds of tortures to punish . . .'

After he had described to me all the seven punishments, I said: 'So be it. But why should I be afraid? Whatever you do, I . . .' Before I had finished my sentence, Li ordered the soldiers to take off my clothes. I was made to kneel naked on the floor. They subjected me to the torture called "blowing the landmine",* and burned my body with incense sticks . . . I thought at first: 'Well, let them burn me to death. In this world death is inevitable, the only question is how.' My two thumbs were almost broken through, just barely hanging together by the skin. My body was already burned into a festering mess, not a single place was good. I was cut and bruised all over.

Then suddenly they stopped beating me, and Li Shaojiu said: 'Liangbi, you want to die, but this is not what I want. Whatever happens, you will have to confess that you are in the AB-*tuan* and to tell us about your network. Otherwise, I will keep you in a state where you are neither living nor dead.'

This was not something that Li Shaojiu, murderous thug that he was, had thought up on his own. He was simply following the instructions of the Front Committee, that Mao personally had approved, which stated: 'Do not kill the important leaders too quickly, but squeeze out of them [the maximum] information . . . [Then], from the clues they give, you can go on to unearth other leaders.'

The same crude methods were applied everywhere. Eighteen months later a CCP investigation concluded:

All the AB-*tuan* cases were uncovered on the basis of confessions. Little patience was shown in ascertaining facts and verifying charges . . . [The] method used . . . was the carrot and stick. The 'carrot' meant . . . extracting confessions by guile . . . The 'stick' meant

---

* This apparently involved a severe beating to the lower part of the body. Such methods were employed not only by the communists, but also in nationalist-ruled areas well into the 1930s. Even modern terms like 'airplane ride' (or 'jetplane ride', as it was called, thirty-five years later, during the Cultural Revolution), which involved tying a person's hands behind the back, and then hanging him, or her, by the arms from a wooden beam, referred to tortures that had been in use for centuries.

thrashing suspects with ox-tailed bamboo sticks after hanging them up by their hands. If that had no effect, next came burning with incense or with the flame of a kerosene lamp. The worst method was to nail a person's palms to a table and then to insert bamboo splints under the fingernails. The methods of torture were given names like . . . "sitting in a sedan chair"; "airplane ride"; "toad-drinking water"; and "monkey pulling reins" . . . Torture was the only method of dealing with suspects who resisted. Torture ceased only after confession.

Like all the others, Duan eventually did confess, but salved his conscience by naming as his accomplices only the seven men who had been arrested with him. Li Bofang, who had a photographic memory, took the opposite tack, trying to confuse his tormentors by writing down almost a thousand names.

Next morning, December 8, Li Shaojiu made further arrests on the basis of the previous night's confessions. Zeng Shan and Mao's secretary, Gu Bo, who now arrived from Huangpi, joined in the interrogations. Before the week was out, 120 people were being held in cells along each side of the courtyard, concealed behind a lattice of narrow wooden slats, about an inch apart, which reached from floor to ceiling like the bars of a cage. Among them were the wives of Li Bofang and two other suspects, who came to the yamen to seek news of their husbands. They were tortured even more brutally than the men: the soldiers cut open their breasts, and burnt their genitals.

Li Shaojiu then left for Donggu, as the Front Committee had instructed, to begin a purge of the 20th Army. There he made a fatal error. One of the men Xie Hanchang had denounced as a fellow AB-*tuan* conspirator was a battalion commander named Liu Di. Liu, like Li Shaojiu, was from Changsha, and managed to convince Li that he had been framed. As soon as he was free, however, he led a mutiny and set out for Futian at the head of a relief column of 400 men. After a battle the following night, in which a hundred of Li's troops were killed, the heavy wooden gates of the yamen were forced open, and the badly injured Action Committee leaders released.

An emergency meeting of the survivors resolved to take the 20th Army across the Gan River to Yongyang, where it would be safe from Mao's reprisals. Banners were put up in the square outside the yamen, declaring: 'Down with Mao Zedong! Support Zhu [De],

Peng [Dehuai] and Huang [Gonglue]!' – and an appeal was sent to the Party Centre to remove Mao from all his posts. When news of this reached Huangpi, the three army commanders issued statements, declaring their solidarity with Mao and denouncing the rebels. But the attempt to split the leadership continued by more devious means, when copies of an incriminating letter were circulated, in which Mao had supposedly instructed Gu Bo to gather evidence that Zhu, Peng and Huang were also AB-*tuan* leaders. The forgery was too crude to be credible, and the Front Committee issued a long, rambling rebuttal, charging the leaders at Yongyang with rebellion against the Party, and conspiring to sow discord among the revolutionary forces. A stalemate then set in: the 20th Army on one side of the Gan River, Mao's forces on the other, both claiming to be the loyal executors of Party policy.

Neither the events at Futian, nor the horrific blood-letting the Red Army had suffered, stopped Mao decisively defeating Chiang Kai-shek's first encirclement campaign. In fact, they may have helped. Bonded by the fury of the purge, those who had withstood it were fused into a tightly disciplined, steel-willed force with extraordinary motivation.

None the less, the existence of a dissident clique in Yongyang could not be tolerated indefinitely. When Xiang Ying reached the base area at the beginning of 1931, his first task was to try to lay to rest the demons that Futian had conjured up. By now Mao, too, his prestige bolstered by the latest victory, felt that the killing had gone too far. Li Wenlin, who had been arrested at Huangpi, was released, albeit on probation, and Li Shaojiu was reprimanded for excessive zeal. On January 16, 1931, the newly formed Central Bureau announced the expulsion of Liu Di and four other rebel leaders, and declared that what had happened in Futian was an 'anti-Party incident'. But it noted that there was as yet no proof that the rebels were all AB-*tuan* members. Over the next six weeks, Xiang Ying began to put out peace feelers, dropping cautious hints that an accommodation might be reached with those who had been misled.

To Mao, these overtures were an implicit disavowal, and he bridled at Xiang's suggestion, the more infuriating because it was so clearly well-founded, that the problem at Futian was partly a factional struggle. On the essential question, however, of whether

the campaign against the AB-*tuan* had been justified, Xiang
supported Mao, as did the majority of the Party. Throughout
January and February, arrests of suspects continued. Even the rebels
at Yongyang, while proclaiming their own innocence, agreed that
this was correct:

> We do not deny [they wrote] that the AB-*tuan* has a widespread
> organisation in Jiangxi and that it has penetrated into the Soviet
> areas, for we have been active fighters against the AB-*tuan*
> ourselves . . . Comrade Duan Liangbi was the first to combat the AB-
> *tuan* in the Jiangxi Special Committee . . . [But now] he too is branded
> a member of the AB-*tuan.*

That the former leaders of the Action Committee, despite the
tortures they had endured, could still endorse the purge, spoke
volumes for the state of mind in the base areas at that time. In March
1931, most of them laid down their arms and returned to face the
music, having been assured, or so they believed, that they would be
treated with clemency.

Unfortunately for them, their return coincided with the news of
Li Lisan's disgrace. The new leaders in Shanghai took an extremely
harsh attitude towards the Futian events, which were now seen as a
manifestation of the 'anti-Comintern, anti-Party Li Lisan line',
aimed at 'wiping out the Red Army and destroying the base area'.
In April, Liu Di was brought before a court martial, chaired by Zhu
De, sentenced to death and beheaded. He was in his early twenties.
Li Bofang and two others were also executed.

The new approach was confirmed at an enlarged Central Bureau
meeting, held under the authority of the Fourth Plenum delegation:

> The AB-*tuan* has become a small party within the Communist Party,
> [carrying out] . . . counter-revolutionary activities under the flag of
> revolution. Why has [it] been able [to do this] recently? The main
> reasons are . . . [Firstly,] landlords and rich peasants have found it
> easy to infiltrate the CCP . . . As the revolution develops . . . these
> elements are bound to betray us . . . [Secondly,] the Party followed
> the mistaken political line of Li Lisan . . . [Thirdly,] in the past, we
> did not pay sufficient attention to the work of purging subversive
> elements. Captured members of the AB-*tuan* were shot on the spot
> instead of being used to dig up further clues . . . [This] also made it
> possible for the AB-*tuan* to expand.

The Front Committee (under Mao) was praised for following a 'generally correct' political line and adopting a class standpoint towards the Futian rebellion. The Central Bureau (under Xiang Ying) was fiercely condemned for its 'conciliation of the Li Lisan line', and for its 'completely wrong' approach to the Futian events, which had been 'divorced from a class standpoint' and had led 'Party organisations at all levels to relax, soften and diminish the struggle against the AB-*tuan*'.

Its conclusion that the leading Futian rebels were all 'important members of the AB-*tuan*... who carried out a counter-revolutionary rebellion under the flag of the Li Lisan line' (rather than just misguided comrades, as Xiang Ying had tried to suggest), and the corollary – that the Li Lisan line and the AB-*tuan* were different sides of the same coin – had enormous advantages for Mao and for the new Party Centre. Mao could now legitimately argue that the purge, far from being directed against factional opponents, was a principled defence of the Party line. The Returned Students in Shanghai, who had been far more influenced by Stalinist practices than previous CCP leaders, saw their priority as the further Bolshevisation of the Party, by which they meant, above all, the rooting out of Li Lisan's supporters and the crushing of localism and dissent – in short, the transformation of the Party into a loyal and obedient Leninist tool. Being able to lump together all forms of opposition under a generic AB-*tuan* label made that task far easier.

The result was that, from April onwards, the purge resumed more ferociously than ever. Despite repeated efforts to centralise investigations through Political Security departments, uneducated, often illiterate, officials in village and township purge committees wielded enormous power. Death came on a whim, at the slightest pretext or no pretext at all. A CCP investigator reported:

> Those who complained about the Party in their sleep, those who refused to help carry provisions on carrying-poles, those who stayed away from mass rallies, those who failed to show up for Party meetings ... were all arrested as AB-*tuan* members. So great was the terror that most people refused to go to a new job even if the transfer were a promotion . . . because the risk of being accused of AB-*tuan* membership was higher if you had newly arrived . . . In the peak period of [the purge], even talking to another person might lead to suspicion of being an AB-*tuan* member. Therefore Party members

refused to attend meetings unless some higher officials were there to witness what was discussed.

[In the late summer] the Jiangxi Political Security Department proposed arresting every rich peasant [in the base area] for investigation on the grounds that they were probably AB-*tuan* members . . . They said quite openly that it was better to kill a hundred innocent people than to leave a truly guilty one at large . . . On account of such weird views, all organs and revolutionary groups won the freedom to arrest, interrogate and execute counter-revolutionaries. The prevailing mood was to hunt down the AB-*tuan* in order to prove your loyalty to the revolution.

When suspects were tortured to reveal details of the 'networks' to which they supposedly belonged, they either denounced acquaintances or tried to remember the names of people they had seen working in Party offices. To protect themselves, officials blackened their name-badges, or stopped wearing them altogether.

During the third encirclement campaign, there was no time even to carry out interrogations. In some units, a roll-call was taken: those who confessed to being AB-*tuan* members were granted an amnesty; those who denied any connection were killed.

In July, the 20th Army units which had fled to Yongyang after the Futian events (and had remained there after the Action Committee leaders gave themselves up in March) were summoned back *in extremis* to the central base area, to help fight off Chiang Kai-shek's pincer movement. On the 23rd they linked up with Mao's forces at Ping'anzhai, about twenty miles north of Yudu. Their commander, Zeng Bingqun, had been in touch with the Central Bureau, and evidently believed that the political cloud over the contingent had been lifted. Instead, his force was surrounded and disarmed as soon as it arrived. Every officer, from Zeng himself to the humblest assistant platoon leader, was arrested. Ordinary soldiers were dispersed among other Red Army units. In the space of a few hours, the 20th Army ceased to exist. The designation would never be used by a Chinese communist army again.

A month later Li Wenlin and the other remaining Action Committee leaders, together with Zeng and most of his officer corps, were sentenced to death before a crowd of several thousand people at Baisha, by a tribunal which Mao himself chaired.

The overall death-toll from the purge in the summer and early autumn of 1931 can only be guessed at. Four hundred officers and men from the 20th Army perished, and probably several hundred from the 35th Army, also locally recruited in Jiangxi, which was purged at about the same time. From other Red Army units, there were many more. In the local Jiangxi Party, 3,400 people were killed in just three of the more than twenty counties. By the beginning of September, a CCP Central Inspector reported that '95 per cent of the intellectuals in the south-west Jiangxi Party and Youth League' had confessed to AB-*tuan* connections. Today the best-informed Chinese historians say merely that 'tens of thousands' died.

As the year drew to a close, and the tensions generated by the nationalist encirclements eased, the purge subsided and Mao's role in it diminished. In December, renewed and, this time, much more serious efforts were made to impose realistic, institutional controls. A 'Provisional Procedure for Handling Counter-revolutionary Cases and Establishing Judicial Organs', intended among other things to 'safeguard the rights of the masses', was promulgated in Mao's name. Low-level officials were deprived of the power to order executions, a system of appeals was instituted and the use of torture was condemned. The new rules were often honoured in the breach, and in any case contained plenty of loopholes. Moreover, it was expressly stipulated that class background should be the determining factor in deciding punishment, an approach which would remain ever after a fundamental fault-line in the Chinese communist legal system. Landlords, rich peasants, and those of 'capitalist origins' were to be sentenced to death; the 'masses' could make a fresh start.

Then Zhou Enlai arrived from Shanghai to take up his post as substantive Central Bureau Secretary, and in January, 1932, for the first time, the scale and conduct of the purge was officially called into question:

> Killing people was regarded as a trifle [the Bureau acknowledged]. The most serious effect of this was that it caused panic in the Party. Even leading organs were affected. This was not a policy . . . of isolating the [Party's] opponents and winning over the masses who had been deceived by their counter-revolutionary influence – it was just the opposite. It damaged our own revolutionary forces and made those on the class battlefront waver. This was a most serious mistake.

But the complaint was merely against *unorganised* killing. Both the Bureau and Zhou Enlai himself continued to insist that the campaign against counter-revolutionaries *per se* remained 'completely correct'. The method needed to be changed, not in order to end it but to make it more efficient.

That spring, executions continued, albeit at a slower pace. In May 1932, Li Wenlin, Zeng Bingqun and three other supposed AB-*tuan* leaders – who, since their 'trial' the previous August, had been paraded before mass meetings in villages all over south-west Jiangxi – were publicly beheaded. Over the next two years, while the purge was idling to a close, the Political Security departments still dealt with 500 cases a month resulting, on average, in 80 to 100 people being shot.

The killings in Jiangxi were part of a wider pattern. In west Fujian, more than 6,000 Party members and officials were executed on suspicion of being covert Social Democrats. At Peng Dehuai's old base on the Hunan–Jiangxi border, 10,000 were killed. In E-Yu-Wan, in the Dabie Mountains about seventy miles north-east of Wuhan, the urbane Beijing University graduate, Zhang Guotao, now a Politburo Standing Committee member and, like Mao, one of the founders of the Party, presided over a purge in which 2,000 'traitors, AB-*tuan* members and Third Party elements' lost their lives. Chen Changhao, his political commissar, explained:

> The revolutionary tide is surging ahead every day . . . The enemy has already seen how useless its airplanes, guns and machine-guns are. Therefore it is making use of the Reorganisationists, the AB-*tuan* and the Third Party to infiltrate our soviet area and the Red Army . . . This is a very vicious plot. It is easy for us to see the enemy attacking with airplanes and guns, but it is not easy for us to see the Reorganisationists, the AB-*tuan* and the Third Party. How vicious the enemy is.

After several thousand counter-revolutionaries were purged in the north-east Jiangxi base area, the leftist leader responsible, Zeng Hongyi, moved to north Fujian, where he killed two thousand more as 'reformists and AB-*tuan*'.

Slowly the purge mentality spread its poison throughout the communist areas. Until 1937, when the political situation changed nationally, beleaguered groups of Red Army men, battling against overwhelming odds, often in unimaginable conditions of deprivation and hardship, turned in on themselves in periodical bouts of blood-letting which, in some cases, killed more of their own comrades than the nationalist armies had.

The pretexts for the purges were invariably the same: differences over land reform; local or ethnic rivalries; and political issues linked to 'the Li Lisan line'. So were the techniques: 'You force him to confess,' the head of the east Fujian security bureau explained, 'then he confesses, you believe him and you kill him; or, he does not confess and you kill him.' The ultimate cause of the purges was always the same, too. They were always about power – the power of individual leaders to enforce their will, and to ensure that followers followed.

The example of Stalinism, and the influence of Stalinist rhetoric, are part of the explanation for what happened in the Chinese Red base areas in the early 1930s, but only a small part. The great blood-purges in Russia did not start until four years *after* Futian, with the murder of Kirov in Leningrad. The way in which the CCP leadership was transformed from an idealistic, ineffectual coterie of well-meaning intellectuals, which had fallen apart at the first push from the Guomindang little more than three years before, into a hardened Bolshevik core-group which, in exceptional times, ordered an exceptional slaughter of men and women who later proved to have been perfectly loyal, had far more to do with the situation within China itself.

The crucial factor was the civil war. In most wars, deserters are shot; prisoners are maltreated to obtain information; basic rights are suspended. In the war between the communists and the nationalists, no rules were honoured.

Early in 1931, the head of the Chinese Politburo's security service, Gu Shunzhang, a formidably effective agent who had been trained by the Russian secret police in Vladivostok, was sent to Wuhan to try to assassinate Chiang Kai-shek. He was disguised as a magician. But the GMD special services identified him from a photograph, and in April he was arrested and persuaded to defect. The French intelligence bureau in Shanghai estimated that as a result of his betrayal, several thousand communists were executed over the next three months. Among them was the Party's figurehead General Secretary, Xiang Zhongfa, who was shot in June.

It was not all one-sided, however. The day after Gu's defection, his family disappeared. Five months later, their naked, headless bodies were discovered, buried under ten feet of earth and concrete, at an empty house in the French concession. The communist agent who had killed them told his GMD captors that they had been executed as a reprisal on the orders of Zhou Enlai. Gu's small son alone had survived, the man said, because he had been unable to bring himself to carry out Zhou's order to kill the child. He then took them to five more houses where further corpses were unearthed, this time of communist cadres whom Zhou had ordered killed to maintain Party discipline. After some three dozen bodies had been unearthed, the settlement police had had enough and ordered the search halted.

Zhou Enlai's extermination of the family of Gu Shunzhang was the rule, not the exception, in a conflict without quarter.

The Guomindang was just as barbarous. In Hubei, the wife of the Red Army leader, Xu Haidong, was seized by the nationalists and sold as a concubine. More than sixty other members of Xu's clan, including children and infants, were hunted down and killed. In November 1930, two months after Mao led the communists' failed attack on Changsha, his wife, Yang Kaihui, was taken to the execution ground outside the city's Liuyang Gate and beheaded on the orders of the GMD Governor. Their children were hidden by relatives and sent secretly to Shanghai, where a few months later, the youngest, four-year-old Anlong, died of dysentery. Nationalist soldiers were sent to dig up the graves of Mao's parents.

In Xu Haidong's base area, E-Yu-Wan, where, in Edgar Snow's phrase, the slaughter attained 'the intensity of religious wars', and in other Red areas in the south, the nationalists followed a policy which they called 'draining the pond to catch the fish': all the able-bodied men were killed, the villages burned and available grain supplies seized or destroyed. Great swathes of forest were cut down, to hem the guerrillas into mountain fastnesses where whatever moved was shot on sight. Villagers who survived were herded into stockaded settlements of wooded huts in the plains, guarded by soldiers and landlord militia. Women and girls were sold as prostitutes or slaves, until foreign missionaries complained and Chiang Kai-shek banned the practice.

Initially, nationalist troops used their victims' heads to keep tally; when this proved impracticable (because of the weight), they cut off ears instead. One division was reported to have collected 700 pounds of ears 'to show its merit'. In Huang'an county, in Hubei, more than 100,000 villagers were killed; in Xin county, in Henan,

80,000. In Peng Dehuai's old base area, on the Hunan–Hubei border, once home to a million people, only 10,000 remained. Twenty years later, ruined villages and human bones were still scattered through the mountains.

Mao himself saw little of such extremes of devastation. By the time the worst butchery reached Jiangxi, the Red Army had moved on. But it informed the social context in which he, and all communist leaders, moved.

All through Chinese history, which, as Mao knew from his reading of the Song dynasty scholar, Si-ma Guang, was but 'a mirror of the present', rebellions had been suppressed with extraordinary ferocity. Chiang Kai-shek's slaughter in the Red areas was a pale reflection of the bloodshed that took place during the Taiping Rebellion. Chiang's troops collected ears; the seventeenth-century general, Li Zicheng, pacified Sichuan by collecting feet, and when his favourite concubine protested at his cruelty, hers were added to the pile. The nationalists exterminated the families of communist leaders; under the Qing, the families of rebellious scholars and generals were slaughtered up to the ninth degree of consanguinity. Even the use of quotas for purge victims, for all its apparent resemblance to later NKVD* practices in Russia, was of Chinese origin.

The vortex of blood and fear in which the communist struggle was played out was the fruit of this legacy. Separated from wives, families, children (when they were not, like Mao, the indirect cause of their deaths), the young men who headed the Party, none more than forty years old, focused all their energies and allegiance on a single goal: the cause. From this remorseless single-mindedness came a fanatical commitment which left no place for the morality of the normal world outside. In the Red Army, whole regiments were made up of communist orphans whose one desire was for class revenge. Hatred was a powerful weapon, whether directed outwards or at enemies within.

Not every leader responded in the same way. Some, like Gao Jingtang, in E-Yu-Wan, took to the purge like ducks to water, generating a climate of isolation and paranoia so extreme that, in 1937,

* The NKVD was the immediate predecessor of the Russian KGB (Committee for State Security). During Stalin's purges in the 1930s, NKVD regional directorates were assigned targets for the numbers of 'enemies of the people' to be arrested and shot.

when the Central Committee tried to renew contact with the guerrillas in the base areas, the first communist envoys to reach them were arrested and shot as spies. Others, like Zhu De's former commissar, Chen Yi, made use of terror sparingly if at all.

Mao's reaction was more complex. On the one hand, he wanted 'iron discipline'; on the other, he continued to hold that the Red Army should be an all-volunteer force, actuated by correct ideas, good leadership and example. To Mao, Bolshevism was far more than simply a means to win power; it was also an ideological, in a sense, a moral force for China's renewal. Intellectually, he came to terms with the contradiction this posed – between discipline and freedom, force and voluntarism – by affirming the unity of opposites (as he had in his student essays, and would again in Yan'an). But in practice they would always be in conflict. That was as true in Jiangxi in the early 1930s as in every other purge and rectification campaign that he would launch during his long life.

At such times, Mao fell back on the lesson he had drawn from the peasant movement in Hunan in the winter of 1926. 'To right a wrong,' he had written then, 'it is necessary to exceed the proper limits; the wrong cannot be righted without doing so.' From that standpoint, the blood-purges were regrettable, in future better avoided, but necessary all the same.

The same was true of the elastic uses to which the term 'AB-*tuan*' was bent. Initially Mao may well have believed, as all the other leaders clearly did, that the AB-*tuan* posed a genuine threat. But he was not so gullible as to go on believing it when no evidence was ever found (other than confessions obtained under torture) that even one of the tens of thousands who were executed was a real AB-*tuan* member. 'Social democrat', 'Reorganisationist', 'Third party' – in the end it no longer mattered: they were just names, capable of being stretched to accommodate whatever kind of political deviance the Party leaders wished to attack. The Central Bureau acknowledged as much when it conceded that there had been what it called 'a mistake in terminology' during the campaign against AB-*tuan*. That, too, Mao must have concluded, was necessary. At any rate, similar 'mistakes' would occur in every political movement that followed.

CHAPTER NINE

Chairman of the Republic

The defeat of Chiang Kai-shek's third encirclement campaign in September 1931 saw the beginning of another and, this time, much more determined attempt by the Party Centre to bring Mao and the Jiangxi base area firmly under its control.

The devastation of the Party's urban networks after the defection of Gu Shunzhang had made the Red areas more important than ever. The Comintern had been insisting for over a year that it was there, rather than in China's cities, that the next stage of the struggle would be played out. The arrest and execution of Xiang Zhongfa, the Party's General Secretary, in June, had made leadership changes imperative, and the growing physical danger of operating in Shanghai argued for dispersal.

Already, in April, senior leaders had been despatched from Shanghai to run the Party committees at E-Yu-Wan and in He Long's west Hunan base area. Three months later, it was decided that Zhou Enlai should embark on his long-delayed journey to Jiangxi, to take over the running of the Central Bureau, while Wang Ming would return to the safety of Moscow as head of the CCP's Comintern delegation. Another Returned Student, Bo Gu, then aged twenty-four, would stay on in Shanghai as acting Party leader until a new congress could be convened. At the same time, plans were set in motion to establish a communist government in the Red districts of Jiangxi (now renamed grandly the Central Soviet Base Area), as a first step towards the relocation of the whole of the Central leadership to the province.

Against this background, Wang Ming, Bo Gu and their Returned Student allies launched a concerted campaign to undermine Mao's authority. At the end of August – even before the third encirclement had been defeated – the Party Centre fired off a long, ill-tempered directive, accusing him (though not by name) of lacking a clear class stand; being too soft on rich peasants; failing to develop the labour movement; ignoring repeated instructions to set up the planned soviet government; failing to expand the base area; and allowing the Red Army to engage in 'guerrillaism'. When this message reached the base area in October, it caused considerable puzzlement, as well as anger. Not only had Mao and his colleagues just successfully fought off an enemy force ten times stronger than their own, but the Returned Students themselves had earlier castigated Li Lisan for pretending that guerrilla warfare was outdated; and the Comintern that summer, in a highly unusual move, had praised Mao personally for his policies in the base area.

To Bo Gu in Shanghai, such niceties were of little account. His concern that autumn was not with doctrine but with power.

In mid-October, he agreed reluctantly that Mao could remain as acting Central Bureau Secretary (a post he had held informally since May) until Zhou Enlai's arrival, but rejected a proposal to promote several of Mao's allies. Shortly after this, when Mao asked for a Politburo member to be sent to head the new soviet government, Bo responded that Mao himself was to take that post. In other words, he was to be kicked upstairs – deprived of the major part of his influence in the Party and the army, and given instead a largely honorific administrative position. At the beginning of November, that was precisely what happened. A base area Party Congress was held, which dissolved the General Front Committee that Mao headed and established in its place a Revolutionary Military Commission, chaired by Zhu De, in which he was merely one of twelve members. For good measure he was roundly criticised (though, again, not by name) for 'narrow empiricism', which meant stressing practical factors at the expense of Party policy.

Two days later, on November 7, the anniversary of the Russian Revolution, six hundred delegates from Jiangxi and the adjoining base areas gathered in the village of Yeping, about three miles east of the little market town of Ruijin, to proclaim the founding of the Chinese Soviet Republic. They met in the medieval splendour of the Clan Hall of the Xie (the common surname of all the village's inhabitants), amid a grove of ancient, gnarled camphor trees, some a thousand years old. Banners marked with the hammer and sickle were strung between the immense, lacquered wooden pillars. A Red Army parade was held, followed by a torchlit procession, punctuated by the deafening explosions and thick blue smoke of firecrackers. 'From now on,' Mao declared, 'there are two totally different states in the territory of China. One is the so-called Republic of China, which is a tool of imperialism . . . The other is the Chinese Soviet Republic, the state of the broad masses of exploited and oppressed workers, peasants, soldiers and toilers. Its banner is that of overthrowing imperialism; eliminating the landlord class; bringing down the Guomindang warlord government . . . and striving for genuine peace and unification of the whole country.'

The First National Congress of Chinese Workers', Peasants' and Soldiers' Soviets, as the new communist parliament was called, named Ruijin as the capital city of the twenty or so Red counties which made up the new Soviet Republic, and appointed Mao state chairman and head of government.

To the uninitiated, it must have seemed he was in an enviable position. His new posts gave him a higher formal status than he had ever had before. The Comintern had made clear that it attached enormous importance to the new 'state' over which he presided. But Mao had seen off too many efforts to neutralise or control him – Zhou Enlai's attempt in July 1927 to send him to Sichuan; Qu Qiubai's proposal, a month later, that he become an apparatchik in Shanghai, Li Lisan's endeavours, in 1929, to make him leave the Fourth Army – to entertain any illusions about what was being done. True, he was now too important simply to be cast out, even by Wang Ming's Returned Students, who had the backing of the Kremlin. But they had been able to move him sideways, out of the main line of decision-making, amputating the roots from which his power stemmed.

The effects were not long in coming.

In January, Zhou Enlai, in one of his first acts after replacing Mao as Central Bureau Secretary, called for a fresh attempt to occupy a major city, in pursuance of the oft-stated goal of 'achieving initial victory in one or several provinces'.

Mao was able to convince his colleagues that Nanchang was too difficult a target. But when the Bureau reconvened, after consultations with Bo Gu in Shanghai, a majority of its members favoured an attack on Ganzhou. This, too, Mao opposed, supported by Zhu De. Ganzhou, he argued, was well-defended, had water on three sides, and was regarded by the enemy as 'a stronghold it cannot afford to lose', while the Red Army still suffered from the same lack of heavy artillery and other siege equipment that had caused the failure of its attempts to take the city the previous year. This time his arguments were rejected. Peng Dehuai, who favoured the plan, was appointed Front Commander and made clear that he relished the prospect of proving Mao wrong.

Ten days later, the Central Bureau held a third meeting, which, in Zhou's absence, Mao chaired. The discussion turned to Japan's invasion of Manchuria the previous September. Bo Gu had interpreted this as 'a dangerous and concrete step towards an attack on the Soviet Union'. Mao begged to differ, arguing that the invasion had triggered a nationwide tide of anti-Japanese feeling which went beyond traditional class divisions and which the Party should try to exploit. This was the germ of an idea – the anti-Japanese united front, bringing together all classes in China in a patriotic effort of national defence – which, not many years later, would play a key role in the CCP's struggle for power. But, in January 1932, it was far ahead of its time. The whole thrust of the Centre's policies was for a sharpening of class struggle, not a blurring of class lines. Mao's colleagues insisted that the primary consideration, as it had been in 1929 during the Eastern Railway dispute, was the threat to Moscow. Tempers flared. Finally, someone told Mao to his face: 'Japan occupied Manchuria to attack Russia. If you can't see that, you're a right opportunist.'* There was a silence. Mao got up and stalked out.

The same day, or soon afterwards, he requested sick leave. It was granted. Wang Jiaxiang, another member of the Returned Student group, took over Mao's sole remaining military post, as head of the Front Army's General Political Department. A week later Mao set out with He Zizhen and a few bodyguards for an abandoned temple on Donghuashan, a low volcanic hill about five miles

---

* This was the term Stalin was then using against Bukharin and other members of the Soviet 'anti-Party bloc'. It was therefore an extremely serious political accusation, implying systematic opposition to Party policy.

south of Ruijin, where he was to spend his 'convalescence'.

It was an austere, lonely place, well suited to Mao's bleak frame of mind. The sanctuary, a single chamber hewn out of the smooth, black rock, with a stone façade and grey-tiled roof, was dark, cold and very wet, with moss growing from the floor. As so often when he was in political difficulties, Mao's depression affected him physically. He Zizhen found him suddenly older, and he started to lose weight. She worried that the damp would make him worse, and put the young bodyguards to live in the main temple, while she and Mao moved into a cave a few yards away, which was smaller but dry, and had a stone basin where they could wash. Water had to be brought up in wooden pails on a bamboo pole from the valley, a hundred feet below, along a narrow path of shallow steps, scooped out of the rock.

There was a fine view across the plain, and to the west three ancient pagodas stood like sentinels on the encircling hills. Mao tried to keep himself occupied by writing out poems he had composed on horseback in happier days in the base area. At irregular intervals, Party documents and newspapers were sent up from Ruijin. He could do nothing but wait, in enforced idleness, for his political wounds to heal.

The new 'provisional Centre' in Shanghai, as Bo Gu's leadership was known, was less irrational than it was afterwards made to appear. The fact that it survived at all was a remarkable achievement. At a time when the Comintern's China operation was completely out of action – following the arrest of its representative, Yakov Rudnik (also known as Hilaire Noulens), an Ukrainian intelligence operative who posed as a Belgian trades unionist – Bo and his colleague, Zhang Wentian, another Returned Student in his early thirties, managed to maintain a network of agents which was able successfully to infiltrate the highest levels of Chiang Kai-shek's military command, and to liquidate GMD special services' operatives and the communist turncoats they recruited.

If they were less successful in providing guidance to the communist base areas, which now had a claimed population of five million, it was mainly because of the continuing influence of the leftist thinking that had animated Li Lisan and, before him, Qu Qiubai.

That was what had led Bo in January to raise anew the issue of attacking large cities:

> We used to avoid attacking large cities. This strategy was correct in the past but is no longer correct because circumstances have changed. Our task now is to expand [our] territory, link up the separate soviet areas to form a single integrated area, and take advantage of the present favourable political and military conditions to seize one or two important central cities so as to win initial victory for the revolution in one or more provinces.

Bo's analysis was more sober than that of his disgraced predecessors. But he reached very similar conclusions. The Great Depression, he wrote, had brought the economy in the nationalist-controlled areas to 'the verge of general collapse', while the Red Army, having been 'tempered on the bloody battlefield of the present civil war' during Chiang's failed encirclement campaigns, was stronger than ever before. The 'balance of domestic class forces' had changed, and policy needed to change, too.

In one sense, this was not unreasonable. For the past three years, Mao, too, had been calling for 'victory in one province'. Doing nothing was not an option: an insurgency which rested on its laurels would quickly collapse. Linking up the different Red base areas, which would necessarily involve occupying cities, was as logical a policy as any. The problem was that Bo demanded rigid adherence to what he called the 'forward, offensive line', and to the overall goal that he had set of occupying Nanchang, Jian and Fuzhou (another Jiangxi city), regardless of tactical imperatives. In addition, there was the disparity of forces. The defeat of Chiang Kai-shek's third encirclement had given the Shanghai leaders a grossly inflated impression of the Red Army's strength. Mao and Zhu De knew that now, no less than a year earlier, they still lacked adequate forces to seize well-defended GMD strongholds, which was why they had opposed the attack on Ganzhou. Bo Gu, Zhang Wentian and their followers saw such doubts as proof of opportunism – a flaw, not in the policy, but in those who were reluctant to carry it out.

One afternoon at the beginning of March, just after the Lantern Festival, Mao's guards saw two horsemen approaching. They turned out be Xiang Ying, who was acting as head of government during Mao's 'sick leave', and a bodyguard.

The attack on Ganzhou, Xiang told him shamefacedly, had been a fiasco. Over a period of three weeks, starting in mid-February, Peng's forces had mounted four exhausting and unsuccessful assaults against the city's defences. Attempts to mine the walls had failed. Two days before, a sortie by nationalist soldiers, which had taken Peng by surprise, had barely been repulsed; and now four divisions of nationalist reinforcements were converging from Jian and Guangdong, threatening to cut off his escape. The Military Commission, Xiang said, wanted Mao to end his sick leave and come at once to give them advice.

Mao did not need to be asked twice. A heavy rainstorm had broken, and He Zizhen asked him to wait. 'You haven't been well,' she fussed. 'If you go out in this, you'll be worse.' He waved her aside. His 'sickness' had gone.

By the time Mao reached the army at Jiangkou, a small market town fifteen miles upriver from Ganzhou, Peng had extricated himself from the trap. However, argument continued over where the Front Army should go next. Mao proposed that they make for north-east Jiangxi and develop a new base area along the northern part of the Fujian border, where the enemy was weak and the hill country favourable to the Red Army's style of warfare. But the majority of his colleagues felt this was too much of a departure from the objectives the Centre had set, which were to threaten Jian and Nanchang. Peng, still smarting from his defeat, supported them. In the end the meting decided that the force should be divided: Peng's Third Army Group would head north along the west bank of the Gan River towards Jian, while the First Army Group, commanded by Lin Biao, tried to occupy a cluster of three county towns in central Jiangxi, about eighty miles south-east of Nanchang. Mao accompanied Lin's army in his new guise of unofficial adviser, and was soon able to persuade him and his commissar, Nie Rongzhen, that Fujian was a far better target. Lin sent a telegram to this effect to the Military Commission and then marched to Tingzhou, just inside the Fujian border, to await further orders. Mao returned to Ruijin where, at the end of March, he presented his case to the Central Bureau.

This time Mao prevailed. Zhou Enlai, who chaired the two-day meeting, had seen his first military venture in the base area, which he had undertaken against Mao's advice, end in an ignominious defeat. Xiang Ying had had the thankless task of summoning Mao back in the midst of that débâcle. Peng Dehuai, who might have objected, was absent.

Yet Mao's success in getting his way that spring had another, deeper cause.

The personal chemistry between himself and Zhou Enlai, which was to be of such extraordinary importance for China over the next half-century, emerged clearly for the first time at this meeting in Ruijin.

Zhou, five years Mao's junior, was a leader of great finesse, cool, controlled, never excessive, always seeking to draw the maximum advantage from whatever the situation offered. He was infinitely malleable in the service of ultimate victory, which he regarded as the only worthwhile end.

Mao was totally excessive, possessed of exceptional vision, strong convictions and unbounded self-confidence, great subtlety of thought and unerring intuition. After Zhou yielded at Ruijin, Mao probed relentlessly, presenting him with one fait accompli after another as Lin's forces, now effectively under Mao's command, marched further and further to the south-east, in a direction precisely opposite to that which the Centre had laid down. In the process he regained, although fleetingly, a good deal of the freedom of manoeuvre which the Returned Students had tried to remove.

Their first goal was Longyan, halfway between Jiangxi and the Fujian coast. It was an area Mao knew well: the Gutian conference had been held there in the winter of 1929. On April 10, they defeated the two regiments garrisoning the town and took 700 prisoners. Ten days later Zhangzhou was taken, the first important city the Red Army had captured since the fall of Jian, eighteen months before.

Mao was elated. Soldiers who fought in the campaign remembered seeing him ride into the city on a white horse, wearing a pale grey peaked army cap, with the communists' five-pointed red star. In a telegram to Zhou Enlai the day after, he described how the local people 'rushed out like mad to welcome us'. Zhangzhou was a rich prize, a major trading centre, thirty miles from Amoy, with a population for more than 50,000. The spoils included half-a-million dollars in cash; arms and ammunition; two nationalist aircraft (which, unfortunately, the communists did not know how to use);

and, almost equally valuable as far as Mao was concerned, a rich haul of books from a middle-school library, which were sent back by road to Ruijin in a requisitioned motor-car.

Bo Gu, however, was greatly displeased.

As details of the Fujian expedition filtered back to Shanghai, the drumbeat of criticism, both of Mao himself, for upsetting the Centre's carefully laid plans for a concerted drive northward, and of the Central Bureau, for allowing it to happen, grew steadily more insistent.

The Bureau was contrite. At a meeting chaired by Zhou Enlai on May 11, which Mao, still in Zhangzhou, did not attend, it made a grovelling self-criticism, in which it admitted to 'very serious mistakes' and promised to 'correct completely' its doubts about the need to take big cities and, more generally, its 'consistent right-opportunist errors'.

This emollient approach typified Zhou's dealings with the Centre that spring, and set a pattern for the weeks that followed. Mao's reaction could hardly have been more different. 'I have taken cognizance of your telegram,' he wrote, after Zhou had passed on to him Bo's criticisms:

> The political appraisal and military strategy of the Centre are wholly erroneous. In the first place, after the three [encirclement campaigns] and the Japanese attack, the ruling forces in China . . . have been dealt a great blow . . . We must absolutely not exaggerate the strength of the enemy . . . Secondly, now that the three campaigns are over, our overall strategy should absolutely never repeat the defensive strategy of fighting on interior lines [i.e., inside the Red base areas]. On the contrary, we should adopt the offensive strategy of fighting on exterior lines [in the White areas]. Our task is to take key cities and achieve victory in one province. One would have thought that destroying the enemy was the prerequisite for this . . . To propose using last year's strategy under present circumstances is right opportunism.

This was a very impudent message indeed. Mao was deliberately throwing back in Bo Gu's face the very reproaches the Centre had made to him. Shanghai had been complaining for months about 'underestimating the revolutionary situation'; failing 'to take advantage of opportunities to develop towards the exterior'; and 'regarding outdated strategy as forever-correct dogma', all of which it had condemned as serious right-opportunist errors.

Bo's reaction is not recorded, but it is safe to assume that he was not much amused. From then on, Mao's relationship with the 'provisional Centre' became increasingly envenomed.

After the foray into Fujian, the Central Bureau made greater efforts to restrain Mao, and he was bombarded with messages urging 'an attacking posture' and strict adherence at all times to the 'forward offensive line'. Zhangzhou was abandoned at the end of May, and Mao's forces moved west to deal with warlord units from Guangdong, which had begun threatening the base area's southern flank. In west Fujian, in early June, he was joined by Zhu De and Wang Jiaxiang, who had been sent to ensure that, this time, he obeyed the Bureau's orders. They marched across southern Jiangxi towards Dayu, the tungsten-mining town near the Hunan border where the Zhu–Mao Army had stopped in January 1929 after its break-out from the Jinggangshan. However, despite Zhou Enlai's injunctions to 'attack the enemy forcefully', it was another month before the Guangdong regiments had been pushed back across the border.

By then, Bo and Zhang Wentian were beside themselves. For six months, they had watched their designs systematically frustrated. The failed attack in January on Ganzhou, then Mao's hijacking of the attempt to march north by taking his troops south to Zhangzhou, and now the Guangdong distraction, meant that the half-year from January to July 1932, arguably the best opportunity the communists would ever have for building the southern Red districts into one strong, integrated area, had achieved nothing. The reason, as the front leadership knew, was that to do more than resist incursions, and attack where the enemy was weakest, was beyond the Red Army's powers. But the Shanghai leaders would not believe that.

Between Bo Gu's rigidity and the imperatives of battlefield survival, dialogue had become impossible.

Against this unpromising background, Zhou Enlai, the eternal deal-maker, tried to engineer a trade-off. Bo would get the offensive he wanted against the northern Jiangxi cities, and Zhou himself would go to the front to lead it – but it would be waged as far as possible in accordance with the Front Army's real capabilities, and Mao would be brought onside by restoring him to his old position as General Political Commissar. Mao's 'experience and strong points' were needed, Zhou argued. If he were reinstated, he would be 'encouraged to correct his mistakes'.

Wang Jiaxiang and Zhu De agreed readily enough. But Ren Bishi and the other Bureau members, who had remained behind in Ruijin to take charge of rear echelon work, had serious misgivings. By the time Zhou secured their agreement, it was almost the middle of August. Bo Gu, ready to try almost anything to get the long-delayed offensive finally under way, gave his approval too.

Mao proposed that the entire Front Army, operating again as a single force, should march north to occupy the same, small cluster of county towns, Le'an, Yihuang and Nanfeng, that were to have been attacked five months earlier, before the expedition into Fujian. They would then try to capture the slightly larger town of Nancheng, which would put them within striking distance of Fuzhou, and 'in a more advantageous position for taking the key cities on the lower reaches of the Gan River and creating the conditions for seizing Nanchang'.

The first stage went like clockwork. Le'an, Yihuang and Nanfeng fell, bringing the Front Army 5,000 prisoners and some 4,000 guns. But the next target, Nancheng, was much more strongly defended. Zhu and Mao ordered a withdrawal while Zhou sent a wireless message to Ren Bishi's rear echelon committee, explaining that they intended to wait until the situation turned in their favour. The withdrawal continued, however, and despite more reassuring messages from Zhou, by early September they had retreated all the way to Dongshao, in Ningdu county, sixty miles to the south. The rear echelon committee, seriously alarmed at the turn events were taking, told them bluntly that this was a mistake and they must head back north without delay. That drew an unusually testy response from Zhou, who said the army was tired; that it was 'absolutely necessary' for it to rest; and that a move at this stage would open the way for an enemy attack on the base area itself.

So began a month of increasingly acrimonious exchanges between the two groups of Central Bureau leaders. No longer was it Mao against the rest. Now Zhou, Mao, Zhu and Wang, on one side, argued with Ren Bishi, Xiang Ying, the base area security chief, Deng Fa, and another Returned Student, Gu Zuolin, on the other.

At the beginning of October, they gathered in a farmhouse in the tiny mountain village of Xiaoyuan, in northern Ningdu, with Zhou Enlai in the chair, to hammer out their differences. It was to be a traumatic and intensely confrontational four days.

The rear echelon accused the front leaders of 'lacking faith in the victory of the revolution and the strength of the Red Army'. The front echelon replied that while the Centre's 'forward offensive line' was correct, it had to be carried out taking due account of practical conditions. Mao, in particular, was outspoken in his own defence. To Ren Bishi, Xiang Ying and the others, that merely confirmed what they had suspected from the start: Mao was the root of the problem and only his removal would solve it.

All the old charges levelled against him during the past year were then brought out again, along with a number of new ones. He was a right opportunist, stubbornly opposing the Centre's correct military line. He flouted organisational discipline (a reference to his outburst in May against the Centre's 'erroneous views'). He had opposed the decision to attack Ganzhou; he had resisted orders to take Fuzhou and Jian; and when eventually he did capture Zhangzhou, he had shown his 'guerrilla mentality' by spending all his time raising money. Mao, the rear echelon charged, favoured a 'pure defence line' of 'luring the enemy in deep' and 'waiting by a tree-stump for the rabbits to dash up and throw themselves against it'. He preferred fighting in remote areas, where the enemy was weakest.

Some of these charges had a basis. Mao did favour a military strategy which was in practice very different from that the Centre had laid down. But as the meeting dragged on, the fact that Mao's views might be correct and the Centre's might be mistaken ceased to be the point at issue. To Xiang Ying, and to the Returned Students, Mao was in breach of Party discipline. Therefore he was wrong.

Reaching an agreement on strategy turned out to be relatively simple. Everyone, including Mao, agreed that the Front Army should concentrate its forces against the enemy's weak points, and pick them off one by one so as to defeat the encirclement before the base area itself was threatened. To Mao, that meant fighting in Yihuang, Le'an and Nanfeng. Others favoured a battle-ground further west. But the principle was sufficiently flexible to accommodate both views.

The real problem arose over what to do about Mao himself. The rear echelon insisted that he be barred from the front altogether. Zhou argued that this was excessive. 'Zedong', he said, 'has many years' experience of warfare. He's good at fighting battles . . . and when he's at the front he makes a lot of useful suggestions which are helpful to our efforts.' The answer, he suggested, would be either for Mao to retain the role of Commissar, but under his (Zhou's) supervision; or for Zhou himself to take over that post while Mao remained at the front as an adviser. Zhu De and Wang Jiaxiang concurred. But Mao was wary of taking responsibility for directing military operations without full power to do so, and the rear echelon also objected. Mao's unwillingness to recognise his errors, they said, meant that if he stayed at the front, he would relapse into his bad old ways. They could have added that Zhou's claimed ability to 'supervise and control' him was not particularly convincing given his track record so far.

In the end Zhou devised a masterly compromise. Mao would give up the Commissar's post and act as a military adviser; but, to mollify Ren Bishi and the other rear echelon leaders, he would take 'indefinite sick leave' until his presence was required. Then, Zhou hoped, once feelings had cooled, he could quietly resume his duties.

Next day, evidently feeling that the outcome might have been worse, Mao set out for the Red Army hospital at Tingzhou, where he arrived to find He Zizhen about to give birth to their second child, a baby boy. But his problems were not to be put behind him so easily. While the Ningdu meeting was in progress, Bo Gu and Zhang Wentian had also met to discuss the situation in Jiangxi. Mao's 'conservatism and flightism', they had ruled, were unacceptable. He must leave the front at once and confine himself to government work, and a resolute struggle would have to be waged against his views. Zhou was blamed for failing to stand up to him, and for not using his authority as Bureau Secretary to ensure that the correct line was carried out.

This bombshell reached Ningdu shortly after Mao left. The meeting immediately reconvened, overturned Zhou's compromise and endorsed the Centre's decisions. When Mao learned what had happened he was furious, accusing his colleagues of 'a judgement in absentia' undertaken in a 'high-handed factional manner'. But there was nothing he could do. On October 12, it was announced that Zhou had been appointed General Political Commissar in his place. For the next two years, Mao was excluded from all significant military decision-making.

*

That winter, for the second year running, Mao celebrated the Chinese New Year in ill-health and political disfavour. His quarters in a small sanatorium, which he shared with two other senior Party officials who were also suffering from political ailments, were more comfortable than the damp temple at Donghuashan; and his standing among the Party at large was unaltered, for the Ningdu decisions were kept secret. But in other respects his situation was worse.

Six times, in the twelve years since he had become a communist, he had been pushed aside: once, of his own volition, when his faith in the movement faltered, in 1924; a second time in 1927, after the failure of the Autumn Harvest Uprising; again in 1928, when the newly formed Hunan provincial committee deposed him as Special Committee Secretary on the Jinggangshan; then in 1929, during the dispute over guerrilla tactics with Zhu De; the fifth time at Donghuashan in January 1932; and now, finally, at Ningdu. On all previous occasions, however, he had either had powerful friends, who eventually came to his aid, or he had withdrawn for tactical reasons, prefiguring a return in strength later on. This time he had been forced out by a Central leadership which was implacably hostile to him and which he had needlessly provoked, after a conflict which had seriously weakened those, like Zhou Enlai, who might otherwise have helped him.

Once again he grew very thin. He Zizhen was alarmed by his sunken eyes and hollow cheeks. The story went round afterwards that he had contracted tuberculosis, but in fact it seems to have been the same neurasthenic depression that always afflicted him at such times. He told her bitterly: '[It's] as if they want to punish me to death.'

Soon after arriving at the hospital, Mao had an encounter which cast another long shadow over the year ahead. The acting Secretary of the Fujian provincial committee, Luo Ming, was also undergoing treatment there. Mao talked to him at length about the first three encirclement campaigns, and urged him on his return home to promote flexible guerrilla operations so as to help the Front Army break Chiang's fourth campaign, then about to get under way. Luo transmitted these proposals to his colleagues, and before long the Fujian committee began developing a Maoist guerrilla strategy.

The growing importance of the Central Soviet Base Area, coupled with intensified police surveillance in Shanghai, meanwhile convinced Bo Gu and Zhang Wentian that the time had come to join the rest of the leadership in Ruijin. While travelling through Fujian, Bo, too, encountered Luo Ming, who told him enthusiastically about the new tactics the provincial committee was now using, far better, in his view, than the 'rigid and mechanical' directives they had tried to follow in the past. Bo was the last person to appreciate a judgement of this kind. As soon as he reached Ruijin, one of his first acts was to launch a sweeping campaign to root out Mao's influence throughout the soviet districts. Luo's words were distorted to try to prove that he was 'following an opportunist line', had made a 'pessimistic and defeatist appraisal' of the revolutionary situation, and even 'openly advocated the abolition of the Party'.

Soon thousands of officials were under investigation for 'following the Luo Ming line', among them four young men, all in their late twenties, who were especially closely identified with Mao: Deng Xiaoping, then Secretary of the Huichang County Committee in southern Jiangxi; Mao's brother, Zetan; his former secretary, Gu Bo; and Xie Weijun, commander of the locally recruited Jiangxi Fifth Independent Division, who had been with Mao since Jinggangshan. In April 1933, they were brought before a denunciation meeting, where they were taunted as 'country bumpkins' who did not understand that there was 'no Marxism in the mountain valleys'. They, in turn, derided their tormentors as 'gentlemen from a foreign house' (in other words, from Moscow). All four were dismissed from their posts, along with many others of Mao's supporters.

By then Mao was back in Yeping, the small village near Ruijin where the leadership had established its headquarters.

His eminence as Chairman of the Republic meant that he himself was untouched directly by the 'Luo Ming' campaign. He also received support from the Comintern, which urged Bo Gu in March to 'take a conciliatory attitude towards Comrade Mao', use 'comradely influence', and give him full responsibility for governmental work. One of the oddities of Mao's position in the late 1920s and early '30s was that, while his relations with the Chinese leaders whom Moscow promoted to head the CCP were often extremely poor, the Russians themselves took an increasingly positive view of his role. From the Sixth Congress in 1928 onwards, Mao was the only major Chinese leader who was consistently in agreement with

Stalin on all three of the key issues in the Chinese revolution: the primary role of the peasantry, of the Red Army and of the rural base areas. In the Kremlin, this did not go unnoticed.

In far-off Jiangxi, however, the practical effects of Moscow's support were diluted. Previously, Mao and He Zizhen had lived with several other Central Bureau leaders in a fine old stone-built mansion, with a sturdy tiled roof and soaring eaves at its four corners, which its landlord owner had abandoned – not to escape the communists but because a woman had died there and the place was considered unlucky. The leaders lived on the first floor in rooms opening on to a covered wooden gallery around a central inner courtyard, decorated with intricately carved beams and delicate latticed windows and screens. Zhou and Ren Bishi, the two full Politburo members, had the best accommodation; Mao had a slightly smaller room, with clay walls and a brick-tiled floor, next to Zhou's; while Zhu De and Wang Jiaxiang occupied the far end. Between them was a conference chamber where bureau meetings were held.

Bo Gu's arrival, and Mao's eclipse, meant all this now abruptly changed. While still a Bureau member, Mao was politically so isolated that sometimes days passed without him seeing his colleagues. Zhou and Zhu De were at the front, and that spring Wang was severely wounded by shrapnel from a mortar shell. The others ostracised him. In April, his exclusion became even more pronounced. The nationalists began regular air raids against Yeping, and Mao and other 'non-essential personnel' were ordered to move to Shazhouba, another village about ten miles to the west. There, his only social contact was with his brothers and with He Zizhen's sister and parents, themselves under political pressure as a result of their relationship with him.

Time weighed heavily on Mao's hands. In the rare intervals of calm on the Jinggangshan, he used to discuss poetry with Zhu De and Chen Yi. They would cap each other's quotations with lines they had learned by heart as young men from the works of the great Tang dynasty writers, Li Bai, Lu You and Du Fu, in the golden age of Chinese poetry, a thousand years before. He Zizhen remembered how Mao's face would light up when literature was mentioned. Reading was such an addiction that he had especially large pockets made on his jackets, big enough to slip a book inside. Usually, she said, he spoke little, but when the subject turned to literary topics he would talk animatedly for hours on end. Once he sat up arguing all night with her about his favourite novel, *The Dream of the Red Chamber*, which, characteristically, he interpreted as a struggle between two factions within a great and powerful household.

Through the summer of 1933 and most of the year that followed, Mao found himself with a surfeit of leisure in which to read and talk, but, beyond his immediate family, no companion with whom to share it. Once again, he could only wait, hoping for better days. This time there was less certainty than ever that better days would come.

As Head of State, and of government – Chairman of the Republic, and Chairman of the Council of People's Commissars – Mao had had overall responsibility, from November 1931 onwards, for civil administration in the base area. This involved the drafting and promulgation of immense numbers of laws and regulations, intended to endow the new Chinese Soviet Republic, notionally at least, with all the administrative machinery necessary for a modern state.

In practice, Mao's chief concern was with the economy. His speeches throughout this period were full of patriotic appeals to the peasantry to 'carry out the spring vegetable planting well', and warnings that 'there must be absolutely no more opium cultivation; cereals should be planted instead.' His job was to ensure that the base area provided the Red Army with food, clothing and other basic supplies, and to control the black-market trade with the White areas in essentials such as salt, which had to be smuggled in from outside. A Red postal service was set up. A People's Bank, headed by Mao's second brother, Zemin, issued banknotes denominated in *guobi* ('national money'), printed in red and black ink on crudely made grass-paper, with an effigy of Lenin in the centre against a frieze of marching workers and peasants with carrying-poles, striding triumphantly forward to a bright, new communist future. The currency was backed by silver, initially expropriated from landlords but later increasingly derived from taxes, imposed on a sliding scale so that the brunt was borne by merchants and rich peasants, and from the forced sale of 'revolutionary war bonds'.

The key economic issue was land reform. In rural China, the possession of land gave life: if you had fields, you could eat; without fields, you would starve. Among a nation of 400 million, 90 per cent of whom were peasants, land redistribution – taking from the rich and giving to the poor – was the primary vehicle carrying the communist revolution forward, the fundamental point of divergence between the CCP and the Guomindang.

Mao's views on this crucial topic were extremely radical. On the Jinggangshan, he had ordered the confiscation of all land without exception, even that owned by middle peasants. Everyone, child or elder, man or woman, rich or poor, including men who were absent serving in the Red Army, was then allotted an identical share, regardless of class background or any other factor. Ownership was held notionally by the state, and once the distribution had been made, the sale or purchase of land was forbidden.

The system of equal distribution according to the number of mouths to feed had the merit of simplicity, Mao argued, and ensured that even the poorest families could survive.* Li Lisan and Bo Gu both disagreed, one finding it too 'leftist', the other, not 'leftist' enough. Li called for land to be distributed on the basis of each family's labour power (which in practice favoured rich peasants). Bo wanted class origin to be the criterion (which had the contrary effect).

Both methods posed an insuperable dilemma. The rich peasants, having more capital and farm animals, were the most productive villagers. Yet in class terms, they were landlords in the making, struggling (as Mao's father had done) to heave themselves one more rung up the ladder, to a more prosperous and, necessarily, more exploitative position. They constituted, in Mao's phrase, 'an intermediate class' in the countryside, a sort of political swing group which, if squeezed too harshly, would instantly switch allegiance. If the communists adopted moderate policies, the economy in the base area boomed, but class struggle faltered; if a class approach were followed, the economy faltered and food shortages ensued. Caught between these conflicting imperatives, policy lurched first

---

* In the land reform movement after 1947, a similar system was used until moves towards collectivisation eliminated individual land-holding altogether. When, after Mao's death, collectivisation was reversed, the result was again similar to the pattern on the Jinggangshan. As of 1999, there was still no freehold land ownership in China, either in the cities or the countryside; and the amount of land contracted out for farming by each peasant family was once more directly proportionate to the number of mouths to be fed.

one way, then the other, in accordance with the prevailing political wind.

That, however, raised a further problem.

If graduated policies were to be applied, as was the case from the end of 1928 onwards, a method of assessment had to be devised to distinguish poor, middle and rich peasants, and landlords. Was a rich peasant one who used hired labourers? Or was usury also a criterion? Should the whole of a rich peasant's land be confiscated? Or only that portion that he could not cultivate himself?

For hundreds of thousands of families, the answers to such questions were, in the most literal sense, the touchstone of survival. Slightly more flexibility here, a slightly harsher policy there, might require no more than a displaced comma in a Party document. In the villages it could make the difference between a family just managing to scrape by, and having to sell a child whom otherwise it could not feed. Mao himself reported, after an investigation in southern Jiangxi:

> [In a] village consisting of 37 households . . . five households had sold sons . . . All five had become bankrupt; consequently they had to sell their sons to repay their debts and buy food. The buyer was either a member of the gentry . . . or a rich peasant [who wished to purchase a male heir]. There are more gentry buyers than rich peasant buyers. The price of a boy ranges from a minimum of 100 [Chinese] dollars to a maximum of 200 dollars. When making this transaction, neither the buyer nor the seller call this business 'selling'; rather they call it an 'adoption'. But the world in general calls it 'selling a child'. An 'adoption contract' is also commonly called a 'body deed' . . .
>
> [When the sale takes place] more than ten relatives and friends might be present [as go-betweens] and are paid a 'signature fee' by the buyer . . . The ages of the boys sold range from three or four years old to seven or eight, or [even] to 13 or 14. After the deal is made, the matchmakers carry the boy on their back to the buyer's house. At this moment the biological parents of the boy always weep and wail. Sometimes couples even fight with each other. The wife scolds the husband for his uselessness and his inability to feed his family, which have forced them to sell a son. Most of the spectators weep too . . .
>
> A child of four or five brings the highest price because such a child can easily 'develop a close relationship'. In contrast, the price of an older child . . . is lower, because it is difficult to develop such a relationship and the boy can easily escape from his adoptive parents . . .

On hearing that a borrower has sold a son, lenders will hurry to [his] house . . . shouting cruelly: 'You have sold your son. Why don't you repay me?' Why does the lender act like this? Because it is a critical moment for his loan. If the borrower does not repay [him] after selling a son, the lender knows that he will never have another chance to get his money back.

The problems of China's peasants fascinated Mao. After his land-mark survey of the peasant movement in Hunan in the winter of 1926, he returned to the subject again and again, on the Jinggangshan in 1927, and from 1930 onward in Jiangxi, when he was developing his arguments against the 'rich peasant line' ad-vocated by Li Lisan and favoured by many provincial cadres. It was better, he wrote in May of that year, to investigate one place in depth, than to make a superficial study of a larger area, for 'if one rides a horse to view the flowers . . . one cannot understand a problem profoundly even after a lifetime of effort'.

The most detailed of these rural investigations was carried out in 1930 in Xunwu, a border county at the junction of Jiangxi with Fujian and Guangdong.

The result was an astonishing document, 60,000 words long, which described in mesmerising detail the daily routine of rural life in the county town and surrounding areas. Xunwu *xian*, a walled town with 2,700 inhabitants, had 30 or 40 brothels, 30 bean-curd stores, 16 general stores, 16 tailors' shops, 10 inns, 8 barber shops, 7 food stores, 7 herb shops, 7 wineshops, 7 jewellery stores, 5 salt shops, 3 butchers, 3 blacksmiths, 2 tobacconists, 2 umbrella-makers, 2 coffin-makers, a furniture-maker, a fireworks maker, a tinsmith and a watch repairer as well as innumerable street stalls, tea-houses, restaurants and periodic markets. Mao omitted opium dens, presumably because they had been closed after the communists took over. He did include, however, a meticulous enumeration of all 131 different types of consumer goods available in the shops, from nightcaps to suspenders and safety razors to conch buttons; of the 34 kinds of cloth, from gambiered gauze to raw silk; and the dozens of different seafoods, fish and vegetables, some, like dried star-fruit and cloud-ear fungus, so rare that only a few pounds were sold each year. He listed the goods which the county exported to neighbouring districts – 200,000 US dollars'-worth each year of rice, tea, paper, timber, mushrooms and camellia oil – and the tracks and paths by which porters and mules transported them. Almost every shopkeeper was identified by name, and his family circumstances, political views and even social habits carefully itemised: thus, the owner of a certain food store 'liked to whore in the past, but now he has stopped on account of his wife (her bride-price was 250 Chinese dollars)'; the proprietor of the town's largest general store 'also likes to use his money for whoring and gambling'.

Prostitutes, who accounted for 6 per cent of the town's population, merited a section of their own. Mao listed the fourteen best-known by name. Most were young, he noted, and came from the district of Sanbiao: 'The people of Xunwu have a saying: "Whores from Sanbiao; glutinous rice from Xiangshan." This means that the women of Sanbiao are very pretty.' The reason there were so many brothels, he explained, was that more and more sons of gentry families were being sent to the new Western-style schools: 'The young masters break away from the warmth of their families when they go to town to study; so they feel quite lonely, and leave a lot of footprints leading to the brothels.'

In the county as a whole, 80 per cent of the inhabitants, including almost all the women, were either wholly illiterate or knew fewer than 200 characters. Five per cent were able to read a book. Thirty people had attended university. Six young men had studied abroad: four in Japan, two in Britain.

The most important section of the report dealt with land ownership. Mao listed twenty great landlords, commencing with Pan Mingzheng, known locally as 'Uncle Shitcrock', whose capital amounted to 150,000 US dollars, an astounding sum in so poor a region, and more than a hundred lesser landowners, each with a detailed note of their wealth, education, family connections and political standpoint. This last, Mao noted, was not wholly a function of class: some of the middle-ranking landlords were progressive, or at least 'not reactionary'. At the top of the scale, the big landlords accounted for 0.5 per cent of the population; small landlords, 3 per cent; rich peasants, 4 per cent. Middle peasants made up 20 per cent, and poor peasants and hired hands the remainder. Later the same year Mao obtained similar figures from a survey in Xingguo county.

On that basis he could argue that the rich peasants were 'an extremely isolated minority' and that his opponents in the South-west Jiangxi Party, by exaggerating their importance (and demanding that they receive favourable treatment), were guilty of 'right opportunism'. The rich peasants, he declared, were 'the bourgeoisie of the countryside' and 'reactionary from start to finish'. Not only should their surplus land be confiscated, but the Party must introduce a policy of 'drawing on the fat to make up the lean' – whereby rich households would have to give up some of their remaining good land in exchange for less fertile holdings owned by poorer families.

In the spring of 1931, however, when Wang Ming and the Returned Students took over, this was judged to be still far too moderate.

Stalin was then ratcheting up his anti-kulak campaign, which would lead to the physical extermination of 12 million Russian 'rich peasants'. Accordingly, the Returned Students decreed that all rich peasants' land and property (not just the surplus) should be confiscated. When redistribution occurred, landlord families would receive nothing, which meant that many starved; rich peasants would get 'relatively poor land' in proportion to their labour power; poor and middle peasants would get the best land based on the number of mouths they had to feed.

To ensure that these harsh new standards had been properly applied, Bo Gu ordered a Land Investigation Movement and, in February, 1933, appointed Mao to head it. There may have been an element in this of making the punishment fit the crime. Mao had been responsible for the previous policy, which was judged to have been too soft: let him now be the one to put it right. But he was in any case the obvious candidate to direct a movement of this kind, for the same reason that Wang Jingwei had chosen him to head the GMD Peasant Institute in 1926, and Chen Duxiu, a few months later, to head the CCP's first Peasant Committee. He knew more than any other Party leader about the dynamics of rural life and was better placed than anyone else to deal with the endless practical problems the land reform kept throwing up.

Rules were needed, for instance, for dealing with ponds; with buildings; with fallow land; with hills and forests; with bamboo thickets; with 'green crops', planted but not harvested, at the time of redistribution.

Then there was the question of whether redistribution should be conducted on the basis of the township, the village, or the district? If the village, clan loyalties overrode class and economic interests, and the reforms were blunted. But redistribution on the basis of a district, which might have a population of 30,000 or more, was too unwieldy to win the peasants' support. And what happened when definitions clashed? What should be done with a small landlord who was recognised as a progressive? Or a poor peasant who abused his class status to become a local tyrant?

That autumn, Mao produced an encyclopaedic set of regulations, which sought to answer such questions. The key distinctions he drew were between landlords, rich and middle peasants. For a family to be classified as rich peasants, at least one person must take part in productive labour for a minimum of four months a year, whereas in a landlord household none did so; and it must obtain at least 15 per cent of its income from exploiting others – by hiring labour, letting fields, or from interest on loans. A middle peasant household was one that obtained less than 15 per cent from such sources. Schoolmasterly examples were given, to show how the sums should be worked out:

> A family with 11 mouths to feed and two people working has 160 *dan* of fields yielding a harvest worth 480 dollars. They have two parcels of hillside tea-oil fields, which bring in 30 dollars a year. They have one pond, producing 15 dollars, while pig breeding and so on generate 50 dollars a year. For seven years, they have hired a farm labourer, the value of whose surplus labour amounted to 70 dollars a year. They made a loan at 30 per cent interest, bringing in 75 dollars a year. They have a son who is a scholar and who bullies people by relying on influence.
>
> Assessment: This family has two people working itself, but hires a labourer and makes substantial loans. Its income from exploitation is more than 15 per cent of its income. Although there are many family members, they have a good deal of money left over after expenses are paid. They are therefore rich peasants and should be given poor land. The scholar, who is a member of the bad gentry, should be given no land at all.

Mao urged that the regulations be applied with 'extreme caution', since determinations of status were 'life or death decisions' for those involved. This was a pious hope. As he well knew, the whole thrust of the movement militated against the rational, finely calibrated approach that he had laid down. Land reform, he wrote, was 'a violent and ruthless class struggle', the aim of which was 'to weaken the rich peasants and wipe out the landlords', and when necessary the 'big tigers' among them should be paraded before public meetings, sentenced to death by the masses and killed.

In such circumstances caution was the exception. The poor peasants who sat in judgement knew that the more 'landlords' and 'rich peasants' they were able to winkle out, the more land they would have to 'redistribute' to themselves. In many districts, terror-stricken middle peasants fled to the mountains, for fear of being reclassified as rich peasants and rendered destitute.

In the event, the movement was cut short, for the entire area was reoccupied by the nationalists less than eighteen months later. But its effects would last far longer. After 1933, in the Red areas, class origin became the ultimate determinant of an individual's worth and fate. From that root grew a poisonous blight that China was still trying to shake off more than half a century later. In many places, well into the 1980s, grandchildren of landlords and rich peasants found that family status still counted far more than ability, intelligence and hard work in deciding what opportunities were open to them, and what doors irrevocably shut. Even when class factors finally became less important, traces of the old hatreds lingered on.

The Land Investigation Movement was accompanied by a paranoid drive to wipe out what were termed 'feudal and superstitious counter-revolutionary organisations'. It had close parallels to the earlier campaign to eliminate AB-*tuan* elements. Mao was once again intimately involved. Large numbers of 'alien class elements', he declared, had concealed themselves within local soviet governments and the armed forces to carry out sabotage. 'It is an urgent task that does not admit of the slightest delay . . . to launch a final attack on the feudal forces and wipe them out once and for all.'

The man chosen to direct the new campaign was the base area's head of Political Security, Deng Fa, a swashbuckling character with an infectious grin, whose twin passions were horse-racing and sharp-shooting. For all his mischievous smile, Deng Fa was a man much feared. His bodyguards carried curved, broad-bladed, executioner's swords, with red tassels on the hilts. In Fujian, in 1931, he had presided over a purge of Social Democrats in which thousands had perished. Now, with Mao's approval, he laid the groundwork for many of the practices which would become indelibly associated with later communist political movements.

Lists of doubtful class elements, 'landlords, local tyrants and evil gentry', were circulated for reinvestigation. 'Denunciation boxes' were set up in towns and villages, where people could place anonymous notes, informing on their neighbours. Legal safeguards were suspended: when people were 'obviously guilty', Mao said, they should be executed first and a report made later. A still more sinister development, also undertaken with his approbation, was to claim that non-existent organisations had been discovered – such as the 'Single-minded Society', the 'Extermination Brigades' (at Yudu), and the 'Secret Watch Brigade' (at Huichang) – as a pretext for rounding up and interrogating those suspected of disloyalty in the areas where they supposedly operated.

Thirty years later, all these techniques, which Mao and Deng Fa pioneered in Jiangxi, continued to flourish under the People's Republic.

The laws drawn up under Mao's chairmanship proved equally enduring. The 'Regulations for the Punishment of Counter-revolutionaries', published in April 1934, listed more than two dozen counter-revolutionary offences, for all but one of which the penalty was death. The crimes listed included, 'engaging in conversation . . . to undermine faith in the soviets' and 'deliberately transgressing laws'. As though that were not enough, a final catch-all clause specified that 'any other counter-revolutionary criminal act', not separately described, would be punished analogously. That article remained part of the Chinese legal code until the early 1990s.

Such practices were not unique to Chinese communism. Catch-all statutes were a legacy of the Chinese Empire, from which the social controls of both the communists and the nationalists stemmed: a Guomindang law of 1931 prescribed the death penalty for 'disturbing the peace'. For both, the purpose of law was political – to uphold orthodoxy, not individual rights.

The election procedures codified at Ruijin at the end of 1931 likewise set a pattern that continued into the People's Republic. The voting age was fixed at sixteen, for both women and men. But the right to vote was limited to 'correct' class categories – workers, poor and middle peasants, and soldiers – while merchants, landlords, rich peasants, priests, monks, and other ne'er-do-wells were explicitly excluded. Candidates were nominated by local Party committees on the basis of class status and of 'political performance', which Mao explained meant having 'the right kind of thinking'. Ability came a distant third. Voting was by a show of hands, and an election was considered successful if 90 per cent of the population took part.

A quarter of those elected, Mao insisted, must be women. This was part of his assault on what he called the 'feudal-patriarchal ideological system' of traditional China. In Hunan, five years earlier, he had noted approvingly the prevalence of extra-marital affairs, and even 'triangular and multilateral relationships', among poorer women 'who have to do more manual labour than women of the richer classes' and therefore had more independence. The sensualist in Mao relished women's sexual liberation.* But his stress on promoting women had a broader purpose. Half a century before it became a fashionable slogan among Western development theorists, Mao understood that to educate a man was to educate an individual, but to educate a woman was to educate a family.

Since the key to women's emancipation was a change in the marriage system, for which Mao had been campaigning ever since the May Fourth movement, the first law to be enacted in the new Chinese Soviet Republic – and the first law enacted by the People's Republic, nearly twenty years later – gave men and women equal rights in marriage and divorce.

Not everyone was pleased. Peasant husbands complained, 'The revolution wants to get rid of everything, wives included.' Some women were so intoxicated by their new freedom that they married three or four times in as many years. To preserve military morale, a special clause was inserted for Red Army soldiers, whose wives could seek divorce only if their husbands agreed. But the communists' core constituency, young men from the poorest families, who, under the old system, would not have been able to buy a wife for years, if at all, were delighted with the new arrangements, as were most peasant women. Mao himself regarded it as one of his greatest achievements. 'This democratic marriage system', he affirmed, 'has burst the feudal shackles that have bound human beings, especially

---

* There is abundant evidence for this in Mao's writings. In his report from Xunwu, which was supposed to be about economic matters, he devoted an inordinate amount of space to changing sexual mores, describing at length how young women had become 'more liberal in their behaviour', staying out late in the mountains on the pretext of cutting firewood, while 'affairs between them and their young male friends . . . increased. Couples "made free" with each other openly in the hills . . . There were married people in almost every township who had new lovers.'

women, for thousands of years, and established a new pattern consistent with human nature.'

While Mao wrestled with the land reform and his other governmental duties, he remained politically in a twilight zone, neither in power nor entirely in purgatory. In the early spring of 1933, Zhou Enlai and Zhu De, ignoring the Centre's 'forward, offensive line', defeated Chiang Kai-shek's fourth encirclement campaign by using tactics broadly similar to those Mao had argued for. Several of Chiang's top divisions were severely mauled, and the Red Army took 10,000 prisoners. Encouraged, Mao attempted in March, a few weeks after leaving hospital, to resume a minor military advisory role, as a member of the rear echelon of the Central Bureau. Bo Gu immediately put a stop to it.

Three months later, Mao asked the Bureau to reconsider the decision it had taken at Ningdu to remove him from the military chain of command, arguing that it had been unjust. Bo retorted that the decision had been entirely correct and that without it, victory over the fourth encirclement would not have been achieved.

During the autumn, Mao's position improved somewhat, as his role in the Land Investigation Movement gave him renewed prominence and the campaign against the 'Luo Ming line' waned. In September, soon after the start of Chiang Kai-shek's fifth encirclement campaign, he and Zhu De became involved in negotiations with the Fujian-based 19th Route Army, whose commanders had become disaffected by Chiang Kai-shek's refusal to take effective action against the Japanese in Manchuria. In October, a truce was agreed, and a secret communist liaison office was set up at the 19th Route Army's headquarters. Four weeks later, the Fujian leaders proclaimed the establishment of a People's Revolutionary Government, independent of Chiang's Nanjing regime.

This could, and should, have been a godsend for the Red Army. That summer, Bo Gu had insisted on an exhausting and ultimately unsuccessful campaign to try to expand the soviet base area northward. Chiang, meanwhile, had assembled a force of half-a-million fresh troops, including many of his crack divisions, with 300,000 auxiliaries. Zhu's men, dispersed, demoralised and weary, were no match for the nationalist onslaught. The town of Lichuan, near the

Fujian border 120 miles north of Ruijin, which guarded the northern entrance to the base area, soon fell, and Zhu's attempts to recapture it were beaten off with heavy losses.

Thus, in November, 1933, when Chiang was compelled to withdraw parts of his main force to meet the threat posed by the Fujian rebellion, it seemed that the communists had been rescued in the nick of time.

However, the Party leaders were suspicious of their new allies' motives and commitment. Even Mao, who, throughout the Jiangxi period, had urged his colleagues to exploit differences between the warlord forces, was wary about how much support the rebels should be given. The upshot was that when Chiang launched a full-scale invasion of Fujian at the end of December, far sooner than his adversaries had expected, the communist leaders hesitated. By the time the Red Army did finally start offering the 19th Route Army limited aid, it was already defeated, and the nationalists were able to return to the main task at hand, the encirclement campaign.

During the two months' respite which the Fujian expedition provided, the Central Committee held its long-delayed Fifth Plenum, which underscored anew the ambivalence of Mao's position. He was elected a full member of the Politburo, a post he had last held in the Party's formative years nearly a decade earlier.* The promotion could hardly have been denied him, given his role as 'Head of State' and the backing he had from Moscow. But he was admitted in eleventh and last place in the rank order. Throughout the four-day meeting, Bo Gu and other leaders criticised his 'right-

---

* Mao was one of the five members of the Bureau of the Central Committee, as the Politburo was initially called, from June 1923 to the end of 1924. He returned to the leadership as an alternate member of the CC in May 1927, and was a Politburo alternate from August to November of that year. In June 1928, he was re-elected a full CC member, a position he held continuously for the next forty-eight years. At the Third Plenum in September 1930, he rejoined the Politburo as an alternate member. From the summer of 1931, following the arrest and execution of Xiang Zhongfa, until the convocation of the Fifth Plenum, the Politburo ceased to function (although, confusingly, its members retained Politburo status). It was replaced by the provisional Centre, whose leaders, Bo Gu and Zhang Wentian, were not Politburo members. In the spring of 1933, they took charge of the base area's Central Bureau, which ceased to exist when the Politburo was formally reconstituted in January 1934.

opportunist views', and when it ended, it was announced that Zhang Wentian would replace him as head of government, leaving him only a figurehead role as Chairman of the Republic.

He showed his contempt for these proceedings, which took place in January 1934, by refusing to attend. This was on the pretext of illness – one of Mao's 'diplomatic disorders', Bo Gu mockingly remarked – though ill-health did not stop him presiding over the base area's Second National Congress a few days later, at which he delivered a speech lasting nine hours.

Later Mao would argue that the Fifth Plenum marked the apogee of the Returned Students' 'left-deviationist line'. Bo's report, which was adopted as the plenum's political resolution, cast caution to the winds, proclaiming that a 'direct revolutionary situation', the prerequisite for nationwide insurrection, now existed in China, and that 'the flames of the revolutionary struggle are blazing across the entire country'. Nothing could have been further from the truth. Even as he spoke, Chiang Kai-shek's troops were resuming their inexorable march south.

The 'blockhouse tactics' the nationalists employed in the fifth encirclement were quite different from those of earlier campaigns. This time they built long lines of stone forts, with crenellated battlements and walls up to 20 feet thick, like the watch-towers of medieval Europe, each able to hold a full company of troops and often only a mile or so apart, linked by newly made roads. These 'turtle shells', as the communists called them, stretched in a great arc, more than 200 miles long, along the northern and western sides of the base area. As the GMD armies inched forward, local troops consolidated their control of the areas in the rear, while the vanguard built a new line of blockhouses, a few miles in front of the old. Chiang's German military advisers ensured that the strategy was executed with teutonic thoroughness. In the year the campaign lasted, the nationalists built 14,000 blockhouses, hemming the Red Army and the population it defended into a steadily dwindling base.

The communists had a German adviser, too. Otto Braun, sent by the Comintern, reached the base area from Shanghai at the end of September 1933. He had spent three years studying conventional warfare at the Frunze Military Academy in Moscow. But the tactic he proposed, known as 'short, sharp thrusts', which called for lightning attacks on nationalist units whenever they left the blockhouses to move forward, proved a total failure. It could hardly have been otherwise: Chiang had forced the communists to fight, on his terms, a positional war of attrition in which his forces had a numerical advantage of more than ten to one. Any tactic based on that premise had to fail. The alternative, which Mao suggested at least twice in 1934, was for the entire Red Army to break out to the north or west, and fight outside the blockhouse area, on terrain better suited to its mobile style of warfare, in Zhejiang or Hunan. Whether, in the long term, given the nationalists' overwhelming strength, that would have succeeded any better, is a moot point, for it was never tested. Bo Gu and Braun rejected not only Mao's ideas but all similar proposals as 'flightist' and defeatist.

As the military pressures escalated, political paranoia resumed. In the army, security officers led execution squads on to the battlefield to 'supervise' the fighting. Geng Biao, a 25-year-old regimental commander, recalled what happened when his troops lost control of a key position. 'I saw [Security Director] Luo Ruiqing coming up, with a Mauser pistol, at the head of an "action team". My heart skipped a beat. Something nasty was going to happen! At that time . . . those suspected [of wavering] would be beheaded . . . Sure enough, [he] came straight up to me and pointed his pistol at my head, demanding loudly: "What the hell's the matter with you? Why did you withdraw?"'

Geng was in luck. He was allowed to fight on, and survived to become, years later, China's Ambassador to Moscow. Others were less fortunate. But it was a far cry from the principles of the all-volunteer army that Mao had proclaimed on the Jinggangshan seven years before.

Civilians fared still worse. Mao's land regulations were abandoned, and a Red pogrom was launched in which thousands of landlords and rich peasants were massacred. Tens of thousands fled as refugees to the White areas. In April 1934, the Red Army suffered yet another disastrous defeat, at Guangchang, seventy miles north of Ruijin. With military encirclement came economic strangulation. Newly recruited peasant conscripts deserted in droves. As signs of collapse multiplied, acts of sabotage, rumoured or real, by secret society members and clansmen hostile to the communist cause, fuelled new efforts to 'ferret out counter-revolutionaries', until the whole area was swept up in a vicious spiral of hatred and despair.

Soon after the Guangchang defeat, probably in early May, Bo Gu and Zhou Enlai realised that the base area might have to be abandoned. The Comintern was informed. Bo, Zhou and Otto Braun formed a 'three-man group' to draw up contingency plans.

Mao knew nothing of this. The Politburo was kept in the dark through the summer. In any case, he wanted no part in decisions which he could not influence and with which he disagreed. After the Fifth Plenum, he stopped attending Military Commission meetings, and spent the whole of May and June on a visit to the base area's southern counties, as far away as possible from where the real battles were taking place. At the end of July, when nationalist bombing raids forced the Party to evacuate Shazhouba, he and He Zizhen moved to an isolated Daoist temple on Yunshishan, 'Cloud Stone Mountain', set amid clusters of pine and bamboo in a landscape of fantastically weathered rocks, a few miles further west. The Politburo and the Military Commission were installed in another village nearby, but his contacts with them were minimal. He was 'out of the loop' because he wanted to be.

Yet already there were straws in the wind that the balance of forces was changing.

That autumn, Mao's political troubles began to affect his health. Dr Nelson Fu, a mission-educated physician who headed the Red Army's primitive hospital service, was sufficiently concerned to assign him a permanent medical orderly. In September, in Yudu, he developed a high fever, and for several days was semi-conscious with a temperature of 105 degrees. Dr Fu made the 60-mile journey there on horseback and diagnosed cerebral malaria, which he cured with massive doses of caffeine and quinine.

The man who ordered Dr Fu to go to Yudu was Zhang Wentian, Mao's successor as head of government and formerly Bo Gu's close ally. After the Guangchang defeat, he and Bo had had a fierce row over Otto Braun's military tactics, which Zhang said took no account of the terrain or the disparity of forces. Bo retorted that he was talking like a Menshevik. Over the next four months, as communist strength, dispersed across six fronts, bled away in a debilitating war of attrition, while Bo promoted the slogan, 'Don't give up a single inch of Soviet territory!', Zhang's disaffection deepened. When Mao was at Yunshishan, Zhang was the only senior leader to visit him. He no longer concealed his frustration with Bo's dogmatism and inexperience.

Wang Jiaxiang, who had been wounded during the fourth encirclement, and now had to be carried everywhere on a litter with mortar fragments embedded in his body, was another Politburo member sympathetic to Mao's cause.

Bo Gu at first gave instructions that the three men should be assigned to different units during the Red Army's 'strategic transfer', as the forthcoming operation was euphemistically termed, but for reasons that are unclear, later relented and let them travel together. It was a political misjudgement which was to cost him dear.

But Zhang and Wang were essentially bit-players. The man Mao really needed to win over was Zhou Enlai. During the disastrous battles at Guangchang, Zhou had been pushed aside, and Bo himself had taken over as General Political Commissar. From then on, Mao cultivated him assiduously. During his tour of the southern counties in June, he sent Zhou a careful briefing on the military situation along the south Fujian front. That autumn, he compiled a handbook on guerrilla warfare, which Zhou arranged to have issued as a Military Commission directive. It was Zhou who had approved Mao's request to go to Yudu in September, where he drew up a security report on the districts which were to serve as the main staging area for the Red army as it gathered for the move west. But Zhou was a cautious man. He had had his fingers burnt once before defending Mao. As long as Bo Gu had the Comintern's backing, he was not disposed to mount a challenge.

Thus, when Mao, accompanied by his bodyguards, set out from Yudu's East Gate, late on the afternoon of Thursday, October 18, 1934, for the crossing point on the Gan River, everything was still to play for.

After seven years of warfare, three of them as Head of State of the Chinese Soviet Republic, his future was as uncertain as ever. All his worldly possessions amounted to two blankets, a cotton sheet, an oilcloth, an overcoat, a broken umbrella and a bundle of books. He crossed the river by torchlight, as darkness was falling, with what mixed feelings at leaving the base area can only be imagined. An armada of small boats plied the wide, slow muddy waters. It took three days before the entire column, more than 40,000 troops and a similar number of Yfsenes and bearers, was safely on the other side. He Zizhen, who was pregnant again, had left Ruijin earlier as part of the nurses' contingent, one of only twenty women, all senior leaders' wives, who were allowed to take part. In order to accompany Mao, she had had to steel herself to leave behind their son, now nearly two years old. Xiao Mao, as the little boy was called, was given to his old wet nurse to be looked after. But in the whirlwind of destruction that engulfed the area after the communists withdrew, he was moved for safety to another family. There, all trace of him was lost. After 1949, an exhaustive search was undertaken. Xiao Mao was never found. With his abandonment, another small part of Mao's humanity withered on the vine.

CHAPTER TEN

In Search of the Grey Dragon:
the Long March North

While the Red Army marched and fought its way across southern
China, half a world away in Europe, the cockpit of the Powers, the
dread forces that had emerged from the carnage of the Great War
were making the opening moves, during that baleful autumn of
1934, in a brutal quest for power that would soon ignite a human
holocaust on an altogether different scale. In the elegant spa of Bad
Wiessee, an hour's drive from Munich, the German Chancellor,
Adolf Hitler, chose the pre-dawn hours of June 30 to launch a
blood-purge of the Sturm Abteilung, the brown-shirted storm-
troopers who had helped him to power but had since become an
obstacle, arguably the final obstacle, to uniting the Nazis, and the
nation, behind the Führer and his ideas. From the murderous seeds
sown that night grew the practice of the Nazi extermination camps
where more than six million Jews, gipsies, homosexuals, communists and other 'undesirables' perished. Five months later, Stalin
followed suit. On the afternoon of December 1, a lone assassin
entered the Communist Party's regional headquarters in Leningrad
and shot dead Stalin's putative, and too popular, rival, Sergei Kirov.
It was the signal for the Great Purge, which, over the next five years,
swept away in a cleansing fire more than a million old Bolsheviks,
Trotskyists, Bukharinites, Red Army commanders, party functionaries, secret police, and opponents, real and presumed, of every
political stripe, and sent ten times that number into labour camps,

where many also perished. On that scale of things, Mao's campaign against the AB-*tuan* in Jiangxi four years earlier was but a distant foretaste, an *amuse-gueule* before a blood-feast.

But the event for which 1934 is remembered above all, the trigger for the infernal machinery of the far greater slaughter to come, occurred in a much more remote land. On December 5, fighting broke out between Ethiopians and troops from Italian Somaliland in a dispute over water wells at Walwal, a small oasis in the Ogaden Desert. Six days later, as Mao and his comrades gathered for the fateful meeting at Tongdao that paved the way for his resumption of power, Mussolini presented an ultimatum demanding reparations. The Walwal Incident, as it was known, became the pretext for Italy's invasion of Abyssinia, which led in turn to the formation of the Axis linking Italy, Germany, and later Japan, and put the last nail in the coffin of the League of Nations, created a decade earlier expressly to prevent such crises escalating into war.

Neither the communists, in China or in Moscow, nor the imperialist Powers themselves, saw clearly where these shifts were leading. But ever since Japan's occupation of Manchuria, in which the other Powers had acquiesced, Russia had felt menaced. It had already been defeated once by Japan, in 1905, and memories were still fresh of the depredations of the Japanese army in Siberia after 1918. From 1931 onward, Moscow and its acolytes began chanting a new tune. The main danger now, they declared, was not that contradictions within the imperialist camp would lead to a new world war, but that the Powers, led by Japan, would wage an imperialist war against Russia. This was the basis for the Comintern slogan, 'Defend the Soviet Union!', which Bo Gu and Li Lisan had echoed so faithfully. It was to be realised by creating a 'united front from below,' in which the world communist movement was to mobilise non-communist support for an anti-imperialist, anti-Japanese crusade, while refraining from formal alliances with bourgeois political parties, regarded as irredeemably compromised.

In the world beyond the base area, the Western democracies' appeasement of Germany, Italy and Japan continued until the underlying political realities had become so hideously distorted by the triumph of fear and greed over principle that communist Russia and Nazi Germany signed a non-aggression pact.

In Ruijin, it was all far simpler. For the next five years, the

Party's propaganda to the White areas was dominated by the claim that the communists would fight Japan, but Chiang Kai-shek would not. The Guomindang, Mao wrote, was acting as the 'running dog of imperialism,' selling out China's national interests by 'shameless non-resistance.' So long as Chiang and his allies were in power, opposing Japan would be impossible; therefore the first task of all true patriots was to overthrow the GMD regime. In April 1932, the Chinese Soviet Republic issued a formal declaration of war against the Tokyo government and called for the formation of an 'anti-Japanese Volunteer Army'. Mao and Zhu De offered to sign a truce with any nationalist commander who agreed to stop fighting the communists and oppose Japan instead. In August 1934, when Red Army units broke out of the base area for a diversionary operation in Zhejiang, the Party described them as an 'anti-Japanese vanguard' on their way to fight the invaders in the north.

Among educated Chinese, these gestures resonated. That Japan's aggression had gone unpunished was a terrible humiliation. However much Chiang Kai-shek might argue that the communists must be dealt with first, he had failed to defend the country's honour.

On the other hand, Chiang held power. The communists did not. As they marched out of Jiangxi, and out of the newspaper headlines, to become little more than a footnote to the great events elsewhere, their calls for unity against the Japanese menace seemed to many increasingly irrelevant. 'Communism in China is dying,' wrote Chiang's amanuensis, Tang Leang-li. The treaty-port press agreed. 'If the government follows up the campaign along the lines adopted in Jiangxi,' the Shanghai *China Weekly Review* concluded, 'the whole thing will collapse into plain banditry.'

Only the Japanese correspondents took a more sombre view, arguing that from the safety of the remote interior, the communists would pose a far more formidable challenge than they ever had from the coast. Japan, of course, had its own agenda. Anything that made the Guomindang's hold on China seem more tenuous comforted its imperial ambitions. Yet the Japanese were right about the communists, just as the communists would prove right about Japan.

*

When the Red Army halted at Zunyi, in January 1935, Mao achieved for the first time a dominant position in the Party leadership because his colleagues recognised that he had been right when everyone else (and Bo Gu, Zhou Enlai and Otto Braun, in particular) had been wrong. Had the base area not fallen; had Bo Gu been less insecure and more willing to heed advice; had the Red Army not been so badly mauled in the botched crossing of the Xiang River; had Braun been less of a dictator, Mao's hour might not have come. They turned to him because every other recourse had failed.

Unlike the many earlier occasions when he had languished in disgrace, to find himself resurrected almost overnight, this time his eclipse had been partial and his return was similarly veiled. Officially, he was, and remained, Chairman of the now abandoned Chinese Soviet Republic. The only formal change in his position was his promotion to the Standing Committee of the Politburo, and his designation as chief military adviser to Zhou Enlai (the role that Zhou had tried, unsuccessfully, to obtain for him at the Ningdu conference, two years earlier). There was also a second, more important, difference. This time he was competing not for a subordinate position, as political commissar of an army or secretary of a border region. Now at the age or forty-one, he was aiming for the top.

If Tongdao was the first step, Zunyi and the meetings that followed in the spring of 1935 were the first stage in a conquest of power which Mao had the good sense to realise could only be accomplished slowly. Between Standing Committee member and leader of the Party yawned a political gulf which others had tried to cross, and failed. Between Zunyi and the north-west, the communists' eventual destination, lay a desperate military campaign that none of them could be confident of winning.

The Red Army, in Zunyi, was down to 30,000 men, from 86,000 who had set out three months earlier. It had not gained a major victory for more than a year. That it had survived at all was due less to its own military prowess than to the instinct for self-preservation of the warlords along the way, who had preferred to stand aside and let the communists pass, rather than risk their strength for their nominal ally, and real rival, Chiang Kai-shek.

Mao's first task, therefore, was to try to restore military morale. This proved even harder than he had thought. The Zunyi

meeting itself came to an abrupt end when the military commanders had to race back to their units to fend off an attack by warlord
troops advancing from the south. In the next five weeks, the Red
Army suffered a further series of dismal reverses. An attempt to
cross the Jinshajiang, the River of Golden Sand, in the upper reaches
of the Yangtse, to set up a new base area in Sichuan, almost turned
into a disaster on the scale of the Xiang River defeat. The army
marched into an ambush by combined Sichuan and Guizhou
warlord units. By the time it had fought its way out, another 3,000
men had been lost.

As the army retreated, with the enemy in hot pursuit, a moment
came that He Zizhen had been dreading. She went into labour with
her fourth child. They stopped at an abandoned hut, and she gave
birth in the litter in which she was being carried. The baby, a girl,
was left with a peasant family nearby. Knowing this time that the
separation would be final, she did not even pause to give the child
a name.

Finally, at the end of February, the communists' luck turned. The
battle of Loushan Pass allowed them to retake Zunyi, capturing
3,000 prisoners and routing two Guomindang divisions led by
one of Chiang's top commanders. Mao's relief, and exultation,
produced one of his loveliest poems:

> The west wind blows cold. From afar,
> In the frosty air, the wild geese call in the morning moonlight,
>   In the morning moonlight,
> The clatter of horses' hooves rings sharp,
> And the bugle's note is muted.
>
> Say not the strong pass has an iron guard,
> Today, with a single step, we shall cross the summit,
>   We shall cross the summit!
> There the hills are blue as the sea,
> And the dying sun like blood.

That spring, the Red Army became once again the 'Zhu–Mao
Army', with Zhu De as Commander-in-Chief, Mao as Political
Commissar, and a new 'three-man group' of Zhou, Mao and his ally,
the wounded Wang Jiaxiang, still carried on a litter, providing
strategic guidance. Its old designation, the First Front Army, was
restored. Orthodox military tactics were abandoned. For the next
two months, Mao engaged in a dazzling, pyrotechnic display of

mobile warfare, criss-crossing Guizhou and Yunnan, that left pursuing armies bemused, confounded Chiang Kai-shek's planners and perplexed even many of his own commanders. Four times they crossed the Chishui, the Red River, between Guizhou and Sichuan, before marching south in a vast arc, passing within a few miles of the provincial capital, Guiyang, where Chiang had established his headquarters, and then threatening Yunnan's chief city, Kunming, 400 miles away in the south-west, only to swing north again, finally crossing the Upper Yangtse where it was least expected, at the beginning of May.

Mao himself called the Guizhou strategy the proudest moment of his military career. In Shanghai, the *China Weekly Review* admitted: 'The Red forces have brainy men. It would be blind folly to deny it.' A Guomindang garrison commander said tersely: 'They had Chiang Kai-shek by the nose.'

Chiang's spokesmen scrambled to cover up the government's embarrassment. It was announced that Zhu De had been killed; that his men were guarding his body, wrapped in a shroud of red silk; that the 'notorious chieftain, Mao Tse-tung' was gravely ill, being carried on a stretcher; that the 'Red remnants' had been smashed. But by then the Red Army was already out of reach, encamped outside the walled county town of Huili, 35 miles north of the river, secure in the knowledge that every boat for a hundred miles had been made fast on the northern bank, and that Chiang's Yunnanese troops had neither the means nor the will for pursuit.

There, at an enlarged Politburo meeting, Mao berated those who had doubted him: Lin Biao and his commissar, Nie Rongzhen, who had complained that Mao's tortuous odyssey was exhausting their men to no purpose and had suggested that Peng Dehuai should take operational command instead; Peng himself, always itching for a fight, who had accepted the idea rather too readily; Liu Shaoqi and Yang Shangkun, who had proposed that the army should stop wandering and try to set up a fixed base; and no doubt others besides. Lin Biao, the youngest, still only twenty-seven, was let off with a scolding. 'You're nothing but a baby!' Mao told him. 'What the hell do you know? Can't you see it was necessary for us to march along the curve of the bow?' Peng, as usual, got most of the blame, and made a mild self-criticism. But, in his hour of triumph, Mao could afford to be magnanimous. His aim at Huili was to unite the Party and military leadership behind him for the trials yet to come.

They, on their side, had to recognise that, once again, he had been proved right and they had been proved wrong.

The campaign had not been without cost. The Red Army now numbered little more than 20,000 men. Yet Mao had extricated them from a situation which many had felt was hopeless. Never again, after Huili, would the corps commanders and the Party leaders accompanying the First Front Army challenge Mao's strategic judgements, or his leadership.

The problem remained, however, where the Red Army should go next. As the 'March to the West' had become the 'Long March', one improvised destination after another had been jettisoned. The Politburo's plans to link up with He Long in north-west Hunan; to set up a new base around Zunyi; to establish soviet areas in southern Sichuan, in the Yunnan–Guizhou–Sichuan border region and now in south-west Sichuan, all had been found wanting. The soldiers, and their officers, needed reassurance that their leaders knew where they were headed. At Huili, at long last, a clear decision was taken. They were to go due north, to link up with Zhang Guotao's Fourth Front Army, which had set out three years earlier from E-Yu-Wan and was now based in northern Sichuan.

In the process, they would perform feats of courage and endurance of which epics are made, weaving a dense myth of invincibility and heroism that their nationalist opponents would try in vain to unravel.

After leaving Huili in mid-May, Mao's forces climbed from the lush subtropical plains of the south into broken, high plateau country, never lower than 6,000 feet where the hillsides were ablaze with Tibetan roses, pink and yellow oleander, azaleas, rhododendrons, and all the other exotic plants which nineteenth-century botanists had brought back from the Himalayas to grace English country gardens. This was the land of the Yi, a fierce Sino-Burmese hill tribe who waged an endless war against encroachments by Han settlers from the plains. The Red Army's Chief of Staff, Liu Bocheng, known as the One-Eyed Dragon, having lost the sight of the other in battle, had grown up in the region, and won safe passage by swearing an oath of brotherhood with the Yi paramount chief, sealed by a libation of chicken's blood. Even with this protection, Yi tribesmen picked off Red Army stragglers, taking their weapons and clothes, and leaving them to starve.

Once that gauntlet had been run, they made for the Dadu River, sixty miles further north. There, seventy years earlier, Shi Dakai, the last of the Taiping princes, had been trapped by the armies of the Qing Viceroy and surrendered. Prince Shi was executed by slicing. His 40,000 troops were slaughtered. For days after, the waters ran crimson with their blood. Chiang Kai-shek, like Mao, knew his history: he ordered his commanders in Sichuan to race to secure the crossing points, so that the communist forces could be hemmed in on the right bank.

By then the Red Army had reached Anshunchang, where there was a ferry. But the river was in spate and there were only three small boats, barely enough to get the vanguard across. Mao ordered Yang Chengwu, a regimental political commissar, to make for Luding, a hundred miles upstream, where an ancient chain bridge spanned the river.

The town lay on the old imperial tribute route from the Tibetan capital, Lhasa, to Beijing. But from Anshunchang there was no road, not even a track. Yang's men went by narrow cliff-paths, which, he wrote later, 'twisted like a sheep's gut around the mountains', while the river seethed menacingly hundreds of feet below. It was slow going, and they had to stop to fight an enemy battalion which was defending a high pass. When it rained, the paths were 'slippery as oil,' Yang remembered, and for much of the time there was thick fog. After they broke camp, at 5 a.m. next day, a courier arrived from the Military Commission. Nationalist troops had been reported on the opposite bank, hurrying northward. They would have to reach Luding, still eighty miles away across trackless mountain ranges, within twenty-four hours.

The stupendous forced march that took them there, and the battle that followed, forged a legend which seared itself into the consciousness of a generation of Chinese. Later it would justly be called 'the most critical single incident of the Long March'. Failure would have meant the Red Army's annihilation.

Yang Chengwu's regiment reached Luding at dawn the following day.

The bridge, a single span of thirteen iron chains, with open sides and a floor of irregularly laid planking, a 'tenuous cobweb of man's ingenuity' linking China to High Asia, as one early traveller called it, was 120 yards long. On the western side, the nationalist commander had ordered the wooden floor-planks removed, leaving only the bare chains swinging free. At the eastern end stood the town gate, set in a 20-foot-high stone wall on which machine-guns had been mounted, commanding the approaches. In Yang's own understated words, 'we were taken aback by the difficulties to be overcome.'

Twenty-two men volunteered for the assault. Edgar Snow, a year later, based his classic account of what followed on the stories of the survivors.

> Hand grenades and Mausers were strapped to their backs, and soon they were swinging out above the boiling water, moving hand over hand, clinging to the iron chains. Red machine-guns barked at enemy redoubts and spattered the bridgehead with bullets. The enemy replied with machine-gunning of his own, and snipers shot at the Reds tossing high above the water, working slowly towards them. The first warrior was hit, and dropped into the current below; a second fell, and then a third . . . Probably never before had the Sichuanese seen fighters like these – men for whom soldiering was not just a rice bowl, and youths ready to commit suicide to win. Were they human beings, or madmen or gods?. . .
>
> At last, one Red crawled up over the bridge flooring, uncapped a grenade, and tossed it with perfect aim into the enemy redoubt. Nationalist officers ordered the rest of the planking torn up. It was already too late . . . Paraffin was thrown on to the planking, and it began to burn . . . But more Reds now swarmed over the chains, and arrived to help put out the fire and replace the boards . . . Far overhead angrily and impotently roared the planes of Chiang Kai-shek . . .

The reality was only slightly more prosaic than the myth which Snow created. The assault force did not 'swing out . . . hand over hand'; they crept crabwise along the chains at each side of the bridge, while a second group laid an improvised floor of planks and branches behind them.

But by whatever means, the miracle was that they crossed. History did not repeat itself. Where the Taipings had perished, the communists broke free. By the beginning of June, the whole army was safely on the eastern bank. Chiang Kai-shek's efforts to bottle them up in the mountains had been foiled.

The leadership then met to discuss where to make for next.

Luding lies at the eastern edge of the Himalayas, in the vast icy shadow of Gongga Shan, which soars up 25,000 feet, thirty miles to the south. The easiest route, eastward towards the plains, was ruled out because it lay too close to Guomindang troop concentrations. Another possibility was to follow the Dadu River to the north-west, which would eventually lead them to the Qinghai–Gansu border region. The problem there was that it lay through hostile country, thickly populated by Tibetans who bore no love for Chinese soldiers.

Mao chose the third way, which led across a series of 14,000-foot passes in the Jiajinshan, the Great Snowy Mountains, to the north-east.

. It started badly. In the foothills, Guomindang aircraft spotted the column with which Mao and other Politburo members were travelling, and strafed and bombed it. None of the leaders was hurt, but one of Mao's bodyguards was killed. From then on, it got worse. Otto Braun remembered:

> We went up over the mountain ridge, separating the Tibetan high-land from China proper, on steep, narrow paths. Rivers in full spate had to be forded, dense virgin forests and treacherous moors crossed . . . Although summer had already begun, the temperature seldom rose above 50 F. At night it sank almost to freezing. The sparse population was made up of . . . national minorities of Tibetan extraction, traditionally called *manzi* (savages) by the Chinese, [ruled by] . . . Lama princes . . . They lay in wait to ambush small groups and strag-glers. More and more, our route was lined with the bodies of the slain . . . All of us were unbelievably lice-ridden. Bleeding dysentery was rampant; the first cases of typhus appeared.

For the rank and file, the crossing of the snow-bound peaks was the hardest part of the whole march. They wore only straw sandals and the thin summer clothing they had brought from the south. Mao remembered one unit losing two-thirds of its baggage animals. They fell, and could not get up. Dong Biwu, the Hubei Party leader, who climbed the mountains in the same group as Mao, remembered that men, too, fell and were unable to get up:

> Heavy fog swirled about us, there was a high wind and half-way up it began to rain. As we climbed higher and higher, we were caught in a terrible hailstorm and the air became so thin that we could hardly breathe at all. Speech was completely impossible, and the cold so dreadful that our breath froze and our hands and lips turned blue . . . Those who sat down to rest or to relieve themselves froze to death on the spot. Exhausted political workers encouraged men by sign and

touch to continue moving . . . At midnight [we] began climbing the next peak. It rained, then snowed, and the fierce wind whipped our bodies . . . Hundreds of our men died there . . . All along the route we kept reaching down to pull men to their feet only to find that they were already dead.

On the worst stretches the going was too rough even for stretcher-bearers, and the wounded had to be carried on men's backs. Among them was He Zizhen. Two months after her baby was born, she had been with the nurses' unit, escorting wounded men, when three Guomindang planes appeared. As they began strafing, she ran to help an injured officer to take cover. She was hit in fourteen places. Mao was told that she would probably die. Tenaciously, He Zizhen survived. But several pieces of shrapnel, including one in her head, were too dangerous to remove, and for weeks she was on the brink of death, drifting in and out of a coma.

Mao's decision to take the back route, the deserted trail across the high peaks, proved well-founded. On June 12, when the First Front Army's vanguard reached the valley beyond, it encountered, near the village of Dawei, in Maogong county, an advance unit of Zhang Guotao's Fourth Army. Initially they took each other for warlord troops and shots were exchanged before they recognised each other's bugle calls. Neither army had had any reliable information about the position of the other.

Mao, Zhu De and the headquarters staff arrived five days later, and a great torchlit rally was held to celebrate the two armies' union. There were folk-dancing and theatricals, and Li Bozhao, the pretty, 24-year-old wife of Yang Shangkun, then a regimental political commissar, later to become China's President, entranced everyone with the Russian sailors' dance, the *yablochka*, which she had learned as a student in Moscow. Mao made a speech, and the troops feasted on provisions the Fourth Army had expropriated from local landlords. Over the next few days, other Fourth Army commanders gathered, followed, on June 24, by Zhang Guotao himself. A powerfully built, stately man, four years Mao's junior, he rode in with a large cavalry escort in the middle of a rainstorm to find Mao and the rest of the Politburo waiting by the roadside to greet him. Another welcoming rally was held, and that night, in Lianghekou, an opium-sodden hill village, even smaller and poorer than Dawei, the leaders held a banquet to mark the joyful occasion.

After eight months of continuous fighting, the exhausted soldiers of the First Front Army were ecstatic over the junction with Zhang Guotao's forces. At last they would be able to rest, and rebuild their depleted strength.

Mao and Zhang were not so sure.

The problem was not ideological or political. It was not that they had different visions of the Chinese revolution, or that they favoured different methods for carrying it out. It was a matter of raw power.

Of the 86,000 men who had set out with Mao from Yudu the previous October, fewer than 15,000 now remained. Zhang Guotao had three or four times that number. Mao's men were in summer rags. Zhang's were warmly clothed. Mao's men were combat-weary southerners, unused to the cold mountain climate, underfed and, even when they could get food, unable to digest the local Tibetan *tsampa*, made from barley flour. Zhang's troops were Sichuanese, fighting on their home terrain, well-provisioned, rested and fit.

This might not have mattered if the Party had had a properly constituted leadership, with a clear chain of command. But in 1935 it did not.

The decisions taken at Zunyi were all open to challenge because only six of the twelve full Politburo members had been present. Zhang Wentian, who had become the provisional Party leader, had never been formally elected to the Central Committee, any more than had his predecessor, Bo Gu: both had originally been co-opted by an emergency procedure in Shanghai, in defiance of normal Party rules. In practice, moreover, since the Huili meeting in May, Mao, not Zhang Wentian, had been the dominant Politburo figure.

Zhang Guotao was Mao's equal in seniority. He too was a founder member of the Party. He, too, had been in and out of the top leadership since 1923. If Mao could achieve de facto primacy, what was to stop Zhang Guotao, a no less ambitious man, from trying to do the same?

In the past, the ultimate arbiter of such matters had always been the Comintern. But for the last eight months, the Comintern had been silent. A few days before the evacuation of Ruijin, police in the French concession in Shanghai had raided a CCP safe house and seized six short-wave transmitters. Direct radio contact with Moscow would not be re-established until the summer of 1936.

The two men began manoeuvring, very cautiously, the moment they learned that their forces had made contact, on June 12. Zhang made discreet overtures to Mao's military commanders. Mao, with breathtaking cynicism, played up the role of Otto Braun as proof of Comintern support. In the ten days before they met at Lianghekou, there was a long exchange of probing telegrams, in which the Politburo, at Mao's urging, proposed setting up a base area in the Sichuan–Gansu–Shensi border region, between the Min and Jialing rivers. Zhang begged to disagree; and Mao politely rejoined: 'Please think it over again.' Face to face, each man invariably referred to the other by the honorific, 'elder brother'. But behind the façade of courtesies, the calculus was brutally simple. Zhang was determined to parlay his overwhelming military strength into political power. Mao controlled the Politburo, and could block him. But at what cost?

After three days of talks, culminating in a formal meeting on June 26, chaired by Zhou Enlai in the lamasery of Lianghekou, its walls black with the smoke of yak's butter from Buddhist votive lamps, a compromise was patched together to which Zhang reluctantly assented. The main forces would head north, as Mao had proposed, and fight an offensive campaign of mobile warfare so as not to become 'turtles in an urn', victims once again of the blockhouse strategy that the nationalists had used to such devastating effect in Jiangxi. Zhang was appointed Vice-Chairman of the Military Commission, under Zhu De. But the crucial issue of unifying the command of the two armies, to which all agreed in principle, was left in practice for another day.

On paper, Mao seemed to have the advantage. Zhang had accepted his plan.

However, the agreement quickly proved hollow. When the First Front Army set out for Maoergai, a small settlement a hundred miles to the north, to prepare for an attack on Songpan, the garrison town which controlled the main pass to Gansu, Zhang's Fourth Army refused to follow. Another Politburo meeting was held. Zhang was offered, and accepted, Zhou Enlai's old post as General Political Commissar, which had been vacant since Zunyi. Yet still the Fourth Army held back. The attack on Songpan failed. As the communist forces crawled northward, more crisis meetings were held and more concessions offered. But never quite enough.

On both sides, suspicion and resentment thickened. The nub of their disagreements was over where the Red Army should go next (and, by inference, who had the power to make that decision). Mao continued to advocate going north. Zhang wanted to go west, or south.

To prevent an open split, the Politburo agreed, at a series of meetings in the Tibetan village of Shawo at the beginning of August, that Zhang's powers should be further enhanced. He and Zhu De would take overall command of the entire Red Army, which would be divided into two columns. They would travel, with the GHQ staff, in the left column, comprising mainly Fourth Army troops. Mao and the rest of the Politburo would move with the much smaller right column, of mixed First and Fourth Army units, led by Zhang's deputy, Xu Xiangqian. In return, Zhang agreed that the army should continue to head northward, across the grasslands, a treacherous expanse of marsh and bog, which, after the failure at Songpan, was now the only route open to them if they wished to reach Gansu.

These arrangements were less of a gamble on Mao's part than they might appear. Ultimate control still rested with the Politburo, which he dominated. In any case, they were not intended as a permanent solution, but merely to stave off for a time the showdown which they all knew was coming.

Ten days later, at a meeting at Maoergai held in Zhang's absence, the Politburo Standing Committee gave instructions to begin secretly collecting evidence for the eventual case against him, and approved (but did not circulate) a Central Committee resolution, describing Zhang's proposal to move west, into the isolated high plateau of Qinghai and southern Ningxia, as 'dangerous and flightist'. It added menacingly: 'This policy stems from fear, exaggeration of the enemy's strength and loss of confidence in our own forces and our victory. It is right opportunism.'

For a while, it seemed the new arrangements would pay off. Despite the Centre's harsh language, and Zhang's continuing reservations, the two columns began moving north along separate routes about fifty miles apart. The stage was slowly being set for what Mao would call, years later, 'the darkest moment of my life.'

The grasslands lie at 11,000 feet in an immense basin, 'an inland Sargasso Sea', as one writer has called it, spreading for five thousand square miles along a vast horseshoe bend in the Yellow River, as it descends from the Himalayas in the west to turn north towards Inner Mongolia. Otto Braun remembered:

> A deceptive green cover hid a black viscous swamp, which sucked in anyone who broke through the thin crust or strayed from the narrow path . . . We drove native cattle or horses before us, which instinctively found the least dangerous way . . . Cold rain fell several times a day, and at night turned to wet snow or sleet. There was not a dwelling, tree or shrub as far as the eye could see. We slept in squatting positions . . . Some did not awaken in the morning, victims of cold and exhaustion. And this was August! Our sole nourishment came from the grain kernels we had hoarded or, as a rare and special treat, a morsel of stone-hard dried meat. The swamp water was not fit to drink. But it was drunk, because there was no wood to purify it by boiling. Outbreaks of bloody dysentery and typhus . . . again won the upper hand.

Some died because their bodies could not assimilate the raw, unmilled grain. Later units, maddened by hunger, picked the undigested kernels from the bloody faeces of those who had gone before, washed them as best they could and ate them.

The rank and file, southern plainsmen, brought up in the bustling villages of the coast, had the will to live sucked out of them by the paralysing emptiness of the place. Ji Pengfei, later China's Foreign Minister, then a young medical orderly, recalled: 'Every morning we had to take a count to see how many were left. We found some who were not dead. Their eyes were open. But they could not rise . . . We got them to their feet, and they slumped back into the bog, dead.' In the crossing of the grasslands, the First Front Army lost as many men as it had in the Snowy Mountains, three months before.

Mao's right column crossed first, taking six days to get from Mowe, at the southern edge of the basin, to Baxi, forty miles across the swamp to the north. Back on dry land, they decisively defeated a Guomindang division which had come over the mountains from the east to block their path, inflicting several thousand casualties.

By then it was the end of August. Mao's troops halted to rest, while Zhang's left column, sixty miles away on the western edge of the basin, launched its own attempt to cross the morass. But when they reached the Gequ, a tributary of the Yellow River, they found it was in flood and decided to turn back. Zhang announced the decision in a fretful, oddly childish wireless signal, in which he blamed Mao for their plight and ordered both columns to head back towards the south: 'Facing the endless grasslands and unable to go forward, we will die here if we do nothing. This place is misery . . . You insisted that we make for [Baxi]. Now look at the result! Going north is not only inopportune, but it will cause all kinds of difficulties.'

That triggered a furious exchange of radio messages. The Politburo insisted that the original plan be respected. Zhang insisted that it be abandoned. Then, on September 8, he issued an order to Fourth Army officers seconded to the First Army to return to their original units.

The Politburo met that night. Zhou Enlai, who had been incapacitated for a month after collapsing at Shawo with hepatitis, joined the discussion from his litter. They approved a telegram, pleading in the most conciliatory terms for Zhang to reconsider: 'We, your brothers, hope that you will think it over again . . . and go north. This is a critical moment for the Red Army. It demands that all of us be prudent.'

Next morning, he appeared to back down.

But something about Zhang's message did not quite ring true. Mao's old rival from Jinggangshan, bull-headed Peng Dehuai, sensed a trap and deployed troops secretly in a protective shield around Politburo headquarters. He asked Mao whether they should take the Fourth Army cadres hostage, in case they were attacked. Mao pondered the question, but said no. Two hours later, the Chief of Staff, Ye Jianying, intercepted a second, secret, message from Zhang. It ordered the commander, Xu Xiangqian, and his commissar, Chen Changhao, both Fourth Army stalwarts, to lead the right column back to the south. Between the lines it was implied that if necessary they should use force against anyone who might try to stop them.

Mao, Bo Gu, Zhang Wentian and Zhou Enlai, met again at Peng's First Army headquarters. They agreed that there was now no choice but to strike out on their own. Lin Biao, whose men were at Ejie, twenty miles to the north-west, was ordered to stay where he was, and await developments.

Later Mao would remember that night as a time when the fate of the Red Army hung by a thread. In the year that had passed since they left Yudu, they had marched nearly 5,000 miles, fighting more than two hundred battles, across some of the most inhospitable terrain in the world. Their illiterate peasant troops had endured hardships that no other modern army had survived. Conventional military science holds that a unit which loses a quarter of its men is finished as a fighting force. By the time the Red Army emerged from the grasslands, more than nine-tenths of those who had set out had been lost. Yet now, just as the end seemed in sight, the pitiful remnants of this extraordinary sacrifice were about to complete their own destruction by unleashing a bloody conflict among themselves.

At 2 a.m., in pitch darkness, Peng's forces silently moved out. Ye Jianying and Yang Shangkun stole away from Xu's front head-quarters to join them, bringing with them a set of maps.

Their flight was soon discovered. Chen Changhao proposed impetuously that troops be sent in pursuit. Xu, dour military man that he was, refused. Instead, another of Zhang's supporters, a brash Returned Student named Li Te, set off with a cavalry escort to try to persuade them to return. Otto Braun, who was with Mao, pulled Li from his horse. The Politburo looked on, bemused, as they screamed at each other in Russian. Mao punctured the tension with an aphorism: 'You don't tie the bride and groom at the altar,' he told Li, 'and you don't stop a family feuding.' Any Fourth Army man who wished to stay behind could do so, he added, but the First Army would go north.

Mao and his colleagues sent one last message to Zhang, ordering him to follow them. It concluded: 'No objections! No delay! No disobedience!' There was no response.

While Xu Xiangqian and the rest of the right column made their way back across the grasslands to meet Zhang and a deeply unhappy Zhu De, who would spend the next year with the Fourth Army as a semi-hostage, the First Army leaders had other, more pressing concerns. Nationalist troops were advancing in strength from the east. Peng took Zhu's place as commander, while Mao returned to his old post of Political Commissar. They now had only 10,000 men. If they allowed themselves to be hemmed in against the marshes, they would risk complete destruction.

At Ejie the situation seemed so desperate that Mao revived an idea he had first raised in Sichuan. If they could break through to the north, they would head for the Soviet Union, and try to set up a new base area, with Russian support, on the border of Outer Mongolia or Xinjiang.

In the end, it did not come to that. Two days' march to the east, at Lazikou Pass, an impregnable, heavily fortified nationalist chokepoint on the Bailongjiang, the White Dragon River, where the valley narrowed to a defile only a few yards across, between sheer cliffs more than a thousand feet high, the Red Army scored another of the astonishing military *tours de force* that would make its name a legend. A twenty-man commando group from Yang Chengwu's regiment climbed the precipitous crags behind, and hurled down grenades from the heights, taking the defenders by surprise. It was the last major battle of the Long March. Four days later, on September 21, the First Army entered Hadapu, in southern Gansu, the first Han town they had seen since leaving Yunnan four months earlier. There, from a GMD newspaper, they learned that a communist base area existed in Shensi. The plan to make for the Soviet Union was shelved. Instead, the army headed east across Ningxia, to Wuqi, near Bao'an, in the parched highlands of China's far north-west.

For the next month, they marched six hundred miles across a lunar landscape of great conical hills of bare cappucino-coloured soil, as fine as talcum powder, carved like tiered wedding cakes into high terraces, so smooth they seemed to have been cut with a knife, and scarred with huge keyhole-shaped ravines, plunging down hundreds of feet into wide flat canyons below. It was poorer than any part of Han China they had seen before. Every two or three years, the harvest failed from drought or floods. The people lived in caves, cut into the soft loess cliffs. But to the Red Army, it seemed like a rest-cure. There were skirmishes with Moslem cavalry, but after the breakthrough at Lazikou the main GMD armies held back. Messengers went ahead to the new base area, which was led by two local men, Liu Zhidan and Gao Gang. They had both been arrested in a purge of suspected counter-revolutionaries, launched by Xu Haidong, a Red Army leader who had reached Shensi a few weeks earlier after fighting his way north from the old E-Yu-Wan base area. The Politburo arrived just in time to order their release.

In this arid, desert country, Mao would spend the next twelve years. On October 22, 1935, a year and four days after he had left Yudu, the March was formally declared to be at an end. Of those who had set out with him, fewer than five thousand remained.

During this immense peregrination, the wider world beyond China's borders was not entirely forgotten. In the south-west, the army had put up slogans, calling on Chinese to unite against Japan. In June, Mao had learned from the Fourth Army that Japanese forces had moved into Mongolia, and had issued a statement condemning Chiang Kai-shek's failure to stop them. But it was not until the First Front Army reached Hadapu, in late September, that Mao became aware that the mood in the country was beginning to change, and Chiang's policy of appeasement was finally wearing thin.

That summer, Japan had forced the Guomindang government to withdraw Chinese troops from the vicinity of Beijing and Tianjin; to dismiss provincial officials regarded as hostile to Japan; and to promulgate a humiliating 'goodwill mandate', banning expressions of anti-Japanese sentiment. Widespread public anger had resulted.

Most of this Mao could only guess at. But what he did learn was enough to convince him that the decision to make for Shensi had been correct. 'Zhang Guotao calls us opportunists,' he told a meeting of regimental commanders in mid-September. 'Well, who are the opportunists now? Japanese imperialism is invading China, and we are going north to resist Japan.' A week later the Politburo Standing Committee declared that north Shensi would become 'a new anti-Japanese base.' To Mao, that decision was a beacon. After a year of haphazard retreat, the Party finally had a new purpose. His instinct to go north, even if for the wrong reasons, had been proved right. Zhang's decision to go south had been wrong. Mao had matured since the day, eight years earlier, when, in a letter to the Politburo, he had written of 'jumping for joy' at a decision which had pleased him. But his elation at the Party's renewed mission, to subdue the eastern Grey Dragon, Japan, was just as strongly felt. In the mountains of southern Ningxia, as he looked out for the first time across the highlands that would take the Red Army to its new home, he expressed his feelings in a poem.

> *High on the crest of Liupan Mountain,*
> *Our banners flap idly in the western breeze.*
> *Today we hold fast the long cord,*
> *When shall we bind the Grey Dragon?*

Mao was not alone in turning his thoughts to Japan in the autumn of 1935. Stalin was watching the rise of west European fascism, and the fledgeling alliance between Berlin, Rome and Tokyo, with growing alarm. At the Comintern's Seventh Congress in July 1935, a new strategy was unveiled: the anti-fascist united front, in which communists and social democrats, formerly deadly rivals, were to join together directly in a common struggle to defend the proletariat, and its champion, the Soviet Union, against the fascist Powers.

In France and Spain, the new policy produced Popular Front governments, bringing together heterogeneous coalitions of anarchists, communists, liberals, socialists and syndicalists.

For the Chinese Party, the road was less clear. On August 1, Wang Ming, the CCP's representative in Moscow, issued a declaration calling for the establishment of a 'unified government of national defence' to resist Japan. In China, however, there were no anarchists, liberals and socialists with whom the communists could make common cause. There was only Chiang Kai-shek's Guomindang; and Chiang, in Wang Ming's words, was a traitor, a 'scum with the face of a man and the heart of a beast', as much an enemy as the Japanese themselves. So while Wang's Moscow declaration reiterated the CCP's long-standing offer to join forces with any White army, including Chiang's own GMD troops, provided they stopped attacking the soviet areas and agreed to fight Japan, in practice it appeared no more likely than before that the offer would be taken up.

News of these developments reached Shensi in November. By then the Red Army had moved south to fight off a Guomindang force from Xian. Another month would elapse before the Politburo met at Wayaobu, a walled county town of one-storey grey-brick houses, fifty miles west of the Yellow River, to discuss the implications of the new strategy.

There, on Christmas Day, 1935, it passed a resolution marking a shift in political line every bit as dramatic as the change in military strategy approved a year earlier. At Zunyi, the conventional warfare tactics of the Returned Student leadership had been jettisoned. Now at Wayaobu, the Russian-inspired dogmatism that had dominated Party decision-making since the Fourth Plenum in January 1931 was swept aside as well.

In its place came pragmatic, flexible policies, designed to win maximum public support with a minimum of ideological baggage.

The CCP, the resolution declared, could not lead the struggle against Japan and Chiang Kai-shek by relying on the working class alone. The rich peasants, the petty bourgeoisie, even the national bourgeoisie, all had their role to play too. Leftism, not rightism, it went on, was now the main danger to the communist cause. Left 'closed-doorism' was shown by reluctance to change tactics to cope with new situations; clinging to policies which were divorced from practice; and 'an inability to apply Marxism, Leninism and Stalinism to the specific, concrete conditions of China, thus turning them into rigid dogmas'. Party members needed to understand that victory would be achieved when people became convinced that they represented the interests of the majority of Chinese, not by slavishly following 'empty, abstract communist principles'. To that end, the land and property of rich peasants would no longer be confiscated. Shopkeepers, small capitalists and intellectuals would enjoy the same political rights as workers and peasants, and their economic and cultural freedoms would be protected. Large-scale capitalists would be treated favourably. The 'Workers', Peasants' and Soldiers' Soviet Republic' would be renamed 'the Soviet People's Republic', to signify that all citizens had a place in it.

The Wayaobu meeting was chaired, and the resolution drafted, not by Mao but by Zhang Wentian. This reflected the formal power structure: Zhang was still acting Party leader. But it was also a political manoeuvre, of the kind at which Mao excelled. As a member of the old Fourth Plenum leadership, who better than Zhang to unveil policies which implicitly condemned everything he and his colleagues had once stood for?

Approved on the eve of Mao's forty-second birthday, the Wayaobu resolution marked the start of his ideological ascendancy in the Party. Two days later, at a rally of activists, he savoured his success:

> The advocates of closed-door tactics say the . . . forces of the revolution must be pure, absolutely pure, and the road of the revolution must be straight, absolutely straight. Nothing is correct except what is literally recorded in Holy Writ. [They say] the national bourgeoisie is entirely and eternally counter-revolutionary. Not an inch must be conceded to the rich peasants. The yellow trade unions must be fought tooth and nail . . . Was there ever a cat that did not eat fish [they ask,] or a warlord who was not counter-revolutionary? . . . It follows, therefore, that closed-doorism is the sole wonder-working magic, while the united front is an opportunist tactic. Comrades, which is right? . . . I answer without a moment's hesitation: the united

front, not closed-doorism. Three-year-olds have many ideas that are right, but they cannot be entrusted with serious national or world affairs because they do not understand them yet. Marxism-Leninism is opposed to [such] 'infantile disorders' found in the revolutionary ranks. Like every other activity in the world, revolution always follows a tortuous road, not a straight one . . . Closed-doorism just 'drives the fish into deep waters and the sparrows into the thickets', and it will drive the millions upon millions of the masses . . . over to the enemy's side.

There was no open criticism at Wayaobu of Bo Gu, Zhou Enlai, or any of the other former leftists. Mao's interest was not to alienate those who had been his adversaries, but to win them over. Zhang's role was to help build a consensus for the hard slog that lay ahead.

Hard slog it was. The Shensi base might be a haven of peace after the hardships of the Long March, but it was so poor that even the wretched hill villages of Guizhou and south-west Sichuan looked rich and fertile by comparison, and it was ringed by enemies. Moslem cavalry patrolled the western marches, towards Ningxia and Qinghai. Yan Xishan's White armies held Shanxi, to the east. Zhang Xueliang's North-East Army, which had been expelled from Manchuria by the Japanese, had just been sent to garrison the south. If the Red Army was to survive, let alone prosper, in its new home, it would have to find provisions and recruits, and to neutralise at least one of the hostile forces encircling it.

Even before the Wayaobu conference, Mao had concluded that the weakest point in Chiang's armoury was Zhang Xueliang's Manchurian force. Zhang was in his early thirties, the son of a bandit leader who in the early part of the century had fought and killed his way to become one of the most powerful warlords in China. The Young Marshal, as he was widely known, to distinguish him from his father, the Old Marshal, was a ruthless, often devious, sometimes naive young man, who had recently kicked a powerful opium habit. But he was also a patriot. The Old Marshal had been assassinated by Japanese agents. Zhang himself had lost his country to the Japanese, partly because Chiang Kai-shek had encouraged him not to resist them. Zhang's troops had lost their homes. They had no interest in fighting communists. They hated Japan.

From late November 1935, Mao deluged the Young Marshal's commanders with offers of a truce and a joint campaign against the Japanese invaders. 'We are Chinese,' he wrote. 'We eat the same

Chinese grain. We live in the same land. The Red Army and the North-East Army are from the same Chinese earth. Why should we be enemies? Why should we kill each other? Today I propose to your honourable army that we cease fighting . . . and sign a peace accord.'

Red Army units were instructed to release captured White officers, and to care for the enemy's wounded. In line with this directive, at the beginning of January 1936, Peng Dehuai released an officer named Gao Fuyuan, who had been captured two months earlier. Gao had been a schoolmate of Zhang Xueliang, and when he returned to Zhang's headquarters at Luochuan, a hundred miles south of Wayaobu, he convinced the Manchurian leader that the communists' offers of co-operation were sincere. A week later, Gao arranged for a message to be dropped to Peng from a nationalist aircraft on a supply run to a Guomindang garrison the communists were besieging. On January 19, Mao's envoy, Li Kenong, arrived at Luochuan to begin negotiations.

It turned out to be surprisingly easy. The Young Marshal received Li next day, and agreed at once to adopt a 'passive' stance in the civil war. The only sticking point concerned Chiang Kai-shek. In Li's negotiating brief, Mao had argued that resisting Japan and opposing the 'national traitors' were two sides of the same coin; one was not possible without the other. This the Manchurian leader adamantly rejected. He was ready for a truce with the communists, but not to come out openly against his own Commander-in-Chief. By the time the year was out, both men would change their stance, with momentous consequences. But for the time being, they agreed to differ. At the beginning of March, Mao told the Politburo that a verbal accord had been reached on a ceasefire, and Zhang's forward garrisons at Yan'an and Fuxian, south of Wayaobu, were to be treated as friendly forces.

Five weeks later, Zhou Enlai slipped into Yan'an to talk to the Young Marshal face to face. The meeting, held in a Christian church, lasted most of the night. When Zhou left, just before dawn, they had agreed that the formation of a national government and a unified anti-Japanese national army was the only way forward. Zhang was not yet ready to take an anti-Japanese stand in public, nor would he defy Chiang Kai-shek if he received a direct order to enter areas under Red Army control. But, short of that, the truce would be strictly observed; permanent liaison officers would be appointed; trade between the Red and White areas would be permitted; and the Young Marshal would use his influence with fellow nationalist commanders to secure safe passage for communist units. He even agreed, Zhou reported, to supply the Red Army with arms and ammunition.

With his southern flank thus secured, Mao was free to pursue the other main task that had been decided at Wayaobu: rebuilding the communists' military strength after the attrition of the Long March.

In December 1935, the First Front Army had barely 7,000 men. The local Shensi forces, led by Liu Zhidan and Gao Gang, and Xu Haidong's E-Yu-Wan army, each had 3,000. Mao's target was to recruit another 40,000, a quarter of them that spring. The only realistic way to do this was to mount an expedition across the Yellow River to Shanxi. That carried the risk, as Peng Dehuai pointed out, that they might not be able to get back. Mao went ahead anyway, leaving behind Zhou Enlai and Bo Gu to watch over the Shensi base.

The venture was christened the 'Eastern Expedition to Resist Japan and Save the Nation'. It made good propaganda. But for all Mao's stirring talk of marching to Hebei to confront the invaders, its objectives were much more limited.

The communists did not come within two hundred miles of Japanese units during the two-and-a-half months, from late February to early May 1936, that they spent in Shanxi, Instead, they skirmished with Guomindang troops in a narrow area, no more than fifty miles from the river, where they raised 300,000 silver dollars by expropriating landlords, and gained about 8,000 men, half of them peasants recruited from the Shanxi villages, the remainder prisoners of war. That brought Mao's forces back to 20,000 men, about the same number as he had had a year earlier, but still far fewer than there would have been had the communist leadership remained united. The irony of the CCP's position in the spring and summer of 1936 was that, even as it successfully pursued a united front with the Young Marshal's North-East Army, its own forces remained irrevocably split. Zhang Guotao was still in Sichuan, and the bulk of the Red Army was with him.

Here, too, however, there were signs of change. In the first weeks after the separation, Zhang had orchestrated a series of Fourth Army political conferences, which 'expelled' Mao, Zhou Enlai, Bo Gu and Zhang Wentian from the Party and elected a new 'Central Committee' and 'Politburo' with Zhang himself as General

Secretary. A message was then sent to Wayaobu, ordering the Shensi-based leaders to cease using the 'false title' of Party Centre, and to refer to themselves in future as the CCP Northern Bureau.

Mao, in contrast, acted with great prudence. At Ejie, the day after the split, he had resisted calls for Zhang's expulsion. Though a resolution was passed, denouncing Zhang for 'crimes of splitting the Red Army' and 'right-opportunist and warlord tendencies', it was not published. When the Long March ended, and Mao consolidated his own position, it was as Chairman of the North-West Bureau of the Military Commission (and, concomitantly, CC Secretary for Military Affairs), with Zhou and Wang Jiaxiang as his deputies, not as Commission Chairman *per se*. Even after the announcement that Zhang had set up a rival leadership, Mao took no action for more than a month. Only in January 1936, when it became clear that Zhang would not retract, did he finally authorise the release of the Ejie resolution, making the break official.

By that time Zhang's star was already on the wane. The Fourth Army's southern campaign had at first been highly successful. But during the winter, Chiang Kai-shek's forces counter-attacked and the tide began to turn. While Mao was off on his 'eastern expedition', Zhang suffered two crushing defeats. The Fourth Army was forced back from the fertile Chengdu plain into the barren, isolated regions bordering Tibet.

In May, when Mao returned to Wayaobu, he made fresh efforts to woo back the errant force, promising to let bygones by bygones if only Zhang and his men would come to join them in the north. 'Between you, Comrade Guotao, and we, your brothers, there are no political or strategic differences,' one emollient Politburo telegram declared. 'There is no need to discuss the past. Our only duty now . . . is to unite against Chiang Kai-shek and Japan.'

Soon afterwards, Zhang's troops were joined by the Second Front Army, formed from units led by Ren Bishi and He Long, who had come together in west Hunan a year earlier. The result was to increase Zhang's military strength, but to dilute his political authority. Gradually the pressure to move north grew stronger. At the beginning of July, the new, combined force reluctantly set off across the grasslands, following the same path to Shensi that Mao's First Army had followed a year earlier, with the same horrific losses. There at last, in October 1936, they were met by First Army troops under Peng Dehuai, who had penetrated into Gansu almost as far as Lanzhou. Yet still the deadly game was not quite over. The Fourth Army's main force, more than 20,000-strong, became stranded on the west bank of the Yellow River, cut off by a GMD army which seized the ferry points. Zhang, in his role of General Political Commissar, ordered it to strike out to the west on a suicidal march through the Gansu corridor, where it was cut to ribbons by Moslem cavalry. A year later, the exhausted remnants of that carnage returned to Shensi. The main group, led by Li Xiannian, consisted of only four hundred men.

A month after Zhang's fateful order, on December 6, 1936, he and Zhu De joined Mao and the rest of the leadership at the Politburo's headquarters in north Shensi for a triumphal celebration of unity restored. Next day, Mao was named Chairman of the Military Commission, with Zhang and Zhou Enlai as his deputies.

The *mise-en-scène* was fictive. Zhang's challenge to Mao was over. So was his political career. For the last year, since the meeting at Wayaobu, Mao had had the final word in the Politburo. Now he had final control, too, over all 40,000 Red Army men who remained after the great migration from south China to the north. The destruction of the flower of the Fourth Army in the Gansu corridor hastened Zhang's political demise. But he was finished anyway. Fifteen months earlier, at Maoergai, Mao had already warned that when the time was right, Zhang would be required to answer for the errors that he had made.

While the long struggle with Zhang Guotao was being fitfully played out, Mao was stalking a bigger quarry. At the beginning of March 1936, a few days after Zhang Xueliang agreed to a truce, the Politburo authorised peace feelers to the government in Nanjing.

The purpose, at that stage, was not to try to win over Chiang Kai-shek. He was still counter-revolution personified, the 'chief traitor and collaborator', to be opposed no less fiercely than Japan. One inner-Party directive stated bluntly: 'everyone wants to see traitor Chiang die a terrible death.' The aim of the communist proposals was rather to undercut Chiang's policy of 'internal pacification first, resistance to Japan second'; to strengthen the hand of the anti-Japanese faction of the Guomindang, led by Chiang's brother-in-law, the former Finance Minister, T. V. Soong; and last, but not least, to satisfy Moscow's demands that no stone be left unturned in the search for united front allies. Russia had re-established diplomatic relations with nationalist China in 1933. As the anti-Comintern Axis strengthened, Russian national interests – as distinct from the interests of Russia's CCP allies – made Chiang a potential partner whose armies, in a future war, were not to be ignored.

The proposals were an artful mixture of substance and spin. They called for an immediate end to the civil war; the establishment of a government of national defence, to send a joint army against Japan; free passage for the Red Army to fight the Japanese in Hebei; the restoration of political freedoms; and internal reforms.

Mao calculated that the communists had nothing to lose. If the talks made progress, the split between pro- and anti-Japanese factions in the Guomindang would widen. If they broke down, they would be made public, which would enhance communist standing among an urban public opinion increasingly enraged by Chiang's appeasement policies. All over China, in 1936, hatred of Japan was burning out of control. In the provinces, angry mobs lynched Japanese travellers. For months, the two countries were on the brink of war. Tens of thousands of students, with secret communist encouragement, staged anti-Japanese demonstrations. Intellectuals flocked to join national salvation associations.

But the talks did not break down. By the summer, a bewildering array of back channels and secret negotiating mechanisms was in place. In Moscow, nationalist diplomats held discreet meetings with Wang Ming at the CCP's Comintern mission. In Nanjing, a communist envoy, disguised as a priest, made contact with Chen Lifu, one of the most powerful men in the Guomindang after Chiang himself. Later Mao sent another, more senior, emissary for talks with Chen in Nanjing and Shanghai. The two sides discussed the possibility of the GMD leaders meeting Zhou Enlai in Hong Kong or Canton.

As the negotiations progressed, Mao's attitude to Chiang Kai-shek, and to the wider implications of Japanese aggression, underwent a gradual change. By April 1936, he had concluded that the old slogan, *Fan-Ri tao-Jiang*, 'Resist Japan, Oppose Chiang', was counter-productive. 'Our stand is to oppose Japan and stop the civil war,' he told Zhang Wentian. 'Opposing Chiang Kai-shek is secondary.' A month later he was wondering aloud whether it made sense to go on lumping together all the imperialist powers as a single bloc, when there were obviously growing strains between Japan, on the one hand, and Britain and the United States on the other.

That led to the decision to allow Edgar Snow to visit the base area, in order to publicise the communist cause in the West. In June, the Red Army gave up Wayaobu, and the Politburo moved its head-quarters to Bao'an, a still more remote and impoverished county town in the very heart of the loess country, where the leaders lived in cave-dwellings, cut into a weathered red sandstone cliff over-looking a muddy river. There Mao told Snow, in a prophetic interview on July 16:

> Those who imagine that by further sacrifices of Chinese sovereignty . . . they can halt the advance of Japan are only indulging in utopian fancy . . . The Japanese navy aspires to blockade the China seas, and to seize the Philippines, Siam, Indochina, Malaya and the Dutch East Indies. In the event of war, Japan will try to make them her strategic bases . . . [But] China is a very big nation, and it cannot be said to be conquered until every inch of it is under the sword of the invader. If Japan should succeed in occupying even a large section of China, getting possession of an area with as many as 100 or even 200 million people, we would still be far from defeated . . . The great reservoirs of human material in the revolutionary Chinese people will still be pouring men, ready to fight for their freedom, into our front lines, long after the tidal flood of Japanese imperialism has wrecked itself on the hidden reefs of Chinese resistance.

All through the summer and autumn of 1936, the CCP multiplied public and private appeals to the Guomindang and its leaders to sign a truce and join forces against Japan. In August, with the encour-agement of the Comintern, Mao proposed that the CCP–GMD united front that had existed in the 1920s be revived, and that an 'All-China United Democratic Republic' be set up, incorporating the Red base areas, which would be subject to the same parliamen-tary system as the rest of the country. 'For a people being deprived of its national freedom,' he told Snow, 'the revolutionary task is not immediate socialism, but the struggle for independence. We cannot even discuss communism if we are robbed of a country in which to practise it.' Mao even agreed to change the designation of the Red Army, so as to make it formally part of the nationalist armed forces, under nominal nationalist command. So long as the reality of the Party's control over communist troops and territory was preserved, almost any concession was possible.

In the end, Mao's optimism proved misplaced. At a secret meeting in Shanghai in November, Chen Lifu upped the ante. There would have to be a ceiling on communist troop strength, he said. At first he proposed 3,000 men; then 30,000. Beyond that he would not budge.

The reason soon became clear. Chiang had become convinced that one last push would rid him of the communists, once and for all. On December 4, traffic was cleared from the highway to Xian's well-guarded aerodrome, and police lined the roadside. The Generalissimo was arriving in state to begin final preparations for what was to be his sixth and last, communist encirclement campaign. For the previous three months, Zhang Xueliang had been imploring him to end the civil war and allow the North-East Army to fight Japan instead. Now Zhang was given an ultimatum: either fight the Reds, or face immediate transfer to the south.

Events then moved with bewildering speed.

On Tuesday, December 8, the Japanese War Minister warned that unless China was more accommodating, fresh conflict was inevitable. Next day, thousands of students marched in protest to Lintong, a hot springs resort near Xian where Chiang had set up his headquarters. The police opened fire, and several young people were injured. On Thursday, the 10th, Mao telegraphed Zhang that negotiations with the nationalists had broken down because of Chiang's 'excessive demands'. Twenty-four hours later, Mao's secretary, Ye Zilong, received Zhang's reply. It was quite short, he recalled, but when he decoded it he came across a phrase, in classical Chinese, containing two characters whose meaning neither he nor anyone else in the Secretariat could work out. He took it to Mao, who looked at it quickly and smiled. 'There's good news on the way', he remembered Mao saying.

Otto Braun, who lived nearby, awoke next morning to find Bao'an abuzz with excitement. The field telephone, linking Mao's office to the Politburo and the Military Commission, rang incessantly. Mao himself, who normally worked at night and slept until midday, was already up. A bodyguard told Braun the news, the incredible, sensational news that was spreading through Bao'an like wildfire: Chiang Kai-shek had been arrested shortly before dawn, and was being held at the headquarters of the North-East Army in Xian on the orders of Zhang Xueliang.

The story, as they gradually pieced it together in the hours that followed, was this. On Friday night, after despatching his mysterious secret telegram to Mao, Zhang had summoned a meeting of about a dozen senior commanders. He ordered them to arrest Chiang's General Staff; to take over the Governor's office; to disarm the police and the Blueshirts, a GMD paramilitary force; and to seize the airport. The head of Zhang's personal bodyguard, a 26-year-old captain, then set off with 200 men for Lintong, where, at 5 a.m., he led the assault on Chiang's quarters. The Generalissimo's guards resisted long enough for him to flee up the rocky, snow-covered hillside behind the resort. There, two hours later, he was discovered in a narrow cave, shivering from the cold, dressed only in a nightshirt, and barely able to talk, having left behind his false teeth in the panic of his flight. From this undignified hiding-place, he was carried down on the young captain's back and driven into the city, where Zhang Xueliang apologised profusely for the treatment he had been made to suffer, assured him of his personal safety, and then repeated the demand that he had been making since the summer: that Chiang change his policy, and resist Japan.

The communists, leaders and soldiers alike, received the news rapturously. At a mass rally that evening, Mao, Zhu De and Zhou Enlai demanded that he be put on trial. '[It was] an occasion to stand up and cheer,' Zhang Guotao wrote later. 'It seemed that all of our problems could be resolved at the drop of a hat.'

At a Politburo meeting next morning, Zhu De, Zhang Guotao and most of the rest of the leadership argued that the captive Generalissimo merited death. Not only had he instigated an atrocious civil war and collaborated treasonably with Japan in a shameful policy of appeasement, but only days before he had finally rejected communist offers of an accommodation, preferring continued 'bandit suppression' to national resistance. In his summing-up, Mao declared that the proper course was to bring Chiang before 'the judgement of the people' so that his crimes might be publicly exposed. At the same time, strenuous efforts should be made to gain backing from the left-wing and centrist factions of the Nanjing government for a national anti-Japanese united front, while guarding against moves by right-wing GMD leaders to put down the Xian mutiny by force.

The Party's position was conveyed to Zhang Xueliang in a series of telegrams that weekend, in which Mao and Zhou Enlai stressed the Red Army's solidarity with the Young Marshal's actions and their determination to make the north-west the main base for a future anti-Japanese war.

Almost at once, however, the CCP's scheme began to unravel.

Zhang made clear that his aim was not to punish Chiang Kai-shek, but, as he put it in a 'Telegram to the Nation', addressed to the Nanjing government on the morning of the coup, to make him 'remedy past mistakes'.

> Ever since the loss of the north-eastern provinces, five years ago, our national sovereignty has been steadily weakened and our territory has dwindled day by day. We suffered national humiliation [again] and again . . . There is not a single citizen who does not feel sick at heart because of this . . . Generalissimo Chiang Kai-shek, surrounded by a group of unworthy advisers, has forfeited the support of the masses of our people. He is deeply guilty for the harm his policies have done the country. We, Zhang Xueliang, and the others under-signed, advised him with tears to take another way. But we were repeatedly rejected and rebuked. Not long ago the students in Xian were demonstrating [for the] National Salvation movement, and General Chiang set the police to killing these patriotic children. How could anyone with a human conscience bear to do this? . . . Therefore we have tendered our last advice to Marshal Chiang, while guaranteeing his safety, in order to stimulate his awakening.

This implied that once the Generalissimo had accepted the mutin-eers' demands, which echoed those the communists had been making – namely that the government should be enlarged to include representatives of all patriotic parties; the civil war should end; political freedoms should be restored; and future policy should be based on 'national salvation' (i.e. resistance against Japan) – he should continue as China's leader.

In Nanjing, meanwhile, his detention had triggered a fierce struggle between his supporters, led by his redoubtable wife, Soong Mei-ling, who urged a peaceful resolution, and a loose alliance of right-wing and pro-Japanese leaders, headed by the War Minister, He Yingqing, who wanted bombing raids against Xian and a full-scale punitive expedition. Soong Mei-ling narrowly prevailed, but it was clear that if peace efforts stalled a military offensive would follow.

Thus, by the time Zhou Enlai reached Xian, on December 17,

after a wearisome journey on muleback from Bao'an, followed by a lengthy wait at Yan'an while Zhang sent a plane to fetch him, the situation had already changed. The balance of forces in Nanjing was turning out to be less favourable than the CCP leaders had hoped. The idea of putting Chiang on trial began to look much less attractive.

At this point Stalin intervened – in such a casual, chauvinistic manner, so contemptuous of Chinese communist interests, that Mao was left speechless with rage.

Far from being a 'revolutionary event', the Soviet leader held, Zhang's mutiny was 'another Japanese plot . . . [whose] purpose is to obstruct the unification of China and sabotage the rising anti-Japanese movement.' This was, on the face of it, such an asinine statement that even the Guomindang found it laughable. In a telegram, which probably reached Bao'an at about the same time as Zhou arrived in Xian, the Comintern's Secretary-General, Georgy Dimitrov, explained that what was meant was that Zhang's action was 'objectively detrimental' to anti-Japanese solidarity, and recommended that the Chinese Party 'try to solve the incident peacefully'. The real reason, it later emerged, was that in November, unknown to Mao, Stalin had decided to make a fresh effort to enrol the nationalist government as an ally, to counter the anti-Comintern Pact that had just been established by Japan and Germany, and secret talks were under way in Moscow on a Sino-Soviet security treaty. Chiang's arrest put all that in doubt. To Stalin, the CCP's concerns were irrelevant: nothing could be allowed to stand in the way of the overriding national interests of the world's leading socialist power.

Friction between Moscow and the CCP leadership was hardly new. But in the past the question of blame had always been obscured. Who could say for certain if Moscow had been at fault, or if successive Chinese leaders had misinterpreted Moscow's line?

Stalin's *ukase* of December 1936 was different. The myth of Soviet infallibility and comradeship was definitively shattered. His intervention was all the more galling because, in the end, it changed nothing. The CCP had already accepted that, given Zhang Xueliang's stance and developments in Nanjing, it had no choice but to seek a peaceful outcome. The effect of Stalin's order was merely to undermine Mao's position, destroying the communists' credibility in the eyes of Zhang Xueliang and, in theory at least, removing much of the incentive for Chiang Kai-shek to come to terms.

By then, however, events had developed a momentum of their own. The Generalissimo himself had come round to the idea of mediation. Soong Mei-ling arrived on the 22nd and, with her brother, T. V. Soong, held talks with Zhang and Zhou Enlai. As suddenly as it had begun, it was all over. On Christmas Day, Chiang flew back to Nanjing. The Young Marshal, to show loyalty, went with him.

What had happened behind the closed doors of the Generalissimo's captivity? Both more *and* less than met the eye.

In his public statements afterwards, Chiang maintained he had steadfastly refused to enter into political negotiations and had signed nothing. Technically this was true. Zhou Enlai told Mao that the negotiations had been with the Soongs, and that only after they had reached agreement on Zhang Xueliang's main demands had the Generalissimo given him a verbal undertaking that he would abide by what had been decided. Mao's judgement was that Chiang remained 'ambiguous and evasive', and that there was no way of knowing whether he would honour an accord which he now denied ever making, and which, even if he had, was obtained under duress.

The first signs were uniformly bad. The Young Marshal, the sacrificial lamb whose bold gesture had made the agreement possible, was court martialled, sentenced to ten years' imprisonment, amnestied, and then placed under house arrest (from which he would not be freed until his ninetieth birthday, more than fifty years later, on Taiwan). Far from pulling back, as Chiang had promised, the nationalists sent up reinforcements. In Nanjing, pressure resumed for a punitive expedition. Zhang's troops began building defensive fortifications, and in January 1937, Mao told the Red Army it must 'firmly prepare for war'. Two months later, the crisis had passed. Chiang and Zhou Enlai resumed contact, at first indirectly, then face-to-face. But the hoped-for united front proved as elusive as before. All through the spring and early summer, the two sides argued over issues ranging from the number of divisions the Red Army should have to the kind of badge they should wear on their caps.

Later, communists and nationalists alike would claim that the Xian incident was a turning-point, a pivotal moment which changed the course of Chinese history. Mao was closer to the truth when he told the Politburo, shortly after Chiang's release, that if a truce with the nationalists came about, it would not be because the Generalissimo had given his word but 'because the situation would leave him no choice'. The events at Xian were a vital catalyst. But they were not the chief factor involved. That was brought into play on July 7, when Japanese troops occupied a key railway junction by the Marco Polo Bridge at Lugouqiao, five miles south-west of Beijing. The Pacific War had begun.

Even then the Generalissimo hesitated. A week after the Japanese attack, he was still unwilling to let the Red Army set out for the front. In a telegram to the CCP Military Commission, Mao urged caution:

> Don't let Chiang get the feeling he's being pushed into a corner. [Our] duty now is to encourage him to take the final step of setting up the united front – and there may still be problems over this. We have reached the moment of truth, which will decide whether our country will live or die. This is the crucial time when Chiang Kai-shek and the Guomindang must change their policy totally. Everything we do must accord with this general line.

The day after Mao signed that telegram, July 15, 1937, Zhou Enlai went to Lushan, the hill resort where the Generalissimo was staying near Nanchang, for their third meeting that year. He handed over a draft declaration, reiterating earlier communist undertakings and pledging the Party's support for the democratic revolution launched by the GMD's founder, Sun Yat-sen. In return, he said, the CCP had only two substantive demands: war against Japan; and 'democracy', a code-word for the legalisation of communist activities.

Still Chiang dragged his feet.

On July 28, Mao issued an ultimatum: The Red Army, with Zhu De as Commander-in-Chief and Peng Dehuai as his deputy, would begin moving towards the front on August 20, whether the Guomindang agreed or not.

Next day, Japanese troops occupied Beijing, followed on the 30th by Tianjin. Ten more days passed. Then, on August 13, they attacked Shanghai, directly threatening Chiang's own power base. The choice could be put off no longer. 'Go and tell Zhou Enlai', he instructed one of his aides, '[the communists] should send their troops at once. They need not wait any more.' Soon afterwards it was announced that the Red Army had been redesignated the

Eighth Route Army of the [GMD] National Revolutionary Army.

Finally, on September 22, the Guomindang published the declaration which Zhou had submitted two months before, and the Generalissimo himself announced that, in the national interest, the united front was being revived.

Chiang's reluctance to cut a deal was understandable. For ten years, he had succeeded in keeping the communists in the wilderness, on the margins of Chinese political life. Now they were back on centre stage, a legal party with a national constituency, a national platform, and a recognised national role. For Mao, the highroad to power was open. As he told a bemused Kakuei Tanaka, Japan's Prime Minister several decades later, it had been opened by the Japanese.

CHAPTER ELEVEN

Yan'an Interlude: the Philosopher is King

Shortly after Chiang Kai-shek's release from Xian, the Red Army moved its headquarters from the impoverished cave-village of Bao'an to more accommodating, and slightly more sophisticated, surroundings, sixty miles further east.

The old walled town of Yan'an which Zhou Enlai had visited secretly the previous year for his first, clandestine meeting with the Young Marshal, stands on the bend of a shallow rock-strewn river, below an ancient white pagoda, built on a promontory as a talisman against the autumn floods. Since Song times, it had been an important local trading centre, where camel caravans came from Mongolia with ponies, wool and furs. Woodcutters brought mule-loads of sawn timber and whole tree-trunks on high-wheeled oxcarts. Salt was smuggled in from the cities to the south. Beside the Bell Tower, a herbalist sold powdered lion's teeth, dried snakes and other homely remedies. During fairs and market days, the dusty streets were clogged with a shouting, brawling throng of humanity, clad in blue homespun with white kerchiefs round their heads, which fascinated the young soldiers fresh from the parched, bare hill country to the west – and provided a welcome change, too, for the Party leaders and their wives, who on high days and holidays would stroll through the town, savouring the noise and colour.

Mao and He Zizhen, who had still not recovered from the shrapnel wounds she had suffered during the Long March, moved

into a wealthy merchant's house in the western part of the walled
city, on the lower slopes of Fenghuangshan, Phoenix Mountain.
Zhang Wentian, as acting Party leader, occupied the central courtyard, which included a large stone-flagged reception hall where
Politburo meetings were held. Zhu De and Peng Dehuai had
quarters in another smaller courtyard nearby, where the Office of
the Military Commission was housed. For them all, it was a big step
up from Bao'an. Mao had a sitting room, where he received visitors,
as well as a spacious study, with latticed paper windows, and a large,
round wooden bath. Yet creature comforts had their limits. The
only heating in the bleak northern winter was from the fire under
the kang; water had to be brought from the well; and Mao's papers,
the very stuff of his political existence, were filed away in makeshift
cabinets fashioned out of Standard Oil drums.

Over the next decade Yan'an's pagoda, its tiered landscape,
its massive crenellated walls and twelfth-century gate, became a
symbol of hope, a beacon for progressive-minded young Chinese
and Western sympathisers alike. Yet, as one sober-minded traveller,
who visited the CCP leaders there in the summer of 1937, noted
prosaically, it was in reality, then as now, a 'rather ordinary Chinese
town in a Shensi backwater'. The aura of romance it exuded, 'of
gallant youth, courage and high thinking', came from the extraordinary collection of people who gathered there.

Michael Lindsay, an aristocratic Englishman whose father was
the Master of Balliol College, Oxford, spent part of the war in
Yan'an training Red Army radio operators. He would remember it
as 'the heroic age of Chinese communism'. The journalist, Gunther
Stein, extolled 'the steady fighting enthusiasm of a primitive pioneer
community . . . They seem to feel, whether we believe it or not,
that the future is theirs.' Thomas Bisson, an American academic,
found an egalitarian commitment, 'a special quality of life'. Only the
occasional sceptic sensed a darker side – the uniformity of thought;
the young bodyguards, armed with Mausers, who hovered, unnoticed, around the top leaders like so many invisible shadows.

The myth of 'the Yan'an Way' – the distinctive brand of
communism which Mao developed during the ten-year interlude
between the end of the first Chinese civil war and the beginning of
the second – would join the legend of the Long March as one of the
most enduring emblems of the system he was to create.

Before that could happen, however, Mao had first to achieve the two long-term goals that he had been consciously striving for ever since his arrival in Shensi, two years before: the consolidation of his political power, and the elaboration of a body of Marxist theory bearing his personal stamp.

They were intimately linked. Every communist leader, from Lenin onward, had based his authority on his theoretical contributions to Marxist doctrine. This was the weakest link in Mao's armour. While his Party rivals, the Returned Students and their leader, Wang Ming, had been soaking up Leninist orthodoxy at Russian universities, he had been away in the wilderness, fighting a guerilla war. Yet there was one way, Mao realised, in which that weakness could be turned into a strength. Ten years earlier, in the winter of 1925, he had called for 'an ideology produced in Chinese conditions'. In China, for two thousand years every regime had had its orthodoxy. The communists, too, needed their own distinctive, Chinese form of Marxism. It would enable the Party to tap into the deep vein of Chinese nationalism; erode the influence of Mao's Russian-trained rivals and formidably buttress his own leadership claims.

He made his first move at Wayaobu, in December 1935.

There, at his urging, the Politburo endorsed the view that Marxism should be applied flexibly to 'specific, concrete Chinese conditions', and condemned 'leftist dogmatism', meaning slavish adherence to Moscow's ideas.

Three months later he was arguing that the Chinese Party should 'run things by itself, and have faith in its own abilities'; the Soviet Union was a friend, but its help was secondary. Soviet and Chinese policies coincided, he declared, 'only where the interests of the Chinese masses coincide with the interests of the Russian masses'.

In June, 1936, the Red Army University was inaugurated in Wayaobu, in a tiny, one-roomed Daoist temple, to serve as a forum where Mao could lecture on political and military affairs. His timing was poor, for the town was abandoned to the nationalists three weeks later. But, following the move to Bao'an, the 'university' was re-established, with Lin Biao as its president, in equally humble surroundings – a natural cave, where the Red Army's top commanders squatted on improvised stone stools, taking notes with the aid of a stylus on 'notepads' of soft stone. That autumn, Mao gave a series of talks there, entitled 'Problems of Strategy in China's Revolutionary War,' in which he developed for the first time the notion of China's distinctiveness, ostensibly in the context of military affairs but actually in a broader sense as well:

> China's revolutionary war . . . is waged in the specific environment of China and so has its own specific circumstances and nature [and] . . . specific laws of its own . . . Some people . . . say that it is enough merely to study the experience of revolutionary war in Russia . . . and the military manuals published by Soviet military organisations. They do not see that these . . . manuals embody the specific characteristics of the . . . Soviet Union, and that if we copy and apply them mechanically without allowing any change, we shall . . . be 'cutting the feet to fit the shoes', and will be defeated . . . Although we must value Soviet experience . . . we must value even more the experience of China's revolutionary war, because there are many factors specific to the Chinese revolution and the Chinese Red Army.

By emphasising the differences between the Soviet Union and China, and affirming the primacy of indigenous experience, 'acquired at the cost of our own blood', Mao was consciously laying the groundwork for the idea of Marxism in a national form. To underline the message, he launched a comprehensive critique of the 'left opportunists of 1931–34' – the Returned Student leadership – whom he accused of behaving like 'hotheads and ignoramuses' and pursuing 'theories and practices [which] did not have the slightest flavour of Marxism about them; indeed, they were anti-Marxist.'

Mao was able to get away with such language because he did not name names, and his remarks were not made in public but to a select audience of the military elite. None the less, he was pushing at the limits of what his colleagues would accept. In February 1937, when his old protégé from Anyuan, Liu Shaoqi, now responsible for the Party's underground work in north China, argued that the whole of the past decade had been a period of 'leftist adventurism', the rest of the leadership cried foul. By the summer, however, the wind had shifted, and when Liu repeated his charges Mao came out openly in his support. 'Shaoqi's report is basically correct,' he told the Politburo. 'He is like a doctor diagnosing our ailments, pointing out systematically the problems we had before.' Although the Party had great achievements to its credit, Mao said, it still suffered from a 'mistaken leftist tradition'. Much more would have to be done if it were to be overcome. The episode marked the start of Liu's rise to become, in the course of the next five years, Mao's most trusted colleague.

While the debate over leftism simmered, Mao resumed his study of Marxism. He had not worked exegetically with philosophical texts since he was a student, twenty years earlier, and found the prospect intimidating. That winter he annotated a number of weighty tomes by a group of Soviet theoreticians, including Stalin's house philosopher, Mark Mitin, and next spring began a twice-weekly lecture course, on Tuesday and Thursday mornings, on dialectical materialism.

It was not a success.

His opening talks, tracing the evolution of European philosophy as a struggle between materialism and idealism, first in France in the seventeenth and eighteenth centuries, then in Germany in the nineteenth, were dreary in the extreme. Mao himself warned his audience, 'These talks of mine are far from adequate, since I have myself only just begun to study dialectics.' In the mid -1960s, he was so mortified at the memory of them that he sought to deny authorship altogether. He did break new ground at one point, by arguing that the particular and the general were 'interconnected and inseparable', which later provided a theoretical basis for contending that general Marxist principles must always exist in a particular national form. But for the most part he came across as a neophyte, bogged down in a a topic he was still struggling to understand.

The next two series were rather better, partly because they were grounded more solidly in Mao's own experience. 'On Practice' developed themes from an essay which he had written during his rural investigations in 1930 in Jiangxi, entitled, 'Oppose Book-worship!'

> If you have not investigated a certain problem, you will lose your right to speak on it. Isn't this too brutal? Not in the least. Since you have investigated neither the actual situation nor the historical circumstances of this problem, and have no detailed knowledge of it, anything you say about it could only be nonsense . . . There are also people who say: 'Show me where it is written in a book' . . . This book-worshipping method of conducting research [is] dangerous . . . We must study Marxist 'books', but they must be integrated with our actual situation. We need 'books', but we must definitely correct book-worship that departs from reality. How can we correct book-worship? Only by investigating the actual situation.

In 'On Practice', this was summed up in the aphorism, 'Practice is the criterion of truth':

> The movement of change in the world of objective reality is never-ending, and so is man's cognition of truth through practice. Marxism has in no way exhausted truth, but ceaselessly opens up [new] roads to [its] knowledge . . . Practice, knowledge, again practice and again knowledge. The pattern repeats itself in endless cycles, and with each cycle the content of practice and knowledge rises to a higher level . . . Such is the dialectical-materialist theory of the unity of knowing and doing.

'On Contradiction' had antecedents in Mao's student days. The unity of opposites, which had prompted, in his notes on Paulsen, the passage: 'Life is death and death is life, up is down, dirty is clean, male is female and thick is thin. In essence the many are one and change is permanence' – he now discovered, like Lenin before him, to be 'the basic law of dialectics . . . the most important theoretical base of the proletarian revolution . . . the fundamental law of the universe and the fundamental law of ideological method'. To formulate correct policies, Mao argued, it was necessary in any given situation to determine what was the principal contradiction, and which was its principal aspect.

Later commentators would claim that he had succeeded in imbuing Marxism-Leninism with 'Chinese national characteristics', by incorporating elements of ancient Chinese thought. Of more immediate importance, he had begun to put in place a theoretical justification for the Chinese Party to seek its own, independent path to communism.

In another important respect, too, Mao cut loose from Stalinist orthodoxy.

Marxism holds that the economic base and the productive forces that operate within it determine the political and cultural super-structure of society. At times, Mao now argued, this relationship could be reversed. 'When the superstructure obstructs the development of the economic base, political and cultural changes become principal and decisive . . . In general, the material determines the mental. [But] we also, and indeed must, recognise the operation of mental on material things.' Here, in Marxist language, was the belief that he had nurtured since childhood in the power of the human will. Decades later, it would provide the ideological underpinning for his two great attempts to transform China by mobilising its spirit – the Great Leap Forward and the Cultural Revolution.

In August 1937, the lecture series came to an abrupt end, as the Japanese advance on Shanghai forced Mao to turn his attention back to more immediate practical issues.

This did not mean he put aside philosophy. That autumn, at his urging, Ai Siqi, the leading figure among the younger generation of academic Marxist theorists, came to Yan'an to start a weekly study circle. One of Ai's followers, Chen Boda, a short, agitated man with an incomprehensible Fujianese accent, made worse by a pronounced stammer, became Mao's political secretary. For the next few years Mao read voraciously every Marxist text he could find – even, in another echo of his schooldays, starting a 'reading diary' in which he noted which books he had read.

Later in life Mao developed a genuine delight in philosophical speculation, and his conversation, whether in private or political discussion, became so studded with arcane analogy and enigmatic references to abstruse debating points that even his Politburo colleagues often scrambled to keep up with him. None the less, it is hard to avoid the impression that philosophy was, for Mao, essentially a point of departure – a springboard into the realm of ideas, rather than intrinsically fascinating in itself. 'On Practice' and 'On Contradiction' were important in establishing his credentials as a theorist, and thus strengthening his claim to Party leadership, but he plainly found them hard work. The writing was pedestrian, lacking his usual trenchancy and flair. Pure theory was a means to an end, not a subject Mao took much joy in.

On November 29, 1937, as the Japanese Kwangtung Army rolled relentlessly southward across the north China plains, an aircraft appeared in the skies over Yan'an and began to circle the primitive airfield. At first, the look-outs thought it was Japanese, on a periodic bombing mission. But then they made out its Soviet markings, and Mao and the rest of the Politburo hurried to the landing-strip. Out of the plane stepped Wang Ming, the owlish, slightly overweight chief of 'Stalin's China Section', whom the Soviet leader was now sending back to stiffen the Chinese Party's commitment to the united front with Chiang Kai-shek. He was followed by a slightly built, scholarly-looking man named Kang Sheng, who specialised in secret police work; and Chen Yun, who had been sent to Moscow two-and-a-half years earlier to inform the Comintern of the decisions taken at Zunyi.

Mao had been forewarned by radio of Wang's imminent return, but the journey, by way of Xinjiang, had taken two weeks, and there had been no way of knowing exactly when he would arrive.

That night, the Red Army cooks prepared a banquet. In the speeches of welcome, Mao hailed Wang's coming as a 'blessing from the sky', while Zhang Wentian praised his achievements in the Comintern. Then the jockeying for position began. Wang was too astute openly to contest Mao's dominance, but he did take issue with him on matters of policy where, he let it be inferred, he had Moscow's support. The crux of their differences, which were given a comprehensive airing at a six-day Politburo meeting starting on December 9, was the united front with the Guomindang.

Mao had set out his strategy three-and-a-half months earlier at a leadership conference in the town of Luochuan, sixty miles south of Yan'an. If China was to defeat Japan, he argued, it was essential to unite all anti-Japanese forces. But within this united front, 'the CCP must be independent, and we must keep the initiative in our own hands'. Politically, that meant the Party should strive to play the 'leading role' in the war effort; and to expand its own ranks. It must also maintain 'a high degree of vigilance' towards the Guomindang, understanding that, alongside unity, there would continue to be rivalry and struggle. Militarily, it meant preparing for a protracted war, in which the Eighth Route Army would rely heavily on guerrilla tactics and avoid positional warfare. 'The basis of guerrilla war', Mao reminded them, 'is to spread out and arouse the masses [to join in the struggle], and concentrate regular forces [only] when you can destroy the enemy. Fight when you know you can win. Don't fight battles you may lose!' The communist main forces, he insisted, must be deployed prudently 'in the light of the actual situation' with a view to preserving their strength.

As the autumn wore on, Mao felt events bore out the wisdom of this policy. Chiang Kai-shek, he believed, was trying to force the Red Army to bear the brunt of the fighting. A campaign was launched to ensure that Party officials defended the CCP's interests, and did not blindly carry out the GMD's bidding. In telegrams to the Red Army commanders, Mao hammered home the message that guerrilla warfare must be 'the sole orientation'; fighting set-piece battles would be 'totally fruitless'. When, in late September, Lin Biao's forces ambushed a Japanese column at Pingxingguan, in northern Shanxi, wiping out a thousand enemy troops, he was torn between elation at the first Chinese victory of the war, which raised the Red Army's prestige and caused a surge of rejoicing throughout China, and anger lest Lin, and others, allow their forces to become dangerously exposed. A few days later, a GMD campaign to concentrate (and thereby, control) the surviving communist guerrilla forces in south China triggered fresh unease about Chiang's intentions. Then came disturbing signs, as one north Chinese city after another yielded before the Japanese onslaught, that the GMD was showing renewed interest in a separate peace with Tokyo. Mao became more convinced than ever that the CCP must keep its own counsel, and 'reject, criticise and struggle against' the Guomindang's 'mistaken policies'.

Wang Ming, fresh from Moscow, took a very different line. Stalin viewed the GMD as an indispensable partner to keep the Japanese at bay (and prevent them turning their attention to Siberia). The Chinese Party, as a loyal member of the Comintern, should therefore do everything possible to further the Soviet–GMD alliance. The key issue, Wang argued, was 'to consolidate and expand the unity between the GMD and the CCP' on a basis not of 'mutual competition' but of 'mutual respect, trust, help and supervision'. Such matters as 'keeping the initiative in our own hands', and which party should play the leading role, were secondary. The guiding principle must be: 'Resisting Japan takes precedence over everything, and everything must be subordinated to resistance to Japan. Everything is subordinate to the united front, and everything must be channelled through the united front.'

When Wang made these points at the December Politburo meeting, Mao retorted that the strategy elaborated at Luochuan was correct. The CCP had to maintain its independence, otherwise it would be reduced to the status of a GMD auxiliary. Unity and struggle were complementary, he went on, reaching into his newly acquired stock of Marxist dialectics. In the context of the united front, there could not be one without the other.

To Zhou Enlai, up to then the chief negotiator with the GMD, and to some of the military commanders, itching for a full-scale anti-Japanese offensive, Wang Ming's argument of 'all hands to the mill' had definite attractions, especially since it plainly had

Soviet backing. Mao is said to have commented later, with the slightly self-pitying melodrama he affected on such occasions, that after Wang Ming's return, 'my authority did not extend beyond my cave'. In fact, he had enough support to block Wang's proposals, and as neither side wanted to force the issue, the meeting ended in stalemate.

Wang's efforts to strengthen his Party base likewise met with mixed success. He, Chen Yun and Kang Sheng, all full members of the Politburo, joined Mao and Zhang Wentian in the Secretariat. But the post of 'acting Party leader', which Zhang had held since early 1935, was allowed to lapse (which prevented Wang seeking it for himself) and, in the interests of 'collective leadership' (another device to restrict Wang's influence), it was agreed that no major CCP document might be issued without the approval of at least half of the membership of the Secretariat or the Politburo. Since Wang left shortly afterwards for Wuhan, where he became Secretary of the Party's Yangtse Bureau and head of the CCP Delegation to the Guomindang, these arrangements meant that Mao and Zhang Wentian remained in effective control of day-to-day decision-making. The Politburo also decided, at the Comintern's urging, to begin preparations for the Party's long-delayed Seventh Congress – a move from which, in theory, Wang stood to gain, for he might reasonably expect it to confirm him at least as second-ranking Party leader. But in practice that did not help him either, for Mao was appointed Chairman of the Preparatory Committee and proceeded to hurry slowly.

The challenge Wang Ming posed was none the less the most serious Mao had faced for almost two-and-a-half years. Wang was the chief representative of the Soviet-trained cohort of the Chinese Party whose influence Mao was trying to break. He was ambitious; he had enormous prestige within the Party at large; and he had backers in Moscow. He viewed Mao as essentially a military figure, whose political mantle he could eventually draw to himself. In 1931, after the Fourth Plenum, Wang had been the pre-eminent Party leader until he handed over his powers to Bo Gu. He had not given up hope of becoming so again.

Initially, Wang's policies appeared to be paying off. In January, German attempts to mediate between China and Japan collapsed, and relations between the CCP and the Guomindang began to show a marked improvement. A communist newspaper, *Xinhua ribao*, was authorised in Wuhan, giving the Party for the first time a legal means of propagating its ideas in GMD-ruled areas. CCP recruitment in the cities grew apace.

But the Japanese advance continued.

Nanjing had fallen. By February, Xuzhou was threatened. The next major target would be Wuhan. The defence of that city, Wang now argued, must be the first priority. If the Japanese could be halted there, final victory would be assured. The united front must therefore be strengthened still further, by establishing 'a unified national army . . . [with] a united command, a united establishment . . . united battle plans and united combat', and by creating a 'national revolutionary alliance', in which all political parties – including the GMD and the CCP – would join together in the common cause.

To Mao, Wang's call 'to defend important positions to stop the enemy's advance' recalled Bo Gu's disastrous slogan, 'Defend every inch of soviet territory!', which had led to the loss of the Red base area in Jiangxi four years earlier.

When the Politburo next met, in late February, he laid out his own, bleak analysis of the future conduct of the war. The Guomindang was corrupt, he said. The CCP lacked the strength to defeat Japan on its own; and the Japanese did not have enough troops to occupy the whole of China. In these circumstances, the conflict would not end soon. Far from defending Wuhan, the correct policy was a strategic withdrawal. To continue the bruising but indecisive battles of recent months was a mistake, Mao warned. China had to preserve its forces for the day when victory might finally be achieved. He did not actually, on this occasion, use the term, 'luring the enemy in deep', but none of his colleagues could have had any doubt as to his meaning: in resisting Japan, China should use the same strategy nationally as the Communists had used in Jiangxi to defeat the Guomindang encirclement campaigns.

Three months later, Mao enlarged on these ideas in two essays which were to become military classics, setting out the guiding principles the Red Army would apply for the next seven years, until the end of the war in 1945.

In 'Problems of Strategy in Guerilla War', he argued that when a large, weak country (China) was attacked by a small, strong neighbour (Japan), part, or even the greater part, of its territory would fall into the enemy's hands. In these circumstances, the defenders should establish base areas in the mountains, as the Red Army had done in Jiangxi, and fight a war of mutual encirclement, resembling a game of chess,* in which each side moved out from its strongholds and tried to dominate 'the spaces on the board' – the vast areas of the countryside where the guerrilla war would be fought.

In the second essay, 'On Protracted War', he tried to prepare the Party, and public opinion at large, now accessible through *Xinhua ribao*, for the long and arduous conflict that such a strategy would entail.

Capitulation, although still much discussed within the Guomindang, was unlikely, Mao argued, because of 'the obstinate and peculiarly barbarous character' of Japanese aggression, which had provoked the unremitting hostility of all sections of the Chinese population. Thus, even though 'certain subjugationists will again crawl out and collude with [the enemy]', the nation as a whole would fight on.† However, a speedy victory was equally improbable. In the initial stage of the war, which might last months or years, China would suffer partial defeats, and Japan would gain partial victories. But as Japan's supply lines became over-extended and war weariness set in, the balance of advantage would change. Subjective factors, Mao maintained, such as people's determination to fight for their homes, their culture and their land, would ultimately prevail:

> The so-called theory that 'weapons decide everything' [is] . . . one-sided . . . Weapons are an important factor in war, but not the decisive factor; it is people, not things, that are decisive. The contest of strength is not only a contest of military and economic power, but also a contest of human power and morale . . .

He went on to cite Clausewitz, whose writings on politics and war he had encountered for the first time that spring:

> 'War is the continuation of politics.' In this sense war is politics, and war itself is a political action. Since ancient times there has never

---

* Mao was referring here to *weiji*, or Chinese chess, in which the object is to safeguard one's own pieces by maintaining blank spaces on the board into which an adversary's pieces cannot penetrate. So long as a player dominates these blank spaces, his pieces cannot be captured even if they are surrounded.

† These turned out to be prophetic words. Six months later, in December 1938, Mao's former GMD patron, Wang Jingwei, broke with Chiang Kai-shek and agreed to set up a Japanese puppet government, based in Nanjing.

been a war that did not have a political character . . . But war has its
own particular characteristics and in this sense it cannot be equated
with politics in general. 'War is a special political technique for the
realisation of certain political objectives.' When politics develops to
a certain stage beyond which it cannot proceed by the usual means,
war breaks out to sweep the obstacles from the way . . . It can therefore be said that politics is war without bloodshed, while war is
politics with bloodshed.

The key to victory, Mao concluded, lay in mobilising China's
people, so as to create 'a vast sea of humanity in which the enemy
will be swallowed up'.

To Wang Ming, this was far too pessimistic.

Once again, the Politburo split. Wang, Zhou Enlai and Bo Gu
lined up on one side; Mao, Zhang Wentian, Chen Yun and Kang
Sheng (who quickly shifted allegiance once he sensed which way
the wind was blowing) on the other. Wang, evidently confident that
Stalin would support him, agreed that Ren Bishi, now Political
Director of the Military Commission, should go to Moscow to seek
new instructions. He then infuriated Mao by claiming publicly, on
his return to Wuhan, that his crusade for its defence had the
communist leaders' unanimous support.

From then on, the leaders in Wuhan and Yan'an increasingly
constituted two distinct loci of communist power, following
conflicting policies and issuing contradictory instructions.

Where Mao denounced the nationalists as venal and compromising, Wang and Zhou Enlai called for closer ties with Chiang
Kai-shek. When Mao instructed them to relocate to the countryside,
on the grounds that Wuhan was indefensible, they urged the city's
inhabitants to emulate Madrid, where the Republicans were
holding out heroically against the Spanish fascists.

In the end, Wang's populism proved his undoing. His appeal
to the population to rise up in the city's defence conjured up in
Guomindang minds the spectre of communist insurrection. In
August, Chiang Kai-shek's police launched a clampdown on communist front organisations, and many of the more active were banned.
The Yangtse Bureau's efforts to expand communist influence by
legal means collapsed.

By then, Wang's cause had suffered an even more serious blow
from a quite different quarter. When Ren Bishi reached Moscow,
he was welcomed by Mao's old ally, Wang Jiaxiang, who had gone

to the Soviet Union to have his war wounds treated and had afterwards stayed on as the CCP's representative to the Comintern. Ren and Wang Jiaxiang had worked together before, as members of the Fourth Plenum delegation to the Jiangxi Soviet in 1931. Both had originally been close to Wang Ming. Both had watched Mao develop into a leader of national stature. Now, they decided together to campaign on Mao's behalf. By July, if not earlier – in any case, several weeks before Wang Ming's policies ran into trouble in Wuhan – Stalin and Dimitrov had agreed that Mao, not Wang, should receive the Kremlin's blessing as the new Chinese Party chief.

In fact, Wang seems to have deluded himself all along about the extent of Soviet backing. Before his departure for China, Dimitrov had warned him not to try to supplant Mao, whose skills as a military leader had long been recognised in Moscow, and whom Stalin had viewed, at least since the Wayaobu meeting in December 1935, as the dominant Chinese Party figure. Ren Bishi did not find it difficult to convince the Comintern that the time had come to lift any ambiguity that remained.

One morning in the second week of September 1938, Mao went to the South Gate of Yan'an to stand beneath the stone battlements of the massive city wall, waiting for Wang Ming to arrive by road from Xian for a Politburo meeting. He had done the same at Bao'an, two years earlier, when Zhang Guotao's defeated forces straggled in from Gansu. It was a gesture Mao would never need to make again. He knew, as Wang did not, that the game was finally over. As the meeting opened, Wang Jiaxiang read out a Comintern statement approving the CCP's efforts to manage the united front under 'complex circumstances and very difficult conditions', and then conveyed two verbal instructions, issued by Dimitrov himself.

> In order to resolve the problem of unifying the Party leadership, the CCP leadership should have Mao Zedong as its centre.

> There should be an atmosphere of unity and closeness.

The two weeks of discussions that followed were devoted to preparing a Central Committee plenum, the first since January 1934, which Mao had decided to convene as soon as Wang Jiaxiang had arrived with the news of Moscow's decision.

Mao spoke twice, on September 24 and 27. As on earlier occasions when his policies had triumphed – at Zunyi, in January 1935; at Huili, after the successful crossing of the Yangtse, four months later; and at Wayaobu – he went out of his way to be magnanimous, insisting that the main point in the Comintern directive was the need to 'safeguard intra-Party unity'. At the same time, he put down various markers. The Comintern's instructions, he said, set out 'guiding principles' not only for the forthcoming plenum but for the Seventh Congress (which, he indicated, would be charged with appraising the Party's past actions and electing a new leadership in accordance with the principles Dimitrov had laid down). The Party must prepare for a military stalemate – the 'protracted war' of which he had written that summer. The united front with the nationalists would be marked by growing struggle.

The Sixth Plenum, which opened on September 29, lasted more than a month.

In his opening speech, Mao sketched out the broad lines of his attack. Wang Ming and his followers, he implied, having been schooled in foreign Marxism, were out of touch with their own culture:

> If a Chinese communist, who is part of the great Chinese nation, bound to it by his own flesh and blood, talks of Marxism in isolation from Chinese characteristics, that Marxism is a mere abstraction. Therefore the sinification of Marxism – that is to say, making sure that its every manifestation has an indubitably Chinese character – is a problem which the whole Party must understand and solve without delay. Foreign stereotypes must be abolished, there must be less singing of empty, abstract tunes, and dogmatism must be laid to rest . . . In this matter there are serious errors in our ranks which must be resolutely overcome.

Thus far, Mao's target was veiled. But to Party veterans, it struck a familiar chord. Years earlier, in Jiangxi, the Returned Students had been known contemptuously as *Yang fanzi*, 'Gentlemen from a Foreign House'.

At the end of October, Wuhan fell, as Mao had predicted it would, dramatising the failure of Wang's strategy. By then, Wang Ming himself had departed to attend a GMD-sponsored conference on united front policy, leaving the plenum to conclude in his absence. It was the signal for Mao to press home his advantage. He ridiculed Wang's slogan, 'everything through the united front', as 'simply binding us hand and foot', and resurrected his own catch-phrase, 'initiative and independence'. Anyone who failed to safeguard that independence, he declared – again sniping at Wang – deserved to be called a 'right opportunist'. Far from demotivating the masses, a long-drawn-out guerrilla war, in which they would take up guns and fight, was precisely the means to awaken their political consciousness:

> Every communist must grasp this truth: '*Political power grows out of the barrel of a gun*'. Our principle is that the Party commands the gun, and the gun must never be allowed to command the Party. Yet, having guns, we can create Party organisations . . . We can create schools, create culture, create mass movements . . . All things grow out of the barrel of a gun . . . It is only by the power of the gun that the working class and the labouring masses can defeat the armed bourgeoisie and the landlords; in this sense we may say that only with guns can the whole world be transformed. We are advocates of the abolition of war . . . but war can only be abolished through war. In order to get rid of the gun, it is necessary to take up the gun. (Emphasis supplied.)

Here was the formula he had first coined at Hankou, in August 1927, which the Party leaders at that time had rejected. Now he charged Wang Ming and the Returned Students with neglecting the importance of military affairs, and with having caused 'serious losses' in the Central Soviet Base Area during the years when they held power.

For Mao, the autumn of 1938 was a watershed. Intellectually, his ideas had matured. His writings showed an ease and self-assurance in assimilating Marxist dialectics to the traditional patterns of Chinese thought that had earlier been absent. From now on, Mao would interpret the world in the same, distinctive, elliptical style, reasoning by opposites, analysing the innate contradictions which, in his words, 'determine the life of all things and push their development forwards'. As he approached his forty-fifth birthday, the main lines of his thought were set: he would continue to refine his ideas, but there would be little more that was radically new.

Politically, his long campaign to dominate the Party had triumphed. Wang Ming was still a force to be reckoned with, but his challenge was at an end. Mao could live with that. In the meantime, he set about consolidating the new powers he had won.

Like Stalin, he chose as his instrument the Party Secretariat, which now took over the day-to-day running of the Party when the Politburo was not in session. Whoever controlled the Secretariat controlled the Central leadership's agenda. Mao became its head, with Wang Jiaxiang, who had done such sterling work for him in Moscow, as his deputy. He rejected a proposal that he become acting General Secretary, while awaiting the Seventh Congress, as Zhang Wentian had done after Zunyi. Mao wanted substantive control; the appearance could come later.

Wang Ming's position was further undermined by a decision to dissolve the Yangtse Bureau, which he headed. Its responsibilities were divided between the Southern Bureau, under Zhou Enlai; a new Central Plains Bureau, headed by Liu Shaoqi; and an upgraded South-Eastern Bureau, under Mao's former adversary, Xiang Ying.

November 1938 saw other changes in Mao's life. Soon after the plenum ended, Japanese bombers, whose sorties against Yan'an had multiplied that year, scored a direct hit on Fenghuangshan. Mao's courtyard was badly damaged. He and the rest of the leadership moved to a cave village at Yangjialing, a narrow valley about three miles north of the Yan'an city walls. But He Zizhen did not go with him. They had separated more than a year earlier. That November, Mao married a willowy young film actress from Shanghai, who had taken the stage name, Blue Apple (Lan Ping), but now called herself Jiang Qing.

The women who shared Mao's life all had their part of misfortune. Miss Luo, the peasant girl his parents chose, suffered the disgrace of rejection and died an early death. Yang Kaihui went to the execution ground proclaiming her loyalty to him, but spiritually crushed by the knowledge that he was living with He Zizhen. She, in her turn, endured extraordinary hardship – forced to abandon three of their four children and losing another, stillborn; sharing Mao's lot in the darkest periods of his political career; and being horribly wounded herself on the Long March – only to find that, when finally they were able to live normally again, they had grown apart.

Edgar Snow remembered He Zizhen in Bao'an as a gentle, unassuming young woman, half Mao's age, who got on with the household chores, making compote from wild peaches, looking after their fourth, and only surviving, child – a baby daughter, Li Min, born shortly after Snow's arrival. On one occasion, he remembered, 'both of them suddenly bent over and gave an exclamation of delight at a moth that had languished beside a candle, [a] . . . lovely thing with wings shaded a delicate apple-green and fringed in a soft rainbow of saffron and rose.' But the image of gentleness was deceptive. As Mao himself recognised, He Zizhen had an indomitable spirit, and a tough, unyielding character, rivalling his own. 'We are like iron and steel,' he told her after one spectacular row. 'Unless we try to compromise with each other, both of us will suffer.' In the event, it was always Mao who had to play the peacemaker. His young wife was too stubborn ever to make the first move.

In the wilds of Jiangxi, and during the perils of the March, they were bound together by a common imperative of political and physical survival. He Zizhen's lack of education – she had left school at sixteen – hardly seemed to matter. She was intelligent, with a quick mind. She loved Mao. And he, in turn, had considerable affection for her.

In Shensi, it was different. Mao spent his nights reading philosophy and his days wrestling with Marxist theory. He was hungry for conversation with fellow intellectuals, and eagerly sought out the students who flocked to Yan'an to join the communist cause. He Zizhen felt excluded.

She was not alone in this. Edgar Snow's wife, Nym Wales, wrote of a 'real crisis in Yan'an in the man–woman relationship', as the women who had made the Long March found their positions threatened by an influx of talented, beautiful young people, bringing with them the loose morals and casual ways of the cosmopolitan cities of the coast. The feminist writer, Ding Ling, and the American, Agnes Smedley, were especially mistrusted for their anarchistic approach to marriage and advocacy of free love – doctrines that sat ill with the puritanical lifestyle the communists enforced in Yan'an. It was in Agnes Smedley's cave, one evening in late May 1937, that Mao's difficulties with He Zizhen came to a head. Wales, Smedley and her interpreter, a young actress named Lily Wu, were making supper when Mao dropped by. They stayed up till 1 a.m. playing rummy, a game which Snow had introduced to the communists in Bao'an a year earlier, and for which Mao, in particular, had developed a real passion. Nym Wales recorded in her diary:

> He was in high spirits that evening . . . Agnes looked up at [him] worshipfully, with her large blue eyes, which at times had a fanatical gleam. Lily Wu was also looking at Mao with hero-worship. A bit later, I was stunned to see Lily walk over and sit beside Mao on the bench, putting her hand on his knee (very timidly). Lily announced that she had had too much wine . . . Mao also appeared startled, but he would have been something of a cad to push her away rudely, and he was obviously amused. He also announced that he had had too much wine. Lily then ventured to take hold of Mao's hand, which she repeated from time to time during the evening.

At the time, no one paid much attention. Nym Wales accepted at face value Lily Wu's explanation that she had had too much to drink. Lily, she wrote, was 'very pretty with long curls, recently arrived in Yan'an and cutting rather a wide swathe', and she was unconventional enough – the only woman in Yan'an to wear lipstick – for Mao also to pass it off as of no consequence.* He Zizhen, however, to whose ears the story quickly came, took a very different view. She bottled up her feelings, she wrote later, until they ate away her heart.

At this point, He discovered that, yet again, she was pregnant. It was the final straw. She was still only twenty-seven years old. She wanted to have a life of her own – not just to go on bearing children for a man from whom she felt increasingly estranged. That summer she told Mao she had decided to leave him.

Only then, it seems, did Mao realise that he had a problem on his hands.

He Zizhen recalled in her memoirs, published after his death, that he pleaded with her to stay, reminding her of how much they had been through together and telling her how much he cared for her. To prove his sincerity, he had both Lily Wu and Smedley expelled from

---

* This begs the question of whether Mao and Lily Wu were in fact having an affair. The balance of the evidence, such as it is, suggests that they were. In her diary, Nym Wales described her 'leaning on Mao's knee in a familiar way'. Agnes Smedley let slip that Lily had been giving Mao 'mandarin lessons'. He Zizhen, while never formally accusing Mao of adultery, charged Ms Wu with 'alienating Mao's affections'.

Yan'an. But to no avail. At the beginning of August, she left for Xian.

There, Mao sent her a traditional wooden cosmetic box, which his bodyguards had made, together with a fruit-knife and other articles she had cherished. Again, he asked her to reconsider. Still she would not change her mind.

When Shanghai, her original destination, fell to the Japanese, she set out across Xinjiang to Urumqi, a thousand miles to the east. Thence, the following spring, ignoring a further plea from Mao and disobeying a direct order from the Party hierarchy to return at once to Yan'an, she travelled on to the Soviet Union, where at last she was able to get proper medical treatment for the shrapnel still lodged in her body.

Far from being a new beginning, He Zizhen's sojourn in Moscow dragged her deeper into despair. The baby boy, Mao's son, born soon after she arrived there, died of pneumonia ten months later. While she was still grieving for him, news came that Mao had re-married. She told friends she wished him well, and threw herself into studying. But the image of her dead son haunted her. She became morbidly depressed, and the local authorities eventually had her committed to a mental asylum. Mao arranged for her to return to China in 1947. She continued to receive psychiatric treat-ment, and for the rest of her life suffered from a persecution complex, convinced that her doctors were trying to poison her.

Shortly after He's departure, Jiang Qing made her entrance.

She was then twenty-three years old, a slender, sophisticated young woman, with a wide, sensual mouth, boyish figure and viv-acious smile, who bore more than a passing resemblance to He Zizhen as she had looked as a teenager, at the time Mao had first met her, nearly ten years before.

Like the Party's security chief, Kang Sheng, Jiang Qing hailed from a small town in Shandong, about fifty miles from the former German treaty port of Qingdao. Her father was a carpenter; her mother worked for a time as a servant in the household of Kang's gentry parents, while moonlighting as a prostitute. By her own account, Jiang grew up amid crushing poverty. When she was still a small child, her mother fled with her from the family home to escape her husband's beatings. At the age of sixteen, she in turn ran away to join a theatre troupe. Three years later, in the spring of 1933, she reached Shanghai, where she became a minor star, eventually graduating to leading roles in leftist films, like *Blood on Wolf*

Mountain, which urged resistance to Japan, and Western dramas, including Ibsen's *The Doll's House*. In the process, she was arrested by the Guomindang as a suspected communist and held for eight months in prison before suddenly being released, supposedly on the intervention of a mysterious, anonymous foreigner. She had numerous well-publicised love-affairs, and married at least twice, the second time to the actor, Tang Na, whom she so enraged that on several occasions he attempted suicide.

Her motives in travelling to Yan'an were mixed. In Shanghai, her acting career had stalled. Her marriage to the mercurial Tang Na was a liability. She was canny enough to work out that if the war with Japan continued, the city would be a prime target. Yan'an, since the Xian Incident, had been the destination of choice for fashionable young Chinese radicals. Her mentor in the Party (and one-time lover), Yu Qiwei, a young White Area communist underground leader who had been instrumental in bringing Edgar Snow to Bao'an, was also making his way there. On every count, it seemed the best place to be.

Like all new arrivals, she had to undergo a screening process. At first, this did not go well. She had no proof that she had joined the Party in 1932, as she claimed, and there were embarrassing questions (which were never entirely laid to rest) about exactly how she had managed to extricate herself from the clutches of her GMD jailers two years earlier.* But in October, Yu Qiwei finally arrived and vouched for her Party credentials, and the following month she was allowed to begin studying Marxism-Leninism at the Party School. Six months later, in April 1938, she moved to the Lu Xun Academy for Literature and Art as an administrative assistant.

There, that summer, she contrived to catch Mao's eye. There are many stories, all more or less scurrilous, and all unverifiable, about how she did so. All that appears certain is that she, not he, took the initiative. They had been formally introduced soon after she

---

* Jiang Qing devoted an immense amount of time and energy during the Cultural Revolution to trying to suppress all record of her activities in Shanghai in the 1930s. This does not, in itself, prove the claims of her enemies (and, supposedly, just before his death, of Kang Sheng) that she bought her way out of prison by agreeing to work for the GMD. But it is clear that she was concerned about unsavoury episodes in her past which might have caused political embarrassment had they come to light.

arrived, but at that point Mao was still bent on repairing his relationship with He Zizhen. Now he encountered her again, probably at a theatrical performance, just as he was finally coming to accept that his wife had indeed left him, and that nothing he could do would bring her back. Nym Wales, reflecting on his dalliance with Lily Wu, had noted: 'Mao was the type of man . . . who especially liked women . . . [He] liked modern-minded women . . .' Mao's bed was empty, and Jiang Qing fitted the bill.

In August, exactly a year after her arrival in Yan'an (and He Zizhen's departure), she was transferred to work as Mao's assistant, nominally attached to the Military Commission. That autumn they began living together openly, and in November Mao gave a series of dinners for fellow Politburo members at which Jiang Qing officiated as hostess. That was the sum of their 'marriage'. There was no official ceremony, and still less any official divorce. Nor was there any truth to the story, widely circulated after Mao's death, that his peers had imposed three conditions before allowing him to 'marry' Jiang Qing: that she should hold no Party post and play no public role, instead occupying herself solely with his private affairs.

Where there was real concern was over Jiang Qing's past. With her promiscuous Shanghai background; the lingering uncertainties over how she had joined the Party; and the persistent rumours that she had made a deal with the Guomindang to get out of jail – was she an appropriate partner for Mao? Xiang Ying, whose South-Eastern Bureau was responsible for Shanghai, was sufficiently alarmed to write to Mao's confidential secretary, Ye Zilong, warning him about the rumours of her conduct circulating in the city. He concluded bluntly: 'This person is not suitable to marry the Chairman.' Others were more circumspect, but entertained similar doubts.

Mao's response came in two parts.

Officially, he maintained that Kang Sheng, as head of the Party's security apparatus, had conducted a thorough investigation, and found that Jiang Qing had no serious problems. Kang, of course, had his own agenda. Supporting his fellow townswoman was not only a way of ingratiating himself with Mao (and with Jiang Qing herself), but also promised him a privileged channel to the Chairman's ear through Mao's pillow companion.

As further reassurance, therefore, Mao decided that his new wife should stay in the background, running his private secretariat, as He Zizhen and Yang Kaihui had before her, with no official responsibilities. Jiang Qing may have bridled at this arrangement, but it suited Mao very well. He was attracted by her youth and sexuality, just as he had been drawn to Lily Wu. But he wanted a helpmate, not a partner in histrionics. For all his intellectualising about the equal status of women, Mao did not brook rivals, least of all in his marriage-bed.

For a while, the doubters were silenced. Jiang Qing knitted Mao pullovers, and cooked for him the spicy Hunanese dishes he liked. His bodyguard at that time, Li Yinqiao, remembered:

> She had jet-black hair, which she wore with a fringe and a hair-band, cut long at the back, delicate eyebrows and bright eyes, a nice nose and generous mouth . . . In Yan'an, we always thought of her as a star. Her calligraphy, especially in cursive script, was good. she liked horse-riding and playing cards . . . She could cut out clothes for herself, and look good . . . At that time she was close to the ordinary people. She cut the bodyguards' hair and taught them how to sew. On the march, she encouraged them, and taught them guessing games . . . In the winter, everyone wore thick clothes. But she cut hers so they fitted her tightly, to show off her figure . . . She was very proud; she liked to be in the limelight. She really liked showing off.

In August 1940, to Mao's delight, she gave birth to a baby daughter, Li Na (who took her surname, like He Zizhen's daughter, Li Min, from Mao's Party alias, Li Desheng). She was his ninth child, of whom four had survived. Child-bearing, however, was not to Jiang Qing's taste, and she made plain she would not submit to the constant pregnancies that He Zizhen had endured. A year later, when she conceived again, she insisted on having an abortion. The operation was botched. She developed a high fever, and soon afterwards found she was also suffering from tuberculosis. She then had herself sterilised.

Mao, who, despite his progressive ideas in other spheres, conserved the traditional Chinese attitude equating numerous offspring with happiness, was not pleased.

Other differences arose, too. Mao frequently worked all night and slept during the day. He Zizhen had gone along with these arrangements. Jiang Qing refused. At Yangjialing, Mao had a bed made up in his study so that he could work in peace. After 1942, when they moved to Zaoyuan (Date Garden), another valley two miles further out from Yan'an, where Zhu De and the Red Army

Command were based, Jiang Qing occupied separate quarters.

To the outside world, she appeared a devoted young wife and mother. But, in private, her relationship with Mao was often turbulent. Her importunities that he intercede with the Party hierarchy to get her special treatment particularly enraged him. Then he would shout at her furiously, calling her a bitch and ordering her out of his presence.

Apart from Kang Sheng, Chen Boda and a handful of others, the rest of the Party elite never entirely accepted her. Mao's bodyguard, Li Yinqiao, recalled being at lunch with her one day when she suddenly screamed out: 'Mother-fucking monsters!' Seeing his stunned expression, she explained hastily that she meant not him but 'those people in the Party' who refused to accept her political bona fides. Twenty-five years later, when she became a power in her own right during the Cultural Revolution, she would have her revenge for these perceived humiliations.

It was to Li Yinqiao, too, that Mao confessed, one day in 1947, his own growing disenchantment with her. 'I didn't marry very well,' he said ruefully. 'I rushed into it too lightly.' Then he sighed. 'Jiang Qing', he said 'is my wife. If she were one of my staff, I'd get rid of her as soon as I could . . . But there's nothing I can do. I've just got to put up with her.' By then, Mao's son, Anying, and Li Min were both living in his household.* He would have been less than human if these flesh-and-blood reminders of earlier, happier marriages had not led him to make mental comparisons that were not to Jiang Qing's advantage. Even without their presence, though, the relationship was turning sour. In public, appearances were maintained. But from the late 1940s on, Mao increasingly sought female companionship elsewhere.

While Mao was, by his own admission, making a mess of his personal life, his political cause prospered as never before.

---

* After the destruction of the Shanghai Party organisation in 1933, Anying, then aged eleven and his younger brother, Anqing, were left to fend for themselves, living on their wits on the streets. They maintained contact with the Party, however, and three years later were sent to Moscow to study. There it was discovered that Anqing was mentally ill. Anying returned to China in December 1945; his brother, four years later.

As he had predicted at the Sixth Plenum, the GMD soon proved itself to be a most unreliable ally. Barely two months later, in January 1939, nationalist party leaders approved a secret decision to 'corrode, contain, restrict and combat' the Communist Party. Mao's counter-order, the same month, read: 'We will not attack unless we are attacked ourselves. But if we are attacked, we will certainly counter-attack.'

Throughout the next year, 'frictions', as the resulting clashes were euphemistically called, multiplied between GMD and Red Army troops.

Neither side was innocent. The communists were expanding their base areas at the GMD's expense; the nationalists were determined to stop them. But neither wanted the alliance to sunder altogether. Mao feared that the GMD, left to its own devices, would sign a separate truce with Japan. Chiang did not want to lose Russian war aid. Nevertheless, the nationalists stepped up restrictions on communist activities in the areas they controlled; and an undeclared blockade was imposed on the border region around Yan'an.

These tensions reached their peak after a major communist offensive, the so-called 'Hundred Regiments Campaign', in the autumn of 1940.

From the standpoint of the war against Japan, this had been a great success. Twenty-six thousand Japanese troops were left dead or wounded. But Chiang saw it as a warning that the communists were growing too strong. That winter, he decided it was time to teach them a lesson. In January, the communist New Fourth Army, made up of former guerrillas from the old southern base areas, was being redeployed to positions across the Yellow River. In Anhui, it was ambushed by a greatly superior GMD force. During a week of fierce fighting, 9,000 communists were captured or killed.

That brought relations to breaking-point. Direct contacts between Yan'an and Chiang Kai-shek's headquarters in Chongqing were suspended, and CCP liaison offices closed in other provincial cities. But even in this extremity, the united front was too valuable for the communists to give up. The legitimacy it conferred had allowed the Red Army to grow from 50,000 to half-a-million men. Party membership was rising so fast that the Politburo had to halt new admissions, because the existing structure could no longer cope with them. To Mao, the front had become a 'magic weapon', smoothing the communists' path to power. Chiang Kai-shek knew that. But his hands were tied, too. The war with Japan, which had brought the alliance into being in the first place, meant that he could not unilaterally end it without reviving charges that he was more interested in fighting the Reds than fighting the Japanese.

In the end, the entry of the Soviet Union into the war in June 1941, and America the following December, left them no choice but to stay together. China became part of an emerging Pacific alliance, which temporarily overrode the imperatives of domestic rivalry. Both sides held their fire, tried to conserve their forces, and prepared for the conflict they both knew would come after Japan's still distant but now foreseeable defeat.

In Mao's case, that meant a new drive to bend the Party to his will.

The method, this time, was to be a reappraisal of Party history, designed to prove even to the most sceptical that Wang Ming and his allies had been wrong, not just over united-front policy, but ever since 1931, while Mao alone had been consistently correct.

In the four years since the war with Japan had begun, a good deal of groundwork had already been done. Mao himself had written, in October 1939, of the need to achieve a common understanding of Party history, so as to consolidate the Party 'ideologically, politically and organisationally', and 'avoid repeating historical mistakes'. Only since Zunyi, he claimed, had the Party been 'soundly on the Bolshevik road'. To Wang Ming, whose supporters had been in power for the four years before Zunyi, the writing was on the wall: Mao wanted nothing less than a wholesale repudiation of the policies they had stood for.

To try to head off this challenge, Wang sketched the basis for a trade-off. He would not dispute Mao's present primacy. But neither should Mao try to negate Wang's own past contributions.

For a time, this compromise seemed to hold. But then, in December 1940, Mao issued a comprehensive list of what he considered to be the Wang Ming group's 'ultra-leftist errors' in Jiangxi:

There was the economic elimination of the capitalist class (the ultra-Left policies on labour and taxation) and of the rich peasants (by allotting them poor land); the physical elimination of the landlords (by not allotting them any land); the attack on the intellectuals; the 'Left' deviation in the suppression of counter-revolutionaries; the monopolising by communists of the organs of political power . . .; the ultra-Left military policy (of attacking the big cities, and denying the role of guerilla warfare) . . .; and the policy within the Party of attacks on comrades through the abuse of disciplinary measures. These ultra-Left policies . . . caused great losses to the Party and the revolution.

Still Mao named no names. And when Liu Shaoqi urged him to characterise the errors as 'mistakes of political line', he prudently refused. 'Melons ripen,' Kang Sheng quoted him as saying. 'Don't pick them when they are not yet ripe. When they are ready, they will just drop off. In struggle, one mustn't be too rigid.'

That autumn, however, as the CCP and the Guomindang drew back from the brink after the New Fourth Army massacre, Mao decided the time had finally come to launch the great political offensive that he had been so carefully preparing.

The Yan'an Rectification Campaign, as it would be called, would last nearly four years. By the time it ended, Mao would no longer be the first among equals. He would be the one man who decided all – a demiurge, set on a pedestal, towering above his nominal colleagues, beyond institutional control.

He opened his attack at an enlarged Politburo meeting, which began on September 10, 1941, with a critique of 'subjectivism', meaning the failure to adapt Party policies to the reality of Chinese conditions. As a general proposition, this had been a theme of Mao's speeches since the spring. Now he became more specific. The 'Li Lisan line' in 1930 had been one such instance, he said. The policies of the Fourth Plenum leadership, from 1931 to 1934, had been still more damaging. Moreover, the problem was not yet over. Subjectivism, sectarianism and dogmatism were still doing a great deal of harm, and a mass movement must be launched to fight them.

By the time the meeting ended, six weeks later, Mao had got almost everything he wanted. Wang Ming and Bo Gu had been condemned for their 'erroneous leftist line' in Jiangxi, and many of their former associates, including Zhang Wentian, had made self-criticisms. The one residual disagreement was over exactly when the Returned Students' errors had begun – at the Fourth Plenum itself, in January 1931, as Mao argued; or, as Wang Ming preferred, the following September, after Wang had returned to Moscow, leaving Bo Gu in charge? But even that had the happy result of dividing the two principal Returned Student leaders.

Several factors had combined to make this breakthrough possible.

By sheer force of repetition, Mao's calls over the previous five years for a distinctively Chinese way had finally instilled themselves into the Party's collective consciousness. He himself exemplified that approach, and by 1941 his record spoke for itself. Since Zunyi, the Party had prospered; before it, under the Returned Students, it had come to the brink of destruction. Moreover, Mao promised his colleagues that the coming movement would be aimed at 'rectifying' mistaken ideas, not the people who held them. The guideline would be 'curing the sickness to save the patient', not the 'harsh struggle and merciless blows' that had characterised previous political campaigns.

Mao would later describe this Politburo meeting in September 1941 as one of the half-dozen crucial steps in his rise to supreme power. It lined up the rest of the leadership behind him (except Wang and Bo, who refused to admit their errors), and endorsed the practical arrangements for the rectification movement he was about to unleash.

Up to this point, all Mao's manoeuvring had been confined to the uppermost echelons of the Party elite. Probably fewer than 150 people, in a Party which by then had 800,000 members, were aware of the struggle that was unfolding. Even Peng Dehuai, a full Politburo member, admitted afterwards that he did not really grasp what was involved until more than a year later. Rank-and-file members had no inkling of what was going on.

But in February 1942, rectification moved into the public domain.

That month Mao gave two major speeches to the Central Party School in which he set out the movement's goals. 'We are communists', he told them, 'so we must keep our ranks in good order, we must march in step.' Then he explained the nature of the music he wanted them to march to:

As an arrow is to the target, so is Marxism-Leninism to the Chinese revolution. Some comrades, however, are 'shooting without a target' . . . at random . . . Others merely stroke the arrow fondly, exclaiming, 'What a fine arrow! What a fine arrow!' but never want to shoot it . . . The arrow of Marxism-Leninism must be used to shoot at the target . . . Why otherwise would we want to study it? We do not study Marxism-Leninism because it is pleasing to the eye, or because it has some mystical value, like the doctrines of the Daoist priests who ascend Maoshan to learn how to subdue devils and evil spirits.

Marxism-Leninism has no beauty, nor has it any mystical value. It is only extremely useful . . . Those who regard Marxism-Leninism as religious dogma show . . . blind ignorance. We must tell them openly, 'Your dogma is of no use,' or, to speak crudely, 'Your dogma is of less use than dogshit.' Dogshit can fertilise fields and man's shit can feed dogs. But dogmas? They can't fertilise fields and they can't feed dogs. What use are they?

In future, he declared, Party officials would be judged by whether they could apply 'the standpoint, concepts and method of Marxism-Leninism' to solve practical problems, not on their ability to 'read ten thousand volumes by Marx, Engels, Lenin and Stalin, and . . . recite every sentence from memory'.

Book-learning in general, ever one of Mao's *bêtes-noires*, came in for a memorable drubbing:

Cooking food and preparing meals is truly one of the arts. But what about book-learning? If you do nothing but read, you have only to be able to recognise three to five thousand characters . . . [and] hold some book in your hand, and the public will provide you with a living . . . But books cannot walk . . . [Reading them] is . . . a great deal simpler than for a cook to prepare a meal, far easier than for him to slaughter a pig. He has to catch the pig. The pig can run. (*Laughter in the hall*) He slaughters him. The pig squeals. (*Laughter*) A book placed on a desk cannot run, neither can it squeal . . . (*Laughter*) Is there anything easier? Therefore, I advise those of you who have only book-learning and as yet no contact with reality . . . to realise your own shortcomings and make your attitudes a bit more humble.

There was much more in the same vein. Empty, abstract speeches which were 'like the foot-bindings of a slattern, long and foul-smelling', 'individualism' which violated Party discipline; and 'foreign formalism' were vigorously denounced:

We must plant our backsides on the body of China. We must study world capitalism and socialism, but if we want to be clear about their relations to the history of the Chinese Party, it's all a matter of where you put your bottom . . . When we study China, we must take China as the centre . . . We have some comrades who have a malady, namely that they take foreign countries as the centre and act like phonographs, mechanically swallowing whole foreign things and transporting them to China.

These strictures were directed less at Wang Ming and his remnant followers, already broken reeds, than at the mind-set they represented. Over the next twelve months, as the Party rank and file, at lecture meetings and in small group discussions, absorbed Mao's ideas and the view of Party history that flowed from them, the intellectual centre of gravity of the Chinese Party shifted. The fount of Marxist-Leninist wisdom was no longer in Moscow but in Yan'an.

In March 1943, the composition of the Party's ruling organs was belatedly brought into line with the new political reality which the Rectification Campaign had produced. Mao was named Chairman of the Politburo, and of a new three-man Secretariat, in which he was joined by Liu Shaoqi, now confirmed, in fact if not yet in name, as second-ranking Party leader, and by Ren Bishi, Wang Jiaxiang's partner in promoting Mao's cause in Moscow five years earlier. Wang himself became deputy head of the Propaganda Department under Mao, while Kang Sheng, whose career had also taken off since he had aligned himself with Mao in 1938, became deputy head, under Liu, of the other key Central body, the Organisation Department. Wang Ming, who had been a member of the top leadership since 1931, was excluded from any decision-making role.

The real innovation, however, lay in the fine print. As before, the Secretariat was empowered to take decisions when the Politburo was not in session. But this time it was explicitly stated that, should its members fail to agree, Mao would have the final say. This was much more than just a matter of giving him a casting vote, or even veto power. It meant that even if both the other members of the Secretariat disagreed, Mao's views would prevail.

In wartime, perhaps, such an extraordinary concentration of authority in the hands of one man may have seemed justified. Mao's colleagues could reassure themselves that the Politburo and the Central Committee, both collegiate institutions, retained ultimate power. But the truth was that a bandwagon was rolling. By then, even Bo Gu had capitulated. Wang Ming, alone, remained the last, defiant hold-out, an example for others to avoid. The rest of the leadership, having watched Mao's rise, and knowing that their own futures would depend on how they handled their relations with him, had little interest in making a stand against what most of them regarded anyway as an inevitable accretion of power.

By 1943, Mao had achieved a status in his own Party that no Chinese communist leader had ever had before.

But his role was still limited to the areas the communists controlled, only a small part of the country as a whole. The next step would entail the fashioning of a mythology of personality and ideas which would enable him, over the next six years, to inspire and direct an armed struggle that would win the support of the population at large, unifying, this time, not merely the Party but all China behind the communist cause.

Like the Cultural Revolution, twenty-five years later, the Yan'an Rectification Campaign was far more than just a struggle for power. It was an attempt to bring about fundamental change in the way people thought.

Its roots lay in the logic of united-front politics, which had required the Party dramatically to broaden its appeal. At Wayaobu, in December 1935, the Politburo had agreed, at Mao's urging, that Party membership should be open to 'all who are willing to fight for the Communist Party's positions, regardless of their class origin'. After the Comintern demurred, that formula was withdrawn. But the open-door approach continued. In order to win over the so-called 'intermediate classes' – the patriotic bourgeoisie, the small and middle landlords and intellectuals – that made up the rank and file of the GMD's political constituency, the CCP moderated its policies. In an article in March 1940, entitled, 'On New Democracy', Mao noted that while socialism remained the ultimate goal, it was still a very long way off. The current task, which would take many years, was to fight imperialism and feudalism.

This policy of class collaboration succeeded beyond all expectations. In the three years from the Marco Polo Bridge incident to mid-1940, Party membership grew almost twentyfold. But many if not most of the new recruits were drawn by patriotism more than communist conviction.

The next problem, therefore, was how to weld this vast, disparate membership into a disciplined political force.

In the early 1930s, the Communist Party had been 'Bolshevised' by fear. But the wave of revulsion that had generated ruled out any repetition, even had Mao wanted it – and by the end of the Long March, he, too, had recognised that there had to be a better way of resolving inner-Party differences. Men who had shared such incredible hardships, he told Xu Haidong in 1935, could not be fundamentally disloyal. Subsequently, various attempts were made to devise new methods, including 'new leaf rallies', where erring comrades confessed their faults and pledged publicly to make a new start. But the answer Mao eventually came up with stemmed from the Classical teachings of his youth.

'If our Party's style is completely orthodox,' he announced at the beginning of the Rectification Campaign, 'the people of the entire nation will learn from us.' The force of virtuous example, as Confucius had written – of 'Redness', as it was termed in Jiangxi, and would be again in the Cultural Revolution – was the key to swaying people's minds. Where Confucius, however, had contended that the masses 'may be made to follow a course of action, but they may not be made to understand it', Mao, as a communist, insisted that 'the masses are the real heroes', capable themselves of generating revolutionary ideas:

> All correct leadership is necessarily 'from the masses, to the masses'. This means: take the ideas of the masses . . . [and] through study, turn them into concentrated and systematic ideas, then go to the masses and propagate and explain these ideas until the masses embrace them as their own, hold fast to them and . . . test [their] correctness in action. Then once again concentrate ideas from the masses and once again go to the masses . . . and so on, over and over again in an endless spiral, with the ideas becoming more correct, more vital and richer each time.

In the Rectification Campaign, this approach was applied within the Party's own ranks. The 'movement of enlightenment' which Mao sought was to be brought about voluntarily, by Party members themselves: 'Communist Party members must ask "Why?" about everything, turn matters over deliberately in their minds and ask whether they conform to reality. They certainly must not follow blindly. Nor must they encourage slavishness.' Yet, at the same time, he insisted on the need for uniformity of thought. 'Submission to Central leadership' was specifically reaffirmed.

Mao's predilection for contradictions of this kind became a hallmark of his political style. It was a fiendishly clever, yet extraordinary simple device, enabling him to modulate the progress of an ideological campaign to accommodate his political needs, to change direction at will, and to lure real or presumed opponents into exposing their views, the better to strike them down.

Rectification had never been intended as a gentle, benign process. It was to be the final struggle, not only against Wang Ming and the ideas he represented, but more broadly against all in the Party who were in any way reluctant to accept the hegemony of Mao's thought. 'Curing the sickness to save the patient' was a fine principle, but Mao had not promised it would be painless. 'The first step', he had explained, 'is to give the patient a powerful shock. Yell at him, "Your're sick!". Then he'll get a fright and break out in a sweat. At that point, he can be put on the road to recovery.' Confucian-style persuasion, moreover, might be the principal method; but, like his imperial predecessors, Mao reserved Legalist coercion for those who refused to submit – not senior leaders like Wang Ming, whose status protected them from crude repression, but lesser, more vulnerable souls, whose plight would serve as a warning to others.

In Yan'an, in 1942, the foremost among these irreductibles was an idealistic young writer named Wang Shiwei.

Sincerity, not to say gullibililty, has been one of the most attractive and enduring characteristics of Chinese intellectuals through the centuries. Among the writers and artists who had flocked to the communist standard since the beginning of the war, Mao's call for inner-Party debate and the questioning of long-held truths provoked an explosion of wall newspapers – with names like *Shiyudi* (Arrow and Target), *Qing qibing* (Light Cavalry), *Tuo ling* (Camel Bells) and *Xibei feng* (Northwest Wind) – like that in the May Fourth Movement, twenty years before.

The feminist, Ding Ling, made a vituperative attack on the Party's hypocrisy towards women. Her colleague, the poet, Ai Qing, complained caustically that Mao's cultural commissars expected him 'to describe ringworm as flowers'. But the most devastating article by far was Wang Shiwei's satirical essay, 'Wild Lily', which appeared in the Party newspaper, *Jiefang ribao* (Liberation Daily), in March. It denounced the 'dark side of Yan'an' – the 'three classes of clothing and five grades of food', which were allocated to senior officials when 'the sick can't get a bowl of noodles, and the young have only two bowls of congee a day' the privileged access to young women enjoyed by those who had political power; the elitism and aloofness of cadres towards the rank and file.

Even now, half a century later, Chinese still disagree whether Mao set a deliberate trap, into which Wang Shiwei, and others, fell, or whether the writers' response took him by surprise.

Typically, he encouraged both interpretations, describing Wang, at one moment, as a sorely needed target for the Rectification Campaign, and, at another, as a distraction, undermining its political purpose. But whether premeditated or not, Wang's calvary became a model in the repression of intellectual dissent, whose lessons would be applied, almost unchanged, to writers and artists in China throughout Mao's lifetime and beyond.

These were spelled out by Mao himself, in May, at a specially called forum on literature and art. Satire and criticism were necessary, he said, but writers and artists must know on which side of the revolutionary divide they belonged. Those (like Wang Shiwei) who devoted their energies to exposing 'the so-called "darkness" of the proletariat' were 'petty-bourgeois individualists', 'mere termites in the revolutionary ranks'. The purpose of art, he went on, was to serve proletarian politics. The 'fundamental task' of writers and artists was to become 'loyal spokesmen' for the masses, immersing themselves in their lives and extolling their revolutionary struggles.

Four days later, Wang was subjected to an ideological show trial, a prototype, albeit in milder form, of the struggle meetings of the 1960s. For two weeks, his Party colleagues debated his errors. Mao's political secretary, Chen Boda, set the tone, likening Wang to a leech and referring to him as 'Comrade Shit-stink', a word-play on the characters that formed his name. The bold poet, Ai Qing, intoned: 'His viewpoint is reactionary and his remedies are poisonous; this "individual" does not deserve to be described as "human", let alone a comrade.' Even the rebellious Ding Ling decided it was wiser to denounce him. In the logic of rectification, it was not enough for Wang merely to be purged. His fellow writers had publicly to humiliate him. His 'trial' marked the beginning of a practice of collective denunication that would remain an essential part of the Chinese Communists' treatment of dissidents for decades to come.

Afterwards, he was dismissed from the Literary Association, which meant he was no longer allowed to write. 'Everyone else', one participant recalled, having 'got rid of their ideological burden' – in other words, having saved their own skins – breathed a sigh of relief and resolved to keep their heads down in future.

Mao, however, was not yet convinced that the writers had learned their lesson. Wang himself had refused to recant, maintaining that what he had written had been intended for the Party's good. According to Kang Sheng, 90 per cent of the Yan'an intellectuals had initially sympathised with him. The Rectification Campaign was therefore extended, and efforts to demonise Wang shifted into higher gear. Already, during his 'trial', he had been accused of Trotskyism, 'anti-Party thoughts', having a 'filthy and disgusting soul' and inhabiting the mental universe of 'a counter-revolutionary shit-hole'. None the less, his case had been treated as that of an erring comrade, who might possibly still be saved. The following October, that changed. Wang was formally accused of being a Guomindang spy, and of leading a Trotskyite 'Five-Member Anti-Party Gang' which had 'sneaked into the Party to destroy and undermine it'. He was subsequently taken into custody by officials of the Social Department, the Party's Security Police, along with some two hundred others regarded as politically unreliable, and detained at a secret CCP prison at Zaoyuan.

The 'Anti-Party Gang' was a frame-up, pure and simple, of the type at which Kang Sheng came to excel. Wang and the other four alleged members, two young married couples, had known each other slightly and shared the same liberal views. That was as far as the 'conspiracy' went. Even Mao, who had approved the operation, tried to shrug it off later as a 'mistake'. Yet it was no less essential to his strategy than other, subtler aspects of the Rectification Campaign. For it showed the Party at large that the leadership's tolerance went only so far, that those who placed themselves beyond the pale – whose cases, as Mao would later put it, changed from being 'contradictions among the people' to 'contradictions between the enemy and ourselves' – would find the Confucian velvet glove replaced by a Legalist chopper.

From the autumn of 1942 onwards, Kang Sheng was given carte blanche for the first (but by no means the last) time to demonstrate his prowess as Mao's axeman.

A 'cadre screening movement' was launched to weed out 'spies and bad elements', on the pretext that the growth of Party membership had allowed Chiang Kai-shek's intelligence services to infiltrate secret agents. 'Spies', Mao warned melodramatically, were becoming 'as thick as fur'. But, as in Wang Shiwei's case, the word 'spy' was broadly construed. Voicing dissident opinions, 'liberalism' towards unorthodox elements, a lack of enthusiasm for rectification, having relatives who were GMD members – all became grounds for suspicion. In December, therefore, with Mao's approval, the 'screening movement' became a 'rescue movement', in which suspects were tortured into confessing in order that they might be 'saved'. This was consistent with Mao's original formula, 'Cure the sickness to save the patient', but distorted into a new, savage form that few in the Party had bargained for.

By July 1943, over a thousand 'enemy agents' had been detained, of whom nearly half had confessed. Kang reported that 70 per cent of recently recruited Party cadres were politically unreliable. At an army communications school, 170 out of 200 students were charged as 'special agents'. Even in the Party Secretariat, the hub of Mao's apparatus of power, 10 officials out of 60 were found to have 'political problems'. There were dozens of suicides, and some 40,000 people (5 per cent of the total Party membership) were expelled.

It was all chillingly reminiscent of Mao's campaign against the AB-*tuan* at Futian in 1930. The death-toll was far lower, but the reliance on torture and confession was essentially the same.

Mao's colleagues thought so, too. Zhou Enlai, who returned to Yan'an from Chongqing in the summer of 1943, challenged Kang's assertions that the underground Party in the White areas was riddled with traitors. That in turn led Ren Bishi to investigate. His report to Mao was never made public, but it was evidently highly critical of Kang's methods, for in August the Chairman started to rein in the Social Department investigators. Two months later he minuted: 'We should not kill anyone. Most people should not be arrested. This is the policy we must stick to.' With that, the 'rescue movement' ended. In December 1943, a year after the movement had begun, it was revealed that 90 per cent of those accused had been innocent and were being rehabilitated, in some cases posthumously.

Mao's reasons for permitting the 'rescue movement' to get so badly out of hand cast a revealing light on his style of rule.

Nationalist pressure was one factor, as it had been at Futian. But far more important was his conviction that a leader should never appear to be soft. In 1943, as he prepared to celebrate his fiftieth birthday, Mao had reached the end of his long apprenticeship in the uses of power. His setbacks in the 1920s and early '30s had taught him that in politics, as in war, the object was to annihilate one's opponents, not to leave them wounded to fight another day. That did not mean a return to the old, discredited policies of 'harsh struggle and merciless blows', which Mao blamed on Wang Ming. But it implied a recognition that persuasion had to be backed up by fear. Revolution was *not* a dinner-party.

Wang Shiwei was the prototypal victim of this conscious ambiguity.

After his arrest, Mao gave orders that he neither be released nor killed. He remained in detention – 'a young man with a grey, deathly look on his face', who spoke 'as if reciting from a textbook' – to serve as a living warning to others in the Party of the fate that would await them should they stray from Mao's appointed path.

In the spring of 1947, when the communists withdrew from Yan'an, He Long was the local military commander. Westerners usually depicted him as the Robin Hood of the Red Army, a dare-devil, romantic figure, who hated the rich and championed the poor. But like his fellow-generals, He Long was a tough, ruthless man. They hated intellectuals like Wang, who whined about literary free-doms while young soldiers were dying at the front. On He's orders one morning, Wang Shiwei was executed, with an axe, in a village near the Yellow River. When Mao was told, he bit his lip but said nothing.

Mao's emergence as the Party's supreme leader was accompanied by a growing personality cult. Already in the late 1920s, the Cantonese-speaking villagers of southern China wove myths about the bandit leader they called Mo Tak Chung, whom the authorities could never kill. But the decision to promote his image nationally as the standard-bearer of Chinese communism had come a decade later with the publication of Edgar Snow's *Red Star over China*. Snow had written that he perceived in Mao 'a certain force of destiny'.

Mao evidently felt that, too. In the winter of 1935, he had revealed the full sweep of his ambition in a poem describing the landscape of northern Shensi. It opened with the lines:

> *A hundred leagues are ice-bound,*
> *A thousand leagues of whirling snow . . .*
> *The mountains dance like silver snakes,*
> *The highlands roll like white wax elephants*
>   *challenging the heavens.*

Mao then turned his thoughts to the Chinese leaders of antiquity who had gazed before him on this same landscape – the founding

Emperors of the Qin, the Han, the Tang and the Song; and Genghis Khan, the Mongol. All had triumphed, he wrote, yet all had been flawed. 'For true heroes,' Mao declared, 'we must look to the present age.'

The comparison was breathtaking.

At a time when the Red Army could muster only a few thousand poorly armed men, Mao already saw himself as the founding figure in a new, communist era, ready to assume the mantle of greatness inherited from the imperial past.

Thus, from the end of the Long March, Mao was predisposed to the idea that he was an exceptional man, ordained to play an exceptional role. From there it was but a small step, once conditions were ripe, to launching a full-blown leadership cult.

In June 1937, the new CCP weekly, *Jiefang* (Liberation), published his picture for the first time. It was a woodcut, with Mao's face illuminated by the rays of the sun, a motif traditionally associated with emperor-worship in China. Six months later, the first collection of his writings were printed in Shanghai. In the summer of 1938 another milestone was passed when Mao's faithful acolyte, Lin Biao, wrote of his 'genius in leadership', a phrase that would become so overworked in the later years of Mao's life that even he would grow sick of it.

At the same time, Mao's relations with those around him underwent a subtle change.

Western visitors in the early days of Yan'an had been charmed by the casualness of the place. Mao would drop in unannounced for dinner or a game of cards. 'There developed', wrote the Comintern adviser, Otto Braun, 'what might almost be called a social life.' Saturday-night dances were held, which Mao – notwithstanding Agnes Smedley's comment that he had 'no rhythm in his being' – particularly relished, because of the opportunities they provided for adoring female company. The American communist, Sidney Rittenberg, recalled arriving late one evening.

I could hear a string bass, a couple of fiddles, and maybe a saxophone and a clarinet tooting away . . . Someone pushed open the door and I peeped inside. There, directly across the room, I saw a lifesized portrait of Chairman Mao Zedong. I recognised immediately the wide forehead and brow, and the tiny, almost feminine mouth. Framed by the doorway, against the whitewashed walls, the leonine head looked stern, almost baleful. The tableau lasted only a split second. Then the band struck up a foxtrot, and the portrait came to life, turned, gestured to his partner, and began gliding across the floor.

Now, behind the façade of easy fellowship – the atmosphere of an American revivalist camp, full of back-slapping and good cheer, as one visitor described it – a new formality developed.

In the spring of 1938, Violet Cressy-Marcks, one of the remarkable generation of intrepid women travellers who spent the inter-war years journeying alone through the Orient, was escorted to Mao's courtyard at Fenghuangshan to find its outer gate guarded by a soldier with a sub-machine-gun, and a second guard, at an inner door, carrying 'the biggest naked sword I had ever seen in my life'. Gone were the days on the Jinggangshan, or even at Ruijin, less than ten years before, when Mao and the other leaders lived among the peasants. Now a pervasive sense of hierarchy set in. Mao no longer visited others; they came to him. Later that year, he requisitioned the only vehicle in town, a donated Chevrolet van, emblazoned with the words, 'Ambulance: Gift of the New York Chinese Laundrymen's National Salvation Association', to serve as his personal transport. The rest of the Politburo walked.

Not everyone welcomed the plethora of superlatives – 'most creative', 'most qualified', 'most talented', 'most authoritative' – which now attached themselves to Mao. Even Liu Shaoqi, who was among his most consistent supporters, issued a cautious warning. In sinifying Marxism, he wrote, 'we must not follow blindly, nor worship any idols'.

But in November 1942, came news from Europe that silenced such hesitations. The battle of Stalingrad, the 'Red Verdun', as Mao called it, was a turning-point in the war, heralding the eventual collapse of the fascist Axis and bringing closer the time when conflict would resume between the Chinese nationalists and the communists.

That redirected attention, in both camps, to the need to build symbolic capital for the coming contest for the country's allegiance. On March 10, 1943, Chiang Kai-shek published his book, *China's Destiny*, setting out his claims to be China's ruler. Mao's elevation to become Chairman of the Politburo, and thus the Communist Party's champion, occurred a few days later. The territory and population each controlled was still heavily weighted in Chiang's favour. But the disparity was growing steadily smaller. Chiang's book was made compulsory reading in schools and universities in the White areas. Mao's writings on the sinification of Marxism became the guiding doctrine in the Red areas.

Two months later, Mao's stature was further enhanced when Stalin, in a gesture to the Western allies, dissolved the Comintern. The CCP was now, in theory and in fact, an independent, national party.

As the personal dimension in the two parties' rivalry became more sharply drawn, the personality cult around Mao reached new heights. In July, Liu Shaoqi, his doubts now stilled, lit the fires of unrestrained adulation. In a hagiographic article, he asserted that the only way to guarantee that the Party would not commit future errors was to ensure that 'Mao Zedong's leadership penetrates everywhere'. That was the signal for his Politburo colleagues, from Zhou Enlai and Zhu De down, to join a chorus of delirious approval. Two American journalists, Theodore White and Annalee Jacoby, visiting Yan'an some months later, reported that Mao 'was set on a pinnacle of adoration', the object of 'panegyrics of the most high-flown, almost nauseatingly slavish eloquence'. Even more striking, they wrote, was the practice of Mao's fellow leaders, 'men of great rank themselves, to make ostentatious notes on Mao's free-running speeches, as though drinking from the fountain of knowledge'.

This was the time when the term 'Mao Zedong Thought' (*Mao Zedong sixiang*) was coined, and when the first versions of his 'Selected Works' were compiled. It was then, too, that the Maoist anthem, 'The East is Red', was written:

> *The East is Red, the sun rises.*
> *In China a Mao Zedong is born.*
> *He seeks the people's happiness.*
> *He is the people's Great Saviour.*

Mao's portrait was painted on village walls and public buildings all over Red China. Schools were named after him: the Zedong Young Cadres' School in Yan'an, the Zedong Youth School in Shandong. Toddlers were taught to chant: 'We are all Chairman Mao's good little children'.

The following winter, labour heroes sent messages, hailing Mao as China's 'star of salvation', a term which, in Chinese minds, conjured up the ancient link between the Emperor and the Heavens. In the spring of 1944, Mao was invited to plant the first grains of millet, as the Emperor, in past ages, had symbolically ploughed the first furrow.

One element, however, was still lacking.

All through Chinese history, the summation of the past had played a crucial part in creating the political basis for a new dynasty's assumption of power. In Mao's case, there was the additional example of Stalin's rule in Russsia. One of the Soviet dictator's first actions after the Great Purge, in which the last of his adversaries perished, had been to issue his own version of Soviet Party history – the *History of the CPSU (Bolshevik), Short Course* – in 1938. This was translated into Chinese and assigned for cadre study in Yan'an a year later. Subsequently it was included among the texts used in the Rectification Campaign, a message not lost on Mao's colleagues.

But the 'clarification of Party history', as it was delicately called, continued to elude him.

The crux of the problem was that Mao, like Stalin – like Chinese leaders through the ages – would brook no rival source of authority. It was not enough that the Party's early leaders, Chen Duxiu and Li Lisan, were already discredited (and Qu Qiubai, had he not died a martyr, would surely have been, too). It was not enough that the political line of Wang Ming and Bo Gu had been repudiated. The exposure and rebuttal of non-Maoist ideas had to be carried through to the end. There was no lack of precedent for this in China's imperial past. The great Qing Emperor, Qianlong, in the eighteenth century, conducted one of the most terrible literary inquisitions of all time to root out seditious thought. Mao, too, felt instinctively that his rule would not be secure until all the intellectual alternatives within the Party had been closed off, and senior officials, starting with his own closest colleagues, had publicly confessed their past errors in supporting the mistaken policies previously associated with his rivals.

It would take another eighteen months before he was finally satisfied that he had the degree of control that he wanted.

From late 1943 until the spring of 1944, Liu Shaoqi, as Mao's point man, led the attack on the Fourth Plenum, which had brought

Wang Ming to power. Everyone who had ever been associated with Wang, starting with Zhang Wentian and Zhou Enlai, made abject self-criticisms – and was criticised by their colleagues in turn.

In Zhou's case, the process was particularly painful. On at least two occasions, Mao himself made blistering attacks on Zhou's record, his lack of principle and willingness to be swayed by whichever group held power. In Jiangxi, Zhou had sided with the Returned Students. After 1937, he had backed Wang Ming. Mao was determined that this time, he should learn his lesson.* Ren Bishi, now one of the Chairman's close allies, was likewise required to repudiate his former ties with Wang Ming. Kang Sheng was criticised for his handling of the 'rescue movement', along with lesser figures like Deng Fa (his predecessor as Security Chief, and the architect of the blood-purge in Fujian in 1931). Apart from absent members, such as Wang Jiaxiang (who was back in Moscow) and Wang Ming (who was ill), every leader went through the ritual of repentance and obeisance to Mao's ideas – with one exception: Liu Shaoqi, who in a foretaste of the hubris that would eventually cause his downfall, claimed to have been on Mao's side all along.

In April 1944, with all opposition stilled, Mao was ready to bring the orgy of self-flagellation to an end. Wang Ming and Bo Gu, he announced, would not be punished for anti-Party crimes, as the Russian Old Bolsheviks had been. Party policy veered back towards conciliation again.

Mao also made a tacit apology for the excesses of the 'rescue movement', bowing to the assembled cadres as a sign of atonement. It was a measure of the depth of hatred which that campaign had aroused that, despite his Olympian stature in the Party by this stage, he had to bow not once but three times before the audience applauded, signifying that his excuses were accepted.

In the new, authorised version of Party history, Mao's struggles

---

* It was evidently this episode that led Dimitrov, the former Comintern chief, to telegram Mao in December with a plea to keep Zhou (and Wang Ming) in the leadership. According to Party historians who specialise in the period, the original texts of Mao's criticisms of Zhou are held in the Central Archives. Mao reportedly sent for them twice to reread after 1949, apparently at times when he was considering a public rebuke to Zhou: in 1956, when Zhou angered him by trying to slow the pace of economic growth; and during the Cultural Revolution.

against the 'wrong views' of Chen Duxiu, Qu Qiubai, Li Lisan, and Wang Ming, and the triumph of his own correct thinking from 1935 on, were depicted as linked elements of a single, continuous whole. The myth that was so created would resonate well into the 1960s, and for many Chinese, beyond: since Mao had always been right in the past, how could he not be right in the future?

A further year elapsed before the formal 'Resolution on Certain Questions of Party History', embodying this principle, was approved by the full Central Committee in April 1945. It had to be revised fourteen times, because almost every senior communist had a personal stake in the interpretation accorded to events in which he had been directly involved. Indeed, so contentious were some of these matters of details that the debate had to be shifted from the Seventh Congress, where it was originally to have been held, to the preceding plenum, which was smaller and more easily controlled. In the interests of unity, Bo Gu was made a member of the drafting committee (signifying that he endorsed the criticism of his own former policies), and Wang Ming was eventually persuaded also to write a letter, recognising his errors. The same sense of unity restored pervaded the Congress itself. At Mao's insistence, Bo and Wang were both re-elected to the Central Committee, albeit in last and last-but-one place. Li Lisan, denounced for his leftist deviations, absent in the Soviet Union where he had been living in disgrace for the last fifteen years, and unaware that the Congress was even taking place, retained his membership too.

Mao became Chairman of the whole Party, instead of merely the Secretariat and Politburo. Liu Shaoqi was confirmed as his number two and putative heir. Zhou Enlai came third in the rank order, although, in a sign that he was still on probation after the Rectification Campaign, Mao allowed him to be placed well down in the Central Committee listing, in a none too subtle reminder that Zhou held office at the will of the Chairman, not because he had a strong following of his own. Zhu De, the Commander-in-Chief, ranked fourth, and Ren Bishi, fifth.

When the Seventh Congress ended, Mao had finally achieved the fusion of power, ideology and charisma he had been seeking since Zunyi. Over the years, the more perceptive of his visitors had sensed obscurely the changes that were at work. Edgar Snow, in 1939, found him acquiring a sage-like serenity. Evans Carlson noted his air of abstraction. But Sidney Rittenberg put it best, when he contrasted Mao with Zhou Enlai. 'With Zhou,' he wrote, 'I felt I was with . . . a comrade. With Mao, I felt I was sitting next to history.'

By the summer of 1944, the tide of war in Europe was flowing strongly in the Allies' favour. Italy had capitulated. American- and British-led forces had landed in Normandy. From the east, the once invincible German army was being pushed back towards its own borders by the Russian juggernaut. In Asia, too, Japan was wavering. A major Japanese offensive was still under way in China, but elsewhere in the Pacific theatre, the Emperor's forces were in retreat. While the High Command in Tokyo began contemplating the unthinkable, the defence of the home islands, Stalin and Roosevelt turned their attention to the shape of the post-war order to come.

On July 22, 1944, an aircraft with US markings appeared over Yan'an. It caused almost as big a sensation as the arrival of Wang Ming, five-and-a-half years before – not least because as it was coming in to land, the left wheel hit a grave-mound just before the runway, causing it to lurch violently downwards and the left propeller to shear off, which then slammed into the pilot compartment, making a huge hole in the fuselage and bringing the plane to a jarring halt. Thus began the so-called Dixie Mission, America's first and last overt attempt (until the early 1970s) to establish official lines of communication with the Chinese communists. Astonishingly, no one was hurt, and after being greeted by Zhou Enlai, the small group of US liaison officers were escorted to their quarters – where a learning experience started for both sides. The Americans had to be reminded not to bawl 'Boy!', whenever they wanted something, but to call politely for their *zhaodaiyuan*, or 'hospitality officer'. The Chinese found themselves for the first time in a quasi-diplomatic relationship with a group of non-communist Westerners. Mao set the tone, giving instructions that the words, 'Our Friends', be inserted into the *Jiefang ribao* headline, welcoming the mission. He and the other leaders were invited to showings of Hollywood musicals on a petrol-driven projector, and for a time films like Charlie Chaplin's *Modern Times* displaced the Saturday-night dances as Yan'an's main social attraction.

The decision to send the US Observer Mission, as the group

was officially named, was part of the triangular manoeuvring between Roosevelt, Stalin and Chiang, as each sought to advance his interests at the expense of the other two.

The Americans were frustrated at the incapacity of the Generalissimo's corrupt, authoritarian and increasingly unpopular regime effectively to prosecute the war. They wanted a settlement between the nationalists and the communists, so that instead of constantly sniping at each other they would join forces to drive out the invader.

Stalin, who feared the creation of an American protectorate in China, wanted treaty relations with the nationalist government that would guarantee Chinese neutrality in any future Great Power struggle, and the recognition of Russia's 'special interests' in Manchuria, notably railway and port concessions. He, too, favoured an agreement between the GMD and the communists.

The Generalissimo himself was adamantly opposed to GMD–CCP negotiations. But, under pressure from both Washington and Moscow, he reluctantly gave in. On November 7, 1944, President Roosevelt's personal emissary, Major-General Patrick J. Hurley, set out for Yan'an to begin a mediation effort.

Unfortunately, no one thought to send word ahead that the General was on his way. When the weekly US plane, bringing the Dixie Mission's supplies, arrived from Chongqing, Zhou Enlai, who happened to be at the airstrip, was startled to see emerge 'a tall, grey-haired, soldierly, extremely handsome man, wearing [a] most beautifully tailored uniform. . . with enough ribbons on his chest to represent every war, it seemed . . . in which the United States had ever engaged'. On being told who the distinguished visitor was, Zhou rushed off to find Mao, and an infantry company was mustered to form an improvised guard of honour. But the day's surprises were only beginning. Hurley, an Oklahoma orphan who had become an oil millionaire, was the incarnation of American capitalism, as vain as a peacock, and loved to play to the cameras. As he took the salute, members of the Mission recalled, he 'drew himself to his full impressive height, swelled up like a poisoned pup, [waved his hat in the air] . . . and pierced the north China stillness with a blood-curdling whooping "Yahoooo!" of the Choctaw Indians'. Mao and Zhu De gaped in astonished disbelief.

Hurley's three-day visit turned out to be an object-lesson in the misunderstanding of China which would characterise US policy until Richard Nixon became President, twenty-five years later.

He offered Mao a draft agreement, replete with sonorous phrases about 'the establishment of a government of the people, for the people and by the people', which he had composed himself, apparently convinced that, if the communists signed on, Chiang, under American pressure, would have no choice but to do the same. The premise was false. The Generalissimo soon made clear that he was not willing to accept key provisions of Hurley's text – such as the legalisation of the Communist Party, and equal treatment for communist and nationalist forces in the allocation of military supplies – and still less Mao's revised version, which proposed a coalition government. Hurley's blunder was made all the more glaring because he had asserted publicly in Yan'an that he found Mao's counter-proposals 'fair and just', and they had both signed the final draft as a gauge of their good faith.

Two weeks later the peace effort stalled. When the Dixie Mission commander, Colonel David Barrett, made a last effort to revive it in December, he was exposed to the full blast of Mao's recriminations:

> General Hurley came to Yan'an and asked on what terms we would co-operate with the Guomindang. We offered a five-point proposal . . . General Hurley agreed that the terms were eminently fair . . . The Generalissimo has refused these terms. Now the United States comes and earnestly asks us to accept counter-proposals which require us to sacrifice our liberty. This is difficult for us to understand . . . If . . . the United States wishes to continue to prop up the rotten shell that is Chiang Kai-shek, that is her privilege . . . We are not like Chiang Kai-shek. No nation needs to prop us up. We can stand erect and walk on our own feet like free men.

Mao's attitude, Barrett reported, was 'recalcitrant in the extreme', and several times he flew into a violent rage. 'He kept shouting, over and over again, "We will not yield any further!", "That bastard, Chiang!", and "If [he] were here I would curse him to his face!" . . . Zhou Enlai backed up in calm, cold language everything that Chairman Mao said. I left the interview feeling I had talked in vain to two clever, ruthless and determined leaders who felt absolutely sure of the strength of their position.'

That was certainly the impression Mao's histrionics were intended to convey. But Barrett's conclusion did the communists too much credit. At the end of 1944, they had 700,000 troops and controlled territory with a population of 90 million. Chiang Kai-shek had 1.5 million troops, and controlled 200 million people. The Guomindang's forces were 'still formidable', Mao warned a few months later, and the Red Army would underestimate them at its peril.

Against this background, General Hurley's peace-making, ham-handed though it was, did Mao an enormous service. It locked Chiang into discussions which helped to legitimise the communist cause, and which he could not break off without antagonising both his American ally and all those Chinese who supported him on patriotic rather than political grounds.

US mediation also gave Mao an opportunity to finesse the communists' image abroad by persuading the foreigners who flocked to Yan'an following the Dixie Mission's arrival that the CCP was a moderate party, made up essentially of agrarian reformers, communist in little more than name. That particular hare had been started by Stalin, six months before, when he told the US Ambassador, Averill Harriman, that Mao and his colleagues were good patriots but 'margarine communists', implying that they were not real Marxist-Leninists (a view which not only fitted well with his efforts to further a CCP–GMD peace accord, but also reflected real doubts about Mao's doctrinal orthodoxy). It was consonant, too, with Mao's 'New Democracy' platform, which stated that the CCP's immediate goal was not Soviet-style communism, but a mixed economy. After the Hurley exchanges, this 'campaign of modera-tion' went into high gear, and took on a strongly pro-American slant. Mao wondered aloud whether 'it might be more appropriate to call ourselves a Democratic Party', dropping the word 'communist' altogether. He opined that the United States was 'the most suitable country' to aid China's modernisation, and startled an American reporter by asking if he thought Sears Roebuck would like to extend its mail order business to China.

All this was wholly disingenuous. But it made effective propa-ganda. By January 1945, the communists were making secret overtures to the State Department, proposing that Mao and Zhou visit Washington for talks with Roosevelt. Chiang's claim to be the only Chinese leader any self-respecting Western government could support suddenly began to look frayed. Mao allowed him-self to hope that the United States might perhaps stay neutral in the communist–nationalist conflict which, following the failure of Hurley's mission, he was convinced must eventually resume.

A month later the Yalta summit muddied the waters again.*

Roosevelt and Stalin agreed to treat Chiang's regime as a buffer, separating a US-dominated Pacific from a Soviet-dominated North-East Asia. As part of the accord, the Soviet leader, unbeknown to Mao, promised not to support the CCP against the nationalist government. Accordingly, both the United States and Russia began pressing their respective clients to accept some form of coalition.

Mao apeared to acquiesce, setting out a comprehensive strategy for an alternative, peaceful route to power in his report to the Seventh Congress. But his scepticism was all too apparent. In a whimsical, off-the-cuff speech to delegates later the same day, he likened Chiang – whom he described as a 'hooligan' – to a man with a dirty face. 'Our policy has been and still is', he declared, 'to invite him to wash his face [in other words, to reform] and not to cut off his head . . . [But] the older one gets, the less willing and likely one is to change one's ways. [So] we say, "if you wash, we can marry, for we still love each other dearly" . . . But we must keep up our defences. When attacked . . . we must resolutely, quickly, thoroughly and completely eliminate the enemy.'

To that end, the Congress called for the expansion of the Red Army from 900,000 (in July 1945) to one million men; preparations for urban insurrections; and increased emphasis on mobile warfare, rather than guerrilla tactics. In coded cables to the military commanders, Mao warned that renewed civil war was inevitable. They must use the time remaining to make the necessary dispositions.

Three months later, as these preparations were in full swing, the Russians finally declared war on Japan. Next day, August 10, Zhu De ordered communist troops to accept the surrender of Japanese units. Chiang then instructed Japanese commanders to surrender only to nationalist forces. Mao dug in his heels, and cabled Stalin for support. Then, on the 15th, the Soviet leader dropped a bombshell. At 3 a.m., Moscow time, only hours before Japan's capitulation, Chiang's Foreign Minister, Wang Shijie, and Vyacheslav Molotov signed a treaty of alliance.

---

* The Big Three (Churchill, Roosevelt and Stalin) met at the Crimean resort of Yalta in February 1945, to define the shape of post-war Europe and to delineate their respective spheres of influence in Asia.

Above Yan'an in the late 1930s, with its distinctive Song dynasty pagoda.

Left Zhang Guotao, whose challenge to Mao collapsed after the destruction of the Fourth Army in Gansu in 1937.

Wang Shiwei, the gifted young writer whose persecution in the Yan'an Rectification Campaign set the pattern for all Mao's subsequent efforts to crush intellectual dissent.

Mao's fourth wife, Jiang Qing, as an actress in Shanghai.

[from left] Zhou Enlai, Mao and Zhu De, in Yan'an in 1946.

Right Mao's reviewing Lin Biao's victorious army after the surrender of Beijing in March 1949.

Below A landlord in North China, on trial before fellow villagers during the land reform after the communist takeover.

Mao proclaiming the People's Republic, from Tiananmen
on October 1, 1949.

Gao Gang, Party boss of
Manchuria, purged in 1954.

[from left] Mao, Bulganin, Stalin and the East German Party chief, Walter Ulbricht,
celebrating the Soviet leader's 70th birthday at the Kremlin in December 1949.

Mao relaxing with his nephew, Yuanxin, and his daughters Li Min and Li Na at Lushan in 1951.

[from left] Jiang Qing; Li Na; Mao; his oldest son, Anying, soon to die in Korea; and Anying's wife, Li Songlin.

Mao with the Dalai Lama *(right)* and the Panchen Lama in Beijing in 1954.

A struggle meeting to criticise bourgeois intellectuals at the start of the anti-Rightist campaign in July 1957.

The parting of the ways: Mao and Khrushchev meet for the last time in Beijing in October 1959.

Peng Dehuai *(second from left)* talking to peasants in Hunan during the Great Leap Forward in 1959.

To Mao, it was a repeat performance of Stalin's perfidy in 1936, when he had demanded Chiang's release during the Xian Incident. Once again the Soviet leader had sold out the CCP for Russia's national interests. Mao had known that the Russians and the GMD were talking. But he had been kept in the dark about the understanding reached at Yalta. Now, finally, it all became clear: if civil war did break out, the CCP would be on its own.

Communist policy changed overnight. All criticism of the Guomindang, and of the United States, stopped. Plans for urban insurrections were put on hold. Red Army units were told to co-operate with US troops in disarming Japanese formations. On August 28, Mao set out for Chongqing aboard a US air force plane, accompanied by General Hurley, for peace negotiations with the nationalists, leaving Liu Shaoqi in charge of the Party in his absence. Pyotr Vladimirov, a Tass Correspondent who served as Moscow's representative in Yan'an, wrote in his diary that Mao looked like a man going to his own crucifixion.

He had a very tough hand to play. Chiang had cast-iron US support and the Soviet Union's benevolent neutrality. As long as the talks lasted, the GMD armies could move gradually to repossess Japanese-held areas while the Red Army was kept at arm's length. If they broke down, Chiang could blame communist intransigence and opt for a military solution.

Their last encounter had been in Canton, when Mao had headed the GMD's Peasant Training Institute, nineteen years before. Nothing had happened since to facilitate a meeting of minds. Their personalities were utterly different: contemporary photographs showed Mao in a baggy blue suit with a round Sun Yat-sen collar and an incongruous, light-grey pith helmet over his long, unkempt hair, while Generalissimo Chiang, immaculately groomed, wore a crisply pressed military uniform. Their politics were diametrically opposed. And, for good measure, they detested each other. Mao, Chiang fumed, was a traitor: if such people went unpunished, no one would obey the government. It particularly galled him that, by agreeing to negotiate, he had been forced to concede – in Mao's words – 'a pattern of equality' between the two parties, which the communists saw as a significant gain.

During the six weeks the talks lasted, the two men met face to face four times; approved a memorandum of understanding, in which they both promised 'resolutely to avoid civil war'; and

Chiang undertook to convene an all-party Political Consultative Conference to discuss a new consititution. Wider agreement was blocked, as in earlier negotiations, by Chiang's insistence, and Mao's refusal, that the CCP place its army and the local governments it led under GMD control as a precondition to an overall settlement.

Far more important, however, was the change in the international context which occurred while the meetings were taking place.

In August, when the Chongqing talks began, the US and the Soviet Union were both officially committed to non-intervention in Chinese affairs. By October, when they ended, 50,000 US marines had started landing on the North China coast, ostensibly to help disarm the Japanese but actually to occupy Beijing, Tianjin and other major cities on the Guomindang's behalf, in order to forestall a Russian move south; while Soviet troops were discreetly conniving in a Chinese communist take-over of Manchuria. Eight months after Yalta, the idea of a neutral China, buffering Soviet and US ambitions, had begun to lose its meaning. The Cold War, conceived in Europe, was rapidly spreading east.

Manchuria became the flashpoint of these new rivalries.

On November 14, nationalist troops, with US military backing, attacked communist units defending Shanhaiguan, the strategic chokepoint at the end of the Great Wall which controls the main land-route north. Six days later, Lin Biao reported that the town was lost and could not be recaptured. The situation was back where it had been in the summer. Both sides were moving inexorably towards full-scale civil war.

Once again, Stalin abruptly cut the ground from under the communists' feet.

This time his concern was to ease the tensions that had developed between the Soviet Union and the US globally over the previous two months. The moment had come, he decided, to show Washington some goodwill – at the CCP's expense. Soviet commanders were instructed to inform their Chinese comrades that they must withdraw from all major cities and communications routes within a week. 'If you do not leave,' one Soviet general warned the north China leader, Peng Zhen, 'we will use tanks to drive you out.' Communist sappers, who were sabotaging the railway lines to slow the nationalist advance, were told to desist or be forcibly disarmed.

By now, the Chinese Party leaders were inured to Soviet treachery. None the less, it was a crushing blow. Normally the most unemotional of men, Peng exploded: 'The army of one Communist Party using tanks to drive out the army of another! Things like this have never happened before.' Yet there was nothing the Chinese Party could do about it. As in August, they had to acquiesce.

Mao played little part in these events. His neurasthenia was back.

For the first time since 1924, when he had retreated in despair to Shaoshan, Mao's political touch had deserted him. He could not see how to go forward.

Having that summer achieved total power and almost godlike status in a Party which was freer than ever of Soviet control, he suddenly found that he was, after all, impotent – bound hand and foot by the overriding interests of the Great Powers. Stalin's treaty with Chiang in August had blocked the civil war for which, psychologically, he had been preparing, and had left him politically naked, to face the Generalissimo in Chongqing. The only policies now open to him – fighting the Guomindang, while trying to avoid becoming embroiled with the US; seeking Soviet support for policies of which the Soviet leaders disapproved – were so flagrantly self-contradictory that they were bound to fail.

While Mao languished in the grip of depression, Liu Shaoqi continued to stand in for him as acting head of the Central Committee. Visitors were told he was suffering from exhaustion. 'All through November,' his interpreter, Shi Zhe, remembered, 'we saw him, day after day, prostrate on his bed, his body trembling. His hands and legs twitched convulsively, and he was bathed in a cold sweat . . . He asked us for cold towels to put on his forehead, but it didn't help. The doctors could do nothing.'

In the end, it was President Truman who got Mao out of his black hole.

Anxieties had been growing in the US Congress over the spectacle of American marines being sucked into a foreign civil war. On November 27, Hurley resigned in a huff after a Congressional resolution urged a US withdrawal. Truman announced the appointment of General George C. Marshall, the architect of the lend-lease programme for Europe, to take his place. The new policy Marshall was to follow had two cardinal objectives: a ceasefire between the nationalists and the communists, leading to a political settlement; and getting the Russians out of Manchuria.

When the news reached Yan'an, Mao saw for the first time in months a glimmer of hope. If the Americans wanted peace in China, they would have to pressure Chiang into halting his offensive against communist positions.

Marshall arrived in Chongqing on December 21. Within ten days, he had persuaded both sides to table truce proposals. Zhou Enlai, on Mao's instructions, accepted the nationalists' principal condition: freedom of movement for government troops to take over Soviet-held areas in Manchuria and to disarm Japanese forces in the south. On January 10, 1946, a ceasefire was signed, which took effect three days later. Meanwhile, in a further gesture to Marshall, Chiang Kai-shek summoned the Political Consultative Conference (PPC), which he had agreed to set up the previous October but had not yet permitted to meet. He intended it as a fig-leaf, to give the government an aura of democratic legitimacy. Instead, an unlikely coalition of communists, third-party figures and GMD moderates took matters out of Chiang's hands, and, building on the momentum generated by the ceasefire accord, approved resolutions calling for, among other things, an elected national assembly, and communist participation in a coalition government, in which the GMD would not be permitted to hold more than half of the ministerial posts.

Mao was ecstatic. His instincts about the Marshall mission had turned out to be correct. The pendulum had swung back from war to political struggle. 'Our Party will soon join the government,' he proclaimed, in a directive at the beginning of February 1946. 'Generally speaking', the armed struggle was over. The major task now, Mao asserted, was to overcome closed-doorism, which led 'some comrades' to doubt that 'a new era of peace and democracy has arrived'.

That night, he gave a banquet for a visiting American journalist, John Roderick of the Associated Press, the first foreign reporter he had seen for several months. It was a festive occasion, and Mao was full of praise for Truman, whose initiative, he said, had made a major contribution to Chinese–American friendship. Roderick was struck by the way he dominated his surroundings, carrying himself with 'an air of self-confidence and authority just short of arrogance'. He was the kind of man, Roderick thought, who would stand out in a crowded room anywhere, exuding an aura of leadership like that 'which must have emanated from men like Alexander the Great, Napoleon and Lenin'.

Sadly for this heroic image, the closed-doorists proved correct. Chiang Kai-shek was not ready to carry out the PCC resolutions, and the United States was not ready to force him to do so. Mao had made a massive misjudgement.

For a few weeks more, the impetus Marshall had created kept the negotiations moving forward. In late February, the two sides astonished themselves by reaching agreement on the integration of communist forces into a new, non-partisan national army – an issue which, even at the height of the wartime united front, had proved intractable.

But soon there were alarming signs that the peace process was starting to unravel.

March was the month of Winston Churchill's 'Iron Curtain' speech, in Fulton, Missouri. Global tensions between the US and the Soviet Union were rising. As the Russians began to withdraw from Manchuria – which had been excluded from the ceasefire in January – Chiang convinced the White House that unless the nationalist armies moved in to reassert Chinese sovereignty, the whole of north-east China would fall under the communists' sway. Mao, still obsessed by the prospect of an imminent political settlement, thought at first that the Generalissimo was just trying to strengthen his negotiating position. But on March 16, as the nationalist advance continued, he referred for the first time to the possibility of warfare resuming. A week later, he instructed Lin Biao to launch a counter-offensive, regardless of the effect on the peace talks. Changchun fell to Lin's forces on April 18; Harbin, ten days later.

The fight for Manchuria had begun, but not yet a general conflict. For another month, Mao continued to urge communist commanders in other areas to hold their fire unless the nationalists attacked first.

The GMD is actively preparing to start a nationwide civil war,' he wrote in a CC directive on May 15, 'but the US is not in favour of it . . . Our Party's policy should [therefore] be . . . to prevent, or at least postpone, it.' Two weeks later, even these remnant hopes had been abandoned. Marshall's mediation effort had been a failure, the Central Committee declared. The 'GMD reactionaries' were ruling China by terror, and the United States was supporting them.

In June, large-scale clashes broke out. A month later, after another brief truce, the fighting spread to engulf the whole of central and northern China.

In retrospect, Mao had had a profoundly unsatisfactory year.

His leadership was intact. To the Party at large, and to the peasantry who made up the bulk of its following, he was still the 'star of salvation', the Red Sun in the East. His colleagues might grumble, out of earshot, over the bewildering zigzags in policy – from war to peace, and back to war again – but no one challenged him. Mao had become indispensable, the irreplaceable guide and symbol of the future of the communist cause.

But his inexperience in dealing with the Powers, which led him to make mistake after mistake the previous autumn and spring, had left him mortified.

Chiang Kai-shek, who headed a recognised government, had had fifteen years to learn how to play them off against each other. Mao led a rebel movement. He had never travelled abroad. He had had no personal contact even with Soviet leaders. Until the arrival of the Dixie Mission, eighteen months before, he had never dealt with a Western official. His naivety in believing that the Americans would force the nationalist government to compromise still rankled, twenty years later, and was among the reasons for his caution in contacts with the Western powers when the question of diplomatic relations arose after Chiang's defeat.

Once the foreign-policy fog cleared, the Soviet withdrawal was complete and the focus of Great Power rivalry switched to Europe, Mao's old sureness of touch returned. Facing an enemy he knew well – the nationalists – on terrain he knew well – the Chinese countryside – he was at ease. In a succession of Central Committee directives, he reiterated the old, tried and tested battle principles which had worked so well in Jiangxi and against the Japanese – luring the enemy in deep, and concentrating strong forces against weak ones. Abandoning territory to preserve troop-strength was 'not only unavoidable but necessary', he told his colleagues that summer, 'otherwise final victory will be impossible'.

Next spring, when Yan'an itself was threatened, his interpreter,

Shi Zhe, asked him despondently what they could do to stop the town falling. Mao burst out laughing. 'That's not clever,' he said. 'We should not try to stop them . . . Chiang thinks when he has seized the devils' lair, he will win. In fact, he will lose everything. [It is written in the Analects:] "If a thing comes to me, and I give nothing in return, that is contrary to propriety." We will give Chiang Yan'an. He will give us China.'

Two weeks later, at dusk on March 18, 1947, the column escorting Mao and other Central Committee leaders left the Red capital, heading north. The Yan'an interlude was over. The final battle had begun.

CHAPTER TWELVE

Paper Tigers

The conflict that raged across China from the summer of 1946 to the spring of 1950 was fundamentally different from any earlier war Mao had fought. On the Jinggangshan, in Jiangxi and in the northwest, the aim had been for the Red Army to secure and defend rural base areas. During the years at Yan'an, it had been, '70 per cent expanding our own forces, 20 per cent resisting the Guomindang and 10 per cent fighting Japan'. Now, for the first time, Mao's objective was not to dominate the countryside but to seize control of China's cities, the teeming proletarian centres from which the communists had been brutally excluded twenty years before.

For the first nine months, the Red Army – now renamed the People's Liberation Army (PLA) – steadily retreated. In Manchuria, where Chiang had deployed the cream of his troops, the communists lost almost all their earlier gains, retaining only Harbin, close to the Soviet border. In east China, they were driven out of northern Jiangsu. The base areas that had been painstakingly reconstituted in the old E-Yu-Wan districts, north of Wuhan, were overrun, and nationalist forces took control of parts of the Shansi–Hebei–Shandong–Henan border region. By December 1946, Chiang was confident enough to tell Marshall that the military threat from the communists would be neutralised by the following autumn, an assessment, which he repeated publicly, with great fanfare, after the fall of Yan'an. The American envoy's admonition that Mao's forces, while retreating, showed no inclination to surrender, fell on deaf ears.

Chiang's strategy was to recapture the main cities and railway lines, north of the Yangtse, and only after these had been secured to move out into the rural areas to occupy county towns, finally using landlord militias to regain control of the villages. Mao ordered his forces to avoid battle unless they were certain of victory, and then to seek the swift annihilation of the forces they attacked:

> When we have encircled . . . one of the enemy detachments (a brigade or regiment), [we] should not attempt to wipe out all the encircled enemy simultaneously . . . and thus divide ourselves . . . making it hard to get results. Instead we should concentrate . . . a force six, five, four or at least three times [larger than] that of the enemy, concentrate the whole or the bulk of our artillery, select one (not two) of the weak spots in the enemy's positions, attack it fiercely and be sure to win . . . When we wipe out one regiment, [the enemy] will have one regiment less. When we wipe out one brigade, he will have one brigade less . . . Using this method we shall win. Acting counter to it we shall lose.

By February 1947, more than fifty nationalist brigades (out of 218 taking part in the campaign) had been put out of action in this way. As in Jiangxi, fifteen years earlier, most GMD troops who surrendered were absorbed into communist units, becoming the PLA's main source of new manpower.

As a security precaution, after leaving Yan'an, the Party leaders divided into two groups. Mao headed what was known as the Front Line Committee, which remained in northern Shensi. Liu Shaoqi took charge of a CC Work Committee in the Jin-Cha-Ji base area, in present-day Hebei, 250 miles to the east. Sidney Rittenberg, who marched with Mao's column, marvelled at the Chairman's tactics but found them terrifying:

> Mao [played] . . . a sardonic cat-and-mouse game with his adversary. [He] deliberately telegraphed his moves, and . . . made it a point never to be more than one day's march ahead of the GMD. He knew that the [nationalist commander] Hu Zongnan would be Chiang's hero if he were able to capture Mao Zedong in person, and Mao played that card for all it was worth. At every encampment he would wait until the scouts brought him the news that the enemy was only an hour's march away before he would methodically put on his coat, mount his horse and lead his little headquarters column off down the trail . . . [Then], when the GMD troops were exhausted . . . and sick

of the whole campaign, Peng Dehuai selected the most vulnerable
cul-de-sac . . . and hurled [his men] against them.

The lore of Old Deaf Ju, which Mao had learned on the Jinggangshan, and which had served him so well on the Long March,
still had its uses. In a telegram to Peng in April, he called it 'the
tactics of wear and tear', designed to fatigue the enemy and deplete
his food supplies.

By this time the nationalist offensive was beginning to bog down.
Mao (and, quite separately, the Americans) had predicted as much
the previous autumn. Chiang's forces were spread too thin, his
communications lines were over-extended. The Generalissimo later
acknowledged that sending his best troops to the north-east, without
first securing the intermediate provinces in north and central China,
had been a major strategic error. Matters were not helped by his
distrust of native Manchurians. When the nationalists brought in
outsiders to administer the region, they lost the support of the local
elite. But the key factor in turning the tide was the ease with which
the PLA adjusted from guerrilla tactics to the use of large mobile
formations. The experience gained in the war with Japan, and the
heightened discipline and 'uniformity of purpose' instilled during
the Rectification Campaign, now paid off handsomely.

That summer, the communist retreat ended, and the counter-
attack began.

Lin Biao launched a three-pronged offensive which severed the
rail-links between Manchuria's main cities and pushed back the
nationalist front line 150 miles to the south. Liu Bocheng, the 'One-
eyed Dragon', attacked across the Yellow River into Hebei, while
Chen Yi did the same in Shandong. Further north, Nie Rongzhen
seized Shijiazhuang, the first major nationalist-held city to fall in
China proper, giving the communists control of the main
north–south railway from Beijing to Wuhan. By December 1947,
Mao was able to announce that 640,000 nationalist soldiers had
been killed or wounded, and more than a million had surrendered.

The war, he exulted, had reached a turning-point. '[A year
earlier] our enemies were jubilant . . . [and] the US imperialists, too,
danced with joy . . . Now [they] are gripped by pessimism. They
heave great sighs [and] wail about a crisis.'

*

All through the spring and summer of 1948, Mao's forces pressed home their advantage. By the end of March, most of Manchuria, apart from Changchun and Shenyang, was in Lin Biao's hands, and the nationalists were cut off both from reinforcement and from the possibility of withdrawal. Further south, PLA commanders recovered much of Shanxi and Hebei, all of Shandong and large parts of Henan and Anhui. In an important symbolic victory, Yan'an fell to communist forces on April 25. Mao began to calculate the number of GMD brigades that would have to be eliminated before final victory could be won. In March 1948, he predicted that nationalist rule would be overthrown by mid-1951. Eight months later, he brought that forward to the autumn of 1949.

The speed with which nationalist resistance crumbled astonished even him.

One factor was the deterioration in the quality of the GMD armies that had followed America's entry into the Pacific War. Nationalist generals lost interest in driving out the Japanese, figuring that, sooner or later, their allies would do it for them. In the words of one of Chiang's commanders: 'Our troops . . . became soft and concerned only with pleasure . . . [They] lacked combat spirit and there was no willingness to sacrifice.' Incompetent leadership made matters worse. The US commander in China, General Wedemeyer, called Chiang's officer corps 'incapable, inept, untrained, petty [and] . . . altogether inefficient'. The Generalissimo himself admitted: 'I have to lie awake nights wondering what fool things they may do . . . They are so dumb . . . that you must imagine everything they can do that would be wrong and warn them against it.' But Chiang's own constant interventions simply stripped his commanders of what little initiative they had.

Poor intelligence compounded the nationalists' difficulties. Kang Sheng's campaigns against GMD special agents, grotesque though they were, made it impossible for Chiang's men to penetrate even low-level communist units. By contrast, the nationalist command was infiltrated by communist sympathisers at every possible level. Chiang's assistant Chief of Staff, General Liu Fei, to all outward appearances a typical GMD career soldier, pompous and bureaucratic, was a communist mole. So was the head of the GMD's War Planning Board, Guo Rugui. In the major battles at the close of the civil war, the PLA commanders knew every nationalist move in advance.

Morale – or the lack of it – was equally important. Chiang's was

a conscript army. Press gangs went out to the villages and carried
men off from the fields, leaving their families to starve. At the reception centres, where they were supposed to receive basic training,
they were held under heavy guard. In some places, even in
midwinter, their clothes were taken away at night to try to stop them
escaping. 'The poor fellows slept naked,' an American observer
reported, 'some 40 or 50 crowded together into a space approximately 10 by 15 feet. The sergeant told us they kept warmer and
slept better . . . close together.' After being enrolled, they were
marched, roped together like prisoners, to their units, often
hundreds of miles away at the front. Frequently they had no food
or water, because their rations had been 'squeezed' by corrupt
officers. In one march, from Fujian to Guizhou, a hundred recruits
arrived out of the thousand that had set out; in another case, only
seventeen were left alive out of seven hundred. Nor were these
atypical cases. One year almost half of the 1.67 million new recruits
perished or deserted before they reached their units. When the
survivors did arrive at the front, many took the first opportunity to
run away. It was not unusual for a nationalist unit to lose 6 per cent
of its men through desertion each month. Those who remained were
chronically malnourished, with no medical treatment available.
Colonel Barrett of the Dixie Mission reported seeing nationalist
soldiers 'topple over and die after marching less than a mile'.

Having been treated like wild beasts, the troops behaved accordingly. Another American officer reported:

> I visited villages [in pro-communist areas] which Chiang's soldiers
> had occupied and looted. Whatever they could not haul away on
> stolen oxcarts and pack animals they rendered useless . . . They had
> mixed corn, wheat and millet with manure to render the grain ined-
> ible. Deep-water wells . . . were filled with earth . . . In a village school,
> the nationalist soldiers had defecated, as they had done elsewhere,
> and had splashed human excrement on the walls. A young woman
> . . . reported to me that she had been dragged from one blockhouse
> to another and raped for many days. An old woman, past 75, was the
> only one in a village evacuated by the nationalists just before we
> arrived. She was sitting, unable to walk, because she too had been
> raped many times.

In some districts, the communists' inability to protect the population
from reprisals of this kind turned the peasants against them. The

nationalists had used the same tactics, to similar effect, in Jiangxi in the early 1930s.

Mao responded by stepping up land reform, which had been put on hold while the united front was in force. 'Local tyrants and evil gentry' were hauled before mass meetings for summary judgement and execution. Class relations in the countryside were deliberately polarised, to give the poorest sections of the peasantry an incentive to commit themselves to the communist cause.

In the cities, the regime fared no better: the tyranny of one-party rule, backed up by the secret police; the repression of liberal dissent; hyperinflation, eroding salaries, as the government printed money to finance the civil war; and pervasive corruption, making legitimate business impossible – all turned against the Guomindang the very groups that previously had been its core supporters.

These were the symptoms of the nationalist disease. But the incurable root lay in the nature of the system of rule Chiang Kai-shek had created. It was too weak and faction-ridden to impose its will by force, too corrupt and careless of public welfare to command broad-based support.

That did not make it a pushover. Alongside disaffected, half-starved regular troops, Chiang had well-trained, well-equipped elite units, which served with courage against Japan and did so again against the communists. The United States poured in arms and equipment worth, by State Department calculations, some 300 billion dollars, more by the communist account. Chiang himself declared in June 1947 that his forces had 'absolute superiority' over the PLA in battle techniques and experience, and were '10 times richer . . . in terms of military supplies'.

Against that, Mao relied on the 'collective will of the masses'. But it was more than enough.

Two years earlier, at the Seventh Congress, he had recounted an ancient folk-tale about the Foolish Old Man of North Mountain, the view from whose door was obstructed by two great peaks to the south. He and his sons took their hoes, and began to dig them away. When another villager mocked him, the Foolish Old Man replied: 'When I die my sons will carry on; when they die, there will be my grandsons, and then their sons and grandsons . . . High as they are, the mountains cannot grow any higher, and with every bit we dig, they will be that much lower. Why can't we dig them away?' As he carried on digging, Mao said, God was moved by his faith and sent down two angels, who carried the mountains away on their backs:

> Today, two big mountains lie like a dead weight on the Chinese people. One is imperialism, the other is feudalism. The Chinese Communist Party has long made up its mind to dig them up. We must persevere and work unceasingly, and we, too, will touch God's heart. Our God is none other than the masses of the Chinese people. If they stand up and dig together with us, why can't these two mountains be cleared away?

For the rest of Mao's life, the story of the Foolish Old Man would serve as a metaphor for his efforts to transform China. Japan's abrupt collapse in August 1945, like the nationalist collapse three-and-a-half years later, merely strengthened his conviction that, beside the power of the human will, all else was secondary. It was not the atom bomb that defeated the Japanese, Mao insisted, it was the struggle waged by the masses:

> The atom bomb is a paper tiger which the US reactionaries use to scare people. It looks terrible, but in fact it isn't. Of course, the atom bomb is a weapon of mass slaughter, but the outcome of a war is decided by the people, not by one or two new types of weapon.
>   All reactionaries are paper tigers . . . Hitler . . . was a paper tiger. So was Mussolini, so was Japanese imperialism . . . Chiang Kai-shek and his supporters . . . are all paper tigers too . . . We have only millet plus rifles to rely on, but history will finally prove that our millet plus rifles is more powerful than Chiang Kai-shek's aeroplanes plus tanks . . . The reason is simply this: the reactionaries represent reaction, we represent progress.

With this invincible certitude in the rightness of their cause, the communist armies began preparing, in the autumn of 1948, for the three climactic battles that would determine China's modern fate.

The overall plan of campaign was drafted by Mao early in September. Lin Biao struck first, at Jinzhou, a heavily fortified junction on the railway line into Manchuria from Beijing, with a force of 700,000 men. After a fierce battle, lasting thirty-one hours, the city fell on October 15. But then events developed in a way Mao had not foreseen. A nationalist relief column, 100,000-strong, set out from Shenyang. Feigning a march south, Lin sent his main force north. The entire column was wiped out. Changchun, which Lin's forces were also besieging, surrendered at the same time. Shenyang, left with half its garrison, followed suit on November 2. Not for nothing was Lin regarded as the communists' greatest commander. In the space of seven weeks, Chiang had lost the whole of Manchuria, and half-a-million of his best troops. Overnight, the military situation was transformed. Not only were the nationalists in wholesale retreat, but, for the first time since the war had begun, the communists outnumbered them.

Zhu De then ordered Lin to make a 600-mile forced march to the south, to encircle Tianjin and Beijing. There his North-Eastern Army joined up with Nie Rongzhen's North China Field Army, giving him a combined force of almost a million men, the largest the communists had ever assembled. The nationalists had 600,000 troops.

Again, Mao drew up a plan of operations. Lin was told that the main task was to cut off the enemy's escape. The nationalists, Mao warned, were 'like birds startled by the twang of a bowstring'. Only when the ring was complete should the attack commence, and then the target should be Tianjin, not Beijing as Chiang would expect.

Meanwhile, the Central Plains and East China Armies, commanded by Liu Bocheng and Chen Yi, had launched the third great battle, 400 miles to the south.

The Huaihai campaign, as it was called, was fought across four provinces – Anhui, Henan, Jiangsu and Shandong – in an area bounded by the Grand Canal in the east, and the Huai River in the south. It lasted just over two months. Each side fielded approximately half-a-million troops, but the communists had the aid of two million peasant auxiliaries, directed by an ad hoc Front Committee, headed by Deng Xiaoping, to provide logistical support. As in Manchuria, the battle began with the destruction of one of Chiang's weaker units. Relief columns were blocked by communist guerrilla action, and when large-scale reinforcements set out, they marched into a gigantic trap which Liu Bocheng had set near Xuzhou. By January 10, when the Huaihai campaign ended, 200,000 nationalist soldiers were dead or wounded, and 300,000 had surrendered.

While Chiang was still reeling from that defeat, Lin Biao tightened the vice around the two northern cities. Tianjin fell on January 15. A week later, the nationalist commander in Beijing, General Fu Zuoyi, negotiated the capital's surrender, ostensibly to save it from communist bombardment. His 200,000 troops were integrated into the PLA, and he himself was later given a sinecure in the new communist government.

The day before Beijing surrendered, Chiang Kai-shek resigned the presidency (while remaining as party leader).

In four months he had lost 1.5 million men. The communists who, two-and-a-half years earlier, had been ready to accept a minor role in a coalition administration, now demanded that he be punished as a war criminal, that the government resign, the constitution be abrogated and the remnants of the nationalist army be absorbed into the PLA. Peace talks opened with Chiang's successor, Li Zongren, but quickly collapsed. On April 21, Liu Bocheng's army began crossing the Yangtse. Nanjing fell three days later; Hangzhou on May 3; Shanghai on May 27. By then Chiang had already decided that he would have to abandon the mainland and transfer his headquarters to Taiwan. There, he would wait for the war that he was certain would one day come between America and Russia, at which point he and his pro-American army would return in triumph to China to reconquer their lost lands.

With the Generalissimo went the nationalist air force and navy, some of the best remaining army divisions and 300 million dollars in gold, silver and foreign currency reserves. Deprived of funds and ammunition, nationalist resistance ebbed away. To all intents and purposes, the battle for China was over.

The nationalist collapse faced Mao, and the Party as a whole, with the challenge of administering, not just a border region or a base area, but a country three times the size of western Europe, devastated by decades of war and containing nearly a quarter of the world's population. Foremost among his concerns was how to deal with the newly conquered cities.

Mao's wariness of urban life had its roots in the experiences of his youth in Beijing and Shanghai. He never quite threw off the feeling of being a country bumpkin, a peasant's son among city slickers. He had studied in one great metropolis, Changsha, and had lived and worked, apparently happily, in two others, Canton and Wuhan. But he would always regard the city as a slightly alien place. Throughout the civil war, Mao's strategy had been to win control of the countryside; the move to the towns could come later. Apart from

one moment of panic, in August 1945, when in a knee-jerk reaction
at the end of the war, he had ordered ill-prepared urban uprisings
in Japanese-occupied cities from Shanghai to Beijing (all of which,
fortunately for him, were called off before any damage was done),
this gradualist approach was maintained until the end of 1948. The
PLA was instructed to 'take medium and small cities and extensive
rural areas first; take big cities later.'

The following March, however, the question of 'shifting the
centre of gravity from the rural areas to the cities' could no longer
be postponed.

That month Mao embarked on a series of speeches, setting out
before the Party hierarchy the economic and political programme
the new regime would follow. Urban living standards must be
raised, he said, to win the loyalty of the urban population. Major
industries and foreign-owned companies would be nationalised, but
other forms of capitalism would continue. China would be ruled by
a coalition government, headed by the Communist Party but
including a number of small progressive parties, mostly splinter
groups formed by ex-GMD leftists, to represent sympathetic non-
communists from the bourgeoisie and the liberal intelligentsia. The
new system was to be known as a 'people's democratic dictatorship',
which, as in the Chinese Soviet Republic, twenty years before, signified that the fruits of democracy would not be shared by all:

> [The reactionaries say:] 'You are dictatorial.' Dear Sirs, you are right,
> that is exactly what we are . . . Only the people are allowed the right
> to voice their opinions. Who are 'the people'? At the present stage in
> China, they are the working class, the peasant class, the petty bour-
> geoisie and the national bourgeoisie. Under the leadership of the
> . . . Communist Party, these classes unite together to . . . carry out a
> dictatorship over the lackeys of imperialism – the landlord class, the
> bureaucratic capitalist class and the GMD reactionaries and their
> henchmen – to suppress them and [ensure] they behave properly . . .
> The democratic system is to be carried out within the ranks of the
> people . . . The right to vote is given only to the people and not to
> the reactionaries. These two aspects, namely, democracy among the
> people and dictatorship over the reactionaries, combine to form
> the people's democratic dictatorship.

For all those who happened to be on the wrong side of this class
divide, these were sobering words. Mao insisted that people would

be punished only if they broke the law. But he also described the judiciary as an instrument of class violence.

None the less, in 1949, the majority of China's citizens, and many foreign residents, too, looked to the advent of communist administration as bringing not repression but release from the graft and rottenness that had marked the final stages of nationalist rule.

Alan Winnington, a British journalist who was with the first PLA detachment to enter Beijing, found the streets lined by a mass of 'shouting, laughing, cheering people'. Derk Bodde, then carrying out research at Qinghua University, wrote in his diary of 'a new feeling of relief' in the city. 'There is no doubt in my mind', he added, 'that the communists come here with the bulk of the population on their side.' The foreign captain of a Hong Kong tramp steamer, one of the first ships into Tianjin after the communist take-over, was dumbfounded to find a port without 'squeeze'. Not only were bribes refused, he reported, no one would accept even a cigarette.

The maintenance of this climate of probity, of hard work and plain living, in a country where, all through history, officialdom had been synonymous with corruption, was of great importance to Mao. The Party, he warned, was heading into uncharted territory where it would face new and unfamiliar dangers:

> With victory, certain moods may grow within the Party – arrogance, putting on airs like a hero, wanting to rest on our laurels instead of striving to make further progress, pleasure-seeking and distaste for hardship . . . There may be some communists who were never conquered by enemies with guns, and were worthy of the name of heroes for standing up against them, but who cannot withstand the sugar-coated bullets [of the bourgeoisie] . . . We must guard against this. The achievement of nationwide victory is only the first step in a Long March of 10,000 li. It is silly to pride ourselves on this one step. What is more worthy of pride lies still ahead . . . The Chinese revolution is a great revolution, but the road beyond is longer and the work to come greater and more arduous . . . We should be capable not only of destroying the old world. We must also be capable of creating the new.

To that end, Mao said, cadres would have to put aside the things they knew well, and master the things they did not know. The Russians, he told them, had also been ignorant of economic construction when their revolution truimphed, but that had not stopped them building 'a great and brilliant socialist state'. What Russia had done, China could do, too.

On the afternoon of October 1 1949, Mao mounted the Gate of Heavenly Peace, overlooking Tiananmen Square in Beijing, and, surrounded by the Communist Party establishment and its progressive allies, formally announced the founding of the People's Republic of China.

Ten days before, at a meeting to approve the new constitution, naming Beijing, the capital of the Ming and the Qing, as the new seat of government (in place of Nanjing), and Mao himself as Head of State, he had proclaimed:

> The Chinese people, comprising one quarter of humanity, have now stood up. The Chinese have always been a great, courageous and industrious nation; it is only in modern times that they have fallen behind ... [Today] we have closed ranks and defeated both domestic and foreign aggressors ... Ours will no longer be a nation subject to insult and humiliation.

Now, in the warm late autumn sunshine, with enormous red silk lanterns swinging in the breeze in front of the incarnadine walls of the Forbidden City, he repeated, in his high-pitched Hunanese brogue, to a crowd 100,000 strong, crammed into the narrow, walled plaza below: 'We, the 475 million Chinese people, have stood up and our future is infinitely bright.'

Beijing's new communist administrators had spent months preparing for this moment, when, as the locals put it, Mao's government would 'put on new clothes'. The plaza itself had been enlarged. Groves of ancient silk trees had been cut down, concrete poured and flagstones laid, and floodlights erected on steel towers. A fading two-storey-high portrait of Chiang-Kai-shek, painted on a steel sheet made by welding together flattened petrol cans, which had ornamented the Gate during the nationalists' rule, had been replaced by an equally large portrait of Mao, hung from the ramparts to one side. The speech-making was followed by a military parade, led by PLA cavalry and long lines of captured American Army lorries and tanks. Then came civilian marchers, chanting, 'Long live Chairman

Mao! A long, long life to Chairman Mao!', while Mao's answering voice floated down from the loudspeakers, giving the response: 'Long live the People's Republic.' As darkness fell, there was a spectacular fireworks display, which could be seen all over the city. Dancers carrying coloured paper lanterns, marked with the hammer-and-sickle and the red star, formed a frieze in the square below, depicting what one poetic soul described as 'a huge fiery ship, the Chinese ship of state, riding on glowing blue-green waves', while the noise of cymbals, trumpets and drums, mingled with the chanting of Mao's name, reverberated across the yellow-tiled roofs of the old imperial city.

Next day the Soviet Union became the first country to recognise the new state. A motley group of minor communist parties and far left luminaries, ranging from the Work Committee of the Communist Party of Thailand to the British Labour Party MP, Connie Zilliacus, sent messages of congratulation. Mao began to prepare for his first visit abroad – to Moscow.

His readiness to leave China, even before the civil war had ended, testified both to his confidence in his colleagues and to the overriding importance he attached to this journey. As 1949 drew to a close, most of south-west China was still in nationalist hands, and an attempt by the PLA to take Jinmen Island (Quemoy), just off the coast of Fujian, had been beaten off with 9,000 communist casualties. In mid-November, Chiang Kai-shek flew back from Taiwan to Sichuan, where the GMD had established a temporary capital. He was still there on December 6, when Mao boarded a special train for Russia.

It also spoke volumes about Mao's foreign policy priorities.

For the new communist government, there was no question of simply inheriting the diplomatic ties bequeathed by the nationalists. Mao wanted a rupture, a clean break, with the Western powers, to expunge the last remnants of a century of humiliation. Earlier that year he had explained to Anastas Mikoyan, a veteran member of the Soviet Politburo whom Stalin had sent on a fact-finding visit to China, that the policy of 'leaning to one side', which the government would follow, involved a degree of diplomatic isolation. Russian help would be welcomed, he said. But until China had 'set its house in order', others would be kept at arm's length. Only when China itself decided that the time was right would imperialist countries be permitted to establish diplomatic missions. Meanwhile their former representatives, and their citizens, would be put under strong pressure to leave.

New China, the new 'Middle Kingdom', would make the barbarians wait at the gates, as old China had before it.

In a speech during the summer, Mao spelled out the implications of these decisions:

> [The reactionaries say:] 'You lean to one side.' Precisely so . . . To sit on the fence is impossible . . . In the world, without exception, one either leans to the side of imperialism or to the side of socialism. Neutrality is mere camouflage and a third road does not exist . . . We belong to the anti-imperialist front headed by the USSR, and we can look for genuine friendly aid only from that front, not from the imperialist front.

Yet there was an important nuance. Mao spoke of *leaning*, not becoming part of a monolithic block. China might belong to a Soviet-led 'anti-imperialist front' (just as the CCP had earlier belonged to a GMD-led 'united front'), but in neither case did that mean that their policies were identical. To Mao, membership of a front included both unity and struggle.

Stalin's betrayals of CCP interests had not been forgotten.

The Soviet leader himself had made sure of that: that spring, he had urged Mao not to send his forces across the Yangtse, but to content himself with controlling the northern half of China. This was prudent, he had explained, to avoid provoking America. But Mao knew, and Stalin knew, that a divided China was in Russia's, not in China's, interest. 'There are real friends and false friends,' Mao told Mikoyan pointedly. 'False friends are friendly on the surface, but say one thing and mean another. They dupe you . . . We shall be on our guard against this.'

Five months later, as the PLA pressed triumphantly southward amid a nationalist rout, Stalin made what amounted to an apology. He told Liu Shaoqi, then visiting Moscow to discuss future Soviet aid: 'Winners are always right. We feel that perhaps we hampered you in the past . . . We didn't know a lot about you, so it's possible that we made mistakes.'

As the clock on the Spassky Tower struck noon, in bitterly cold weather on December 16, 1949, Mao's train pulled into the

Yaroslavsky Station, near the Kremlin Wall, its stuccoed, gilt-and-gingerbread façade picked out in white and ochre paint, ablaze with red flags.

He was apprehensive. A few days earlier, in Sverdlovsk, while walking on the station platform, he had suddenly staggered, his face chalk-white and pouring sweat. After he had been helped to his carriage, the Russians were told he had a cold. It was an attack of neurasthenia. Stalin, for all his faults, was still to Mao the communist pontiff. The relationship they forged in the coming weeks would determine whether 'leaning to one side' could be translated into practical policy.

To the Soviet leaders, Mao was an enigma – the second most powerful communist leader in the world, and one of very few who had gained power without significant Russian help. Was he simply a communist original (who, in that case, would not fit easily into the Soviet scheme of things)? Or might he become another Tito whose defiance had led, a year earlier, to his excommunication from the communist camp?* Stalin, too, wanted to put the relationship on a proper footing.

That night, at 6 p.m., the doors of the St Catherine's Hall in the Kremlin swung open, and Mao found Stalin and the entire Soviet Politburo drawn up to receive him. It was, and was intended to be, an exceptional gesture for an exceptional guest.

The Russian leader greeted him effusively as 'the good son of the Chinese people.' But the underlying tensions surfaced moments later, when the Soviet leader, thinking that Mao was about to allude to their differences,† cut in with the same words he had used to Liu Shaoqi: 'You're a winner now, and winners are always right. That's the rule.' A stilted conversation followed, in which Stalin asked Mao

---

* George Kennan and others in the US State Department argued in the late 1940s that Mao, like Tito, would prove resistant to Soviet control, and that it was in the US interest to promote their differences. Mao himself later accused Stalin of having viewed him as 'a second Tito' in 1949.

† Mao had started telling the Soviet leader: 'I was criticised and pushed aside for a long period, and had nowhere to express my views . . .' He probably intended to go on to thank him for the Comintern's support during those difficult years (and, in the process, subtly to remind him of the indignities he had suffered at the hands of Moscow's Chinese protégés). But, at this point, Stalin interrupted.

what he wanted his visit to achieve. 'Something that doesn't [just] look good, but tastes good,' Mao replied. The KGB chief, Lavrentii Beria, giggled when that was translated. Stalin insisted on knowing what it meant. Mao declined to be more explicit, and by the time the two-hour meeting ended, the Soviet leader was reduced to asking whether China had a meteorological service, and if Mao would agree to his works being translated into Russian.

In fact, Stalin knew full well exactly what Mao wanted. China expected Russia to abrogate the Sino-Soviet Friendship Treaty concluded with Chiang Kai-shek and to negotiate a new alliance, appropriate to the relationship between fraternal communist powers.

This Stalin was reluctant to do. The pretext was that the agreement with Chiang flowed from the Yalta accords with Britain and the US. Therefore, he told Mao, 'a change in even one point could give England and America the legal grounds to raise questions about [other points]', such as Soviet rights to former Japanese territory in the Kuriles and South Sakhalin. This was bunkum – and designedly so. It was Stalin's way of telling Mao that if he wanted a new relationship with Moscow it would have to be on Russia's terms. The existing treaty would remain formally in effect, and, in accepting it, Mao would be recognising Stalin's primacy. The most the Soviet leader would add, by way of sugaring the pill, was that there was nothing to stop the two governments informally modifying its contents.

Mao was familiar was that game.

In 1938, when Stalin had endorsed his leadership, the symbolic quid pro quo had been that Mao publicly acknowledge that Stalin had been correct in viewing the Xian Incident as a Japanese-inspired plot. Mao had paid the requisite lip-service. With Stalin, he said later, it was 'a relationship between father and son, or between a cat and a mouse'.

But this time the stakes were far higher. Relations with Russia were the cornerstone of Mao's policies towards the rest of the world. If they continued to be based on Chinese subservience, what had the revolution achieved? If Russia insisted on perpetuating outdated treaty accords, why should capitalist countries agree to put their relations with China on a new footing?

Mao dug in his heels. In his usual elliptical fashion, he avoided confronting Stalin directly, focusing instead on a seemingly minor issue – whether or not Zhou Enlai should come to join him in Moscow. (If Zhou came, it would mean the Russians agreed to negotiate a new treaty; if he did not, the old treaty would continue.)

For the next two weeks, the talks were suspended.

Mao was left to stew, half prisoner, half cosseted guest, in the ponderous elegance of Stalin's personal dacha, in a birch forest a few miles west of Moscow. On December 21, he attended ceremonies marking the Soviet leader's seventieth birthday, and made an appropriately fulsome speech. But this was a purely formal occasion; and the Russians then abruptly cancelled talks which had been tentatively scheduled for the 23rd. Mao exploded in anger. 'I have only three tasks here,' he shouted at his Soviet minders, pounding the table. 'The first is to eat, the second is to sleep, and the third is to shit.' Yet when Stalin telephoned him, two days later, Mao was evasive and refused to broach political issues. When he, in turn, telephoned Stalin, he was told the Soviet leader was out.

This byzantine battle of wills, as each man waited for the other to blink first, might have continued indefinitely had not Western journalists, puzzled by Mao's apparent disappearance, begun to speculate that he might be under house arrest. That prompted Stalin to send a Tass correspondent to interview him. Mao then indicated that he was ready to remain in Moscow for as long as it took to get an agreement. Soon afterwards, Stalin backed down. On January 2, 1950, Molotov was despatched to inform him that Zhou could come to Moscow: the old treaty would be scrapped, and a new one concluded in its place. 'But what about Yalta?' Mao enquired mischievously when he and Stalin next met. 'The hell with that!' the Soviet leader replied.

Exactly what made him change his mind is unclear. Mao thought Britain's impending decision to recognise the Beijing government played the key role, by fuelling Stalin's paranoia that China might tilt to the West. But perhaps he simply recognised that, on this issue, Mao would not give way.

In any event, six weeks later, on February 14, the two foreign ministers, Zhou and Vyshinsky, signed the new 'Treaty of Friendship, Alliance and Mutual Assistance', with Stalin and Mao looking on. That night, in another break with precedent, the Soviet leader attended a reception Mao hosted in the ballroom of the Metropol Hotel. It was so unusual for him to leave the Kremlin that Russian security officials insisted on placing a bulletproof glass

partition between the leaders and their guests, with the result that
no one could hear the toasts until Mao asked that it be removed.

Appearances were again deceptive. The detailed negotiations
had been painfully difficult. Stalin's interpreter, Nikolai Fedorenko,
remembered the room where they were held as being like 'a stage
where a demonic show was being acted out'. Mao pressed for a cast-
iron Soviet commitment to come to China's aid in the event of a US
attack, only for Stalin to finagle by adding the condition that a
state of war must have been declared. He was still more incensed
by Stalin's demands for special privileges in Xinjiang and
Manchuria. Stalin, for his part, remained convinced that Mao was
an ersatz communist, a Chinese version of the nineteenth century
Russian peasant leader, Pugachev. 'He mistrusted us,' Mao
complained later. 'He thought our revolution was a fake.'

None the less, a modus vivendi had been achieved. As Mao
began the long rail journey home, he could take satisfaction in the
fact that a solid foundation had been laid for China's new place in
the world. With the civil war all but over, the government could now
turn its attention to rebuilding the shattered economy, and taking
the first, giddy steps on the road to socialism.

Four months later, at 4.40 a.m. on June 25, 1950, the Korean War
broke out.

Mao had been forewarned. The North Korean leader, Kim Il
Sung, had flown to Beijing six weeks earlier to tell him that Moscow
had approved a military offensive to reunify the peninsula. Stalin,
wily as ever, had laid down a condition: Kim must first get Mao's
approval. 'If you get kicked in the teeth,' the Soviet leader had told
him, 'I shall not lift a finger.' The implication was that Mao would
then have to bail the Koreans out. In his discussions in China, Kim
had omitted that part of the conversation.

In Beijing, the war was deeply unwelcome. Not only was there
uncertainty over how America would react, but the Chinese were
themselves at that stage preparing to invade Taiwan. Mao had been
suspicious enough of Kim's story to send a message to Stalin, asking
him to confirm that he had approved the attack. This Stalin did, but
took care in his reply to place the ball squarely in Mao's court: a
final decision, he said, must be taken by 'the Chinese and Korean
comrades together'. If the Chinese disagreed, the decision should

be postponed. That left Mao with no real choice. A hundred thousand Koreans had fought alongside Chinese troops in Manchuria. How could he now tell Kim that he must not try to 'liberate' his own land? The North Korean was informed that China acquiesced.

But mistrust on both sides continued. Kim decreed that the Chinese should be kept in the dark about the date of the attack, and excluded from the military planning.

To Chiang Kai-shek, the war was a godsend. Six months earlier, Truman had made clear that the US would not intervene to protect the nationalists, should Taiwan be attacked. In April, Chinese troops had made a large-scale amphibious landing on the island of Hainan, off the coast of Guangdong, crushing nationalist resistance in two weeks and killing or wounding 33,000 GMD soldiers. It looked like, and was, a dress rehearsal for the invasion of Taiwan itself. The next step would be attacks on Quemoy and the other offshore islands, followed by the final assault, to take place the following year.

Korea changed all that. The US might turn a blind eye to what all sides agreed was a continuation of the Chinese civil war. It could hardly do the same when a Soviet client-state in the northern part of the Korean peninsula undertook armed aggression against what was in effect a US protectorate in the south. On June 27, Washington announced that it would send troops to support South Korea's Syngman Rhee, and, for good measure, that the US Seventh Fleet would neutralise the Taiwan Straits.

Mao's initial response was limited. Chinese anti-aircraft units were moved to the North Korean side of the border to defend the bridges across the Yalu River, and reinforcements were sent from the south to Manchuria, on the grounds that, as one Chinese commander put it, 'one must prepare an umbrella before it rains'. The plan to attack Quemoy was put on indefinite hold.

At the end of July, however, as the North Korean forces continued their triumphant march southward, Mao began to grow alarmed. He could see, as Kim Il Sung could not, that the Korean lines were becoming overextended and vulnerable to an American counter-attack. At a Politburo meeting on August 4, Mao raised for the first time the possibility that Chinese forces might have to intervene directly to help the North Koreans, even at the risk of US nuclear retaliation. The problem, he told his colleagues, was that if the Americans won, their appetite would grow with eating. China would face the threat of US air raids against Manchurian and east China coast cities; amphibious attacks by nationalist units across the Taiwan Straits; even, perhaps, a combined operation involving the French forces fighting Ho Chi Minh's armies across China's southern border in Vietnam.

Two weeks later, Mao's fears deepened. One of Zhou Enlai's military analysts was convinced that the US Commander, General Douglas MacArthur, would make his move at Inchon, on the narrow waist of Korea, just south of the 38th parallel, the nominal dividing line between North and South. When Mao looked at the map, the young analyst convinced him too. He ordered the PLA to deploy another half-million men along the Manchurian border, and to begin planning for a war lasting at least a year.

At the same time, he sent Kim an urgent warning.

Strategically the United States was indeed a paper tiger, he said. But tactically 'the United States is a real tiger and capable of eating human flesh'. The Koreans should regroup and prepare to beat off an amphibious assault: 'From a tactical point of view, sometimes retreat is better than attack . . . Your enemy is not an easy one. Don't forget, you are fighting the chief imperialist. Be prepared for the worst.'

Kim ignored him. So did Stalin. On September 15, the Inchon landings began, and the North Korean army disintegrated. In Pyongyang, there was panic. Kim sent two of his top lieutenants to Beijing with a frantic plea for help. Stalin added his voice, offering Soviet air cover if Mao would send in ground forces to prevent a Korean collapse.

The next few weeks were the worst Mao had faced since the traumatic months following the Japanese surrender in 1945. He barely slept. On the one hand, he told Gao Gang, whom he had placed in charge of war-preparedness in Manchuria, there appeared to be no way to avoid intervention. On the other, China desperately needed peace for economic reconstruction. The country had been ravaged by war ever since the fall of the Qing dynasty, almost forty years earlier. The communists still had to recover Tibet and Taiwan and, within China proper, an estimated one million bandits were roaming the countryside; industry was in ruins; there was massive unemployment in the cities, and famine in the central plains.

Even in Beijing, food was in short supply. Incidents of sabotage, attributed to GMD agents, multiplied. The stock of goodwill the regime had acquired by ending nationalist corruption, stabilising the currency and restoring basic services had already been used up.

None the less, by the end of September, the die was cast.

Mao's military planners estimated that China would lose 60,000 dead and 140,000 wounded in the first year. The Americans enjoyed superior weaponry; but the PLA was better motivated, had greater reserves of manpower, and was better at the 'jigsaw warfare' which would occur when there was no stable front. The Chinese armies should therefore adopt the traditional Maoist tactic of 'concentrating superior forces against weaker ones' and fighting battles of annihilation, to maximise US casualties and erode American public support for continuing the war. The optimum time for Chinese entry, they concluded, would be shortly after US units crossed the 38th parallel into the North, because at that point the American supply lines would be stretched to the maximum, Chinese forces would still be close to their rear base, and politically Chinese intervention would be easy to justify.

On September 30, the first South Korean units crossed into North Korea. Twenty-four hours later, as the Chinese leaders celebrated the first anniversary of the People's Republic, Kim sent a special plane to Beijing with a hand-carried message, admitting that he was on the verge of defeat. 'If attacks north of the 38th parallel continue,' he wrote grimly, 'we shall not be able to survive relying merely on our own strength.'

Next day, Mao told an enlarged meeting of the Secretariat:*

> The question now is not whether but how fast we should send troops to Korea. One day's difference will be crucial . . . Today we will discuss two urgent questions: when our troops should enter Korea, and who should be the commander.

But if, for Mao, intervention had become inevitable, it did not mean that the rest of the leadership immediately rallied to his views. When the full Politburo met, on October 4, the majority was against him, for the same mixture of economic and political reasons that he himself had weighed in August.

* The Secretariat, in 1950, also served as the Politburo Standing Committee. Besides Mao himself, it comprised Liu Shaoqi, Zhou Enlai and Zhu De. The fifth member, Ren Bishi, had suffered a stroke and died later that autumn, being replaced by Chen Yun.

Lin Biao was particularly sceptical. If Kim were going to be defeated, he argued, China would do better to draw a defence line at the Yalu River, and let the North Koreans mount guerrilla actions from Manchuria to recover their lost land. Mao was unimpressed. That way, China would abandon the initiative, he replied. 'We would have to wait [on the Yalu] year after year, never knowing when the enemy will attack.' Lin had been Mao's first choice to command the Chinese intervention force, but had declined on grounds of ill-health. Now Mao proposed instead that the command should to to Peng Dehuai. Peng had arrived at the meeting late, having flown in from Xian. But he agreed with Mao's analysis that the United States would not be stopped by concessions, and when the discussion resumed, the following afternoon, his support helped secure a consensus in favour of military action.

Two days later, the first US troops – the American First Cavalry Division – crossed the 38th parallel, and Washington persuaded the UN to endorse Korean unification as its final goal. On Sunday, October 8, Mao issued the formal decree creating a Chinese expeditionary force to go to North Korea's aid. It would be known as the Chinese People's Volunteers, to underline that its mission was in the nature of a moral crusade, based on communist solidarity, and, more importantly, to maintain the fiction that Beijing's intervention was unofficial, and could not therefore justify American retaliation against Chinese cities. The force was to start crossing the Yalu River on October 15.

Then abruptly, three days before the expedition was to begin, Mao ordered all troop movements halted and summoned Peng back to Beijing 'to reconsider the [intervention] decision'.

The problem, as ever, was Moscow. A crisis had erupted over Soviet military support. On October 1, Stalin had cabled Mao from his Black Sea villa at Sochi, where he was vacationing: 'I see that the situation of our Korean friends is getting desperate . . . I think that you should move at least five or six divisions towards the 38th parallel at once.' In Mao's mind, this tripped an alarm. The problem was not Stalin's request. What worried him was the Soviet leader's silence about the undertakings the Russians had given, in the panicky days after Inchon, to provide Soviet air cover and military supplies.

Mao decided to bluff. He replied that a majority of the Chinese Politburo opposed intervention, and that he was sending Zhou Enlai for urgent consultations.

They met in Sochi on October 10. On Mao's instructions, Zhou presented what amounted to an ultimatum. China, he told Stalin, would respect the Soviet Union's wishes. If the Russians were willing to provide air cover and a massive infusion of weaponry, the Chinese would intervene. Otherwise, Mao would defer to Stalin's judgement and call the whole thing off. Then he sat back to wait for the old dictator's response.

To Zhou's horror, Stalin simply nodded.

If the Chinese felt it was too difficult to intervene, he said in substance, North Korea would have to be abandoned. Kim Il Sung could resort to partisan warfare from bases in Manchuria.

Zhou's hand had been trumped. In the ten hours of talks that followed, ending with a drunken banquet that broke up at 5 a.m., he was able to obtain some fresh assurances, conveyed to Mao in a cable which both he and Stalin signed, that Russia would provide needed weaponry and air defence for Chinese cities. But there would be no Soviet air cover over Korea, at least for the first two months. Stalin's excuse was that the Soviet air force needed time to prepare. In fact he had got cold feet. Even with Chinese help, he decided, North Korea might well be defeated. If Soviet pilots took part, the risk of conflict with the Americans was too great.

For Mao, this decision to renege on military commitments made only weeks earlier was the bitterest of all Stalin's betrayals.

At Xian in 1936 and in Manchuria in 1945, all that had been at stake were the political interests of a Chinese Party still struggling for power. But now China was a sovereign state, and Russia a treaty ally. 'Lean to one side' or not, the Soviet Union, Mao concluded, would never be a partner China could trust.

As usual, in the end the Chinese leaders had to yield. Mao's bluff had been called. China was far too deeply committed for there to be any real possibility to change course. The Politburo agreed. On Friday, October 13, Mao cabled Zhou to tell him that the intervention would go ahead anyway. Stalin, despite himself, was impressed. 'So the Chinese really are good comrades!' he was quoted as saying. Mao's troubles were still not over. The army commanders in the north-east were deeply alarmed by the prospect of exposing their men to American bombardment without air cover of any kind. On the 17th, they sent Peng Dehuai a joint message, proposing that China's entry into the war be postponed until the following spring. But with the South Koreans already at the gates of

Pyongyang, that was not an option. Next day, after hearing Peng's report, Mao told his colleagues: 'No matter what the difficulties, we should not change [our] decision . . . nor should we delay it.' At Mao's proposal, it was agreed that the Volunteers should begin moving into Korea under cover of darkness on the 19th. Thirty hours later, at around midnight, the Chief of the General Staff, Nie Rongzhen, informed him that the troops were crossing the Yalu as planned. For the first time in weeks, Mao had a proper night's sleep.

Once the decision-making was over, the war itself was brutally simple.

After initial defensive skirmishing in late October and early November, Peng ordered a general retreat. MacArthur then launched an all-out offensive to reach the Yalu River, under the slogan, 'Get the boys home by Christmas!'. As the Americans would soon discover, Mao was playing his old game of 'luring the enemy in deep'. At dusk on November 25, the Chinese counter-attacked. Ten days and 36,000 enemy casualties later (including 24,000 US troops), Peng's forces took Pyongyang.

It was not a perfect campaign. Chinese casualties were high, and the men suffered appallingly from the cold and from lack of food. None the less, seven weeks after entering the war Peng's volunteers had recaptured virtually all of North Korea.

At this point, Peng proposed a halt until the following spring. Mao pressed for a further advance. The Russians had begun providing limited air cover and, with the campaign now succeeding, Stalin had promised improvements in military resupply. Peng dragged his feet, but, at Mao's urging, reluctantly ordered a new offensive to start on New Year's Eve, when there would be a full moon, facilitating night operations, and the Americans would be busy with year-end festivities. Five days later, Chinese and North Korean forces captured the South Korean capital, Seoul, now a deserted shell of burnt-out buildings and rubble-filled streets, and forced the Americans back a further eighty miles to the south. But then, again, Peng halted. Kim Il Sung was furious and complained to Stalin. The Soviet leader, however, supported Peng's decision.

A month later, the Americans counter-attacked. Peng proposed a withdrawal, trading territory for time, following Mao's own hallowed precept which had served the communists so well against

Chiang Kai-shek and Japan. But Mao forbade it. He wanted to hold on to Seoul and the 38th parallel, whose capture had become a powerful symbol, both at home and abroad, of Red China's new-found strength.

In cable after cable, Peng tried to explain why this was unrealistic. 'Boots, food and munitions have not been provided,' he told Mao. 'The men cannot march barefoot in the snow.' With temperatures falling to –30 centigrade, thousands died of exposure.

For the first time in Mao's long career, he had allowed political considerations to cloud his military judgement.

In the end, not only was Seoul abandoned, but with it the eastern part of the 38th parallel and a large swathe of territory further north. In little more than four months, the Chinese Volunteers lost 140,000 men. The Americans built a strongly fortified defence line along the 38th parallel, and the war settled into seesaw battles around the two sides' existing positions. Truce talks opened in July 1951, but neither side was yet willing to admit that it had had enough. Not until two years later, after the death of Stalin and the election of Dwight D. Eisenhower, a Republican, as the new US President, were the Americans and the Chinese ready, over the objections of both their Korean clients, to end the blood-letting and allow an armistice to be signed.

Peng and the other Chinese commanders, who had experienced at first hand the effects of advanced military technology, came away from Korea convinced that warfare had fundamentally changed. Peng would spend the next five years as Defence Minister trying to transform the PLA into a modern, professional force.

Not Mao. To him, the fact that poorly-armed Chinese troops had fought the cream of the US Army to a standstill merely confirmed his belief that will-power, not weapons, decided the outcome of wars. 'We have won a great victory,' he exulted that autumn:

> We have taken the measure of the US armed forces. If you have never taken them on, you are liable to be scared of them . . . [Now we know] US imperialism is not terrifying, nothing to make a fuss about . . . The Chinese people are now organised, they are not to be trifled with. Once they are provoked to anger, things can get very tough.

Mao's impatience in the early stages of the conflict for quick, dramatic results was part of a wider pattern. Now that China had 'stood up', he yearned for a renewal of its ancient grandeur. Korea, like Vietnam, had been for centuries a tributary state. In the autumn of 1950, China had gone to war not merely to prevent a hostile, pro-American government taking power just across the Yalu River. National security, in a deeper sense, required the restoration of that suzerain relationship. For the same reason, Mao had sent military advisers to work with Ho Chi Minh's armies. Vietnam, too, had to be brought back into the Chinese fold.

After the war in Korea, America was no longer the only 'paper tiger' in Mao's book. China's attitude to the Soviet Union underwent a sea change. By preventing a North Korean defeat, China had come to Russia's rescue. Stalin's successors viewed Mao's regime with new respect, tinged with some apprehension. If a weak China could act so boldly, what future for its partnership with Russia once it became strong? To Mao, on the other hand, Moscow's stock had fallen. Not only had the Russians been devious, by manoeuvring China into a conflict it would have preferred to avoid, but they had shown themselves undependable and, ultimately, weak.

Outwardly, nothing changed. China was desperate for Soviet aid to rebuild its economy. In the Cold War of the 1950s, there was nowhere else it could turn. But the seeds of contempt had been sown.

When the final tally was made, China had suffered almost 400,000 casualties in Korea, including 148,400 dead. Among the latter was Mao's eldest son, Anying.

Since returning from Moscow, five years earlier, Anying had worked among the peasantry – renewing his Chinese roots, as his father put it – and then at a Beijing factory, where he became Deputy Secretary of the Party branch. In the autumn of 1950, with Mao's agreement, he volunteered for duty in Korea. Peng Dehuai turned down his request to serve with an infantry regiment, thinking that it was too dangerous, and named him instead to a post on his own staff as a Russian-speaking liaison officer. On November 24, 1950, less than five weeks after Chinese units crossed the border, Peng's head-quarters, in an abandoned gold-mine, were attacked by US bombers. Peng himself and most of his staff took refuge in a tunnel. Anying and another officer were trapped in a wooden building on the surface. It was hit by an incendiary bomb. Both men were killed.

That afternoon, Peng sent Mao a telegram, announcing the young man's death and proposing that he be buried on the battle-field, like all Chinese soldiers in Korea. When Mao's secretary, Ye Zilong, received it, he telephoned Zhou Enlai, who contacted other leaders. They authorised the burial, but decided that, with the war at a critical juncture, Mao should not be told.

So it was that, three months later, when Peng next saw Mao in Beijing, and blurted out how ashamed he was at not having protected Anying better, Mao was brutally confronted with news for which he was totally unprepared – that his eldest son had died. He crumpled, Peng remembered, trembling so violently that he could not light his cigarette. For several minutes, they sat in complete silence. Then Mao lifted his head. 'In revolutionary war,' he said, 'you always pay a price. Anying was one of thousands . . . You shouldn't take it as something special just because he was my son.'

The revolution had already taken Mao's siblings: his adopted sister, Zejian, had been executed with Yang Kaihui in 1930; his youngest brother, Zetan, had died in Jiangxi, in a clash with nation-alist troops in 1935; the second brother, Zemin, was killed by the Xinjiang warlord, Sheng Shicai, in 1942. His other surviving son, Anqing, was mentally unstable. His daughters, Li Min and Li Na, were both under Jiang Qing's influence, a connection he found increasingly distasteful.

Anying's relationship with his father had not been easy. Mao was a demanding man, who insisted that his children behave irre-proachably and receive the same treatment as everyone else. His bodyguard, Li Yinqiao, remembered him telling them: 'You're Mao Zedong's child, and that's hard luck for you!' Yet, since the young man's return to China, the two had grown close. When he died at the age of twenty-eight, the one remaining human bond capable of evoking in Mao a deep, personal loyalty, was severed.

The bloodshed that marked the birth of New China was not limited to the Korean War. The civilian death-toll in the political and economic movements that accompanied it was many times higher.

In the spring of 1950, Mao had begun to mobilise the Party for the immense effort necessary to install communist rule in the vast areas of central and southern China, with a population of more than 300 million, that the PLA had occupied in the course of the previous twelve months. The first step, he had decreed, was to 'stabilise social order'. This required 'resolutely eliminating bandits, spies, bullies and despots', along with nationalist secret agents, who, he said, were spreading anti-communist rumours; sabotaging economic work; and murdering Party workers. There was some basis for these charges. That year, 3,000 officials had been killed in the country-side while trying to collect grain taxes.

The original intention was to proceed cautiously. 'Chief culprits' were to be punished; others might be shown leniency.

The Korean War changed all that. All over China, hundreds of thousands of people marched in anti-American demonstrations. A huge hoarding was erected in the centre of Beijing, showing Truman and MacArthur, green-faced and unshaven, reaching out towards China with claws dripping blood, being repulsed by a stalwart Chinese Volunteer. People were encouraged to send small gifts to the soldiers at the front, accompanied by inspirational messages, along the lines: 'I saved this cake of soap for you so that you can clean off the enemy's blood, sprinkled on your clothes, and prepare for another battle.' Workers gave part of their wages for the war effort; peasants pledged to increase production, and donate the extra harvest. To encourage activism, they were told that weapons bought in this way would be inscribed with the donors' names.

Foreigners played their part, too, but as negative examples. An Italian, long resident in China, was accused of plotting to assassinate Mao at the October 1st parade. He was convicted of heading a US espionage network, aided by his neighbour, a Japanese. After a summary trial, the two men were driven, standing on the back of an open jeep, across the city to an execution ground by the Temple of Heaven. There they were shot. Two other foreigners, an Italian bishop and a French bookshop owner, were imprisoned as alleged accomplices. That the plot was a fabrication was irrelevant. Blazoned across several pages of the Party newspaper, *Renmin ribao* (People's Daily), it helped to justify the imposition of ever harsher social controls.

Subsequent Chinese claims that the US was using germ warfare in Korea, and that the American military were shipping Chinese prisoners of war to Nevada to test the effect of nuclear weapons, piled on further pressure. In every corner of the country, Chinese seethed with indignation at imperialist atrocities. Those who did not seethe were suspected of being disloyal.

In this superheated atmosphere, the campaign to suppress
counter-revolutionaries burned white-hot. In the space of six
months, 710,000 people, most of them linked in some way, however
tenuous, with the departed Guomindang, were executed or driven
to suicide.

At least a million-and-a-half more disappeared into the newly
established 'reform through labour' camps, purpose-built to accommodate them.

Mao himself fine-tuned the operation, issuing a steady stream of
directives from the winter of 1950 until the following autumn. Thus,
in January 1951, when the campaign was apparently flagging, he
insisted that death sentences be carried out, arguing: 'If we are weak
and indecisive, and excessively indulgent . . . of evil people, it will
bring disaster.' Two months later, he applied the brakes. 'Rashness
presents the major danger,' he now warned. 'It doesn't make much
difference if a counter-revolutionary is executed a few days sooner
or a few days later. But . . . making wrong arrests and executions
will produce very bad effects.' In May, he advocated suspended
death sentences, because otherwise 'it will deprive us of a large pool
of [prison] labour power'. A month later, the movement needed
to be encouraged again. 'Persons who . . . have to be executed to
assuage the people's anger,' Mao declared, 'must be put to death for
this purpose.'

Land reform lurched violently to the left, too.

Mao laid down a new guideline of 'not correcting excesses
prematurely'. In almost every village, at least one and sometimes
several landlords were dragged before mass meetings, organised by
Party work teams, and either beaten to death on the spot by enraged
peasants or reserved for public execution later. By the time the land
reform was completed, at the end of 1952, upwards of a million
landlords and members of their families had been killed. Even that
figure is only a guess. The actual death-toll may have been two,
possibly even three, times higher. Within three years of the
founding of New China, the landlords as a cohesive class, which had
dominated rural society since Han times, had simply ceased to exist.

In contrast to Soviet practice, Mao insisted that the major role in
these movements be played, not by the public security organs, but
by ordinary people. The rationale was the same as it had been in
Hunan in 1927 and in the soviet base areas in the 1930s: peasants
who killed with their bare hands the landlords who oppressed them

were wedded to the new revolutionary order in a way that passive spectators could never be.

The Party faced a still greater challenge in trying to bring about a comparable social transformation in the cities – to cleanse our society', as Mao put it, 'of all the filth and poison left over from the old regime.'

To that end, starting in the autumn of 1951, Mao launched in quick succession three more political campaigns: the 'Three Antis' (anti-corruption, anti-waste and anti-bureaucratism), the purpose of which, he explained, was to prevent 'the corrosion of the cadres by the bourgeoisie'; the 'Five Antis' (anti-bribery, anti-tax evasion, anti-fraud, anti-embezzlement, anti-leakage of state secrets), aimed at the capitalist classes whose 'sugar-coated bullets' caused the corrosion in the first place; and a thought reform movement, modelled on the Yan'an Rectification Campaign, designed to remould urban intellectuals, especially those trained in the West, so as to enforce conformity and eradicate bourgeois ideas.

Again, the primary actors were not state or Party agencies but the men and women who were themselves the targets of each campaign and the 'broad masses' mobilised to judge them. In the 'Three' and 'Five Antis', workers denounced their bosses; cadres exposed each other; children were encouraged to inform on their parents; wives turned against their husbands. Activists set up 'tiger-hunting teams', to drag out actual and presumed offenders for humiliation before mass meetings.

A climate of raw terror developed. Minor offenders, Mao declared, should be criticised and reformed, or sent to labour camps, while 'the worst among them should be shot'. For many, the psychological pressure became unbearable. The two campaigns together took several hundred thousand more lives, the great majority by suicide, while an estimated 2 billion US dollars, a staggering sum at that time, was collected from private companies in fines for illicit activities. Surviving cadres, private businessmen and the urban population as a whole, had received a memorable lesson in the limits of communist kindness.

The bourgeoisie, Mao explained in the summer of 1952, was no longer to be regarded as an ally of the proletariat. It was now the principal object of struggle waged by the working class.

Intellectuals were treated differently. They were to be cleansed of bourgeois ideology, especially individualism, pro-Americanism, objectivism (indifference to politics) and 'contempt for the toiling masses'. These issues were discussed in small groups whose participants would make repeated self-criticisms, until, layer after layer, anything resembling independent thought, incompatible with Maoist orthodoxy, had been stripped away.

Sooner or later Mao would have moved to assert Party control over the urban population, whether or not war had broken out in Korea. The death-toll would not necessarily have been lower had he done so in peacetime. The power of the landlords would still have had to be broken; the functionaries, the capitalists and the intellectuals brought into line. The same pervasive system of compulsory registration with the police, of designated residence under the scrutiny of neighbourhood committees, of personnel dossiers held by security departments attached to every town-dweller's work unit, would have been enforced even without a foreign war.

None the less, for the Chinese communists, the Korean conflict did have a silver lining.

It produced a sense of regeneration and national pride which forced grudging respect even among those who otherwise had little sympathy for the new regime. The perception of heroic sacrifice on the battlefield helped to explain extreme measures at home. The external threat from America fuelled internal transformation. Above all, it allowed Mao to go faster. By the autumn of 1953, four years and at least two million deaths after the proclamation of the People's Republic, the Maoist state was more securely entrenched than had seemed imaginable when he and Zhou Enlai had set off from their temporary headquarters near Shijiazhuang to enter newly conquered Beijing, feeling, as Mao put it, 'like students in the old days, going to the capital to take the [imperial] examinations'. By his own lights, Mao had passed the first test handsomely. After so many years of revolution and war, the cost in human suffering had become irrelevant.

CHAPTER THIRTEEN

The Sorcerer's Apprentice

Economics were not Mao's strong point.

The surveys he had carried out in Jiangxi in the early 1930s had focused on class relations in the countryside, not the dynamics of rural trade. Even when his avowed aim was to describe the commercial life of a small market town, the result was an exhaustive listing of hundreds of obscure local products, meticulously compiled, but with painfully little understanding of what made the economy grow, generating employment and prosperity, or what, in bad times, made it falter.

In Yan'an, a decade later, Mao's New Democracy platform, conditioned by the political needs of the united front and the war against Japan, envisaged a mixed economy with a strong capitalist component. The two substantial innovations which the communists made in the economic field in the early 1940s, the introduction of co-operatives and a movement for economic self-sufficiency in the Red Army, were likewise politically motivated – the one as a step away from individual peasant ownership towards a collectivised system, the other a means of lessening the burden the military imposed on the civilian population. Both continued in the People's Republic. When the PLA occupied Tibet, in the winter of 1951, Mao's prime concern was that the army produce enough food to meet its own needs. Otherwise, he warned, it would be impossible to win over the Tibetans and eventually they would rebel.

Mao's stress on self-sufficiency was a product of the peasant economy in which he had been reared, reinforced by his experience in Red base areas that were under constant threat of enemy blockade. Economic autarky, both at the provincial and the national level, was an article of faith. China's historical experience had taught that foreign countries were exploitative, and should be kept at arm's length. Throughout the Maoist period, foreign trade was held to a minimum, and the balance of payments kept firmly in the black. China accepted foreign loans only from the Soviet Union, and then, apart from military supplies during the Korean War, only in limited amounts. When, in 1949, the Russians offered a five-year credit totalling 300 million dollars, even at that time a very modest sum, it was widely attributed to Stalin's niggardliness. Mao himself was privately relieved that China's borrowings would remain small.

Shortly before nationwide victory, Mao spoke publicly of his concerns about the economic tasks ahead. 'We shall have to master what we do not know,' he warned. 'We must learn to do economic work from all who know how, no matter who they are . . . We must acknowledge our ignorance, and not pretend to know what we do not know.'

Three years later, when he and his colleagues were confronted with the task of drawing up a comprehensive development strategy for their vast, newly pacified country, they did precisely that – and called in Russian experts to help. A Five-Year Plan was worked out, modelled on Soviet practice, with more than a hundred large Soviet-built heavy industrial plants at its core.

Mao would afterwards complain that 'dogmatism' had taken hold at that time. 'Since we didn't understand these things and had absolutely no experience,' he grumbled, 'all we could do in our ignorance was to import foreign methods . . . It didn't matter whether a [Russian] article was correct or not, the Chinese listened all the same and respectfully obeyed.' But in 1953 Russian guidance was exactly what Mao wanted. That spring he personally urged officials to 'whip up a high tide of learning from the Soviet Union throughout the whole country'.

Only in two major respects did China stray from the Soviet path. In place of a Stalinist programme of forced collectivisation, Mao laid down a voluntary, step-by-step approach. Villagers were first encouraged to form Mutual Aid Teams, in which a handful of families joined together to pool draught animals, tools and labour power; then came lower-level Agricultural Producers' Co-operatives (APCs), whose members were remunerated in proportion to the amount of land and labour they contributed; and, finally, higher-level APCs, where the land and equipment of a whole village became collective property and members were paid on the basis of labour alone. Similarly, in commerce and industry, the 'general line for the transition to socialism', which Mao put forward in the summer of 1953, retained substantial elements of the New Democracy platform. To build a socialist economy, he declared, would take 'fifteen years or a little longer' in the cities, and eighteen years in the countryside. In the meantime, China's private business-men (whose spirit had by then been crushed by the violence of the 'Five Antis' campaign) were to transform their enterprises into partnerships with the state, from which they would be permitted to continue drawing a quarter of the profits.

It all sounded eminently reasonable. Too reasonable, no doubt, for a country of festering class hatreds, led by a group of revolution-aries devoted to radical change. In any event, it turned out to be too reasonable to last.

Already in 1951, a dispute had developed over the pace of the transformation they were trying to accomplish. That year, the Finance Minister, Bo Yibo, supported by Liu Shaoqi, had spoken out forcefully against pushing rural collectivisation too fast. Twelve months later, with Mao's approval, Gao Gang, now a senior Politburo member and Party chief of Manchuria, presented the opposite view. Rapid collectivisation was imperative, he said, because if the 'spontaneous tendency of the peasants towards capitalism' went unchecked, China would have a capitalist, rather than a socialist, future. Afterwards, the two men clashed again, this time over tax policy. Bo proposed equal treatment for state and private firms. Gao charged that he was advocating 'class peace'. Again, Mao supported Gao. Bo, he said, had been struck by a 'spiritual sugar-coated bullet' which had caused him to succumb to the influence of bourgeois ideas. If the Party's cause were to triumph, such 'right-opportunist deviations' must be corrected and 'the question of the socialist road versus the capitalist road must be clarified'.

Thus, the battle lines were drawn. The dilemmas posed in these obscure debates of the early 1950s – economic growth vs. sponta-neous capitalism; ideological imperatives vs. objective reality; the socialist vs. the capitalist road – would resonate through all the great political upheavals of the years ahead: the anti-Rightist campaign;

the Great Leap Forward; and the Cultural Revolution. The seeds of turmoil were sown, not towards the end but at the very beginning of Mao's rule.

The dispute between Bo and Gao also provided the springboard for the first major power struggle in the Chinese leadership since Mao had ousted Zhang Guotao and Wang Ming in the late 1930s.

Gao was a rising star in the communist hierarchy. Six or seven years younger that Liu Shaoqi and Zhou Enlai, he was unsophisticated, energetic, capable – and, more important, Mao liked him. He was also highly ambitious. In Manchuria, he had gone out of his way to cultivate Russian officials, and apparently used this channel to spread rumours that Liu and Zhou were pro-American. Liu was also the true target of his attacks on Bo Yibo. In the late autumn of 1952, when Mao summoned Gao to Beijing to head the State Planning Commission, a crucially important task at a time when China was preparing the transition to a planned economy, he and Liu evidently liked each other no better. By the following spring, Gao was casting about for ways to supplant him.

Mao encouraged Gao in this, though to what extent wittingly is unclear. He was irritated with Liu and Zhou because of what he saw as their foot-dragging over the transition to a socialist system. That winter he groused about them privately to Gao, who became convinced that the Chairman was giving him the go-ahead to take a higher-profile role himself.

Other factors concurred. Mao was finding his state duties wearisome. In 1952 he began speaking of 'withdrawing to the second front', by which he meant leaving the day-to-day running of the Party and government to his younger colleagues, so that he could concentrate on major strategic and theoretical issues. This did not imply any diminution of Mao's control. On the contrary, during this period, his domination of decision-making grew still more pronounced. In May 1953, he was infuriated to discover that Yang Shangkun, who headed the CC's General Office, the nerve centre of the Party, had issued directives without his prior approval. 'This is a mistake and a breach of discipline,' he thundered. 'Documents and telegrams sent out in the name of the Central Committee can be despatched only after I have gone over them, otherwise they are invalid.' His reaction showed how profoundly his conception of his role had changed. In 1943, Mao's colleagues had given him the power, in exceptional cases, to overrule the rest of the Secretariat.

Now, ten years later, he was arrogating to himself blanket authority over everything: his colleagues were allowed to do nothing without his explicit accord.

To Gao Gang, the talk of a 'second front' was a signal to act fast, before Mao's withdrawal allowed Liu to entrench himself as his successor. He drew further encouragement from events in Moscow, where, after Stalin's death, the comparatively youthful Georgii Malenkov inherited his mantle, while older Politburo members, like Molotov and Kaganovich, were passed over. If Malenkov could do that in Russia, Gao asked himself, why could he not do the same in China?

The result was a palace conspiracy.

First Gao won over the east China leader, Rao Shushi, to whom he held out the prospect of the premiership. Then, by an extraordinary stroke of luck, he obtained a copy of a draft list for a new Politburo, prepared by one of Liu Shaoqi's associates in the Central Committee apparatus as a working document ahead of the next Party Congress. It proposed increasing the representation of men who, like Liu, had spent most of the civil war period in the Guomindang-controlled 'White' areas, including, notably, Bo Yibo, at the expense of those who had fought in the Red areas. Armed with this smoking gun and claiming to have Mao's backing, Gao set about working up support among indignant ex-Red area colleagues.

Peng Dehuai fell into the trap. So did Lin Biao. But Deng Xiaoping, after beginning to negotiate with Gao about the future allocation of Party posts, sensed something amiss and sent a report to Mao. Chen Yun, who had honed his political antennae in Moscow watching Stalin at work during the purges, also jibbed. He, too, informed the Chairman, who told both men to say nothing.

Mao then set an ambush of his own. When the Politburo met in December, he announced that he intended to spend several weeks resting in the south, and proposed that, as usual, Liu should act in his place. Gao rose to the bait. Why not, in the Chairman's absence, he suggested, rotate the responsibility among other senior Politburo members? Mao indicated that he would consider the idea, and over the next few weeks Gao lobbied his colleagues frantically for other leadership changes, including his own promotion to Vice-Chairman, or alternatively, General Secretary.

By December 24, when the Politburo reconvened, Mao had heard enough. He accused Gao of unprincipled factionalism, carrying out 'underground activities' and attempting to enhance his personal power. The conspiracy collapsed.

In the months that followed, the winners and losers received their due rewards.

Gao was convinced that Mao had betrayed him, and in February 1954 attempted to kill himself. In August he tried again, with poison, and succeeded. Rao Shushi was arrested, to die of pneumonia, still in prison, twenty years later.

Peng Dehuai and Lin Biao were exonerated, after pleading that they had thought Gao was acting with Mao's approval (though both men's relations with Liu remained definitively soured). Deng Xiaoping was appointed Secretary-General of the Central Committee, and afterwards was promoted to the Politburo. Chen Yun also prospered. At the Eighth Congress, two years later, he became a Party Vice-Chairman, while Deng was named General Secretary.

By the spring of 1954, the Gao Gang–Rao Shushi anti-Party 'sinister wind', as Mao called it, had blown itself out. Officially, it had no wider significance. Yet if, as was plainly the case, Mao had sowed the idea in Gao's mind that Liu and Zhou were expendable, he must have had his reasons. Both men were supremely competent, dedicated to Mao personally no less than to the communist cause. He had only to give the order and they would have done whatever he wished. In retrospect, it is clear that he never had any intention of getting rid of them. But destabilising his two closest colleagues was another matter. Mao found in Gao Gang's ambition an instrument to keep them off-balance – to force them to try to read his mind better, to stay more attuned to his thinking. Gao had not been so stupid as to misread Mao's intentions entirely: he merely went too far.*

---

* In the mid-1980s, Hu Yaobang, then CCP General Secretary, proposed to Deng Xiaoping that the case of Gao Gang and Rao Shushi be reopened. Deng was reportedly furious and forbade any further discussion. Key documents, including the minutes of the December 24, 1953, Politburo meeting, are still sealed, and published accounts within China remain silent about Mao's role. It is not clear whether Deng's reluctance to re-examine the case was a result of the post-Mao leadership's decision to treat the years prior to 1957 as a period when Mao made no major errors; or whether it was because of the light it might throw on Deng's own conduct during Gao's purge.

The purge cast a long shadow. That Peng Dehuai, Lin Biao and, initially, Deng Xiaoping, could all have believed that Mao was plotting behind the backs of Liu and Zhou spoke volumes about the level of trust which his imperial style of leadership had fostered. Mao's eminence and sense of national mission meant that his only remaining loyalty was to his vision of China's future. His colleagues – men and women with whom, in some cases, he had spent thirty years in shared struggle – were being reduced to tools in the working out of his dreams.

The debate over the pace of change which Bo Yibo had initiated ended with no clear consensus over how quickly collectivisation should proceed. Mao's instincts were to go faster. But each time he forced the pace, over-eager local officials coerced the rural population into ill-prepared co-operatives where socialism was regarded as 'eating from one big pot', the poor lived off the rich until their resources were exhausted, and then the whole venture collapsed under a mountain of debt.

In the spring of 1953, a campaign was launched, with Mao's blessing, against 'rash advance'. But as soon as the situation stabilised, 'spontaneous capitalism' appeared: the better-off peasants began hiring labour, lending money, and buying and selling land. That sparked a new campaign, this time against 'rash retreat'. Collectivisation roared ahead again – with even more deleterious results: rich peasants slaughtered their livestock, rather than share them with poorer neighbours. Then, in 1954, severe flooding along the Yangtse reduced the summer harvest. Local cadres, determined to show their mettle, insisted that grain procurement be maintained. Food riots broke out. In the southern provinces, the peasants cursed the communists as worse than the Guomindang.

Accordingly, in January 1955, Mao slammed on the brakes for the third time. The collectivisation drive, he admitted, was out of step with the objective capabilities of the peasantry. The new policy would be a 'three-word scripture: "Stop, contract, develop."' The number of APCs had already increased from 4,000 in the autumn of 1952 to 670,000 that winter, one in seven of all peasant households. Mao now decreed that there should be no further expansion for the next eighteen months. Liu Shaoqi authorised a plan to disband more than a quarter of existing APCs in the interests of stabilisation, and grain procurement was sharply reduced.

Had Mao been willing to leave it at that, all might have been well. In April, however, he set off on an inspection tour in the south to see things for himself. There, egged on by local officials, whose own interests were intimately linked to the collectivisation campaign – and who were therefore only too happy to tell Mao what he wanted to hear – the Chairman concluded that peasant resistance had been overstated.

Only Deng Zihui, a trusted ally since the late 1920s, whom Mao had appointed to oversee the collectivisation drive, had the courage to dig in his heels and tell the Chairman he was mistaken.

Deep down, Mao knew Deng had a point. In a revealing admission, he conceded: 'The peasants want freedom, but we want socialism.' Yet Mao was too hooked on his vision of socialised agriculture to allow material obstacles, even when he acknowledged their existence, to stand in his way. The problem, Deng told his subordinates grimly, was that the Chairman thought '[material] conditions for running co-operatives are unnecessary'. His objections were brushed aside. 'Your mind needs to be shelled with artillery,' Mao raged at him, and at a conference of provincial secretaries in July he proceeded to do just that:

> A high tide in the new socialist mass movement is imminent throughout the countryside. But some of our comrades, tottering along like a woman with bound feet, are complaining all the time: 'You're going too fast, much too fast.' Too much carping, unwarranted complaints, boundless worries and countless taboos – all this they take as the right policy to guide the socialist mass movement in the rural areas.
>
> No, this is not the right policy. It is the wrong one . . .
>
> [This] is a . . . movement involving a rural population of more than 500 million and has tremendous worldwide significance. We should lead this movement actively [and] enthusiastically . . . instead of dragging it back by whatever means.

With Mao's own doubts stilled, and all opposition silenced, the targets were raised exponentially. He himself spoke of collectivising half the rural population by the end of 1957. Provincial officials were determined to go still faster. In July 1955, 17 million households belonged to APCs. Six months later, the figure had reached

75 million, 63 per cent of the peasant population. Mao told his secretary that he had not felt so happy since the victory over Chiang Kai-shek. As he prepared to celebrate his sixty-second birthday, he gloated:

> In the first half of 1955, the atmosphere was foul and dark clouds threatened. But in the second half there has been a complete change, and the climate is entirely different . . . This [co-operativisation movement] is a raging tidal wave, sweeping away all demons and monsters . . . By the time the year ends, the victory of socialism will be largely assured.

In fact, by December 1956, only 3 per cent of the peasantry still farmed as individuals. The socialist transformation of agriculture, which was not to have been completed until 1971, had been accomplished fifteen years early.

Ideologically it was a tremendous success. Politically it was a mixed blessing. Economically it held the seeds of disaster, for it convinced Mao, and other leaders, that, given the will to succeed, material conditions need not be decisive.

Collectivisation sapped the energies of the countryside for a generation to come, causing a levelling-down of rural society which stifled independent initiative, demotivated the most productive, rewarded the least capable, and replaced the rule of the landlords and literati with rule by the Party branch, whose members enjoyed power and privilege unconstrained by the fear of banditry and rebellion that, for centuries past, had kept their predecessors in check.

With the rural areas in socialist hands, Mao returned his attention to the cities where, he declared, the bourgeoisie was now isolated and should be dealt with 'once and for all'. His promise of only two years earlier, that a mixed economy would continue until the mid-1960s, was conveniently forgotten:

> On this matter we are quite heartless! On this matter, Marxism is indeed cruel and has little mercy, for it is determined to exterminate imperialism, feudalism, capitalism and small production to boot . . . Some of our comrades are too kind, they are not tough enough, in other words, they are not so Marxist. It is a very good thing, and a significant one too, to exterminate the bourgeoisie and capitalism in China . . . Our aim is to exterminate capitalism, obliterate it from the face of the earth and make it a thing of the past.

That speech was made at a closed meeting of Party leaders in October 1955. In his encounters with Chinese businessmen, Mao understandably took a subtler line, which some unnamed wit among the Shanghai capitalists summed up as the 'how to make a cat eat pepper' approach.

Liu Shaoqi, it was said, advocated firmness: 'You get somebody to hold the cat,' he said, 'stuff the pepper into its mouth, and push it down with a chopstick.' Mao was horrified. Force, he declared, was undemocratic: the cat must be persuaded to eat voluntarily. Then Zhou Enlai tried. 'I would starve the cat,' said the Premier. 'Then I would wrap the pepper with a slice of meat. If the cat is sufficiently hungry, it will swallow it whole.' Again Mao shook his head. 'One must not use deceit,' he said. 'Never fool the people!' His own answer, he explained, was very simple. 'You rub the pepper into the cat's backside. When it starts to burn, the cat will lick it off – and be happy to be permitted to do so.'

Accordingly, rather than nationalise by decree, Mao asked his private sector interlocutors what they would advise him to do. The businessmen, whose backsides still burned from the peppering they had received in the 'Five Antis' campaign, fell over each other to tell him that nationalisation was what they longed for – the quicker, the better.

Even so, the speed of the take-over was astonishing.

On December 6, 1955, Mao stated that all private businesses should be taken over by the state before the end of 1957, twelve years ahead of his original schedule. In practice, all private commerce and industry in Beijing was converted to joint state–private ownership in the first twelve days of the New Year. To mark the achievement, Mao and the rest of the leadership presided over a celebratory rally attended by 200,000 people in Tiananmen Square on January 15. Other major cities hurried to follow suit. By the end of January 1956, the urban economy had followed the rural areas into the straitjacket of Party and state control.

That, in turn, was the signal for another gravity-defying leap forward.

Declaring that 'rightist conservatism' was the main obstacle to progress, Mao now set several new targets. Within the next few decades, he said, China must become 'the number-one country in the world', surpassing the United States in cultural, scientific, technological and industrial development. 'I don't consider [American achievements] as anything so terrific,' he went on breezily. If America produced 100 million tons of steel annually, 'China should produce several hundred million tons'.

As a first step, he called for the First Five-Year Plan to be fulfilled ahead of schedule, and unveiled a Twelve-Year Agricultural Plan proposing a doubling of grain and cotton production. The slogan, 'more, faster, better', which he had used in the last months of 1955 during the high tide of collectivisation, was modified to become, 'more, faster, better and more economically', as though that somehow made it more rational. Saltationist socialism, as one foreign scholar called it, had established itself as Mao's favoured model for economic advance.

On February 25, 1956, Nikita Sergeyevich Khrushchev, who had succeeded the ephemeral Malenkov twelve months earlier, stood before his peers in the baroque white-and-gold banqueting hall in the Kremlin where the Soviet Party's 20th Congress was being held, and told them what they all knew in their hearts but had never expected to hear: that Stalin, before whom they had trembled for so long, had been a brutal psychopath, animated by 'a persecution mania of unbelievable dimensions', whose personality cult had concealed a capricious, despotic rule; whose 'military genius' had brought Russia to the verge of defeat by Germany; and whose sickly suspicion and mistrust had sent millions of innocent men and women to cruel and unnecessary deaths.

The Secret Speech, as it became known, was delivered in closed session, from which representatives of fraternal parties were barred, the day before the Congress ended. A week later, Deng Xiaoping, who, with Zhu De, had headed the Chinese delegation, flew back to China with a copy, which was hurriedly translated.

Given Mao's own problems with Stalin, he might have been expected to welcome the Soviet dictator's posthumous come-uppance. In one important sense, he did: such criticisms, he said, 'destroyed myths, and opened boxes. This brings liberation . . . [allowing people to] speak their minds and to be able to think about issues.' Overall, however, Mao had serious doubts about Khrushchev's approach. At a meeting with the Soviet Ambassador in late March, he spoke a great deal about Stalin's errors towards China, but very little about the cult of personality – the nub of

Khrushchev's attack – emphasising instead that Stalin had been 'a great Marxist, a good and honest revolutionary', who had made mistakes 'not on everything, but [only] on certain issues'. These views were reflected soon afterwards in an editorial in the *People's Daily*, entitled 'On the Historical Experience of the Dictatorship of the Proletariat', which, nearly six weeks after Khrushchev had spoken and long after the rest of the communist bloc had endorsed the new Soviet line, set out for the first time publicly the Chinese Party's position:

> Whatever the mistakes [that have been made], the dictatorship of the proletariat is, for the popular masses, always far superior to . . . the dictatorship of the bourgeoisie . . . Some people consider that Stalin was wrong in everything: this is a grave misconception . . . We should view Stalin from an historical standpoint, make a proper and all-round analysis to see where he was right and where he was wrong and draw useful lessons therefrom. Both the things he did right and the things he did wrong were phenomena of the international communist movement and bore the imprint of the times.

Under Stalin's leadership, it insisted, the Soviet Union had made 'glorious achievements' in which he had 'an ineffaceable share', while his 'mistakes' had been confined to the latter part of his life.

The editorial was the first step in the slow unravelling of the Sino–Soviet alliance. It made clear that, in future, China would copy Soviet experience only selectively. It raised questions, even though implicitly, about the role of Stalin's subordinates, now his successors, in the crimes of which he was accused – triggering, not long afterwards, an acrimonious exchange between Mikoyan and Peng Dehuai. 'If we had spoken out, we would have been killed!' the Armenian admitted. 'What kind of communist is it that fears death?' came Peng's disdainful reply. But, most important of all, the *People's Daily*'s comments signalled a fundamental change in the Chinese attitude to Moscow. It was written from the standpoint not of a junior partner but of an equal. Mao was sitting in judgement on the hasty actions of a neophyte Soviet leadership.

Far more than ideological differences, it would be this assertion of equality, on the one hand, and the efforts of Khrushchev and his colleagues to maintain the old 'elder brother' relationship, on the other, that would bring Beijing and Moscow, before the decade was out, to the point of no return.

As 1956 unfolded, Mao's concern that Khrushchev was 'throwing out the communist baby along with the Stalinist bathwater', as one contemporary writer put it, seemed amply justified. After riots during the summer in Poland, the Soviet-backed leadership in Warsaw, which Khrushchev had personally installed only half a year before, was replaced, over strong Russian objections, by a new 'liberal' group, headed by one of Stalin's victims, Wladyslaw Gomulka. Soon afterwards, a still graver challenge to Moscow's dominance came from Hungary, where the Stalinist First Secretary, Matyas Rakosi, was deposed by reformists led by Imre Nagy.

In Poland, Mao supported Gomulka, on the grounds that the root of the problem was the same Russian 'great power chauvinism' that China had had for so long to endure. Liu Shaoqi was despatched to Moscow, where in October he persuaded Khrushchev not to resort to armed intervention. But when Hungary announced that it was leaving the Soviet bloc military alliance, the Warsaw Pact, Mao took a very different view. Supporting the right of a brother party to choose its own path to socialism was one thing; sitting with folded hands in the face of counter-revolution was another. Again, Liu put pressure on Khrushchev – this time to send in troops to put down the revolt by force.

The mess the Soviet leaders had made in their own east European backyard further lowered them in Mao's estimation.

On November 15, 1956, shortly after the Russian army occupied Hungary, he gave the new Chinese Central Committee, elected at the Eighth Congress a few weeks earlier, the benefit of his reflections on the past year's events:

I think there are two 'swords': one is Lenin and the other Stalin. The sword of Stalin has now been discarded by the Russians . . . We Chinese have not thrown it away. First we protect Stalin, and second, at the same time, we criticise his mistakes . . .

As for the sword of Lenin, has it not also been discarded to a certain extent by some Soviet leaders? In my view, it has been discarded to a considerable extent. Is the October Revolution still valid? . . . Khrushchev's report at the 20th Congress of the CPSU says it is possible to seize state power by the parliamentary road, that is to say, it is no longer necessary for all countries to learn from the October Revolution. Once this gate is opened, by and large Leninism is thrown away . . .

How much capital do [the Russians] have? Just Lenin and Stalin.

Now [they] have abandoned Stalin and practically all of Lenin as well – with Lenin's feet gone, or perhaps with only his head left, or with one of his hands cut off. We on our part stick to studying Marxism-Leninism and learning from the October Revolution.

That was far harsher than anything Mao had said before, even in the privacy of the Politburo. Although his remarks were kept secret, they inspired a second *People's Daily* editorial, published at the end of December under the title, 'More on the Historical Experience of the Dictatorship of the Proletariat'. The road of the October Revolution, and specifically the violent seizure of power by the proletariat from the bourgeoisie, it declared, were 'universally applicable truths'. Any attempt to 'evade this road' was revisionist.

When Zhou Enlai visited Moscow in January 1957, he found, unsurprisingly, that the Soviet leaders were 'displeased'.

By then, four major areas of dispute had emerged between the two Parties – all stemming from the 20th Congress. First came the assessment of Stalin: Mao insisted that he was 'three parts bad, and seven parts good'. Next, there was the argument over Khrushchev's 'parliamentary road to socialism', which was closely linked to the third issue, peaceful co-existence. Imperialism, in Mao's view, was unremittingly hostile towards the socialist camp. The December editorial had concluded: 'The imperialists are always bent on destroying us. Therefore we must never forget . . . class struggle on a world scale.' For China, this made perfect sense: its UN seat was still occupied by Taiwan;* its last sustained contact with America had been on the battlefield in Korea. The Soviet leaders felt quite differently. They dealt with the United States and the other capitalist powers, at the UN and through diplomatic channels, as a matter of routine. For the Kremlin, a judicious mixture of competition and contact with the West was far

---

* Following the communist victory in 1949, Chiang Kai-shek's regime on Taiwan, with the support of the United States, continued to occupy China's UN seat. On Stalin's orders, the Soviet Union boycotted meetings of the Security Council from January to October, 1950, ostensibly in protest against the nationalists' presence. The effect was in fact to perpetuate the exclusion of the People's Republic, in keeping with Stalin's aim of maximising Chinese dependence on, and subjection to, Moscow. After China's entry into the Korean War, Beijing's debarment was ratified by annual votes of the General Assembly until 1971, when Taiwan, in its turn, was excluded.

more attractive than the sterile immobilism of the Cold War.

Last and in some ways most troubling for the Russians – because it was impossible to tell where it might lead – was Mao's stress on contradictions. This had never sat well in Moscow. Stalin himself had criticised it as un-Marxist. Yet here was Mao now proclaiming that Stalin's abuses of power showed that contradictions arose even under socialism. In December, the *People's Daily* had affirmed the existence of 'contradictions in socialist countries between different sections of the people, between comrades within the Communist Party, [and] between the government and the people', as well as 'contradictions between socialist countries, [and] contradictions between Communist Parties'. From the Russian standpoint, which held that monolithic unity was the highest possible good, that was a can of worms that no one wished to see opened. The communiqué issued after Zhou Enlai's visit was adamant: 'There have been and are no essential contradictions . . . in the relations between socialist states. Even if in the past there were . . . shortcomings, they are now being rectified and eliminated.'

Despite these differences, there was little at the beginning of 1957 to suggest an imminent rupture.

While Zhou complained of the Soviet leaders' unwillingness to face up to their own mistakes, their 'subjectivity [and] narrow-mindedness . . . and [their] tend[ency] to patronise others and interfere with other brotherly parties' and governments' internal affairs', he was careful to add that 'in spite of all the above, Sino–Soviet relations are far better now than during Stalin's era'. Mao, too, was relatively sanguine. 'Not all Soviet farts are fragrant!' he noted. Khrushchev had a swollen head and was blinded by power, and if the Russians persisted in their errors, 'it is certain that, one day, it will all have to be brought out into the open'. But disputes between communist parties were inevitable, and Beijing and Moscow would continue to seek common ground.

Throughout the first half of the 1950s, China's intellectuals had been treated as one of the 'black classes', hostile or at best lukewarm towards the communist revolution.

The thought reform movement which accompanied the Korean War was punctuated by personalised attacks against named individuals and their works, among them the philosopher, Hu Shi, whose lectures Mao had attended as a library assistant in Beijing. There were a number of campaigns against films, such as *The Secret History of the Qing Court,* set during the Boxer Rebellion, which was denounced for capitulation to imperialism; and *The Life of Wu Xun,* about a nineteenth-century beggar who used his savings to build schools for the poor, accused of promoting capitulation to feudalism. Another major effort to bring the intellectuals into line involved the liberal thinker, Liang Shuming, who had had the temerity to criticise the communists for taxing the peasants too heavily. At a meeting of the Central Government Council, to which Liang had been invited as a guest, Mao pilloried him for more than an hour:

> Mr Liang styles himself a 'man of integrity' . . . Do you really have 'integrity'? If you do, then make a clean breast of your past history – how you opposed the Communist Party and the people, how you assassinated people with your pen . . . There are two ways of killing people: one is to kill with the gun and the other with the pen. The way which is most artfully disguised and draws no blood is to kill with the pen. That is the kind of murderer you are.
>
> Liang Shuming is utterly reactionary, yet he flatly denies it . . . What service did you do, Liang Shuming? In all your life, what service have you ever done for the people? Not the slightest, not the least bit . . . Liang Shuming is an ambitious schemer, a hypocrite.

It was using a sledgehammer to crack a nut. To Mao, any expression of heterodox thought might carry the seeds of future opposition. Liang escaped with a verbal drubbing. But two years later, when Mao decided that the intellectuals needed a sterner lesson, the abrasive glove of persuasion gave way to overt repression.

In a case that bore strong parallels to the persecution of Wang Shiwei, at Yan'an, a left-wing writer named Hu Feng was accused of leading a 'counter-revolutionary clique' and imprisoned. During the second half of 1955, a countrywide witch-hunt was conducted for 'Hu Feng elements', provoking numerous suicides in literary and academic circles. Like Wang, a decade earlier, Hu's offence had been to refuse to submit to the Party's will. Like Wang, his fate offered a terrifying warning to the intelligentsia generally of the perils of failing to toe the Party line.

It should therefore have been no surprise that when, in April 1956, Mao called for a new blossoming of intellectual debate under the slogan, 'Let a hundred flowers bloom, let a hundred schools of thought contend,' it fell on very stony ground indeed. After the bludgeoning they had received over the previous six years, the last thing Chinese intellectuals wanted was to have to stick their necks out publicly and start speaking their minds again.

A variety of factors had combined to bring about this abrupt – and, at the time, wholly unconvincing – change of course.

China was at peace. The Party was securely in control. The transition to a socialist economic system was already far advanced. The exceedingly tight grip the regime had maintained on every aspect of national life, justifiable, perhaps, in the early years, had become counter-productive. The main theme of Mao's speeches that spring was the need to decentralise power. 'Discipline that stifles creativity and initiative should be abolished,' he said at one point. 'We need a little liberalism to facilitate getting things done. To be strict all the time won't work.'

Sooner or later, a thaw of this kind would have begun regardless of other causes. As Mao would have put it, it was part of the dialectic inherent in all things. 'If war is not brewed during times of peace, how can war come so suddenly? If peace if not brewed during war, how can there be peace so suddenly?'

But in the early part of 1956, two additional forces began pushing the Party towards liberalisation. One was the shortage of skilled manpower – above all, of scientists and engineers – which was blocking Mao's plans to speed up economic development. To try to remedy this, intellectuals' salaries were raised; they were allotted better apartments; attempts were made to woo back Chinese professors living in the US and Europe. But Mao soon recognised that, if the problem were to be resolved, Party bureaucrats would have to stop interfering in academic matters they did not understand; and intellectuals would have to be given more latitude to work as they thought best. The second force was the Secret Speech, and China's decision as a result to stop mechanically copying Soviet methods. In education, in factory management, in fields as diverse as genetics and music, Chinese intellectuals and managers suddenly found themselves, for the first time in years, with a margin of freedom in which to experiment.

In the summer of 1956, none of these changes could be described as dramatic. The most visible effect of relaxation was to lend new colour and vitality to the spartan austerity of Chinese daily life.

Young women began wearing flowered blouses. Foreigners reported the occasional *cheong-sam*, the traditional Chinese long skirt, slit decorously to an inch above the knee. Dances were permitted, to the music of Gershwin and Strauss. The *People's Daily* went from four pages to eight, and Liu Shaoqi admonished Chinese journalists to make their stories less boring.

Politically, the repercussions were minimal. The personality cult around Mao survived essentially intact. The only significant change came at the Eighth Congress in September, when references to 'Mao Zedong Thought' as the Party's guiding ideology were excised from the CCP Constitution.* But that was treated as a glitch occasioned by the changes taking place in the Party's leadership structure as Mao began to implement his plan, under discussion since 1952, to withdraw to the 'second front'. He was beginning to feel his age, he had written to Sun Yat-sen's widow, Soong Chingling, earlier that year. 'One must recognise the symptoms that one is on the downward side of things.' A new post of Honorary Party Chairman was created but left vacant, to await the time (generally expected to come in 1963, as Mao entered his seventieth year), when Liu Shaoqi would assume his mantle.

Then came the crisis in Poland and the Hungarian revolt.

Communist regimes everywhere watched, horrified, fearing that the contagion would spread, as the socialist bloc threatened to implode. China was no exception. In the winter of 1956, Mao made speech after speech, reassuring the Party, and its non-communist allies, that there was little chance they would be exposed to similar unrest.

He went on to ask what had caused the storms in eastern Europe. Part of the answer, he told the Central Committee, was that the Communist Parties in Poland and Hungary had failed to do a proper job of eliminating counter-revolutionaries. China had not made that error. But the other factor was bureaucratism, which had led Party

---

* Liu Shaoqi, whom Mao had delegated to take charge of the Congress proceedings, sent him the amended text of the constitution for approval. However, he received it in the early hours of the morning – after he had already taken his nightly sleeping pill – and evidently did not notice the deletion. By the time he realised its significance, the text had already been passed. During the Cultural Revolution, this became a key charge against Liu.

cadres in both countries to become estranged from the masses. This problem China had not solved:

> Right now there are certain people who behave as if they can sit back and relax and ride roughshod over the people now that they have the country in their hands. Such people are opposed by the masses, who [want to] throw stones at them and hit them with their hoes. From my point of view, this is what they deserve and I find it most welcome. There are times when nothing but a beating can solve the problem. The Communist Party has to learn its lesson . . . We must be vigilant, and must not allow a bureaucratic work-style to develop. We must not form an aristocracy divorced from the people. The masses are justified in removing anybody who has a bureaucratic work-style . . . I say it's better to remove such people; they ought to be removed.

The answer, Mao said, was another rectification campaign – but in a form which would provide a safety valve for popular discontent. The problem in Hungary, he argued, was that the Party there had failed to deal in a timely fashion with the contradictions between rulers and ruled, with the result that they had festered and become antagonistic. 'If there is a pustule it must emit pus,' he went on. 'It is precisely from such things that we must learn our lesson.' It followed that in China, workers should be allowed to strike because 'this will be helpful in solving contradictions among the state, the factory directors and the masses', and students should be allowed to demonstrate. 'They are just contradictions, that's all. The world is full of contradictions.'

Thus, by the end of 1956, the two major elements of what was to become the Hundred Flowers Campaign – a rectification movement to make the Party more responsive to the wishes of the people; and a relaxation of controls to allow the venting of public dissatisfaction – had both already been decided. The only uncertainty was over when it should start (Mao had suggested the following summer), and how sweeping it should be.

At this juncture, a new factor intervened.

Some of the younger writers, encouraged by continuing signs of cultural liberalisation, had at last plucked up their courage and begun to test the limits of the Party's new tolerance. Conservatives were outraged. On January 7, 1957, a group of cultural commissars in the PLA published a letter in the *People's Daily*, complaining of a resurgence of traditional literary forms at the expense of socialist realism, and that the principle of art serving politics, which Mao had enunciated at Yan'an, was being honoured in the breach. The avalanche of favourable comment that followed showed their views were widely shared.

As always, when Mao felt his aims being thwarted, he dug in his heels.

Publicly, his response was low-key. Five days after the letter appeared, he sent a selection of his poems, written in the classical style, for inclusion in the inaugural issue of the magazine *Shikan* (Poetry). The implicit message was that, contrary to the PLA group's assertions, traditional literary forms still had their place in China.

In private, Mao was more forthright. The critics had got it wrong, he told a conference of senior Party officials later the same month. There was not too much freedom but too little. Writings hostile to Marxism, such as the works of Chiang Kai-shek, should be published openly in China, because 'if you haven't read anything written [by him], you won't be able to do a good job of opposing him'. Circulation of *Cankao xiaoxi* (Reference News), a compendium of Western news reports for restricted use by senior officials, should increase a hundredfold in order 'to publicise imperialist and bourgeois [thinking]'. Even men like Liang Shuming should be free to spread their ideas: 'If they have something to fart about, let them fart! If it's out, then one can decide whether it smells bad or good . . . If the people think their farts stink, they will be isolated.'

It was wrong to quarantine things, Mao declared. Better by far to 'vaccinate' the masses by exposing them to harmful ideas, so as to strengthen their political immunity. The guiding principle should be:

> Truth stands in contrast to falsehood and is developed out of the struggle against it. Beauty stands in contrast to ugliness and is developed out of the struggle against it. The same is true of good and bad things . . . In short, fragrant flowers stand in contrast to poisonous weeds, and are developed out of the struggle against them. It is a dangerous policy to forbid people to meet face to face with false, ugly and antagonistic things . . . Such a policy would lead to . . . people being incapable of facing the outside world, and unable to meet the challenge of a rival.

Within the Party, the use of 'negative teaching material' had been current since the 1930s. But this time Mao was proposing that the same method be applied among the population as a whole. If disturbances resulted, he maintained, that was nothing to be afraid of:

> Wouldn't it be a little strange if we communists, who have never feared imperialism or Chiang Kai-shek's Guomindang . . . were now to be afraid of students causing trouble and peasants raising a fuss over the co-operatives? Fear is no solution. The more afraid you are, the more ghosts will come to visit you . . . I think that whoever wants to cause trouble should be allowed to do so for as long as he wants. If a month is not sufficient, give him two months. In short, don't stop the show until he's had enough. If you stop the show too hastily, one of these days he will cause trouble again . . . What good will come out of this? The good will be that we will expose problems fully and distinguish right from wrong . . . We can't just stifle everything all the time . . . Contradictions have to be exposed before problems can be solved.

Mao's audience of provincial Party secretaries, the men who would have to manage 'trouble' in the event that it arose, was distinctly underwhelmed. A few weeks later he conceded that '50 or 60 per cent' of the Party disagreed with him, and 90 per cent of high-ranking cadres. His blasé statements that 'in a population of 600 million, I would think of it as normal if every year there were a million people making trouble', and that even, in a worst case, if large-scale disorders did result, 'We'd just go back to Yan'an, that's where we came from anyway!', can only have alarmed them still more.

Ten or twelve years earlier, their opposition might have given Mao pause. By 1957, he was beyond that. Both of the major decisions he had taken since the founding of the People's Republic, disregarding the doubts of his colleagues – to enter the war in Korea, and to speed up collectivisation – had been triumphantly vindicated. If the Party was reluctant again this time, it simply made him want to push all the harder. In his speeches that spring, he paraphrased a favourite statement of Lenin's, which he had first quoted in 1937: 'The unity of opposites is temporary; antagonistic struggle is absolute.' Harmony was transient; strife was eternal. The student who, forty years earlier, had written, 'it is not that we like chaos, but simply that . . . human nature is delighted by sudden change', now told his colleagues: 'It is good if life is a bit more complicated, otherwise it is too boring . . . Should there be only peace and no trouble . . . [it] would lead to mental sluggishness.'

There were other, more practical reasons for Mao's determination to press ahead. The shortage of engineers and technicians, which had helped trigger the liberalisation movement in the first place, was merely the tip of the iceberg. China had a proletariat of 12 million, and a petty bourgeoisie (including the peasantry) of 550 million. To develop the economy, all their energies were needed. But that, Mao argued, required a policy of mutual supervision, in which petty-bourgeois intellectuals were free to criticise the communists, and they, in turn, 'educated' the petty bourgeoisie.

These ideas were given formal expression for the first time before a wider public on February 27, 1957, in a speech entitled, 'On the Correct Handling of Contradictions among the People'. It lasted four hours, and was delivered before an invited audience of nearly two thousand people, including scientists, writers, and leaders of the democratic parties.

Mao began by speaking in laudatory terms of the process of self-transformation, of being 'steeled' in the communist cause, that intellectuals had undergone. Thought-remoulding, he said, was still necessary, but in the past it had been 'a bit rough, [and] people were hurt'. From now on, the policy would be different.

> [The slogan of] 'Let a hundred flowers bloom, a hundred schools of thought contend' . . . was put forward in recognition of the various different contradictions in society . . . If you want to grow only [fragrant flowers] and not weeds, it can't be done . . . To ban all weeds, and stop them growing, is that possible? The reality is that it is not. They will still grow . . . It is difficult to distinguish fragrant flowers from poisonous weeds . . . Take, for example, Marxism. Marxism was [once] considered a poisonous weed . . .The astronomy of Copernicus . . . the physics of Galileo, Darwin's theory of evolution were all, at the start, rejected . . . What is there to fear from the growth of fragrant flowers and poisonous weeds? There is nothing to fear . . . Among the bad flowers there might be some good flowers . . . [like] Galileo [and] Copernicus. [Conversely], flowers that look Marxist are not always so.

The use of 'crude methods' to solve ideological problems, Mao added, did more harm than good. What if agitation ensued? 'I say,

let them agitate to their hearts' content . . . I, too, created distur-
bances at school because problems could not be resolved . . .
Expulsion is the Guomindang way. We want to do the opposite of
Guomindang methods.'

The speech was not published at once, but tape-recordings were
played to gatherings of intellectuals and Party cadres in cities all
over China.

Reactions were mixed. One man was allegedly 'so stimulated by
Chairman Mao's address that he could not sleep for one whole
night'. Robert Loh, a Shanghai businessman, remembered: 'I was
in a daze. After Mao's speech anything seemed possible. For the first
time in many years, I allowed myself to hope.' But most were wary.
As the Chinese proverb has it: 'A man who has been bitten by a
snake is afraid of a piece of rope.' The anthropologist, Fei Xiaotong,
wrote of 'early spring weather', which brought the risk of sudden
frosts. The historian, Jian Bozan, was blunter. Intellectuals, he
said, did not know whether to trust Mao or not. 'They have to guess
whether [his] call is sincere or just a gesture. They have to guess to
what extent, if the call is sincere, flowers will be allowed to blossom,
and whether the [policy will be reversed] once the flowers are in
bloom. They have to guess whether [it] is an end, or just a means
. . . to unearth [hidden] thoughts and rectify individuals. They have
to guess which problems can be discussed, and which problems
cannot be discussed.' The result, he added, was that most had
decided to remain silent.

Their prudence would have been yet more marked had they
known what Mao had said in the secrecy of the Party conclaves that
had preceded the public launching of the Hundred Flowers
Campaign. In public, he had declared that the bourgeoisie and the
democratic parties had made 'great progress'; in private, he said
they were untrustworthy. In public, he had spoken of the students
'loving their country'; in private, he complained that 80 per cent of
them had bourgeois backgrounds, so there was 'nothing strange'
if they opposed the government. In public, he had insisted that
'poisonous weeds' must be allowed to grow; in private, he said they
would be cut down and turned into fertiliser. In public, he had said
there were 'only very, very few' counter-revolutionaries; in private,
that they must be 'resolutely suppressed'. In public, he had spoken
of allowing disturbances; in private, of allowing 'bad people' to
'expose and isolate themselves'.

To Mao's dialectical mind, these were just two sides of the same coin. 'In a unity of opposites,' he explained, 'there is always one aspect that is primary and the other secondary.' The problem was that, with Mao, which was which could change.

Throughout March and April, Mao laboured to get the Hundred Flowers Campaign off the ground. It proved a herculean task. Beyond the ambiguities in his own position (which, to the extent that the intellectuals sensed them, fed into their misgivings), the middle and lower ranks of Party officialdom remained deeply hostile. They, after all, were the natural targets of any anti-bureaucratism campaign, and once rectification started, they would be at the receiving end of the agitation and disturbances Mao promised.

At the summit of the hierarchy, the Politburo was curiously silent. The 'Hundred Flowers' was Mao's show. 'I am alone with the people,' he would say later, and in a sense he was. So long as his colleagues supported him in public (which they did), it hardly mattered if Liu Shaoqi and the Beijing Party leader, Peng Zhen, were privately lukewarm, or that Zhou Enlai and Deng Xiaoping were personally enthusiastic. 'Blooming and contending', as it came to be called, was not susceptible to administrative fiat. People had to be persuaded to speak their minds, and grass-roots Party officials had to be persuaded to let them do it.

To that end, Mao undertook a three-week-long train journey through eastern China, in which he acted, in his own words, as a 'wandering lobbyist'. Half his time was spent trying to convince Party cadres that the coming movement would be 'calm and un-hurried', 'ultra-fine drizzle, not torrential rains', and would not be permitted to expand into large-scale mass struggle. The other half was devoted to calming the fears of non-Party groups. In the process, the rationale for the campaign – and the means by which it would be conducted – became more sharply defined.

Now that class struggle against the landlords and the bourgeoisie was basically at an end, Mao explained, differences between the Party and the people had naturally come to the fore. 'In the past we fought the enemy alongside the people. Now, since the enemy is no longer there . . . only the people and we remain. If they don't argue with us when they have grievances, who can they argue with?' If these differences were to be resolved, people had to be encouraged to think for themselves. 'If we . . . do not allow [this], our nation will be sapped of its vitality.' The method used would be criticism and self-criticism, with the democratic parties playing the leading role. '[They must make] sarcastic comments revealing our shortcomings,' Mao declared. 'We must brace ourselves and let them attack . . . The Communist Party has to let itself be scolded for a while.'

At face value – and, in the end, most intellectuals did take it at face value – this was a heady prospect, especially when Mao went on to speak of permitting, at least in academic and press circles, a significant erosion of the Party's monopoly of power. Up till now, he acknowledged, a non-communist might be the president of a university, or the editor of a 'non-Party' newspaper, but in reality power was always held by a deputy who was a Party member. In future, non-communists should have 'position and power in fact, not just in form. From now on, no matter where, whoever is the chief is in charge.'

By mid-April, Mao's efforts were beginning to bear fruit.

He had found it necessary to promise Party officials that, as a general rule, 'blooming and contending' would be limited to criticisms which 'strengthened Party leadership', and would not be permitted to produce 'disorganisation and confusion'. He had also referred to the intellectuals' fears that the Party was setting a trap – and alert cadres would have noticed that he did *not* deny that this might be the case. Fortified by these assurances, the hierarchy stopped dragging its feet.

Even the *People's Daily*, whose silence on the new policies had faithfully reflected the Party's doubts, now fell into line, though not until Mao had summoned the editor, Deng Tuo, to a blistering session of reproaches, which he delivered in his bedroom, sprawling on his outsized bed, covered in piles of books. One of Deng's deputies, Wang Ruoshui, a neat, fastidious man, who was called midway through to join them, remembered being struck by the slovenliness of the scene, as the Chairman, now a flabby figure, well past middle age, raged at them in his nightrobe: 'Why are you keeping the Party's policies secret? There's something fishy here. In the past, this paper was run by pedants. Now it's being run by a corpse.' Glaring at Deng, he went on: 'If you can't shit, get off the privy and make way for someone who can!' When the beleaguered editor offered to resign, Mao waved the offer aside. Wang was ordered to write an editorial promoting the 'Hundred Flowers', which appeared on April 13. From then on, the word began to spread among the population at large that non-communist criticisms of the regime would be welcomed.

A week later, the Politburo met, and decided to bring forward the official start of the campaign. Provincial leaders were told to report on the status of 'blooming and contending' within fifteen days. But Mao was not willing to wait even that long. In practice, he said, rectification had 'already been going on for two months'. While Chinese celebrated the May Day holiday, the 'Hundred Flowers' slogan was blazoned across the front page of the *People's Daily*, followed by every other newspaper in the country as, within the Party and outside it, the movement got formally under way.

The 'Hundred Flowers' was the most ambitious attempt ever undertaken in any communist country to combine a totalitarian system with democratic checks and balances. Even Mao was unsure what it would produce. 'Let's try it and see what it's like,' he said at one point. 'If we acquire a taste for it, there will be no more worries.' What would happen if the Party did not 'acquire a taste for' being criticised was left discreetly unsaid.

As May unfolded, non-communist academics, writers and artists, members of the democratic parties, businessmen, and even some workers and rural officials, gradually plucked up their courage and decided to speak out – or more often were persuaded to do so against their better judgement.

Although the Central Committee had stated that participation by non-communists must be voluntary, local Party officials were under strong pressure to ensure that 'blooming and contending' in their units was seen to be a success. Wu Ningkun, an American-educated professor of English at an elite Party school, remembered being approached by a senior colleague, who complained that, at faculty meetings, 'no one seems willing to air their views . . . Chicken feathers and garlic skins [i.e. trivia] are all that has been brought up.' After several further proddings, Wu recounted, 'I had no reason to question their sincerity, so I spoke up.' A woman cadre in the Changsha Police Department was told that if she wanted to join the Party, she should show willing and 'come up with something'. One of the leaders of a merchants' association in Beijing's main shopping street, Wangfujing, was urged by the local Party Secretary to speak out, 'to set an example for the others'. They, too, racked their brains and complied. So did millions of others.

The main thrust of the criticism that ensued was that the communists, whom the intelligentsia had welcomed in 1949 as liberators from Guomindang misrule, had developed, after less than eight years in office, into a new bureaucratic class which monopolised power and privilege and had alienated itself from the masses. Mao, it turned out, had not been wrong in the lessons he drew from the Hungarian revolt: in the eyes of non-communists, Party officials had indeed become 'an aristocracy divorced from the people'. One of the most trenchant critiques came from Chu Anping, editor of the influential non-Party newspaper, *Guangming ribao*, who observed that the communists had turned China into a 'family domain, all painted a single colour'.

Lesser figures were still blunter. Party members behaved as 'a race apart', one professor wrote. They received preferential treatment, and regarded the rest of the population as 'obedient subjects, or to use a harsh word, slaves'. An economics lecturer complained: 'Party members and cadres who wore worn-out shoes in the past now travel in saloon cars and put on uniforms made of wool . . . Today the common people avoid the Party like the plague.' He went on:

If the Communist Party distrusts me, it's mutual. China belongs to [all of its] 600 million people, including those who are counter-revolutionaries. It does not belong to the Communist Party alone . . . If you [Party members] work satisfactorily, all well and good. If not, the masses may knock you down, kill you and overthrow you. This cannot be described as unpatriotic, for the communists would no longer be serving the people. The downfall of the Communist Party would not mean the downfall of China.

Another constant theme was the Party's mistreatment of intellectuals, who were regarded as 'dog-shit one moment and 10,000 ounces of gold the next'. If the Party needed you, a journalist wrote, it did not matter if you were a murderer; if it didn't need you, it would cast you aside no matter how faithfully you worked. An engineer complained that intellectuals were more subdued than under the Japanese occupation. Party members snooped around, reporting back to personnel offices on the behaviour of their non-communist colleagues. The result was that 'no one dares to let off steam even privately in the company of intimate friends . . . Everyone has learned the technique of double-talk; what one says is one thing, what one thinks is another.'

On May 4, only three days after the movement had been launched, Mao issued a secret directive, in which he said that, although some of the views being expressed were wrong, they should not be rebutted for the time being. 'We should not stop it in the middle,' he wrote. 'If there is no pressure from society, it will be very difficult for us to get the results from rectification that we want.' For 'at least a few months', therefore, criticism was to continue unchecked. Then, once the Party had been rectified, the movement could be enlarged and criticism extended to the democratic parties, the intellectuals and society at large.

But as the torrent of popular anger, mistrust and bitterness swelled, Mao began to have second thoughts.

On May 15, in a memorandum entitled 'Things are turning into their opposites', issued for restricted circulation to officials of Central Committee rank and above, he signalled that his attitude was changing. In it, for the first time, Mao applied the term 'revisionism' to events at home. The revisionists, he said, denied the class nature of the press; they admired bourgeois liberalism and democracy, and rejected Party leadership. Such people were the main danger within the Party, and they were now working hand in glove with right-wing intellectuals. It was these non-Party 'Rightists' (another term he now used for the first time) who were responsible for 'the current spate of wild attacks':

> The Rightists know nothing about dialectics – things turn into their opposite when they reach the extreme. We shall let the Rightists run amuck for a time and let them reach their climax . . . Some say they are afraid of being hooked like a fish . . . [or] being lured in deep, rounded up and annihilated. Now that large numbers of fish have come to the surface of themselves, there is no need to bait the hook . . . There are two alternatives for the Rightists. One is to . . . mend their ways. The other is to go on making trouble and court ruin. Gentlemen Rightists, the choice is yours, the initiative (for a short time) is in your hands.

This was not quite as dramatic a shift in Mao's position as it might seem. Already, in early April, discussing the harmful views that would be expressed, he had told Party cadres in Hangzhou: 'This is not setting an ambush for the enemy, but rather letting them fall into the snare of their own accord.' What was new was the change in emphasis. The focus of Mao's attention was moving ominously from 'flowers blooming' to the uprooting of 'poisonous weeds'.

Since the document was secret, the public at large, as well as the 'Rightists' themselves, remained in ignorance of these developments.

The movement next spread to the campus at Beijing University, where a 'Democracy Wall', covered in posters several layers deep, was set up outside the canteen. Student orators harangued crowds of thousands on subjects ranging from multi-party elections to the respective merits of socialism and capitalism. The movement found its *Pasionara* in a 21-year-old literature student named Lin Xiling, who accused the Party of practising 'feudal socialism' and urged sweeping reforms to guarantee basic freedoms. Student associations were formed with names like 'Bitter Medicine', 'Voices from the Lowest Level', 'Wild Grass' and 'Spring Thunder', which published mimeographed journals and sent activists to 'exchange experience' with out-of-town colleagues.

After another week had passed, Mao spoke again, this time publicly. At a meeting with a Youth League delegation, he warned: 'Any word or deed at variance with socialism is completely wrong.' This was immediately written up in giant, white characters on the side of a building at the campus.

But the fire the Chairman had lit was not to be put out so easily. Student leaders called openly for an end to Communist Party rule. Their teachers, inspired by their example, stoked the flames still higher. Mao's rule was 'arbitrary and reckless', a Shenyang professor declared. If there was no democracy in China, it was the fault of the Party Centre. Others spoke of a 'malevolent tyranny' employing the 'fascist methods of Auschwitz'. In Wuhan, middle-school students took to the streets and stormed local government offices. Trouble was also reported from Sichuan and Shandong.

On June 8, less than six weeks after rectification had begun, Mao launched the Party's counter-offensive.

'Certain people,' said the *People's Daily*, were using the rectification campaign as a pretext to try to 'overthrow the Communist Party and the working class, and to topple the great cause of socialism'. Mao himself, in a Central Committee directive the same

day, spoke of a small section of the Party having been rotted by reactionary views – which meant, he added approvingly, that 'the
pus is being squeezed out'. Ten days later, his 'contradictions'
speech in February was published for the first time – but in a heavily
revised version, which set out six criteria for distinguishing 'fragrant
flowers' from 'poisonous weeds'. These effectively restated
the assurance Mao had given privately to Party officials before the
movement started – namely that criticisms were acceptable only if
they strengthened, not undermined, Party leadership.

Finally, on July 1, in another *People's Daily* editorial, Mao accused
the Ministers of Forestry, Luo Longji, and of Communications,
Zhang Bojun, both leaders of a small coalition party called the
Democratic League, of forming a counter-revolutionary alliance to
promote an 'anti-communist, anti-people, anti-socialist bourgeois
line'. The implication was that the 'Hundred Flowers' policy had
been correct, but had been sabotaged by a small group of extremists
unreconciled to the communist victory who wanted to turn back
the clock.

All this was both dishonest and wise after the event. The
'Luo–Zhang Alliance' was a fabrication – another in the long line
that had begun with the 'Extermination Brigades' in Yudu in
1934, and continued with the 'Wang Shiwei counter-revolutionary
conspiracy' in 1943 and the 'Hu Feng clique' in 1955 – the sole
purpose of which was to justify the clampdown that was already
under way. In the same way, *Guangming ribao*, which Mao now
accused of serving 'as a mouthpiece for the reactionaries', had
merely done as he had asked. So had most of the 'Rightists'. The
six criteria were so restrictive that, if they had been in the original
speech, 'blooming and contending' would never have started
at all. In fact Mao had said repeatedly, in the course of the
campaign, that no limits should be laid down, because 'the people
[themselves] have the ability to distinguish . . . [We must] trust them
. . . to discriminate.'

Why, then, did he decide that a crackdown was necessary?

There is no simple answer. The 'Hundred Flowers' was not, as
Mao's victims and supporters both claimed, a carefully contrived
trap from the start, an example of the Chairman's cunning in 'luring
the snake out of its hole'. Nor was it a 'colossal blunder', as most
Western scholars argue.

Mao had always mistrusted intellectuals; their behaviour at Yan'an had strengthened his conviction that they were fundamentally unreliable, and nothing that had happened since, in the repeated remoulding campaigns of the early 1950s, had done anything to alter that view. He did not suddenly decide, in the spring of 1957, that they were trustworthy after all. He believed from the outset that there would be some cases, if only a few, of 'extremists' transgressing reasonable bounds, who would have to be uprooted. Hence his refusal to give a blanket assurance that there would be no retaliation. Hence, too, a revealing slip of the tongue at a Party conference in March, nearly two months before the movement began, when, in speaking of the struggle against bourgeois ideology, he referred to intellectuals as 'the enemy', rather than potential allies to be won over.

On the other hand, the economic base of Chinese society had been transformed, and therefore, in Marxist theory, the ideological 'superstructure' should follow suit.

Throughout the 'Hundred Flowers' period, Mao used the metaphor of hair and skin, arguing that now the old, bourgeois, economic 'skin' had died, the intellectuals, the ideological 'hair', had no choice but to shift their allegiance and graft themselves on to the new 'skin' of the proletarian economy.

The unstated question all along was how numerous the 'extremists' would be and how much pressure they would exert. Here Mao made not one but two misjudgements. He underestimated the volume and bitterness of the criticisms, and the cadres' ability to withstand them. What had started as an attempt to bridge the gap between the Party and the people (and had been only incidentally an effort to expose and punish a small number of anti-communist irreducibles) was turned on its head. It became a trap not for the few but for the many – for the hundreds of thousands of loyal citizens who had taken the Party at its word.

This wholesale reversal was entirely of Mao's making. Yet he evidently undertook it with some reluctance. He said later that he had been 'confused by false appearances' at a time when the Party, and society at large, were panicking about the risk of large-scale unrest. In speeches the following summer and autumn, he made clear that he continued to believe the original 'Hundred Flowers' policy was correct. The 'Rightists,' he said, were counter-revolutionaries, but they should be treated leniently. 'Extreme policies [in the past] did not bring good results. We ought [this time] to be a bit more far-sighted.'

Leniency, in Mao's lexicon, was a relative term.

The 'Rightists' were not shot. Indeed, the more senior among them, including Luo Longji, Zhang Bojun and another minister, Zhang Naiqi, were all amnestied two years later. But 520,000 smaller fry – one in twenty of all non-communist intellectuals and officials in China – underwent labour reform or were exiled to the countryside to learn class consciousness from the peasants. In many units, local Party secretaries ordered that a fixed quota be applied: 5 per cent of the cadres had to be designated as 'Rightists'. Those with suspect backgrounds, or who had fallen foul of the Party hierarchy at some time in the past, were invariably chosen first.

The professor of English, Wu Ningkun (educated in the West), was arrested and spent three years in prison camps, first in Manchuria, then near Tianjin. The woman police cadre in Changsha (who had criticised her section chief) was sent for labour reform in the suburbs; her husband then divorced her in a fruitless effort to prevent the 'Rightist' label being applied to him and their children. The leader of the merchants in Wangfujing (a capitalist) spent the next twenty years in and out of penal institutions. They, and half-a-million others like them, saw their lives and those of their families pitilessly destroyed. Unlike the landlords and the counter-revolutionaries, they were punished not for their actions (past or present, real or imagined), but solely for their ideas.

Mao himself was sensitive to that charge. 'These people not only talk, they also act,' he claimed. 'They are guilty. The saying, "Those who speak up shall not be blamed" does not apply to them.' It was a poor defence.

The tragedy of the 'Hundred Flowers' was that Mao genuinely did want the intellectuals to 'think for themselves', to join the revolution of their own free will rather than being forced to do so. His goal, he told Party cadres, was 'the creation of a political environment where there will be both centralism and democracy, both discipline and freedom, both unity of purpose and personal ease of mind and liveliness'.

Yet that formula, in practice, proved utterly self-defeating. By the mid-1950s, Mao was so convinced of the essential correctness of his own thought that he could no longer comprehend why, if people had the freedom to think for themselves, they would think what *they* wanted, not what *he* wanted – that, so long as they retained a spark of intellectual independence, they would produce ideas of which he disapproved and which he would find it necessary to suppress. In practice, discipline always won out; independence of mind was crushed. The uprooting of 'poisonous weeds' would lead to total stultification.

There was another, more immediate result, too.

The intellectuals were scorched so badly in the anti-Rightist campaign that they would never believe Mao again. A quarter of a century later, when the old merchant from Wangfujing lay dying, his last words to his family were: 'Never trust the Communist Party!' The very people whom Mao needed most to build the strong, new China he had been dreaming of since his youth had been definitively alienated.

In the eight years since the establishment of the communist regime, Mao's life had changed out of all recognition. It was not simply that he had more power. As supreme leader of 600 million people, he became an august, detached figure, enveloped in an imperial aura, distant from his own colleagues and isolated from those he ruled.

A month after the proclamation of the People's Republic, he had taken up residence in Zhongnanhai (literally, 'Central and Southern Lakes'), a walled estate containing the dwellings of former Manchu princes and traditional, courtyard mansions, set amid a park within the *enceinte* of the Forbidden City and separated from it by the artificial lakes from which it derives its name. It had fallen into disrepair when the nationalists were in power and had their capital in Nanjing, but in 1949 the old palaces were refurbished for use by Politburo members and modern, three-storey blocks were built as offices for the Central Committee and the State Council. Mao and his immediate entourage occupied a former imperial library, built for the Emperor Qianlong in the eighteenth century, a splendid, grey-tiled edifice, whose name, Fengzeyuan, the Hall of Beneficent Abundance, was carved in the Emperor's own calligraphy on a wooden board above its massive, gabled south gate. In the inner courtyard, shaded by ancient pines and cypresses, Mao had his

private quarters, the Juxiang shuwu, or Study of Chrysanthemum
Fragrance, comprising a vast high-ceilinged room which served as
his bedchamber, study and salon, all in one; a large dining room;
and, beyond it, Jiang Qing's bedroom, connected by a covered
walkway to her living quarters, which were in a neighbouring
building. Mao's daughters, Li Min and Li Na, lived in the next courtyard, looked after by Jiang Qing's elder sister; while Mao Zemin's
young orphaned son, Mao Yuanxin, had rooms nearby.

For Mao, as for the Chinese emperors before him, Zhongnanhai
was a cocoon. In place of eunuchs, he was surrounded by secretaries
and bodyguards. For his protection, there were three concentric
rings of special service troops, discreet but omnipresent. His food
came from a designated, secure farm, and was tasted before he ate
as a precaution against poison. After Ren Bishi's death in October
1950, Mao, and all the other top leaders, were assigned personal
physicians. Whereas in Yan'an and Shijiazhuang, he had been free
to move about as he wished, albeit with a security escort, in Beijing
he could not stir without every detail of his route being planned and
reconnoitred in advance. When he did travel, it was aboard an
armoured special train. He rarely flew, lest the nationalists on
Taiwan try to sabotage or shoot down his plane.*

In the first years, Mao tried from time to time to break out from
the protective screen his minders threw up around him. Usually it
ended badly.

His chief bodyguard, Li Yinqiao, remembered one such occasion,
in Tianjin, when Mao insisted on having lunch at a restaurant.
Word was sent ahead. The management cleared the place of other
customers, and it was invested by plain-clothes police. But when
Mao stopped at an upstairs window, to look out at the street
below, he was spotted by a woman hanging out washing on a
balcony opposite. Her excited cries brought crowds so dense that
it took the local garrison command six hours to persuade them
to disperse sufficiently for Mao to leave. Whenever afterwards he

---

* This was less far-fetched than it might sound. In 1955, an airliner that was to have
taken Zhou Enlai to Indonesia was blown up in mid-air by a bomb which had been
placed aboard by a nationalist agent in Hong Kong. Zhou changed his travel plans
after Chinese intelligence got wind of the plot. Several other members of the
Chinese delegation, who were allowed to go ahead with the trip, lost their lives
when it crashed.

wanted to break away from the route his security officers had prepared, this incident would be brought up as a reason for not doing so.

Mao's isolation was exacerbated by the absence of a family around him. Anying was dead, and Anqing in a psychiatric hospital in Dalian. Jiang Qing was bedridden for most of the 1950s – initially with psychosomatic ailments, whose nature neither Chinese nor Russian doctors were able to discover, and later with cervical cancer – and made several extended journeys to Moscow, the longest lasting over a year, to undergo medical treatment. Mao was only too pleased to be rid of her and, when she begged permission to return, insisted that she stay on until she was completely cured. According to his doctor, Li Zhisui, by 1955 they were already leading separate lives: whatever affection they had once felt for each other had long since evaporated. Even Li Yinqiao, who tried to be charitable, concluded that by the mid-1950s, the marriage was on the rocks. They ate, slept and worked apart. On the rare occasions when they did spend time together, Jiang got on Mao's nerves and he would grumble to his guards afterwards that he never wanted to see her again.

Their estrangement made him nostalgic for his former wives: for He Zizhen, whom he met again for the first time in twenty-one years; and for Yang Kaihui, whose memory now drew from him a romantic, astonishingly beautiful poem, which he entitled 'The Immortals'. It was addressed to an old friend, Li Shuyi, the woman who, thirty years earlier, had sat up, nursing her infant son, as the Horse Day massacre began. Li's husband, Liu Zhixun, had been killed not long after Kaihui. In Chinese, their names signify 'willow' and 'poplar', a play on words which Mao entwined with the legend of Wu Gang, a Sisyphus-figure condemned to cut down an ever-lasting cassia tree on the moon:

> *I lost my proud poplar, and you your willow;*
> *Poplar and willow soar to the highest heaven,*
> *Wu Gang, asked what he has to offer,*
> *Presents them humbly with cassia wine.*
> *The lonely goddess in the moon spreads her ample sleeves*
> *To dance for these good souls in the endless sky.*
> *Of a sudden comes word of the Tiger's defeat on earth*
> *Tears stream down like an upturned bowl of rain.*

The tears (at Chiang Kai-shek's defeat) were bitter-sweet, reflecting Mao's own mood that summer as he cast his mind back to earlier, simpler times.*

Into the gap left by present loneliness and a past which could never be recaptured, Mao brought, first, a succession of mistresses, and then, in his sixties, the earthier, more anonymous pleasures of physical companionship with much young women.

The tradition of Saturday-night dances in Yan'an had survived the move to Zhongnanhai. From the dance-floor, Mao and his young partners would gravitate to his study, where they would make love beside the piles of books stacked on his vast bed. The girls came from dance troupes organised by the cultural division of the PLA, chosen both for their looks and their political reliability. Mao's lovemaking, like his dancing, was clumsy, according to one former partner, but varied and indefatigable. The French politician, Maurice Faure, once remarked of Mitterrand: '*il a besoin des fluides feminines.*' Mao was the same.

Among the vast collection of historical and literary tomes lining his shelves were copies of the ancient Daoist manuals by which Chinese literati, since immemorial times, had initiated their male descendants into the arts of the bedchamber. They included a Han dynasty text, 'The Secret Methods of the Plain Girl', which had particular relevance for older men:

> The union of man and woman is like the mating of Heaven and Earth. It is because of their correct mating that Heaven and Earth last forever. Man, however, has lost this secret. If a man could learn [it], he would obtain immortality . . . The principle of this method is to have frequent intercourse with young girls, but emit semen only on rare occasions. This method makes a man's body light and will expel all diseases . . . All those who seek to prolong their life must seek life's very source.

The Chinese are a practical people, behind their outward prudery more tolerant of sexual licence than the Americans or the British. If Mao indulged himself, no one thought much the worse of

---

* A few weeks after writing 'The Immortals', Mao invited Chen Yuying, the maid-servant who had worked for Kaihui and himself in Changsha, to visit him in Beijing. They talked for two hours, and before she left, he told her: 'Seeing you today, it seems as if I have seen Kaihui again.'

him. Even Jiang Qing suffered his philandering in silence. The only real criticism of such behaviour in China, and that not voiced till long after his death, was over Mao's hypocrisy: in a country where illicit sex was grounds for sending an ordinary citizen to a labour camp, the Chairman could, and did, fill his bed with as many young women as he wished. The 'Plain Girl' and the other old texts offered a fig-leaf of classical authority, justifying his libertine ways as gathering *yin*, the female essence, to replenish his *yang*, in a millennial tradition of conserving male potency and health. His bodyguards had a simpler explanation: he had power, and it was his right.

The arrangement suited both sides. Mao's young women were not concubines in the old imperial sense. They were more like groupies, congregating around the Chairman as some young women in the West seek out racing drivers and pop singers. For a while, they basked in the reflected glory of his bed, proud beyond measure of their good fortune. Then Mao's aides ensured they were married off to good communist husbands.

Among his entourage, some surmised that he was becoming obsessed with old age, fending off intimations of mortality. But Li Yinqiao probably had it best when he said Mao surrounded himself with young people to escape from solitude. Young women served that purpose. So did the young men who were his body-servants. In the last twenty years of his life, Mao himself acknowledged, they became his surrogate family. He saw far more of them than of his own daughters, who spent most of their time at boarding school. The bodyguards gave him his nightly sleeping pills and massaged away his insomnia; they helped him to dress; they served his meals; they watched his every move. But they were an impermanent family, whose members could be dismissed at a whim; a simulated family, involving no responsibilities, no worries and no binding ties.

Beyond this tight, small circle, Mao, in his years of untrammelled power, was cut off from all normal human contact. His relations with the rest of the Politburo were exclusively political. Where Stalin had caroused late into the night with his cronies, Mao withdrew further and further into the seclusion of his own thoughts. Friendship was ruled out. 'The relationship between man and "god" is one of prayer, and of the answer to prayer,' wrote Li Yinqiao, years later. 'There can be no exchange between them on an equal footing.'

Before, much of Mao's attention had been devoted to military affairs – civil war, war with Japan, civil war again and then war in Korea. After 1953, only politics remained.

The 'Hundred Flowers' movement had been Mao's first attempt to break away from the rigid top-down command system of Soviet communism, and to find a distinctive Chinese path for the state he now ruled. Khrushchev had disapproved. In private, Mao retorted that the Russians' minds were petrified, they were abandoning Marxist-Leninist fundamentals.

When the experiment came to a bruising end amid the anti-rightist campaign, he began hankering once more after the old tried-and-tested strategy of mass mobilisation, used to such good purpose in the collectivisation movement.

He had attempted to apply this principle to the economy in the spring of 1956. But the so-called 'Little Leap Forward' had foundered, as local cadres set impossibly high targets, and peasants and disgruntled workers downed tools in protest. When Zhou Enlai had urged a slower pace, Mao had reluctantly stood aside. An editorial in the *People's Daily* on the theme of 'opposing rash advance', which had been sent for his approval, was returned, marked in his handwriting with the two words: 'Not read'.

At the time he had explained away this setback by arguing that in economic construction, as in warfare, advance was never in a straight line, but came in successive waves. 'There are ups and downs,' he said, 'with one wave chasing another . . . Things must develop and go forward in accordance with the laws of the waves.' The 'Little Leap' had failed, he suggested, because it coincided with a 'trough' in China's economic advance; at a more propitious moment of the cycle, it might succeed far better.

In the autumn of 1957, Mao decided that the moment had come to try again.

This time, most of the rest of the leadership agreed. The Soviet model was perceived to be failing. The co-operatives were not generating the agricultural surpluses necessary to finance a Soviet-style industrialisation programme; the intellectuals, needed to run it, had shown themselves unreliable; and Soviet financial aid, to help pay for it, was not available – because the Russians were using their money to shore up their client states in eastern Europe. A consensus was emerging that an alternative means would have to be found to jump-start China's economy, translating surplus rural labour power into industrial capital.

Alongside these practical imperatives, the political context had changed.

Throughout the 'Hundred Flowers' in the spring, Mao had repeated constantly the formula approved by the Eighth Congress, that class struggle was 'basically over'. After the anti-Rightist campaign started in June, he argued that while 'large-scale turbulent class struggle' was 'in the main at an end', class struggle *per se* was very much alive. The principal contradiction in Chinese society, he now held, was not economic, as the Congress had wrongly claimed, but the old, elemental fault-line between 'the socialist and capitalist roads'. In short, the stage had been set for a renewed upsurge of Leftism.

At a Central Committee plenum in October, Mao envisaged a radiant future based on economic revolution in the countryside. China, he said, would attain the highest crop yields in the world. Steel production would reach 20 million tons annually within fifteen years (four times the 1956 production level). More bizarrely, he also insisted that the 'Four Pests' must be eliminated, making China 'a country of the four "noes": no rats, no sparrows, no flies and no mosquitoes'. Citizens everywhere rallied to his call. A visiting Russian expert recalled:

> I was awakened in the early morning by a woman's blood-curdling screams. Rushing to my window, I saw that a young woman was running to and fro on the roof of the building next door, frantically waving a bamboo pole with a large sheet tied to it. Suddenly, the woman stopped . . . but a moment later, down in the street, a drum started beating, and she resumed her frightful screams and the mad waving of her peculiar flag . . . I realised that in all the upper stories of the hotel, while-clad females were waving sheets and towels that were supposed to keep the sparrows from alighting on the building.

The plan worked. Hecatombs of sparrows fell dead from exhaustion. Another foreigner reported some months later that in four weeks he saw not a single sparrow, and flies, usually singly, on only fifteen occasions. Unfortunately, Mao had ignored warnings that sparrowcide would cause the crops to be infested with caterpillars (which the birds usually ate). The following year the target was changed to bedbugs instead.

Revolutionary élan at home was matched by events abroad. On October 4, while the CCP plenum was in session, the Soviet Union launched the first sputnik at a time when, as Mao put it, the United States 'hadn't even launched a potato'.

Shortly afterwards, Khrushchev spoke of surpassing Western levels of meat and dairy production, insisting that this was 'not an arithmetical matter; it is a political issue' – a phrase which was music to Mao's ears, for he had just told his own Central Committee that, in the duality of politics and technology, 'politics is primary and [always] takes first place'. The following month, while Mao was visiting Moscow to take part in the Conference of World Communist Parties, the Soviet leader announced plans to overtake the United States in the production of iron, steel, coal, electric power, oil and many types of consumer goods, within fifteen years. Not a man to let pass a challenge, Mao promptly informed the assembled leaders of world communism that China would overtake Britain in fifteen years.

Then he gave them his views on the current state of the world by referring to a saying from the novel, *The Dream of the Red Chamber*. 'Either the East wind prevails over the West wind, or the West wind prevails over the East wind':

> At the moment I sense that the international situation has come to a turning-point . . . It is characterised by the East wind prevailing over the West wind. That is to say, the forces of socialism have become overwhelmingly superior to the forces of imperialism . . . I think we can [say] that we have left the Western world behind us. Are they far behind us? Or just a tiny bit behind us? As I see it – and maybe I am a bit adventurist in this – I say that we have left them behind us once and for all.

In this overheated, not to say euphoric state of mind, Mao flew back to Beijing in late November to confront the economic challenges at home. The direction had been set. By promising to overtake Britain, Mao had committed China to producing 40 million tons of steel by the early 1970s (twice the already high figure approved at the CC plenum less than two months before), as well as surpassing British production of cement, coal, chemical fertiliser and machine tools. The only question was how.

To find the answer, Mao set off on a four-month-long tour of the provinces, which took him from south China to Manchuria; westward to Sichuan in March; then by Yangtse river-steamer to Wuhan; and finally to Hunan and Guangdong in April.

Ostensibly, he was 'seeking truth from facts' by carrying out grass-roots investigations before proceeding to formulate new policies, just as he had in Jiangxi in the 1930s. But there was a crucial difference. In the 'Chinese Soviet Republic', a quarter of a century before, he had been free to investigate as he wished. In the People's Republic, in 1958, his every move was choreographed days or weeks in advance. 'Going to the grass roots' now meant meeting provincial first secretaries and visiting carefully selected model farms where everyone had been briefed to tell Mao only what the provincial authorities wanted him to hear. He still got no accurate, first-hand information. Instead, he had the illusion of being well-informed, which was to prove far more dangerous than ignorance.

At each stage of Mao's peregrination, he summoned a leadership conference, at which the theoretical basis for the 'Great Leap Forward' was gradually put in place.

At Hangzhou, on January 4, 1958, he propounded for the first time his view of 'uninterrupted revolution' (a concept which, he was quick to explain, had nothing to do with the Trotskyite heresy), whereby the 'socialist revolution' (collectivisation of the means of production), which had now been completed in China, would be followed seamlessly by a 'revolution in ideology and politics' and by 'technological revolution'. The latter term, he made clear, signified a new 'high tide' in production.

Ten days later, in Nanning, he vented his rage against those who had persuaded him to abort the 'Little Leap', eighteen months before. 'I am the "chief culprit" of rash advance,' he announced defiantly. 'You are against rash advance. Well, I am against opposing it!' Zhou Enlai made a self-criticism, confessing that he had 'wavered about policy' and had committed 'right conservatist errors'. In Chengdu, in March, Mao castigated the planning ministries, for adhering slavishly to Soviet practices, and the Party, for exhibiting a 'slave mentality' towards 'experts' in general and bourgeois experts in particular. A month later, in Hankou, he went further, declaring that bourgeois intellectuals constituted an exploiting class which must be struggled against, and that

China should not be shackled by the economic laws they had devised:

> We must break down superstition, believing in – yet also disbelieving
> – the scientists . . . Whenever a problem is discussed, we must also
> discuss ideology. When we study a problem, we must subdue the
> [facts] by [adopting] a viewpoint, and activate the affair at hand with
> politics . . . How can [anything be resolved] when only numbers are
> discussed, without politics? *The relationship between politics and numbers*
> *is like that between officers and soldiers: Politics is the commander.*
> (Emphasis supplied)

The exaltation of political will was familiar enough, but Mao had rarely affirmed quite so brazenly that facts and figures could be ignored. In the late spring of 1958, he was on an adrenalin high, pumped up by the limitless vista of a bright communist future in which nothing would be able to withstand the concerted efforts of 600 million people.

His confidence had been fired by a nationwide irrigation movement launched the previous winter. In the space of four months, 100 million peasants had dug ditches and reservoirs to water almost 20 million acres, far in excess of the initial target. It was only necessary to 'lift the lid, break down superstition, and let the initiative and creativity of the labouring people explode', he told the Second Session of the Eighth Congress, which officially launched the Great Leap in May, and miracles could be achieved. He added, almost as an afterthought, 'No, we are not insane!'

Insane or not, the targets set that year for both agricultural and industrial production rose exponentially.

At the Chengdu meeting, in March, Mao had urged provincial leaders to stay within the realm of the possible. 'Revolutionary romanticism is good,' he told them, 'but it's no use if there's no way to put it into practice.'

By May, he had increased that year's steel target from six to eight million tons, and cut the length of time needed to overtake Britain by half (to seven years) and the United States to fifteen years, the same as Khrushchev had proposed for Russia. Indeed, China might get there first, Mao suggested, and 'reach communism ahead of schedule'. After that, all restraint was cast to the winds. In the autumn, the 1958 steel estimate was raised to 10.7 million tons, and three weeks later to '11 or 12 million'. By then Mao envisaged annual steel output in 1959 of 30 million tons (surpassing Britain); in 1960, 60 million (surpassing Russia); in 1962, 100 million (surpassing the USA); and 700 million tons – several times the production of the whole of the rest of the world – by the early 1970s. The 1958 grain target rose in tandem, first to 300 million tons (half as much again as the previous record harvest), then to 350 million.

The aim, as ever, was to make China great. 'Although we have a large population,' Mao told the Politburo, 'we have not yet demonstrated our strength. When we catch up with Britain and America, [even US Secretary of State] Dulles will respect us and acknowledge our existence as a nation.' Nor was that all. The new Communist China would also be elegant. 'The French', Mao noted, 'have made their streets, houses and boulevards very beautiful: if capitalism can do it, why can't we?' It would be replete with creature comforts, too. Tan Zhenlin, once one of Mao's battalion commanders on the Jinggangshan, who had replaced his contemporary, the sober-minded Deng Zihui, as agricultural supremo, unveiled a vision of plenty which put Khrushchev's 'goulash communism' to shame:

> After all, what does communism mean? . . . First, taking good food and not merely eating one's fill. At each meal one enjoys a meat diet, eating chicken, pork, fish or eggs . . . Delicacies like monkey's heads, swallow's nest and white fungus are served, 'to each according to his needs' . . . Second, clothing. Everything people want should be available. Clothing of various designs and styles, not [just] a mass of blue garments . . . After working hours, people will wear silk, satin . . . and overcoats lined with fox furs . . . Third, housing . . . Central heating will be provided in the north and air conditioning in the south. Everyone will live in high-rise buildings. Needless to say, there will be electric light, telephone, piped water [and] television . . . Fourth, communications . . . Air services will be opened in every direction and every county will have an airport . . . Fifth, higher education for everyone . . . The sum total of all these means communism.

Tan was not alone in such extravagant speculations. Mao himself envisaged asphalt highways which would also serve as airstrips, with each township having its own planes and its own resident philosophers and scientists. 'It's like playing mahjong,' he exclaimed delightedly as he contemplated China's riches piling up: 'You just double your stakes!' The rest of the leadership concurred. Even the down-to-earth Deng Xiaoping foresaw every Chinese owning a bicycle, and women wearing high heels and lipstick.

How did this extraordinary sea change in attitudes come about?

How could Mao, who, in order to win power, had spent the whole of his adult life making finely calibrated judgements about what was possible and what was not, suddenly suspend all rational criteria to espouse a utopian dream which even the most cursory reflection ought to have shown to be impossible? How could men like Zhou Enlai and Bo Yibo, who had held out against much more modest targets only a year earlier, now support plans which, it should have been obvious at the time, were the sheerest fantasy?

Even now, almost half a century later, it is not easy to give a complete answer.

The catalyst was undoubtedly Russia's successful launch of the sputnik, which awoke Mao to the possibilities opened up by technological advance. Science, once his interest had been aroused, fascinated him, but in a medieval rather than a modern sense. He read avidly, but less for new insights than to comfort his own view of the world. His speeches were soon peppered with scientific analogies illustrative of his political ideas: the structure of the atom demonstrated the contradictions inherent in all things; the proliferation of chemical elements showed that 'matter always changes and converts into its opposite'; metabolism was an example of the tendency of everything to split. To Mao, scientific progress justified his long-held belief that mind could triumph over matter (or, as he had put it in 1937, 'the operation of mental on material things'). Like a latter-day philosopher's stone, it would transmute China's poverty-stricken reality into a glowing new world without scarcity or hunger. Not for him the rigorous discipline of analysis and proof. China had had no Galileo, no Copernicus, no Darwin or Alexander Fleming, to foster a spirit of sceptical enquiry. Modern science, like modern industry, was a recent, alien import, with no roots in Chinese culture, and Mao freely admitted he knew nothing about either. It was the concept that he seized on – the prospect of unbounded progress through technical revolution.

In a country with a tradition of scientific and industrial expertise, the targets advanced in the Great Leap would have been dismissed as the idle dreams they were.

But not in China. Within the Politburo, only Chen Yun asked awkward questions on economic matters, and from the beginning of 1958, he was systematically sidelined. Zhou Enlai may have had reservations. But if so he kept them to himself: he had already had his fingers rapped once for opposing Mao's desire for 'bold advance'.

Among the other leaders, Liu Shaoqi had his own reasons to champion the Chairman's cause. His relationship with Zhou contained a greater element of rivalry than either man admitted. The Great Leap was to be run by Liu's Party apparatus, not Zhou's State Council: whatever was bad for the one stood to benefit the other. Moreover, Mao had informed the members of the Politburo Standing Committee two years earlier that, as part of his withdrawal to the 'second front', he intended to step down as Head of State. At the Second Session of the Eighth Congress, in May, it was officially announced that Liu would succeed him. If Liu had doubts about the Great Leap – and there is no evidence that he did – the prospect of marking his assumption of the highest office of state with a dramatic upsurge in economic growth was evidently enough to make him close his eyes to them.

The rest of the Politburo was composed of old-guard loyalists, like Lin Boqu, who had been with Mao in Canton in the mid-1920s, and Li Fuchun, now Chairman of the State Economic Commission, whose association with him went back to the days of the New People's Study Society; recently promoted men, such as the first secretaries of Shanghai and Sichuan, whose appointments Mao had sanctioned precisely because of their enthusiasm for the Leap; and military figures, led by Lin Biao (newly elevated to the Politburo Standing Committee) and Defence Minister Peng Dehuai, who had learned the hard way over the years that on all major issues, Mao was invariably right.

None of these men, in 1958, was prepared to challenge him. Most were as convinced as he that a new era of prosperity was at hand. The only group which might have disabused them – the bourgeois intellectuals – had been discredited.

That summer, Mao knew what he wanted; he knew why; but he still did not know how to accomplish it. The month of May found him still asking plaintively: 'Apart from the Soviet method, is it possible to find something even faster and better?'

In fact, although he had not recognised it, the germ of the answer was already at hand. The previous winter's irrigation movement had begun a chain reaction of mergers of co-operatives, in order to permit cadres to mobilise the vast quantities of manpower necessary to build networks of dykes and canals.

Here were the ready-made building blocks for the communist society to come. In late June, Mao reached back into his memory to find a name, and a concept, dating from pre-Marxist days, which would take this process a step further. What was needed, he said, was a form of 'large commune' combining agriculture, industry, commerce, culture, education and self-defence. The name derived from the Paris Commune of 1871, whose 'deep significance' he had noted in an article in 1926; the concept came from the experiments in communal living that he had dabbled in as a young student-teacher during his anarchist days at the end of the First World War.

On August 9, 1958, Mao formally proclaimed, 'People's communes are good', a verdict enshrined three weeks later by an enlarged Politburo meeting at the seaside resort of Beidaihe, on the Yellow Sea coast north of Tianjin. The commune, the Politburo asserted, was 'the best organisational form for the building of socialism and the gradual transition to communism'. Mao's secret police chief from Yan'an days, Kang Sheng, who had remained one of the Chairman's confidants, put it more succinctly in a jingle he wrote, which was sung that autumn by peasants throughout China:

> *Communism is Paradise,*
> *The People's Communes are the way to get there.*

Mao himself was yet more reckless. 'The communist spirit is very good,' he told his colleagues at Beidaihe. 'If human beings only live to eat, isn't that like dogs eating shit? What meaning is there to life if you don't . . . practise a bit of communism? . . . We should put into practice some of the ideals of utopian socialism.' The way forward, he argued, lay in a return to the 'supply system' which the communists had used in Yan'an. Progressively, China would shift towards a non-monetary economy, where food, clothing and housing would all be supplied free. 'Eating in public mess halls without paying for it is communism,' he declared. Eventually even money itself might be abolished.

Over the next two months, the Leap, which had been inexorably gathering momentum since the spring, exploded into a frenzy of activity that changed the face of the Chinese countryside for ever.

Some 500 million people, many of them still struggling to adjust to living in co-operatives, which had been established only two or three years before, found that they now belonged to something called a *renmin gongshe*, literally, 'people's communal organisation', in which they were to share weal and woe with thousands of complete strangers formerly scattered in separate villages. The commune became the basic unit of rural society and the presumptive model for the rest of the country as well. 'In future', Mao said, 'everything will be called a commune, [including] factories . . . and cities.'

For many, especially richer households, the transition was painful.

Private plots and livestock were confiscated, usually without compensation. In south China, even remittances from relatives overseas were siphoned off for the communal pot. Families were forced to hand over their cooking implements, on the grounds that the mess halls had made them redundant. 'Happiness Homes' were promoted for the elderly, and boarding kindergartens for the very young. Parents were urged to give up 'bourgeois emotional attachments' in favour of a collectivised, militarised lifestyle, in which the ideal family unit was an able-bodied couple, willing and able to work Stakhanovite hours as members of a shock brigade.

Officially everyone was supposed to have at least six hours' sleep every two days, but some brigades boasted of working four or five days without stopping. Since no one could keep that up, there was widespread faking. The peasants left lanterns alight in the fields all night while they slept, with a look-out to give the alarm should a cadre come along. Material incentives were decried and supposedly rendered unnecessary by the system of free supply, but many communes found that their members refused to work without them. Only the most advanced units could offer the '10 guarantees' which were the system's ultimate goal, assuring their members 'meals, clothes, housing, schooling, medical attention, burial, haircuts, theatrical entertainment, money for heating in winter and money for weddings'.

Much of this was animated by nostalgia for the simplicity and fervour of the early years of the communist revolution.

Party cadres were ordered to toil alongside the masses. Mao himself, together with Premier Zhou Enlai and other Politburo members, set the example by being photographed 'toiling' at the site of a new reservoir near Beijing. PLA officers, from generals down, were ordered to spend a month a year serving in the ranks.

A militia drive was launched under the slogan, 'Everyone a soldier', and peasants worked in the fields with antiquated rifles stacked beside them.

At the core of the Great Leap, however, lay the targets for steel and grain production.

When it became clear that the country's medium and large steel plants would be unable to meet the new targets, Zhou Enlai, whom Mao had placed in charge of the steel drive, proposed a mass campaign using 'backyard furnaces', similar to the small, native iron-smelting plants used in the countryside to make farm implements.

The results were immediate and spectacular. The Chinese countryside became a lattice of smoking chimneys. Sidney Rittenberg, who had joined the Party in Yan'an and now worked for Radio Beijing, was an enthusiast. 'Every hill, every field', he wrote, 'glowed with the light of the home-made ovens turning out steel in places where not a thimbleful of metal had ever been produced before.' Albert Belhomme, another American who had embraced the communist cause, saw it rather differently. When his paper mill in Shandong was ordered to build furnaces, 'members of the Party street committees went from house to house, confiscating pots and pans, ripping up iron fences and even tearing locks off doors . . . They tore the radiators out of our shop at the mill and melted them down.' An English visitor to Yunnan, in the far south-west, described how, in one village where four improvised blast furnaces had been rigged up, he found 'a furious, seething, clattering scene of frenzy . . . People carried baskets of ore, people stoked, people goaded buffalo carts, people tipped cauldrons of white-hot metal, people stood on rickety ladders and peered into furnaces, people wheeled barrows of crude metal.' The commune chairman explained that they had learned steel-making from reading a news-paper article.

The same scenes were replicated in every town and village in China. In Beijing, factories, government offices, universities, even the writers' association, set up primitive foundries. The editors of *Beijing Review* reported:

> In response to the government call . . . we, too, turned to making steel in our own courtyard . . . Some brought in broken pans, pots and kettles; others contributed old bricks and limestone; still others turned in all sorts of odds and ends. In a matter of hours, a rever-

beratory puddling furnace, Chinese style, was built . . . The only person in the group who could claim some technical know-how was a young man who had visited several office-built furnaces before our furnace went into operation.

In September 1958, 14 per cent of China's steel production came from small, local furnaces; in October, the figure was 49 per cent. When the movement was at its peak, 90 million people, close to a quarter of the active population, abandoned their normal pursuits to take part.

The result, inevitably, was an acute shortage of agricultural labour, putting at risk the autumn harvest. In October, schools were ordered closed, and students and other non-essential personnel, including shop assistants, sent to work in the fields. Once again, peasant shock brigades toiled through the night.

Mao, and the rest of the leadership, were convinced that an exceptional crop was being gathered in. Close planting, combined with deep ploughing techniques, on experimental plots had produced reports of phenomenal yields. One enterprising model peasant conned Deng Xiaoping into believing that he had obtained the equivalent of 200 tons an acre. Even 'normal' high-yielding fields were said to produce 30 tons, and ordinary fields, 9 to 15 tons – in a country where the average yield, even in good years, had up till then been *one ton per acre.* The Politburo spoke of production increases of 'one hundred per cent, several hundred per cent, over one thousand per cent and several thousand per cent.' By the onset of winter, some of the claims were becoming so extravagant that even Mao started to doubt them. But he was still confident enough in the astounding surge in productivity his green revolution had supposedly unleashed to propose that two-thirds of China's arable land be afforested or allowed to lie fallow.

The drawback of intensive farming was that it required high labour inputs. That led Mao to the fateful decision to abandon China's birth control programme, ultimately, perhaps, the gravest of all the consequences of the Great Leap.

Meanwhile China's leaders, in a collective suspension of disbelief, savoured what they were all convinced would be a radiant future.

When the Central Committee met in Wuhan in December, Mao announced that grain production would be a staggering 430 million tons, more than twice the previous best harvest. In the interests of 'prudence', the publicly-announced figure was 15 per cent lower; and though the steel target of 10.7 million tons had also been fulfilled, Mao acknowledged that only nine million tons (later revised downward to eight million) were of acceptable quality. That led him to the remarkable admission that the Beidaihe steel figures had been unrealistic. 'I made a mistake,' he told the plenum. 'I was [too] enthusiastic at that time, and failed to combine revolutionary fervour with a practical spirit.' But his very willingness to criticise himself in this way was the clearest proof that he believed the Leap to have been a huge success. That was obvious, too, from the new steel targets he proposed: although lower than at Beidaihe, they were still resolutely upbeat: 20 million tons in 1959, and 60 million in 1962.

As 1958 drew to a close, Mao looked back with satisfaction on what had been achieved. 'During this [past] year, there have been so many good things,' he mused. 'Trails have been blazed. Many things have been realised, about which we did not even dare to dream before.' His vision of China pioneering its own path to communism was beginning to come true. The Russians were being left behind.

Two years earlier, at the start of the Little Leap, he had written of the Chinese people being 'poor and blank'. This was an advantage, he maintained, because 'once a piece of paper has been written on, you cannot do much more with it'. Throughout the Great Leap Forward, poverty and 'blankness' remained a constant theme. As he put it in an article in April:

> China's 600 million people have two remarkable peculiarities; they are, first of all, poor, and secondly blank. That may seem like a bad thing, but it is really a good thing. Poor people want change, want to do things, want revolution. A clean sheet of paper has no blotches, and so the newest and most beautiful words can be written on it, the newest and most beautiful pictures can be painted on it.

That statement, with its stupendous arrogance, its megalomaniac ambition to mould, like putty, the lives and thoughts of almost a quarter of mankind, provided an alarming glimpse into Mao's mind as old age approached. Hubris on such a scale presaged catastrophe. It was not long in coming.

*

The Russians watched these developments with mounting disquiet. Already, in November 1957, Mao's visit to Moscow for the Conference of World Communist Parties had left a residue of unease. On his arrival there, Khrushchev had greeted him with an offer too good to refuse: a secret agreement to provide China with nuclear weapons technology, including a sample atom bomb, in return for Mao's support of the Soviet leader personally, and of continued Russian primacy in the international communist movement. On both counts he had been happy to oblige. The 'new' Khrushchev, who wanted to surpass America, was better to his liking than the author of the Secret Speech; and Mao had never disputed that international communism needed a leading core (though he might have added that it did not always have to be Russia).

The nuclear agreement was to push the already shaky Sino–Soviet relationship a big step closer to the abyss.

Buoyed up by his conviction that 'the East wind prevails over the West', Mao gave the leaders of world communism an apocalyptic vision of their future triumph. If peace could be maintained, he said, the socialist camp would become invincible. But there was also another possibility:

> Let us speculate. If war broke out, how many people would die? There are 2.7 billion people in the entire world, and one-third of them may be lost . . . If the worst comes to the worst, perhaps one-half would die. But there would still be one-half left; imperialism would be razed to the ground and the whole world would become socialist. After a number of years, the world's population would once again reach 2.7 billion and certainly become even bigger.

There was nothing particularly new in this: Mao had expressed the same view to Nehru in 1954, when tensions over Taiwan had led America to hint at possible nuclear weapons use, and he repeated it in even more cataclysmic terms to a Finnish diplomat a few months later. 'If the US had atom bombs so powerful that . . . they would make a hole right through the earth,' he told the astonished envoy, 'that would hardly mean anything to the universe as a whole, though it might be a major event for the solar system.' It was one thing, however, to engage in such airy speculations in private conversation, quite another at a meeting attended by communist functionaries from more than sixty countries. To them, Mao's words were chilling. The Soviet leadership found itself wondering whether a man who spoke of nuclear armageddon with such total unconcern could really be trusted with an atomic arsenal of his own. But by then, the technology agreement had been signed.

The following spring, Mao plunged into the Great Leap Forward, secure in the knowledge that nuclear partnership with the USSR would spare China the need for a costly build-up of conventional forces.

Meanwhile, Khrushchev cast about for ways to increase Soviet leverage over Beijing's atomic weapons policy. To that end he proposed a further broadening of military co-operation, including an agreement to set up a jointly-owned ultra-long-wave radio station to communicate with the Soviet submarine fleet in the Pacific (70 per cent of the cost to be met by Russia, the remainder by the Chinese side), and another for a joint Soviet–Chinese nuclear submarine flotilla.

To his amazement, Mao reacted very badly. At a meeting with the Russian Ambassador, Pavel Yudin, in late July, the Chairman poured out in venomous terms his accumulated resentment at what he viewed as Moscow's high-handedness:

> You never trust the Chinese! You only trust Russians. To you, Russians are first-class citizens, whereas Chinese are among those inferior peoples who are stupid and careless. That's why you came up with this question of joint ownership and operation. Well, if that's what you want, why don't you have it all – let's have joint ownership and operation of our army, navy, air force, industry, agriculture, culture, education! Would that be all right? Or you can have the whole of China's 10,000 kilometres of coastline, and we'll just keep a guerrilla force. Just because you have a few atomic bombs, you think you are in a position to control us by seeking leases. How else can you justify your behaviour? . . . These remarks of mine may not sound so pleasing to your ear . . . [But] you have extended Russian nationalism right up to the Chinese coast.

To Mao, 'joint ownership' smacked of the unequal treaties imposed during China's humiliation at the hands of the Western powers, and of the Soviet Union's demands in 1950 for special privileges in Manchuria and Xinjiang. Khrushchev, he told Yudin, had had the good sense to annul the accords which Stalin had imposed, yet now he was himself behaving in exactly the same way.

Khrushchev recalled in his memoirs that Yudin's report on this meeting came 'like a thunderbolt out of a clear blue sky', and there is no reason to disbelieve him. Less than ten days later, he flew secretly to Beijing, accompanied by the Defence Minister, Rodion Malinovsky, to try to sort out the mess.

He failed. Not only was Mao intransigent, refusing to countenance arrangements even for shore leave in China for Soviet submariners, but, in a mischievous symbolic snub, the naval talks were held beside an open-air swimming pool which Mao had had built at Zhongnanhai, where they sunned themselves, as Khrushchev remembered, 'like seals on the warm sand', and the Russian leader, who could not swim, was forced to suffer the indignity of wallowing about in the water buoyed up by a rubber float.

Three weeks later, another major row blew up, this time concerning Taiwan.

In January 1958, the PLA had begun preparing for a renewed Chinese attempt to occupy the islands of Quemoy and Matsu. That summer, a left-wing coup in Iraq, which led the United States and Britain to send troops to the Middle East, had given Mao the opportunity he had been waiting for. On July 17, he told the Politburo that an attack on the nationalist outposts would divert American attention from the Iraqi imbroglio and show the world that China was serious about supporting national liberation movements. The initial plan was for the bombardment of Quemoy and Matsu to begin nine days later – shortly before Khrushchev's arrival – but in the event it was delayed until late August. By then, the Soviet leader had proposed a four-power summit with the Americans, British and French, to defuse Middle East tensions, which led the *People's Daily* to comment caustically on 'the nonsensical idea that peace can be achieved only by currying favour and compromising with the aggressors'.

As it turned out, Mao had misjudged American resolve. After a disagreeable ten days, in which the US dropped heavy hints about the use of nuclear weapons, the Chinese were forced to back off. Khrushchev, having assured himself that Russia no longer risked being dragged in, promised China maximum assistance. Two months later, the crisis ended with the PLA announcing, in the best Beijing opera tradition, that it would continue the bombardment of the island, but only on even-numbered days.

The short-term effect of these disputes was to remind both China and the Soviet Union that it was in their national interests to maintain a normal working relationship. China cooled its rhetoric about an imminent leap into communism, which had exasperated the Russians; and Khrushchev approved a five-billion-rouble loan for Chinese industrial development projects.

But behind the façade of renewed amity, their mutual mistrust deepened. To Khrushchev, Mao's refusal to permit closer military co-operation despite Moscow's agreement to help China build atomic weapons, his cavalier attitude to nuclear destruction and his wild flights of doctrinal unorthodoxy, made him an erratic, ungrateful and unpredictable partner. To Mao, the priority Khrushchev accorded to improving relations with the United States was a betrayal of the international communist movement and the revolutionary cause it was pledged to promote. The Russian leader's conversation that winter with a prominent American politician, Senator Hubert Humphrey, in which he poured scorn on the Chinese communes, was just one more example, in Mao's eyes, of Moscow's dereliction of basic socialist solidarity.

Throughout the spring of 1959, the campaign to consolidate the Great Leap, which Mao had initiated at Wuhan in December, steadily continued. The backyard furnace movement was abandoned in recognition that much of what it produced was unusable – leaving the rural landscape pockmarked with rusting hulks of congealed metal, Byronesque monuments to a national folly. By early summer Mao had agreed that the 1959 steel target should be cut back again, from 20 to 13 million tons, and it was beginning to sink in that the previous year's grain production, while good, had been grossly exaggerated. 'Just as a child plays with fire . . . and knows pain only when it is burnt,' he acknowledged ruefully, 'so, in economic construction, we declared war on nature, like an inexperienced child, unfamiliar with strategy and tactics.' Provincial leaders were ordered not to push the peasants too hard. Otherwise, Mao warned chillingly, the CCP might end up like the ancient Qin and Sui dynasties, which had succeeded in unifying China only to lose power a few decades later because of the harshness of their rule.

It was still a matter of fine-tuning, not of changing basic principles; communism might not be realised tomorrow, Mao said, but it was achievable in fifteen to twenty years 'or perhaps a little longer'. None the less, it seemed that some sense of reality was finally returning.

In this relatively sober frame of mind, the Central Committee gathered in July at the hill resort of Lushan, just south of the Yangtse. On the way, Mao visited his old home at Shaoshan for the first time since 1927. What he was shown there strengthened his conviction that the Leap was succeeding, but also that the adventurist notions of utopian Leftists in the provinces needed further damping down – and soon after reaching Lushan he began to apply himself to that purpose.

Mao, however, was not the only Chinese leader to have returned to his roots that year. The Defence Minister, Peng Dehuai, had gone back several months earlier to his native village, Niaoshi, not far from Mao's birthplace in the same county, Xiangtan, also for the first time since the 1920s, but had come away with very different impressions.

What had stayed in Peng's mind was the detritus of the steel campaign – lumps of pig-iron rusting uselessly in the fields; the shells of deserted houses, stripped of their timbers to feed the furnaces; and fruit trees cut down for the same purpose. At the so-called 'Happiness Homes' for the aged, he had found spindly old people, subsisting on minimal rations without even blankets to keep them warm. 'The old can grit their teeth,' one elderly man said, 'but babies can only cry.' The peasants were mutinous, Peng had concluded. They hated the militarisation of daily existence, the enforced communal eating in the mess halls, the destruction of family life. The cadres were under constant pressure to outdo rival communes, leading to systematic exaggeration of crop yields, often by a margin of 10 or 20 times. The alternative, they had told him, was to be branded as Rightists.

Peng was not Mao's favourite colleague. They had clashed too often in the past – going back all the way to the winter of 1928, when Peng and his small army of fellow-Hunanese had been left behind on the Jinggangshan, and Mao had failed to execute a promised diversionary manoeuvre to allow them to break out. The Defence Minister's loyalties were to the Party, not to Mao as an individual.

In Shaoshan, the Chairman had been moved to write a poem, eulogising the 'waves of growing rice and beans, and heroes everywhere going home in the smoky sunset'. Peng, too, had set his thoughts in verse on his last night in Hunan. But he had seen 'scattered millet . . . and withered potato plants', and had made a solemn vow to 'speak out on behalf of the people'.

In fact, however, Peng did no such thing. In the first half of 1959, he uttered not so much as a word of criticism of the Great Leap. This may have been partly because his attention was taken up by the rebellion in Tibet, which broke out in March; and partly because Mao himself, by then, was preaching the virtues of moderation in a way that promised to correct the more egregious errors. But the main reason was the sheer difficulty, even for a man of Peng's stature, who had been at Mao's side for three decades, to call into question policies with which the Chairman was so intimately involved.

Five years earlier, Gao Gang had overstepped the bounds Mao had fixed and it had cost him his life. In 1955, Deng Zihui had opposed Mao – on technical, rather than political grounds – over the speed of collectivisation; Deng had survived but had lost most of his power. The following year, Zhou Enlai questioned the Little Leap, only to find himself forced to make a cringing self-criticism eighteen months later. Nor was the fate of those who spoke out during the 'Hundred Flowers' an encouragement to candour.

By 1959, it had become obvious that the only person who could safely criticise Mao and his policies was Mao himself; others did so at their peril. Back in Beijing, Peng's enthusiasm for 'speaking out' waned. Like other leaders who had doubts, he kept them to himself.

At this point, a new factor came into play.

Serious food shortages had begun to appear. At first they were confined to the cities. Rice rations were reduced. Vegetables and cooking oil disappeared. Then, as the government stepped up procurement to feed the industrial workforce, swollen by the Leap, the countryside went short. The 1958 harvest had not been 375 million tons, nor even 260 million, which was the government's new best estimate, but actually (though it would not be admitted until after Mao's death) only 200 million tons. That was still a record. But the leadership's grandiose claims that China had entered an era of plenty where people could eat as much as they wished had led the peasants to do just that: they had literally eaten themselves out of house and home. In many parts of China, penury set in.

Peng was better informed than most about the true state of the harvest. Military transport was being used to take relief grain to the worst-hit areas, and within the PLA there were already ominous rumblings as the overwhelmingly peasant recruits received news from home that their families were going hungry.

Meanwhile, as part of an effort to put the Leap on a more rational footing and combat exaggerated production claims, Mao had started urging officials to express their views frankly. 'An individual sometimes wins over the majority,' he had told the Central Committee in April. 'Truth is sometimes in one person's hands alone . . . Speaking out should involve no penalty. According to Party regulations, people are entitled to their own opinions.' He had cited the example of the Confucian bureaucrat, Hai Rui, of the Ming dynasty, a model of probity who had been dismissed from office for upbraiding a sixteenth century emperor. China, Mao declared, needed more Hai Ruis. From June onward, Party propagandists began producing anthologies, articles and plays extolling the Ming official's virtues. On July 2, the day the Lushan conference opened, Mao renewed his assurance that no one would be punished for 'making criticisms and offering opinions'.

Peng had originally intended to skip the meeting. He had just returned from a six-week-long tour of eastern Europe, and he was tired. But, at Mao's urging, he went, and, once there, soon decided that this was the right place and the right moment to fulfil his pledge of the previous winter and 'speak out'.

The Defence Minister, as was his custom, did not mince words. At a group discussion with officials from north-west China, he declared that 'everybody is responsible for the mistakes committed during the [Great Leap] . . . including Comrade Mao Zedong'. A week later he resolved to take his concerns to Mao himself. But when he appeared at Mao's quarters, on the morning of Monday, July 13, he was told the Chairman was still sleeping. That night, therefore, he set out his views in a 'letter of opinion', had his aide-de-camp write out a clean copy, and next morning, not without some nervousness, despatched it for Mao to read.

Peng's letter mixed considerable praise for the achievements of the Leap – notably the unprecedented growth rate, which, he wrote, proved that Mao's strategic line was 'in the main . . . correct' – with criticisms of specific failings. Taken individually, these were unexceptionable. Mao may not have relished hearing that 'petty-bourgeois fanaticism' had generated Leftist errors; that in the backyard steel movement there had been both 'losses and gains' (implying that the former predominated); that 'we have not sufficiently understood the socialist laws of proportionate and planned development'; and that economic construction had been handled less successfully than the PLA's shelling of Quemoy or the suppression of the revolt in Tibet. However, all these were things he could perfectly well have said himself. The problem was that, cumulatively, their effect was devastating. To Mao, the burden of Peng's message was that the Great Leap, even if justified in theory, had in fact led to disaster. Woven through his text were passages linking the Chairman personally with errors that had been made, including one where he took issue with Mao's claims that 'politics is the commander':

> In the view of some comrades, putting politics in command can take the place of everything else. They have forgotten [that] it is aimed at ... giving full play to the enthusiasm and creativity of the masses in order to speed up economic construction. [It] cannot take the place of economic principles, still less can it be a substitute for concrete measures in economic work.

But more galling than anything Peng wrote was the way in which he had arrogated to himself the right to sit in judgement. Mao's praise of Hai Rui notwithstanding, punctual criticism of policy errors was one thing, 'upbraiding the emperor' quite another.

Three days later, on July 17, the conference secretariat, on Mao's instructions, distributed the text of Peng's letter to all delegates. This was generally interpreted at the time as a sign, if not of Mao's approval, at least that Peng's views were an acceptable basis for discussion. Over the next few days, several other Central Committee members – including Zhang Wentian, Mao's ally in the mid-1930s, who had remained a Politburo alternate – made speeches supporting his views. Two more Politburo members, Li Xiannian and Chen Yi, indicated agreement with it, and a number of others were hesitating.

At this point, Mao spoke, and the bottom fell out of Peng's world.

Like most of the Chairman's speeches in later years, it was a rambling, somewhat disjointed statement, full of half-finished thoughts tangential to his main theme. But he made two ominous points. Peng Dehuai's letter, he said, constituted an error of political

line, like those committed earlier by Li Lisan, Wang Ming and Gao
Gang. Peng and his supporters were Rightists. Others, too, were 'on
the brink'. Those who were wavering, he warned, must make up
their minds quickly on which side they wished to stand. Secondly,
Mao said, if there were nothing but criticism, communist power
would collapse. If that happened, he would 'go away, go to the
countryside, to lead the peasants and overthrow the government'
again, in order to re-establish the regime. He added menacingly, in a
direct challenge to the PLA marshals, who were Peng's natural
allies: 'If you, the PLA, don't follow me, I'll go and found a [new]
Red Army. [But] I think the PLA will follow me.'

After Mao had finished speaking, Peng walked home, as he wrote
later, 'with a heavy heart'. He lost his appetite and lay on his bed for
hours, staring into space. His bodyguard called a doctor, who
concluded that Peng must be ill. The Defence Minister disabused him.
'If I've got a sickness,' he said, 'it's nothing that can be cured now.'

The conference ended on July 30. Next day, Mao convened an
enlarged meeting of the Politburo Standing Committee to decide
Peng's fate.

Once again Khrushchev had simplified his task. Six weeks
earlier, on the eve of the planned shipment to China of the sample
atom bomb which the Soviet leader had promised Mao, the
Russians had informed Beijing that they were cancelling the nuclear
technology agreement. Now, in the same week that Peng had issued
his 'letter of opinion', Khrushchev publicly condemned the
communes. Mao lost no time in circulating at Lushan an approving
account of the Russian leader's remarks issued by Taiwan's Central
News Agency. What better proof could there be that Peng and his
supporters were 'objectively' aiding China's enemies – if, indeed,
not actually colluding with them? Peng and Zhang Wentian, after
all, had both just visited Moscow.

Against this background of innuendo, Mao had no difficulty
persuading his colleagues that they were confronted by an anti-
Party conspiracy, and that Peng and his 'military club' should be
cast into outer darkness.

The operative question was no longer whether the Chairman was
right, but whether anyone had the courage to tell him he was wrong.
Certainly not the malleable Zhou Enlai, for whom avoidance of
confrontations with Mao was the basic premise of political survival.
Not Liu Shaoqi, either: he had not forgiven Peng for giving Gao

Gang a sympathetic hearing in 1953. Chen Yun was away on sick leave, and Deng Xiaoping, conveniently, had broken his leg playing table tennis. Lin Biao detested Peng, and would do whatever Mao asked of him. Of all the inner core, only the venerable Marshal Zhu De, now in his seventies, was rash – or honest – enough to speak on Peng's behalf, counselling moderation – and he was afterwards required to make a self-criticism for his pains. The others formed a political lynch-mob. The verbatim record of the Standing Committee meeting, taken down by one of the Chairman's secretaries, Li Rui, himself to be purged shortly afterwards, offers a revealing glimpse of the snakepit that life at the top in Mao's China had become:

MAO: When you speak of 'petty bourgeois fanaticism', you are mainly pointing the spearhead at the central leadership organs. It's not at the provincial leaders, or even at the masses. This is my observation . . . In fact you are pointing the spearhead of attack at the centre. You may admit this, or, more likely, you may not. But we think you are opposing the centre. You were prepared to publish your letter in order to win people over and to organise them [against us] . . .

PENG: When I wrote about petty-bourgeois fanaticism . . . I should have recognised that this is a political problem. I did not grasp it very well.

MAO (interrupting): Now that the letter has been made public, all the counter-revolutionaries have come out to applaud it.

PENG: This was a letter I sent to you personally . . . I wrote on it, 'Please check and see if I am right, and give me your comments'. My whole intention concerning this letter was that it might have some reference value, and I wanted you to consider it.

MAO: That's not true . . . Whenever there is a problem, you are not straightforward about it . . . People [who don't know you] think you are simple, frank and outspoken. When they first know you, that's all they see. [But later] they realise . . . you are devious. No one can see what's in the bottom of your heart. Then they say you are a hypocrite . . . You are a Right opportunist. [You said in your letter] the Party leadership is no good. You want to usurp the proletarian banner.

PENG: The letter was sent to you personally. I carried out no [factional] activities.

MAO: You did.

PENG ZHEN: In the group discussions, you said everyone should take responsibility for what happened, including Comrade Mao Zedong . . . Who were you attacking then? . . .

HE LONG: You have a very deep prejudice against the Chairman. In your letter you show you are full of preconceived ideas . . .

ZHOU ENLAI: You have adopted a Right-opportunist stance. The target of your letter was the Party's general line . . .

MAO: You wanted to bring about the disintegration of the Party. You have a plan, you have an organisation, you have made preparations, you have attacked the correct line from a Rightist standpoint . . . [You say that] at [Yan'an], I fucked your mother for forty days. So this time, there are still twenty days to go. For you to be satisfied, you want to fuck my mother for forty days this time. I tell you, you've fucked enough* . . .

PENG: If you all think this way, it's very difficult for me to say anything . . . [But] you need not worry, I won't commit suicide; I will never be a counter-revolutionary; I can still go out and work in the fields.

On August 2, the Central Committee met to confirm the Standing Committee's verdict. A few of Peng's junior military colleagues spoke up for him (and were promptly purged as a result). The Defence Minister humiliated himself with a speech of self-abasement in which he denounced his letter to Mao as 'a series of absurdities', and confessed to damaging Mao's 'lofty prestige' from motives of 'exceedingly wrong personal prejudice'. The speech was a pointless gesture, which he afterwards regretted.

The CC, in its resolution, accused him of heading a 'Right-opportunist anti-Party clique'; of making 'vicious attacks' on Mao; of having focused on 'transient and partial shortcomings' in order to 'paint a pitch-black picture of the present situation'; of having formed an 'anti-Party alliance' with Gao Gang; and of engaging in 'long-standing anti-Party activities'. As if that were not enough, he, Zhang Wentian, and the other members of the alleged clique, were described as 'representatives of the bourgeoisie' who had wormed their way into the Party during the civil war period.

Yet then came a contradiction. Having detailed a list of offences which more than justified expulsion from the Party (and, in the case

---

* Mao was replying here to an earlier remark of Peng's, in which the Marshal had referred to criticisms to which he had been subjected (apparently related to the Hundred Regiments Campaign) before the Seventh Congress in 1945. 'You fucked my mother at Yan'an for forty days,' Peng had said. 'I've been fucking your mother in Lushan for only eighteen days and you've already come out to stop me!'

of a low-level official, would have meant a long term in a labour camp, or·even execution), the Central Committee ruled that the 'conspirators' could not only keep their Party membership, but Peng and Zhang Wentian, while losing their governmental responsibilities, would retain their Politburo posts.

This was presented as an example of Mao's long-established policy of 'curing the sickness to save the patient'. In fact, it had more to do with Peng's stature within the PLA and among the Party rank and file. Even for Mao, it was not easy to discredit one of the great heroes of the Revolutionary War, who had led the Chinese Volunteers in Korea; a man with a reputation for incorruptibility, who lived as an ascetic and was morally unassailable. Outwardly, the Chairman had no choice but to appear magnanimous, even as, in private, he continued to fume over Peng's 'surprise attack'.

A month later, Lin Biao, whom Mao had been grooming since 1956 as Peng's eventual successor, was named Defence Minister in his place. Lin was in poor health, and had played little public role since 1949. But he was a Mao loyalist, and he set to work with a will to extirpate Peng's influence from the military, which, in the 1950s and '60s, no less than during the civil war, remained the bedrock on which Mao's political power was based. Peng moved out of his home in Zhongnanhai, and for the next six years lived a hermetic existence under virtual house arrest in a building in the grounds of the old Summer Palace, on the northern outskirts of Beijing. Although he had retained his formal rank, he never attended another Politburo meeting, or any other official function. His career was finished.

It was not simply personal cowardice and political self-interest that had made Peng's colleagues line up to savage him. If the Politburo operated in this way, it was Mao who made it do so.

Criticising the Chairman did not *have* to be synonymous with overthrowing Party rule. Since 1949, it had not always been like that. Yet now, after months of urging people to speak out, pledging that there would be no retribution – the moment someone did so, Mao could not stomach it. Zhang Wentian had complained at Lushan, in a passage that had especially angered Mao, that all the problems of the Great Leap had a single basic cause – the lack of inner-Party democracy, which meant that one man decided everything. 'One would be labelled a sceptic, a tide-watcher, or a "white flag" to be pulled down, if one made a few differing remarks,' he had told the conference. 'Why? Why are negative views not tolerated? . . . What is there to be afraid of?'

Why indeed? Why could Mao not accept the criticism which he himself solicited?

In Peng's case, there were specific factors at work. Within the pressure-cooker of the inner circle, the Chairman was open to influence by those whose views reinforced his own. During the crucial two days when he was deciding how to respond to Peng's letter, Kang Sheng and Ke Qingshi, the left-wing Shanghai First Secretary, who had both been in the forefront of the Leap and were thus particularly vulnerable to any change of policy, artfully fuelled his suspicions that the Defence Minister was orchestrating a concerted campaign of opposition. Moreover, the fact that it was the cussedly independent-minded Peng, with whom Mao had been quarrelling for decades, rather than a more congenial figure, who dared to criticise his policies, made his reaction all the fiercer.

The very day the letter was distributed, he told his staff: 'Where Peng Dehuai is concerned, I have always had a rule. If he attacks, I attack back . . . [With him] it is 30 per cent co-operation, 70 per cent conflict – and it has been like that for 31 years.'

Yet, even without these aggravating circumstances, Mao would no doubt have acted in the same way. As the 1950s drew to a close, in his mind 'disagreement' became identical with 'opposition' – whether it was the disagreement of the intellectuals, in the Hundred Flowers movement, or disagreement within the Party.

After the 'Hundred Flowers', he had warned that class struggle between the proletariat and the bourgeoisie would continue in Chinese society for many years to come. Now he asserted that this was true within the Party as well:

> The struggle at Lushan was a class struggle, and a continuation of the life-and-death struggle between the two major antagonistic classes, the proletariat and the bourgeoisie. This kind of struggle will continue . . . in our Party for at least another 20 years and possibly for half a century . . . Contradictions and struggle will go on and on for ever, otherwise the world will no longer be worthy of its being. The bourgeois politicians say the philosophy of the Communist Party is a philosophy of struggle. That is correct, only the modes of the struggle vary according to the times.

Thus were laid the foundations for the notion, which would dominate the last years of Mao's life, that there was a 'bourgeoisie' inside the Party, which must be ferreted out, regardless of cost, if revolutionary purity was to be preserved.

Just as the 'Hundred Flowers', through the anti-Rightist Campaign, silenced China's intellectuals, so the Lushan conference, through the purge of Peng Dehuai, silenced Mao's Party colleagues. Zhu De had asked the Standing Committee: 'If people like us don't speak up, then who will dare to talk?' Now he had the Chairman's answer. Never again in Mao's lifetime would a Politburo member openly challenge his policies.

There was one, further, depressing parallel. The anti-Rightist Campaign had claimed half-a-million victims. The campaign against 'Right opportunism', as the movement against critics of the Leap was known, triggered a political blood-letting more than ten times larger: six million people, most of them Party members or low-level officials, were criticised and struggled against for allegedly opposing Mao's policies. In Sichuan, 80 per cent of basic-level cadres were dismissed. As in 1957, local Party secretaries assigned their subordinates quotas of purge-victims to round up. In some areas, whole groups were accused, rather than individuals. Once again, there were numerous suicides. 'Everybody was in a state of danger,' one provincial First Secretary recalled, 'mothers and fathers, husbands and wives, dared not speak to each other.'

Far worse, however, was to come.

The attack on alleged 'Rightists' produced, as it had done two years earlier, a fresh upsurge of Leftism. Mao's efforts of the first half of the year to moderate the Great Leap went abruptly into reverse. To prove that Peng had been wrong, the policies which he had condemned were revived with redoubled vigour. Once again, Mao dreamed aloud of cornucopian production figures: 650 million tons of steel annually by the end of the century, perhaps 1,000 million tons of grain.

This renewed vision of plenty coincided with a further sharp deterioration in the food supply. Floods in the south coupled with drought in the north made the 1959 harvest the worst for several years. The government announced that 270 million tons had been gathered in; the true figure, not disclosed until after Mao's death, was 170 million. Hunger had not ended in China in 1949. Most winters there were still pockets of starvation in one province or another. In 1959, amid the celebrations marking the tenth anniversary of the founding of Red China, hundreds of millions of people went hungry. For the first time since the communist victory, mass famine loomed.

Then relations with the Soviet Union – still, despite mutual tensions, China's only major ally – took an abrupt turn for the worse. The Tibetan revolt that spring, and the subsequent flight of the Dalai Lama, had caused friction with India; and in August, less than ten days after the end of the Lushan plenum, a border clash occurred in which an Indian soldier was killed. Khrushchev, to Mao's fury, adopted an attitude of neutrality. A month later, after returning from a triumphal visit to the United States, which consecrated the policies of peaceful coexistence that China so detested, he flew to Beijing, ostensibly to attend the tenth-anniversary celebrations, but in fact to make one last attempt to get the relationship back on a normal footing. It was doomed from the outset. The Russian leader's decision to abrogate the nuclear co-operation accord; his wooing of American imperialism; his insistence in recent months that Taiwan be recovered only by peaceful means; not to mention the Indian dispute – were all, in Mao's view, so many acts of deliberate betrayal.

For three days, the two sides argued. Nothing was resolved.

The suspicion that had begun to form in Mao's mind back in 1956, that the Soviet leadership was abandoning 'the sword of Leninism', now crystallised into certainty. Just as in Stalin's day, he decided, Russia would always put its own interests first and those of China, second. For Khrushchev, too, the visit marked the final parting of the ways. Mao, he concluded, was bellicose, duplicitous and nationalistic. The basis for a fraternal relationship simply no longer existed.

In February 1960, at a Warsaw Pact meeting in Moscow, the two sides aired their differences over peaceful coexistence before the east European members of the bloc. In April, in an article to mark the ninetieth anniversary of Lenin's birth, which Mao himself revised, the *People's Daily* set out the ideological basis for China's stance. As long as imperialism existed, it said, wars would occur; peaceful competition was a fraud, perpetrated by 'the old revisionists and their modern counterparts'. Both sides began canvassing support among other communist parties. Inevitably, an open clash followed. At the Romanian Party Congress in June, Khrushchev, for the first time, denounced Mao by name as 'an ultra-Leftist, an ultra-dogmatist and a left revisionist' who, like Stalin, had become 'oblivious of any interests but his own, spinning theories detached from the realities of the modern world'. Peng Zhen, representing China, responded in kind. Khrushchev, he said, was behaving in a 'patriarchal, arbitrary and tyrannical' manner in order to impose non-Marxist views.

Three weeks later, the Soviet leadership officially informed China that, with immediate effect, all Russian experts were being withdrawn and all Russian aid was being terminated. Factories were left half-built; blueprints torn up; research projects abandoned. Nearly 1,400 Soviet specialists and their families boarded special trains to Moscow.

If Khrushchev's intention had been to force Mao to back down, as his aides asserted, he had miscalculated grievously. Even those Chinese leaders who harboured private doubts about the communes and Mao's Great Leap Forward strategy now rallied to their defence. Russia's treachery proved that Mao's insistence on China finding its own independent path to communism had been amply justified. Never again would it allow itself to become reliant on a foreign power.

Nevertheless, the Soviet action inflicted enormous economic damage at a time when China was least able to deal with it.

By July it was already clear that the 1960 harvest would be even worse than the previous year's. This was partly attributable to the weather. One hundred million acres, more than a third of all cultivated land, were in the grip of the worst drought for a century. In Shandong, eight of the twelve main rivers were bone-dry. Even the Yellow River fell to a point where men could wade across its lower reaches, something not seen within living memory. Then came floods. Another 50 million acres were devastated. After a winter of hunger, the peasantry had neither the strength to fight back, nor – more crucially – the means to do so because of the disruption caused by the frenzy of the Leap. 'The people are too hungry to work, and pigs are too hungry to stand up,' one young soldier complained. 'The commune members are asking: "Is Chairman Mao going to let us starve?" ' That year, China did starve. All the grain that could be gathered amounted to a paltry 143 million tons. Even on the outskirts of Beijing, people ate bark and weeds. The annual death-rate in the capital, the best-supplied city in China, rose two-and-a-half times. In parts of Anhui, Henan and Sichuan, where Leftist provincial secretaries had promoted the Leap most strongly, a quarter of the population died of hunger. Men sold their wives, if there were buyers – and women were pleased to be bought, because purchase meant survival. Banditry reappeared. Cannibalism was rife, as it had been during the famines of Mao's youth. Peasants ate each other's children, to avoid eating their own.

Detailed figures, showing the extent of the catastrophe nationally, were withheld even from members of the Politburo; only the Standing Committee was informed.

In 1959 and 1960, some 20 million Chinese starved to death, and 15 million fewer children were born, because women were too weak to conceive. Five million more perished from hunger in 1961. It was the worst human disaster ever to befall China – worse even than the great famine of 1870; worse than the Taiping Revolt.*

As Mao contemplated the ruins that his delusions had brought about, he began gloomily to implement his long-delayed promise to retire to the 'second front'. The Great Leap had ended in an apocalyptic failure. His grandiose dream of universal plenty had been metamorphosed into an epic of pure horror. At the end of 1960, he set aside once and for all the idea of making China a great economic power, never to concern himself with it again.

---

* In 1980, Hu Yaobang, the first Chinese leader officially to acknowledge the existence of the famine, put the death-toll at 20 million. That figure was based on contemporary documents compiled for the Standing Committee. Subsequently some Western and Chinese writers have suggested a total death-toll of 40 or even 60 million. Those estimates, however, have been arrived at by taking figures from the worst-hit areas and extrapolating them to the country as a whole, and correlate poorly with the overall demographic trend-lines for the period. In the absence of conclusive proof to the contrary, a figure of 20 to 30 million extra deaths remains by far the most credible. It is, in all conscience, enough.

CHAPTER FOURTEEN

Musings on Immortality

It was to take five years to restore even a semblance of normality after the haemorrhaging away of wealth and population that Mao's stupendous folly had caused.

The first year of recovery – or, as it was officially termed, of 'adjustment, consolidation, improvement and filling out' – was taken up with a desperate scramble to find whatever stopgap measures might serve to keep the People's Republic from falling apart. In Sichuan, and in three other western provinces, as well as Tibet, the PLA had to be called out to suppress armed rebellions, launched by starving peasants. In Henan, the militia, which had been created to give the communes a means of self-defence, went on the rampage, committing armed robberies, rapes and murders. The peasants referred to the militiamen as 'bandit kings', 'tiger bands' and 'beating-up gangs'. There and in Shandong, where the excesses of the Leap had been most stark, government authority in many districts disintegrated altogether. Liu Shaoqi warned that China was facing a descent into anarchy, similar to that which the Soviet Union had experienced during the civil war in the early 1920s.

To reduce the pressure on urban food supplies, 25 million city-dwellers were forced to move to the countryside – a feat that Mao described admiringly as 'equivalent to deporting the population of a medium-sized country like Belgium'. Even then, massive grain imports were needed to feed those who remained. In 1961, nearly six million tons of wheat were purchased abroad, mostly from

Australia and Canada, some even from the United States, laundered through Europe. Imports would remain at that level into the 1970s.

Alongside these punctual steps, Liu and his colleagues began to re-examine the false assumptions on which the Great Leap had rested.

The difficulty, as always, was Mao.

His retirement to the 'second front' had not meant relinquishing power, merely exercising it in a different manner. Whereas before, the Chairman had set the pace and everyone else had followed, now he expected the other members of the Politburo Standing Committee to take the lead – but only in ways that were consonant with his own thinking. Peng Dehuai had learned to his cost that Mao alone was permitted to question the policies he had framed. Now Liu and Deng Xiaoping, in their turn, discovered the perils of being on the 'first front'. 'Which emperor took this decision?' Mao demanded in March 1961, after Deng had proposed (without first securing his agreement) that agricultural policy should be handled differently in the north and the south.

The result was extreme caution. Rethinking the 'newborn things' of the Great Leap Forward – the communes, the collective mess halls, the system of free supply – was resolutely avoided until it became clear which way the Chairman's own mind was working. Thus, in March 1961, the Central Committee strongly reaffirmed the value of communal eating arrangements. But when, a month later, Mao endorsed a report stating that the mess halls had become 'an impediment to developing production and a cancer in relations between the Party and the masses', his colleagues instantly changed course. Within days, the Chairman's new line was being echoed by Liu Shaoqi, then making an inspection tour of Hunan; by Zhou Enlai, visiting Hebei; followed in quick succession by Deng Xiaoping, Peng Zhen and Zhu De. The repercussions were even felt in the labour camps, where China's prison population was set to making aluminium kitchen utensils, to replace the iron ones smelted down in the backyard steel campaign, so that peasant households might once more have the means to cook for themselves now that collective catering was at an end.

In June, the supply system disappeared as well. The amount of land that could be allocated for private plots was increased. The principle of 'more pay for more work' was restored, along with the Leninist slogan, 'He who does not work shall not eat' – a grim warning indeed at a time of mass starvation. Rural fairs and markets, which had been banned during the Leap, were authorised again, and pedlars and street-traders reappeared.

Finally, in September, Mao made one last concession.

During the summer, with the leadership's approval, many communes had been subdivided to about a half, or a third, of their original size, in an attempt to make them less unwieldy. Now Mao informed his colleagues that he had decided that the basic management unit, which assigned each household its labour and shared out the fruits of the harvest, should also be made smaller, reverting from the 'brigade', grouping several villages, to the 'production team', equivalent to the original one-village co-operatives set up five or six years before. The aim was to restore the peasants' motivation by linking their rewards directly to their own efforts and those of their neighbours, rather than making them pool their resources with families from other communities.

It was a far cry from the principles Mao had set out in 1958. Then he had proclaimed that the superiority of the communes was that they were 'first, big; and second, publicly owned'. Now the best he could hope for was that the concept of the commune might be preserved against the onslaughts of famine and nationwide demoralisation.

Once again, however, the Chairman's pre-emptive retreat turned out to be not enough.

Part of the problem was that there had been so many twists and turns in the recent past that local cadres were reluctant to change course, even if the Politburo ordered them to, lest the wind shift yet again and they find themselves being denounced as Rightists.

Others – not only at the local level but including Politburo radicals like Kang Sheng; Ke Qingshi in Shanghai; and the Sichuan leader, Li Jingquan – were so closely identified with Leftist policies that any overt repudiation of the Great Leap would leave them politically exposed. Accordingly, they dragged their feet – Li Jingquan even to the point of defending the mess halls after Mao himself had condemned them.

Both groups, moreover, noted that the Chairman remained deeply ambivalent about the change in direction that events had imposed. Not only did he refuse to admit that the previous policies had been mistaken – the furthest he would go was to say that no one was immune from error – but the new plans which were worked out that year to revive commerce and industry, and to encourage new efforts in science, education, literature and the arts, all contained inherent ambiguities (and had to, in order to obtain Mao's approval), allowing them to be given either a radical or a moderate interpretation, depending on the prevailing political wind. Zhou Enlai summed up the unstable compromise on which the new policies were based by urging officials 'on the one hand to wage class struggle, on the other to consolidate the united front' – a squaring of the ideological circle which he knew quite well was impossible.

In these circumstances, Mao's colleagues continued to adhere rigorously to the parameters the Chairman had laid down.

The steel and coal targets were cut back to levels which, for the first time since 1957, had some connection with reality. Industrial workers were permitted bonuses again, and factory managers given back their old powers. Deng, Liu and the Foreign Minister, Chen Yi (though not the ever-prudent Zhou Enlai) all elaborated on Mao's tacit admission that mistakes had been made – with both Deng and Liu quoting the peasants in areas they had visited as saying the famine was due '30 per cent to natural calamities, 70 per cent to human failings'. But no one said what the mistakes were, and still less who had made them.

The impasse, therefore, continued.

For the rest of the autumn, Mao, as befitted his new role on the 'second front', remained silent. His colleagues urged greater realism, but in such equivocal terms that no one was convinced. Lower-level officials held their fire, awaiting clearer signals.

The result was that, by December, there was still no sign of the economy bottoming out. In Anhui and other hard-hit provinces, cadres began experimenting with so-called 'household responsibility systems', under which land was contracted out to families to farm individually. Zhu De, on a visit to his native Sichuan, found cases of peasants abandoning the communes to grow crops on their own, and asked whether, in the current extremity, such expedients should not be officially approved, since 'even if you don't write it in, it will happen anyway'.

To Mao, that raised the spectre of collectivisation in the countryside unravelling altogether.

Accordingly, in January 1962, he summoned a Central Committee work conference in Beijing, to be attended not just by the two or three hundred senior officials normally present at such gatherings, but by more than 7,000 cadres, drawn from county and commune Party committees all over China.

The idea behind this exceptional meeting was that it should mark a turning-point. But where Mao wanted the conference to call a halt to the erosion of the socialist values, Liu Shaoqi and the other 'first front' leaders saw it as a moment of truth, when, at long last, lessons could be drawn from past errors and the Party would make a fresh start on the basis of consensus policies which the local cadres in attendance would convey directly and convincingly to the grass roots.

Liu set the tone with a report which lavished fulsome praise on Mao's correct guidance 'at every critical moment' before coming abruptly to the nub of the matter. 'It is necessary to point out', he acknowledged, 'that the primary responsibility for the shortcomings and errors in our work in these past few years lies with the Party Centre.' That provoked demands from the floor for a precise attribution of blame. Neither Liu, nor anyone else, was prepared to commit himself in open session. But a few days later, in committee, the north China leader, Peng Zhen, was more forthright. The Party Centre, he said, included Mao, Liu Shaoqi and the rest of the Politburo Standing Committee. To the extent that they were responsible, they should share the blame. Mao himself, Peng went on, was not immune from mistakes. It was he who had spoken of making the transition to communism in 'three or five years', and who had been behind the setting-up of the now abandoned mess halls. Even if the Chairman had been 'only one-thousandth part mistaken', it would be 'odious if he did not make a self-criticism'.

Ten days later, Mao gave his response:

> Any mistakes that the Centre has made ought to be my direct responsibility, and I also have an indirect share of the blame because I am the Chairman of the Central Committee. I don't want other people to shirk their responsibility. There are some other comrades who also bear responsibility, but the person primarily responsible should be me.

As a 'self-criticism', this was perfunctory in the extreme. Not only did Mao fail to acknowledge any personal errors of judgement, but there was no hint of an apology, no expression of remorse for the millions who had died, no admission of the true extent of the calamity that his policies had brought about. Instead, he sought to relativise his fault, insisting that at all levels of the leadership 'everyone has his share of responsibility', and urging others to face their mistakes, too.

> Those of you who ... are afraid of taking responsibility, who do not allow people to speak, who think you are tigers, and that nobody will dare to touch your arse – whoever has this attitude, 10 out of 10 of you will fail. People will talk anyway. You think that nobody will really dare to touch the arses of tigers like you? They damn well will!

Minimal though it was, Mao's acknowledgement of liability electrified the meeting. He did not need to say more: in a Party which had learned to regard him as infallible, it was extraordinary enough for him to admit to any failings at all.

For the next week, tiger after tiger, from Zhou Enlai and Deng Xiaoping down, ritually flagellated themselves with detailed confessions of error. When the meeting ended, on February 7, there was a new sense, in the Politburo and among the regional delegations, that a page had been turned, and that it would at last be possible to give effect to the moderate, pragmatic policies that had evolved over the previous year.

For Mao, the '7,000-cadre big conference', as it was afterwards known, had been a thoroughly disagreeable experience. He had not enjoyed criticising himself (while recognising that it was essential in order to draw a line under the past). He had been dismayed by the hostility shown by grass-roots delegates to Great Leap Forward policies, and by demands from the hall for an explanation of why the disaster had occurred. 'They complain all day long and watch plays at night, they eat three full meals a day – and fart; that's what Marxism-Leninism means to them,' he grumbled. He had relished even less the strictures of Peng Zhen – though the changed circumstances resulting from three years of famine and economic ruin meant that he could no longer respond as he had in the case of Peng Dehuai. The meeting had produced, too, a worrying undertow of support for the disgraced marshal's rehabilitation, now that his critique of the Leap had proved so well justified. Liu Shaoqi, who knew his own position would be at risk if Peng were vindicated, had vigorously squashed any suggestion that he be allowed to return, but in such a way as to let the audience understand that Peng's criticisms had been correct – his errors had been 'colluding with Russia' and 'plotting against the Party leadership'.

Liu's own speech to the conference had troubled Mao as well.

While dutifully reciting the mantra that 'since 1958, our successes are primary, shortcomings are secondary', he had acknowledged, as Mao never would, that in parts of the country the reverse had been true, and had put the ratio of achievement to failure nationally not at 9:1, as Mao did, but at 7:3.

More than any of this, however, the Chairman was concerned that the meeting had done nothing to reassert basic socialist truths. 'If our country does not establish a socialist economy,' he had warned the delegates, 'we shall become . . . like Yugoslavia, which is actually a bourgeois country.' There had been no response. Amid economic collapse, preserving socialist shibboleths was not uppermost in most delegates' minds.

Accordingly, when the meeting ended, Mao withdrew to Hangzhou, where he spent the spring and early summer, leaving, for the first time, the triumvirate of Liu Shaoqi, Zhou Enlai and Deng Xiaoping in sole charge of Party and state matters.

In part, Mao was sulking: he had no wish to be involved in policies of which, deep down, he disapproved. In part, he was testing the waters: putting his colleagues in control on their own would show what stuff they were made of. But there was also a parallel with Mao's behaviour much earlier in his political career, when in the 1920s and '30s, at critical moments, he had withdrawn, voluntarily or involuntarily, to await more propitious circumstances in which to effect his return.

He did not have to wait long.

In March, he sent his personal secretary, Tian Jiaying, to his home village of Shaoshan to see at first hand how the peasants were faring. Tian was astonished to find that all they wanted to talk about was the 'household responsibility system', of which both he and Mao strongly disapproved. Since collectivisation in 1955, they explained, the harvest had declined in each successive year. By farming on their own, they could reverse that trend. By May, Tian had been converted: family farming might be politically incorrect, but, in the desperate straits in which China found itself, it was the best way to increase production and it was what the peasants wanted. Chen Yun and Liu Shaoqi concurred. At a meeting of the Secretariat in June, Deng Xiaoping quoted a Sichuanese proverb: 'It doesn't matter if the cat is black or white; so long as it catches the mouse, it is a good cat.' Deng Zihui, the agricultural supremo who had clashed with Mao over the setting-up of co-operatives, drew up a national programme for putting the 'responsibility system' into effect. In many areas, the peasants had already gone ahead anyway. That summer, 20 per cent of China's fields were being farmed on an individual basis.

When Tian informed Mao of his findings, the Chairman's response echoed his words to Deng Zihui, seven years earlier: 'The peasants want freedom; but we want socialism.' There were times, he told Tian drily, when 'we cannot completely heed the masses', and this was one of them.

For a few weeks longer, Mao held his fire. The situation in the countryside was still too critical for even him to risk rocking the boat. But at the beginning of July, when it became clear that the summer harvest would be better than in either of the previous two years – and that, therefore, agriculture was recovering without the ideological compromises that 'responsibility systems' would entail – he intervened decisively. Without bothering to inform the 'first front' leaders on the Politburo Standing Committee, he returned to Beijing, where he ordered Chen Boda, his former political secretary in Yan'an, now a Politburo alternate and a leading radical, to draw up a Central Committee resolution on strengthening the collective economy. As word leaked out that the Chairman was back, and on the warpath again, his colleagues ran for cover.

Deng Xiaoping issued a panicky instruction for the 'black cat, white cat' phrase to be deleted from the written texts of his speeches. Chen Yun left on sick leave, where he would languish for the next fifteen years, returning to work only after Mao's death. Liu Shaoqi got away with criticising himself for failing to prevent the other leaders' mistakes. Even the ultra-cautious Zhou Enlai was upbraided for falling prey to pessimism. 'We've been discussing difficulties and darkness for two years now,' Mao fumed. 'It's become a crime to look on the bright side.'

Private farming, however, was not the Chairman's only grievance. He was also unhappy with the conciliatory stance Liu had adopted towards the United States and the Soviet Union. This had been prompted by a paper drawn up by Wang Jiaxiang, the Returned

Student who, in the late 1930s, had helped to convince Stalin of
Mao's claims to the leadership, and now headed the Party's
International Liaison Department. At a time of acute internal strain,
Wang had argued, China should try as much as possible to avoid
international complications. Liu and Deng agreed. The spring
brought faint signs of an easing of tension with India and the Soviet
Union, and in June an understanding was reached with the
Americans to avoid renewed conflict over Taiwan.

To Mao, all this oozed betrayal.

On the very first occasion that he had ceded control to the men
he had hand-picked to lead China when he himself passed on,
they had shown themselves, on two crucial issues – opposing imperialism and 'its running dog, revisionism', abroad; and preventing
capitalism at home – at best, capable of massive misjudgements; at
worst, guilty of unprincipled compromises for short-term practical
ends.

The Chairman launched his counter-attack at the annual
summer work conference at Beidaihe. The 'responsibility systems',
he declared, were incompatible with the collective economy.
The Party, therefore, faced a stark choice: 'Are we going to take
the socialist road or the capitalist road? Do we want rural co-
operativisation or don't we?' It was the same tactic that he had
employed at Lushan, when he had confronted the Central
Committee with an equally Manichaean choice between Peng
Dehuai and himself. With Mao, there was never a middle road.

Having thus transferred the question of farming practices from
the economic to the political arena, Mao raised again, as he had in
January, the example of Yugoslavia as a country which had
'changed colour' by abandoning its socialist economy. Class
struggle, he reminded his audience, continued under socialism, and,
as developments in the Soviet Union had shown, 'the capitalist class
can be reborn'. The same thing, he implied, might one day happen
in China.

A month later, at the Central Committee's Tenth Plenum, Mao
reverted to those themes:

In our country, we must . . . admit the possibility of the restoration
of reactionary classes. We must raise our vigilance and properly
educate our youth . . . Otherwise, a country like ours may yet move
towards its opposite. Therefore, from now on, we must talk about this

every year, every month, every day . . . so that we have a more
enlightened Marxist-Leninist line on the problem.

Mao added, reassuringly, that there was to be no repetition of
what had happened at Lushan, when 'all [Peng Dehuai's] mother-
fucking messed up the conference and practical work was affected'.
This time, after tens of millions of famine deaths, not even he was
willing to put class struggle in a position where it might again abort
economic recovery. None the less, he declared, right-opportunism,
or 'Chinese revisionism', as he now called it, existed 'within the
country and within the Party', and had to be combated.

So ended Liu Shaoqi's brief effort to put Chinese policy on a
more rational basis, guided not by class struggle but by economic
imperatives.

No one in the Politburo attempted to rein in Mao's pyromaniac
ideological urges, any more than they had tried to curb his powers
at the moment of his greatest weakness, at the '7,000-cadre big
conference', the previous January. As a result, the notion that a
bourgeoisie might emerge within the Party, which Mao had first
raised at Lushan in August 1959, was once again placed centre
stage, now explicitly linked to a rejection of degenerate Soviet
communism in a simple, four-character slogan: *Fan xiu, fang xiu* –
'Oppose revisionism (abroad), prevent revisionism (at home)'. That
fatal nexus would inform Mao's thinking, and dominate the politics
of China, for the last fourteen years of his life.

The first outward sign of the new Leftist spin that Mao had so
effortlessly imparted to Chinese policy-making in the autumn of
1962 came in the Himalayas. Armed clashes had broken out in
July after Indian troops began establishing checkpoints along the
disputed border between Tibet and India's North-east Frontier
Agency. In October, after Nehru had spoken incautiously of 'freeing
occupied Indian territory', Mao decided the time had come to
teach 'that representative of the reactionary national bourgeoisie'
a lesson. In a series of engagements, involving some 30,000 Chinese
troops, Indian units were decisively defeated, and by the time the
Chinese declared a unilateral ceasefire, on November 21, Nehru
had been compelled to make a humiliating appeal for help to
the West.

In the early stages of the conflict, Khrushchev had been more supportive than in China's last spat with India, in 1959. But he was then embroiled in a crisis of his own, in Cuba, where the CIA was about to discover the emplacement of Soviet missiles, and he needed Chinese support. Once the Cuban débâcle was behind him, the Soviet leader reverted to his more usual, pro-Indian stance – causing Mao's disgust to redouble, not only at Khrushchev's betrayal of socialist solidarity but at the ill-judged mixture of adventurism and capitulation with which he had affronted the Americans. Within days, Sino-Soviet polemics, which had been muted since the Russians had excommunicated Albania at the end of 1961, resumed in full flood, culminating, a year later, in a series of nine immensely long open letters – known as 'The Polemic on the General Line of the International Communist Movement' – in which, for the first time, the Chinese attacked the Soviet Party by name (and the Russians responded in kind).

Renewed militancy abroad was matched by militancy at home.

The decision to ban private farming led, in the winter of 1962, to a number of provincial initiatives which were soon afterwards brought together, with Mao's personal imprimatur, under the name, the Socialist Education Movement. Its *raison d'être* was simple. If the peasantry, and the local cadres who led them, were still hankering after capitalism in the form of 'responsibility systems', they needed to relearn the virtues of the collective economy and the superiority of socialism.

In its initial form, the movement was directed against cadre corruption, and such anti-socialist behaviour as arranged marriages, geomancy, sorcery, Buddhist and Daoist rites, and ancestor-worship. Meetings were held at which older commune members were encouraged to 'speak bitterness', dilating on the miseries of the old society in order to persuade younger peasants that, even in times of famine, life under the communists was preferable. Party propagandists created a new role model, a PLA soldier named Lei Feng, who had spent his military career washing his comrades' bedding, helping the cooks to clean cabbages and old ladies to cross roads, under the motto, 'It's glorious to be a nameless hero', before dying selflessly for the good of the revolutionary cause. Lei was the quintessential rustless screw, whose devotion, unswerving loyalty and obedience to Mao and to the Party was catalogued in a diary of nauseating servility:

I felt particularly happy this morning when I got up, because last night I had dreamed of our great leader, Chairman Mao. And it so happens that today is the Party's 40th anniversary. Today I have so much to tell the Party, so much gratitude to the Party . . . I am like a toddler, and the Party is like my mother who helps me, leads me, and teaches me to walk . . . My beloved Party, my loving mother, I am always your loyal son.

But the movement had to have a harder edge than merely 'speaking bitterness' and emulating Lei Feng. At a Central Committee work conference in February 1963, Mao asserted that the only way to prevent revisionism was by class struggle. 'Once [this] has been grasped,' he declared, 'everything will be solved.' Accordingly it was agreed that a nationwide campaign should be launched to carry out 'Four Clean-ups' in the countryside (to check production team accounts, granaries, housing, and the allocation of work-points), and 'Five Antis' in the towns (against embezzlement, graft, speculation, extravagance and red tape). Three months later, another work conference at Hangzhou drew up a formal programme for the movement, in which Mao depicted in apocalyptic terms what was at stake if the slide towards revisionism were not stopped:

> If things were allowed to go on this way, the day would not be too far off – a few years, over 10 years, or a few decades at the most – when the resurgence of a nationwide counter-revolution becomes inevitable. It would then be a certainty that the Party of Marxism-Leninism would turn into a party of revisionism, of fascism. The whole of China would then change colour . . . The Socialist Education Movement is . . . a struggle that calls for the re-education of man . . . [and] for a confrontation with the forces of feudalism and capitalism that are now feverishly attacking us. We must nip their counter-revolution in the bud!

After this call to arms, Mao once more retired to the sidelines to see how the 'first front' leaders would cope with the new mission he had entrusted to them.

It was a delicate assignment. Rural capitalism was to be suppressed, but rural markets and private plots, judged essential for economic recovery, encouraged. Mass criticism, to cleanse corrupt cadres, was to be promoted, but without any deleterious effect on production.

As the movement progressed, those issues paled into insignificance against the sheer scale of the task the Party leaders found they faced. Initially Mao had employed his usual rule of thumb to suggest that perhaps 5 per cent of the rural population had 'problems' that needed correcting. By the spring of 1964, both he and Liu Shaoqi were talking in terms of a third of rural production teams being controlled by hostile forces. Not only was cadre corruption almost universal, but so many grass-roots officials had been purged in one political campaign or another in the course of the preceding ten years that there were no more 'clean' local leaders to draw on. Outside cadres, seconded to oversee the movement, found themselves having to replace one group of flawed officials with another equally dubious group because no one else was available.

To deal with that situation, Liu Shaoqi unleashed, in September 1964, the most sweeping purge of rural Party organisations ever undertaken in China.

One-and-a-half million cadres were mobilised, organised into work teams of 10,000 people or, in some cases, several tens of thousands, and despatched to selected counties for a minimum of six months, to act like a human wave, cleansing leadership groups from the village level up. The targets of the campaign were expanded to include ideology, politics and organisation, as well as economic offences. Violence was universal. Even in the initial moderate stages, 2,000 people died in one trial group of counties in Hubei, while in Guangdong, 500 committed suicide. Later, in the words of one lowly Party cadre, 'all hell broke loose'. The Hubei First Secretary, Wang Renzhong, one of Mao's favourite provincial leaders, urged a 'violent revolutionary storm', in which most lower-level Party branches would collapse and power would be temporarily ceded to poor peasant associations. Liu Shaoqi himself spoke of the upheaval lasting five or six years.

It was a prospect which should have entranced Mao, as an apostle of class violence. As 1964 drew to a close, he and Liu seemed closer in their thinking than at almost any time since the younger man had become Mao's heir apparent. But, as so often, appearances were misleading.

Mao's original decision in 1952 to withdraw to the 'second front' had been taken partly in order that he might escape the routine duties of Head of State, which he detested, and concentrate on strategic issues; and partly to give his putative successors experience in running the Party and state while he was still there to guide them. Events in the Soviet Union soon made this second reason primary. Malenkov, Mao said later, had failed to endure because Stalin had never allowed him to exercise real power in his lifetime. For that reason, he explained, 'I wanted [Liu Shaoqi and the others] to have their prestige established before I died.'

The Soviet Union's bad example did not end there. Khrushchev, in Mao's eyes, turned out to be an even less worthy candidate to continue the revolutionary cause, discarding not only 'the sword of Stalin' but 'the sword of Lenin' as well. Under his leadership, the Soviet Union became a revisionist state, practising capitalism. The inheritance of Marx and Lenin had been squandered – all because of Stalin's failure to groom revolutionary successors to carry on his cause.

Up till 1961, Mao seems to have been in no doubt that Liu Shaoqi was the right choice to act as steward of his own revolutionary legacy. Liu was organisation personified, a remote, intimidating man, with no real friends, no outside interests and little sense of humour, whose phenomenal energy was channelled in its entirety into the service of the Party – which in practice meant making possible whatever it was that Mao wanted to happen. He was exacting with himself and his family; eschewed privilege of any kind; and cultivated a puritanical public persona which spoke of eighteen-hour workdays and a code of conduct so absolute that when he found out he was being paid an extra one yuan (at the time, about 30 pence) a day because he worked after midnight, he insisted on reimbursing every last penny through deductions from his salary.

When, in September of that year, Mao told Field Marshal Montgomery that Liu was his designated successor, it was made known widely among the upper echelons of the Party, apparently to prepare the ground for his withdrawal, at the next Party Congress, to become honorary Party Chairman, as foreshadowed by the 1958 constitution.

Each May Day and National Day, Liu's portrait was printed in the *People's Daily*, side by side with Mao's, and of equal size. His writings were studied alongside Mao's (as they had been during the Yan'an Rectification Campaign twenty years before), and at the

Chairman's suggestion, work started on preparing an edition of his 'Selected Works', an honour up till then accorded only to Mao himself. One of Liu's essays from the 1930s, entitled 'How to be a Good Communist', was reissued as a pamphlet in an edition of 18 million copies.

This did not mean there were no frictions between them. Unlike the pliant Zhou Enlai, who made a religion of loyalty to Mao, or the sycophantic Lin Biao, Liu had a mind of his own (which was what had led the Chairman to choose him as his deputy in the first place). At times – as in 1947, when Mao reproached him for excessive Leftism in the land reform movement; or in 1953, when he sought to use Gao Gang to curb Liu's independence – Liu's tendency to go his own way irritated him. But there was nothing to suggest that a breach was in the offing.

That began to change in the spring of 1962.

Liu's criticisms of the Great Leap Forward at the '7,000-cadre big conference' were one factor. Far more important was his lack of steadiness in the five months of Mao's withdrawal. If Liu lost his nerve so easily when the economy failed to respond – authorising emergency measures that involved a sell-out of fundamental communist values – how could he be trusted to defend Mao's policies when the Chairman was no longer around? It was as though, by withdrawing, he had given Liu enough rope to hang himself, and his heir apparent had promptly obliged. For the next two years, Mao would reserve judgement, but his faith in the younger man had been shaken.

The plan for him to retire as Honorary Party Chairman was never heard of again. Instead in a poem the following January, as he entered his seventieth year, he celebrated anew his implacable determination to move China along his chosen path:

> *So many deeds cry out to be done,*
> *And always urgently;*
> *The world rolls on,*
> *Time presses.*
> *Ten thousand years are too long,*
> *Seize the day, seize the hour!*
> *The Four Seas are rising, clouds and waters raging,*
> *The Five Continents are rocking, wind and thunder roaring,*
> *Away with all pests!*
> *Our force is irresistible.*

The 'pests' were the Khrushchevite revisionists, with perhaps just a sideways glance at revisionists nearer home. But the subtext was Mao's realisation that he would have to lead from the front himself, because he could rely on no one else to do so in his place.

Mao's doubts about Liu showed up in other ways, too.

Starting from the summer of 1962, he began to develop alternative instruments of power, to act as a counterweight to the Party machine, controlled by Liu, as first Party Vice-Chairman; Deng Xiaoping, as General Secretary; and Deng's deputy, Peng Zhen.

That year, his wife, Jiang Qing, who had been kept away from the limelight since their marriage in Yan'an, twenty-five years before, began for the first time to play a public role. In September, her picture appeared on the front page of the *People's Daily* when Mao received President Sukarno of Indonesia. Three months later, when the Chairman triggered another onslaught against one of his favourite targets, China's intellectuals – this time on the pretext of eliminating revisionism from the nation's cultural life – Jiang Qing was ready and waiting to take up the cudgels on his behalf. Their personal relationship had ended long before. But politically she was his to command; her loyalty was beyond question; and she wanted nothing more in life than to prove her usefulness to him. As she put it, many years later: 'I was Chairman Mao's dog. Whoever he told me to bite, I bit.' From April 1963 onwards, with Mao's encouragement and discreet help from Zhou Enlai, she began to nip the heels of Liu's cultural commissars and of the playwrights and film-makers, historians and philosophers, poets and painters that they favoured, until the whole of China's intellectual life took on the same, monotonous Maoist coloration as the 'revolutionary model operas' which she eagerly promoted.

Zhou Enlai himself, ever anxious to defend his corner of the Chairman's affections against Liu's depredations, became another indispensable part of Mao's new inner circle. The Shanghai Party leaders, under Ke Qingshi and his protégé, Zhang Chunqiao, served as a radical ginger group to promote policies of which the more conservative Beijing leaders disapproved. Mao's amanuensis, Chen Boda, took on a higher profile. So did Kang Sheng, who became the Chairman's informant on Deng Xiaoping's Secretariat. He soon showed that he had not forgotten his old tradecraft as secret police chief in Yan'an by setting up a 'Special Case Group' to investigate what he claimed was a covert attempt to promote the rehabilitation of Gao Gang. In a chilling foretaste of the tactics Kang would use against Mao's enemies in the great upheavals that lay ahead, thousands of people were interrogated and a senior vice-premier purged on the sole evidence of an unpublished historical novel, set in Gao Gang's old base area in Shensi, one of whose leading characters was said to resemble him.

But the most important of Mao's placemen was Lin Biao, who, since his appointment in 1959, had worked single-mindedly to transform the PLA into the acme of ideological rectitude, the incarnation of Mao's view that men were more important than weapons, where politics was always 'the supreme commander, the soul and guarantor of all work', and Mao Zedong Thought was 'the highest peak in today's world . . . [and] the apex of contemporary thought'. It was Lin who published the main article in the *People's Daily*, eulogising the fourth volume of Mao's *Selected Works*, when it appeared in 1960; and Lin, a year later, who suggested that a handy compendium of the Chairman's aphorisms be compiled for soldiers to learn by heart, a proposal which led, in 1964, to the appearance of the 'Little Red Book' – the future bible of Chinese youth, talisman and touchstone of Mao's personality cult. Soon afterwards, in an attempt to revive the egalitarian simplicity of the early days of the Red Army, ranks and insignia were abolished; officers could be distinguished from other ranks only by the four pockets on their jackets, where ordinary soldiers had two. By then, the PLA was being held up as a model for the entire nation, exemplifying boundless loyalty, devotion and self-sacrifice.

None of Mao's moves up to the spring of 1964 indicated any definite conclusion about Liu's fitness as a successor. He continued to bracket Liu's name with his own as the two principal representatives of 'Chinese Marxism-Leninism'.

But the following summer, his doubts hardened.

One factor was evidently the realisation that, despite their apparent unity of views, Liu's aims in the Socialist Education Movement were different from his own. Deng Xiaoping told a Sri Lankan diplomat in February 1964 that he hoped Mao would not notice what they were doing because if he did he would surely disapprove. Liu wanted to use the movement to make the Party in the rural areas a reliable, disciplined instrument to enforce orthodox Marxist-Leninist economic policies. Mao wanted to combat revisionism by unleashing the energies of the masses.

As Mao took stock of this divergence, he was reminded of Liu's behaviour in the first half of 1962, and began to reflect anew on some of the things his heir apparent had said at that time, including a remark to the '7,000-cadre big conference' about Mao's 'three Red banners' – the Party's general line; the Great Leap Forward; and the communes. 'We will continue the struggle to uphold the three banners,' Liu had affirmed, 'but there are still some issues that are not clear. We will sum up experience again in five or ten years' time. Then we may be able to resolve them.' At a time when Mao was deeply involved in the Chinese Party's polemic with Moscow, it was a small step to start wondering whether Liu's words contained an implicit threat to reverse China's policies after his death, as Khrushchev had done after Stalin. Mao remembered something else, too. In 1959, Kang Sheng had said that Stalin had erred, not by repressing 'counter-revolutionaries' too harshly but by not repressing them harshly enough. It was his failure to 'dig out' people like Khrushchev that had allowed them to discredit him. Again, the question was posed: would Mao make the same mistake?

By July 1964, these ideas had crystallised to a point where Mao approved a passage, in the ninth and last of the Chinese 'open letters' to the Soviet Party, which referred specifically to the issue of succession:

> In the final analysis, the question of training successors for the revol-
> utionary cause of the proletariat is one of whether or not . . . the
> leadership of our Party and state will remain in the hands of prole-
> tarian revolutionaries, whether or not our descendants will continue
> to march along the correct road laid down by Marxism-Leninism, or,
> in other words, whether or not we can successfully prevent the emer-
> gence of Khrushchev's revisionism in China . . . It is an extremely
> important question, a matter of life and death for our Party and our
> country.

In retrospect, those lines offer a startling insight into the way Mao's mind was working. At the time, however, none of his colleagues saw anything untoward. Nor, apparently, did they pay attention to a subsequent paragraph, which spoke of successors being formed through mass struggle and tempered in 'great revolutionary storms'.

Then, in October, came the overthrow of Khrushchev, accused by his successors of ruling by personal whim and imposing

'hare-brained schemes' on the long-suffering Russian people.
Whether Mao drew a conscious parallel between his old adversary's
comeuppance and the charges that could be made regarding his
own style of rule is unclear. But, given the differences he now
discerned between Liu Shaoqi's aims and his own, it must at the very
least have made him feel vulnerable. A month later, Khrushchev's
successors rebuffed a Chinese attempt to renew the dialogue
between them, providing final confirmation that the Sino-Soviet
schism was irrevocable and the world communist movement
shattered into two unequal and irreconcilable halves.

Mao's claim to revolutionary immortality would now rest, more
than ever, on the forging of a distinctive Chinese way from which
true revolutionaries everywhere would draw their inspiration. This
had been implicit in the nine 'open letters', which had been written
on the basis that the fount of revolutionary knowledge – 'Mekka',
as Sneevliet had called it, forty years earlier – had been transferred
from Moscow to Beijing. As 1964 drew to a close, it became, for
Mao, explicit – the ultimate goal to which he would devote the final
years of his life.

His aim was no longer to make China rich. That was Liu Shaoqi's
logic.

Revolutionary zeal was in inverse proportion to affluence. 'Asia
is more progressive politically than Britain and the United States,
because Asia's living standards are much lower,' he had written
some years earlier. 'Those who are poor want revolution . . . [In
future] we countries in the East will become rich. When the
[Western countries'] living standards fall, their people will become
progressive.' The unstated corollary, Mao now realised, was that if
China became prosperous it would cease to be revolutionary. It was
politically impossible to say so outright – few Chinese would will-
ingly embrace continued penury in pursuit of abstract ideological
goals – but in practice, in the choice between affluence and revolution, Mao came down on revolution's side.

To make China a realm of 'Red virtue', in which class struggle
would transmute human consciousness, generating a revolutionary
continuum that would shine out like a beacon to the peoples of the
world, Liu, and those who thought like him, together with the orthodoxy they represented, would have to be swept aside.

In this illuminated frame of mind, Mao attended a series of top-
level leadership meetings in late November and December, during

which his behaviour was even more wilful and eccentric than usual.

On November 26, while discussing long-term defence planning, he suddenly expostulated: 'you [Liu] are first deputy chairman, but something unexpected could happen at any time. Otherwise, once I die, you may not succeed. So let's change over now. You be Chairman. You be the First Emperor.' Liu cautiously declined, unfazed by Mao's grumbling that he no longer had the strength for the job and no one listened to him any more. Two weeks later, the Chairman spoke blackly of a capitalist class emerging within the Party and 'drinking the blood of the workers'. On that occasion, the phrase, 'leaders taking the capitalist road', was used for the first time. Then, on December 20, he again spoke of Liu, rather than himself, being in charge. This time he argued that the Socialist Education Movement would have to be refocused – no longer aimed at corrupt cadres and peculating peasants, but at extirpating from the Party hierarchy, through the cleansing fire of mass struggle, all trace of revisionist thought. The 'wolves', the 'power-holders', would have to be dealt with first, Mao warned menacingly; the 'foxes' – the petty offenders – could be handled later.

Unusually, Liu held his ground. He agreed with Mao that some provincial Party committees had become 'rotten', and that the 'backstage Party bosses' of corrupt officials should be targeted as a priority. But he made clear that he felt this should be done within the context of a movement whose principal focus remained the elimination of corrupt practices, rather than an ideological onslaught against 'revisionism'.

Mao showed his displeasure at a banquet in the Great Hall of the People to celebrate his seventy-first birthday, on December 26, when, without naming names, he charged that Liu's views were non-Marxist, and that Deng was running the Party Secretariat as an 'independent kingdom'. Two days later, in a still more extraordinary outburst – reminiscent of his threat, five years earlier, to go to the hills and found a new Red Army if his colleagues sided with Peng Dehuai – he held up a copy of the Party constitution, and after stating icily that he had as much right to express an opinion as any other Party member, implied that Deng was attempting to stop him attending leadership meetings and Liu was trying to prevent him from speaking. No less ominously, he recalled the dispute he had had with Liu and the rest of the Standing Committee in 1962 over 'responsibility systems'. That had been 'a kind of class struggle', Mao declared. Now, a new struggle was looming, whose main task would be 'to rectify the power holders within the Party taking the capitalist road'.

That incendiary phrase was included in new guidelines for the movement issued in mid-January. There was one slight change of wording: instead of 'power-holders', the term, 'persons in authority', was used. In the original draft it was explicitly specified that such renegade communists might be found even in the Central Committee. But Zhou Enlai, who evidently had a shrewd idea of how the Chairman's mind was working, managed to get that modified to 'Central Committee departments'.

Liu Shaoqi himself, and most of the rest of the leadership, put down his remarks as the rumblings of a cantankerous old man, an ageing megalith, still capable of striking sparks, but increasingly imprisoned by the revolutionary dreams of his past. The crisis seemed to blow over. But Liu's fate had been sealed. All that remained was for Mao to find an appropriate means to dispose of him.

CHAPTER FIFTEEN

Cataclysm

In February 1965, the Chairman despatched Jiang Qing to Shanghai. Her mission was to lay the ideological powder-trail which, at the opportune moment, he would light, triggering the tortuous events that would plunge China into the fiery chaos of the Great Proletarian Cultural Revolution.

The device which Mao chose to provoke the coming storm had originated six years earlier in his call to Party members to emulate the Ming bureaucrat, Hai Rui. Peng Dehuai had taken him too literally, and was purged for his pains. But the movement continued, and in 1959 and 1960 a number of plays were written to illustrate Mao's theme, including one by a well-known scholar named Wu Han. Some of Mao's inner circle, including Jiang Qing, had argued that Wu's play, which was entitled, *The Dismissal of Hai Rui*, was an allegorical defence of Peng. Mao, who liked Wu's work, at first discounted the charge. But, at the beginning of 1965, he realised its uses.

Wu Han was not simply a historian. He was also a deputy mayor of Beijing and, as such, a protégé of Peng Zhen. Peng was both First Secretary of the municipal Party committee in the capital and deputy head of the Central Committee Secretariat, the core of the CCP's national machine. Like many of the top leaders, he was a remote, rather solitary figure, whose isolation made him vulnerable.

An attack on Wu, Mao realised, could serve as the thin end of a political wedge to split open Peng Zhen's empire. And behind Peng stood Liu Shaoqi.

In Shanghai, Jiang Qing enrolled the services of a radical left-wing journalist named Yao Wenyuan, who had first come to Mao's notice as a hammer of bourgeois intellectuals during the anti-Rightist Campaign. In conditions of extraordinary secrecy – Yao pretended to be ill, and retired to a sanatorium to work – she commissioned from him a 10,000-word diatribe denouncing Wu's play as a 'poisonous weed'.

The writing took all summer. The article went through ten drafts, three of which Mao worked on himself. When it was finally ready in August, the Chairman waited another three months, during which he took the additional precaution of sending Peng Dehuai himself, who had been under house arrest in the capital since 1959, to work in a minor defence post in Sichuan.

On November 10, 1965, when both Peng Zhen and Wu Han were travelling outside Beijing, Yao's essay was published in the Shanghai newspaper, *Wenhuibao*. On Mao's instructions, it contained no direct reference to the Peng Dehuai affair. That was kept in reserve. Instead, Yao accused Wu Han of having portrayed Hai Rui's support of the peasantry in such a manner as to generate sympathy for the idea of private farming (which was, of course, the issue that had fuelled Mao's dispute with Liu Shaoqi). The play, he declared, should therefore be viewed as part of 'the struggle of the capitalist class against the dictatorship of the proletariat . . . Its influence is great and its poison widespread. If we do not clean it up, it will harm the people's cause.'

In the Beijing Party committee, Yao's broadside caused consternation.

Ad hominem attacks were supposed to have been forbidden under guidelines laid down by the Propaganda Department earlier in the year. It was impossible to discover who had authorised it, and Peng Zhen, on his return, ordered the Beijing press, including the *People's Daily*, not to reprint it. A few days later he refused to permit its distribution in pamphlet form, leading Mao to complain retrospectively that Peng's control of Beijing was so tight that 'not even a needle could slip through or a drop of water penetrate'.

The Chairman could perfectly well, at that stage, have simply ordered the article to be republished. But he was still unwilling to reveal his hand. Instead, therefore, he brought into play his conciliator, Zhou Enlai. On November 28, Zhou summoned a meeting in Beijing, at which, after listening to the objections of Peng's colleagues that Yao had resorted to 'abuse and blackmail', he laid down that the correct approach, in literary matters of this kind, was 'to allow the freedom of criticism and counter-criticism'. Two days later, accompanied by an editorial note to that effect, which Zhou himself approved, Yao's article finally appeared in the literary section of the *People's Daily*.

The needle had been slipped in.

On the same day that Yao Wenyuan's article was published in Shanghai, Mao announced to the Politburo Standing Committee the dismissal of Yang Shangkun, the Zunyi veteran who headed the CC's General Office. The pretext was that Yang had authorised the bugging of Mao's train in 1961. But Mao had been aware of Yang's role for four years and had not taken any action. If he moved now it was because the General Office was the Party's communications centre, and he needed to ensure that it was in reliable hands. Yang was replaced by Wang Dongxing, the pudgy commander of the Central Guards Division, known as the 8341 Unit, responsible for the leaders' security. Wang had been a member of the Chairman's entourage for more than twenty years, and his devotion to Mao was unquestioned.

Four weeks later, another high official was purged. Luo Ruiqing's career stretched back to the 1930s in Jiangxi. When Lin Biao had become Defence Minister, Mao had appointed Luo to serve as his Chief of Staff. But the two men had fallen out over the issue of whether the PLA should be primarily a professional or a political force, and Luo had unwisely suggested that Lin should 'spend more time resting' in order to conserve his health. When the issue was raised in the Standing Committee, Mao agreed, at Lin's urging, that Luo should be suspended, and an 'investigating group' was formed, under Zhou Enlai and Deng Xiaoping, to 'persuade' Luo to confess that he had tried to push the Defence Minister aside.

Thus, by mid-December 1965, Mao's senior colleagues were struggling to make sense of a succession of inexplicable events. The Chairman had fired one Party veteran, Yang Shangkun, ostensibly for errors committed several years before. He had acquiesced in the impending purge of another, Luo Ruiqing, apparently to please Lin

Biao. And he was encouraging an obscure literary campaign, which might, or might not, presage a full-scale attack against the Beijing Party organisation.

Liu Shaoqi, for one, was taking no chances. From the end of November on, with that fine instinct for self-preservation which all Mao's subordinates shared, he distanced himself from Peng Zhen, determined that whatever political fallout might come, it should not fall on him.

In this tense climate, Mao made his second move.

Just before Christmas, in Hangzhou, he told Chen Boda and a small group of radicals from the Party journal, *Red Flag*, that Yao Wenyuan's article (in which he still admitted playing no part) had missed the point. The real problem with Wu Han's play lay in the last three words of its title: 'Hai Rui *dismissed from office*'. 'The Jiaqing Emperor dismissed Hai Rui from office,' Mao said. 'We dismissed Peng Dehuai from office. Peng Dehuai is indeed Hai Rui.' The importance of this statement was that it meant that Wu Han's case would in future be regarded as a political rather than a literary issue.

January was marked by a stalemate. Mao's remarks had not been publicised, even within the Politburo, and when one of Chen Boda's staff wrote an article, detailing for the first time (without identifying the source) the Chairman's explosive allegation that Wu had sought Peng Dehuai's rehabilitation, Peng Zhen got his allies in the Propaganda Department to block publication. But he was unable to halt the attacks on Wu altogether. February brought more bad news. Jiang Qing, with Lin Biao's encouragement, had begun working with the PLA's Cultural Affairs Department to promote a new movement against feudal and capitalist thinking. The implication was that the campaign against Wu Han was about to move into higher gear.

At this point the Beijing leader made a desperate, if belated, attempt to regain the initiative.

For the previous eighteen months, he had headed a Central Committee 'cultural revolution group', which Mao had set up to combat revisionism in the arts. At Peng's suggestion, this body now approved new guidelines for dealing with ideological disputes. The 'February Outline', as it became known, affirmed that a 'gigantic struggle' was under way 'between Mao Zedong Thought, on the one hand, and bourgeois ideas on the other', and acknowledged that Wu

Han had committed political errors. But it also maintained that, as Zhou Enlai had laid down in November, academic quarrels should be resolved by scholarly, not political, means.

On February 8, Peng and the rest of the group flew to Wuhan, where they reported to Mao. The Chairman did not explicitly endorse the 'Outline', but neither did he voice any objection. He asked Peng Zhen whether he thought Wu Han was an 'anti-Party element', and again expressed concern about the significance of 'dismissed from office'. But he added that if there were no evidence of organisational links between Wu and Peng Dehuai, the historian might continue to serve as deputy mayor.

Peng returned to Beijing, believing that he had weathered the storm.

In the weeks that followed, there were some minor ructions. Mao complained that the *People's Daily* was only a 'semi-Marxist news-paper'. He groused to Zhou and Deng Xiaoping that Peng Zhen was running Beijing as an 'independent kingdom'.

More worrying, had Peng known about it, was Mao's approval of a programmatic document, drawn up after the cultural forum held by Jiang Qing and the PLA, which stated that, since 1949, 'we have been under the dictatorship of a black anti-Party, anti-socialist line which is diametrically opposed to Chairman Mao's thought'. Since Peng had been in charge of culture since July 1964, he was implicated; so was the Propaganda Department, run by an alternate member of the Politburo, Lu Dingyi; so, too, more generally, was the entire post-1949 cultural establishment. Here, for the first time, clearly stated, was the prospect of a wholesale rejection of existing cultural values.

Before making his next move, Mao waited until the end of March, when Liu Shaoqi had left the country on a month-long tour of Asia. He then let it be known that he wanted to see the 'February Outline' repudiated on the grounds that it 'obscured class lines'. Wu Han and like-minded intellectuals were 'scholar tyrants', he declared, protected by a 'Party tyrant', Peng Zhen. He threatened to dissolve not only Peng's 'cultural revolution group' but the Central Committee Propaganda Department, which he referred to as 'the palace of the King of Hell', and even the Beijing Party committee itself.

Mao's views were formally conveyed by Kang Sheng to a meeting of the Secretariat, presided over by Deng Xiaoping, on April 9.

Kang listed Peng's 'mistakes' in handing the Wu Han affair; Chen Boda listed his 'crimes' in matters of political line going back to the 1930s. It was decided to refer the case to the full Politburo for decision. Two weeks later, when Liu Shaoqi returned from Burma, the last stop on his Asian tour, he found a summons awaiting him to proceed straight to Hangzhou, where Mao had called a Standing Committee meeting to pronounce on Peng Zhen's fate. There the Chairman informed him that Peng and his alleged associates were to be purged, and that Liu himself was to deliver the verdict at an enlarged meeting to be held, in Mao's absence, in Beijing the following month.

This gathering began on May 4 and lasted more than three weeks.

Kang Sheng, seconded by Chen Boda and the leading Shanghai radical, Zhang Chunqiao, again acted as prosecutor. The existence of the 'Peng Zhen–Lu Dingyi–Luo Ruiqing–Yang Shangkun anti-Party clique', he asserted, proved that revisionism had emerged within the Central Committee, just as Mao had predicted during the debates over the Socialist Education Movement sixteen months before. Its members must be publicly criticised and removed from all their posts. Zhou Enlai accused the four of 'taking the capitalist road'. Lin Biao spoke melodramatically of 'the smell of gunpowder' and 'the decided possibility of a coup involving killings, seizure of power and restoration of the capitalist class'.

On May 16, the meeting approved a Central Committee circular, ostensibly issued to replace the now discredited 'February Outline', but actually the first official salvo of what was to become known (in Chinese) as the 'Great Revolution [to establish] Proletarian Culture' – the Cultural Revolution. It had been a month in gestation, and Mao himself had revised it no fewer than seven times. The central political issue, the circular declared, was 'whether to carry out or to resist Comrade Mao Zedong's line on the Cultural Revolution'. Peng Zhen and his allies were not the only traitors. There were other 'people in authority taking the capitalist road' who must also be cleared out:

> These representatives of the bourgeoisie who have sneaked into our Party . . . are actually a bunch of counter-revolutionary revisionists. When the time is right, they will try to seize power, turning the dictatorship of the proletariat into a dictatorship of the capitalist class. Some of these people have already been exposed by us; others have

not. Some are still trusted by us, and are being groomed as our successors, people of a Khrushchev type who are nestling right beside us. Party cadres at all levels must pay special attention to this point.

The circular announced the abolition of Peng Zhen's 'cultural revolution group' and the formation of a new body of the same name, headed by Chen Boda, with Jiang Qing, Zhang Chunqiao and two others as his deputies, and Kang Sheng as adviser. Peng and his cohorts were cast into outer darkness – imprisonment in some cases, house arrest in others – and a Central Case Examination Group set up to investigate their 'anti-Party conduct'.

Thus, by mid-May 1966, Mao had signalled to the Party at large the broad aim of the great upheaval that he was so painstakingly preparing: the removal from power of 'capitalist-roaders' who were planning to betray the socialist cause. He had put in place a headquarters to direct it, bypassing the Politburo and the mainstream Party chain of command, whose membership replicated precisely the quincunx of radical influence that he had begun assembling in 1962 – apart from Lin Biao, for whom he had other plans. But it was far from clear, even to those closest to him, why he had set about it in the way he had, and still less what the final outcome would be.

One consideration which had led Mao to act in so devious and convoluted a manner was deniability.

Had the initial attack on Wu Han gone awry, he could have blamed it on the excessive zeal of Jiang Qing, whose public role in cultural affairs would have made her a credible scapegoat. He was equally prudent in making Liu Shaoqi deliver the *coup de grâce* to Peng Zhen, while he himself stayed away. The rest of the leadership could hardly turn round and complain that Peng had been treated unfairly when they themselves had done the dirty work.

But there was also a more fundamental reason.

At the time of the last leadership clash, in 1959, the Chairman had been able to swing the rest of the Politburo behind him by turning it into a vote of confidence in himself. His adversary, Peng Dehuai, was an irascible, pig-headed old soldier, whose sharp tongue had made more enemies than friends. It had been relatively simple for Mao to depict him as a threat to Party stability. This time, the grounds for his action were, by any objective criterion, not just flimsy but totally non-existent. Mao wished to purge Liu Shaoqi, whose prestige was second only to his own, and the General Secretary, Deng Xiaoping – neither of whom had presented any overt challenge to his policies, and who both had the support of most of the older generation of the leadership. There was no conceivable basis on which, in a straightforward debate, Mao could have persuaded his colleagues that Liu and Deng should go.

Since a frontal assault was out of the question, the Chairman fell back on the guerrilla tactics he knew best. 'War is politics', he had written. 'Politics is war by other means.' It evidently never entered Liu's head that Mao's actions might be the prelude to a larger conflict. He saw only that the Chairman was bent on launching a new movement to revolutionise culture, and that Peng Zhen had got in the way.

Had the rest of the leadership joined together at that point to stop him, they might conceivably have averted the disaster bearing down on them. But to do so would have required them to confront Mao face to face, in the Politburo Standing Committee. None had the stomach for that kind of fight.

The same mixture of cowardice and self-interest that had made possible Peng Dehuai's fall at Lushan was still more pronounced in 1966. The sanctification of Mao and his writings, promoted assiduously by Lin Biao, had by then reached such undreamed of heights that to oppose him directly had become unthinkable. In any case, Mao left nothing to chance. Liu Shaoqi's absence until the eve of the Hangzhou meeting meant that there was no time to organise resistance, even had anyone wished to. The subsequent Politburo session in Beijing was enlarged, on Mao's instructions, to include sixty of his hand-picked supporters. Although they could not vote, their presence made reasoned discussion impossible.

Yet there were warning signs that should have told the leadership that this latest movement would be unlike any Mao had launched before. The language of the polemics was more extreme, more emotionally charged – geared to whipping up a mob to frenzy rather than making a political case. Personal and political motives were from the start inextricably mixed. Mao's use of Jiang Qing, and of a coterie of personal trusties, reinforced this trend. Lin Biao opened one Politburo meeting with an accusation that a political opponent had slandered his wife – by claiming that she was not a virgin when they married.

There was one other development in May that might have alerted Liu Shaoqi to the plot that Mao was brewing.

Yao Wenyuan published a new polemic, this time attacking not only Wu Han but two of his collaborators – Deng Tuo, the one-time *People's Daily* editor whom Mao had excoriated in 1957 for failing to publicise the 'Hundred Flowers'; and a novelist named Liao Mosha – who had worked with him in the early 1960s on a weekly satirical column entitled 'Notes from a Three-family Village'. The column, Yao now claimed, had used Aesopian language to attack Mao by innuendo in the time-honoured Chinese tradition of 'pointing at the locust tree in order to revile the mulberry'.

The charge was almost certainly unfounded. Although, with hindsight, pieces with titles like 'The Royal Way and the Tyrant's Way' and 'Amnesia' (describing a mental disorder for which the only cure was 'complete rest') seemed written in such a manner that they could only apply to Mao – no one in China made that connection *at the time*, any more than anyone at the time had seen 'Hai Rui Dismissed from Office' as a defence of Peng Dehuai. Instead the essays were read as witty caricatures of lower-level officials whose stupidities had contributed to what were euphemistically called the 'three years of natural disaster' – which was no doubt all they were.

But the point of Yao's article lay elsewhere.

If a Politburo member, Peng Zhen, had been able to install a 'black anti-Party, anti-socialist line' opposing the Chairman's cultural policies; and if a group of Party writers had been able, for four years, to lampoon him with impunity in the public prints of the capital – why had the man Mao had placed in charge of the Party, Liu Shaoqi, done nothing to stop it?

There were only two possible answers. Either Liu was incompetent, or he was in league with Mao's opponents.

Having completed his preliminary dispositions, Mao set in motion the next stage of his infernal machination.

On May 14, Kang Sheng sent his wife, Cao Yiou, to Beijing University to make contact with the Party Secretary of the Philosophy Department, a woman named Nie Yuanzi. Ten days later, after Cao had given her assurances of high-level backing, Nie and a group of supporters wrote a wall-poster accusing the university president,

Lu Ping, of having suppressed Mao's directives on the Cultural Revolution, and pasted it up on the same wall, outside the university canteen, where the 'Hundred Flowers' movement had blossomed, nine years earlier. It urged students and lecturers 'resolutely, thoroughly, cleanly and completely to eliminate all demons and monsters, and all Khrushchev-type counter-revolutionary revisionists, and to carry the socialist revolution through to the end'.

The University Party Committee, which Lu Ping chaired, went into overdrive. By next morning, hundreds more posters had appeared, most of them condemning Nie's group.

On June 1, the promised 'high-level backing' arrived.

Mao in person endorsed Nie's poster, and ordered it broadcast by radio stations throughout China. The *People's Daily*, which had been taken over two days before by Chen Boda, denounced the university as 'a stubborn anti-Party and anti-socialist bastion' and Lu Ping as the leader of a 'black gang'. Nie became an instant celebrity. Telegrams of support poured in from all over the country. Students from other Beijing colleges flocked to the university to see her, and to seek guidance on how to deal with recalcitrant Party committees at their own institutes of higher learning.

Secondary-school pupils in the capital, led by the offspring of the elite (who heard from their parents of the political convulsions under way), moved even faster.

At the end of May, an enterprising, forever nameless pupil at the Qinghua University Middle School had coined the term *hongweibing* – 'Red Guard'. The movement to which this gave rise spread through Beijing's schools like wildfire, fuelled by a campaign to adulate Mao that became more extravagant and outlandish with every passing day. Lin Biao had started it with a speech to the Politburo on May 18, when he asserted: 'Chairman Mao is a genius . . . One single sentence of his surpasses 10,000 of ours.' The *People's Daily* then took up the cry: 'Chairman Mao is the red sun in our hearts. Mao Zedong Thought is the source of our life . . . Whosoever dares to oppose him shall be hunted down and obliterated.' Mao's works, it said, were 'more precious than gold'; 'every sentence is a war drum, every utterance a truth'.

Liu and Deng watched these developments with dismay and growing bafflement.

Already during the spring, there had been a foretaste of the ruthlessness with which the anti-revisionist witch-hunt would be pursued. The former Chief of Staff, Luo Ruiqing, had leapt from an upper floor window in a suicide attempt. He had lived, but broke both his legs: the struggle sessions against him had continued. After the publication of Yao Wenyuan's article, Deng Tuo took his own life. Less than a week later, it was the turn of Mao's secretary, Tian Jiaying. He was told he was being dismissed as a Rightist; that night, he, too, killed himself. Suicides had long been a common feature of political movements in China; but there had been no case of a senior Party official taking his own life since Gao Gang, in 1954. The deaths of Deng Tuo and Tian Jiaying were widely seen as the traditional Chinese scholar's way of protesting against injustice.

To these grim events within the political establishment was now added spiralling turmoil in colleges and schools.

Liu and Deng knew full well – having witnessed the effects nine years earlier, during the 'Hundred Flowers', not to mention their own youthful experience as student agitators – how quickly campus disorders, once ignited, could set the whole country aflame. This time, moreover, Chen Boda, evidently with Mao's approval, was publishing incendiary editorials which stoked the fire still higher. The usual recourse in such circumstances was to send in outside work teams, which carried out rectification and reorganised defective Party committees. This had already been done, as a stop-gap measure, at Beijing University. But was it what the Chairman wanted?

Liu and the other 'first front' leaders were out of their depth.

Mao was then in Hangzhou. He had not set foot in the capital since the previous November. Liu telephoned to ask him to return and take charge of the movement himself. Mao replied that he would remain in the south a little longer, and they should deal with the situation as they thought best. A few days later, Liu and Deng flew down to seek instructions directly. Mao gave the same response. This time he did vouchsafe that the use of work teams was not excluded, only 'whether they should be sent or not sent, they must not be sent in hastily'. The phrase was ambiguous, and designedly so.

None the less, on that basis, teams of Party cadres and Youth League members were despatched to all institutions of higher learning in the capital and other large cities, under instructions to restore order and bring the movement under their control.

This orthodox, top-down approach sat ill with the fiery exhortations being pumped out by the *People's Daily* and other newspapers. It also failed to acknowledge the students' genuine grievances. At Chinese universities, on the eve of the Cultural Revolution, the problems which the 'Rightists' had raised during the 'Hundred Flowers' had not only not gone away; they were now, in most cases, far worse. Mao's charges that Party bureaucrats at the universities behaved like 'scholar tyrants' resonated among those who had had to suffer their arbitrary whims. Incompetent staff members were protected; originality was repressed; cronyism and nepotism were rampant. The preferred method of teaching was still 'duck-stuffing' – as it had been in the 1930s – since rote-learning carried less political risk. Party and Youth League members got the plum job assignments; and, because the economy was still floundering, there were far fewer of those to go round.

Within days, conflicts developed. The work teams treated the student rebels as 'anti-Party and anti-socialist elements'. The radicals retorted that Liu's men were 'black gangsters' in league with the ousted Party committees. By late June, nearly forty teams had been manhandled out of the campuses. In response, Liu branded thousands of students as 'Rightists' and struggle sessions were organised against their leaders. Faculty members who supported them were detained as counter-revolutionaries.

In retrospect, it is hard to understand how Liu and Deng could have misjudged so fundamentally Mao's intentions.

At the time, however, the enormity of what the Chairman was contemplating was beyond the comprehension not only of his adversaries but even of his allies. That he had decided to unleash the masses against the Party itself was too far-fetched for any in the Politburo to believe. When radicals at Beijing University staged a struggle meeting at which Lu Ping and sixty other 'black gang elements' were forced to kneel, wearing dunce's caps, their faces blackened, clothes ripped, and wall-posters plastered all over their bodies, for students to pummel and kick, to yank their hair and bind them with ropes, before parading them through the streets, not only Liu Shaoqi but also Chen Boda and Kang Sheng declared it to be a 'counter-revolutionary incident' whose authors must be severely punished.

While Mao concealed his hand, each tried to make sense in his own way of the events that were unfolding. To Liu and Deng, it was a sinister re-run of the 'Hundred Flowers', to 'lure the snake out of its hole' and expose those who retailed capitalist ideas, while at the same time teaching a lesson to youths who were hoodwinked by them. Chen Boda and Kang Sheng understood that Mao was out to curb the power of Liu Shaoqi, but saw it as part of a renewed effort to radicalise policy, not as the start of an onslaught aimed at demolishing the Party system.

The time was fast approaching when they would all be disabused.

Mao's trap was about to be sprung. As he had told Kang Sheng, in Yan'an, a quarter of a century before: 'Melons ripen. Don't pick them when they are not yet ripe. When they are ready, they will just drop off.'

On July 16, Mao swam for over an hour in the Yangtse near Wuhan, drifting nine miles downstream with the current. It was a demonstration of vigour, a metaphor for throwing himself back into the fray. Photographs of the 72-year-old Chairman's exploit were printed in all Chinese newspapers, and newsreels shown at cinemas.

Two days later, without informing Liu Shaoqi, he flew back to Beijing.

That night, in a further snub, Mao, closeted with Chen Boda and Kang Sheng, refused to receive the Head of State.

Next morning he told Liu that sending the work teams had been a mistake. Jiang Qing went to Beijing University, where she told radical students: 'Whoever does not join us in rebellion, let him stand aside! Those who want revolution, stand with us!' Chen Boda declared that the mass struggle session against Lu Ping had, after all, been a revolutionary, not a counter-revolutionary, event. On the 25th, Mao called for the work teams to be withdrawn altogether, describing Liu's policy as 'an error of political line'. Two days later, Jiang Qing, Chen Boda and Kang Sheng led the entire Cultural Revolution Group to Beijing Normal University where, at a mass rally, they called on the students to 'overcome all obstacles, liberate their thinking and carry out a thoroughgoing revolution'.

Shortly afterwards, at a meeting of Cultural Revolution activists in the Great Hall of the People, Liu criticised himself for the work teams' errors. But now there was an edge of resentment to his words, a dawning realisation that Mao had set him up. 'You ask us how this [cultural] revolution should be run,' he told the activists. 'I tell you frankly, we don't know ourselves. I believe that many comrades of the Party Centre and many members of the work groups do not know.' The result, he added pointedly, was that 'even when you have made no mistakes, someone else says you have'.

On August 1, the Chairman convened a Central Committee plenum – the first for almost four years – to approve the political and ideological basis on which the Great Proletarian Cultural Revolution should be conducted. In his political report, Liu again acknowledged mistakes in the work teams' approach. But, as before, he suggested that these resulted more from a lack of clarity (on the part, he implied, of Mao) than from any fundamental error in line. The debate that followed made clear that there was a good deal of sympathy for his views.

Accordingly, three days later, Mao convened an enlarged meeting of the Politburo Standing Committee, where he likened the sending of the work teams to the suppression of student movements by the northern warlords and Chiang Kai-shek's Guomindang. Liu and Deng had carried out 'an act of suppression and terror', he said, adding menacingly: 'There are "monsters and demons" among people present here.' When Liu retorted that he was ready to assume responsibility, since he had been in charge in the capital at the time, Mao sneered: 'You were exercising dictatorship in Beijing. You did a fine job!'

This inflammatory statement was immediately circulated as a conference document. Like his speech at Lushan, condemning Peng Dehuai, seven years before, Mao's anger left the plenum transfixed.

Next day, in case the message had still not got through, he spelt it out again in a wall-poster, entitled 'Bombard the Headquarters!'. Since mid-June, Mao asserted, certain 'central leading comrades', who had opposed him on two previous occasions – in 1962 (over private farming) and in 1964 (over the Socialist Education Movement) – had been resisting the Cultural Revolution and trying to install a bourgeois dictatorship. 'They have inverted right and wrong, and confused black and white,' he claimed. 'They have encircled and suppressed revolutionaries, and stifled opinions different from their own. They have practised White terror, glorifying capitalism and denigrating the proletariat. How venomous!' The poster's title reinforced the attack by implying that the unnamed 'leading comrades' had formed a bourgeois headquarters within the Party.

Mao's poster confirmed what Liu had begun dimly to apprehend some days earlier: the Chairman had decided to get rid of him.

His allies in the Politburo, led by Deng Xiaoping, and his supporters in the Central Committee, waited for the axe to fall on them. It did not: Mao was still taking no chances. On his instructions, Chen Boda, Kang Sheng, the Public Security Minister, Xie Fuzhi, and other radical spokesmen concentrated all their fire on Liu. Few of those present understood what the Head of State was supposed to have done wrong. But nor did anyone try to defend him. For thirty-two years, since the start of the Long March, no one had picked a fight with Mao and won. August 1966, with the Chairman stirring up mayhem in the leadership and the country at large, did not seem the best time to start.

That afternoon, Mao sent a plane to fetch Lin Biao from Dalian, where he had gone with his family to escape the summer heat. Zhou Enlai met him at the airport and, as they drove into Beijing, briefed him on what was going on. Then the Chairman himself received him, and informed him that he was to become deputy leader of the Party in Liu's place. Lin, who was only too well aware of the danger of such a dizzying promotion, tried to refuse, pleading poor health. But Mao's mind was made up.

On August 8, the CC meekly passed – by unanimous vote – a document, to which Mao himself had put the finishing touches, known as the 'Sixteen Points'. It was the blueprint for the *daluan*, the 'great chaos', that would engulf China for the next three years.

The Cultural Revolution, it declared, was 'a great revolution that touches people to their very souls', an 'irresistible general trend', which would vanquish bourgeois and feudal ideology, and instil a 'proletarian world outlook', exemplified by 'the great Red banner of Mao Zedong Thought'. It was a revolution from the bottom up, in which the masses would liberate themselves. 'Trust the masses,' Mao exhorted the Party, 'rely on them, and respect their initiative, cast out fear and don't be afraid of disturbances.' He had said much the same in 1957. But this time his shock troops were 'revolutionary young people', 'daring and courageous path-breakers'. Their task was different, too, from that of the bourgeois intellectuals he had unleashed during the 'Hundred Flowers'. The target now was not the sloth and arrogance of bureaucratic cadres, but 'all those people in authority who are taking the capitalist road'.

Mao was not quite ready to say openly that Liu Shaoqi was their

chief. But when the plenum elected a new Politburo – on the basis
of a list drawn up, not, as the rules required, by the Party's
Organisation Department, but by Jiang Qing, in accordance with
Mao's private wishes – Liu slipped from second to eighth place in
the rank order.

The 'first' and 'second' fronts disappeared. Lin Biao became
Mao's sole deputy, with the title of Vice-Chairman. Premier Zhou
Enlai, as before, ranked third, but, like the ailing Chen Yun and Zhu
De, was now merely a Standing Committee member. They were
joined by Mao's radical allies, Chen Boda and Kang Sheng, and
by the Guangdong leader, Tao Zhu, who had replaced Peng Zhen
in the Secretariat. Deng Xiaoping found himself promoted –
despite his association with Liu – from seventh to sixth place in the
hierarchy. His case was merely postponed.

On the day the plenum opened, August 1, Mao had written a letter
expressing 'warm support' for the Red Guards at Qinghua
University Middle School, where the movement had been
launched. It was the signal for Red Guard organisations, which until
then had been confined to the capital, to spread all over China.

Two weeks later, a million Red Guards, some from as far away
as Sichuan and Guangdong, converged on the capital for the first of
ten gigantic rallies in Tiananmen Square. At midnight on August
17, detachments of schoolchildren and college students, singing
revolutionary songs and carrying red silken banners and portraits
of the Chairman, began marching down Changan dajie, the
Avenue of Eternal Peace, to take up their positions. Mao's appearance was timed to coincide with the first rays of the rising sun.
Shortly after 5 a.m., he walked out from the Forbidden City and
mingled briefly with the crowd, before retiring to the pavilion above
the gate to meet Red Guard representatives.

To underscore the mood of militancy, the Chairman, like the rest
of the Politburo, wore a green PLA uniform – something he had not
done since the despatch of Chinese forces to Korea in 1950.

The meeting opened with the playing of the Maoist anthem, 'The
East is Red'. Chen Boda and Lin Biao whipped up the fervour of
the crowd, praising Mao as the 'Great leader, Great teacher, Great
helmsman and Great commander'. Then a girl student from a
Beijing middle school pinned a Red Guard armband to Mao's

sleeve, triggering scenes of delirium among the young people crammed into the square below. Mao himself said nothing. He did not need to.

> Let me tell you the great news – news greater than heaven [ran one typical letter home] . . . I saw our most, most, most, most, dearly beloved leader, Chairman Mao! Comrades, I have seen Chairman Mao! Today I am so happy my heart is about to burst . . . We're jumping! We're singing! After seeing the Red Sun in Our Hearts I just ran around like crazy all over Beijing . . . I could see him ever so clearly, and he was so impressive . . . Comrades, how can I possibly describe to you what that moment was like? . . . How can I possibly go to sleep tonight! I have decided to make today my birthday. Today, I started a new life!!!

An orgasm of devotional enthusiasm swept feverishly through the streets. A few independent spirits saw through the divine charade, like the student who wrote a few weeks later: 'The Great Cultural Revolution is not a mass movement, but one man moving the masses with the barrel of a gun.' But the vast majority did not. Mao had found his new guerrilla army to assault the political heights. A whole generation of young Chinese was ready to die, and to kill, for him, with unquestioning obedience.

And kill they did.

It began within days of the August 18 rally. One of the first victims was the eminent writer, Lao She, author of *Rickshaw Boy* and *Teahouse*. With some thirty other cultural figures, he was taken to the courtyard of the former Confucian Temple in Beijing. There they were given *yin-yang* haircuts (with one half of the head shaven, the other left uncut); black ink was poured over their faces; and signs labelling them as 'ox demons and snake spirits' hung around their necks. Then they were made to kneel as the Red Guards beat them with stakes and leather belts. Lao She, who was sixty-seven, lost consciousness. When he was sent home, in the early hours of next morning, his clothes were so thick with congealed blood that his wife had to cut them from his body. Next day he drowned himself in a shallow lake, not far from the Forbidden City.

Thousands of lesser victims met similar fates. There was scarcely a housing block in Beijing where the Red Guards did not beat at least one person to death. Over four days at the end of August, in one small suburban area, 325 people were killed, ranging from a six-week-old baby (the child of a 'reactionary family') to an old man in his eighties.

The rapidity with which peaceable, idealistic young students were transformed into avenging furies astounded older people. To Mao, it was a sign of the Chinese people's 'fighting spirit'. How many times before, from the May Fourth movement in 1919, to the 'Hundred Flowers' forty years later, had apparently tranquil campuses erupted in a matter of hours to become seething cauldrons of political agitation? This time, the most powerful man in the land, the Chairman himself, had personally pointed the way, recalling (in the 'Sixteen Points') that revolution was 'an act of violence whereby one class overthrows the power of another'. Lin Biao had urged them to 'smash the Four Olds' – 'old thought, old culture, old customs and old practices'. The Security Minister, Xie Fuzhi, had told the police to give the Red Guards free rein:

> Should Red Guards who kill people be punished? My view is that if people are killed, they are killed; it's no business of ours . . . If the masses hate bad people so much that we cannot stop them, then let us not insist . . . The people's police should stand on the side of the Red Guards, liaise with them, sympathise with them and provide them with information, especially about the five black categories – the landlords, rich peasants, counter-revolutionaries, bad elements and Rightists.

It was rarely put that bluntly. But Xie's statement simply echoed Mao's own words in 1949, when, in explaining the nature of the 'people's democratic dictatorship', he had declared: 'the state apparatus, including . . . the police and the courts . . . is the instrument by which one class oppresses another. It is an instrument . . . [of] violence.'

Violence, revolution and power were the trinity by which Mao had struggled to realise his political vision all through his long career.

In the 1960s, violence served the same purpose as it had in the Hunan peasant movement in 1926, in the 'land investigation movement' in Jiangxi in the 1930s, and during the land reform of the 1940s and 1950s. The Red Guards who tortured and killed in the Chairman's name – like the peasants who had beaten to death their landlords – were committing themselves to the Maoist cause irrevocably. Ken Ling, a Red Guard in Fujian, described his own initiation as a sixteen-year-old middle-school student:

> Teacher Chen, over 60 years old and suffering from high blood-pressure, was . . . dragged up to the second floor of a classroom building and . . . beaten with fists and broomsticks . . . He passed out several times, but was brought back to consciousness . . . with cold water being splashed on to his face. He could hardly move his body; his feet were cut by glass and thorns. He shouted, 'Why don't you kill me? Kill me!' This lasted for six hours, until he lost control of his excrement. They tried to force a stick into his rectum. He collapsed for the last time. They poured cold water on him again. It was too late . . . People began to run away, one after the other. The killers were a little frightened. They . . . summoned the school doctor, [who] . . . finally wrote on the death certificate: 'Death due to a sudden attack of high blood pressure . . .' When [his wife] rushed to the scene, she was forced to confirm this cause of death before being allowed to take the body . . .
>
> After a night filled with dreadful nightmares, I mustered enough courage to go to school the next day to witness more of this torture . . . After 10 days or so, I became used to it; a blood-smeared body or a shriek no longer made me feel uneasy.

Teachers with bourgeois connections; members of the 'democratic parties'; those from the 'five black categories' (later enlarged to seven to include traitors and spies; and finally to nine, by the addition of capitalists and 'stinking intellectuals') – in short, the 'usual suspects' – were among the first to be targeted, often with the tacit encouragement of Party committees, which sought in this way to draw the Red Guards' fire away from themselves. Very soon, with support from the police and from sympathisers in the military, the killings became systematic. After the Cultural Revolution, another teacher, crippled by his students, described what that had meant:

> On the athletic field, every few days, several teachers would be taken out and shot in public . . . Some teachers were buried alive. On the roof of that building over there, four teachers were ordered to sit on a pack of explosives and [forced] to light them themselves. [There was] a tremendous sound, and nobody could be seen – only legs and arms were in the trees and [scattered] over the roof . . . [Altogether] about one hundred [school officials] were killed.

To adolescents, there could be no more potent symbol of the overthrow of the old order than the physical destruction of those set in authority above them. 'It is right to rebel', Mao had written in December, 1939. The phrase was resurrected by the *People's Daily*, and the Red Guards made it their own. By publicly humiliating their victims, when they did not actually kill them, they ensured that none could remain indifferent to the extraordinary changes that Mao was bringing about. Like the 'people-beating meetings' staged in certain Beijing theatres, the Red Guards' terror had an educational, as well as a punitive, role.

Before long, the revolution began to devour its offspring.

The rebels split first on class lines, between the children of workers, peasants and soldiers, and those from less desirable backgrounds; then through factional cleavages, as rival groups were manipulated by competing political and military forces at provincial and national level. The violence turned inwards. By mid-autumn, many Red Guard units had set up 'reformatories' and 'detention centres', where wayward members were disciplined and enemies punished. Fifteen-year-old Gao Yuan recalled finding some of his friends after their schoolmates had tortured them:

> Some lay on the floor bound with ropes. Some were strung from beams . . . The discovery of Songying [a seventeen-year-old girl] was the biggest shock. She lay unconscious on the floor in a pool of blood. Her pants had been stripped off. Her blouse was torn, revealing her breasts. She had been beaten so badly that her whole body was purple . . . Her tormentors had pushed dirty socks and twigs into her vagina, causing heavy bleeding . . .

Another boy, Zongwei, lay dying on a bed. Gao rushed to get the school doctor:

> As she slit open [his] trouser legs with scissors, she flinched. When I looked at Zongwei's bare legs, I knew why. They were riddled with holes the diameter of a pencil, surrounded by strings of loose flesh the consistency of shredded pork. Blood and puss oozed from the wounds. 'What in hell did they use on him,' Dr Yang muttered. Looking round the room, I found the answer to her question: the pokers used to tend the stove.

Among the many thousands who died that autumn was the young man who had written so ecstatically of seeing Mao in Tiananmen

Square. Less than three weeks afterwards, he was severely beaten and committed suicide.

The Central Cultural Revolution Group made half-hearted attempts to stop the Red Guards' internecine killings. Mao showed little concern; excesses were inevitable.

The Red Guard leaders were doing no more than he himself had done, when he had ordered the purge of the AB-*tuan* and the 'suppression of counter-revolutionaries' at Futian. It was not the best way of dealing with opponents or with renegades, but it was a necessary, perhaps, to a degree, even a desirable part of the 'great revolutionary storm' by which the 'young Generals' were to be tempered as successors, just as Mao's generation had been, thirty years before.

The parallel with the early stages of the Chinese revolution was deliberate. Both for Mao and for his young followers, the Cultural Revolution was in part an attempt to recreate the glory days of his own struggle for power.

At the end of August, the Chairman endorsed a nationwide 'networking movement', inspired by the Long March, under which Red Guards were given free train passes to travel all over the country, spreading the gospel of the Cultural Revolution, while provincial youths came to the capital to be fired by the Red Guard rallies at which Mao presided. In the process, millions of young Chinese visited his birthplace at Shaoshan; the first Red base area on the Jinggangshan; and other revolutionary sites, often making the journey on foot to relive the experiences of their revolutionary forebears.*

Similarly the campaign against the 'Four Olds' emulated the iconoclasm of the decade that had ended in the May Fourth movement.

Where Mao and his student friends had sheared off Manchu pigtails, the Red Guards declared war on 'Hong Kong-style haircuts, Hong Kong-style clothing, cowboy trousers, winkle-pickers and high-heeled shoes', in order, as one group put it, 'to stop up every

---

* Millions of others took advantage of the free transport to go sightseeing, travelling to scenic spots like the Three Gorges, and to Xinjiang and Inner Mongolia. That, Mao understood. He had done the same himself, while travelling from Beijing to Shanghai in the spring of 1919, and afterwards accounted the experience one of the more worthwhile undertakings of his youth.

orifice leading to capitalism, and [to] smash every incubator of revisionism'. Correction stations were set up at street corners to shave
offending heads. Where, half a century before, Chen Duxiu's 'new
culture movement' had ushered in a change of language, from the
classical to the vernacular, now there was a 'movement' to change
names: old 'feudal' shop signs were discarded in favour of terms like
Weidong (Defend Mao Zedong), *Hanbiao* (Defend Lin Biao), *Yongge*
(Permanent Revolution) and so on. Children changed their given
names to *Hongrong* (Red Glory) or *Xiangdong* (Face the East). The
road outside the Soviet Embassy became 'Anti-Revisionism Street';
the Beijing Union Hospital, established in 1921 by the Rockefeller
Foundation, the 'Anti-Imperialism Hospital'. The Red Guards even
changed the traffic lights, so that red became the signal for 'go',
until Zhou Enlai told them that red got people's attention better
and therefore should remain 'stop'. It was Zhou, too, who sent
troops to guard the Forbidden City, when Red Guards came with
pickaxes to smash its ancient sculptures. Other historic sites were
less fortunate. All over China, city gates and temples were demolished, tombs desecrated, bronze statues and artefacts melted
down, mosques and monasteries vandalised, paintings and sutras
destroyed, monks and nuns defrocked.

But where Mao's generation had contented itself with ransacking
public places of worship (and Mao himself had opposed even that,
arguing that the people would take action themselves when they
judged the time was right), the Red Guards ransacked private
homes. Between a quarter and a third of all dwellings in Beijing were
subjected to Red Guard searches in the autumn of 1966. Antiques;
calligraphy; foreign currency; gold and silver; jewellery; musical
instruments; paintings; porcelain; old photographs; the manuscripts
of famous writers; scientific notebooks – all were suspect, liable to
be confiscated, stolen or smashed on the spot. In Shanghai, such
searches yielded 32 tons of gold; 150 tons of pearls and jade; 450
tons of gold and silver jewellery; and more than six million US
dollars in cash. Serious offenders, usually from one of the 'black
classes', had their homes sequestered and were driven out of the
city; minor culprits merely lost their possessions. Even such diver-
sions as cultivating pot plants, keeping cagebirds and pet dogs and
cats, which Mao had criticised, were condemned as legacies of
feudalism.

Books were a special target. As a student, Mao had proposed that 'all the anthologies of prose and poetry published since the Tang and Song dynasties [should] be burned' (including presumably, his personal favourites, like *The Dream of the Red Chamber* and *Water Margin*), on the grounds that 'the past oppresses the present' and the essence of revolution was 'replacing the old with the new'.

But, in 1917, Mao had merely proposed. In 1966, the Red Guards acted.

In cities all over China, the accumulated haul from the sacking of temples and libraries, bookshops and private homes, was piled up in main squares. Ken Ling remembered the scene in Amoy at the beginning of September:

> The piles contained many different things: wooden ancestor tablets, old Guomindang paper currency, brightly coloured Chinese-style dresses . . . mahjong tiles, playing cards, foreign cigarettes . . . But most of all, idols and books. All the books that had been removed from the city libraries . . . were there – the yellow, the black, and poisonous books. Most of them were old hand-sewn volumes. *The Golden Lotus . . . The Romance of the Three Kingdoms, Strange Tales from a Chinese Studio* – all awaited burning. Shortly after 6 p.m., 50 kilograms of kerosene were poured on the piles, which were then set afire. The flames leapt three stories high . . . [They] burned for three days and nights.

Later on, old books were sent to be pulped. In this way, many unique copies of Song and Ming dynasty texts were lost for ever.

The greatest difference, however, between the iconoclasm of Mao's youth and that of his Red Guard successors, half a century on, was that his generation had rebelled to liberate itself from the straitjacket of Confucian orthodoxy, triggering an explosion of free thinking in which every new idea, every fashion, every social doctrine, was permitted.

The Red Guards curtailed even the vestigial freedoms that then existed, imposing a new, Maoist orthodoxy more rigid than any that had gone before. Their object was to expunge the old, to 'burn the books and bury the scholars alive', as the Emperor Qin Shihuang had done, two thousand years before, so that China would become, in Mao's phrase, 'a blank sheet of paper', ready to be inscribed with the holy writ of Marxism-Leninism-Mao Zedong Thought.

To fill the vacuum left by the 'Four Olds', the 'Four News' were devised – 'new ideology, new culture, new customs, new habits'.

In practice, that meant the exaltation of Mao and his ideas to the exclusion of everything else. He was no longer venerated; he was worshipped.

At workplaces each morning, people stood in formation and bowed three times before Mao's portrait, silently 'asking instructions' for the tasks of the day ahead. They repeated the same ritual each evening, to report on what they had accomplished. Red Guards told their victims to pray to Mao for forgiveness. At city railway stations, passengers had to carry out a 'loyalty dance' on the platform before they were allowed to board the train. In country districts there were 'loyalty pigs', branded with the character *zhong* (loyalty) to show that even dumb beasts could recognise Mao's genius. Mao's works were referred to as 'treasure books', and special ceremonies were held whenever a consignment went on sale. Activists learned Mao's essays by heart, and festooned themselves with Mao Zedong lapel badges. Switchboard operators greeted callers with the words, '*Mao zhuxi wansui!*' ('Long live Chairman Mao!'). Business letters opened with quotations from Mao's writings, printed in bold type. The 'Little Red Book' of his aphorisms was ascribed the power to work miracles. Chinese newspapers reported how medical workers armed with it had cured the blind and the deaf; how a paralytic, relying on Mao Zedong Thought, had recovered the use of his limbs; how, on another occasion, Mao Zedong Thought had raised a man from the dead.

None of this was wholly new to China. Mao himself, as a schoolboy, had bowed before a portrait of Confucius each morning. In the 1920s, Guomindang members had started their meetings by bowing to a portrait of Sun Yat-sen. Chiang Kai-shek had tried, unsuccessfully, to introduce a similar cult of himself. Loyalty dances had been performed at the Tang Court, twelve hundred years before. As a sign of reverence, the Emperor's words were always placed higher, and in larger characters, than those of any other man (a cause, in the nineteenth century, of endless diplomatic bickering with the Powers).

But the irony was that to bring into existence his new world, the Chairman had reached back to his roots, to the bedrock of his thought, to the days when China was ruled by a Son of Heaven – the 'Red Sun in Our Hearts' – to forge an emperor-system whose limitless power, once harnessed to revolutionary goals, could build the Red utopia to which he pinned his dreams.

As 1966 drew to a close, the whole of China seemed to be marching to Mao's step.

His imperial status, his deification, the fanaticism of the Red Guards, created a climate of militancy and menace so overpowering that no one could oppose him. The Chairman was elated. At his seventy-third birthday party, he proposed a toast to 'the unfolding of an all-round nationwide civil war'. Zhou Enlai summed up the new guiding principle by which all Party leaders must act: 'Whatever accords with Mao Zedong Thought is right, while whatever does not accord with Mao Zedong Thought is wrong.'

Within the Central Committee, as within the Party at large, radicals were in the minority. Most officials were appalled by the prospect of yet another upheaval that would imperil their positions. The Chairman himself had no illusions on that score. 'When you are told to kindle a fire to burn yourselves, will you do it?' he had asked sceptically back in July. 'After all, you yourselves will be burned.' Hence his decision to enrol the young as his new revolutionary vanguard.

By October 1966, the terror tactics of the Red Guards – whose attentions had shifted from their teachers to higher-level education officials and then to the provincial Party committees – were beginning to put pressure on some of Liu Shaoqi's key supporters. That month Liu and Deng Xiaoping made self-criticisms at a Central Committee work conference, where for the first time they were accused of trying to restore a 'capitalist dictatorship'. Shortly afterwards the Party Organisation Department secretly distributed wall-posters, which were prominently displayed in the centre of Beijing, denouncing the two men by name. Officially, they retained their leading posts. But on National Day, when Liu, as Head of State, stood next to Mao, waving to the crowd, Sidney Rittenberg, who was on the platform with them, remembered his eyes being 'beady with fear'.

None the less, Mao was forced to recognise that the Red Guards alone lacked the strength to bring about the decisive shift in the balance of political forces that he wanted. In August he had spoken confidently of 'a few months of disorder' being enough to bring about the downfall of almost all the provincial Party leaders. Now it was clear that it was going to take much longer.

He responded by soft-pedalling his animus towards the veteran cadres – even, in one remarkable speech, apologising for the mischief he had caused:

> No wonder [you] old comrades did not understand too much. The time was so short and the events so violent. I myself had not foreseen that the whole country would be thrown into turmoil . . . Since it was I who caused the havoc, it is understandable if you have some bitter words for me . . . [But] what's come has come . . . Undoubtedly you have made some mistakes . . . but they can be corrected and that will be that! Whoever wants to overthrow you? I don't, and I don't think the Red Guards do either . . . You find it difficult to cross this pass, and I don't find it easy. You are anxious and so am I. I cannot blame you, comrades.

On the same occasion, he insisted that Liu and Deng were not in the same category as Peng Zhen. They had acted openly, he said. 'If they have made mistakes, they can change . . . Once they have changed it will be all right.'

Meanwhile he took a number of steps to shore up the radicals.

The Red Guards were instructed to broaden their class base. The early Red Guard slogan, 'If the father is a hero, the son is courageous; if the father is reactionary, the son is a bastard', was denounced as 'historical idealism', no better than feudalism. Millions of youths, who had previously been excluded from the movement and had little love for the traditional 'Red classes' of the Party hierarchy, now rallied to the radicals' cause.

Several leaders whose ardour in pursuing 'capitalist-roaders' was judged to be insufficient were purged as a warning to others to show more enthusiasm.

Wang Renzhong, the left-wing Hubei Party chief, whom Mao had personally chosen as one of the deputy heads of the Cultural Revolution Group, went first – accused of suppressing 'exchanges of experience' among Red Guards. Then Tao Zhu, who ranked fourth in the hierarchy – behind Mao, Lin Biao and Zhou Enlai – was charged with being a 'faithful follower of the Liu–Deng line'. He had adopted what Mao considered too restrictive a view of the Cultural Revolution and had tried to defend veteran cadres. To the Red Guards, that made him an 'uncompromising emperor-protector' and a 'high-level two-faced rogue'. Marshal He Long, also a Politburo member, was accused of being in league with Peng

Zhen. Even eighty-year-old Zhu De was denounced in wall-posters as 'an old swine' and a 'black commander' who had consistently opposed Mao's proletarian line. At a slightly lower level, about a score of Central Committee members working in the capital were brought before Red Guard struggle meetings, where they were made to wear dunce's caps and endured verbal and physical abuse.

Finally, in December, Mao allowed the Cultural Revolution Group to bring back Peng Dehuai from Sichuan. He was held at a military barracks for questioning about his links with Liu Shaoqi and Deng Xiaoping.

The choice of victims was determined partly by personal factors (Chen Boda had a long-standing grudge against Tao Zhu; Wang Renzhong had offended Jiang Qing; He Long's wife and Lin Biao's wife, Ye Qun, had loathed each other since Yan'an) and partly by political self-interest – Lin regarded fellow veterans like He and Zhu De as an impediment to achieving complete control of the PLA himself. But, for all of them, there was a single, overriding cause. The Shanghai radical, Zhang Chunqiao, explained:

This Cultural Revolution is precisely to pull down all of these old fellows, sparing no one. Zhu De, Chen Yi, He Long – there's not a single good egg among them! . . . Zhu De is a big warlord; Chen Yi is an old careerist . . . He Long is a bandit . . . Which one is worth keeping? Not one of them should be kept.

All represented the 'old thinking' which the Cultural Revolution was pledged to destroy. A few, like Zhu De, were spared physical maltreatment, because Mao personally forbade it. But for the most part the Chairman obeyed the precept he had laid down for his followers: 'Trust the masses, rely on them and respect their initiative.' He rarely initiated arrests himself (which allowed him, if he wished, to disavow them later) but instead let the radicals act as they thought fit.

As the pressure on the Party veterans mounted, Mao instructed the Cultural Revolution Group to intensify the movement against Liu and Deng.

At a meeting with the Qinghua University Red Guard leader, Kuai Dafu, on December 18, Zhang Chunqiao passed on the Chairman's views. 'Those two at the Party Centre . . . still won't surrender,' he explained. 'Go after them! Make them odious! Don't do it halfway.' The following weekend, thousands of students, preceded by loudspeaker vans, marched to the main shopping areas in Beijing, where they plastered the walls with slogans, urging the two men's overthrow. Jiang Qing persuaded the Head of State's daughter by a previous marriage, Liu Tao, who was also studying at Qinghua, to join the campaign – warning that if she refused it would show her lack of 'revolutionary sincerity'. On January 3, 1967, a poster signed by the girl and her brother, entitled, 'Witness the Despicable Soul of Liu Shaoqi', was put up inside the walls of Zhongnanhai. Red Guard organisations made copies and sent it all over the country. The same day, some thirty members of a rebel group called the 'Zhongnanhai Insurrectionists', which had been formed, with Mao's encouragement, by young staff members and bodyguards from the Central Committee offices, burst into the Head of State's house, where they berated him for three-quarters of an hour and made him recite quotations from the 'Little Red Book'.

Three days later, the Red Guards struck again. This time a hoax telephone call sent Liu's wife, Wang Guangmei, rushing to a Beijing hospital, where she had been told that another daughter, Pingping, was awaiting surgery after a traffic accident. On arrival, she found no injured child, but a crowd of Qinghua rebels, who took her to their campus and staged a struggle meeting against her.

Meanwhile, with Mao's authorisation, the Central Case Examination Group, which had been set up seven months earlier to investigate Peng Zhen and his colleagues, formed a special team to examine Wang Guangmei's past. She came from a wealthy family and had been educated at an American mission school. To Kang Sheng, whom Mao had asked to resume responsibility for political security matters, that immediately raised the possibility that she could be shown to be an American spy. Later, another 'Special Case Group' was formed to try to prove that Liu had betrayed the communist cause while working as an underground leader in the White areas in the 1920s.

A week after the hospital incident, Mao invited Liu for the last time to the Study of Chrysanthemum Fragrance.

Mao enjoyed his triumphs; he liked to savour them.

He enquired solicitously after Pingping's health (knowing full well that the 'accident' had been a fabrication), and reminisced about old times. Liu asked Mao to allow him to resign all his official positions and return with his family to Yan'an, or to his native village in Hunan, to work on a commune as a peasant. The Chairman did not answer. He sat silently, chain-smoking, and when Liu got up to leave said merely: 'Study well. Take good care of yourself.' Five days later, on January 18, the special telephone line linking Liu with other members of the Politburo, including Mao and Premier Zhou, was cut. His isolation was complete.

That winter, Mao added one more, crucial weapon to the radicals' armoury.

Alongside the expansion of the Red Guards, militant factory and office workers, in many cases fired by personal grievances against the Party committees of their work units, began forming their own rebel groups. At the beginning of November, a young textile worker in Shanghai, 33-year-old Wang Hongwen, set up the 'Workers' Revolutionary General Headquarters' to co-ordinate radical workers' groups in the city. When the municipal authorities refused to recognise the new body, Wang despatched a delegation to Beijing. The Shanghai Party committee had the train on which they were travelling stopped before it could leave the city, whereupon the workers lay across the tracks – blocking rail movement for more than thirty hours. Zhang Chunqiao, who was sent in as a troubleshooter, immediately endorsed the General Headquarters' demands and instructed the Shanghai First Secretary, Cao Diqiu, to make a public self-criticism. Two days later, Mao approved Zhang's action, and proclaimed that workers in all commercial, industrial and government offices had a legitimate right to establish mass organisations.

The workers' groups, however, like the student Red Guards before them, soon split into rival factions – 'revolutionary rebels', who sought the overthrow of all existing power structures, and 'proletarian revolutionaries', who wanted to preserve Party leadership, albeit in a more radical form.

From late November, the Shanghai General Headquarters, backed by the Cultural Revolution Group in Beijing, engaged in an increasingly violent power struggle with its conservative rival, the Shanghai Red Detachment, tacitly supported by the city Party committee. On December 30, tens of thousands of workers fought running street battles outside the Party committee's offices. Strikes broke out. The port was paralysed, with more than a hundred foreign ships waiting to be unloaded. Rail transport came to a halt. Workers who had been sent to the countryside in the famine after the Great Leap Forward began demanding the right to return. Starting on January 3, 1967 – the day that the campaign against Liu Shaoqi and his wife went into high gear in Beijing – Wang Hongwen's rebels seized control of Shanghai's main newspapers, first the *Wenhuibao*, then two days afterward, the Party paper, *Jiefang ribao* (Liberation Daily).

At that point, Mao himself intervened, sending Zhang Chunqiao and Yao Wenyuan to the city with a directive stating that the Shanghai Party committee would inevitably fall, and 'a new political authority' should be established in its place – whereupon the balance tilted definitively in the rebels' favour. Two days later, several hundred thousand people gathered in the central square for a rally at which the General Headquarters announced that it no longer recognised the Party committee's authority and that 'revolutionary rebels' in the city government would assume responsibility for day-to-day affairs.

The 'seizure of power' in Shanghai became a model for the rest of the country. Mao called it a 'great revolution' of 'one class overthrowing another'. He cited an old proverb: 'Don't think that because Butcher Zhang dies, we will have to eat pork with the bristles still on it.' The sense was that the country could keep going even if the provincial committees did fall. Over the next three weeks, rebel groups seized power in seven other provinces and cities, including Beijing itself, Anhui, Guangdong and Heilongjiang.

There was a problem, however. The unseating of Party committees was one thing; what to put in their place was quite another.

Neither Mao, nor the rebel groups themselves, had really thought this question through. Zhang Chunqiao was initially preoccupied with warding off challenges from rival Red Guard groups and revolutionary factions, and it was not until February 5, 1967, that, with backing from local PLA units, he felt sufficiently in control of the situation to be able to proclaim the establishment of the Shanghai People's Commune.

In taking this step, Zhang was convinced he had Mao's full support. A few days earlier, Chen Boda had telephoned to say that the Chairman was about to approve the setting-up of a Beijing Commune, and that Shanghai should do the same. The 'Sixteen Points' had called explicitly for 'a system of general elections, like that of the Paris Commune', to establish local organs of power to serve as a bridge between the Party and the masses. As the most important of all the 'newborn things' produced during the Great Leap Forward, the communes symbolised the originality of the Chinese revolution. Mao himself, in 1958, had looked forward to the day when 'everything will be called a commune . . . [including] cities and villages'.

Unexpectedly, however, the Chairman changed his mind. Other cities and provinces were told not to follow Shanghai's example, and Zhang and Yao Wenyuan were summoned to Beijing to hear Mao's explanation.

> A series of problems arises, and I wonder whether you have thought about them [he said]. If the whole of China sets up people's communes, should the 'People's Republic of China' change its name to 'People's Commune of China'? Would others recognise us? Maybe the Soviet Union would not recognise us, whereas Britain and France would. And what would we do about our ambassadors in various countries? And so on.

The reasoning was spurious – and Mao knew it. A name-change would make no difference whatever to China's international relations. None the less, this was what was broadcast by the Red Guards, and soon came to be generally accepted as the reason for the 'commune' form of organisation being rejected. It implied *force majeure*: whatever Mao's own preferences might be, external constraints ruled it out.

The reality was rather different. The Shanghai leaders' move had forced Mao to look into the abyss – and he did not like what he saw.

A system based on the Paris Commune, with free elections and unrestricted political activity, meant allowing the masses to rule themselves. This was the logic of his injunction to 'trust the masses and rely on them' – the logic, in fact, on which the entire Cultural Revolution had been based. But where would that leave the Party? As he put it to Zhang Chunqiao: 'There must be a Party somehow! There must be a nucleus, no matter what we call it.' Truly free elections were a utopian dream. Doing away with leaders and 'over-throwing everything' might look progressive, but in fact it was reactionary and would lead to 'extreme anarchism'.

In one view, Mao lost his nerve, just as he had, ten years earlier, when he had clamped down on the 'Hundred Flowers', only to acknowledge afterwards that he had been 'confused by false appearances' and might have acted prematurely.

Another way of putting it would be that he demonstrated, once again, the skills of a consummate politician. Age had done nothing to dull the acuteness of the Chairman's political antennae. The Cultural Revolution might appear to be a descent into madness, but Mao had moved at each stage with the greatest circumspection. He had made clear from the outset that destruction would have to be followed by rebuilding – that 'the great disorder', as he had put it in July 1966, would eventually have to yield to 'great peace'. That was why he had stayed in the background, letting others do the dirty work, while he kept clean hands – ready to rally, and to rehabilitate, the survivors when the time came to build a new Party on the ashes of the old. It was a pretence to which even his victims, like He Long and Peng Dehuai, subscribed, for they knew that Mao alone had the power, if he wished, to save them; it was in their interests, as well as his, to believe that he was innocent of the horrors perpetrated in his name.

Whether from prudence or fear, or a judicious mixture of both, the outcome was that the visionary ideology of the Shanghai Commune was abandoned.

The Cultural Revolution had reached its Rubicon, the moment at which it lost its compass, when the ideals which had inspired it, no matter how misbegotten they were, became irredeemably tainted. Faced with a choice, Mao had preferred a flawed instrument of rule to no instrument at all. On his proposal, Zhang Chunqiao announced the establishment of a new organ of power, to be known as the Shanghai Revolutionary Committee, formed from a 'three-in-one alliance' of revolutionary rebels, PLA representatives and veteran cadres. The same name had been used for the provisional communist administrations set up in towns and villages after the Autumn Harvest Uprising, forty years before.

Despite Mao's sleight of hand in attributing the change of course to diplomatic pressures, not everyone was fooled. As the revolutionary committees multiplied, ultra-Leftists among the Red Guards spoke darkly of 'capitalist restoration'. To most Chinese, it did not seem like that. But, from February 1967 onward, the Chairman was in ideological retreat and the struggle against the 'capitalist-roaders' became increasingly focused on issues of raw power.

*

Notwithstanding the long-term implications for Mao's dream of a 'realm of Red virtue', the immediate and visible effect of the power seizure in Shanghai was to give a potent, new impetus to the spiral of revolutionary violence.

In the provinces, Red Guards and revolutionary workers redoubled their efforts to topple provincial committees. The first secretaries of Shanxi and Yunnan committed suicide, and the Anhui leader, Li Baohua, was driven through the centre of Beijing on the back of an open truck, like a criminal being taken to execution. A new directive from the Chairman was published, urging 'proletarian revolution groups' to seize power. Crowds gathered outside the West Gate of Zhongnanhai to demand that Liu, Deng Xiaoping and other Central leaders be dragged out and brought before struggle meetings. The Coal Minister, Zhang Linzhi, was forced by Red Guards to wear an iron hat weighing 60 kilograms and afterwards beaten to death.

At the same time, the PLA, which until then had been largely insulated from the disorders, began to be sucked into the morass. In January, Mao had approved the dismissal of Liu Zhijian, the head of the PLA's Cultural Revolution Group, signalling the start of a short-lived drive to ferret out military supporters of Liu Shaoqi's 'bourgeois reactionary line'. His case illustrated a dilemma which the Chairman would wrestle with for the next eight months. Should the army be permitted to engage in the Cultural Revolution on the same basis as civilian groups? Or was there an overriding need, for national security reasons, to maintain war preparedness and military discipline?

Liu's crime, for which he paid with seven years in prison, was to have tried to dissuade cadets from the country's military training colleges from harassing regional army commanders. In this, he had had the support of Ye Jianying, who was in day-to-day charge of the Military Commission, and of three other PLA marshals – Chen Yi, Nie Rongzhen and Xu Xiangqian. To Jiang Qing and Chen Boda, Liu and, by implication, the marshals, as well, were 'obstructing the Cultural Revolution'.

Mao equivocated. Three days after Liu's dismissal, he approved a Central directive prohibiting 'any person or organisation from attacking the organs of the PLA'. But, in the absence of clear Central backing, it was honoured in the breach. Army cadets seized leaders of the Nanjing military region and staged a struggle meeting against them, prompting a warning from their commander, General Xu Shiyou, that if it happened again he would order his men to open fire. Other incidents occurred in Fuzhou and Shenyang. Then, to help the radicals in Shanghai, Mao issued an order for the PLA to 'support the Left'. That brought still closer the prospect of the army becoming embroiled in the politics of warring Red Guard factions, which was the last thing senior officers wanted.

In short, by late January 1967, the veterans who led the PLA in the military regions, many of whom had been with Mao since the days of the Long March, were thoroughly disgruntled.

Trouble flared up first in Xinjiang, where a regimental PLA commander sent troops to subdue radicals in the town of Shihezi, leaving several hundred people wounded. In Sichuan, a force of radical Red Guards and rebel workers which attacked an army barracks was disarmed and its leaders arrested. In the remote province of Qinghai, bordering on Tibet, the military district commander despatched soldiers to surround the offices of the local Party newspaper where radicals had 'seized power' and beaten to death a number of journalists. When they refused to surrender, he ordered an assault in which more than 170 people were killed and a similar number wounded. In Wuhan, after another dispute involving a 'power seizure' at a Party newspaper, a thousand radicals were detained, some of whom were imprisoned, others released after making public confessions. Similar incidents occurred in seven other provinces.

Parallel to the 'February Crackdown', as these events came to be known, a 'February Adverse Current' developed. Mao himself inadvertently lit the fuse, by lashing out at Jiang Qing and Chen Boda for their role in the purge of Tao Zhu. He had approved of Tao's removal. But he objected to their having taken the initiative without consulting him first. Chen was 'an opportunist', he fumed. Jiang Qing was 'ambitious but incompetent'. Even Lin Biao, who had initially tried to protect Tao, was accused of failing to keep the Chairman informed. The conservatives in the Politburo (the four marshals and several vice-premiers), already deeply unhappy over the purge of senior cadres, took this as a signal – wrongly, as it turned out – that Mao was losing patience with the radicals' excesses. At a Military Commission meeting in January, when that subject had been broached, Ye Jianying had banged the table so hard that he broke a bone in his hand. Now, at a joint session of the

Politburo and the Cultural Revolution Group on February 14, Ye warned again, supported by Xu Xiangqian and Chen Yi, of the danger of anarchy. Did the proclamation of the Shanghai Commune, he asked, mean that the Party and the army were redundant? No one answered.

Two days later, Vice-Premier Tan Zhenlin, one of Mao's oldest associates, who had chaired the first Workers' and Peasants' Soviet at the Jinggangshan base area in 1927, picked a quarrel with Zhang Chunqiao.

'Masses this and masses that!' Tan raged. 'You don't want the leadership of the Party. You insist on the masses liberating themselves, people teaching themselves and conducting revolution themselves. What is that but metaphysics?' He went on: 'Forty-year veterans of the revolution have had their homes burst into and dear ones dispersed . . . This is the cruellest instance of struggle in Party history.' Next day, he poured out his bitterness towards Chen Boda, Jiang Qing and the rest of the Cultural Revolution Group in a letter to Lin Biao:

> They are completely ruthless; one word and a life can be snuffed out . . . Our Party is ugly beyond repair . . . They will push you over the edge, even for a minor offence. And yet . . . can they take over? I doubt it . . . The Premier is big-hearted . . . He can wait it out. But how long are we to wait? Until all of the old cadres are downed? No, no, ten thousand times no! I will rebel!

Mao's first impulse was to dismiss these strictures as 'old soldiers sounding off'. But, on reflection, he decided otherwise. Of the twenty-one members of the Politburo appointed six months before, four had been overthrown (Liu, Deng, Tao Zhu and He Long), and four were inactive or neutral (Chen Yun, Dong Biwu, Liu Bocheng and Zhu De). Over the previous few days, seven of the remaining thirteen had come out against Cultural Revolution policies.

At midnight on February 18, Mao summoned Ye Jianying and two of the other critics – Li Xiannian, who was in charge of finance; and Li Fuchun, the Planning Minister – along with Zhou Enlai and two leading radicals.

'What kind of Party leadership do you want?' he asked with an old man's petulance. Why didn't they bring back Wang Ming? Or let the Americans and the Russians run China? If they wished to restore Liu Shaoqi and Deng Xiaoping, he fumed, he would go back to the Jinggangshan to start another guerrilla war. It was the same threat that Mao had made eight years earlier at Lushan. But, this time, there was an element of play-acting. After delivering his ultimatum, he stormed out in a huff.

In fact, on the three basic questions at issue – the role of the Party; of the army; and of the veteran cadres – the Chairman had considerable sympathy for the arguments that Ye and his colleagues had raised. Two weeks earlier, he had condemned the Shanghai rebels for putting forward the principle of 'suspecting everyone and overthrowing everyone'. He had laid down that veteran cadres were to be included in the 'three-in-one alliances' on which the new revolutionary committees were to be based – and what was true of the provinces was no less true for the Centre. He knew, too, that there was a limit beyond which it would not be prudent to test the loyalty of the military elite. For all these reasons, he was disinclined to press the marshals too hard. Only Tan Zhenlin, who had infuriated Jiang Qing by comparing her with the Empress Wu, a Tang dynasty consort regarded as one of the most evil women in Chinese history, was held to be beyond redemption and disappeared from sight.

Over the next month, the old guard were made to attend all-night study meetings at which their errors were condemned by members of the Cultural Revolution Group. In the streets outside, Red Guard posters called for their overthrow. But, unlike Tao Zhu and He Long, they were not purged. At the end of April, Mao summoned all of them, except Tan, to a 'unity meeting' at which he noted that they had not 'plotted secretly', and tried to soothe ruffled feelings.

None the less, their action had important repercussions.

After February 1967, the Politburo ceased to function. Mao was not willing to take the risk of a majority uniting against him. In its place, he convened enlarged meetings of the Standing Committee or of the Cultural Revolution Group, now chaired by Zhou Enlai.

At the same time the wall-poster campaign against the veterans put the traditional military hierarchy on the defensive, while encouraging a fresh upsurge of Leftist militancy. Mao himself became convinced that the military leaders' efforts to restore stability in the 'February Crackdown' had been excessive. Officers who had shown special zeal in repressing radical assaults – including the Qinghai commander – were denounced as ultra-Rightists and court-martialled. Lin Biao, who had earlier supported the regional commanders' efforts to limit radical disruption, now began to warn of 'an armed Liu–Deng line'. On April 1, Mao approved a directive condemning the 'arbitrary stigmatising of mass organisations'. Military units, which previously had been permitted to open fire to suppress 'reactionaries' – a catch-all term which was applied to almost any rebellious group – or as a last resort in self-defence, were now prohibited from using their weapons against radicals in any circumstances.

Factional violence rapidly escalated. Large quantities of weapons were stolen, including arms consignments being sent by rail to Vietnam. At Yibin, on the Upper Yangtse, pitched battles broke out involving tens of thousands of people. At Chongqing, rival groups used anti-aircraft guns to bombard each other's positions. In Changsha, they used missiles. Thirteen-year-old Liang Heng found himself in the middle of one such firefight:

> I went out to buy kerosene to use when there were shortages of elec-tricity . . . Then suddenly, too suddenly, 50 or 60 men carrying machine-guns ran past the gate of the *Hunan Daily* [building] toward me. A short man in black carried the flag with the words, 'Young People's Bodyguard Squad' on it, the name of one of the groups in the [radical] Xiang River Wind and Thunder faction . . . When the men were almost abreast of me they opened fire, aiming off down the road into the distance . . .
>
> The enemy was out of sight, but it responded with force . . . The flagman fell in front of me and rolled over and over like a lead ball. The flag never touched the ground. Someone caught it and raised it, hardly breaking stride. Then he crumpled and rolled, and someone else seized it and carried it forward . . .
>
> At last . . . they retreated to the nearest shelter . . . [where] other 'Bodyguard Squad' members were waiting with trucks and stretchers . . . Those still unharmed reloaded madly, breaking open huge wooden crates and spilling the long pointed bullets in random hillocks on the ground . . .
>
> In the meantime, three shining black cannon had been taken off the trucks and the Rebels were trying to get the soldiers to show them how to use them. The soldiers were refusing . . . Finally [they] decided to go ahead [anyway]. They shot three times, but each time the shell went wildly astray . . . At the time, I found this vaguely amusing, but later . . . a worker . . . told me how he had shot and killed his best friend at a distance of two feet because he did not know how to use a machine-gun . . .
>
> Someone they called Commander Tang [then arrived], a

distraught young man with two guns in his belt and a small contingent of bodyguards. 'Quickly, quickly,' he was saying furiously. 'Retreat, retreat . . .' They piled into the trucks, a bloody collection of bandages and filth, the motors roared, and they were gone . . .

The city shook the whole day, and that evening the sky glowed a queer orange . . . The next day we learned that members of the [radical] 'Changsha Youth' organisation had levelled anti-aircraft missiles at the Xiang Embroidery Building on May First Square in an attack on the [conservative] Workers' Alliance. The entire block-long four-storey building had burned to the ground.

The 'all-round nationwide civil war' which Mao had toasted the previous winter had become a reality.

At this juncture, the Chairman set out for a two-month-long tour of the provinces, to see for himself how the Cultural Revolution was progressing. His first stop was in Wuhan, where armed clashes had been occurring between a conservative workers' group, known as the 'Million Heroes', which was supported by the regional military commander, Chen Zaidao, and the radical 'Workers' General Headquarters', whose leaders had been in prison since the 'February Crackdown'. In the worst incident, in June, more than a hundred people had been killed and some 3,000 wounded.

Mao's presence was kept secret, and exceptional security was in force. The entire staff of the East Lake state guest-house, where he stayed, was changed on the eve of his arrival in case it had been infiltrated by counter-revolutionaries.

On Monday, July 18, after two days of talks with local leaders, Mao concluded that Chen had committed errors and must make a public self-criticism, while retaining his command; the 'Workers' Headquarters' should be regarded as the core group of the Left; and the 'Million Heroes' should be encouraged to unite with them. They were, after all, workers, he said, and there should be no fundamental conflict of interest. This was announced that night by Wang Li, the Cultural Revolution Group's propaganda chief, and a summary of his remarks, in which he described the 'Million Heroes' as a conservative group, was broadcast over the city's street loudspeaker system. Next day, the Security Minister, Xie Fuzhi, gave a more detailed account to the Military Region Party Committee.

Chen Zaidao accepted Mao's verdict. The 'Million Heroes', unaware that it came from the Chairman himself, did not.

The following night, thousands of the group's followers com-

mandeered army lorries and fire trucks and drove in convoy to the
Military Region headquarters, demanding that Wang Li come out
and talk to them. When he failed to appear, they went to the East
Lake guest-house and stormed the building where he was staying –
totally unaware that Mao was less than a hundred yards away.
Supported by uniformed troops from a local regiment, they broke
into Wang's room, dragged him out into a car and took him to a
struggle meeting, where he was severely beaten and one of his legs
was broken. For the next three days and nights, several hundred
thousand people – members of the 'Million Heroes' and their
supporters, including large numbers of fully armed soldiers
– paraded through the city in a show of strength, calling for
the dismissal of Wang Li and Xie Fuzhi, and the overthrow of the
Cultural Revolution Group radicals.

Mao was never in any danger. Even if he had been, it probably
would not have bothered him greatly. Three months earlier he had
horrified his staff by insisting that the masses must be allowed to
storm Zhongnanhai if they wished.

But for the radicals, it was a heaven-sent opportunity to press for
a nationwide campaign to root out conservative resistance in the
army once and for all.

Lin Biao and Jiang Qing portrayed the Wuhan events as a full-
scale mutiny. Mao himself, who was flown out to Shanghai in the
early hours of Thursday morning – breaking, for the first and last
time in his life, the rule imposed by the Politburo in 1959, forbidding
him to travel by air for fear of an accident – pooh-poohed that idea,
pointing out that if Chen Zaidao had wanted to stage a rebellion he
would not have been permitted to leave. None the less, the fact that
he had been pressured into a precipitate departure as a result of
military unrest irritated Mao greatly.

Wang Li was released next day, and flew back with Xie Fuzhi to
Beijing, where the two men were given a heroes' welcome. Lin Biao
presided over a rally of a million people in Tiananmen Square,
attended by the whole leadership (except the marshals, who were
pointedly not invited), to denounce the Wuhan military region for
'daring to use barbaric, fascist methods to besiege, kidnap and beat
up the Centre's representatives'.

Chen Zaidao was summoned to the capital and stripped of his
command. But, on Mao's instructions, he was not designated a
counter-revolutionary; and when thousands of cadets tried to drag

him out for a struggle meeting, the Beijing garrison commander, Fu Chongbi, hid him for two hours in a lift, immobilised between two floors of the guest-house where he was staying, until they had dispersed. The defeated 'Million Heroes' were less fortunate. Their radical opponents from the 'Workers' Headquarters' launched a pogrom which, in Wuhan alone, left 600 workers dead. In the province as a whole, an astounding 184,000 people were seized, beaten and maimed.

Despite Mao's personal confidence in Chen Zaidao, he gave his full backing to Lin Biao's efforts to 'drag out that small handful [of capitalist-roaders] within the armed forces' – an expression first used by Lin's son, Lin Liguo, in an article in the *People's Daily* the day after the Wuhan events. The Chairman had been growing alarmed at the military weakness of the Left, and in mid-July had proposed to Zhou Enlai that workers and students should be armed. Zhou had taken no action, but shortly afterwards Jiang Qing publicised the slogan, 'Attack by reasoning, defend by force', which was widely used by radical groups to justify armed struggle.

On August 4, in a private letter to Jiang Qing – which she read out to a meeting of the Standing Committee – Mao went further. It was imperative to arm the Left, he wrote, because the great majority of the army was backing conservative workers' groups. The stealing of arms by workers was 'not a serious problem'. The masses should be encouraged to take the law into their own hands.

In this febrile climate, the Party journal, *Red Flag*, published an editorial to mark the fortieth anniversary of the founding of the Red Army on August 1, which made clear that the struggle against capitalist-roaders in the army was the next major national task.

When Mao read it, he changed his mind.

Just as he had after the proclamation of the Shanghai Commune, he now decided, for the second time, that the Cultural Revolution had reached a Rubicon. For the second time, he ordered a retreat.

Mao himself liked to explain such reversals in terms of dialectics: when a thing reaches its extreme, it turns into its opposite. Thus, in February 1967, he had moved to preserve the principle of Party rule against the day when he would want to rebuild it. Now, six months later, with the Party hierarchy virtually destroyed, he recognised an overriding imperative to preserve the one instrument of power that remained: the army. This time, it was not the fear of anarchy that had given him pause, but the politician's instinct for the possible. In the trade-off between radical activism and military stability that he had been juggling with since the winter, he had pushed the radicals' cause to the limit. The moment had come for the pendulum to swing decisively back the other way.

On August 11, he sent word to Beijing that the policy of 'dragging out capitalist-roaders in the army' was 'unstrategic'. That was enough for Lin Biao and Jiang Qing to drop it like a hot brick and start casting around for scapegoats. Soon afterwards, Mao returned the *Red Flag* editorial with the fateful words, 'poisonous weed', scrawled on it. It had been written by the hero of the Wuhan events, Wang Li, the editor of *Red Flag*, Lin Jie, and another Cultural Revolution Group propagandist named Guan Feng. All three were arrested. Wang was charged in addition with stirring up dissension at the Foreign Ministry, where, in late July, an ultra-Leftist group had seized control and had tried to oust Chen Yi. That had led to a Red Guard attack on the British Legation, which had been burned to the ground in reprisal for arrests of radicals in Hong Kong, and to lesser incidents at the Burmese, Indian and Indonesian missions. These had angered Mao because they showed that China was failing to meet its international obligations. It strengthened his determination to ensure that the army, if nothing else, should remain a disciplined force.

In February, the Chairman had justified the retreat from the Shanghai Commune on a diplomatic pretext. In August, to protect the army, a different device was employed.

The wave of radical attacks was blamed on a shadowy ultra-Leftist organisation called the 'May 16 Group'. It was not wholly fictitious: a Red Guard groupuscule of that name, with about forty members, had been formed that spring at the Beijing Iron and Steel Institute, and had distinguished itself by making wall-poster attacks on Premier Zhou Enlai as the 'backstage boss' of the 'February Adverse Current'. Other radical groups were making similar accusations at that time, tacitly encouraged by followers of Jiang Qing, who already saw Zhou as an impediment to her political ambitions. However, Mao had ordered Chen Boda to issue a statement that Zhou was a member of the Chairman's 'proletarian headquarters', and the agitation stopped. By August, the 'May 16 Group' had virtually ceased to exist – and, in any case, it had no connection with Wang Li and Guan Feng, or any of the other senior figures who were later named as its leaders. But that was of no importance. What mattered was the concept it represented. From September 1967 onwards, when Mao personally branded it a 'conspiratorial counter-revolutionary clique' with 'unspeakably evil purposes', 'May 16' became a catch-all weapon for wiping out any manifestation, suspected or real, of political dissent.

That month the Chairman approved a directive, forbidding weapons seizures by Leftist rebels and once more authorising troops to fire in self-defence. On his instructions, Jiang Qing delivered a speech, condemning armed struggle and denouncing the idea of 'seizing a small handful in the army' as 'a wrong slogan' and 'a trap' set by right-wingers in order to ensnare the left. 'We must not paint the PLA black,' she went on. 'They are our own boys.' The army commanders' problems were not over. But the threat that had hung over the military since the beginning of the year had finally been lifted.

The repudiation of the 'February Adverse Current' in the spring of 1967 had not only triggered an upsurge of radical attacks against the army. It had also signalled the start of a new stage in the criticism of Liu Shaoqi, and of the bourgeois ideology he was held to represent.

It began on April 1, 1967, with a long article in the *People's Daily*, written by a Cultural Revolution Group propagandist named Qi Benyu, which broke new ground by attacking Liu directly (though still not by name) as 'the top Party person in power taking the capitalist road'. The article, entitled 'Patriotism or National Betrayal', had been revised by Mao himself. Like many Cultural Revolution polemics, the topic was extremely obscure – a film made in 1950, set in the time of the Emperor Guangxu, which Mao had once denounced as treasonous because it denigrated the Boxer Revolt but which Liu was said to have approved. The burden of the article was that the Boxers, like the Red Guards, were revolutionary, and that Liu's support of the film was a paradigm for his many other acts of betrayal. On April 6, the 'Zhongnanhai Insurrectionists' staged another raid on Liu's home – the first since January – and questioned him about Qi Benyu's charges. Next day, the Head of State put up a wall-poster outside his house, denying any traitorous intent. It was torn down after a few hours, and on the 10th his wife, Wang Guangmei, was taken to a struggle meeting before thousands of Red Guards at Qinghua University, where she was humiliated by being made to put on a silk dress, silk stockings and high-heeled shoes (which she had worn during a State Visit to Indonesia), as well as a necklace made of ping-pong balls, to symbolise her supposed bourgeois tastes.

The media barrage continued. In May, Liu's book, *How to be a Good Communist*, was denounced as 'a big anti-Marxist-Leninist and anti-Mao-Zedong-Thought poisonous weed'. The Chairman himself described it as 'a deceitful work, a form of idealism, opposed to Marxism-Leninism'.

The climax came in July. On the eve of Mao's departure for Wuhan, Red Guards from the Beijing Institute of Aeronautical Engineering, backed by the Cultural Revolution Group, set up a 'Collar Liu Shaoqi Frontline Command Post' outside the West Gate of Zhongnanhai. Dozens of loudspeaker vans blared out Maoist slogans day and night. By July 18, several hundred thousand people had gathered in the streets outside, vowing to fast until Liu was 'dragged out'. This was not done, because Mao had expressly forbidden it. But that evening the 'Zhongnanhai Insurrectionists' held an 'accusation meeting' within the leadership compound, at which Liu and his wife were made to stand silently for two hours, bowing from the waist, while their accusers harangued them. Mao's doctor saw them being beaten and kicked, while soldiers of the Central Guard Unit stood by and watched: Liu's shirt had been torn open, and people were jerking him around by the hair. Two-and-a-half weeks later, the process was repeated. This time the couple had to stand in the Red Guards' 'jetplane' position, bending forward with their arms stretched back behind them, while Liu was interrogated anew about his alleged 'national betrayals'. Deng Xiaoping and Tao Zhu and their wives were subjected to similar indignities.

It was mild stuff compared to the treatment meted out to lesser officials. None the less, Liu was seventy years old. He was forced to kneel before Red Guard posters, with rebels pulling his hair and pushing his head to the ground. His left leg was injured, and afterwards, as he was frog-marched back to his residence, his face was swollen and a bluish, ashen colour.

On August 7, he wrote to Mao, resigning as Head of State.

He received no reply. Soon afterwards he was separated from his family. Wang Guangmei was imprisoned. Their children were sent to work as peasants in the countryside. The accusation meetings ceased. From then on Liu was held in solitary confinement at his home, while the Central Case Examination Group continued to assemble 'evidence' of treachery that would justify his formal dismissal.

This body took on growing importance as the swirl of movements that constituted the Cultural Revolution became ever more complex. It was chaired by Zhou Enlai and answerable directly to Mao. But in practice it became the personal empire of Kang Sheng. Alongside the Red Guards and the rebel worker detachments, who were the revolution's foot soldiers, and the PLA, whose 'support for the Left' made up for the radicals' numerical weakness – Kang's political police provided the edge of cold steel which ensured that, in all circumstances, 'proletarian dictatorship' would triumph.

From the spring of 1967 onwards, the Examination Group's remit, initially limited to the investigation of Peng Zhen and his associates, and then of Liu and Wang Guangmei, was dramatically enlarged.

One of the first new cases Kang devised was that of the so-called '61 Renegades'. This involved a group of senior Party officials, including the former Finance Minister, Bo Yibo, and the Organisation Department head, An Ziwen, who had been imprisoned in the 1930s in Beijing. With the agreement of the then Party leader, Zhang Wentian, and of the rest of the Politburo (including Mao), Liu Shaoqi, as head of the North China Bureau, had authorised them to renounce their Party membership as a means of winning release. The matter had been reviewed at the Seventh Party Congress in 1945, and it had been agreed that Liu had acted correctly.

When Kang initially suggested that the case should be reopened, Mao demurred. But, by February 1967, he had overcome his scruples. A month later, the Cultural Revolution Group approved a directive, labelling the sixty-one officials 'a clique of traitors', and accusing them of having 'betrayed the Party' as the price of their freedom. Mao, Zhou Enlai, Kang himself and the rest of the leadership all knew perfectly well that the charge was a complete fabrication. But it was useful, both to discredit Liu among the Party rank and file, and as a means of removing some of his principal supporters.

Unlike Stalin, Mao appears to have taken no interest in the sordid details of his victims' treatment. Kang had a free hand, employing a mixture of Red Guard violence and the subtler tortures of trained professional interrogators. Bo Yibo kept a record of his torment, written on scraps of newspaper that he scattered in his cell, guessing correctly that his persecutors would preserve them – and that, one day, when the political wind changed, they would become a part of the indictment against them:

> I received another round of severe beatings today [he wrote]. I am now covered in wounds and injuries, and my clothes are all in tatters. At one point, because I became dizzy and moved my body a couple of times, I was hit . . . and kicked over and over again . . . [Another time] my two arms were held behind my back, twisted, and when they put me on the 'jetplane', they forced me to keep my legs wide apart, while pressing my back down as far as it would go but keeping my head up and at attention. Then they took turns pulling my hair while kicking and beating me . . . I can no longer hold a pen steadily. How can I write a confession?

Two more 'Special Case Groups' were formed to deal with Peng Dehuai and He Long. In July 1967, Peng was beaten so severely, in an attempt to make him confess that he had plotted against Mao, that the interrogators broke four of his ribs. He Long died of diabetic complications after being denied medical treatment.

Other investigations followed – into the Party's underground networks in the 1920s and '30s. In east Hebei, 84,000 people were arrested, of whom 2,955 were executed, tortured to death or committed suicide. In Guangdong, 7,200 people were interrogated, and 85, including a provincial vice-governor, beaten to death. In Shanghai, 6,000 people were detained. Most were accused of working for the nationalists (an easy enough charge to make about a period when the CCP and the Guomindang had formed a united front), and about half were labelled traitors. Another small 'renegade clique', similar to Bo Yibo's, was unearthed in Xinjiang. In the north-east, an even more fantastic story was concocted, in which it was claimed that a group of senior army officers were 'remnant followers' of the Manchurian leader, Zhang Xueliang, and had plotted against Lin Biao: they, too, were purged. In Yunnan, 14,000 Party cadres were executed in an investigation to 'ferret out traitors'. But the most extraordinary case of all was in Inner Mongolia. There 350,000 people were arrested; 80,000 people were beaten so badly they were permanently maimed, and more than 16,000 died, in an effort to prove that the veteran provincial leader,

Ulanfu, a Politburo alternate, had established a rival 'black party' to compete with the CCP for power.

None of these cases had any basis in fact. All were based on confessions, extracted by torture, and on the weaving together of isolated incidents, taken out of context, to produce a web of paranoid suspicion. In Mao's new 'all-round nationwide civil war', he had reverted to the logic, and the methods, of the old – to the practices of the 1930s during the frenzied blood-purges in the beleaguered Red base areas. Terror was again the means by which Red China would be cleansed, ready for the creation of the new utopia.

By the autumn of 1967, the first, firestorm year of the Cultural Revolution was drawing to a close. Liu Shaoqi had been vanquished. His allies had been purged, and Kang Sheng's ever-widening net was sweeping up their supporters, imagined or real. The Red Guards and rebel worker detachments had broken the hold of veteran Party officials in the provinces.

In the triad of 'struggle, criticism, transformation', on which all Mao's political movements were based, the time for struggle was over; criticism would continue; but the priority was now transformation – replacing the old with the new.

Amid the chaos of a country, all of whose main institutions except the army, the secret police and the economic ministries, had been effectively destroyed, this was easier said than done. In September 1967, during his tour of the provinces, Mao issued a new directive, requiring rival Red Guard and workers' factions to unite and form 'grand alliances'. In Beijing and Shanghai, this was done fairly quickly – though violent factional strife continued among university Red Guards. In other provinces, the army was instructed to maintain a policy of neutrality while rival Red Guard organisations despatched delegations to the capital, where, under the watchful eyes of the Cultural Revolution Group, they were ordered to negotiate until they resolved their differences.

To promote unity, the opposing factions were no longer described as 'radicals' and 'conservatives'. Instead, local names were used. Thus, from Anhui there was the 'good' faction (*hao pai*) and the 'fart faction' (*pi pai*) – so-called because the radicals had said the power seizure in the province was 'good', while the conservatives said it was 'as good as a fart'. But even with that encouragement, and the personal intervention of leaders as highly placed as Jiang Qing and Kang Sheng, it took fourteen months before the Anhui groups reached agreement. Up to the autumn of 1967, only six provinces had been able to establish Revolutionary Committees. Everywhere else the Red Guards and other mass organisations were still arguing about which of them should take part and which of the veteran provincial leaders, whose participation was required under Mao's 'three-in-one' formula, they could agree to support.

Meanwhile, to put steel into the Chairman's call to order, the campaign against the ultra-Leftist 'May 16' group was vastly expanded. That winter, Qi Benyu was arrested, joining his former colleagues, Wang Li and Guan Feng, as one of the three 'black hands' who had supposedly acted as the group's backstage bosses. Over the next four years, 10 million people would fall under suspicion as 'May 16' elements, and more than three million people would be detained – one in twenty-five of the adult urban population. At the Foreign Ministry, where Wang Li's influence was alleged to have been strongest, more than half of the 2,000 diplomats and officials were purged under the 'May 16' banner. The sheer scale of the movement meant that the main investigative role had to be taken by the army, which also had the leading role in a parallel campaign, launched in the spring of 1968, for 'the cleansing of class ranks'. That resulted in the arrests of another 1.84 million people, most of them alleged 'spies', 'bad elements', 'newly emerged counter-revolutionaries' and other undesirables. Tens of thousands of nameless men and women were beaten to death or committed suicide. The survivors were sent to labour camps.

Others, whose offences were linked directly to Cultural Revolution activities, were detained under new public security regulations which made it a counter-revolutionary crime to criticise Mao, Lin Biao, or, by extension, any of the other radical leaders. The regulations had been promulgated in January 1967, but were not applied until efforts to restore order began in earnest at the end of that year.

Despite this battery of repressive weaponry, the Chairman did not have it all his own way. The campaign against the ultra-Leftist 'May 16' group encouraged conservatives to question certain aspects of the Cultural Revolution Group's policies. Ninety-one Chinese ambassadors and other senior diplomats signed a wall-poster supporting the Politburo moderates who had been denounced during the 'February Adverse Current'. A Red Guard group did the same. Xie Fuzhi, whom Mao had named to head the Beijing Revolutionary Committee, was accused of extreme Leftism. Similar attacks were made on radical leaders in Shanghai and Sichuan.

Mao's counter-offensive, when it came, was from an unexpected quarter.

Lin Biao had made skilful use of the various movements in the Cultural Revolution to strengthen his control over the army. In 1967, he had been the beneficiary of a particularly bizarre sequence of events, when a PLA dance troupe, whose members supported the radicals, rioted during a performance by a rival, conservative troupe. It turned out that several of the girl dancers in the conservative troupe were regular visitors to Mao's bed, and quickly persuaded the Chairman of the justice of their cause. Lin Biao (and the rest of the Cultural Revolution Group) promptly switched allegiance – and the affair became the pretext for a purge which enabled him to oust the head of the PLA's General Political Department, the independent-minded General Xiao Hua.

At the beginning of 1968, Lin decided he also wished to replace Yang Chengwu, whom he had appointed two years earlier to succeed the disgraced Luo Ruiqing as Chief of Staff. As a young battalion commander, Yang had been responsible for two of the epic feats of the Long March – the crossing of the Dadu River, and the storming of Lazikou Pass – which had passed into PLA legend. Like Xiao Hua, he had shown that he had a mind of his own, which to Lin made him, ipso facto, suspect. Lin had doubts, too, about the reliability of two other senior officers. Fu Chongbi, the Beijing garrison commander, had protected Chen Zaidao after the Wuhan incident; while Yu Lijin, the Political Commissar of the PLA air force, had fallen out with the Air force Commander, Lin's ally, Wu Faxian.

To Mao, the fact that the three men had lost Lin's trust, at a time when he needed scapegoats to serve as targets in a new campaign against Right-deviationism, was enough to seal their fate.

On March 21, 1968, Jiang Qing and Kang Sheng made speeches, claiming that 'certain people' were trying to 'reverse the verdict' on the 'February Adverse Current'. The following day, it was announced that Yang, Yu and Fu had committed 'serious mistakes' and had been dismissed. Four days later, wall-posters appeared, accusing the three men of fomenting a resurgence of 'right-conservatism'. That marked the start of a nationwide movement to oppose the 'Rightist wind of reversing correct verdicts'.

Soon afterwards, Yang was replaced as Chief of Staff by Huang Yongsheng, commander of the Canton Military Region and one of Lin's most loyal supporters. Later the same month Mao gave orders that the functions of the Standing Committee of the Military Commission should be transferred to its General Office, headed by Wu Faxian and staffed entirely by Lin's aides. From then on, Ye Jianying, Xu Xiangqian and the other veteran marshals lost any role in military decision-making.

Lin Biao would never achieve complete mastery of the PLA. Its size – five million men – and its growth from different base areas, each with its own chain of command and its own network of historical loyalties, meant that, with the exception of Mao (and, for a period, Zhu De), no single individual could control it. None the less, in 1968, Lin was as close as he would ever be to dominating the military, and the PLA itself achieved an unprecedented role in the conduct of the nation's affairs.

That summer, Mao moved decisively to restore order in Shensi, then in the grip of full-scale civil war, and in Guangxi, where heavy weaponry had been looted from shipments bound for Vietnam and factional fighting had reduced parts of the provincial capital, Nanning, to rubble. Troops were sent in to separate the warring parties. On July 3, the Chairman issued a directive, calling for an immediate end to the violence. Military Control Commissions were installed in the worst-affected counties to punish those who resisted. In Guangxi, that sparked a wave of indiscriminate slaughter and, in some areas, political cannibalism: alleged traitors were killed and their livers eaten, in the same way as forty years earlier, Peng Pai's followers in Hailufeng, further up the coast, had killed and eaten their adversaries at 'banquets of human flesh' – with those who refused to take part being branded as 'false comrades'.*

---

* Similar incidents took place in Cambodia under Khmer Rouge rule in the mid-1970s. In each case, the motive appears to have been the same – to obtain from the participants a physical proof of loyalty that went beyond conventional constraints.

The army was also entrusted with re-establishing discipline in the country's schools and universities, where 'workers' propaganda teams' were sent to prepare for the resumption of classes, suspended for the previous two years while students rebelled.

This gave rise to another bizarre incident, less gruesome but in inspiration no less atavistic than the events in Guangxi.

At the end of July, Mao despatched a team of 30,000 workers and PLA men to Qinghua University, where radical Red Guards had refused to lay down their arms. The fighting duly ended, though not before ten people had died and more than a hundred had been wounded. As a token of support, Mao sent the work team a gift of mangoes, which he had received a few days earlier from a visiting Pakistani delegation. These were treated with all the reverence prescribed in the *Liji*, the Book of Rites dating from the fifth century BC, a period of China's antiquity whose precepts the Cultural Revolution was supposed utterly to have swept away. Like holy relics – a tooth of the Buddha, or a nail from the Cross – the mangoes were venerated, and eventually, when they were half rotten, preserved by being coated in wax, while 'replicas' were distributed to other organisations.

The reopening of the schools helped to restore civil peace, but it did nothing to resolve the problem of the millions of youths who should have graduated during the previous two years and instead had spent their time roaming the country as Red Guards.

Even before the Cultural Revolution, youth unemployment in the cities had necessitated a voluntary rustication programme for school-leavers. The political turmoil since had made jobs still harder to find. Industrial output had fallen nearly 14 per cent in 1967, and continued to decline the following year.

In the autumn of 1968, therefore, the rustication programme was revived on an expanded basis – but this time it was compulsory. Over the next two years, five million young people would be sent to the countryside. In a parallel programme, several million cadres and intellectuals were ordered out of the cities to live in rural 'May 7 Cadre Schools' – so-called because Mao had put forward the idea of work-study among the peasants in a letter to Lin Biao on May 7, 1966. That most peasants wanted nothing to do with the new arrivals, regarding them as yet another unwelcome burden, was beside the point. To Mao, it was a neat solution: ideologically, it fulfilled his cherished ideal of breaking down barriers between town and country; politically, it forced the bureaucracy, the 'new class' which he believed had degenerated because of the softness of urban life, to seek renewal through manual labour; and socially, it removed from the cities both the former Red Guards and many of their former victims.

Here, too, the military played a key role.

Many of the rusticated youths wound up working on army-run farms in the border regions. Army officers oversaw the 'cleansing of class ranks' at the cadre schools. Military work teams were installed in every government department and ministry, in factories and newspaper offices.

But the full extent of the PLA's dominance was shown most clearly in the provincial administration. Half the members of the new revolutionary committees were PLA officers, as against less than a third from Red Guard and rebel worker detachments, and only 20 per cent, veteran cadres. In the standing committees – which served as the provincial governments – almost three-quarters of the members were army men. At the grass roots, the proportion was still more striking: in a run-of-the-mill province like Hubei, where disruption had not been out of the ordinary, an astounding 98 per cent of county-level revolutionary committees were chaired by PLA officers. In practice, most of China was under military rule.

That, however, was the price of ending the descent into anarchy. The devastation of the social tissue had been too deep to admit of any other solution.

At the beginning of September 1968, it was announced that the last of the twenty-nine provincial revolutionary committees – in Tibet and Xinjiang – had been established. The Cultural Revolution Group proclaimed that 'the entire country is Red' and, at a mass rally two days later, Zhou Enlai declared: 'We have finally smashed the plot of the handful of Party persons in power, taking the capitalist road.' The stage was at last set for the political denouement which Mao had begun preparing nearly four years before.

On October 13, 1968, the Central Committee, or what was left of it, gathered in Beijing to begin its Twelfth Plenum. More than two-thirds of its original membership had been purged, and of those that remained, only forty full members were present – too few to constitute a quorum. To remedy that, Mao named ten additional members (in violation of Party statutes, which required the promotion of alternates, in accordance with their rank order), and packed the meeting with some eighty PLA officers and leaders from the newly formed revolutionary committees, who participated in the debates but did not have the right to vote.

The plenum had three main tasks: to ratify the overthrow of Liu Shaoqi; to confirm the designation of Lin Biao as Mao's new successor – a state of affairs that had been implicit since August 1966, when Lin had become sole Vice-Chairman, and which Mao had explicitly acknowledged in November 1967; and to condemn the 'February Adverse Current' and its sequel, the 'Right-deviationist wind' of March 1968.

Of these, by far the most important was the resolution damning Liu. Jiang Qing, who had taken personal charge of the 'Special Case Group' carrying out the investigation, had compiled three large volumes of evidence – based entirely on confessions obtained through torture – which purported to show that he had betrayed the Party to the Guomindang on at least three occasions: in Changsha in 1925; in Wuhan in 1927; and in Shenyang in 1929. To obtain even those flimsy charges of treachery four decades before, Kang Sheng's investigators had had to interrogate 28,000 people, most of whom were later imprisoned as counter-revolutionaries. One key witness, Meng Yongqian, who had been arrested with Liu in 1929, was questioned continuously for seven days and nights to force him to admit that they had turned traitor while in captivity. When he recovered, he retracted his 'confession' – but this was concealed.

Jiang Qing herself evidently recognised that these were slim pickings, and in her report she listed other, more recent, examples of Liu's perfidy – including collusion with 'the US secret agent, Wang Guangmei'; sending 'valuable information' to the CIA in Hong Kong; and opposing 'Chairman Mao's proletarian revolutionary line'. Evidence to back up these charges would be published later, she said, though in fact it never was.

None the less, the plenum voted 'to expel Liu Shaoqi from the Party, once and for all'; to dismiss him from all his posts as 'a renegade, traitor and scab . . . [and] a lackey of imperialism, modern revisionism and the Guomindang reactionaries'; and 'to continue to settle accounts with him and his accomplices'. It was not quite a unanimous vote. Zhou Enlai, Chen Yi, Ye Jianying and the other veteran leaders all raised their hands obediently to condemn their erstwhile colleague. But one elderly woman CC member refused to go along with the charade and abstained. She was purged afterwards too.

Lin Biao's nomination as Mao's successor was also approved – without dissent.

The one issue on which serious differences did arise was the treatment of the Politburo moderates. Jiang Qing and Kang Sheng wanted the next Party Congress – for which the plenum was preparing – to reduce substantially the role of the old guard leaders. To that end, with Lin Biao's agreement, they instructed their supporters to launch concerted attacks on them when the plenum broke up into group discussions. Zhu De was accused to his face of being 'an old right-wing opportunist', who had opposed Mao's leadership since their days on the Jinggangshan; Chen Yun was said to have resisted the Great Leap Forward; the four marshals, by instigating the 'February Adverse Current', had sought to reverse the verdict on Liu Shaoqi, Deng Xiaoping and Tao Zhu.

Mao was unimpressed. The veterans, he insisted, had merely exercised their right to express their opinions. Even Deng Xiaoping, he added, was not in the same category as Liu Shaoqi.

In Deng's case, Mao had held this view since the start of the Cultural Revolution. In 1967, he had already rejected a proposal from Kang Sheng to establish a separate 'Special Case Group' to investigate Deng's past, agreeing only that the team investigating He Long – a relatively minor inquiry – might set up a subgroup for that purpose. Now he dismissed the Cultural Revolution Group's suggestion that Deng, as well as Liu, should be expelled from the Party. It was an insurance policy. 'That little man . . . has a great future ahead of him', he had once told a foreign visitor. Deng was never officially attacked by name during the Cultural Revolution. Mao preferred to keep him in reserve, just in case the unexpected should happen and he might need his talents again.

Six months later, when the Ninth Congress met to bring the Cultural Revolution to a triumphal close, the Chairman was equally prudent.

The leaders who had taken part in the 'February Adverse Current', all except Tan Zhenlin, retained their positions as Central Committee members, and two of them, Ye Jianying and Li Xiannian, were reappointed to the Politburo. Three other veterans – Zhu De; the 'One-eyed Dragon', Marshal Liu Bocheng, now totally blind; and Dong Biwu, who, besides Mao, was the only surviving founder member of the Party – kept their Politburo posts, and two younger professional soldiers – Xu Shiyou and Chen Xilian, the Military Region commanders in Nanjing and Shenyang – entered the Politburo for the first time.

In one sense, these seven were political ballast.

Power lay with the Standing Committee, whose core membership had stayed unchanged since the spring of 1967 – Mao; Lin Biao, now officially described not only as the Chairman's successor but as his 'close comrade-in-arms'; Zhou Enlai; Chen Boda and Kang Sheng – and with the two radical clans within the leadership, led by Lin and Jiang Qing. Jiang had the support of the Shanghai radicals, Zhang Chunqiao and Yao Wenyuan, and the Security Minister, Xie Fuzhi – all of whom became full Politburo members. Lin's group comprised his wife, Ye Qun; the Chief of Staff, Huang Yongsheng; the air-force commander, Wu Faxian; and two other senior generals, who were similarly promoted.

Yet the Chairman's decision to make room for the moderates was important. It was not simply a gesture of magnanimity, rather, Mao was attempting – as he had at the Seventh Congress in 1945 – to fashion a coalition representing the different interest groups that made up the communist polity. He was lucid enough to know that, even at a time of radical dominance, men like Zhu De and Liu Bocheng (and still more, Zhou Enlai) had a political constituency which Lin Biao and his followers could not reach. Fifty years of political infighting had taught Mao not to put all his eggs in one basket.

There was a more fundamental, reason, too.

Officially the Cultural Revolution had been an outstanding success. Mao was credited with raising Marxism-Leninism 'to a higher and completely new stage', creating a guiding philosophy for 'the era when imperialism is heading for total collapse and socialism towards worldwide victory'. His aphorisms had become so rooted in the nation's consciousness that, in everyday conversation, they had acquired the status given to quotations from the Confucian Classics in the speech of earlier generations. The Ninth Congress had affirmed class struggle as the Party's 'basic line throughout the period of socialism', and had laid down that future generations should conduct policy under the rubric of 'continuing the revolution under the dictatorship of the proletariat'.

But, after three years of turmoil, how much had actually been achieved?

Liu Shaoqi had been definitively purged. Deng Xiaoping and Tan Zhenlin were under house arrest. Two other senior leaders, He Long and Tao Zhu, had died in captivity. Thousands of lesser figures at all levels of the Party hierarchy had been removed from power, and many of them, too, were in jail. About half-a-million people had been killed – a figure which would double as the purge of 'May 16' elements and the 'cleansing of class ranks' unearthed fresh 'counter-revolutionaries' and sent them to their deaths. All outward manifestations of bourgeois thought and behaviour had been crushed.

In Liu's place, Mao had put Lin Biao. In one respect, he was a better choice of successor; he was almost ten years younger. But he was chronically sick, to the point where even Mao referred to him contemptuously by the soubriquet, 'Forever Healthy'. Lin suffered from a nervous disorder – akin to Mao's neurasthenia – which caused him to sweat profusely. Unlike Mao, he was also a hypochondriac. He hated meeting people, and the ordeal of having to receive a foreign delegation left him drenched in perspiration. While undergoing medical treatment in the Soviet Union in the early 1940s, he had become addicted to morphine, and had never entirely quit the habit. He developed an aversion to sunlight. In his office the blinds were perpetually drawn. He refused to go out in the wind. Indoors, the temperature had to be maintained at a constant 21 degrees centigrade, summer and winter alike.

Even by the standards of a leadership where personal friendships were the exception, Lin's behaviour was irrationally antisocial. He lived in semi-seclusion in a heavily guarded mansion at Maojiawan, in the north-western quarter of Beijing. Visitors were discouraged, and he never visited others, often declining to see even his own military subordinates. He refused to read documents himself, instead getting his secretaries to give him an oral summary, which was not allowed to take up more than thirty minutes a day.

None of these eccentricities disqualified Lin from becoming Mao's successor. The role of Party Chairman was not executive but strategic. In Mao's eyes, Lin's supreme merit was that, ever since they had met on the Jinggangshan in 1928, he had been a totally loyal follower. He had an impressive intellect. Alone among Mao's subordinates, he peppered his major speeches with apt historical allusions (which he employed a team of researchers to find for him), and when he was not wallowing in panegyrics on the Chairman, he was capable of articulating Mao's views with a cogency and clarity that none of the others could equal. Politically, he had the prestige that came from being the most brilliant of the communists' civil war commanders. Ideologically, he adhered religiously to the precepts of Mao Zedong Thought.

But Lin was not a charismatic leader, and it must have been clear to Mao that he would need to be well seconded.

Therein lay the difficulty. When the Chairman looked around the auditorium in the Great Hall of the People where the Ninth Congress was being held, he could hardly fail to notice that two-thirds of the 1,500 delegates were wearing green PLA uniforms. Nearly half of the new Central Committee was from the army. Fewer than a fifth were veteran cadres. The newcomers might be politically and ideologically sound, but very few were of the calibre of the first-generation leaders they had replaced.

In the country at large, the success of the Cultural Revolution was even more problematic. It had been essentially an urban phenomenon. Most of China's 600 million peasants, far from being 'touched to their very souls' – as revolutionary propaganda had it – heard only distant rumours of the tumult in the cities.

Outwardly, China had become a sea of collectively-owned grey buildings, of collectively-farmed fields, of uniform blue cotton clothes – where the only colour came from the red flags on buildings and the bright jackets and leggings of small children. Ornament of any kind was forbidden. Culture had been reduced to Jiang Qing's eight revolutionary model operas. There were no markets, no street stalls, no pedlars. Every bicycle was black.

But to eradicate the individualism of the spirit – to achieve a 'proletarian revolution of the mind', as Mao put it – was a much more uncertain undertaking.

In 1966, he had written that cultural revolutions would have to be unleashed 'every seven or eight years' to renew the nation's revolutionary élan and halt the onset of bourgeois degeneration. Now, in April 1969, he repeated that the task had not yet been completed, and 'after a few years' it might have to be done all over again.

Mao never admitted, then or later, that the Cultural Revolution had fallen short of his original design. None the less, it is hard to believe that a man of his questioning, dialectical bent could not see that the new 'realm of Red virtue' whose birth pangs had been marked by such terror, cruelty and pain, was of stultifying shallowness. If he did, he did not let it show. The Cultural Revolution had provoked a collective demonstration of the worst instincts of a nation; even Lin Biao, in private, dismissed it as a 'Cultureless Revolution'. But Mao had other concerns. Revolution, he was fond of saying, was not a dinner-party. The overriding priority was the perennity of class struggle.

In the service of that cause, China had become a vast prison of the mind. The old world had been smashed. Mao had nothing to put in its place but empty, Red rhetoric.

In the end, the void was filled with unwitting help from Moscow.

On the night of August 20, 1968, Soviet troops invaded Czechoslovakia to crush the 'Prague Spring' and overthrow the reforming communist government there. To justify their action, the Russians argued that all Soviet-bloc states had a duty to defend the socialist system wherever it was threatened. This 'Brezhnev doctrine', as it was called, was formally limited to Europe. But to Mao, it provided a basis for a possible Russian attack on China.

The following spring, he decided to pre-empt that.

Minor incidents had been occurring haphazardly along the Sino-Soviet border for several years. The clash that took place on March 2, 1969 was premeditated, however. Three hundred Chinese troops, wearing white camouflage outfits, advanced under cover of darkness across the ice of the Ussuri River on to Zhenbao (Damansky) Island, a disputed speck of territory on the river frontier 150 miles south of the Siberian city of Khabarovsk. There they dug foxholes in the snow, and lay in ambush. Next morning, a Chinese decoy party moved ostentatiously on to the island. When a Russian patrol arrived to intercept them, the Chinese opened fire. The Soviets then brought up reinforcements and succeeded in driving the Chinese back, losing more than thirty men dead and wounded. Another, bigger battle in the same area two weeks later ended with sixty Russian and several hundred Chinese casualties.

Mao's plan was of breathtaking simplicity. If the Soviet Union had become China's main enemy, then the United States, on the principle that 'my enemy's enemy is my friend', had become a potential ally – even if it was engaged in a brutal and destructive war on China's southern frontiers against another of Beijing's allies, Vietnam.

The fighting on Zhenbao Island was the beginning of a prolonged Chinese effort to convince the newly elected US President, Richard Nixon, that Beijing's foreign policy priorities had undergone a fundamental change. The Russians, in ignorance of Mao's objectives, unintentionally strengthened his case by stepping up military pressure to try to force China to negotiate. All through the spring and summer, border incidents multiplied – accompanied by heavy hints from Moscow of Warsaw Pact intervention and the possible use of nuclear weapons (just as the Americans had brandished the nuclear threat during the Taiwan Straits crisis in 1958). The Kremlin began a massive build-up of Soviet forces in Mongolia. China approved a 30 per cent increase in military spending. In August a civil defence programme was launched in Beijing and other large cities, in which millions of people were mobilised to dig air-raid shelters for use against nuclear attack.

Having made his political point, Mao agreed, after a suitable show of reluctance, to a meeting in September between Zhou Enlai and the Soviet Premier, Andrei Kosygin – held symbolically at Beijing airport to underline that the Middle Kingdom was still determined to keep the barbarians at the gate. They reached an understanding to maintain the status quo along the frontier; to resume border negotiations; and to avoid further military clashes.

With that, the crisis was defused.

While it lasted, it created an appropriately militant backdrop for the holding of the Ninth Congress. Four hundred million people, half of China's population, were said to have taken part in demonstrations against the 'new tsars'. In the longer term, the escalating rhetoric aimed at 'Soviet social-imperialism' provided a new political focus for the nation's energies (just as, twenty years earlier, anti-American rhetoric had galvanised China at the time of the Korean War).

It also allowed Mao to tie up loose ends. In mid-October, Lin Biao, on the authority of the Politburo, ordered a 'red alert', in which a million troops were deployed in rehearsal for a possible Soviet attack. This was not totally far-fetched. Although the border crisis had eased, China had just carried out its first successful underground nuclear test, sparking concerns that the Russians might launch a surgical strike against Chinese nuclear facilities. Whether the Chairman really believed, as was claimed later, that they might also stage a punitive bombing raid on Beijing is another matter. But it provided him with a pretext for dispersing the veteran Party leaders, and at the same time removing from the capital – three years after their fall – Liu Shaoqi and Deng Xiaoping.

Deng was sent with his wife to Jiangxi, where he lived under guard in an army barracks and spent his days working part-time in a nearby tractor repair plant.

Liu had been bedridden since the summer of 1968, when he had contracted pneumonia. He had lost the power of speech and was being fed intravenously. His thinning hair, which had turned white, had not been cut for two years and was a foot in length. On Mao's instructions, he was taken out of Zhongnanhai on a stretcher on October 17 and flown to Kaifeng, the capital of Anhui. There he was held in an empty unheated building at the Municipal Party Committee headquarters. He developed pneumonia again, but permission to send him to hospital was refused. He died on November 12, four years almost to the day after Mao had launched the campaign against him.

The Chairman did not give a direct order for Liu's death, any more than he ordered the deaths of He Long or Tao Zhu, or of Peng Dehuai who died several years later in a prison hospital.

But he did not move a finger to prevent them.

CHAPTER SIXTEEN

Things Fall Apart

Six weeks after Liu Shaoqi's death, Mao celebrated his seventy-sixth birthday. He was a heavy smoker and suffered from respiratory problems. But, that apart, his health was good. His doctor, returning after a year's absence, found that he was still waited on by a harem of young women, and would sometimes invite 'three, four, even five of them simultaneously' to share his great bed.

With age, he had grown increasingly capricious and unpredictable. He had always expected his subordinates to stay in tune with his thinking – if not to anticipate him, at least not to get out of line. All the major victims of the previous two decades, Gao Gang, Peng Dehuai, Liu, Deng and Tao Zhu, had fallen because they failed that test. But now it was growing even harder to fathom the Chairman's true intentions. Not only would he push a policy to its extreme and then abruptly reverse it – as he had with the Shanghai Commune, and with the purge of 'capitalist-roaders' in the army in 1967 – which invariably left his supporters wrong-footed; but, more often than in the past, he would deliberately conceal his real views, or cloak them in utterances of Delphic ambiguity, in order to see how others would react.

A whiff of paranoia began to emanate from the Study of Chrysanthemum Fragrance. 'In his later years', one Politburo radical wrote, 'almost nobody trusted him. We very seldom saw him, and . . . when we [did], we were terrified of saying something wrong in case he took it as an error.'

The result was that all Mao's colleagues assumed the role, and the habits, of courtiers.

Zhou Enlai was best at it. It was he who, in March 1969, realising that the Chairman's ruling to exclude Jiang Qing from the new Politburo was merely to avoid the appearance of nepotism, put her name (and that of Ye Qun) on the list anyway. It was Zhou, too, who, in his speech to the Ninth Congress, spoke of Mao having developed Marxism-Leninism 'creatively' and 'with genius', terms which the Chairman had deleted from the new Party constitution. Again, he judged correctly. What Mao found unacceptable in the CCP's public statutes was one thing; what might please him in a speech confined to the Party faithful was quite another.

But good judgement alone was not enough. Mao's suspiciousness required that he be constantly reassured of the loyalty of his inner circle.

Zhou survived because he would betray anyone he thought necessary to maintain the Chairman's trust. When his adopted daughter was tortured by Red Guards and then thrown into prison, where she eventually died from maltreatment, Zhou was told – but refused to take any action to protect her. To do otherwise, he reasoned, would expose him to charges of putting family before politics. The most vicious attack on Deng Xiaoping by any leader during the Cultural Revolution was contained in a minute appended to a 'Special Case Group' report, not by Jiang Qing or Kang Sheng – but by Zhou.* In statements to the Cultural Revolution Group, he denounced exceptionally harshly the failings of the veteran cadres. Even his chief bodyguard, a close companion of many years' standing, was abandoned the moment Jiang Qing, on a whim, took against him; Zhou's wife, Deng Yingchao, urged that the man be arrested because 'we don't want to show any favouritism towards him'.

---

* In the 1980s Deng Yingchao, asked Hu Yaobang, then General Secretary of the CCP, to authorise the destruction of the offending minute, which had been preserved in Zhou's personal files in the secret section of the Central Archives. Hu agreed, and the original was destroyed. But, unknown to him, a copy was kept. Deng Xiaoping himself was aware of Zhou's conduct, but in 1979 exonerated him on the grounds that he would otherwise have been overthrown, which would have made the situation still worse. That has remained the official view ever since.

The Cultural Revolution Group, in the late 1960s, was even more a nest of vipers than the Politburo a decade before.

This was partly due to the amoral nature of the movement itself, which sapped whatever vestiges of probity might have remained. But the presence of Jiang Qing certainly did not help. In middle age, she had become shallow, vindictive and totally self-centred. Many of those who had been kind to her early in her career were now hunted down and imprisoned to ensure that they could not divulge details of her actress past. When she learned that Chen Boda had contemplated suicide after Mao had criticised him, she laughed in his face, telling him, 'Go ahead! Go ahead! Do you have the courage to kill yourself?' Kang Sheng, whose own career had profited from his early support of her liaison with Mao, viewed her as dangerous and unreliable. Lin Biao could not abide her, and became so enraged during one meeting at Maojiawan that he told Ye Qun (out of Jiang's hearing, however): 'Get that woman out of here!' Even Mao lost patience with her. But, like Zhou, she was useful to him. And, because she was a conduit to Mao, she was useful to others. The Shanghai radicals clung to her with limpet-like devotion, acting as front men in her unremitting efforts to undermine Zhou Enlai. So, to a lesser extent, did Kang Sheng and Xie Fuzhi.

Before 1969, these personal animosities were subsumed by the larger struggle to eliminate 'capitalist-roaders' and promote the radical cause.

But after the Ninth Congress they became institutionalised. Within the new Politburo, Jiang Qing and Lin Biao had roughly equal support. In theory, Lin was stronger. He controlled the army, which in turn controlled China. However, Jiang Qing had a privileged relationship with Mao, who controlled everything. In Lin's eyes, that was an uncertain weapon. The Chairman did not always take his wife's side.

Since there were no policy differences between them, the only ground for their rivalry was power. They fought their battles by palace conspiracies, whose sole and unique purpose was to win the Chairman's favour. Thus was the basis established for a succession of events which, over the next two years, would blow apart all Mao's carefully laid plans to ensure that his policies survived him.

*

It began simply enough. Liu Shaoqi's disgrace and death had created a vacancy for the post of Head of State. In March 1970, as part of the general rebuilding of the Chinese polity after the Cultural Revolution, Mao set out guidelines for a revised state constitution, under which that office would be abolished and the ceremonial functions attached to it would devolve to the Standing Committee of the National People's Congress, the Chinese parliament. This was approved by the Politburo and, soon afterwards, by a Central Committee work conference.

Lin rarely attended Politburo meetings, and was therefore absent when these decisions were taken. Five weeks later, however, on April 11, he sent a message to Mao, urging him to reconsider and take back the post himself on the grounds that otherwise 'it would not be in accordance with the psychology of the people' – in other words, as the incarnation of the Chinese revolution, the Chairman should be surrounded by the full panoply of state honours. Next day, Mao turned him down. 'I cannot do this job again,' he told the Politburo. 'The suggestion is inappropriate.' Later that month he reiterated that the post did not interest him.

None the less, Mao was intrigued.

That Lin should have made such a suggestion was wholly out of character. Where Zhou Enlai made a religion of loyalty, Lin's fetish was passivity. 'Be passive, passive and again passive,' he had told his friend, Tao Zhu, who came to him for advice shortly before his fall. He was so cautious that he had actually formulated as a personal guideline the principle, 'Don't make constructive suggestions' – on the grounds that anyone who did so would be held responsible for the results. 'At any given time, in all important questions,' he told the Ninth Congress, 'Chairman Mao always charts the course. In our work we do no more than follow in his wake.'

Mao's political antennae were humming for other reasons, too. Since the announcement that Lin had become his 'close comrade-in-arms and successor', the reclusive Marshal had become more confident – 'self-important', in the view of one of his secretaries. Mao had noticed. 'When [they] fart,' he said angrily to his staff, '[it's] like announcing an imperial edict.' He had been struck, too, during his travels in the provinces by the number of military uniforms everywhere. 'Why do we have so many soldiers around?' he kept grumbling. He knew the reason, of course: it had been his own decision to use the PLA to restore order. But that did not make him like it. Then there was the puzzle of Lin's relationship with the fourth-ranking member of the leadership, Chen Boda. Just before the Ninth Congress, Chen had fallen out with his erstwhile colleagues in the Cultural Revolution Group and had transferred his allegiance to Lin and Ye Qun. Mao instinctively mistrusted such alliances.

Accordingly the Chairman blurred his signals. Instead of issuing a categorical ruling which would have ended the discussion once and for all – as he very easily could have done – he allowed a measure of doubt to subsist. That had always been one of Mao's favourite techniques: he placed his colleagues before a situation where they had to make a choice, and then stood back and waited to see which way they would jump.

Lin persisted. With his backing, the issue of the state chairmanship was raised again in May, and in July, after which Mao disowned the idea for a fourth time.

By then, it had become enmeshed in the rivalry between Lin's and Jiang Qing's supporters in the Politburo. In August, this took on a new dimension. Wu Faxian, backed by Chen Boda, proposed writing into the state constitution a reference to Mao having developed Marxism-Leninism 'creatively', 'comprehensively' and 'with genius'. These were the terms the Chairman had deleted from the Party statutes a year earlier. But Wu now argued that it would be wrong to use Mao's dislike of boastfulness in order to minimise the importance of his theoretical contributions. Kang Sheng and Zhang Chunqiao, who had initially objected, were evidently intimidated by this tortured argument and next day the proposal was passed.

Mao kept his own counsel. The cult of his personality had been an invaluable tool to mobilise the country against Liu Shaoqi. But now that Liu had fallen, it had lost its usefulness. So why was Lin determined to prolong it? To the Chairman's mistrustful mind, the Defence Minister's emphasis on his theoretical 'genius' and on Mao Zedong Thought – and his insistence of dignifying him with the title of Head of State – began to look suspiciously like an attempt to kick him upstairs.

There was some basis for this. The original succession plan, under which Mao was to become Honorary Chairman of the Party, had been swept aside when Liu Shaoqi fell. The idea that he should retreat into an elder statesman role, in an honorific capacity as Head of State, must have seemed to Lin a sensible alternative.

It was not something the Defence Minister could propose directly: he knew Mao well enough to realise that any such suggestion, unless it came from the Chairman himself, would be anathema. But Mao's blurred signals made him believe that the concept of an exalted office, to highlight Mao's unique status in China, might in the end prove acceptable – if, indeed, it was not what he had wanted all along. After all, Zhou Enlai had shown that it was sometimes best not to rely on what the Chairman said, but to intuit the way his mind was working and carry on accordingly.

What Lin failed to realise was that Mao had been so badly burned by his first experience of retiring to the 'second front' that any hint of a repetition was totally unacceptable.

The result was a massive political misjudgement.

On August 23, 1970, the Defence Minister delivered the keynote speech at a Central Committee plenum at Lushan, the same ill-fated mountain resort where the career of his predecessor, Peng Dehuai, had ended eleven years before.

Mao had approved in advance an outline of what Lin had to say, which included a conventional paean of praise to the Chairman's greatness and a proposal that the new state constitution find an appropriate way of honouring his unique position. If he was unhappy that Lin, in his oral remarks, had again used the word 'genius', he did not show it. With his agreement, the text was distributed as a conference document.

Next day, when the plenum divided for group discussions, all Lin's followers made the 'genius' issue the main theme of their speeches.

The bombshell, however, was dropped by Chen Boda, who launched into an excited attack on 'a certain person', who, he charged, was opposing the use of the term 'genius', in a covert attempt to disparage Mao Zedong Thought as the nation's guiding ideology. When other members of the group demanded that he name the guilty party, he indicated that he was referring to Zhang Chunqiao.

From a leader of Chen's seniority, this was a very serious charge indeed. He then stoked the flames still higher by asserting that 'certain counter-revolutionaries' were 'overjoyed' at the idea that Mao might refuse the state chairmanship. That caused pandemonium. Chen's group drafted a bulletin, urging Mao to become Head of State with Lin as his deputy, and warning against the activities of 'swindlers in the Party' (a reference to Zhang). As word spread to other groups, a second letter was drawn up, also urging Mao to accept the state chairmanship.

At one level, this was merely a typical courtiers' squabble. Jiang Qing described it later as 'a *literati* quarrel'.

To the Chairman, however, it had weighty implications. To promote Lin Biao's scheming, Chen had rashly launched a factional attack to try to bring down a man whom Mao regarded not merely as his wife's ally but as a key member of his own political camp.

On the afternoon of August 25, he called an enlarged Standing Committee meeting, at which he accused Chen of violating Party unity. He ordered that discussion of Lin's speech, which had served as the springboard for Chen's action, be terminated. Finally, after six months of uncertainty, he quashed once and for all the idea that he would ever agree to be state chairman. Chen, who had been at Mao's side since 1937 and had played a pivotal role in promoting his ideas, was then denounced for 'launching a surprise attack', 'trying to blast Lushan to pieces' and using 'rumour-mongering and sophistry' instead of Marxism-Leninism. On Mao's orders, Chen was taken to Qincheng high security prison, outside Beijing. Two months later, a campaign was launched within the Party, accusing him of being an 'anti-Party element, sham Marxist, careerist and plotter'.

Lin's wife, Ye Qun, and three of his Politburo allies – Wu Faxian; the head of the PLA General Logistics Department, Qiu Huizuo; and the Navy Commissar, Li Zuopeng – were told to make self-criticisms before the Central Committee.

In formal terms, Lin himself emerged unscathed.

Yet the row that had broken out at Lushan had sown a grain of doubt that would grow to poison his relationship with Mao as insidiously and just as surely as if he had challenged him head on. The Chairman had no special desire to see his succession plans fall through a second time. He therefore stayed his hand – 'shielding' Lin, as he put it later – in the hope that the Defence Minister would find a way to retrieve the situation. Theoretically, this was still possible. Lin could have gone to Mao and made a grovelling self-criticism for promoting the 'genius' and 'Head of State' issues, while blaming Chen Boda (and, perhaps, Ye Qun) for the factional attack on Zhang Chunqiao. That is certainly what Zhou Enlai would have

Members of the Politburo Standing Committee in a rare, unposed shot at the '7,000-cadre big conference' in January 1962. [from left] Zhou Enlai, Chen Yun, Liu Shaoqi, Mao and Deng Xiaoping.

Swimming in the Yangtse.

Above Jiang Qing *(centre)*, appearing with Mao in public for the first time in September 1962 to greet the wife of Indonesia's President Sukarno.

Left Mao's propagandist, Yao Wenyuan.

Opposite above [from left] Mao, with Lin Biao, Liu Shaoqi, Zhu De and Dong Biwu during the 1966 National Day celebrations.

Opposite below In Tiananmen Square, reviewing Red Guards at one of the ten gigantic rallies held at the outset of the Cultural Revolution to encourage China's youth to rebel.

Above Magic talisman: the 'Little Red Book'.

Opposite above Red Guards giving the *yin-yang* haircut to the Governor of Heilongjiang at a struggle meeting in September 1966. The placard around his neck labels him 'a member of the reactionary gang'.

Opposite below Smashing ancient stone carvings at the Confucian Temple in Qufu, during the campaign against the "Four Olds".

(top, from left) Lin Biao with Edgar Snow and Mao on Tiananmen during the 1970 National Day celebrations. 18 months later, US-China relations had progressed to a point where *(below, from right)* Henry Kissinger and President Richard Nixon would meet Mao, with interpreter, Nancy Tang and Zhou Enlai, at the Chairman's residence in Zhongnanhai.

Above The Chairman's inner sanctum, dominated by his vast bed, in the Study of Chrysanthemum Fragrance.

Below Mao with his last companion, Jiang Yufeng, nine months before his death, in December 1975.

The memorial meeting for Mao in Tiananmen Square on September 18 1976. [from left] Marshal Ye Jianying; Hua Guofeng (reading the eulogy); Wang Hongwen; Zhang Chunqiao and Jiang Qing.

done. But, whether because he was too confident in his new status as the Chairman's successor, or because of the climate of generalised mistrust existing within the leadership, he did not.

That would turn out to be his second major misjudgement.

In October, when Mao read the written self-criticisms that Ye Qun and the three generals had prepared for the Central Committee, his attitude hardened. All four had made pro-forma admissions of error, but blamed it on their 'low level of understanding' and conspicuously failed to explain why they had acted in concert. The Chairman vented his irritation in angry marginal comments. Ye Qun, he wrote, 'refuses to do as I say, but dances immediately when Chen Boda blows his trumpet'; Wu Faxian 'lacks an open and upright character'.

At this point Mao decided to begin whittling down the military power which Lin Biao had acquired. In December, the Central Committee held a work conference, chaired by Zhou Enlai, at which the Beijing Military Region was 'reorganised'. Two of Mao's allies replaced Lin's followers (who were accused of being supporters of the disgraced Chen Boda) as Regional Commander and Political Commissar. Three months later, Ye Qun and the others produced a second self-criticism, which Mao found as unsatisfactory as the first. He then added new members to the General Office of the Military Commission – 'mixing in sand', as he put it afterwards – to dilute Lin's control.

In another revealing decision that winter, he dismissed his young partners from the PLA dance troupes, lest they turn out to be Lin's spies.

But beyond the inner circle, not the slightest hint was allowed to seep out that anything untoward was afoot. Even those closest to Mao, like Zhou Enlai and Jiang Qing, were uncertain how seriously the Chairman was taking Lin's problem. Not only to the country at large, but to members of the Central Committee, the Defence Minister was as much his 'successor and close comrade-in-arms' as he had ever been. Nor did anyone outside the Politburo know that the four generals were in trouble. They retained their posts, and went about their normal duties.

Lin himself seems to have had the keenest intuition of what might lie ahead. By March 1971, he had become morbidly depressed. That month, his 25-year-old son, Lin Liguo, who had a senior post in the air force, began holding secret discussions with a small group of fellow officers on ways of safeguarding Lin's position. The Defence Minister was apparently unaware of these meetings. However, one of the documents the group drew up included a devastatingly accurate assessment of Mao's political tactics which clearly reflected Lin's views:

> Today he uses this force to attack that force; tomorrow he uses that force to attack this force. Today he uses sweet words and honeyed talk to those whom he entices, and tomorrow he puts them to death for some fabricated crimes. Those who are his guests today will be his prisoners tomorrow. Looking back at the history of the past few decades, is there anyone he supported initially who has not finally been handed a political death sentence? . . . His former secretaries have either committed suicide or been arrested. His few close comrades-in-arms or trusted aides have also been sent to prison . . .

The group referred to Mao as B52 because, like the US long-range bombers then being used against North Vietnam, he set off explosions from a great height.

Lin Liguo and his colleagues concluded that the Defence Minister's position was not yet under threat, and that the likeliest eventuality was still an orderly succession when Mao died. They examined the possibility of Lin seizing power beforehand, and drew up a rough contingency plan for that purpose, called Project 571. However, the consensus was that this was to be avoided if at all possible because, even if it succeeded, politically there would be 'a very high price' to pay.

None the less, the fact that such discussions were being held at all – even if without Lin Biao's knowledge – testified to a deep malaise within the Defence Minister's camp.

At the end of April 1971, events took a more ominous turn. With Mao's authorisation, Zhou told the three generals, Wu Faxian, Li Zuopeng and Qiu Huizuo, together with the Chief of Staff, Huang Yongsheng, and Ye Qun, that they were suspected of factional activities and 'mistakes of political line'. Mao also created a new power base for Jiang Qing and her allies, who were given control of the two key Central Committee departments responsible for propaganda and personnel matters.

As the year advanced, Lin became more and more withdrawn. He stopped working and his behaviour became increasingly eccentric. On May Day, he pleaded ill-health as an excuse not to attend the celebrations. Zhou persuaded him to change his mind, but when finally he arrived – contrary to protocol, after Mao – the Chairman, irritated by his lateness, ignored him. After a short while, Lin left without their having exchanged a word or even a glance.

At some point in the early summer, Mao decided that a confrontation could no longer be avoided.

In July he told Zhou Enlai: 'The Lushan affair is not finished, the problem is not at all solved. There is a sinister scheme. [The generals] have a backstage boss.' That month, Lin and his family went to Beidaihe to stay at their seaside villa. In mid-August, Mao set off aboard his special train for Wuhan, where he held the first of a series of meetings to canvass support from political and military leaders in the provinces. Everywhere he went, his message was the same: at Lushan, there had been a full-fledged line struggle, in essence identical to the struggles against Liu Shaoqi, Peng Dehuai and Wang Ming. 'A certain person', he said, 'was anxious to become state chairman, to split the Party and to seize power.'* The only difference this time was that no conclusions had yet been drawn. What, therefore, should be done? 'Comrade Lin Biao', Mao answered his own question, would have to bear 'some responsibility'. Some of his group might be able to reform; others would not. Past experience had shown, the Chairman noted drily, that 'it is difficult for someone who has taken the lead in committing major errors . . . to reform'.

It was a measure of how few real allies Lin had in the provincial military commands that not until the night of Monday, September 6 – a full three weeks after Mao started his tour –

---

* Mao's charge that Lin wanted to become Head of State himself became a key theme in the subsequent campaign against him. The only known evidence is a confession by Wu Faxian, obtained under duress, parts of which have been shown to be false and which, even if it were true, was based on hearsay from Ye Qun. It is possible that, as the official Chinese version insists, Lin did want the post and had urged Mao to take it as a cover for his own ambitions. But, given Lin's dislike of ceremonial, that appears highly improbable. It is also possible that, even if Lin did not want it, Mao suspected that he did. On balance, though, by far the likeliest explanation is that Mao felt the charge of trying to usurp power would resonate more strongly with his audience than a convoluted allegation that Lin had been trying to nudge him into honorific idleness.

did word reach Beidaihe of what the Chairman had been saying.

The following six days were utterly surreal.

Lin himself spent much of his time discussing his children's marriage plans. During the Cultural Revolution, he had asked Xie Fuzhi to organise a search in Beijing and Shanghai for good-looking high-school girls as candidates to wed Lin Liguo – just as, under the Empire, young women of good family had been sought as imperial concubines. Several hundred girls were interviewed, but in the end Liguo had taken as his fiancée a young woman from a PLA dance troupe. A similar search had been undertaken to find a husband for Lin Liheng, Lin Biao's daughter, but Ye Qun had disapproved of her choice and she had twice tried to commit suicide. She, too, was now about to become engaged.

As the Vice-Chairman's political career slipped away from him, it was these family matters that absorbed his attention.

In their discussions, Lin Liguo argued that they must act decisively. Either Mao had to be stopped by force; or Lin should move to Canton to set up a rival regime. If that failed, he could flee abroad, perhaps to the Soviet Union. Lin Liheng proposed that her father should retire to an honorary post like Zhu De.

The Defence Minister himself remained curiously aloof, as though he had already decided that every possible course open to him was doomed.

On the morning of Wednesday, September 8, he agreed to write a note, enjoining his supporters to 'act according to the orders of Comrades Liguo and Yuchi' – a reference to Zhou Yuchi, one of his son's air-force colleagues – but that was as far as he would go.

The previous day Lin Liguo and his fellow officers had begun frantically discussing ways to kill Mao, and had agreed that the best prospect was to attack his special train.

Various plans were considered – most of them so juvenile they might have come from a child's comic strip: flame-throwers were to be used; or an anti-aircraft gun, aimed to shoot horizontally; an oil depot near the tracks would be blown up; an assassin armed with a pistol would shoot him. Not only was no attempt made to carry out any of these hare-brained schemes, but the conspirators never even reached the stage of making serious preparations.

Appearances notwithstanding, Lin Biao was not plotting against Mao. Mao was closing in on Lin.

On Wednesday evening, the Chairman received word of unusual

activity at the PLA air-force headquarters. His personal security was reinforced. Soon afterwards, he left Hangzhou for Shanghai. But instead of spending several days there, as had been planned, he received the Nanjing commander, Xu Shiyou, on Saturday morning, and then set out immediately for Beijing, not stopping until his train reached Fengtai, a suburban station on the southern outskirts of the capital, on Sunday afternoon. There he spent two hours with the Beijing Military Region Commander, Li Desheng, whom he briefed on much the same lines as he had the provincial commanders in the south.

While Mao was at Fengtai, Lin Biao and a tearful Ye Qun were attending their daughter's engagement party at their residence in Beidaihe.

Lin Liguo, on learning of Mao's precipitate return, held a panic-stricken meeting with his fellow air-force officers, at which it was decided that the best option was for his father to move to Canton. Immediately afterwards he commandeered an air-force Trident to fly to Beidaihe, where he arrived at about 8.15 p.m. just as Mao was returning to Zhongnanhai.

The Defence Minister and his family were to have spent the evening watching films with the newly engaged couple and their friends.

Instead, Lin Biao closeted himself away with his wife and son. How much he had known of Lin Liguo's plans up to that point is unclear. Perhaps very little. When his daughter, Liheng, realised later that evening that her mother, whom she hated, and her brother, whom she liked no better, were preparing to flee and to take her father with them, her immediate assumption was that he was being kidnapped. In this, she was certainly wrong. Lin Biao knew, at the very least, that Ye Qun and Lin Liguo had acted rashly, and that the whole family faced terrible retribution. That evening he finally shook himself out of his inertia and agreed to move to Canton. But whether he shared his son's optimism about setting up a rival regime there is a different matter. He may well simply have seen it as a staging post to Hong Kong and eventual exile abroad.

Shortly after 10 p.m., Lin Liheng, still convinced that her father was being manipulated, slipped away to warn the head of the guard unit charged with Lin's security.

Half an hour later, Zhou Enlai was called out of a meeting in the Great Hall of the People to take an urgent telephone call. He was told that an air-force jet was at Beidaihe without authorisation, and that, according to Lin Biao's daughter, the Defence Minister was to be taken to an unknown destination, possibly against his will.

Zhou immediately telephoned Wu Faxian and told him to have the plane grounded.

When this news reached Lin Biao, he realised the game was up. It was then that he decided that they should make straight for the nearest border – which meant heading north, to Russia.* In an attempt to disarm suspicion, Ye Qun telephoned the Premier to inform him that they were planning to move next day to Dalian. At midnight, Lin Biao's armoured limousine pulled away from their residence, sped past a cordon of guards who tried ineffectually to stop them, and headed for the airport. On the way one of Lin's secretaries leapt from the moving vehicle and was shot and wounded.

Despite Zhou's order, the Trident had been partly refuelled. Lin, Ye Qun, Lin Liguo, another air-force officer and their driver clambered aboard, and at 12.32 a.m. on Monday, September 13, with its navigation lights turned off and the airport in total darkness, the aircraft took off.

Zhou ordered a total ban on aircraft movements throughout China, which remained in force for the next two days. He then went to report to Mao.

While he was there, Wu Faxian telephoned to say that Lin's plane was heading for Mongolia and to ask whether it should be shot down. Mao responded philosophically: 'The skies will rain; widows will remarry; these things are unstoppable. Let them go.'

At 1.50 a.m. the aircraft left Chinese airspace.

Mao moved, for security reasons, to the Great Hall of the People, where, at 3 a.m., the Politburo convened, to be informed of his return to the capital and the sensational news of Lin's flight.

Thirty hours later, Zhou was awakened to be handed a message from China's Ambassador in Ulan Bator. The Mongolian Foreign Ministry had issued an official protest because a Chinese air-force

---

* This enabled Mao to claim later, as part of the campaign of denigration of the Defence Minister, that Lin had been opposed to an improvement in relations with America. No evidence has ever been produced to support this allegation. Lin's few public statements on the subject followed the standard Chinese line. He had virtually no interest in foreign policy, which was the exclusive province of Mao and Zhou Enlai.

Trident had violated Mongolian airspace in the early hours of Monday morning, and had crashed near the settlement of Undur Khan. All nine people on board had been killed.

An examination of the site showed that the plane had run out of fuel, overturned and caught fire while trying to make an emergency landing in the steppe. The bodies, which were identified by Soviet KGB forensic experts, were buried nearby.

Of all the Chinese leaders Mao purged during his years of power, only Lin Biao attempted to resist. Peng Dehuai and Liu Shaoqi had gone meekly to their fates, maintaining to the last their unswerving devotion to the Party. Neither had attempted to defend himself; neither tried to hit back. Even Gao Gang, who made a kind of protest by committing suicide, had first confessed his errors.

Lin was different. In the end, the only defence he could find was what Mao called the 'last and best' of the '36 stratagems' from the military manuals of Chinese antiquity: to run away. But he did not abase himself. Nor did he submit to Mao's will.

The Chairman was shattered.

His doctor, who was present when Zhou broke the news of Lin's flight, remembered years later how his face collapsed in shock. Once the initial crisis had passed, and the Defence Minister's allies – including the four unfortunate generals, Wu Faxian, Lin Zuopeng, Qiu Huizuo and Huang Yongsheng, who had been as much in the dark as everyone else – had been placed under arrest, Mao took to his bed, suffering from deep depression. He remained there for nearly two months, with high blood pressure and a lung infection. As ever, it was psychosomatic. But this time, he did not bounce back. In November, when he emerged to meet the North Vietnamese Premier, Pham Van Dong, Chinese who saw the television pictures were shocked at how much he had aged. His shoulders were stooped, and he walked with an old man's shuffle. People said his legs looked like wobbly, wooden sticks.

In January 1972, Chen Yi died. Two hours before the funeral, Mao decided that he would attend, disregarding the entreaties of his aides who feared that the subzero weather would be too much for his frail health. They were right. After standing through the ceremony, Mao's legs were trembling so badly he could barely walk.

It was widely rumoured afterwards that that month he had a

stroke. In fact he suffered from congestive heart failure, which he made worse by refusing medical treatment. But the root of the problem remained political. Although Mao had been preparing, in August and early September, for a confrontation with Lin Biao, he had not decided exactly how the problem should be resolved: whether simply to demote him within the Politburo; to criticise him inside the Party, but allow him to remain a nominal member of the leadership, like Peng Dehuai in 1959; or to purge him altogether – a possibility, given careful preparation, but the least desirable option because of its effect on public opinion. By fleeing, Lin Biao had taken the initiative out of the Chairman's hands.

In one sense, his task was made easier by the discovery of the activities of Lin Liguo.

Although Mao had sensed a security risk, and had taken pre-cautions accordingly, details of the young air-force officers' plotting had emerged only after Lin's flight. Juvenile though the conspiracy was, it enabled Mao to paint the Defence Minister as a traitor, who had attempted to stage a *coup d'état.*

This was the line pursued in briefings to Party officials which began in mid-October, to be followed by meetings in factories and work units to inform the population at large.

It was not an easy story to sell. Even the credulity of the long-suffering Chinese was strained by the revelation that yet another of Mao's closest colleagues had proved to be a villain. What did it say about the Chairman's judgement if Liu Shaoqi (a 'scab and renegade'), Chen Boda (a 'sham Marxist') and Lin Biao (a 'counter-revolutionary careerist'), all of whom had been at Mao's side for decades, were suddenly, one after the other, unmasked as hidden enemies? The 'Hundred Flowers' and the anti-Rightist Campaign had cost Mao the trust of China's intellectuals. The chaos and terror of the Cultural Revolution had destroyed the faith of the Party hier-archy and tens of millions of ordinary citizens. Lin Biao's fall was the last straw. After 1971, general cynicism prevailed. Only the young (and not all of them), and those who had profited from the radical upsurge, still believed in Mao's revolutionary new world.

The combined effects of illness and political failure brought the Chairman close to despair. For the first time since the autumn of 1945, when Stalin had betrayed him in the confrontation with Chiang Kai-shek, he felt like giving up. One afternoon in January 1972, he told an appalled Zhou Enlai, whom he had placed in charge of the day-to-day work of the Central Committee, that he could no longer carry on and Zhou should take over. In 1945 it had had been an American, Harry Truman, who had lifted Mao's depression by launching the Marshall mission to mediate in the Chinese civil war. This time, too, an American would get him out of his black hole. For Mao, and for the Chinese people, the fate of Lin Biao was soon to be eclipsed by an even more astonishing and unthinkable event: after twenty years of unblinking hostility, the US President, Richard Nixon, was to pay an official visit to Beijing.

The clashes on Zhenbao Island in March 1969, and the tension between Beijing and Moscow the following spring and summer, had certainly got Washington's attention. Even beforehand, some US leaders had begun to think aloud about a more productive relationship with Beijing. A year or so earlier, Nixon had written of the need to wean China from its 'angry isolation', a phrase which he had repeated in his inaugural address. There had been talk of trying to move towards a triangular relationship. But until the border conflict raised the spectre of a Sino-Soviet war, no one could see how that might be done.

The first hesitant signals began in July that year. The United States modified its ban on American citizens travelling to China. Three days later, China released two American yachtsmen who had strayed into Chinese waters. In August, the Secretary of State, William Rogers, stated publicly that the US was 'seeking to open up channels of communication'. Romania and Pakistan were asked to relay private messages. In October, as Sino-Soviet tensions eased, Nixon made a more substantial gesture: the Chinese were informed that two US destroyers, which had been making symbolic patrols in the Taiwan Straits since the Korean War, were to be withdrawn.

So began what Kissinger called an 'intricate minuet', which twenty-one months later would make him the first US official to travel to Beijing since 1949.

Along the way there was farce: when Walter Stoessel, the US Ambassador in Warsaw, approached his Chinese counterpart at a reception to express interest in talks, he watched his interlocutor back away and run down a staircase, terrified of a contact for which he had no instructions. There was tragedy: an American business-man, who had spent fifteen years in Chinese prisons as a spy, committed suicide shortly before he was to have been released as a gesture of goodwill. There were setbacks: contacts virtually stopped for six months in 1970 because of the US offensive in Cambodia. And there was bafflement: on National Day in Beijing that year, Zhou Enlai brought Edgar Snow and his wife, who were then visiting China, to be photographed with Mao on Tiananmen. It was an unprecedented gesture: no foreigner had ever been so honoured. 'Unfortunately,' Kissinger confessed later, 'what they conveyed was so oblique that our crude Occidental minds completely missed the point.' Only long afterwards did he realise that Mao was signalling that the dialogue with America had his personal support.

Mao's elliptical way of doing things soon defeated his purposes a second time. In an interview with Snow in December, he alluded to Nixon's remark, two months earlier, that 'if there is anything I want to do before I die, it is to go to China'. Mao told Snow: 'I would be happy to talk with him, either as a tourist or as President.' Afterwards, Snow was given the official Chinese transcript of the conversation, but asked to delay publication for several months. Mao's assumption was that Snow would send a copy of the transcript to the White House. He did not – and again the Chairman's message did not get through.

The following spring, therefore, Mao made a gesture which even the obtuse Americans could not fail to understand.

In March 1971, a Chinese table-tennis team participated in the World Championships in Nagoya, Japan. They were the first Chinese sportsmen to travel abroad for years. On April 4, one of the US team taking part, a nineteen-year-old Californian, mentioned casually to a Chinese player that he would love to visit Beijing. This was reported back to Zhou Enlai, who raised it with Mao next day. They decided not to pursue it. But that night, after taking his sleeping pills, Mao called his head nurse and told her drowsily, just before he fell asleep, to telephone the Foreign Ministry with instructions to invite the American players at once.

Ping-pong diplomacy, as it was called, took the world by storm.

The US players were given a dazzling welcome. Zhou himself received them in the Great Hall of the People, and declared that they had opened a new chapter in the two countries' relations which marked a 'recommencement of our friendship'.

Three months later, Kissinger followed. His journey was kept secret – thanks to a subterfuge about a stomach upset which supposedly confined him to bed in Pakistan. On his return, an exuberant Nixon announced on American television that a high-level dialogue with China was under way and he himself would go there next spring. To flesh out the details, Kissinger returned to Beijing in October – this time in the full glare of publicity – and agreed the basis for the Shanghai communiqué, which was to be the crowning achievement of the presidential visit, fixing the pattern of Chinese–US relations for the rest of the century and no doubt beyond.

Mao was preoccupied with the Lin Biao affair during Kissinger's first trip, and bedridden, suffering from depression, during the second. None the less, it was his caustic instruction that the two sides avoid 'the sort of banality that the Soviets would sign, but neither mean nor observe' that gave the communiqué its force. Differences were stated 'explicitly, sometimes brutally', which underlined their common interest in opposing Soviet hegemony. Only the crucial issue of Taiwan remained wrapped in ambiguity.

> The United States acknowledges that all Chinese on either side of the Taiwan Strait maintain there is but one China, and that Taiwan is a part of China. The United States does not challenge that position. It reaffirms its interest in a peaceful settlement of the Taiwan question by the Chinese themselves.

As Kissinger left for home at the end of this second visit, the United Nations General Assembly voted to expel Taiwan and seat the People's Republic in its place. An era in post-war politics was over.

By January 1972, the diplomatic preparations for Nixon's trip had been completed.

But the central personage of the drama was missing. Mao's physical condition was deteriorating, and he was still refusing to allow his doctors to treat him. On February 1 – three weeks before Nixon was due to arrive – he relented, only to collapse, unconscious, next day after choking on phlegm from his infected lungs. A combination of antibiotics and the prospect of meeting China's 'most respected enemy' pulled him back from the brink. However, his throat remained swollen, making it difficult for him to talk, and his body was so bloated from the build-up of fluid that a new suit and shoes had to be made. In the week before Nixon arrived, his staff helped him to practise sitting down, getting up and walking about in his room, to exercise his muscles again after the months he had spent confined to his bed.

When the great day came, Mao was on tenterhooks. He sat by the telephone listening to minute-by-minute reports of the President's progress from the airport, where he had been greeted by Zhou Enlai; through the empty streets of Beijing, cleared of traffic for the occasion; to the state guest-house at Diaoyutai. No meeting with Mao was on the schedule. But he now sent word that he wanted to see the President at once. At Zhou's insistence, Nixon was allowed to rest and have lunch. But then he and Kissinger were swept off in a cavalcade of Red Flag limousines to Zhongnanhai, where Mao was impatiently waiting. In his memoirs, Kissinger gave an awed description of the scene that met them:

> [In] Mao's study . . . manuscripts lined bookshelves along every wall; books covered the table and the floor; it looked more the retreat of a scholar than the audience room of the all-powerful leader of the world's most populous nation . . . Except for the suddenness of the summons, there was no ceremony. Mao just stood there . . . I have met no one, with the possible exception of Charles de Gaulle, who so distilled raw, concentrated will power. He was planted there with a female attendant close by to help steady him . . . He dominated the room – not by the pomp that in most states confers a degree of majesty on the leaders, but by exuding in almost tangible form the overwhelming drive to prevail.

Nixon's account was more matter-of-fact. But he, too, was bowled over by what Kissinger called, in words almost identical to those Sidney Rittenberg had used at Yan'an, thirty years earlier, 'our encounter with history'.

Mao took Nixon's hand in both his own and held it for almost a minute.

One of them presided over the citadel of international capitalism, backed by the strongest economy and military forces in the world; the other was uncontested patriarch of a revolutionary communist state of 800 million people, whose ideology called for the overthrow of capitalism wherever it might appear.

The photograph in the *People's Daily* next day told China, and the world, that the global balance of power had been transformed.

Their talks lasted over an hour, far longer than the brief courtesy call that had initially been planned. Mao startled Nixon by telling him that he preferred dealing with right-wing leaders because they were more predictable. Nixon emphasised that the biggest threat they both faced came not from each other but from Russia. Kissinger, ever the diplomatist, was struck by Mao's deceptively casual conversation, embedding his thoughts in tangential phrases which 'communicated a meaning while evading a commitment . . . [like] passing shadows on a wall'. Zhou worried about Mao getting tired. Nixon had been told that the Chairman was recovering from bronchitis, and after Zhou had looked at his watch several times, the President brought the meeting to a close.

After that, everything else was anticlimax. Nixon and Zhou laboured over the nuts and bolts of the Chinese–American relationship. But the tone had already been set.

To Mao, Nixon's visit was a triumph. Others, whose nations' historical role in China was not less, would soon follow: Kakuei Tanaka, to establish diplomatic relations with Japan; the British Prime Minister, Edward Heath. But nothing would ever again in Mao's life equal the moment when the leader of the Western world came to the Forbidden City bearing in tribute a shared concern about a common enemy. In 1949, Mao had argued that China should not be in too much of a hurry to establish ties with the Western powers – that it should complete its 'house-cleaning' first, and then determine, at a time of its own choosing, which countries it wished to admit. For years, as Western leaders sought to isolate Red China, that had seemed a hollow excuse. But now the first among them had come to Beijing, seeking co-operation on a basis of equality. China had indeed stood up. It was a moment to savour.

Yet it also marked a massive retreat.

Nixon had put his finger on it in an article he wrote a year before his election. The United States, he said, needed to engage with China, 'but as a great and progressing nation, not as the epicentre of world revolution'. That was indeed what happened. In opening the door to America, Mao had responded to geopolitical necessity – the need for a common front to contain the expansionist impulses of Russia. The price had been the abandonment of his vision of a new Red 'Middle Kingdom' from which the world's revolutionaries would draw hope and inspiration. In its place came cold-eyed balance-of-power politics aimed at guaranteeing not revolution but survival.

At his meeting with Nixon, Mao acknowledged this himself. 'People like me sound like a lot of big cannons,' he said. 'For example, [we say] things like "the whole world should unite and defeat imperialism . . ."' – at which point he and Zhou laughed uproariously.

Mao could rationalise such statements by his usual argument that all progress stemmed from contradictions, and that there could be no advance without retreat. None the less, retreat it was. Another of his favourite themes of the 1960s – the notion that China, by the force of its example, would spur a worldwide revolutionary upsurge – had been irredeemably compromised.

The collapse of Mao's plans for his succession and the eclipse of revolutionary by geopolitical concerns were not the only holes being punched into the Cultural Revolution and its policies.

In the autumn of 1971, when Mao toured central China to rally support among the provincial military commanders, he had complained that veteran cadres who had been unjustly purged had still not been rehabilitated. The following November, two months after Lin Biao's death, he said the denunciation of the marshals and others involved in the 'February Adverse Current' had been wrong; they had merely been 'opposing Lin Biao and Chen Boda'. At Chen Yi's funeral in January 1972, he gave further signs of distancing himself from the attacks on the old guard.

Encouraged by these developments, Zhou Enlai began a full-scale effort to rebuild the administration and restore economic production.

He was in a stronger position than he had been for many years. Of the five members of the Standing Committee, Lin was dead; Chen Boda was in prison; and Kang Sheng had cancer. That left just him and Mao. Even disregarding the Chairman's anguished outburst from his sickbed, asking him to take over, the tide was running vigorously in the Premier's favour. The disgrace of Lin Biao had put Jiang Qing and her fellow radicals on the defensive. China's admission to the United Nations and the Nixon visit had shown that pragmatic policies brought results. Zhou's discovery, during a routine medical check-up in May, that he, too, was suffering from cancer, simply made him more determined. He knew now that this was the last chance he would have to place his own seal on China's progress – to nudge the country on to a path of orderly, balanced development that would assure its people a better and happier future.

The Premier's strategy was to use the movement against Lin Biao – officially known as the 'campaign to criticise revisionism and rectify working style' – for an all-out offensive against ultra-Leftist policies and ideas. In April, the *People's Daily* fired the opening salvo, describing veteran cadres as 'the Party's most treasured possession' and urging that they be rehabilitated and given appropriate positions. Chen Yun, the doyen of old-guard economists, reappeared in public (although, prudently, he pleaded that his poor health would not permit him to resume work). Expertise was emphasised again. A Beijing radio station began broadcasting English-language lessons. For the first time since 1966, China sent students abroad. Zhou criticised the Foreign Ministry for failing to change its Leftist ways, using the ingenious argument that unless ultra-Leftism were denounced, Rightism would surely re-emerge.

But even a thicket of straws in the wind could not hide the fact that Mao had conspicuously refrained from giving Zhou public support. Pragmatism abroad was one thing. Demolishing Cultural Revolution policies at home was another. In November 1972, the Chairman decided that the pendulum had swung too far.

The trigger was a page of articles in the *People's Daily* condemning anarchism. The themes it raised were familiar: the persecution of veteran cadres, the trashing of the role of the Party, the waste and destruction of the 'great chaos' – which it blamed on ultra-Leftism. But cumulatively the articles called into question all that the Cultural Revolution stood for. On December 17, Mao announced that Lin's errors, while 'Left in form', were henceforward to be viewed as 'Right in essence', and that Lin himself had been an ultra-Rightist, who had plotted conspiracies, splits and betrayal. Criticising ultra-Leftism was 'not a good idea'.

Two days later Zhou Enlai showed the stuff of which he was made.

He repudiated his previous statements, echoed Mao's revised view of Lin, and cast his unfortunate allies at the *People's Daily* to the wolves.

From then on, the campaign underwent a sea change. Where Zhou had tried to use it as a lever to undo Cultural Revolution policies, the radicals made Lin a scapegoat for the movement's excesses. The new line was spelt out in a New Year's Day editorial, which commended the Cultural Revolution as 'much needed and very timely for consolidating the proletarian dictatorship, preventing capitalist restoration and building socialism'.

However, the Chairman was not about to reverse himself completely.

The pendulum might have swung too far. But there was a limit to the extent it would be allowed to swing back. The last four years of Mao's life would be taken up with an effort, so inherently contradictory that it was almost schizophrenic, to maintain an unstable balance between his radical yearnings and the country's all too evident need for a more predictable, less tortured future.

The conflict was shown most dramatically over the succession.

In 1972, as Mao contemplated the ruins left by Lin Biao's defection, he had few options. Zhou Enlai – moments of panic apart – was too old, too moderate and, in the final analysis, too weak, to be considered a possible heir. Jiang Qing was a loyal radical but, as Mao well knew, she was almost universally detested – greedy for power, haughty, vain and incompetent. Yao Wenyuan was a propagandist, no more able to command others than a man like Chen Boda. Among the younger Politburo members, the only possible candidate was Zhang Chunqiao. He was fifty-five years old. His fidelity to the Cultural Revolution was unquestioned. He had proven qualities of leadership. Mao had even once mentioned him as a potential successor to Lin.

But Mao did not choose Zhang Chunqiao.

Instead, in September 1972, he summoned from Shanghai one of Zhang's deputies, Wang Hongwen, whose Workers' General Headquarters had engineered the Cultural Revolution's first 'seizure of power' almost six years before.

Wang, now a Central Committee member, was a tall, well-built man, who, at the age of thirty-nine, retained some of the earnestness of youth. He came from a poor peasant family; had fought in the Korean War; and afterwards had been assigned to a textile mill. To Mao, that meant he combined the three most desirable social backgrounds – peasant, worker and soldier. He was not told why he had been brought to the capital, and was mystified when the Chairman in person received him and plied him with questions about his life and views. Evidently he passed with flying colours, for Mao set him to studying the complete works of Marx, Engels and

Lenin – a task far beyond his meagre educational accomplishments and which he found excruciatingly boring. He also found it hard to adjust to Mao's night-owl work habits and made homesick phonecalls to his Shanghai friends, complaining how tedious life was. None the less, at the end of December, two days after Mao's seventy-ninth birthday, Zhou Enlai and Ye Jianying introduced him at a conference of the Beijing Military Region Party Committee as 'a young man the Chairman has noticed', adding that it was Mao's intention to promote people of his generation to vice-chairmanships in the Central Committee and the Military Commission.

This was not mere caprice on Mao's part. Liu Shaoqi and Lin Biao had both had the stature to carry the whole Party with them. Zhang Chunqiao did not. He was too deeply involved in radical factionalism (and too close to Jiang Qing) to command the loyalty of the Party mainstream, and too sectarian in his attitudes to work together with moderate leaders who could.

Wang was an outsider, a dark horse, who, because he had been far from the capital, was not tarred with the same factional brush.

In March 1973, he began the next stage of his apprenticeship in power when, on Mao's instructions, he started attending Politburo meetings. So did two other neophytes: Hua Guofeng and Wu De. Hua had first caught Mao's eye in the 1950s as Party Secretary of the Chairman's home county of Xiangtan. After the Cultural Revolution he had been appointed First Secretary of the Hunan Provincial Party Committee before moving to Beijing to become acting Security Minister when Xie Fuzhi died of cancer. Wu De had succeeded Xie as First Secretary of the Beijing Party Committee. Both were older than Wang: Hua was fifty-one; Wu, sixty. Like him, both had impeccable radical credentials and were sufficiently middle-of-the-road to build support across factional lines. They were there as a backstop, in case Mao's primary strategy should miscarry.

That left just one more piece of the puzzle for the Chairman to put into place.

On April 12, a short, stocky man with a bullet head and slightly greying hair attended a banquet for the Cambodian Head of State, Prince Sihanouk, in the Great Hall of the People, looking as though he had never been away. Deng Xiaoping, the 'number-two Party person in authority taking the capitalist road', had been quietly rehabilitated a month earlier to resume work as a vice-premier.

Deng was then nearly sixty-nine years old, almost twice Wang Hongwen's age. His return had been prompted partly by Zhou's cancer, which had made it urgent to find an understudy, and partly by a shrewdly worded appeal, which he had sent the Chairman the previous August, praising the Cultural Revolution as 'an immense monster-revealing mirror' that had exposed swindlers like Lin Biao and Chen Boda (and mentioning, in passing, that he would like to get back to work himself). But the fundamental reason for Deng's reinstatement was Mao's awareness that Wang would not be able to assume the succession without help. The Chairman's grand design was that they should work together, Wang heading the Party and Deng the government, until the younger man acquired the knowledge and experience, ten or fifteen years down the road, to run China on his own. Deng had the prestige to keep the army in check; Wang, Mao knew very well, did not. Deng had the ability to keep the administration turning; Wang, again, did not. But if Wang could be established before Mao died as the inheritor of his Party mantle, his youth and commitment to Cultural Revolution values looked like being the Chairman's best hope of ensuring that his ideological legacy would outlive him.

With this aim in view, Wang was given a starring role at the Tenth Party Congress, an oddly abbreviated, ritualistic gathering, held in total secrecy in the Great Hall of the People from August 23 to 27, 1973. He chaired the Election Committee, with Zhou Enlai and Jiang Qing as his deputies; he introduced the new, revised Party constitution (eliminating the reference to Lin Biao as Mao's successor); and, in the new Politburo, to the astonishment of Party and non-Party members alike, he took third place in the hierarchy, behind Mao himself and Zhou, with the rank of Vice-Chairman.

Deng was restored to the Central Committee – though not, at that stage, to the Politburo, apparently to avoid detracting from the lustre of Wang's consecration. His moment would come later.

The Congress also put flesh on the bones of Mao's new formula of having a mix of radicals and veteran cadres to rule China after his death. In the Politburo and the Standing Committee, there was an approximate balance between Jiang Qing's group, on one side, and the old guard, headed by Zhou Enlai and Ye Jianying, on the other. As well as Deng, a number of other prominent veterans were re-elected to CC membership, including Tan Zhenlin, who had fallen foul of Jiang Qing at the time of the 'February Adverse

Current'; the Inner Mongolian leader, Ulanfu, who had survived a regional purge in which tens of thousands of his followers had been killed and injured; and Wang Jiaxiang, Mao's early supporter at Zunyi, who had fallen foul of the Chairman by advocating moderation towards the United States and Russia in the early 1960s.

That autumn, Mao sent Deng and Wang Hongwen on a tour of the provinces to see how they could work together. On their return, Deng told him, with characteristic bluntness, that he saw a risk of warlordism. Twenty-two out of the twenty-nine provincial Party committees were headed by serving army officers.

Mao had reached the same conclusion. In December 1973, he ordered a reshuffle of the commanders of China's eight military regions. He told the Politburo and the Military Commission that in future there must be a clearer division of responsibilities between military and political work, and that Deng, whom he described as 'a man of rare talent', should from now on participate in meetings of both bodies, while also assuming the duties of Chief of the General Staff.

The following April, Mao chose Deng to lead the Chinese delegation to the United Nations, where he unveiled the Chairman's latest thoughts on international affairs, the so-called 'Three Worlds' theory, under which the two superpowers, the United States and the Soviet Union, were viewed as the 'first world'; the other industrialised nations, communist and capitalist alike, as the 'second world'; and the developing countries as the 'third world'.

Two months later, when a very sick Zhou Enlai entered hospital for long-term cancer treatment, Mao designated Wang Hongwen to take day-to-day charge of the work of the Politburo and Deng to head the work of the government.

Thus, by June 1974, the Chairman had put in place the political partnership that he hoped would continue his work after him. It was all still highly provisional. Deng was not even a member of the Politburo. Wang existed politically only because Mao had created him. Yet it seemed that a consensus, however fragile, was finally being established for the orderly succession which had eluded Mao twice before.

Once again it would turn out to be a house of cards.

The fatal flaw in the logic of Mao's arrangements came from the tension inspired by his contradictory impulses towards radicalism and reason. As long as he himself had the whiphand – as he did in 1973 and 1974 – the rival halves of the leadership that mirrored this ideological conflict could be made to work together in an uneasy coalition. But as his strength ebbed away, his physical weakness meant that he was less often present to impose his authority and the two groups grew into warring factions.

Instead of dominating this struggle, as Mao had hoped, Wang and Deng were both sucked into it.

As so often, it was Mao himself who chose the terrain. In May 1973, he had proposed to a Central Committee work conference a campaign to criticise Confucius (who had, of course, died 2,500 years earlier). The pretext was that Lin Liguo had likened Mao to Qin Shihuang, the First Emperor of Qin, who had 'burned the [Confucian] books and buried the scholars alive'. Mao generally welcomed that comparison. But this time he had chosen to interpret it as meaning that Lin Biao and his followers – since they opposed Qin Shihuang – were supporters of Confucius, and therefore of the feudal landlord system that the Sage had extolled in his writings. However, things were not quite what they seemed. By associating Confucius with Lin Biao, Mao was playing the old game of 'pointing at the locust tree in order to revile the mulberry'. The true target of the new movement was neither Confucius nor Lin Biao, but Zhou Enlai.

The connection with Zhou was never openly admitted. However, Mao had dropped a broad hint at a meeting with Wang Hongwen and Zhang Chunqiao that summer, when he reiterated the need to criticise Confucius while, almost in the same breath, grumbling that the Foreign Ministry was not discussing 'important matters' with him, and that if this continued, 'revisionism is bound to occur'. The Ministry was Zhou's responsibility. It was there, a year earlier, that the Premier had spoken out against ultra-Leftism. Mao had not forgotten. The anti-Confucius campaign was his way of warning Zhou, and by implication the rest of the old guard, against any further attempt to call into question the Cultural Revolution's achievements.

The attacks, coming on top of the Premier's illness, sapped his strength. When Kissinger visited Beijing, on his sixth visit to China in November 1973, he found Zhou 'uncharacteristically tentative'. The old bite and sparkle were missing. During their discussions on Taiwan, Kissinger wrote later, he sensed, for the first time, a willingness to envisage the normalisation of US–Chinese relations without a formal rupture between Washington and Taibei (an impression which Mao appeared to confirm the following day). However, something in their exchanges – exactly what, the Chinese transcripts do not make clear – led the two Foreign Ministry officials attending the talks (Mao's grand-niece, Deputy Foreign Minister Wang Hairong, and Nancy Tang, the head of the Ministry's American and Oceanic Department) to report to the Chairman that the Premier had made 'unauthorised statements'. In December, Mao ruled that Zhou should be criticised, whereupon a Politburo meeting was called at which Jiang Qing accused him of treason and of 'being too impatient to wait to replace Chairman Mao', a singularly absurd allegation against a man in an advanced stage of cancer. She then called for a full-scale line struggle to be waged against him, similar to those against Liu Shaoqi and Lin Biao.

At that point, Mao intervened, telling Zhou and Wang Hongwen that the only person impatient to replace him was Jiang Qing herself. Zhou had made errors, he indicated, but his position was secure.

None the less, very soon afterwards the Premier relinquished responsibility for foreign affairs (which passed to Deng Xiaoping), and the campaign to 'criticise Lin Biao and Confucius', which until then had been relatively restrained, became a full-fledged national movement.

To Mao, its purpose was unchanged: to combat revisionism and protect the Cultural Revolution's achievements. To Jiang Qing and her allies, it was a means of undermining the Premier – and thus of blocking the rise of Deng Xiaoping, whom the radicals now saw as the main impediment to their taking power after Mao's death.

The result was a welter of far-fetched historical innuendo, accompanied by petty attacks on Zhou's policies – based on symbolic incidents, such as a student handing in a blank examination paper to protest against the new emphasis on academic standards – under the rubric of 'going against the tide'. The aim was to foment a new surge of unrest, in the same way as Mao's statement, 'It is right to rebel', had mobilised the Red Guards seven years before – and it became sufficiently threatening, with armed clashes reported from some areas, that the Chairman found it necessary to issue a directive, giving provincial Party committees responsibility for the movement and banning the establishment of mass organisations.

Mao was displeased by these attempts to hijack the campaign for factional ends, and on March 20, 1974, wrote reproachfully to Jiang Qing, whom he regarded, rightly, as the moving spirit behind the radicals' actions:

> For years I have advised you about various things, but you have ignored most of it. So what use is it for us to see each other? . . . I am 80 years old and seriously ill, but you show hardly any concern. You now enjoy many privileges, but after my death, what are you going to do? . . . Think about it.

Mao's reference to his poor health was an uncharacteristic admission of his decline since Nixon's visit, two years earlier. He had lost more than two stone; his clothes hung off his thin shoulders and his whole body sagged. The least physical effort tired him. When he attended the Tenth Congress, oxygen tanks had to be installed in the car which took him on the three-minute drive to the Great Hall of the People; in his rooms there; and even at the podium where he spoke. He drooled uncontrollably. His voice had become low and guttural, and his speech was almost incomprehensible even to those who knew him well.

Kissinger remembered the struggle it cost him to emit each thought: 'Words seemed to leave his bulk as if with great reluctance; they were ejected from his vocal cords in gusts, each of which seemed to require a new rallying of physical force until enough strength had been assembled to tear forth another round of pungent declarations.'

Then Mao's eyes began to fail. Cataracts were diagnosed. By the summer of 1974 he was almost blind, barely able to distinguish a finger held up in front of his face until an operation on his right eye restored partial sight a year later.

His ailments made him increasingly reclusive. Three years earlier he had taken as his companion an intelligent, somewhat haughty young woman named Zhang Yufeng, whom he had met while she was working as an attendant on his special train before the Cultural Revolution. Now she began to act (and later took over on a permanent basis) as his confidential secretary, in the process acquiring considerable influence. After Mao's sight failed, she read Politburo documents aloud to him. Because no one else could understand what he said, she passed on his instructions. When he could no longer eat solid food, she fed him. She helped to wash and bathe him.

Yet, even in his physical decay, Mao wielded untrammelled power, as he showed dramatically over the next few months in his treatment of Deng Xiaoping and Wang Hongwen.

To Mao's disgust and annoyance, his young Shanghai protégé, instead of establishing himself as an independent force in the leadership, had foolishly (if predictably, given his background) aligned himself with Jiang Qing and the rest of the radical group.

At a Politburo meeting on July 17, 1974, the Chairman reiterated his dissatisfaction with his wife, who, he said, 'does not represent me, she only represents herself', and for the first time rebuked Wang and the other radicals for forming 'a small faction of four people', an appellation later to become familiar as the 'Gang of Four'.

Immediately afterwards he left Beijing for Wuhan and Changsha, where he spent the following autumn and winter. At that point, his doctors discovered that in addition to all his other maladies – which included bedsores, a lung infection, a diseased heart and anoxia (insufficient oxygen in the blood) – Mao was suffering from Lou Gehrig's disease, a rare, incurable, nervous disorder which causes paralysis of the throat and respiratory system. The medical team estimated that he had, at most, two years to live.

Mao was not told of their prognosis. But his growing enfeeblement must have made clear to him that if he were going to make further adjustments to the succession arrangements, it had better be done sooner rather than later.

Once that decision had been taken, events moved swiftly.

On October 4, Mao appointed Deng Xiaoping First Deputy Premier, making him the automatic successor to Zhou Enlai. Jiang Qing was outraged, and at a Politburo meeting two weeks later she and the other radicals launched a concerted attack on Deng's foreign trade policies which ended only when he got up and walked out. Next day Wang Hongwen flew to Changsha, where he informed Mao that he had come secretly on behalf of Jiang Qing, Zhang Chunqiao and Yao Wenyuan, without telling the rest of the Politburo, because they were concerned about the activities of Deng and Zhou Enlai. Zhang Chunqiao, they felt, was better qualified to lead the government than Deng; and Zhou, while claiming to be ill, was plotting secretly with other veteran leaders, creating an atmosphere of usurping power, like that at Lushan in 1970.

If Mao needed proof that his successor-designate was a fool, Wang could not have done better. He was sent away with a stinging rebuke, and a warning not to be misled by Jiang Qing in future.

Over the next two-and-a-half months, Mao's wife attempted on three more occasions to persuade him that Deng was a liability and that he should promote her supporters instead. The only effect was to make the Chairman more determined. As well as naming Deng senior Vice-Premier, he decided that he should also have the posts of Vice-Chairman of the Party and the Military Commission, and be confirmed as Chief of Staff. Jiang Qing, he minuted, was ambitious, and wanted to be Party Chairman herself. 'Don't organise a cabinet from behind the screen,' he told her. 'You have provoked too much enmity.' In contrast, he praised Deng as 'a person of extraordinary ability with a firm ideological standpoint.'

At the beginning of January 1975, Mao's decisions were ratified by a Central Committee plenum, at which, for the last time, Zhou Enlai presided. It marked a watershed. From then on, meetings of the leadership would be chaired not by Zhou or Wang Hongwen, but by Deng.

To all intents and purposes, Mao had given up on Wang.

He had not abandoned completely the idea of a leadership coalition. But the young Shanghai radical would have no role in it; he had shown himself too stupid. Jiang Qing was out of the question, too. In a self-criticism she had sent to the Chairman in November, she had written: 'I am muddle-headed and unable to handle correctly and realistically objective situations.' Mao agreed. She was loyal, but wildly ambitious, incompetent – and exasperating. He had once told a perplexed Henry Kissinger that China was a very poor country but 'what we have in excess is women'. If America liked to import some, he would be delighted; then they could create some disasters over there and leave China in peace. In January 1975, Mao had no illusions that Jiang Qing would be the kiss of death for any succession arrangement in which she was given a part.

That left only Zhang Chunqiao. It was Mao's doubts about Zhang that had caused him to promote Wang Hongwen in the first place. However, someone had to be found to act as a counterweight to Deng. So Zhang was appointed Second Vice-Premier and head of the PLA General Political Department.

The formation of the new government and the restoration of the offices of state,* five years after the Cultural Revolution had formally drawn to a close, directed Mao's thoughts to the economy. In the process, he reflected anew on the dangers of revisionism, quoting Lenin's dictum that 'small-scale production engenders capitalism . . . continuously, daily, hourly'. That triggered a fresh crackdown on peasants' private plots and rural markets. None the less, Mao made clear that the priority was 'unity, stability and development'. With his support, Zhou Enlai presented to the National People's Congress a programme for 'modernising agriculture, industry, defence and science and technology before the end of the century, so that our national economy will be . . . in the world's front ranks'. Deng, supported by Li Xiannian and Ye Jianying, spent the next ten months working indefatigably to put that into practice. Jiang Qing and her allies obstructed his efforts, but Mao was unsympathetic.

The campaign to criticise Confucius and Lin Biao waned. Zhou was too ill for it to be worth the radicals' while any more.

Instead, Zhang Chunqiao and Yao Wenyuan launched a new movement against 'empiricism', a code-word for Deng's emphasis on solving practical problems rather than giving attention to politics and ideology. But Mao lashed out at their 'poor understanding of Marxism-Leninism', declaring that dogmatism was just as bad as empiricism, and that the real problem, revisionism, included both.

On May 3, 1975, shortly after his return from Changsha to Beijing, he reiterated this before the Politburo, which he now chaired for the last time. He upbraided the radicals again, in the presence of their colleagues, for forming a 'Gang of Four', and drew a parallel between their conduct and that of his old adversary, Wang Ming. Ominously, he repeated the warning he had given at Lushan, before the purge of Chen Boda: 'Practice Marxism, not revisionism; unite and don't split; be open and above-board, don't intrigue and conspire.'

That summer marked the nadir of the radicals' fortunes.

In late May and June, Jiang Qing and her three allies, on Mao's orders, all made self-criticisms before the Politburo. At about this

---

* The only exception was the State Chairmanship, which, under the new constitution, was abolished. Instead, the functions of Head of State devolved to the Chairman of the National People's Congress, who, from January 1975 until his death, eighteen months later, was Zhu De.

time, Mao learned that Roxane Witke, an American feminist and sinologist, was preparing a book about Jiang, on the basis of interviews which she had given, without his authorisation, some three years earlier. That drove him into another fury. 'She is ignorant and ill-informed,' he railed. 'Drive her out of the Politburo immediately! We'll separate and go our different ways.' Kang Sheng, on his deathbed with cancer, took Mao literally, and wrote the Chairman a letter in which he claimed to have discovered proof that Jiang and Zhang Chunqiao had both been GMD agents in Shanghai in the 1930s. But no one dared to deliver it; Kang died shortly afterwards and Mao was never told.

Jiang Qing, however, was nothing if not persistent. She knew, as Mao did, that she and her fellow radicals were the only ones he could trust to keep alive the Cultural Revolutionary flame after he died. Curse her though he might, he needed her.

In September, the radicals launched one more attempt to show that Deng's modernisation effort ran counter to Mao's 'proletarian line'. That summer, the Chairman had spent several weeks listening to readings from one of his favourite novels, *Water Margin*. The story relates the exploits of a group of bandits, the '108 heroes of Liangshanpo', whose leader, Song Jiang, eventually betrayed his patron, Chao Gai, and accepted an amnesty from the Emperor. Mao had commented that Song Jiang was a revisionist, and that the value of the book lay in its description of capitulationism.

That became the pretext for a flood of abstruse, supposedly scholarly, articles implying that Deng's efforts to restore economic order were a capitulation to capitalism and a betrayal of the Cultural Revolution. The climax was reached when Jiang Qing told a conference a month later: 'Song Jiang made Chao Gai a figurehead. Are there people making Chairman Mao a figurehead? I believe there are!'

The Chairman scrawled on the text of her speech, 'Shit! Wide of the mark!', and forbade its distribution.

Yet the tide was slowly turning. Notwithstanding Mao's contemptuous rejection of the laboured polemics the radicals were producing, he was becoming concerned that Deng was going too far. There was too much emphasis on improving living standards, not enough on class struggle. The Chairman's nephew, Mao Yuanxin, who took over at the end of September as his liaison officer with the Politburo, replacing Wang Hairong, played on these fears, insinuating that Deng planned to abandon the Cultural Revolution and its values once the Chairman was no longer alive to defend them.

Deng himself sensed the changing mood. In October 1975 he told a group of senior cadres: 'Some say [we represent] . . . the old order . . . Let them say whatever they like . . . The worst that could happen is you could be overthrown a second time. Don't be afraid. If you've done a good job it's worth being overthrown for it!' Mao's staff noticed the change, too. That month the Chairman became restless and irritable.

In the end, a minor incident triggered the crisis. Mao asked Deng to chair a Politburo discussion to evaluate the Cultural Revolution, which he viewed, employing his usual rule of thumb, as having been 70 per cent successful and 30 per cent mistaken. Deng politely declined, ostensibly because he had been 'absent' for most of it, but actually, as Mao immediately realised, because he did not wish to be associated with a judgement that would put the Cultural Revolution in a positive light. Mao never alluded directly to this incident. But afterwards he told his nephew: '[Among] some senior comrades . . . I discern two attitudes to the Cultural Revolution: one is discontent; the other is . . . denial.'

From there, it was a small step for Mao to declare that 'the capitalist-roaders are still on the capitalist road'.

A seemingly unrelated dispute at Qinghua University, where the Party Secretary was an ally of Jiang Qing, led the Chairman to accuse Deng of supporting those who, under the pretext of attacking radical education policies, were actually 'directing the spearhead at me'. In late November, his views were conveyed to the Politburo and the Military Commission at a meeting chaired by one of the few top leaders who was a member neither of the radical nor of the old-guard faction, the Security Minister, Hua Guofeng. On Mao's instructions, the gathering was told that 'there are some people who are not satisfied with the Cultural Revolution [and who] . . . want to settle accounts with it and to reverse the verdict'. It was the signal for a new campaign against a 'Right deviationist wind of reversing correct verdicts', with Deng as the principal target.

By the end of the year hints of the new line were beginning to appear in the press, and for all practical purposes Deng had been stripped of his responsibilities. Yet again, Mao's succession strategy had foundered. Wang Hongwen was a broken reed, and Deng, left to his own devices, had proved untrustworthy.

At this juncture, Zhou Enlai died.

Like many long-expected events, when it came it had profound and immediate repercussions. Politically, the choice of a new premier could be delayed no longer. Emotionally, the mass out-pouring of grief that the news of his passing provoked – as though the flood walls of cynicism, which, since the Cultural Revolution, had held back genuine popular feeling, had abruptly sundered – signalled an attachment to Zhou personally, to the values he was thought to represent and to the policies he had promoted, which the regime would ignore at its peril. From January 9, 1976, when his death was announced on radio and television, the people of Beijing took wreaths and white paper flowers to the Monument to the People's Heroes in Tiananmen Square in a spontaneous gesture of respect. Two days later, when the cortège carried his body to be cremated, a million people lined the streets to bid him a last farewell.

Mao had never felt any personal affection for Zhou, and he showed none at his death. The staff in Zhongnanhai were forbidden to wear black mourning armbands. There was no official lying-in-state. Press coverage was kept to a minimum, and factories and work units were discouraged from holding memorial meetings.

At the funeral ceremony, in the Great Hall of the People, on January 15, Deng was allowed to give the eulogy, but it was to be his last public appearance. Mao was too sick to attend, which saved him having to make the choice to stay away; instead he sent a wreath.

The next step was to name the new Premier. The population at large, along with the rest of the world, unaware that a new campaign was brewing, confidently expected Deng to be appointed. The radicals, better informed, pinned their hopes on Zhang Chunqiao.

Mao named neither man.

Instead, on January 21, he informed the Politburo that he intended to support Hua Guofeng.

This was not quite as astonishing a move as it was made out to be at the time. Mao had tapped Hua as a possible successor – should

Wang Hongwen fail to come up to his expectations – in the spring of 1973. Later that year Hua had joined the Politburo, and in January 1975, Mao had named him one of China's twelve vice-premiers. He was an amiable, phlegmatic man, who had shown himself a capable government administrator, and had the talent – rare in the upper ranks of the CCP hierarchy – of getting on well with his colleagues. Equally germane, as Mao had recognised when he had asked him to chair the meeting at which Deng had been criticised the previous November, he was neutral. Unlike Wang and Deng, Hua might prove capable of remaining above the factional strife.

Nevertheless, the Chairman proceeded cautiously. When the public announcement of Hua's promotion was made on February 3, it was only on an acting basis. Deng was still officially First Deputy-Premier. Although a full-scale movement was under way to criticise him as an 'unrepentant capitalist-roader', he had not been identified by name as its target – and Mao had made clear that he viewed his case as 'non-antagonistic', meaning that he might yet be redeemed. Hua, Deng and the radicals were all part of the succession equation, but in the opening months of 1976, Mao had still not decided exactly how they fitted together.

To Deng, that spring, there was a curious air of *déjà vu*. Ten years earlier, in the opening months of the Cultural Revolution, he had been in a very similar situation – nominally still a member of the Politburo Standing Committee, yet under fierce radical attack, while Mao, inscrutable and sardonic, held his fate in his hands. This time, however, there was a crucial difference. In 1966, Mao had been still vigorous, masterminding an immense upheaval which would change China for ever. In 1976, he was dying.

The Chairman's mind was clear. But he could no longer stand unaided; his right side was partly paralysed, and he could barely speak.

Nixon, who visited him in February, wrote that 'it was painful to see him' as he uttered 'a series of monosyllabic grunts and groans'. Zhang Yufeng had learned to lip-read. But on bad days even that was no help, and Mao had to scribble his thoughts on a notepad before she could grasp his meaning. She afterwards wrote a moving description of how they celebrated his last Chinese New Year:

> There were no visitors, no family members. Chairman Mao spent his last Spring Festival with those who served him. I had to feed him his

New Year's Eve dinner with a spoon, since he could not use his hands. It was hard for him even to open his mouth and swallow. I helped him from the bed to the sofa in his study. For a long time, he rested his head on the chairback without uttering a word . . . Suddenly, from somewhere in the distance, we heard firecrackers. In a low, hoarse voice, Mao asked me to explode some for him . . . A faint smile crept over his old and weary face when he heard the fire-crackers in the courtyard.

The realisation that Mao's death could only be months away convinced Deng to stand firm. Where, in the autumn of 1966, he had admitted his errors and made a full self-criticism, he now showed his accusers his contempt. At a Politburo meeting called in March to criticise him, he turned off his hearing aid and refused to answer, claiming that he could not hear what they were saying.

The stalemate was finally broken by those whom Mao had always claimed were the true heroes moving history forward, but whose wishes he had so often ignored – the people. They were no longer quite the same people as they had been before the Cultural Revolution. The constant injunctions 'to rebel' and 'to go against the tide' had finally succeeded in undermining the tradition of blind faith in authority that had characterised earlier generations of Chinese.

At a time of mind-numbing propaganda campaigns, effete political movements and unreadable newspapers, Zhou Enlai had been, for many, an authentic popular hero, the more cherished precisely because he had not been imposed by the regime but had won a place in their hearts by his own perceived merit. In the spring of 1976, there was widespread anger in China at the cursory treatment given to his funeral in the press and the brevity of the official mourning. The result was a spontaneous movement, beginning in late March, to honour Zhou's memory at Qingming, the Festival of the Dead, which falls in early April. As a precautionary measure, the radicals ordered the closure of the cemetery where he had been cremated, and commemorative activities were officially discouraged.

The flame to ignite this tinderbox was supplied on March 25 by the Shanghai newspaper, *Wenhuibao*, which, on the instructions of Zhang Chunqiao, published a front-page article implicitly accusing Zhou of having been a capitalist-roader.

That provoked demonstrations in several Yangtse Valley cities, including Nanjing, where hundreds of students pasted up slogans attacking Zhang Chunqiao and honouring the memory of Mao's first wife, Yang Kaihui, in a none too subtle jibe at Jiang Qing. They were quickly covered up and the perpetrators accused of 'counter-revolutionary restoration'. The official media were forbidden to mention the incident. But the students had daubed slogans on railway carriages and long-distance buses. On March 31, news of their action reached Beijing, where unofficial memorial rites were already in full swing in Tiananmen Square. From then on the eulogies and poems became increasingly hostile, attacking not only the 'mad empress', Jiang Qing, and the 'wolves and jackals' who were her allies, but also Mao himself. The city authorities announced a ban on wreath-laying. It was ignored. By Sunday, April 4, the day of the Qingming festival itself, so many thousands of wreaths had been laid in memory of Zhou that they formed a vast mound, burying the base of the Monument to the People's Heroes and reaching 60 feet up its sides. An estimated two million people had visited the square by nightfall.

In the evening, the Politburo met. Deng was absent, as were his main allies, Ye Jianying, Li Xiannian and the Guangzhou Military Commander, Xu Shiyou. Several speakers, including the Mayor of Beijing, Wu De, accused Deng of fomenting the unrest. This was untrue. But it reflected a realisation that, with Mao's health now so precarious, the groundswell of popular support for Zhou and his policies would strengthen Deng's position immeasurably if it were allowed to continue. None of those present wanted that.

The meeting therefore concluded that the demonstrations were 'reactionary', and that the wreaths should be removed. Mao was informed and, with his agreement, the square was cleared overnight.

Early next morning, a sullen, mutinous crowd, numbering several tens of thousands, gathered outside the Great Hall of the People, to demand that the wreaths be returned. As the day wore on, their mood grew uglier. A police van was overturned, and several jeeps and other vehicles set on fire. A building which the police were using as a command post was also burned down. At 6.30 p.m., Wu De broadcast an appeal over the loudspeaker system, urging people to disperse. Many did. But about a thousand irreductibles remained. Three hours later, the floodlights were suddenly turned on, and as martial music played over the loudspeakers, police and troops moved in, making several hundred arrests.

That night, the Politburo met again and agreed that 'a counter-revolutionary incident' had taken place, for which Deng Xiaoping should be held responsible.

Two days later, Mao handed down his decision.

The rioting was condemned as 'a reactionary event'. Deng was stripped of all his posts, but allowed to keep his Party membership 'to see how he will behave'. Mao had evidently not entirely abandoned hope that he might one day play a useful role again. Deng himself had by then already slipped away from Beijing to go into hiding in Canton, where he remained until the autumn, secure under the protection of Xu Shiyou despite intensive efforts by the radicals to locate him.

But the most important decision was that Hua Guofeng was confirmed as Premier and appointed First Vice-Chairman of the Party. Mao's mind was finally made up. Hua would be his fourth, and last, choice as successor.

Three weeks later, on April 30, 1976, the Chairman sanctified the new arrangement with a scribbled six-character phrase, which Hua would afterwards cite as his legitimation: *Ni banshi, wo fanxin* – 'With you in charge, I am at ease'.

The next four months were a death-watch.

On May 12, after a brief meeting with the Singapore Prime Minister, Lee Kuan Yew, Mao suffered a minor heart attack. He recovered, and two weeks later received Pakistan's Premier, Zulfikar Ali Bhutto, for a few minutes. But he looked exhausted, his face expressionless, with half-closed eyes. Afterwards, he decided there should be no more meetings with foreign leaders. At the end of June, he had another heart attack, this time more serious. Then, on July 6, Zhu De died, at the age of eighty-nine. Three weeks later came the great earthquake at Tangshan, in which a quarter-of-a-million people perished. Beijing was shaken. From the Study of Chrysanthemum Fragrance Mao was wheeled in a hospital bed inside Zhongnanhai to a more modern building nearby which was said to be earthquake-proof.

Some time that summer, probably in June, he summoned Hua, Jiang Qing and several other members of the Politburo to his bedside. There he told them, as if delivering a last testament:

In my life, I have done two things. First I fought Chiang Kai-shek for several decades, and drove him to a few small islands . . . We fought our way to Beijing, and at last to the Forbidden City. There are not many people who do not recognise those achievements . . . The second thing I have done you all know. It was to launch the Cultural Revolution, which now has the support of few and is opposed by many. But this matter is not ended yet. It is a legacy which must be handed down to the next generation. How should it be handed down? If not in peace, then in turmoil. If this is not properly handled, there will be bloodshed. Heaven alone knows what you will do.

As his life ebbed away, Mao had few illusions that the legacy of the Cultural Revolution would survive intact. With his heart, he hoped. But his head, lucid to the end, told him that, even if something were salvaged, the essence of his vision would perish with him.

Jiang Qing, in her arrogance and stupidity, helped to ensure that happened.

Mao had dealt the radicals a strong hand. Their main rival, Deng Xiaoping, had been removed. Deng's ally, Ye Jianying, while still Defence Minister, had lost day-to-day control of the Military Commission. There was a sufficient community of interest between Hua and themselves for a modus vivendi at the old guard's expense.

But Jiang Qing and Zhang Chunqiao, pumped up with their own power and importance, had no interest in a tactical alliance. Jiang saw herself as Party Chairperson, a Red Empress to succeed Mao just as Empress Lu of the Han dynasty, two thousand years earlier, had succeeded the Han founder, Liu Bang. Zhang would be her Prime Minister and Wang Hongwen the Head of State. Hua, 'a nice gentleman of Malenkov's ilk', as she called him witheringly, was an obstacle to these plans. Throughout the summer – with Mao too ill to know what she was doing, let alone control her – she worked relentlessly to undermine him.

That drove Hua into the arms of her opponents. In July, after Jiang Qing attacked him at a State Council planning meeting, he discussed with Wang Dongxing, as head of the Central Guards Regiment which controlled the leaders' security, possible ways of getting rid of her. Ye Jianying had similar talks with Marshal Nie Rongzhen and a group of senior generals.

Independently they reached the same conclusion. Nothing could be done as long as Mao was alive.

On September 2, the Chairman had another massive heart attack. On the evening of the 8th, the members of the Politburo filed slowly past Mao's bed. As Ye Jianying was about to leave the room, Zhang Yufeng called him back. Mao's eyes were open, and he tried to speak. But only a hoarse sound came. Three hours later, just after midnight, in the early morning of September 9, the imperious will faltered. The line being traced by the electrocardiograph became flat. It was over.

Epilogue

When the news was broadcast by Beijing Radio, it caused shock and apprehension, but not grief. There was none of the outpouring of emotion that marked the disappearance of Zhou Enlai. The extinction of a titan brings no personal sense of loss.

However, history rarely wraps up its work neatly. Mao had left unfinished business.

On the night of Wednesday, October 6, exactly four weeks after his death, Hua Guofeng summoned Wang Hongwen, Zhang Chunqiao and Yao Wenyuan to a Politburo meeting in the Great Hall of the People.

Wang arrived first, to find Hua and Ye Jianying waiting. As he entered, four soldiers from Wang Dongxing's Central Guards Regiment sprang out from behind a screen and seized him. Hua read out a brief statement: 'You have entered into an anti-Party and anti-socialist alliance . . . in a vain attempt to usurp the leadership of the Party and to seize power. Your offence is serious. The Centre has decided that you shall be taken into custody for a full examination.' Zhang Chunqiao and Yao Wenyuan were afterwards detained in the same manner. An hour later, Jiang Qing was arrested at Zhongnanhai, where she had moved back with her staff shortly before Mao died. As she was being taken away, popular legend has it that one of her servants spat at her.

None of the four attempted to resist. There were no disturbances after their arrests. Less than a month after his passing, Mao's great experiment was at an end.

It was a prospect that already haunted him in the early 1960s, when he first began to have doubts about Liu Shaoqi. But at that time he was still convinced that, whatever the setbacks along the way, the ultimate triumph of communism was ineluctable. 'If our children's generation go in for revisionism,' he told the Central Committee, 'so that although they still nominally have socialism, it is in fact capitalism, then our grandsons will certainly rise up in revolt and overthrow their fathers, because [otherwise] the masses will not be satisfied.' Four years later, in 1966, he was less sanguine. If the Rightists came to power after his death, he wrote then, their regime would 'very probably' be short-lived. 'The Rightists may prevail for some time by using my words, but the Leftists may also use my words to overthrow them.' In his last years, even that confidence slipped away.

At one level, Mao's prescience was uncanny. For two years after his death, there was indeed a 'war of words', in which the Cultural Revolution's beneficiaries, led by Hua and Wang Dongxing, used Mao's writings to fight off the efforts of the movement's old-guard victims to win control of the Chairman's ideological legacy. Deng, whose rehabilitation Hua delayed but was unable to prevent, did establish a regime which, while 'nominally socialist', was capitalist in every other respect. Mao had been right about Deng Xiaoping: improbable though it had seemed at the time, he was a 'capitalist-roader' all along – and the moment he was in a position to do so, he began dismantling the socialist system Mao had built and putting a bourgeois dictatorship in its place. There was indeed a bourgeois class within the Communist Party and the country did indeed 'change its political colour'.

The only point on which Mao was wrong was the reaction of the masses. Far from rebelling against capitalism, the overwhelming majority of China's people responded to Deng's new policies with unconcealed delight.

Stripped of pejorative jargon, the 'capitalist road' for China meant putting prosperity first and ideology last. The result was an unparalleled surge of economic development, creating a professional and business elite whose aspirations and way of life – from cellular telephones to Porsches – became increasingly indistinguishable from those of its counterparts in Hong Kong, Singapore and Taiwan. The new wealth trickled down, generating inequalities along with opportunities. Corruption and crime sky-rocketed, along with drug use, Aids and prostitution. In an amazingly short space of time, China acquired most of the problems, and many of the joys and freedoms, which normal countries have.

Deng Xiaoping might order the slaughter of hundreds of students in Tiananmen Square, shattering the illusions of Western liberals, but Chinese who compared his rule with the mindless terror that had preceded it had no doubt which they preferred.

The losers in political struggles no longer disappeared into oblivion. Hua and Wang Dongxing, despite having opposed Deng's return, went into honourable retirement. Jiang Qing committed suicide in prison in 1995. But her ally, Yao Wenyuan, was released after serving a fifteen-year sentence and allowed to return to his old home in Shanghai. So were Chen Boda and other Cultural Revolution luminaries, including the alleged leaders of the ultra-Left 'May 16' group. China had not become a democracy. But it was a livelier, more tolerant place. The curtain of fear that stifled even the tiniest freedoms in Mao's day had been lifted.

In these circumstances, where so much that Mao had done was being reversed and implicitly condemned, his successors did not find it easy to make a judgement on his historical role. After more than a year of discussion, the CCP Central Committee approved a resolution in 1981 which affirmed that, despite 'gross mistakes' during the Cultural Revolution, 'his merits are primary and his errors secondary' in the proportion of seven to three, the same rule of thumb that Mao himself applied to Stalin. Chen Yun had put it more poignantly, two years earlier, telling his colleagues: 'Had Mao died in 1956, his achievements would have been immortal. Had he died in 1966, he would still have been a great man. But he died in 1976. Alas, what can one say?' None the less, the 'seven/three' formula suited the Party's needs. It allowed Deng and the old guard to repudiate whichever of Mao's policies they disliked without inviting a challenge to the legitimacy of Communist Party rule.

China has been locked into that assessment ever since. Having abandoned its ideology, the CCP could not allow itself the luxury of negating the myth of its founder.

Political constraints aside, to evaluate the juggernaut who wrenched China from its medieval torpor and forced it into the contours of a modern nation is a formidable task.

The achievements of Mao's great contemporaries, Roosevelt, Churchill and De Gaulle, are measured against those of their peers. Even Stalin built on Lenin's accomplishments. Mao's life was played out on an altogether vaster canvas. He was unquestioned leader of almost a quarter of mankind, inhabiting an area the size of Europe. He wielded powers equalled only by the most awesome of Chinese emperors, in an era when China's history was so compressed that changes which, in the West, had taken centuries to accomplish, occurred in a single generation. In Mao's lifetime, China made the leap from semi-colony to Great Power; from millennial autarky to socialist state; from despoiled victim of imperialist plunder to Permanent Member of the UN Security Council, complete with H-bombs, surveillance satellites and ICBMS.

Mao had an extraordinary mix of talents: he was visionary, statesman, political and military strategist of genius, philosopher and poet. Foreigners might sniff. In a memorable put-down, Arthur Waley, the great translator of Tang dynasty poetry, described Mao's poems as 'not as bad as Hitler's paintings, but not as good as Churchill's'. In the judgement of another Western art historian, his calligraphy, while 'strikingly original, betraying a flamboyant egotism, to the point of arrogance, if not extravagance . . . [and] a total disregard for the formal discipline of the brush', was 'essentially inarticulate'. Most Chinese scholars disagree. Mao's poems, like his brushwork, seized the tormented, restless spirit of his age.

To these gifts, he brought a subtle, dogged mind, awe-inspiring charisma and fiendish cleverness.

The philippic penned by Lin Biao's son – 'Today he uses sweet words and honeyed talk to those whom he entices; tomorrow he puts them to death for fabricated crimes' – unconsciously echoed the judgement two thousand years earlier of an adviser to Qin Shihuangdi, the greatest of China's founding emperors. 'The King of Qin is [like] a bird of prey . . . There is no beneficence in him, and he has the heart of a tiger or a wolf. When he is in difficulties, he finds it easy to humble himself. But when he has achieved his aim, he finds it just as easy to devour human beings . . . If [he] realises his ambitions concerning the Empire, all men will be his slaves.'

Mao knew by heart the lessons of the dynastic histories. It was not chance that led him to choose, among all his imperial predecessors, the First Emperor of Qin – who throughout Chinese history had been feared and reviled as the epitome of harsh rule – as the man against whom he wished to measure himself. 'You accuse us of acting like Qin Shihuangdi,' he once told a group of liberal intellectuals. 'You are wrong. We surpass him a hundred times. When you berate us for imitating his despotism, we are happy to agree! Your mistake was that you did not say so enough.'

To Mao, the killing of opponents – or simply of those who disagreed with his political aims – was an unavoidable, indeed a necessary, ingredient of broader political campaigns.

He rarely gave direct instruction for their physical elimination.* But his rule brought about the deaths of more of his own people than any other leader in history.

The victims of the land reform, of his political campaigns – the 'movement to suppress counter-revolutionaries'; the 'Three Antis'; the 'Five Antis'; the anti-Rightist Campaign; the movement against 'Right opportunism'; the Socialist Education Movement; the Cultural Revolution; the campaign against 'May 16' elements; and the 'cleansing of class ranks', to mention but the most important – and of the famines triggered by the Great Leap Forward, have been exceeded only once – by all the dead of the Second World War.

By comparison, Stalin's liquidation of the kulaks and his destruction of the Russian intelligentsia in the labour camps, claimed 12 to 15 million victims; Hitler's holocaust, less than half that number.

Those parallels, while persuasive, are in one important sense false, however. Stalin set out deliberately to encompass the physical extermination of all who stood in his way. During the Great Purge, he and Molotov personally signed NKVD lists containing the names of thousands of high officials for arrest and execution. Hitler's 'final solution' was designed to extirpate in the gas chambers an entire racial group – the Jews – whose genetic stock besmirched his new Aryan world order.

---

* Mao's direct involvement in the hunting down and execution of presumed opponents was limited to the period from 1930–31 in the Jiangxi base area. In the Yan'an Rectification Campaign, he gave instructions that 'no cadre is to be killed', but, in practice, allowed Kang Sheng to drive Party dissidents to suicide. This pattern was repeated throughout his leadership of the People's Republic.

The overwhelming majority of those whom Mao's policies killed were unintended casualties of famine. The others – three or four million of them – were the human detritus, of his epic struggle to transform China.

That was cold comfort for his victims; nor did it diminish in any way the egregious misery that Mao's colossal effort of social engineering caused. But it put him in a different category from other twentieth-century tyrants. Just as, in law, there is a capital distinction between murder, manslaughter, and death caused by negligence, so in politics there are gradations of responsibility, related to motivation and intent, for leaders who bring massive suffering to their peoples.

Stalin cared about what his subjects did (or might do); Hitler, about who they were. Mao cared about what they thought.

China's landlords were eliminated as a class (and many of them were killed in the process); but they were not exterminated as a people, as the Jews were in Germany. Even as his policies caused the deaths of millions, Mao never entirely lost his belief in the efficacy of thought reform and the possibility of redemption. 'Heads are not like chives', he said. 'They do not grow back again.'

What was achieved at the cost of such bloodshed and pain?

Mao's own judgement, that his two major accomplishments were his victory over Chiang Kai-shek and the launching of the Cultural Revolution, offers a partial answer, though not quite in the sense he had intended. The one reunified China after a century of division and restored its sovereignty; the other gave the Chinese people such an overdose of ideological fervour as to immunise them for generations to come. Mao's tragedy and his grandeur were that he remained to the end in thrall to his own revolutionary dreams. Where Confucius had taught harmony – the doctrine of the mean – Mao preached endless class struggle, until it became a cage from which neither he nor the Chinese people could escape. He freed China from the straitjacket of its Confucian past. But the bright Red future he promised turned out to be a sterile purgatory.

So culminated a process of national disillusionment that had begun at the time of Mao's birth, when nineteenth-century reformers, responding to the clash with the West, for the first time challenged the beliefs that had kept the Chinese system frozen in immobility for the previous two thousand years.

After Mao, there was no new emperor – merely a succession of fallible leaders, not better and not worse than in any other country.

Blind faith and ideology died. People began thinking for themselves. The old world had been smashed; the new had been found wanting. After a century of turmoil, China was ready to make a fresh start.

Revolution has more to do with tearing down the old than with painstakingly constructing the new. Mao's legacy was to clear the way for less visionary, more practical men to build the shining future that he could never achieve.

Twice before in Chinese history, radical despotisms have ushered in long periods of peace and prosperity. The First Emperor of Qin unified the feudal princedoms in the third century BC but his dynasty survived for only fifteen years. He paved the way for the Han, the first Golden Age of Chinese antiquity, which endured four centuries. In the sixth and early seventh centuries AD, the Sui, who reunified China after a time of division and instability known as the Six Dynasties and the Three Kingdoms, ruled for thirty-nine years. They were followed by the Tang, the second Golden Age, which lasted for three centuries.

Mao ruled for twenty-seven years. If the past, as he believed, is indeed a mirror for the present, will the twenty-first century mark the start of a third Chinese golden age, for which the Maoist dictatorship will have opened the way?

Or will it be his fate to be remembered as a flawed colossus, who brought fundamental change on a scale that only a handful of others had managed in all the years of China's history, but then failed to follow through?

In December 1993, during celebrations marking the centenary of Mao's birth, a private soirée was held at Maxim's, in the business district of the new capitalist Beijing. It is a carbon copy of the restaurant on the Rue Royale in Paris, with the same heavy *belle époque* panelling, rococo silverware and velvet hangings, and similar prices. The two hundred invited guests were a cross-section of the city's moneyed aristocracy: private entrepreneurs in dark suits with foreign labels sewn ostentatiously on to the cuffs, and chunky gold watches on their wrists; stars of China's new film industry; actresses with curled hair; willowy fashion models. Among them was a Mao look-alike named Gu Yue, who had played the eponymous hero in a hagiographic television series depicting the communists' struggle for power. The official entertainment that night, to create the right mood of nostalgia and irony, was one of Jiang Qing's dreary revolutionary operas. After it was over, Gu and half-a-dozen friends, mellowed by champagne and cognac, climbed on to the stage and began to chant together the old Red Guard refrain, 'Mao Zedong Thought lights the way ahead'. As they did so, they blundered about like blind men bumping into each other in the dark. The audience collapsed. The leader they had once revered was now a laughing-stock.

For others, Mao became an icon. Taxi-drivers hung his portrait from their windscreens, suspended like an image of the Buddha on a chain of rosary beads. China's teenyboppers, too young to be burdened with memories of what life under the Chairman was really like, swapped Mao badges and memorabilia. Pop singers parodied his poems; painters reworked his image; designers put him every-where, from dresses to eiderdowns.

In the countryside, Mao's smooth, unfathomable face continues to hold pride of place in innumerable homes. In Hunan, a temple with a 20-foot-high statue of him, flanked by seated effigies of Zhou Enlai and Zhu De, commissioned by local peasant associations from a sculptor at the Buddhist monastery on Wutaishan, attracted tens of thousands of visitors every day – until the Party ordered it closed for encouraging 'feudal superstition'.

The wheel had gone full circle. Mao had entered the pantheon of gods and folk-heroes, outlaws and brigands, who had peopled the dreams of his childhood at the start of his own long life of rebellion, a hundred years before.

History is laid down slowly in China. A final verdict on Mao's place in the annals of his country's past is still a very long way off.

Dramatis Personae

Mao Zedong (1893–1976).

1st marriage =	Miss Luo	(m. 1908)
	(unconsummated)	
2nd marriage =	Yang Kaihui	(b. 1901, m. 1920–30, d. 1930)
	ch: Anying	(1922–51)
	Anqing	(1923–)
	Anlong	(1927–31)
3rd marriage =	He Zizhen	(b. 1909, m. 1928–38, d. 1984)
	ch: Xiao Mao	(1932–lost in 1934)
	Li Min	(1936–)
	[son]	(1939–40)
	Two children abandoned as infants	
	(1929 and 1935)	
4th marriage =	Jiang Qing	(b. 1914, m. 1938–76, d. 1991)
	ch: Li Na	(1940–)

Bo Gu (1907–46):   Moscow-trained member of the 'Returned Student' faction who was de facto Party leader from 1931 until 1935. Sidelined after the Zunyi conference but remained a CC member until his death in an aircrash.

Bo Yibo (1908–):   Youth leader in Shanxi who developed close ties to Liu Shaoqi. After 1949, held a series of high-level posts with responsibility for the economy. Purged during the Cultural Revolution. Rehabilitated after Mao's death.

Cai Hesen (1895–1931):   One of Mao's closest friends at First Normal School in Changsha. Founder member of New People's Study Society.

Central Bureau (later Politburo) member from 1923–7; afterwards Secretary of the CCP's North China Bureau. Arrested by British police in Hong Kong and handed over to the nationalist authorities in Canton for execution.

Chen Boda (1904–89):   Mao's political secretary at Yan'an, later a key member of the Chairman's private brains trust. Head of the Cultural Revolution Group from May 1966; ranked fourth in the leadership at the time of the Ninth Congress. Purged in 1970. Sentenced to eighteen years' imprisonment in 1981 for political crimes; released early because of ill-health.

Chen Duxiu (1879–1942):   Radical intellectual whose journal, *New Youth*, prepared the ground for the May Fourth Movement in 1919. One of the two founding fathers (with Li Dazhao) of the Chinese communist movement. CCP General Secretary from 1921–7; afterwards led a Trotskyist opposition group.

Chen Yi (1901–72):   Nanchang Uprising participant. With Mao on Jinggangshan. One of ten PLA marshals appointed in 1955. Politburo member; Foreign Minister from 1958. Participated in the 'February Adverse Current'. Criticised during the Cultural Revolution but not purged. Died of cancer.

Chen Yun (1905–95):   Shanghai printing worker. Zunyi veteran. Politburo member from 1934. Became a CC Vice-Chairman in 1956 with overall responsibility for economic matters. Withdrew on pretext of ill-health during radical upsurges and thereby survived the Cultural Revolution unharmed. Resumed an active political role after Mao's death.

Chiang Kai-shek (1887–1975):   Japanese-trained army officer who rallied to Sun Yat-sen's nationalists in 1922 and, over the next eight years, led the Guomindang (GMD) to nationwide victory. President of the GMD regime on Taiwan from 1949 until his death.

Deng Xiaoping (1904–97):   Zunyi veteran. General Secretary and Politburo Standing Committee member from 1956. Purged early on in the Cultural Revolution as the 'number-two Party person in authority taking the capitalist road', but allowed to keep his Party membership. Rehabilitated in 1973; purged again in 1976; rehabilitated a year later to become China's paramount leader from 1978 until his death.

Deng Zihui (1896–1972):   With Mao at Ruijin. In charge of agricultural collectivisation in the early 1950s. Repeatedly criticised as a 'right conservative' after 1956, but survived the Cultural Revolution without being purged.

Gao Gang (1905–54):   North-west China CCP leader who rose to become sixth-ranking member of the leadership. Purged after a failed attempt to topple Liu Shaoqi in 1953; committed suicide a year later.

He Long (1896–1969): Participated in the Nanchang Uprising. One of ten PLA marshals appointed in 1955. Politburo member and Vice-Chairman of the CC Military Commission. Purged at the start of the Cultural Revolution. Died from deliberate medical neglect.

He Shuheng (1870–1935): One of Mao's teachers at First Normal School in Changsha, a founder member of the New People's Study Society and of the CCP. With Mao at Ruijin. Stayed behind in Jiangxi at the time of the Long March, was captured and killed.

Hua Guofeng (1921–): CCP Secretary of Xiangtan, Mao's home county. Appointed Hunan First Secretary after the Cultural Revolution, and picked by Mao as a possible successor in 1973. Became Party Chairman after Mao's death, but lost a power struggle with Deng Xiaoping in the winter of 1978 and went into semi-retirement three years later.

Jiang Qing (1914–91): Shanghai actress. Married Mao at Yan'an in 1938. Began playing a significant political role in the early 1960s. As Mao's wife, she became a major force during the Cultural Revolution. A Politburo member from 1969, she headed the leftist 'Gang of Four', all of whom were arrested four weeks after Mao's death. Received a commuted death sentence in 1981 for political crimes. Committed suicide in prison.

Kang Sheng (1898–1975): CCP Security chief in Shanghai in the early 1930s, later given intelligence training in Moscow. A member of the Politburo from 1935. Mao's hatchetman in Yan'an and during the Cultural Revolution. In 1973 he became CC Vice-Chairman, ranking fifth in the hierarchy. Died of cancer; expelled from the Party posthumously for political crimes.

Li Lisan (1899–1967): Met Mao while a student in Changsha in 1917; they disliked each other. As de facto Party leader from 1928, Li vigorously opposed Mao's guerrilla strategy in Jiangxi, demanding that the Red Army attack cities as part of a nationwide insurrection. Dismissed on Stalin's orders in the autumn of 1930, he spent the next fifteen years as an involuntary exile in Russia. After 1949 held minor posts; committed suicide during the Cultural Revolution.

Li Weihan (1896–1984): A member of the New People's Study Society. He succeeded Mao as Hunan Party Secretary in 1923. Elected to the Politburo in 1927; later occupied a succession of lesser posts. Criticised but not purged during the Cultural Revolution.

Li Xiannian (1909–92): Political Commissar in Zhang Guotao's Fourth Army. Long-serving Vice-Premier and Finance Minister from the mid-1950s. Survived the Cultural Revolution unscathed. After Mao's death, became a Party Vice-Chairman and Head of State.

Lin Biao (1907–71):   Participated in the Nanchang Uprising. With Mao on Jinggangshan. Zunyi veteran. Politburo member since 1956. CC Vice-Chairman in 1958, Defence Minister a year later. Brilliant military strategist and chronic hypochondriac. Architect of extravagant Mao cult of the 1960s. Designated as Mao's successor at the outset of the Cultural Revolution in 1966; confirmed as such in the Party constitution of 1969. Lost Mao's confidence in 1970. Died in an aircrash a year later while fleeing to the USSR.

Liu Shaoqi (1898–1969):   Moscow-trained Hunanese communist who spent much of his pre-1949 career in the Party underground in north and central China. Zunyi veteran. Worked with Mao at Anyuan in 1922 and again in Yan'an. Second-ranking Party leader and heir apparent from 1943. Succeeded Mao as Head of State in 1959. Purged in the Cultural Revolution as the 'biggest Party person in authority taking the capitalist road'; expelled from the CCP as a 'renegade, scab and traitor' in 1968. Died a year later from deliberate medical neglect. Buried under a false name. Posthumously rehabilitated after Mao's death.

Liu Bocheng (1892–1986):   Legendary Red Army commander known as the 'One-eyed Dragon'. Zunyi veteran. One of ten PLA marshals appointed in 1955; entered the Politburo a year later. Totally blind and politically inactive from the mid-1960s, but remained a nominal member of the leadership until after Mao's death. Survived the Cultural Revolution unharmed.

Luo Ruiqing (1906–78):   Red Army political security officer in the early 1930s. Minister of Public Security; afterwards PLA Chief of Staff under Lin Biao. Purged in December 1965 amid preparations for the Cultural Revolution. Broke both legs in a failed suicide attempt three months later. Rehabilitated in 1975.

Nie Rongzhen (1899–1992):   Participated in the Nanchang Uprising. Zunyi veteran. Headed the Jin-Cha-Ji north China base area during the war against Japan. One of ten PLA marshals appointed in 1955, responsible for China's nuclear weapons programme. Despite playing a leading role in the 'February Adverse Current', came through the Cultural Revolution unscathed.

Peng Dehuai (1898–1974):   With Mao on Jinggangshan. Zunyi veteran. Front commander during the anti-Japanese war; Chinese commander in the Korean War. Politburo member since 1945. Dismissed in 1959; purged in December 1966. Died in a prison hospital from deliberate medical neglect. Buried under a false name. Posthumously rehabilitated after Mao's death.

Peng Shuzhi (1895–1983): Moscow-trained Hunanese communist. Politburo member from 1925–27, expelled from the Party two years later after founding a Trotskyist opposition group. Died in exile in Los Angeles.

Peng Zhen (1902–97): Leader of the underground Party in north China in the 1930s and '40s; close ally of Liu Shaoqi. Politburo member from 1945, later Mayor of Beijing. Purged at the outset of the Cultural Revolution. Survived ten years in prison. Rehabilitated after Mao's death.

Qu Qiubai (1899–1935): A talented literary figure who found himself, almost by accident, de facto Party leader from August 1927 to June 1928. Like Li Lisan, he urged a policy of nationwide insurrection. Sidelined in 1931. Stayed behind at the time of the Long March; captured and executed by the nationalists.

Ren Bishi (1904–50): A member of the Russian Studies Society set up by Mao in Changsha in 1920. Studied in Moscow. Returned to head the CCP Youth League. Joined the Politburo in January 1931, remaining a member until his death from a stroke. After 1943 he ranked fifth in the Party hierarchy.

Sun Yat-sen (1866–1925): Led the campaign for republican government which paved the way for the overthrow of the Manchu Empire in 1911. Served briefly as China's first President before yielding power to Yuan Shikai. A year later he founded the Guomindang (Nationalist Party), which formed a tactical alliance with the fledgeling CCP in 1923. Died in Beijing while trying to negotiate with the northern warlords.

Tan Yankai (1880–1930): Literary scholar from a progressive Hunan gentry family who served three times as a provincial Military Governor between 1911 and 1920. He afterwards rallied to Sun Yat-sen and in 1927 became Chairman of the GMD Political Council.

Tan Zhenlin (1902–83): With Mao on Jinggangshan. In the 1950s, Vice-Premier in charge of agriculture. Politburo member from 1958. Harshly criticised for his role in the 'February Adverse Current', he dropped from view after 1967. Re-emerged at the Tenth Party Congress six years later.

Tao Zhu (1908–69): South China Party leader, promoted to the Politburo Standing Committee at the start of the Cultural Revolution in August 1966. That autumn ranked fourth in the Party hierarchy. Purged four months later. Died of cancer while in custody. Posthumously rehabilitated after Mao's death.

Wang Hongwen (1933–92): Shanghai textile-mill cadre who led the rebel 'power seizure' in Shanghai in January 1967. Picked by Mao as a possible successor in 1972. Became a CC Vice-Chairman and third-ranking Party leader in 1973. Arrested with Jiang Qing and the other members of the 'Gang of Four' a month after Mao's death. Sentenced to life imprisonment in 1981 for political crimes. Died of liver cancer.

Wang Jiaxiang (1906–74):   Trained in Moscow with Wang Ming, but broke with the other 'Returned Students' in the early 1930s to become one of Mao's leading supporters. After 1949, served as a vice-Foreign Minister. Purged in the Cultural Revolution, re-emerged at the Tenth Party Congress in 1973.

Wang Jingwei (1883–1944):   Close associate of Sun Yat-sen. In 1910 led an unsuccessful attempt to assassinate the Prince Regent. After Sun's death, became the top GMD civilian leader, in which capacity he acted as Mao's patron. Defeated in a power struggle with Chiang Kai-shek, but retained a strong factional following within the party. In the winter of 1938, he broke with Chiang and left to head a Japanese puppet government in Nanjing.

Wang Ming (1904–74):   Leader of the Moscow-trained group of 'Returned Students' whom the Comintern placed at the head of the CCP in January 1931. After reaching Yan'an in 1937, he became Mao's main rival for the Party leadership. His defeat less than a year later set the stage for a lengthy campaign by Mao against Left-deviationism and dogmatism (blind support of Soviet policies). Wang lost his Politburo rank in 1945 but remained a member of the CC until the late 1950s, when he left China to live in exile in the USSR.

Wang Zuo (1898–1930):   Leader of a bandit force on Jinggangshan. Enrolled his men under Mao's banner in the spring of 1928. Killed with Yuan Wencai in an internecine Party feud.

Wu Faxian (1915–): Commander of the PLA air force. One of four senior military officers (with Huang Yongsheng, Li Zuopeng and Qiu Huizuo) who constituted Lin Biao's faction in the Politburo after the Ninth Congress in 1969. All were purged after Lin's death; sentenced to long prison terms for political crimes in 1981, but released early on grounds of ill-health.

Xiang Ying (1889–1941):   A communist labour organiser who rose to become third-ranking CCP leader in 1928. He slowly lost power after Wang Ming and his allies took control of the Party in January 1931. Stayed behind at the time of the Long March to lead the resistance in the Central Soviet Base Area.

Xiang Zhongfa (1880–1931):   Titular CCP General Secretary from 1928 to 1931, when Li Lisan and Wang Ming were de facto Party leaders. Betrayed to the GMD by a communist turncoat and executed.

Xie Fuzhi (1909–72):   Minister of Public Security from 1959, Politburo member from the Ninth Congress. Chairman of Beijing Revolutionary

Committee. Seconded Kang Sheng in persecuting old-guard leaders during the Cultural Revolution. Died of cancer; expelled posthumously from the Party for political crimes.

Xu Xiangqian (1901–90):   Led Red guerrilla base north of the Yangtse in the early 1930s. One of ten PLA marshals appointed in 1955. Vice-Chairman of CC Military Commission. Criticised during the Cultural Revolution but not purged.

Yang Shangkun (1907–98):   Zunyi veteran. Director of the CC General Office until November 1965. Purged at the outset of the Cultural Revolution. Rehabilitated after Mao's death; subsequently became Head of State.

Yao Wenyuan (1925–   ):   Radical literary critic who came to prominence during the anti-Rightist campaign. Drafted for Mao the polemic which set in motion the Cultural Revolution. Politburo member from 1969. Arrested with the rest of the 'Gang of Four' a month after Mao's death. Sentenced to twenty years' imprisonment in 1981 for political crimes, later released on parole. Now living in Shanghai.

Ye Jianying   (1897–1986):   A nationalist army officer who joined the CCP in 1927. Took part in the Canton Uprising and then served for many years as Red Army Chief of Staff. One of ten PLA marshals appointed in 1955 and a key leader of the CC Military Commission. Joined the Politburo in 1966. Passed through the Cultural Revolution unscathed (despite playing a major role in the 'February Adverse Current'). After Mao's death, was instrumental in securing the arrests of the 'Gang of Four' and the return to power of Deng Xiaoping.

Yuan Wencai (1898–1930):   Leader of a small bandit force at Maoping, at the foot of the Jinggangshan. Joined the CCP in 1926 and enrolled his men under Mao's command a year later, becoming Chairman of the Soviet border area government. Shot dead by local rivals in an internecine Party feud.

Zhang Chunqiao (1917–   ):   Radical propaganda official in Shanghai who rose to become Deputy Head of the Cultural Revolution Group and Chairman of the Shanghai Revolutionary Committee. A member of the Politburo from 1969 and of its Standing Committee from 1973. Detained with the rest of the 'Gang of Four' a month after Mao's death. Received a commuted death sentence in 1981 for political crimes.

Zhang Guotao (1897–1979):   Student leader at Beijing University. Founder member of the Party, CC member from 1921, Central Bureau (later Politburo) from 1925. Headed the E-Yu-Wan Red base area, north of the Yangtse. After a power struggle with Mao during the Long March, lost most of his army. Sidelined politically from 1937; defected to the Guomindang a year later. Died in exile in Canada.

Zhang Wentian (1900–76):   Moscow-trained 'Returned Student' who served as deputy to Bo Gu from 1931–4, but switched support to Mao shortly before the Long March. Played a key role in securing Mao's ascendancy at Zunyi. Afterwards became provisional Party leader (until November 1938). Sidelined after 1949. Dismissed with Peng Dehuai after the Lushan plenum. Imprisoned during the Cultural Revolution. Posthumously rehabilitated.

Zhao Hengti (1880–1971):   Military Governor of Hunan from 1920–26. Ordered Mao's arrest and execution during peasant uprisings in 1925. Died in Taiwan.

Zhou Enlai (1898–1976):   Founded CCP European branch in France. Alternate member of the Politburo in 1927; full member continuously from 1928 until his death, longer than any other Party leader. Initially hostile, then ambivalent relationship with Mao until Zunyi, where he supported Mao's leadership against Bo Gu and the Comintern adviser, Otto Braun. Backed Wang Ming in 1938; thereafter made a religion of loyalty to Mao. Too useful a politician for Mao to purge. Premier from 1949 until his death. Played a vital role in implementing the Great Leap Forward and the Cultural Revolution. Died of cancer.

Zhu De (1886–1976):   Participated in 1911 Revolution under the Yunnan Military Governor, Cai E. Became a minor warlord. Joined the CCP in Europe. One of the leaders of the Nanchang Uprising. With Mao on Jinggangshan. Commander-in-Chief of the Red Army. Politburo member from 1945 until his death. Withdrew into an elder-statesman role after 1949. Protected on Mao's orders during the Cultural Revolution. Chairman of the National People's Congress (de facto Head of State) from 1975–6.

Notes

Since the late 1970s, a flood of new material about Mao's life and times has become available inside China. The effects of this have been twofold: firstly, it has, to a considerable extent, invalidated interpretations of Chinese politics current in Western writings prior to Mao's death; and, secondly, because little of the new research has been published in translation, any serious attempt to grapple with Mao's character and policies must rely heavily on Chinese-language sources. This is particularly true of the period prior to 1960, where the present Chinese authorities have allowed Party researchers substantial access to previously closed archives while remaining infinitely more cautious in regard to the final decade, from 1966 to 1976, when Mao's policies were in complete contradiction with those being pursued today. Recent Western scholarship, by contrast, has concentrated on the post-1960 period. In these notes, English-language references have been cited wherever reliable translations or secondary sources exist. The initial reference gives full bibliographical details; thereafter, the first reference to the same work in each subsequent chapter provides a short-form title. In the case of Chinese-language documentary collections, the full title is repeated. Other abbreviations are employed as follows:

CHOC	Cambridge History of China
JYMZW	Jianguo yilai Mao Zedong wengao (Mao Zedong's Manuscripts since Liberation)
NCH	North China Herald
SW	Selected Works
ZZWX	Zhongyang zhonggong wenxian xuanji [Selected Central Committee Documents]

PROLOGUE

Page

1   *December 12, 1934*: Pang Xianzhi (ed.), *Mao Zedong nianpu* [Chronological Biography of Mao Zedong], Renmin chubanshe, Beijing, 1991, vol. 1, pp. 439–40. The more commonly given date, December 11, is incorrect. The Party History Research Centre of the CCP CC, in its *History of the Chinese Communist Party: A Chronology of Events, 1919–1990* (Foreign Languages Press, Beijing, 1991, p. 93), states that the Red Army 'seized the passage to Hunan on the 11th'. The Tongdao meeting was convened the following day. See also Ma Qibin, Huang Shaoqun and Liu Wenjun, *Zhongyang geming genjudi shi*, Renmin chubanshe, Beijing, 1986, pp. 528–9, Guofang daxue dangshi zhenggong jiaoyanshi, *Changzheng xintan*, Jiefangjun chubanshe, Beijing, 1986, pp. 39–40; and Braun, Otto, *A Comintern Agent in China: 1932–39*, C.M. Hurst, London, 1982, pp. 92–3.
    A Faded Slogan: Exhibited at Zunyi Museum, January 1995.
    Wedding Party: Salisbury, Harrison, *The Long March*, Harper & Row, New York, 1985, p. 109 and p. 364, n. 10.
2   *His dark, inscrutable face*: Smedley, Agnes, *Battle Hymn of China*, Victor Gollancz, London, 1944, pp. 121–3.
3   *More than three weeks passed*: *North China Herald* [NCH], Shanghai, Nov. 14 1934. See also Garavente, Anthony, 'The Long March', *China Quarterly* [CQ], 22, pp. 102–5; Yang, Benjamin, *From Revolution to Politics*, Westview Press, Boulder, CO, 1990, p. 103; and Salisbury, pp. 92–3. The nationalists captured Ruijin soon after the communists pulled out on October 10. But while Chiang knew the Red Army was on the move, he could not tell whether it was abandoning the base or merely regrouping for a fresh offensive. *The battle lasted more than a week*: The best account of the engagement is in Salisbury, *Long March*, pp. 91–104.
4   *House-moving operation*: Yang, Benjamin, 'The Zunyi Conference as One Step in Mao's Rise to Power', CQ, 106, p. 264.
    The eight or nine weary men . . . of Guizhou: After the meeting ended, at 1900 hours on December 12, the Military Council issued the following order: 'Top Priority. The Hunan enemy troops and the main force of [the warlord] Tao Guang are closing in on Tongdao. Other enemy forces are continuing to make their way towards Hongjiang and Jingxian [on the Guizhou/Hunan border further north]. They are trying to stop us going north. Therefore prepare to enter Guizhou . . . Tomorrow, the 13th, our Red Army should continue its westward deployment . . . The First Army should . . . occupy Liping' (*Nianpu*, 1, pp. 439–40).

5   *We went up a mountain*: Agnes Smedley, *The Great Road*, Monthly Review Press, New York, 1956, pp. 313–14. *Horses fell to their deaths*: Martynov, Aleksandr, *Velikii Pokhod*, Izdatelstvo Inostrannoi Literatury, Moscow, 1959, pp. 170–6. *Zhu De remembered*: Smedley, *Great Road*, pp. 315–16.

8   *Mountains!*: Gu Zhengkun (ed.), *Poems of Mao Zedong*, Peking University Press, Beijing, 1993, pp. 68 and 70. *The Politburo met*: *Nianpu*, 1, pp. 440–1. *Changzheng xintan*, pp. 41–2. Li Weihan, *Huiyi yu yanjiu*, Zhonggong dangshi ziliao chubanshe, Beijing, 1986, pp. 350–1. Braun, p. 93.

9   *On tactics, the resolution*: Text exhibited at Liping Museum in January 1995. *Houchang*: *Changzheng xintan*, pp. 43–4; *Wenxian he yanjiu*, no. 1, 1985, pp. 20–1; *Nianpu*, 1, p. 442. The text of the Houchang Resolution was exhibited at Zunyi Museum in January 1995.

10   *Issue of January 15, 1935*: Exhibited at Zunyi Museum in January 1995.

11   *Twenty men gathered*: Much of the detail of the Zunyi meeting is still a matter of sinological controversy. Yang, CQ, 106, pp. 235–71; and Thomas Kampen, 'The Zunyi Conference and Further Steps in Mao's Rise to Power', CQ, 117, pp. 118–34, provide the most reliable published accounts of the proceedings. See also *Zunyi huiyi ziliao xuanbian*, Guizhou chubanshe, Guiyang, 1985; and Braun, pp. 94–108. *A handsome, rectangular, two-storey building*: The meeting-place is now a museum, as is the house where Mao stayed. Salisbury [*Long March*, p. 118] was curiously misled about the leaders' accommodation, stating that 'Bo Gu and Otto Braun were . . . living in isolation from the rest'. In fact, Bo and Braun were less than 100 yards from the CCP HQ. Mao, Wang and Zhang were the ones on the far side of town. *It was obvious that Mao wanted revenge*: Braun, p. 96.

12   *'Painstakingly prepared'*: Ibid., p. 98. *The fundamental problem, Mao said*: No text of Mao's speech has been preserved, but the two versions of the resolution approved at the meeting are clearly based on it (Yang, *CQ*, 106, pp. 262–5; and Chen, Jerome, 'Resolutions of the Zunyi Conference', CQ, 40, pp. 1–17). *Chen Yun*: See Kampen, p. 123; and Yang, CQ, 106, pp. 265–71, especially the phrase, 'Comrade Bo Gu . . . did not apparently put this factor in a secondary place' (p. 267).

14   *'Most of those at the meeting'*: Braun, p. 104. *Over the next few months*: Ibid., pp. 108–18; *Nianpu*, 1, pp. 445–59; Kampen, pp. 124–34. *Georgy Dimitrov pleaded*: *Dangshi ziliao tongxun*, no. 10, 1987, p. 39. *Mao was aboard his private train*: Li Zhisui, *The Private Life of Chairman Mao*, Chatto & Windus, London, 1994, pp. 365–9.

15 *He was accompanied*: Ibid., pp. 355–64. See also Salisbury, Harrison, *The New Emperors*, HarperCollins, London, 1992, pp. 134, 217–19, 221. When I lived in Beijing in the early 1980s, Mao's sexual proclivities were common knowledge, and a subject of much amusement (mixed with envy), among the sons and daughters of the communist elite. *I wash my prick*: Dr Li quotes Mao as saying: 'I wash myself inside the bodies of my women'. According to one of his former partners, Mao used the phrase frequently and not in the bowdlerised form given by Dr Li. *Mao's doctor takes up the story*: Ibid., p. 366.

16 *Bugged and secretly tape-recorded*: Ibid., pp. 292–3 and 365–69.

17 *Under unfavourable conditions*: Yang, CQ, 106, p. 263. *War is politics*: The phrase is from Lenin (and Clausewitz). Mao made it one of the central themes of his essay, 'On Protracted War' (SW, 2, pp. 152–3) in 1938. His formulation was: 'War is politics . . . Politics is war without bloodshed while war is politics with bloodshed.'

CHAPTER ONE: A CONFUCIAN CHILDHOOD

19 *Winter solstice*: Bodde, Derk, *Annual Customs and Festivals in Peking*, Henri Vetch, Peiping, 1936, p. 87. *Nineteenth day*: Siao, Emi, *Mao Tse-tung: His Childhood and Youth*, Bombay, 1953, p. 2. *By tradition*: Dore, Henri, SJ, *Recherches sur les Superstitions en Chine*, vol. 1, Shanghai, 1911 [Variétés Sinologiques no. 32], pp. 8–17; Cormack, A., *Chinese Births, Weddings and Deaths*, Peking, 1923, pp. 2–5.

20 *Mao's Family*: The main source of information about Mao's home life during his childhood is his own account given to Edgar Snow in the summer of 1936, when he was 42 years old (Snow, *Red Star over China* [rev. edn], London, Pelican Books, 1972, pp. 151–62). Secondary sources include the books by the Xiao brothers, who became Mao's close friends when he was in his early twenties (Emi Siao, *Mao Tse-tung*; and Siao [Xiao] Yu, *Mao Tse-tung and I were Beggars*, Syracuse University Press, New York, 1959). Those parts of Xiao Yu's book dealing with Mao's earliest years appear to be largely fictional. The semi-official biography by Li Rui (*The Early Revolutionary Activities of Comrade Mao Tse-tung*, M.E. Sharpe, White Plains, NY, 1977) in so far as it deals with Mao's childhood is based on Mao's reminiscences to Snow.
Wealthiest and most fertile: Xiangtan county was at this time among the most productive in Hunan, itself the third richest rice-growing province in China (McDonald, Angus W., Jnr, *The Urban Origins of Rural Revolution*, University of California Press, Berkeley, 1978, pp. 7 and 275).

21 **Thought to be doing well**: Yang Zhongmei, *Hu Yaobang: a Chinese biography*, M. E. Sharpe, Armonk, New York, 1988. p. 5. **Large, rambling farmhouse**: The house had an additional wing, comprising a further three rooms, which were occupied by the family of the labourer Mao's father employed.

A great fortune: On the basis of Mao's figures, the family had a cash income from farming of at least 50 silver dollars a year when they owned two-and-a-half acres of land (25 piculs of surplus rice, at 2,000 cash a picul) and, subsequently, more. In a year of shortage, when prices rose, they probably earned two to three times that amount. This was supplemented by the profits from his father's rice-trading, and interest paid on the mortgages he bought.

Becoming a landlord: Mao came close to acknowledging this when he told Red Guard leaders in July 1968: 'My father was bad. If he were alive today he should be [struggled against].' (*Miscellany of Mao Tse-tung Thought*, pt II (JPRS-61269-2], Joint Publications Research Service, Arlington, VA, February 1974, p. 389).

Xiangtan: O'Sullivan, Mortimer, 'Report of a Journey of Exploration in Hunan from 14th December 1897 to March 1898' Shanghai, North China Herald Office, 1898, p. 4. Other sources suggest the population was about 300,000. **Famously unwilling**: Quan Yanchi, *Mao Zedong: Man not God*, Foreign Languages Press, Beijing, 1992, pp. 90–4.

22 **Earthiness**: Dr Zhisui Li in the 1960s (*Private Life of Chairman Mao*, pp. 77 and 103) and Edgar Snow in the 1930s both noted that he had 'the personal habits of a peasant' (*Red Star over China*, pp. 112–13). His former bodyguard, Li Yinqiao, described him as 'a rustic' (Quan Yanchi, p. 90). **A total apathy**: Little, Archibald J., *Through the Yang-tse Gorges, or Trade and Travel in Western China* [3rd edn], London, 1898, pp. 167–8. **Steaming towel**: Li Zhisui, pp. ix, 100 and 107. Li Yinqiao confirms Mao's aversion to washing, stating that he used soap only 'to remove grease or inkstains from his hands' (Quan Yanchi, p. 96). See also Siao Yu, pp. 85–6, 152 and 257. **Using a toothbrush**: Quan Yanchi, p. 65; Siao Yu, p. 86; Li Zhisui, p. 103. **Uninvited guest**: Snow, pp. 112–13. **Specially built latrine**: Quan Yanchi, pp. 111–12. **When Mao was six**: In Mao's own account of his early life (Snow, pp. 151–62), it is unclear whether his age is counted by the Western or the Chinese system (which adds a year). I have assumed the former. Six is the usual age at which peasant children start helping their parents. **Four or five silver dollars**: Williams, S. Wells, *The Middle Kingdom* [rev. edn], New York, 1883, vol. 1, p. 525.

23 **Royal road**: Macgowan, Rev. John, *Lights and Shadows of Chinese Life*, Shanghai, North China Daily News and Herald Press, 1909, pp. 57–8. **Population was too poor**: Williams, p. 544. Smith, Arthur

H., *Chinese Characteristics*, Shanghai, 1890, p. 386. **Mao's father**: Williams, p. 542: 'Tradesmen, mechanics and country gentlemen . . . put their sons into shops or counting houses to learn the routine of business with a knowledge of figures and the style of letter-writing; they are not kept at school more than three or four years, unless they mean to compete in the examinations.' **Apprenticeship**: Snow, pp. 153–6, 159. **Village school**: Macgowan, pp. 59–63. Smith, *Chinese Characteristics*, p. 220, also notes that 'great harshness is certainly common' among schoolteachers.

24   **Mao's teacher**: Snow, p. 153. **Incense board**: Emi Siao, p. 15. **Three Character Classic**: *Chinese Repository*, vol. 4, Canton, July 1835, pp. 105–18.

25   **Textbooks were printed**: Macgowan, p. 64. *Chinese Repository*, 4, p. 105. **After being informed**: Smith, Arthur H., *The School System of China*, East of Asia, vol. 3, p. 4, Shanghai, 1904. **Incomprehensible cacophony**: Williams, 1, pp. 526–7. **The teacher did not explain**: Ibid., p. 541. Macgowan, p. 66. Justus Doolittle, *Social Life of the Chinese*, New York, 1865, p. 378. **Six books**: *Chinese Repository*, 4, pp. 153–60, 229–43, 287–91, 344–53; 5, pp. 81–7, 305–16; 6, 185–8, 393–6, 562–8. Williams, pp. 527–41.

26   **Without ever learning to read**: Smith, *Chinese Characteristics*, p. 323. Claude Cadart and Cheng Yingxiang, *L'Envol du Communisme en Chine (Mémoires de Peng Shuzhi)*, Paris, 1983, pp. 14 and 36–7. **Mao was about ten**: For the duration of primary schooling, see Williams, 1, p. 541; Macgowan, p. 66; Cadart and Cheng, p. 37. Mao himself recalled that by the time he left the school he was already reading *Water Margin* and other popular historical romances (Snow, pp. 153–6). **Diligence has merit**: From the *Three Character Classic* (*Chinese Repository*, 4, p. 111). **The Four Books**: Snow, p. 153. **Even Mao's father**: Ibid., pp. 154 and 156.

27   **Men must rely**: From *Odes for Children* (*Chinese Repository*, 4, p. 288). **Initially from novels**: Snow, p. 156. **Records of rule and misrule**: *Sanziqing*, Beijing, 1979 (mimeographed), lines 258–63. This translation is based on *Chinese Repository*, 4, p. 110. **To dislike the Classics**: Snow, p. 156. **Lenin and Marx**: Vsevolod Holubnychy, 'Mao Tsetung's Materialistic Dialectics', CQ, 19, 1964, pp. 16–17. **He knew better**: Mao did not read a Marxist book until he was 26.
Zemin: Professor Lucian Pye has based an entire book on the premise that Mao's character and behaviour throughout his adult life were decisively influenced by his feelings of abandonment on the birth of his younger brother. The argument is cleverly pursued, but fails to explain why every other firstborn child in China, deprived of maternal affection by the appearance of a sibling, did not also turn into a revolutionary leader (Pye, Lucian W., *Mao Tse-tung: The Man*

in the Leader, Basic Books, New York, 1976). There is in fact no evidence that Mao was more affected by his brother's birth than any other normal child.

Four other children: 'Mao Zedong's funeral oration in honour of his mother' (Oct. 8, 1919), in Schram, Stuart R. (ed.), *Mao's Road to Power*, vol. 1: *The Pre-Marxist Period: 1912–1920*, New York, 1992, p. 419.

28   *Exemplary tales*: *Chinese Repository*, 6, pp. 130–42. *The term 'filial'*: Smith, *Chinese Characteristics*, p. 202. *My father invited*: Snow, pp. 154–5.

29   *His father perpetually nagged*: The strongest evidence for this is Mao's statement that the only way to silence his father was to ensure that he could find nothing to criticise. The same thing is hinted at elsewhere; at one point Mao refers to his father's 'favourite accusations' against him, implying systematic fault-finding.

An extra pair of hands: 'A daughter-in-law is regarded as a servant for the whole family, which is precisely her position, and in getting a servant it is obviously desirable to get one who is strong and well-grown' (Smith, *Chinese Characteristics*, p. 292). *A family's annual income*: Williams, p. 787.

He never slept with her: Snow, p. 172. Mao himself says simply, 'My parents . . . married me.' But marriage in China at that time consisted not of a single ceremony but of a whole series of steps, starting with an exchange of horoscopes and the choice of a propitious day, and continuing with exchanges of gifts and the payment, by the bride-groom's family, of the marriage portion. The couple were considered to be married only after the bride had moved into her parents-in-law's home, where she would now live, had sipped wine with her new husband and, together with him, had kowtowed to Heaven and Earth and to the ancestral tablets (ceremonies still practised in rural China in the 1990s).

Unemployed law student: Snow, p. 157. *One account suggests*: Oral sources, Shaoshan, May 1999.

Mao's mother eventually left: In June 1915, Mao told Xiao Yu that he had no particular desire to return home for the summer holiday (Schram, *Mao's Road*, 1, p. 62); Xiao himself, commenting on this incident, wrote that Mao 'had no warm sentimental feeling for his home' (*Mao Tse-tung and I*, p. 84). She fell ill the following year (Schram, 1, p. 92), and apparently returned to Xiangxiang in the autumn of 1917. By August 1918, Mao was writing to his maternal uncles: 'I am deeply grateful that my mother has lived in your house for a long time.' She came to Changsha for medical treatment in the summer of 1919 (Ibid., pp. 174 and 317).

Emotional oration: Ibid., p. 317.

30   *To enrol at a junior middle school*: Snow, pp. 157 and 159–60. The

school, in the neighbouring county of Xiangxiang, was officially classed as an 'upper primary school'. *Mao's father ... school fees and living expenses*: Ibid., pp. 160, 168, 170 and 175. *Family scholar*: Ibid., p. 156.

31   *Distinct type of the Chinese race*: O'Sullivan, p. 2. *Turbulent and pugnacious*: NCH, April 22, 1910. *No Manchu*: O'Sullivan, p. 7. *The closed province*: Parsons, William B., 'Hunan: the Closed Province of China', in *National Geographic Magazine*, vol. XI, New York, 1900, pp. 393–400. *Griffith John*: 'Hunan: A Record of a Six Weeks' Trip', NCH, June 12 and 19, July 3, 10 and 17, 1891. *Keenness ... apathy*: O'Sullivan, p. 2; Hillman, Lt.-Com. H.E., RN, *Report on the Navigation of Tung Ting Lake and the Siang and Yuan Rivers (Upper Yangtse) with descriptions of the three principal towns, Changsha, Siangtan, Chang Teh, in the province of Hunan, China*, London, HMSO, 1902, p. 17. The unanimity of early Western writers about the character of the Hunanese and the contrast with other parts of China is striking. *Jesuits*: *Lettres Edifiantes et Curieuses*, vol. 22, Paris, 1736, pp. ix et seq.

32   *Independence and aloofness*: NCH, April 22 1910. *British sphere of influence*: Sir Claude Macdonald, British Minister at Beijing, to the Zongli Yamen, 19 February 1898, quoted in Little, pp. xxi–xxiv. *News was exchanged*: Cadart and Cheng, pp. 28 and 50.

33   *Vague rumours of the Boxers ... two years after it occurred*: Ibid., pp. 42–3; Snow, p. 161. Peng Shuzhi was two years younger than Mao. His village, Tongluocun in Shaoyang county, was smaller and more remote than Shaoshan but apparently no worse informed. Unlike Mao, Peng recalls a proclamation of the Emperor's death being posted up within weeks.
Words of Warning: Schram, Stuart R., *Mao Tse-tung* (rev. edn), Penguin, Harmondsworth, 1967, p. 21. Mao probably obtained this book from a cousin (Schram, *Road to Power*, 1, p. 59).
Telephones, steamships and railways: A small, private electricity plant, commissioned by the provincial Governor, functioned intermittently in Changsha from 1897. Telegraph service to Xiangtan was established the same year, despite strong opposition from conservative gentry who feared the poles would disrupt the *fengshui*, the geomantic harmony of wind and water. The first foreign steamer, the German tug *Vorwaerts*, reached Xiangtan in 1900. Mao may have heard rumours of the 'foreign fireboat', but he cannot have seen it until he first visited the city at the age of 17. Changsha had a telephone system by 1910; the railway came seven years later. (Preston, T.J., 'Progress and Reform in Hunan Province', *East of Asia*, vol. 4, pp. 210–19, Shanghai, 1905; NCH, April 29 1910, p. 249; Hillman, p. 3; O'Sullivan, pp. 6–7.)

Pamphlet: Snow, pp. 156–7 and 159. ***Tales of rebels***: Ibid, p. 156.

34   ***Food riots***: Ibid, p. 158. Mao implies that the uprising (of which he gives a somewhat distorted account) took place when he was about 14, in 1908. It was in fact two years later. ***British consul . . . cornering the market***: NCH, June 10 1910, p. 616; July 1 1910, pp. 23–4; Esherick, Joseph W., *Reform and Revolution in China: The 1911 Revolution in Hunan and Hubei*, University of California Press, Berkeley, 1976, p. 130. ***By early April***: NCH, April 22 and 29 1910. A worker's monthly ration of 45 catties of rice then cost two silver dollars, at a time when the poorest labourers earned less than one silver dollar a month, from which they also had to feed their families. ***People eating bark***: Esherick, p. 126.

    A water-carrier and his wife: Report from Xiangtan, dated April 22, in NCH, May 6 1910. The same story was reported from Hankou (Wuhan), in NCH, April 29 1910. The best account of the riots is in Esherick, pp. 130–8. The incident involving the water-carrier's suicide is confirmed in contemporary reports from the Japanese consul in Changsha.

    No different from a war: Esherick, p. 133. ***A mob gathered . . . burned to the ground***: NCH, April 29 1910.

35   ***Another 17 buildings***: NCH, May 6 1910. ***Qing government's . . . lamp-posts***: NCH, April 29 and May 13, 1910. ***It made a deep impression***: Snow, p. 158.

    A few weeks later: Mao says this incident took place in Shaoshan (ibid, pp. 158–9), but had a rebellion broken out in Mao's own small village, he would surely have described it differently. The *North China Herald* (June 17 and July 1 1910) reports what are apparently the same events as occurring at Huashi, in Xiangtan county, close to Liushan.

36   ***Seized by hungry villagers***: Snow, p. 159. ***I had never before***: Ibid, p. 160. ***Dongshan Upper Primary School***: Emi Siao, p. 18; and Xiao Yu, pp. 20–1.

    Five months' board: Mao says simply, 'I went to the school with my cousin and registered.' Xiao Yu (pp. 21–6) gives a highly-coloured account of Mao, arriving alone with a bundle of belongings on a carrying-pole and pleading with the headmaster to accept him, if only for a five-month trial period. A more credible explanation is that Mao arrived at the school in August 1909, when only five months of the school year remained. Mao himself says he entered the school at 16, which would date his arrival to the spring of 1910; but since, by his own account, he spent nearly two years there, it must have been earlier than that. Xiao Yu says Mao was 15 when he went there.

37 *Childish pig-headedness*: Xiao Yu's description of Mao's behaviour here has a ring of truth to it (pp. 27–30). *The sparrow sings*: Snow, p. 161.

38 *I read and reread ... Kang Youwei's reforms*: Ibid, pp. 161–2.

CHAPTER TWO: REVOLUTION

39 *Bomb exploded*: Esherick, *Reform and Revolution in China*, pp. 179–82; NCH, Oct. 14 1911, p. 105. *Forward Together Society*: Esherick, pp. 153–5.

40 *Xin Han, Mie Man*: NCH, Oct. 21 1911, pp. 143 and 152. *Eight hundred Manchu corpses*: Ibid, p. 143; *The Times*, London, Oct. 15 1911.
    Descendants of Holy Han: NCH, Nov. 11 1911, p. 354. *The Manchu government*: Ibid., Oct. 28 1911, p. 227. *The Times reported*: *The Times*, London, Oct. 14 1911.

41 *Only in Beijing*: NCH, Oct. 14 1911, p. 103; Oct. 21, p. 143; and Nov. 11, p. 360 (on the hunting down of Manchu women at Yichang). The seriousness with which the Throne viewed the rising is reflected in the abject imperial edict issued on October 30 (NCH, Nov. 4, p. 289). *By riverboat*: Siao, Emi, *Mao Tse-tung: His Childhood and Youth*, p. 22. Mao himself claimed that he walked all the way to Changsha (Snow, *Red Star over China*, p. 163). *A magnificent place*: Snow, p. 163.
    First sight of the city: For accounts of early twentieth-century Changsha, see Hume, Edward H., *Doctors East, Doctors West: An American Physician's Life in China*, Allen & Unwin, London, 1949; Parsons, William B., *An American Engineer in China*, McClure, Phillips, New York, 1900; and Hobart, Alice Tisdale, *The City of the Long Sand*, Macmillan, New York, 1926. Further information appears in O'Sullivan, Mortimer, 'Journey of Exploration', and in Stokes, Anson Phelps, *A Visit to Yale in China: June 1920*, Yale Foreign Missionary Society, New Haven, 1920.

42 *No rickshaws*: Dr Hume says 'jinrickshas' became popular in Changsha only after the 1911 revolution (p. 113). According to Stokes, there were still few in 1920 (p. 6). *Sweetmeat-seller*: Hume, p. 98.

43 *I was exceedingly excited*: Snow, p. 163. *Changsha had been seething*: Esherick, pp. 141 and 162.

44 *Attitude to the queue*: Snow, pp. 163–4. *Similar scenes*: Esherick, p. 162, quoting *Minli bao*, Jan. 4 1911. *Two other events ... schools went on strike*: Esherick, pp. 165–8; Snow, p. 164. *He went to listen*:

Schram, *Mao's Road*, 1, pp. 405–6 (Aug. 4 1919). ***Anti-Manchu rallies continued . . . impending collapse***: Hume, pp. 160 and 235.

45   ***First confused reports***: Esherick, pp. 199–201. ***The passengers spoke***: NCH, Oct. 14 1911, p. 105; Oct. 21, pp. 144–5 and 152. ***That weekend it was down***: On October 12 the Japanese consul in Hankou reported that the telegraph lines to Changsha were 'cut off' (NCH, Oct. 14 1911, p. 104). On October 14 they were still 'badly impaired' (NCH, Oct. 21, p. 131). ***A run on the provincial banks***: NCH, Nov. 4 1911, p. 295. ***The British consul***: Bertram Giles, Telegram no. 22 of Oct. 16 1911, FO228/1798, Public Records Office, London. ***Japanese steamer***: Esherick, p. 200. ***Distinct change in the situation***: Giles, Despatch no. 44 of Nov. 2 1911, FO228/1798. ***He made a stirring speech***: Snow, pp. 164–5. ***Countermeasures***: Esherick, p. 200; Giles, Despatch no. 44; NCH, Nov. 4 1911, p. 288.

46   ***The first attempt . . . very differently***: Giles, Despatch no. 44. ***I went to borrow***: Snow, p. 165. ***At 9.30 a.m. I was informed***: Giles. Despatch no. 44. ***Discrepancies***: See also Schram, *Mao Tse-tung*, p. 33.

47   ***But the militia commander . . . lying in the street***: Giles, Despatch no. 44. NCH, Nov. 4 1911, p. 288. ***In Hubei***: Esherick, pp. 182–6. ***The situation in Changsha***: Ibid, pp. 204–10; McCord, Edward A., *The Power of the Gun: The Emergence of Modern Chinese Warlordism*, University of California Press, Berkeley, 1993, pp. 74–6. ***Hunan's secret societies***: Esherick, pp. 58–65 and 155–7. ***Consul Giles reported***: Giles, Despatch no. 44; see also Esherick, p. 209.

48   ***The soldiers rushed into the city***: Giles, Despatch dated Nov. 17 1911, FO228/1798. ***Mao saw the two men's bodies . . . dissatisfied with them***: Snow, p. 166. ***The whole Empire is seething***: NCH, Nov. 4 1911, p. 289. ***Early in November . . . fled to Manchuria***: NCH, Nov. 11 1911, pp. 361–2, 364 and 366. ***Only four provincial capitals***: Up to the end of the first week in November, the revolutionaries had occupied Wuchang, Changsha, Xian (which fell the same day as Changsha) and Yunnan-fu. Fuzhou and Canton followed a week later. ***Troops loyal to the Throne . . . students hid in terror***: NCH, Nov. 11 and 18 1911.

49   ***Mao revived his earlier plan***: Snow, p. 166. ***Recruitment in Hunan***: McCord, p. 120. The British consul estimated that by the end of November, 50,000 Hunanese soldiers had left Changsha for Wuchang, Shasi, Chenzhou and Sichuan, and 20,000 to 30,000 remained (Giles, Despatch no. 49 of Dec. 1 1911, FO228/1798). ***Possibly the bloodiest***: NCH, Dec. 2 1911, p. 594. ***Consul Giles reported***: Giles, Despatch no. 50 of Dec. 20 1911, FO228/1798. ***Mao's regiment***: I have assumed that Mao was attached to the 50th Regiment since, at the time he signed up, the 49th was in Hubei (Esherick, p. 238). Giles (Despatch no. 50) appears to have confused

the two units. **They regard destruction**: Li Yuanhong, quoted in McCord, p. 135. **The company to which**: Emi Siao, p. 28. **Chair-bearers, ruffians**: McCord, p. 135. **Mao made himself popular . . . pedlars to carry it**: Snow, p. 166.

50   **While some of the men . . . full seven dollars**: NCH, Feb. 24, p. 506, and May 18, 1912, p. 467. **I protested strongly**: Giles, Despatch no. 50. **Farmers and peasants . . . the Manchus return**: Hume, p. 165.

51   **Bugles were blown**: NCH, Jan. 13 1912, p. 105. **An expeditionary force**: NCH, Feb. 17 1912, p. 441; Snow, p. 167. **Wholesale demo-bilisation**: McCord, pp. 119–20; McDonald, *Urban Origins*, pp. 22–3. **Thinking the revolution was over**: Snow, p. 167.

CHAPTER THREE: LORDS OF MISRULE

52   **Hunan's new Governor . . . theatres and brothels**: Esherick, *Reform and Revolution*, pp. 237–49. **Modern schools**: *Selected Works of Mao Tse-tung* (SW), vol. 4, Beijing, 1967, p. 412. **The new men really do**: NCH, Dec. 30 1911, p. 872. **Teenage girls . . . lily feet**: Hume, *Doctors East, Doctors West*, pp. 159 and 165–6. **Exotic new world for shaven Chinese heads**: NCH, Dec. 30 1911, p. 872; Jan. 20 1912, p. 173.

53   **I did not know exactly . . . all future advertising**: Snow, *Red Star over China*, pp. 167–70. Mao told Snow he entered the Normal School in 1912 (p. 174), but in this, as in many other cases, he is a year out.

55   **Already at Dongshan**: Ibid, p. 162. **In the provincial library**: Li Rui, *Early Revolutionary Activities*, p. 8; Snow, p. 169. **Studying capitalism**: *Miscellany of Mao Tse-tung Thought*, pt II, pp. 496–7. **Comprehensive Mirror**: Often translated as the *General Mirror for Aid in Government*. See de Bary, Theodore (ed.), *Sources of Chinese Tradition*, Columbia University Press, New York, 1960, pp. 493–5. **He paints**: *Mémoires concernant l'Histoire . . . des Chinois*, Tome 1, Paris, 1776, p. 86.

56   **Xiang River Daily**: Snow, p. 166. **Chinese Socialist Party**: Scalapino, Robert A., and Yu, George T., *The Chinese Anarchist Movement*, University of California Press, Berkeley, 1961, p. 38; Dirlik, Arif, *Anarchism in the Chinese Revolution*, University of California Press, Berkeley, 1991, pp. 121–3. **His political ideas began to take shape**: Snow, p. 170. **Two professors**: Schram, *Mao's Road*, 1, pp. 9n and 487–8. **Yuan the Big Beard**: Snow, p. 171.

57   **Mao's marginal notes**: Schram, 1, pp. 175–313 (Winter 1917). **Shang Yang**: Ibid., pp. 5–6 (June 1912). **A hundredfold**: Ibid., p. 63 (June 25 1915). **Slavish in character**: Ibid., p. 139 (Sept. 23 1917). **Many undesirable customs**: Ibid., p. 132 (Aug. 23 1917).

58   **Extraordinary shame**: Ibid., p. 66 (Summer 1915). **Remonstrate with the government**: Ibid., p. 67 (July 1915). **Repeatedly the barbarians**:

Ibid., pp. 61–65 (May and June 1915). *Without a war*: Ibid., p. 103 (July 25 1916). *Our nation is*: Ibid., p. 113 (April 1 1917).

59 *Students feel that exercise is shameful*: Ibid., pp. 121 and 124 (April 1 1917). *If we do not have the will*: Ibid., pp. 117 and 120 (April 1 1917). *Will is the truth*: Ibid., pp. 133–4 (Aug. 23 1917). *If man's mental*: Ibid., p. 138 (Sept. 16 1917). *Ultimately the individual*: Ibid., pp. 201; 204–5, 208, 251 and 273 (Winter 1917). [See also pp. 280–1.] These remarks have been conflated from a much broader body of text because Mao repeatedly returned to the same idea from different viewpoints at different points in his notes.

60 *The power of the will*: Ibid., p. 310 (Winter 1917). *Great and powerful men*: Ibid., p. 77 (Sept. 6 1915). *The truly great person*: Ibid., pp. 263–4 (Winter 1917). *There is only movement*: Ibid., p. 118 (April 1 1917). *Throughout the ages*: Ibid., p. 69 (July 1915). *A long period of peace*: Ibid. pp. 237–8 and 247 (Winter 1917).

61 *Scholarly issues*: Ibid., p. 130 (Aug. 23 1917). *I have come to the conclusion*: Ibid., p. 62 (June 25 1915). *One ought to concentrate*: Ibid., pp. 77–9 (Sept. 6 1915). *Disorganised and unsystematic*: Ibid., pp. 128–9 (Summer 1917).

62 *He was not so sure*: Ibid., p. 132 (Aug. 23 1917). *All nations inevitably go through*: Ibid., p. 249 (Winter 1917). *All the anthologies*: Ibid., p. 139 (Sept. 23 1917). *Iron Pig*: The term 'Xinhai', like all cyclical year-names, is not normally translated. 'Xin' is the eighth of the celestial stems, whose affinity is iron; 'hai' is the tenth of the twelve terrestrial branches represented by zodiacal animals and denotes the year of the pig.

63 *There was a huge fire*: Snow, p. 169. *When Yuan capitulated*: See NCH, May 8 1915, p. 422; June 5, p. 715. *Wang Fuzhi Society*: Li Rui, p. 25. *Anti-restoration writings*: Ibid., p. 50; Schram, 1, p. 85 (Winter 1915).
    In Hunan, secret society members . . . disputed his position: McDonald, *Urban Origins*, pp. 26–8. For the mutiny, see also NCH, May 20 and 27 1916; on Tang's disguise, NCH, Sept. 23, p. 617, and Hume, p. 241; on the blood-letting, *North China Daily News*, Shanghai, July 20 and 21 1916. The same newspaper reported in a despatch dated July 29 that 'the situation in Hunan has improved' (July 31).

64 *Letter to his classmate . . . in France*: Schram, 1, pp. 92 (June 24), 93 (June 26) and 7 (July 18 1916). *An American missionary doctor*: Hume, pp. 238–40.

65 *Amphitheatre used for athletics events*: McDonald (p. 25) says this took place in 'the long-disused Provincial Examination hall'. The hall had been demolished years earlier, and new buildings belonging to the Hunan Education Association erected in their place (Hume, p. 160). *At least 5,000 people*: Li Rui, p. 47. McCord (*Power of the*

Gun, p. 196, n.125) quotes two Chinese sources as giving figures of 15,000 and 16,000 deaths. Mao (Schram, 1, p. 95) says 'well over 10,000'.

Independent accounts: The Shanghai newspaper, *Shibao*, called Hunan 'a world of terror' (March 14 1914, quoted in McCord, p. 198, n.136). Hume (p. 240) said Tang's rule was 'a reign of terror'. Hunan members of parliament telegraphed President Li Yuanhong after Tang's fall with 'a very powerful, indeed shocking, indictment' of his 'rule with an iron hand' (*North China Daily News*, 15 July 1916), and subsequently impeached him (*Shibao*, Nov. 29 1916).

As they would not name: NCH, May 15 1915, p. 449. *Even by such standards . . . current affairs*: McCord, pp. 193 and 195–8; see also NCH, Sept. 23 1916, p. 616. The quotation beginning 'Detectives are everywhere' is from *Shibao*, July 31 1914. *His own school*: Li Rui, p. 47.

66   *I still maintain*: Schram, 1, pp. 94–8 (July 18 1916). *The fact that Tang killed*: Ibid., p. 95.

67   *Promulgating laws*: Ibid., p. 6 (June 1912). *Disgust at the squabbling*: Ibid., pp. 100–1 (July 25 1916). *One of the three pre-eminent figures*: In 1917, Mao wrote: 'Those that can be called men today are three in number: Yuan Shikai, Sun Yat-sen and Kang Youwei' (ibid., p. 131; see also p. 76 [Sept. 6 1915]).

No more than tyrants: In his marginal notes on *System der Ethik* (ibid., Winter 1917, p. 276), Mao wrote Yuan's name against Paulsen's line: 'What makes a tyrant a tyrant is that . . . he seeks only pleasure and power.' By September 1920, Mao was speaking of 'Bandit Yuan' and 'Butcher Tang' (ibid., p. 552, Sept. 6–7 1920; see also p. 529, n.14). *A first-rate teacher*: Ibid., p. 141, n.1 (September 1917). *At that time*: Siao Yu, *Mao Tse-tung and I*, pp. 37–40.

68   *Except for the sages*: Schram, 1, p. 63 (June 25 1915). *He circulated a notice*: Mao told Edgar Snow he inserted it as an advertisement in a Changsha newspaper (*Red Star* p. 172). He told friends at the time he had merely 'posted [it] in several schools' (Schram, *Mao's Road*, 1, pp. 81–2 and 84). *Inviting young people*: Snow, p. 172. *At the Provincial Women's*: Li Rui, p. 74; Schram, 1, p. 81 (Sept. 27 1915). *Three and one half replies*: Snow, p. 172. *Half-a-dozen young people*: Mao wrote that autumn that 'five or six people responded' (Schram, 1, p. 84, Nov. 9 1915). *It was a serious-minded little group*: Snow, p. 172.

69   *Every morning*: Li Rui, p. 29. *We tramped through the fields*: Snow, p. 173. *When I think of his greatness*: Schram, 1, p. 69 (July 1915). *It is truly difficult*: Ibid., p. 60 (April 5 1915). *The student newspaper recalled*: *Beijing daxue yuekan*, Jan. 28 1920. *Throughout my life*: Schram, 1, p. 84 (Nov. 9 1915). *Many heavy thoughts*: Ibid., p. 72

(August 1915). *His obstinacy . . . prevent him being expelled*: Li Rui, pp. 44–6.

70   *You do not have the capacity*: Schram, 1, pp. 73–4 (August 1915). *Xiao Yu remembered him*: Siao Yu, p. 36. *He possessed only a blue . . . other professors did*: Li Rui, pp. 41–2. Snow (p. 175) quotes Mao as saying he spent 160 dollars while at the Normal School (actually in the six-and-a-half years from 1912 to 1918, since he specifically includes the period when he paid his 'numerous registration fees'). *Almost half his income*: Snow, Ibid.; Li Rui, p. 23. *He was equally diligent*: See Schram 1, pp. 9–56 (Oct.–Dec. 1913); pp. 141–2 (September 1917) and pp. 175–310 (Winter 1917). *Natural sciences*: Snow, p. 170; see also Schram, 1, p. 62 (June 25 1915).

71   *In the past I had some mistaken ideas*: Schram, 1, p. 62 (June 25 1915). *This is no place to study*: Ibid., p. 84 (Nov. 9 1915). *In the early morning*: Ibid., p. 85 (Winter 1915). *Half a year on*: Ibid., p. 105 (July 25 1916). *Who does not want to seek advancement*: Ibid., p. 130 (Aug. 23 1917). *Student of the Year*: Li Rui, pp. 52–3. *He criticised a teaching manual*: Schram, 1, p. 129 (Summer 1917).
      A month-long walking tour: Mao told Edgar Snow he got the idea for this trip, which took them through five counties, from an article in the *Minbao* (Snow, p. 171; see also Siao Yu, pp. 96–202). Despite Mao's assertion that 'peasants fed us and gave us a place to sleep', their contacts were almost entirely with local gentry, merchants and officials.

72   *Thrashed a wake*: Schram, 1, p. 159 (1917). *Only the Qing Viceroy*: Ibid., pp. 106 and 131 (Dec. 9 1916 and Aug. 23 1917). *Superior men*: Ibid., p. 135 (Aug. 23 1917). *Elected head of the Students' Society*: This election was apparently separate from the 'Student of the Year' contest which took place in June (ibid., p. 145, Nov. 1917). Mao became 'General Affairs Officer' of the society, which made him its de facto head under the nominal responsibility of the school proctor (ibid., p. 143n; Li Rui, pp. 54–5). *One of its first decisions*: Schram, 1, p. 145 (Nov. 1917). *Such initiatives . . . that one attends for ever*: Ibid., pp. 145–6.

73   *Of the little progress*: Ibid., p. 68 (July 1915). *He commented approvingly*: Ibid., p. 235 (Winter 1917). *In the educational system*: Ibid., p. 115 (April 1917). *Seven of Mao's fellow students*: Ibid., p. 157 (Winter 1917). *Sixty or so Changsha workers*: 85 people attended the first day's classes, of whom 30 per cent were adolescents (ibid., pp. 152–3, November 1917).

74   *These principles were*: Ibid., pp. 143–56. Even so progressive a publication as *New Youth* did not switch completely to the vernacular until January 1918. *The buying of Chinese-made*: Ibid., p. 142. In planning the evening-school courses, Mao stressed that the history lessons,

which he taught himself, should try to inculcate 'patriotic spirit'
(p. 149). *Tan proceeded to . . . as a foreigner*: McCord, pp. 245–56;
NCH, Sept. 15 1917, p. 594; Oct. 20, p. 85.

75   *Three days after taking up*: McCord, pp. 256–7. See also NCH, Oct. 6
1917, pp. 17–18, Oct. 13, pp. 72 and 85–6; Oct. 20, pp. 152–3; Nov. 3,
pp. 253–4 and 272–3. *Martial law was proclaimed*: Schram, 1, p. 144
(Oct. 30 1917). *But the combatants . . . remarkably lightly*: McCord,
pp. 257–9; NCH, Nov. 10 1917, pp. 333–4; Nov. 24, p. 463; Dec. 1,
pp. 518–20. *During these stirring times*: Li Rui, pp. 48 and 50–1;
Schram, *Mao Tse-tung*, p. 43. *The three heroes*: Schram, Mao's Road,
1, p. 19, n.52.

76   *Hidden in a latrine*: Snow, pp. 169–70. In a letter to Xiao Yu during
the unrest in July 1916, Mao wrote, 'I was in Xiangtan and too timid
to venture to the capital, so I waited for the reports of friends before
making the trip. I was truly frightened.' (Schram, 1, p. 97). *First
Normal School Record*: Li Rui, p. 48. *The following March*: McCord,
pp. 259–63. *With nightfall . . . twenty-four hours later*: NCH, April
6 1918, p. 21; April 13, pp. 78–9.*Cruel, sadistic dictator*: Hume,
p. 260. *Honour of women*: NCH, April 13 1918, p. 80. *Mrs S, 20
years of age*: NCH, April 20 1918, p. 137.

77   *Pingjiang*: Ibid., NCH, April 13 1918, p. 79. *Liling*: NCH, May 25
1918, pp. 452–3; McDonald, pp. 31–2. *Angry editorials*: NCH, June
1 1918, pp. 501–2. *Wu Peifu . . . Anfu rivals*: McCord, pp. 263–4 and
284. *Mao's college played . . . his own pocket*: Li Rui, pp. 48–9 and
59; Schram, 1, pp. 167–8 (May 29 1918). *Network of informers . . .
who has disappeared*: NCH, May 18 1918, pp. 398–9.

78   *Much secret terror*: Ibid., Sept. 14 1918, p. 626. *At the beginning of
June*: Li Rui, p. 85. *No clear idea . . . Mao did not have*: Schram, 1,
p. 136 (Aug. 23 1917). Although this was written nine months before
Mao graduated, evidently nothing had happened in the interim to
change it. *He spent the next few weeks*: Li Rui, pp. 85–6.
New People's Study Society: Li Rui, pp. 75–6. Mao told Edgar Snow
(*Red Star*, p. 173) that the society was set up in 1917, but this appears
to be yet another example of his faulty chronology. Xiao Yu's claim
that he was elected secretary is indirectly confirmed by Li Rui, who
writes that Mao 'modestly declined' the post but omits to say who
was appointed instead (Xiao having become in the 1950s a non-
person in China). Mao, according to Li, was deputy secretary. See
Schram, 1, pp. 81–2 and 164, n.1; Siao Yu, pp. 71–6.
You should know: Letter from Luo Xuezan to his grandfather
(summer 1918), displayed at the 'Centenary of Mao's Birth' exhibi-
tion, Natural History Museum, Beijing, December 1993.

79   *Classical term*: See Li Rui, p. 76. *The pupils bowed each night*:
Schram, 1, p. 152 (November 9 1917). *Increasingly critical*: In

August 1917, for instance, Mao wrote that Confucian good deeds such as building bridges and repairing roads were 'laudable'; in 1918, that they had 'no value at all' (Ibid., pp. 135 and 211). *Our country's three bonds*: Ibid., p. 208 (Winter 1917). *The churches, the capitalists*: Ibid., p. 208 (Winter 1917). *Fundamental change*: Ibid., p. 132 (Aug. 23 1917). *All phenomena in the world*: Ibid., pp. 249–50 and 306.

80   *Those who wish to move the world*: Ibid., pp. 131–2 (Aug. 23 1917). *Luo Zhanglong*: Ibid., p. 164, n.1. *Mao's old teacher . . . to find out more*: Li Rui, p. 87.

81   *Sightseeing*: Schram, 1, p. 174 (August 1918).

CHAPTER FOUR: A FERMENT OF 'ISMS'

82   *Beijing is like a crucible*: Schram, *Mao's Road*, 1, p. 83 (Nov. 9 1915). *Serious doubts*: Ibid., pp. 172–3 (Aug. 11 1918). See also Siao Yu, *Mao Tse-tung and I*, pp. 215–16; and Smedley, *Battle Hymn of China*, p. 123.

83   *I felt that I did not know enough*: Snow, *Red Star over China*, p. 176. See also Li Rui, *Early Revolutionary Activities*, p. 85. *Professor Yang . . . an assistant*: Snow, p. 176; Siao Yu, p. 210. *A position as a staff member*: Schram, 1, p. 317 (April 28 1919). *My office was so low*: Snow, p. 176. *When he tried to ask a question*: Schram, *Mao Tse-tung*, p. 48.

84   *Fu Sinian*: Snow, p. 176. *Eight dollars a month . . . wanted to turn over*: Snow, pp. 176–7; Siao Yu, p. 210. See also Kates, George, *The Years That Were Fat*, Harper, New York, 1952, pp. 20–2; and Strand, David, *Rickshaw Beijing*, University of California Press, Berkeley, 1989, pp. 29–30. *Shao Piaoping*: Snow, p. 177. See also Li Rui, p. 95. *Chen Duxiu*: Snow, pp. 179–80. *Latest new theories*: Li Rui, p. 93. *Looking for a road*: Snow, p. 177. *My mind was a curious mixture*: Ibid., p. 174.

85   *Jiang Kanghu*: Dirlik, *Anarchism in the Chinese Revolution*, pp. 135–6. *Kang Youwei*: See Wakeman, Frederic, Jnr, *History and Will*, University of California Press, Berkeley, 1973, pp. 115–36. *All under heaven*: Schram, 1, p. 135 (Aug. 23 1917). *I am sure*: Ibid., pp. 237–9 (Winter 1917). *Sage-king*: See Wakeman, pp. 140–6. *From Liang Qichao . . . moving history forward*: Ibid., pp. 15–52 (Liang Qichao); pp. 156–7 (liberalism); pp. 238–43, 251 and 257 (Wang Yangming); pp. 82–5 (Wang Fuzhi). See also Li Rui, pp. 17–19 and 24–7.
Embraced a concept: Mao's acceptance and subsequent rejection of Kang Youwei's utopianism in the autumn and winter of 1917 are one example; his views on immortality are another. Having written in December 1916: '[it is] the amount of one's achievement which is really immortal' (ibid., p. 107), a year later he condemned as 'stupid' the idea

of trying to leave behind a reputation (ibid., p. 240; see also p. 253).
The clarity that comes: Schram, 1, p. 130.

86 *Shanghai anarchist magazine*: Several articles appeared in the first
two issues of *Laodong* (labour), in March and April 1918 (Luk,
Michael Y. M., *The Origins of Chinese Bolshevism*, Oxford University
Press, 1990, pp. 18–19). See also Dirlik, Arif, *The Origins of Chinese
Communism*, Oxford University Press, 1989, pp. 26–8. Li Dazhao
published a comparison of the French and Russian revolutions
in *New Youth* in July 1918, but it was less specific and drew less
attention than his November article.
Li Dazhao published: de Bary, *Sources of Chinese Tradition*, pp. 863–5.
Vigorously promoted ... they had in mind: Dirlik, *Anarchism*, pp. 176–7.
See also Scalapino and Yu, *The Chinese Anarchist Movement*, and Zarrow,
Peter, *Anarchism and Chinese Political Culture*, Columbia University
Press, New York, 1990. *There will be no congress*: de Bary, pp. 864–5.
Beijing University: Dirlik, *Anarchism*, pp. 172–5; Chow Tse-tung, *The May
Fourth Movement: Intellectual Revolution in Modern China*, Harvard
University Press, Cambridge, MA, 1960, p. 97. See also Li Rui, p. 96. The
'Society of Cocks Crowing in the Dark' was founded in 1912. Although
Liu Shifu died in 1915, his supporters remained active until 1922; it
was they who started the magazine *Laodong* in the spring of 1918.

87 *Communism, anti-militarism*: Scalapino and Yu, p. 40. *To Mao,
anarchism*: Snow, p. 177. *There is one extremely violent party*:
Schram, 1, p. 380 (July 21 1919).

88 *China's capital in 1918*: Strand, pp. 1–46; LaMotte, Ellen N., *Peking
Dust*, Century Publishing, New York, 1919, pp. 16–21; Franck,
Harry, *Wandering in North China*, Century, New York, 1923,
pp. 196–203. George Kates, in *The Years That Were Fat*, describes the
city in the early 1930s, but in most respects it was little changed.
Sickly and stunted: Strand, p. 42. *A cacophony*: Kates, p. 87. *In the
parks*: Snow, pp. 177–8.

89 *Smoke hangs in the sky*: Schram, 1, p. 93 (June 26 1916). *He had
copied*: Ibid., p. 9.
In March 1919 ... in Shanghai: By his own account, Mao left Beijing
on March 14 and arrived in Shanghai two days later. He reached
Changsha on April 6 (ibid., p. 317). The steamer taking his friends
to France reportedly left on March 19 (Li Rui, p. 97), so it is possible
that, after leaving Shanghai, Mao stopped for a few days in Nanjing.
However, most of the places he told Edgar Snow he saw during this
trip (pp. 178–9), he actually visited a year later. See also Zhong
Wenxian, Mao Zedong: *Biography, Assessment, Reminiscences*, Foreign
Languages Press, Beijing, 1986, p. 41n.
His mother had already arrived ... a few months later: Zhong
Wenxian, p. 234. *The previous autumn*: Schram, 1, p. 174 (August

1918). *In a letter to his uncles*: Ibid., p. 317 (April 28 1919). *He wrote, more candidly*: Ibid., p. 504 (March 14 1920).

90   *He pretended to Edgar Snow*: Snow, p. 175. *Part-time job*: Li Rui, p. 97. *New political storm*: The best account of the May Fourth Incident and the events that led up to it is in Chow Tse-tung, pp. 84–116. See also NCH, May 10 1919, pp. 345–9 and May 17, pp. 413–19. *Throughout the world*: Kiang Wen-han, *The Chinese Student Movement*, New Republic Press, New York, 1948, p. 36.

91   *We now approach*: Chow Tse-tung, pp. 107–8. *Down with the nation-selling clique*: NCH, May 10 1919, p. 348. *A mock funeral inscription*: Chow Tse-tung, p. 108 (translation amended). *An eyewitness reported . . . their driver for speeding*: NCH, May 10 1919, pp. 348–9; Chow Tse-tung, pp. 111–15; Dirlik, *Anarchism*, pp. 148–9. Westerners in China had grave misgivings about Japan's ambitions, which they saw as a threat to their own interests (NCH, May 17, pp. 418–9).

92   *In Hunan*: McDonald, *Urban Origins*, p. 97. *Pitifully few*: 30,000 demonstrated in Jinan; 20,000 in Shanghai; 'more than 5,000' in Nanjing; 4,000 in Hangzhou (NCH, May 17 1919, pp. 413–14; Chow Tse-tung, p. 130). *Economic boycott*: McDonald, pp. 97–103, and Li Rui, pp. 103–4. See also NCH, May 17 1919, pp. 415–7; May 24, p. 507.

93   *Zhang himself noted*: NCH, June 28 1919, p. 837. See also NCH, June 21, p. 765. *Fiery appeal*: Siao, Emi, *Mao Tse-tung: His Childhood and Youth*, pp. 69–70.
      Merely symptoms: Mao barely mentions either problem in the *Xiang River Review*. A year later, he would write that movements like the boycott were 'only expedient measures in response to the current situation', and that China's real needs went 'way beyond' such punctual concerns (Schram, 1, p. 611, Nov. 1920).
      Xiangjiang pinglun: McDonald, pp. 103–4; Li Rui, pp. 104–5. *Today we must change*: Schram, 1, pp. 318–20 (July 14 1919).

94   *The Great Union*: Ibid., pp. 378–89 (July 21, 28 and Aug. 4 1919).

95   *Four hundred or more*: Chow Tse-tung, pp. 178–82; McDonald, p. 105. *Hu Shi*: Li Rui, p. xxix. *Lo Jialun*: *Xin chao*, vol. 2, no. 4, p. 849 (May 1 1920); See Schram, Stuart R., *The Political Thought of Mao Tse-tung*, Pall Mall Press, London, 1963, p. 104. *He continued to view*: Schram, *Mao's Road*, 1, p. 372 ('moving inexorably eastward' and 'whether or not to retain the nation'); p. 319 ('oppression'); pp. 379–80 ('classes of the wise and ignorant').
      A dialectical relationship: Ibid., pp. 234–5: 'Where the river emerges from the Tong pass, because Mount Hua is an obstacle to it, the force of the rushing water is much greater . . . Great power faces great obstacles, and great obstacles face great powers.'

His assessment of Germany's defeat: Ibid., p. 367 (July 21 1919). See also pp. 357–66 (July 21); pp. 334, 337–8 and 343 (July 14).

96 *Japan and Germany*: Ibid., p. 392 (July 28 1919). *Governor Zhang, fanned*: Li Rui, pp. 125–6. *Students' Association*: McDonald, p. 106. *A wickedly mischievous petition*: Schram, I, pp. 396–8 (July 30 1919).

97 *Despite Mao's claim*: Ibid., p. 377 (July 21 1919). *Confiscated*: Li Rui, p. 116. *Bayoneted to death*: Schram, 1, p. 479 (Jan. 19 1920); see also McDonald, p. 106. *Xin Hunan . . . was banned*: Schram, 1, p. 418 (Sept. 1919); see also pp. 414–15 (Sept. 5). *Gentlemen, we are women*: Ibid., p. 383 (July 28 1919).

98 *Particularly ghastly case*: Ibid., pp. 421–49 (Nov. 16–28 1919), esp. pp. 421–2 ('darkness of the social system'); pp. 434–8 ('shattered jade' and 'act of courage'). *Mr Peng wonders*: Ibid., p. 428 (Nov. 21 1919).

99 *The role of scholars*: Ibid., pp. 611–12 (Nov. 1920). *On December 2*: McDonald, pp. 108–9; NCH, Dec. 20 1919; Li Rui, p. 127.

100 *A leading Changsha banker*: NCH, Oct. 25, pp. 215–16. *After eighteen months*: Ibid., Oct. 4 1919. *Resume opium cultivation*: Ibid., Nov. 22 1919, pp. 482–3. *Two weeks after the confrontation*: McDonald, pp. 110–12; Li Rui, pp. 127–9. *People's News Agency*: Snow, p. 179; Schram, 1, p. 457 (Dec. 24 1919). *Notable scoop*: Schram, 1, pp. 457–9, 463–5 and 469–71 (Dec. 24 and 31 1919, Jan. 4 1920). *Hail of petitions*: Ibid., pp. 457–90 and 496–7 (Dec. 24 1919 to Feb. 28 1920). *They held a meeting . . . Zhang was dismissed*: McDonald, pp. 112–13. *They could do nothing more*: Mao initially planned to leave at the end of February (Schram, 1, p. 494, Feb. 19 1920), then put it off till March and finally set out in April. *When Zhang fell*: NCH, May 29 1919, p. 509, and June 12, p. 649 (Wu Peifu's departure); June 19, p. 708 (million dollars); June 26, p. 774 (munitions dump and 'greatest day of rejoicing').

101 *Problem Study Society*: Schram, 1, pp. 407–13 (Sept. 1 1919).
My Marxist Views: Meisner, Maurice, *Li Ta-chao and the Origins of Chinese Marxism*, Harvard University Press, Cambridge, MA, 1967, pp. 90–5 and 280, n.2. Dirlik suggests that the first part of the article, although dated May 1919, was not published until September (*Origins of Communism*, p. 47), in which case Mao could not have read it until after the founding of the 'Problem Study Society'.
He started to realise: Schram 1, p. 453 (Dec. 1 1919). *Core relationship . . . economic independence*: Ibid., pp. 432–3 (Nov. 21 1919). *If society was to change. . . working people as toilers*: Ibid., pp. 453–4 (Dec. 1 1919).

102 *Repudiate the unequal treaties*: Chow, pp. 209–14. The 'Karakhan Declaration', setting out this policy, was issued on July 25 1919, and published in Soviet newspapers three weeks later. But it was not officially confirmed in Beijing until March 21 1920.

Mao tried to learn: Snow, p. 181, and Schram, 1, pp. 493–518 passim. Ibid., p. 506, March 14 1920 ('number-one civilised country'); p. 494, Feb. 19 1920 (talked to Li Dazhao); p. 518, June 7 1920 (to learn Russian); pp. 504–7 (deeply ambivalent . . . 'our craving for it') and pp. 494, 506–7 and 518 (resolved his dilemma).

Very little Marxist literature: Dirlik, *Origins of Communism*, pp. 32–8 and 98–110. *Mao was about to leave for Shanghai*: He left on April 11 and reached Shanghai on May 5 (*Nianpu*, 1, p. 57). *Li Dazhao*: Snow, pp. 182–3. *Deeply impressed me*: Ibid., pp. 180 and 183. *New Village' movement*: Luk, pp. 30–1. *Which envisaged . . . to spread Bolshevism*: Schram, 1, pp. 450–6 (Dec. 1 1919). See also pp. 458–500 (March 5 1920).

103 *Several such schemes*: Luk, pp. 30–1. See also Chow Tse-tung, pp. 190–1. Mao's friends, Deng Zhongxia and Luo Zhanglong (a founder member of the New People's Study Society), participated in the 'Morning Garden;' community, founded by Beijing University students in the autumn of 1919. It collapsed early in 1920 (see Schram, 1, p. 494, Feb. 19 1920).

Mao conceded: Schram, 1, p. 518 (June 7 1920). *Self-study University*: Ibid,. p. 494 (Feb. 19 1920) and p. 506 (March 14 1920); Womack, Brantly, *The Foundations of Mao Zedong's Political Thought, 1917–35*, University Press of Hawaii, Honolulu, 1982, pp. 25–6; Li Rui, pp. 170–1. *Cultural Book Society*: Schram, 1, pp. 534–5, July 31 1920; pp. 583–7, Oct. 22 1920 and pp. 589–91, Nov. 10 1920; and Womack, p. 25. *Three great contemporary philosophers*: Schram, 1, p. 519, June 7 1920. *Years later, in Bao'an*: Snow, p. 181. *He admitted to a friend*: Schram, 1, p. 505 (March 14 1920). *I am too emotional . . . live a disciplined life*: Ibid., pp. 518–9 (June 7 1920). *Chinese culture*: Ibid., p. 505.

104 *Water Margin*: Ibid., p. 586 (Oct. 22 1920). *I stopped at Qufu*: Snow, pp. 178–9.

105 *Mao was initially sceptical*: Schram, 1, p. 501 (March 12 1920). *Less than three weeks later . . . self-determination*: Ibid., pp. 510–11 (April 1 1920). For Peng Huang's role, see p. 503 (March 12). *A model . . . the whole country*: Ibid., p. 523 (June 11 1920).

106 *From now on the essential*: Ibid., pp. 526–30 (June 23 1920). *With his brothers in Shaoshan*: Ibid., p. 543 (Sept. 3 1920); *Nianpu*, 1, p. 82. *Xiong Xiling*: McDonald, Angus W., Jnr, 'Mao Tse-tung and the Hunan Self-government Movement', CQ, 68, April 1976, pp. 753–4.

107 *Mao returned to Changsha . . . new progressive forces*: Schram, 1, pp. 543–53, Sept, 3, 5 and 6–7, and p. 580, Oct. 10 1920. *In mid-September*: McDonald, 'Mao Tse-tung', pp. 754–5. *Constitutional convention*: Schram, 1, pp. 559 (Sept. 27), 565–71 (Oct. 5–6); pp. 573–4 (Oct. 8 1920). *Petition to this effect*: Ibid., pp. 577–8 (Oct.

10 1920); McDonald, 'Mao Tse-tung', p. 765. *Citizens of Changsha*:
Schram, 1, p. 572 (Oct. 7 1920). *Two days later*: McDonald, 'Mao
Tse-tung', p. 765; NCH, Oct. 23 1920, p. 223.

108   *The document was the work*: NCH, Nov. 6 1920, pp. 387–8. *Tan was
having ... people's rule was quite another*: Schram, 1, pp. 544 (Sept.
3), 546 (Sept. 5), 556 (Sept. 26), 558 (Sept. 27), 561–2 (Sept. 30), 572
(Oct. 7) and 578 (Oct. 10). *National Day march*: McDonald, 'Mao
Tse-tung', pp. 765–6; Li Rui, p. 144.

109   *Tan was repaid*: Li Rui, pp. 145–6; McCord, pp. 301–2; McDonald,
'Mao Tse-tung', p. 767. *Total self-rule*: Schram, 1, p. 562 (Sept. 30
1920). *To no avail ... carve out a new path*: Ibid., p. 595 (Nov. 25
1920). *Soul-searching*: Ibid., pp. 608 and 610 (November 1920).
What was needed ... in November 1920: Schram, 1, pp. 491–2, Feb.
19 1920 ('dedicated group'); pp. 505–6, March 14 1920 (common
goals); 2, p. 26, Winter 1920 ('vain glory'); 1, p. 612, Nov 1920
('political stage'); p. 524, May 16 1920 ('overthrow and sweep away')
and p. 556, Sept. 20 1920 (an ism required).

110   *We really must create*: Ibid., 1, p. 600 (Nov. 25 1920). *Already, that
July*: Ibid., 2, p. 29, Winter 1920 ('sixteen members'); pp. 5–14, Dec.
1 1920 (Montargis). Li Rui says fourteen members attended
(pp. 149–50). *I don't think anarchism*: Schram, 2, p. 7 (Dec. 1 1920).

111   *China's first 'communist group'*: *History of the CCP, Chronology*,
pp. 6–7; Van de Ven, Hans J., *From Friend to Comrade: The Founding of
the Chinese Communist Party, 1920–27*, University of California Press,
Berkeley, 1991, pp. 21. ('revolutionary means must be used') and 59.
Russian Studies Society: Schram, 1, pp. 554–5, Sept, 23 1920. *A dozen
young Hunanese*: Peng Shuzhi says there were sixteen Hunanese
students (Cadart and Cheng, *L'Envol du Communisme en Chine*, p. 196),
but some of these, like Liu Shaoqi, were in Shanghai already.
Marxist Study Circle: Cadart and Cheng, pp. 153–62. He Minfan's
role is contentious. He contributed to the Cultural Book Society in
November 1920 and January 1921 (Schram, 2, pp. 49 and 58), and
in March 1921 played a leading role in the China-Korea Mutual Aid
Society of Changsha, which Mao and others set up to support the
Korean struggle for independence from Japan (*Nianpu*, 1, p. 82). Peng
Shuzhi, who detested Mao, described He Minfan as Chen Duxiu's
main interlocutor in Changsha. However, Zhang Guotao (Chang
Kuo-t'ao), an equally hostile source, says Chen wrote directly to Mao
to encourage him to establish the Changsha group (*The Rise of the
Chinese Communist Party*, University Press of Kansas, KC, 1971, vol,
1, p. 129). Since Mao had been in contact with Chen since 1918, had
spent time working with him in Shanghai and was well known as a
New Youth contributor and as editor of the *Xiang River Review*, this
seems much more likely. Chen may, however, as Peng claims, have

asked He Minfan to recruit students to go to Russia. The Russian
Studies Society, the Wang Fuzhi Society and the Wang Fuzhi
Academy were all closely linked.
Socialist Youth League: Schram, 1, p. 594, Nov. 21 1920. *Russian
'terrorist tactics'... that would work*: Schram, 2, p. 9 (Dec. 1 1920).
Hans Van de Ven gives a totally different translation of this passage
(p. 52). *The Russian method*: Schram, 2, pp. 62 and 68 (Jan. 1–2 1921).

112 *The alternative, advocated by Xiao Yu ... the views of Cai Hesen*:
Ibid., pp. 8–11 (Dec. 1 1920). *On New Year's Day*: Ibid., pp. 59–71
(Jan. 1–2 1921).

113 *By now the Marxist Study Circle... the same time*: Nianpu, 1, pp. 73, 75
and 79. There has been much scholarly debate over whether a Changsha
'communist group', separate from the Youth League, ever formally
existed. The evidence that it did is overwhelming (see Zhang Guotao, 1,
pp. 130–1; Cadart and Cheng, pp. 155–6). Moreover, had there been no
Changsha group, Mao and He Shuheng could hardly have attended the
First Congress in July 1921 as its representatives (*Nianpu*, 1, p. 86; Saich,
Tony, (ed.), *The Rise to Power of the Chinese Communist Party: Documents
and Analysis*, M. E. Sharpe, New York, 1996, p. 14).
The instrument to defeat capitalism: Saich, pp. 11–13. *Explicitly
rejecting anarchism*: Schram, 2, pp. 35–6 (Jan. 21 1921).

114 *I did not know*: Snow, p. 178. *Reduced to taking in washing*: Li Rui,
p. 134. *In September he was appointed Principal*: Nianpu, p. 67. *He
married Yang Kaihui*: Ibid., p. 76. *Every new radical group*: Dirlik,
Anarchism, p. 120 and Scalapino and Yu, pp. 37–8 (Six Noes Society);
Schram, 2, p. 20 (New People's Study Society). *Memorial poem*:
Schram, 1, p. 64 (June 25 1915).

115 *Irresistible sexual desire*: Ibid., pp. 263–4 (Winter 1917). *Basic
human instincts*: Ibid., p. 256. *Mao fell in love*: Snow, p. 181. *Meals
at the professor's home*: Siao Yu, p. 51. *Power of the human need for
love*: Schram, 1, pp. 445–6 (Nov. 28 1919). *Tao Yi*: Ibid., p. 491; Siao
Yu, pp. 52–3. *Back courting Kaihui*: Li Rui, p. 164. *Mao was lost in
admiration*: Schram, 1, pp. 608–9 (Nov. 26 1920).

116 *Criterion of marriage*: Schram, 1, pp. 443–4 (Nov. 27 1919).
Clearwater Pond: Nianpu, 1, p. 88.

CHAPTER FIVE: THE COMINTERN TAKES CHARGE

117 *On Friday, June 3 1921 ... received no reply*: Saich, Tony, *The Origins
of the First United Front in China: The Role of Sneevliet (Alias Maring)*,
E. J. Brill, Leiden, 1991, 1, pp. 31–3. *Powerfully built*: Zhang Guotao,
Rise of the Chinese Communist Party, 1, p. 139. *Shanghai*: By far the
best description of the city in the 1920s is to be found in Harriet

Sergeant's splendid book, *Shanghai* (Crown Publishers, New York, 1990).

118   *Mr Andresen*: Saich, 1, p. 35. *Hendricus Sneevliet ... first represen-tative of the Comintern*: Ibid., 1, pp. xxv and 21. *Mekka*: Ibid., 1, pp. 254 and 263–5.
Initial contact ... news agency correspondents: Ibid., 1, pp.43–7 and 52; Dirlik, *Origins of Chinese Communism*, pp. 191–5; Saich, *Rise to Power*, p. 25. Peng Shuzhi quotes a detailed account by Li Dazhao of a visit to Beijing by a Russian emissary named (in French transcrip-tion) 'Hohonovkine' [perhaps Khokhonovkin] in January 1920 (Cadart and Cheng, *L'Envol du Communisme en Chine*, pp. 162–5). There is independent confirmation that Li discussed with Chen Duxiu that month the possible formation of a party (Dirlik, pp. 195 and 293, n.14).

119   *This foreign devil*: Zhang Guotao, 1, pp. 137 and 139. *At the end of June*: *Nianpu*, 1, p. 85. *Amid great secrecy*: Li Rui, *Early Revolutionary Activities*, p. 166. *Founding Congress*: Zhang Guotao, 1, pp. 136–51; Saich, *Origins*, 1, pp. 60–69; Van de Ven, *From Friend to Comrade*, pp. 85–90.

120   *The programme of our party*: Chen Gongbo (Ch'en Kung-po), *The Communist Movement in China*, Octagon, New York, 1966, p. 102.

121   *Long live the Chinese Communist Party*: Saich, *Rise to Power*, p. 16. *Furious and radical decisions*: Chen Gongbo, p. 82. *Independence, aggression and exclusion*: Ibid., p. 105; see also p. 102. *Lenin's thesis*: Saich, *Origins*, 1, pp. 12–21. *Refused to acknowledge Moscow's supremacy*: Ibid., 1, p. 102; see also p. 105. *When, in September, Chen Duxiu*: Ibid., 1, pp. 73–7.

122   *He made a report*: On the first day, 'the Congress listened to reports concerning the activities of the local small groups' (Saich, *Rise to Power*, p. 14). Only the reports of the Beijing and Canton groups have survived (ibid., pp. 19–27). *Ten of the fifty-three*: Ibid., p. 14; Zhang Guotao, 1, p. 141. *Official note-takers*: *Nianpu*, 1, p. 85. *Zhang Guotao remembered him*: Zhang Guotao, 1, p. 140. *None of the partic-ipants*: See Saich, *Origins*, 1, pp. 64–7. *He told his friend Xiao Yu*: Siao Yu, *Mao Tse-tung and I*, p. 256. *English lessons*: *Nianpu*, 1, p. 87. *Hunan branch of the CCP*: *Ibid.*, p. 88. *At least thirty members*: Chen Gongbo, pp. 102–3; Saich, *Rise to Power*, pp. 27–8. *One of three to meet the target*: Saich, p. 77, n.22.

123   *An immense red flag*: This account is of the 1922 rally (*Minguo ribao*, Nov, 15 1922, reprinted in Wieger, Leon, *Chine Moderne*, vol. 3: 'Remous et Ecume', Xianxian, 1922, pp. 433–4). It corresponds closely to Mao's description in Snow, *Red Star over China*, pp. 180–1, the only significant difference being that Mao dates the episode, wrongly, to 1920. A description of the 1921 rally, which had an

identical format and was also broken up by the police, is given in the *Nianpu* (1, p. 89).

Self-study university: Li Rui, pp. 170–3; *Nianpu*, 1, p. 86; Schram, *Mao's Road*, 2, pp. 88–92 and 93–8. *School's stated objectives*: Schram, 2, pp. 91 and 97; see also pp. 156 and 162–3 (April 10 1923). *Mao gave up his job*: *Nianpu*, 1, p. 87.

Unconventional ideas: He Minfan was deeply shocked when, one particularly hot day, Mao 'went about his teaching duties and visited his colleagues, wearing nothing but a towel around his waist, in other words virtually naked, walking about our dignified establishment as though it were the most natural thing in the world.' When He remonstrated with him, Mao allegedly retorted: 'How can you make such a fuss about such a small thing? What would be so scandalous even if I were naked? Think yourself lucky I'm wearing a towel.' Although both He himself and Peng Shuzhi, who related the incident in his memoirs, had a strong bias against Mao, the story has the ring of truth (Cadart and Cheng, pp. 159–60).

124   *Chief aim*: Chen Gongbo, p. 103. *One-and-a-half million*: Chesneaux, Jean, *The Chinese Labour Movement: 1919–27*, Stanford University Press, 1968, pp. 41–7. *Beijing match factory*: Wieger, *Chine Moderne*, vol. 4: *L'Outre d'Eole*, Xianxian, 1923, pp. 434–7.

125   *Hunan Workingmen's Association*: Li Rui, pp. 192–4; Shaffer, Lynda, *Mao and the Workers: The Hunan Labour Movement, 1920–23*, M. E. Sharpe, Armonk, 1982, pp. 45–9. *Labour secretariat*: *Nianpu*, 1, p. 86; Saich, *Origins*, 1, pp. 70–2. *2,000 members*: Schram, 2, p. 176 (July 1 1923). *Pang was a Xiangtan man*: Li Rui, p. 195.
Trip itself was inconclusive: Ibid., p. 197; Shaffer, pp. 44–5 and 85. There is no evidence that the Workingmen's Association established a presence at Anyuan at this time; however, the rival Mechanics' Union, a smaller group founded in November 1920, did set up a branch there in September. It was this group that invited Mao to pay a second visit to Anyuan three months later.
Mao to contribute an article: Schram, 2, pp. 100–1 (Nov. 21 1921). *Huang and Pang secretly*: Li Rui, p. 197. *Mass rally*: *Nianpu*, 1, p. 90. *But then, in January 1922 . . . Association was banned*: Wieger, 4, pp. 441–3; Shaffer, pp. 54–6; Li Rui, p. 197; McDonald, *Urban Origins*, pp. 164–5; NCH, Feb. 25 1922, p. 512.

126   *Sun Yat-sen . . . telegrams of protest*: Shaffer, pp. 56–7; NCH, April 29 1922, p. 299. *Mao spent most of March*: *Nianpu*, 1, pp. 92–3. *Inexcusable*: NCH, Feb. 25 1922, p. 512. *Unfortunately the general public*: NCH, April 29 1922, p. 299. *Mao's next move: Nianpu*, 1, p. 23; Shaffer, pp. 57–61; Li Rui, pp. 184–7.

127   *Anyuan*: Shaffer, pp. 71–89. See also *Nianpu*, 1, pp. 91, 95 and 98; McDonald, pp. 166–8; and Li Rui, pp. 199–206. *Meanwhile Mao*: In

late April, he went to the Shuikoushan lead and zinc mines (*Nianpu*, 1. p. 93); in May with Yang Kaihui to Anyuan; and 'in early summer' to Yuezhou (p. 95). *Agitation among railway workers*: Saich, *Rise to Power*, pp. 27–8. *Railwaymen's Club*: *Nianpu*, 1, pp. 94–5. *It was at Yuezhou*: McDonald, pp. 172–8; Li Rui, pp. 229–38. See also Shaffer, p. 91; Chesneaux, pp. 190–1; and Schram, 2, pp. 122–4 (Sept. 8 and 10 1922).

Incendiary telegram: Schram, 2, pp. 125–6 (Sept. 12 1922). Changsha labour groups unleashed a barrage of appeals, including one, apparently not written by Mao, which urged the workers to 'overthrow the evil and violence of the warlords' and 'smash these bone-crushing, marrow-sucking robbers' (*Hunan jinbainian dashi jishu*, Hunan renmin chubanshe, Changsha, 1979, pp. 493–4; translation in McDonald, p. 177).

Governor Zhao let it be known: Li Rui, p. 234; McDonald, p. 175.

128   *Word of these events*: Shaffer, p. 91. The account of the strike which follows is taken from Shaffer, pp. 88–98; McDonald, pp. 169–72; and Li Rui, pp. 206–10. *More than a thousand delegates*: McDonald, p. 177; Li Rui, pp. 238–9. *Dispute among masons*: Shaffer, pp. 109–43; McDonald, pp. 180–6; Li Rui, pp. 213–29. Unless otherwise indicated, the account that follows is drawn from these three sources. *In July they asked the Temple Board*: *Hunan jinbainian dashi jishu* (pp. 496–504) says the workers started petitioning for a wage increase in May 1922, and that notices were posted that it would come into effect on June 1. In fact the workers were using the old lunar calendar, under which 'the first day of the sixth month' was July 24 (NCH, Nov. 4 1922, p. 288).

129   *Mao himself drafted its charter*: Schram, 2, pp. 117–19 (Sept. 5 1922).

On October 4: Shaffer (pp. 116–17) and McDonald (p. 181) claim that the magistrate overruled the increase soon after it was enforced. It was not until October 4, 'the fourteenth day of the eighth month', that he issued a notice formally rescinding the increase (NCH, Nov. 4 1922, p. 288). The aim of the strike then became to get this notice withdrawn (Schram, 2, pp. 129–31, Oct. 24 1922).

130   *We, the masons*: Schram, 2, p. 127 (Oct. 6 1922).

131   *Right to carry out summary executions*: See NCH, Jan. 14 1922, p. 83. *About 10 p.m. I wandered*: Ibid., Nov. 4 1922, p. 288.

132   *Barest living wage*: Ibid., Nov. 11 1922, p. 370.

133   *The government capitulated*: Ibid. *Yang Kaihui . . . gave birth to a son*: *Nianpu*, 1, p. 103. *The strike epidemic*: McDonald, pp. 186–7; Li Rui, pp. 255–9. *All-Hunan Federation of Labour Organisations*: *Nianpu*, 1, pp. 103–4. See also Li Rui, pp. 259–61. *Mao himself served*

as nominal leader: McDonald, p. 188. *Joint delegation . . . to meet Governor Zhao*: Schram, 2, pp. 132–40. See also Li Rui, pp. 263–5.

134 *Shuikoushan*: Shaffer, pp. 164–92; McDonald pp. 188–91; Li Rui, pp. 239–44. *Shanghai . . . was so tightly controlled*: Zhang Guotao, 1, pp. 271–3. See also Saich, *Origins*, 1, pp. 148–9.

Even in Hunan: See Schram, 2, pp. 141–4 (Dec. 14 1922). The *Dagongbao*, in an article which Li Rui says was written by Mao's ally, the editor-in-chief, Li Jiangong, implicitly accused Mao of using the workers for 'ideological experiments' (Li Rui, pp. 248–53), a charge which Mao angrily rebutted.

Wu Peifu: Saich, *Origins*, 1, pp. 121–32 and 149; Zhang Guotao, 1, pp. 273–7; Chesneaux, pp. 191–2. See also Saich, *Rise to Power*, p. 35.

That summer the Secretariat: Schram, 2, pp. 111–16 (July 1922).

Adolf Joffe: Wilbur, C. Martin, and How, Julie Lien-ying, *Missionaries of Revolution: Soviet Advisers and Nationalist China, 1920–1927*, Harvard University Press, Cambridge, MA, 1989, pp. 54–7 and 60–3; Saich, *Origins*, 1, pp. 126–9.

135 *Against this background . . . two hundred others were wounded*: Chesneaux, pp. 206–10; Saich, *Origins*, 1, pp. 151–4; McDonald, pp. 195–7; Zhang Guotao, 1, pp. 277–91. *Work stoppages*: Chesneaux, pp. 212–19. *In Hunan*: Ibid., p. 221; McDonald, pp. 199–200; Li Rui, p. 262. *Angry telegrams*: Schram, 2, pp. 147–54. *Mao sent his brothers*: McDonald, pp. 171–2 (Mao Zemin); *Nianpu*, 1, p. 111 and Li Rui, p. 244 (Mao Zetan). *60,000 people*: McDonald, p. 201. *Zhao declared martial law*: Ibid., pp. 202–5. *Arrest warrants*: Despite the assertions of McDonald (p. 205) and Li Rui (p. 270), it appears that no arrest warrant was issued for Mao (see *Hunan jinbainian dashi jishu*, pp. 516–20).

136 *Chen Duxiu had invited him . . . delayed until mid-April*: *Nianpu*, 1, pp. 109–10 and 113. *Second, much more serious, dispute*: Saich, *Origins*, 1, pp. 79–85. *At the beginning of April 1922*: Ibid., pp. 256–7. Those who approved the resolution are not listed by name, but Mao was the only 'comrade from Changsha' then in Shanghai. The *Nianpu* (1, p. 93) says he returned from there during 'the second 10 days of April'.

137 *Grudging acceptance*: Saich, *Rise to Power*, pp. 34–8. See also Saich, *Origins*, 1, p. 90, n.21. *A temporary alliance*: Saich, *Rise to Power*, pp. 38–40. *Party's new constitution*: Ibid., pp. 43 and 49.

138 *Paid-up membership*: History of the CCP, Chronology, p. 14.

Mao did not attend: Snow, pp. 184–5. The *Nianpu* quotes Mao's explanation to Snow without comment (1, p. 96n); it lists no other activities by him between July 5 and August 7. Given that Mao had been in Shanghai only three months earlier, and that secrecy became a real issue in the CCP only after January 1923 (*Nianpu*, 1, p. 109 and

Schram, 2, p. 155; Zhang Guotao, 1, p. 296), it is hard to take his story at face value.

Canton Party committee: Zhang Guotao, 1, p. 247.

Directive from the Comintern: 'Instructions to a Representative of the ECCI in South China' (August 1922), in Pantsov, Alexander, and Benton, Gregor, 'Did Trotsky Oppose Entering the Guomindang "From the First"?' (*Republican China*, XIX, 2, pp. 61–3). The directive, from Karl Radek, instructs the communists merely to 'set up groups of supporters inside the Guomindang'; the 'bloc within' formula, as the CCP eventually adopted it, may in fact have come from Sneevliet himself. See also Saich, *Origins*, 1, p. 117 (vigorous opposition); Ibid., p. 338 (Sun Yatsen himself); Ibid., pp. 119–20 (Xiangdao zhoubao); Wilbur and How, pp. 54–7 (Adolf Joffe).

Forced to operate underground: 'Chen Duxiu's Report to the Third Party Congress' (June 1923), in Saich, *Origins*, 2, pp. 572–3.

Internal divisions: Saich, *Origins*, 2, p. 612. There were two major splits in the summer and autumn of 1922: Zhang Guotao formed what was termed a factional 'small group' (ibid., 2, pp. 115–16; Zhang Guotao, 1, pp. 250–2; Cai Hesen, 'Zhongguo gongchandangde fazhan [tigang]', in *Zhonggong dangshi baogao xuanbian*, Zhonggong zhongyang dangxiao chubanshe, Beijing, 1982, p. 43); and the Canton Party committee rejected the decision of the Hangzhou plenum on co-operation with the GMD, leading in November to the resignation of Chen Gongbo and the expulsion of Tan Zhitang (Cai Hesen, p. 69; Chen Gongbo, pp. 10–12; Zhang Guotao, 1, p. 249).

'Born, or more correctly, fabricated': Saich, *Origins*, 2, p. 611 (June 20 1923). Earlier he had written to Bukharin that the Chinese movement was 'very weak and a little artificial' (ibid., 2, p. 476, March 21 1923). **Joffe had stated publicly**: NCH Feb 3 1923, p. 289.

139 **Special praise**: Saich, *Origins*, 2, p. 577. Sneevliet also reported to the Comintern the same month that 'Hunan has the best organisation' (ibid., p. 617). In a note to Zinoviev in November 1922 (ibid., pp. 344–5), he had described Hunan as having both the best Party committee and the best Youth League branch (with 230 members, compared with 110 in Shanghai, 40 in Canton, 20 in Jinan and 15 in Anhui).

At the end of his Latin: Ibid., 2, p. 590. **China's future**: Ibid., 1, p. 449. **Third Congress**: Ibid., 2, p. 642 (forty delegates); 2, p.573 (420 members). See also ibid., 1, pp. 175–86 and 2, pp. 565–6; Zhang Guotao, pp. 296–316; and Van den Ven, *From Friend to Comrade*, pp. 122–6.

Mao, Cai Hesen: This point is contentious. Sneevliet reported that the vote was carried by 21 to 16, and 'among these 16 [opposition] votes were [the] six from Hunan'; he then identified the Hunan 'representative' as Mao (Saich, *Origins*, 2, p. 616). Zhang Guotao recalled in his memoirs that he, Cao and Mao were Sneevliet's principal opponents (1, p. 308); Mao (and Cai Hesen) submitted to the majority decision, Zhang wrote, only after the vote had been taken (p. 311). Stuart Schram relies on Sneevliet's note of Mao's remark, 'we should not be afraid of joining [the Guomindang]', to argue that Mao supported the Comintern line (*Mao's Road*, 2, pp. xxix–xxx). But the question of 'joining' had already been settled at Hangzhou in August 1922; the debate at the Third Congress was over the conditions and conse- quences of doing so, and here Mao had strong reservations.

Mao's assessment . . . Everyone must keep this in mind: Schram, 2, pp. 157–61; Saich, *Origins*, 2, pp. 448–9, 580 and 590; and Zhang Guotao, 1, pp. 308–9.

140   *Did not share his pessimism*: Saich, *Origins*, 2, p. 590. *Narrowly approved*: Ibid., 2, p. 616. See also Zhang Guotao, 1, p. 310. *The Congress documents*: Saich, *Rise to Power*, pp. 76–9. *Mao was elected*: *Nianpu*, 1, p. 114; Saich, *Origins*, 2, pp. 642–3.

141   *Li Hanjun . . . resigned in disgust*: Saich, *Origins*, 2, pp. 539–40 and 643. *Chen Duxiu could no longer complain*: Ibid., p. 576.

No more real grasp of Marxist theory: Sneevliet told Zinoviev in June 1923 that 'the only comrade who is able to analyse reality in a Marxist fashion' was Qu Qiubai, a 23-year-old journalist who had just returned to China after spending two years in Moscow. Qu was elected a Central Committee alternate at the Third Congress (Saich, *Origins*, 2, p. 615).

Centralised national-revolutionary army: *Nianpu*, 1, p. 115. *Mao joined the Guomindang*: Sneevliet (Saich, *Origins*, 2, p. 659) and the *Nianpu* (1, p. 115) both indicate that Mao was a GMD member by June 25 1923. See also Li Yongtai, *Mao Zedong yu da geming*, Sichuan renmin chubanshe, Chengdu, 1991. *Sun rejected*: Saich, *Origins*, 2, pp. 657–61, 678 and 690; *Nianpu*, 1, p. 115. *Nothing can be expected . . . throwing away money*: Saich, *Origins*, 2, p. 696.

142   *This revolution*: Schram, 2, pp. 178–82 (July 11 1923). *Central Bureau returned to Shanghai*: Saich, *Origins*, 2, pp. 554–5 and 695–8; *Nianpu*, 1, p. 116. *Trojan Horse strategy*: Saich, *Origins*, 2, pp. 679 and 695. The Guomindang at that time had no organisation outside the south. The Hunan GMD network Mao built was so strongly pro-CCP that a later GMD historian spoke of its existence as a 'communist plot' (McDonald, p. 138).

143   *Mao went secretly to Changsha*: *Nianpu*, 1, p. 118. *Hunan was once again . . . in Zhao's hands*: McDonald, pp. 53–8. *Opéra-bouffe war . . . long knife to behead them*: Hobart, *City of the Long Sand*, pp. 237–8. *The villages were subjected*: McDonald, p. 58. *Mao still thought*: Schram, 2, pp. 192–4 (Sept. 28 1923).

144   *The liberal elite . . . Students Union banned*: McDonald, pp. 58–9.
Inventory of Zhao's crimes: Schram, 2, pp. 183–5 (Aug. 15 1923). *Mao Shishan*: Ibid., p. 194.
Mao and the Socialist Youth League leader . . . total secrecy: Mao informed the GMD's General Affairs Department that he and Xia Xi had begun discussing how to establish a provincial Party organisation at the end of September, and that a secret preparatory organ for the Changsha branch would be created 'within the next few days' (Schram, 2, p. 193, Sept. 28 1923; see also Saich, *Rise to Power*, p. 85). According to the *Nianpu*, the Anyuan, Changsha and Ningxiang branches were founded between mid-September and December, 1923.
Thirtieth birthday: The CPC CC's Directive no. 13, announcing that the GMD Congress would be held in January, was dated December 25. It is not known on what day Mao left Changsha, but he set out from Shanghai for Canton on January 2 1924 (*Nianpu*, 1, pp. 119–20). *Love-poem*: Schram, 2, pp. 195–6 (Dec. 1923).

145   *Undergone a transformation*: Wilbur and How, pp. 87–92; Holybnychy, Lydia, *Michael Borodin and the Chinese Revolution, 1923–25*, Columbia University Press, New York, 1979, pp. 212–19; Cadart and Cheng, p. 335 (treated royally) and p. 340 (Counsellor Bao).

146   *Mao had arrived via Shanghai*: *Nianpu*, 1, p. 121; McDonald, p. 137. According to Wilbur and How (p. 97) and other sources, provincial delegations in general comprised three members named by Sun and three members elected from the local branches. The Hunan delegation was apparently larger because it included men like Lin Boqu, who was already working in Canton as deputy head of the Guomindang's General Affairs Department (Lo Jialun et al. [compilers], *Geming wenxian*, vol. 8, Taibei, 1953, pp. 1100–3).
The congress approved: Wilbur and How, pp. 93 and 97–9. *Wang Jingwei . . . commented*: Zhang Guotao, 1, p. 332. *New GMD Central Executive Committee*: Ibid., p. 100.

147   *Mao moved back to Shanghai*: *Nianpu*, 1, pp. 118 and 123. *Customs Declaration Office*: Luo Zhanglong, 'Zhongguo gongchandang disanci quangguo daibiao dagui he diyici guogong hezuo', pt 2, in *Dangshi ziliao*, no. 17, 1983, p. 14. *Guomindang Shanghai Executive Committee*: *Nianpu*, 1, pp. 122–3. This body had five full members, led by Wang Jingwei and Hu Hanmin, and five alternates including Mao and Qu Qiubai. *French concession*: Cadart and Cheng, p. 374; Peng Shuzhi, in Evans, Les, and Block, Russell (eds), *Leon Trotsky on China*, Monad Press, New York, 1976, p. 44.
Voitinsky: Voitinsky returned to China in April 1924 and attended the CCP plenum in Shanghai a month later (Glunin, V. I., 'The Comintern and the Rise of the Communist Movement in China', in

Ulyanovsky, R.A., The Comintern and the East: *The Struggle for the Leninist Strategy in National Liberation Movements*, Progress Publishers, Moscow, 1981, p. 267).
Friction between the two parties intensified: Wilbur and How, pp. 100–5; Zhang Guotao, 1, pp. 338–45. *Mao, Cai Hesen and Chen Duxiu*: Wilbur and How, p. 105.

147n *Disproportionately well represented*: Glunin, V. I., 'Politika Kominterna v Kitae', in Ulyanovsky, R. A. (ed.), *Komintern I Vostok: Kritika Kritiki – Protiv Falsifikatsii Leninskoi Strategii i Taktiki v Natsionalnovo-osvoboditelnovo Dvizhenii*, Glavnaya Redaktsiya Vostochnoi Literaturi, Moscow, 1978, p. 243.

148 *Secret Central Committee circular*: Schram, 2, pp. 215–17 (July 21 1924). *Pithy Chinese folk-saying*: Cadart and Cheng, p. 373.

149 *Morose and apathetic*: Ibid., pp. 374 and 381. *Money stopped arriving*: Nianpu, 1, p. 130.
Neurasthenia: See Schram, 2, p. 214 (May 26 1924), where Mao speaks of his 'mental ailment growing worse'. The *Nianpu* (1, p. 134) quotes a passage from the (apparently unpublished) diary of He Erkang on July 12 1925: 'After the [GMD branch] meeting ended at 1.15 a.m., Mao wanted to return home to rest. But he said he was suffering from neurasthenia . . . and he knew he wouldn't be able to sleep. The moon was already high. So we walked two or three li, then we were tired and stopped, and went to [the nearby village of] Tangjiawan to rest.' He suffered a relapse in September (ibid., p. 137). See also Li Zhisui's description of Mao's symptoms in *Private Life*, pp. 109–10.
Relations with the rest of the CCP leadership: The best evidence for this is Mao's exclusion from the leadership at the Fourth Congress the following January. Zhang Guotao and Qu Qiubai, who were also away when the Congress was held, were both elected to the CC and the Central Bureau in absentia.
Fourth Congress . . . was postponed: Van de Ven, pp. 143–4. For Mao's organising role, see *Nianpu*, 1, pp. 128–9. *Towards the end of December*: Nianpu, 1, p. 130. Yang Kaihui had joined him in Shanghai at the beginning of June (ibid., p. 127). *Mao's neurasthenia was always political*: Li Zhisui, p. 110.

150 *Mao celebrated . . . family and fellow villagers*: Nianpu, 1, pp. 131–2. *When Lenin*: Lenin, V. I., *Collected Works*, Progress Publishers, Moscow, 1966, 31, pp. 241. *Second CCP Congress*: Saich, *Rise to Power*, pp. 40–3. *A friendly army*: Ibid., p. 59. *Party's thinking had evolved*: Ibid., p. 77.

151 *Peng Pai*: Galbiati, Fernando, *Peng Pai and the Hailufeng Soviet*, Stanford University Press, 1985, pp. 44–151. *Peng was not yet a Party member*: Zhou Enlai wrote, in a memorial article for Peng, that he

had engaged in peasant work 'before entering the Party', which he joined 'in 1924' (Yi Yuan [pseud: Zhou Enlai], Peng Pai tongzhi zhuanlue', in *Beifang hongqi*, no. 29, August 1930).

Did not even get a mention: Zhang Guotao, 1, p. 309. On July 15 1923, Sneevliet referred to Guangdong merely as one of four provinces (with Hunan, Shandong and Zhejiang) 'where there are comrades who have contact with the peasant population' (Saich, *Origins*, 2, p. 656): clearly he had no inkling of what Peng Pai had achieved.

That spring he had sent: *Nianpu*, 1, p. 112. **Zhang Guotao remembered**: Zhang Guotao, 1, pp. 308–9. Zhang's recollection (which is reproduced without comment in the *Nianpu*, 1, p. 114) reads too pat. But, given their mutual antagonism, it is hard to see why he should give Mao credit for raising the peasant issue at the Congress unless it were true. **Chen Duxiu . . . local tyrants**: Saich, *Origins*, 1, p. 184; *Zhonggong zhongyang wenjuan xuanji* [ZZWX], 1, Beijing, 1992, p. 151. **National Revolution in China**: Kara-Murza, G. S. and Mif, Pavel, *Strategiia i taktika Kominterna v Natsionalno-kolonialnoi Revolyutsii na primere Kitaia*, Moscow, 1934, pp. 114–16, 344.

151n **Yuebei**: McDonald, pp. 218–24; Li Rui, pp. 279–81. The Hunan CCP provincial committee was aware of the movement, but reported in November that it was 'unable to send capable people to supervise it' because the war had disrupted river and road transport (Saich, *Rise to Power*, p. 89).

152 **Party workers . . . do not like the rural areas**: Galbiati, p. 115. **So lacking in energy . . . politics and current events**: *Nianpu*, 1, pp. 131–2. The first peasant association in Shaoshan was formed in February 1925 (*Hunan lishi ziliao*, no. 3, Changsha, 1958, pp. 1–10). On Mao Fuxuan, see Li Rui, p. 283.

Unit of British-officered settlement police: This account of the May 30th Incident is taken from Wilbur, C. Martin, 'The Nationalist revolution: from Canton to Nanking, 1923–28', in the *Cambridge History of China* [hereafter CHOC], vol. 12, Cambridge, pp. 547–9. See also McDonald, pp. 206–8; Chesneaux, pp. 262–80.

153 **When the news reached Changsha . . . their home districts**: McDonald, pp. 209–10.

154 **In mid-June . . . and at a fair price**: *Nianpu*, 1, pp. 132–5. The drought was clearly the crucial trigger for peasant involvement (see Chesneaux, p. 278, and McDonald, pp. 210 and 231). **First such movement**: Jin Chongji, *Mao Zedong zhuan*, Zhongyang wenxian chubanshe, Beijing, 1996, p. 123. **Twenty peasant associations**: Snow, p. 186; *Nianpu*, 1, p. 132. **Word of Mao's activities . . . closed sedan chair**: *Nianpu*, 1, p. 135.

155 *In a poem*: Schram, 2, pp. 225–6. It was evidently written between
Mao's arrival in Changsha on August 29 or 30 and his departure for
Canton ten days later. *Chinese politics*: See Wilbur, CHOC, 12,
pp. 547–53 and 556–7.

156 *As he conferred with Xia Xi*: *Nianpu*, 1, p. 136. *They taught Sun Yat-
sen's Three Principles*: Ibid., p. 132. *More to helping the
Guomindang*: Ibid., pp. 33–5. *I believe in Communism*: Schram, 2,
p. 237 (Nov. 21 1925).

157 *Peasant Department*: This was set up at the First Party Congress in
January 1924. The Peasant Movement Training Institute followed in
July 1924 with Peng Pai as its first Principal. *Mao slipped out of
Changsha*: *Nianpu*, 1, p. 136. *Burning all his notes . . . in
hospital*: Ibid., p. 137. *Air of great optimism*: Snow, p. 186. *Head
of the GMD Propaganda Department*: *Nianpu*, 1, p. 137. *Western
Hills Group*: Wilbur, CHOC, 12, pp. 556–9. *Convictions are
wavering . . . no neutral ground*: Schram., 2, pp. 263–7 (Dec. 4 1925).
This statement, drafted by Mao on November 27, was approved by
the GMD CEC, and issued to 'all comrades throughout the country
and overseas' as the party's response to the Western Hills Group
meeting.

158 *Joint rule of 'all revolutionary forces'*: Ibid., 2, p. 237 (Nov. 21 1925)
and pp. 321 and 325 (Jan. 10 1926). *Grey mask of neutrality*: Ibid.,
2, p. 295 (Dec. 20 1925). See also pp. 290–2 (Dec. 13 1925) and
pp. 326–7 (Jan. 10 1926). *Analysis of all the Classes*: Ibid., 2,
pp. 249–62 (Dec. 1 1925).

159 *By the end of 1925, Chiang Kai-shek*: Ibid., pp. 553–7. *Lurch to the
left*: Ibid., p. 559. *Resolution on Propaganda*: Ibid., pp. 342–4 (Jan.
16 1926).

160 *Notion that the peasant movement*: The 'Resolution on the Peasant
Movement' declared that the national revolution was, 'to put it
bluntly, a peasant revolution' (ibid., pp. 358–60, Jan. 19 1926).
Unnerving: Chiang himself, like Tan Yankai, welcomed the
peasant movement as a component of the national revolution,
but no more (see Wilbur and How, p. 797). Borodin acknowledged
in February 1926 that there would be tremendous difficulty in
persuading the Guomindang to support an agrarian revolution (i.e.,
a social revolution in the countryside), and that to do so it might be
necessary to split the party and drive out the conservatives (ibid.,
p. 216).
Suddenly under pressure . . . battle lines were drawn: Ibid., pp. 248–9
and 250–2. *Neatly summed up*: Vishnyakova-Akimova, Vera V., *Dva
Goda v Vosstavshem Kitae*, Moscow, Izdatelstvo Nauka, 1965, p. 190.
In the early hours of March 20: Ibid., pp. 237–8; Wilbur and How,
pp. 252–7 and 703–5; Zhang Guotao, 1, p. 495; Isaacs, Harold, *The*

Tragedy of the Chinese Revolution, Stanford University Press, 1961, pp. 91–4.

161 ***Over almost as soon as it began***: Wilbur and How, pp. 254–5. ***Mao disagreed***: *Nianpu*, 1, p. 159. Zhou said later that the coup caught them 'totally unprepared' (Zhou Enlai, *Selected Works*, Foreign Languages Press, Beijing, 1981, p. 179). Zhou was then one of the three leaders of the Canton CCP committee, with Tan Pingshan and the Party Secretary, Chen Yannian (Zhang Guotao, 1, p. 454). ***Chiang's forces were too strong***: This was also the line advanced later by the Party Centre in Shanghai (Saich, *Rise to Power*, pp. 232–3). ***Mao and others complaining***: Zhang Guotao, 1, p. 498.

162 ***Several other key posts***: On December 15 1925, Mao had been named one of seven members of the Council of the GMD Political Study Group, which began work the following February, training party cadres; on February 5 1926, he was appointed to the GMD Peasant Movement Committee; and on March 16, he was named Principal of the Peasant Movement Training Institute (*Nianpu*, 1, pp. 146 and 156–9).
The CCP had been angling for: In May 1924, a CCP CC resolution stated: 'The CP's responsibility is to make the GMD unceasingly propagandise the principles of opposing imperialists and warlords... To achieve this objective, we must in practice be able to join the GMD Propaganda Department' ('Resolution concerning the problem of CP work in the GMD', in Saich, *Rise to Power*, p. 120).
No contact with the Party Centre: Neither the *Nianpu* (1, pp. 130–8) nor Mao's semi-official biographer, Jin Chongji (pp. 91–106) mentions any contact. Nor technically would there have been any reason for it, since he had held no leadership post since December 1924.
Ideology that has been produced... social basis: Schram, 2, pp. 340–1 (Jan. 16 1926). ***Xiangdao***: Chen Duxiu's protégé, Peng Shuzhi, was editor. He was notorious for his dry scholasticism, and it may well have been Peng that Mao had in mind when he wrote in January: 'Academic thought... is worthless dross.' ***Chen Duxiu refused***: Snow, pp. 186–7. ***Internecine squabbles***: Zhang Guotao, 1, pp. 484–93.

163 ***Mao deliberately kept in the background***: Ibid., p. 510. See also Evans and Block, pp. 53–4, and *Nianpu*, 1, p. 164, neither of which refer to Mao playing any part in the discussions.
After a month of acrimonious... Northern Expedition: See Wilbur and How, pp. 267–73 and 717–19, Zhang Guotao, pp. 507–19. The plenum also proposed the establishment of a Joint Conference, comprising five leaders of the GMD, three from the CCP and a representative of the Comintern (Borodin), to resolve future inter-party disputes. Tan Pingshan, Qu Qiubai and Zhang Guotao were

named from the communist side, but no meeting was ever held (Zhang Guotao, 1, p. 521).

Chen Duxiu proposed: Evans and Block, pp. 54–5. *Stalin insisted*: Ibid., pp. 53–5. See also Zhang Guotao, 1, pp. 517–19. *Borodin's sardonic phrase*: Zhang Guotao, 1, p. 519; Chen Duxiu, in Evans and Block, p. 601.

164 *On May 28*: *Nianpu*, 1, pp. 164–5. He also relinquished his membership of the Political Study Group Council; and of the Propaganda Committee under the GMD Propaganda Department, to which he had been appointed on April 27 (ibid., pp. 162 and 165).

But he retained: Ibid., pp. 159, 163 and 165. The *Nianpu* states that Mao 'and other CCP members' were removed from the GMD Propaganda Committee on May 28, but makes no reference to his leaving the Peasant Movement Committee. In March 1927, when the committee was re-established in Wuhan, Mao became a Standing Committee member (ibid., 1, p. 183).

Chiang's recognition: A senior Soviet adviser noted: 'Those Guomindang members who reputedly belong to the centre or even to the right . . . [in some cases] meditate deeply on the solution of the agrarian problem. As an instance, General Chiang Kai-shek may be quoted' (Wilbur and How, p. 797).

He had given lectures: *Nianpu*, 1, pp. 147–8, 157 and 161. *Russian advisers were adamant*: Wilbur and How, pp. 216–17. *Mao shared that view*: Schram, 2, p. 370 (March 30 1926). *July 9 1926*: Wilbur and How, p. 312. *To take advantage of events in Hunan*: McDonald, pp. 232–6. *Hunan was in southern hands . . . installed himself in Changsha*: Wilbur and How, pp. 311–14.

165 *Mao . . . went to the parade ground*: *Nianpu*, 1, p. 166. Apart from the GMD CEC plenum which preceded it, this was the only 'political' event Mao attended for four-and-a-half months, from May 31 to October 15. *Instead he immersed himself*: *Nianpu*, 1, pp. 165–9. *Playing a significant part*: Angus McDonald gives a carefully balanced account of peasant support for the Northern Expedition in Hunan and concludes that, while fragmentary, it gave the military campaign significant political legitimacy (pp. 264–79). *He sent fifty students*: *Nianpu*, 1, p. 167. *A month later, he published . . . root and branch*: Schram, 2, pp. 287–92 (Sept. 1 1926).

166 *Central problem of the national revolution*: Ibid., p. 387. *Real foundation*: Ibid., p. 304 (January 1926). *Borodin had seized on*: According to Wilbur and How (p. 216), Borodin wrote that 'the chief bulwark of imperialism in China . . . was the medieval landowning system, and not the warlords'. Mao's phrase had appeared in *Zhongguo nongmin* two or three weeks earlier.

167 *Events moved swiftly, too . . . fell in December*: Ibid., pp. 318–29,

344–5 and 771–6; Wilbur, CHOC, 12, pp. 581–9. *In September, the Canton committee*: ZZWX, 2, pp. 373–6. *Unprincipled congeries*: Saich, *Rise to Power*, pp. 210–13. Borodin and other Russian advisers shared the Canton group's views (Wilbur and How, pp.796–7). *Chen Duxiu found himself yet again*: Saich, *Rise to Power*, pp. 213–28.

Mao's sympathies: See Mao's subsequent criticisms of the GMD-Left's military weakness (ibid., p. 225). All those who worked in Canton, from Borodin down, concluded that the GMD-Left was unreliable: there is no reason to think Mao was an exception. A few weeks later, moreover, he voted with his feet, returning to CCP head-quarters in Shanghai instead of accompanying the GMD-Left to Wuhan.

Despaired at the hypocrisy: Schram, 2, pp. 397–401.

168   *On November 4*: Saich, *Rise to Power*, pp. 213–19.

Qu Qiubai: Qu shared Mao's interest in peasant issues, and in August had lectured at the Peasant Movement Institute (Li, Bernadette [Li Yuning], *A Biography of Chu Chiu-p'ai*, Ph.D. dissertation, Columbia University, New York, 1967, pp. 178–9); he had been sufficiently impressed by Mao's article to make enquiries about it from the GMD Propaganda Department (*Nianpu*, 1, p. 169). In the spring of 1927, Qu again supported Mao against Chen on peasant policy (Li Yuning, p. 194).

A few days later: *Nianpu*, 1, p. 173. *On November 15*: Schram, 2, pp. 411–13. *Mao set out for Wuhan*: *Nianpu*, 1, p. 173. *Storm-clouds gathering . . . might throw at him*: Wilbur and How, pp. 359–62 and 375; Zhang Guotao, 1, pp. 556–62.

169   *The result was the creation*: Wilbur and How, pp. 362–3, 373–5 and 393–4; CHOC, 12, pp. 599–603. *At a CC Plenum*: Saich, *Rise to Power*, pp. 219–28.

170   *Phenomenal growth*: Glunin, in 'Politika Kominterna v Kitae' (p. 243), based on unpublished Comintern archives, says the CCP had 1,500 members in May 1925; 7,500 in January 1926; and 11,000 in May 1926. According to Samuil Naumov's 'Brief History of the CCP', written in November 1926, CCP membership had by then reached 'approximately 30,000' (Wilbur and How, p. 444). By the Fifth Congress in April 1927, the Party claimed nearly 58,000 members. See also Wilbur and How, pp. 810–13 (unit commanders). *Mao put his finger on it*: Saich, *Rise to Power*, p. 225. Although Mao prudently attributed his observation to 'comrades in Gaungdong', it clearly represented his own view (see also *Nianpu*, 1, p. 174). *As the weeks passed*: Wilbur and How, pp. 806–9. *Mao, too, in public . . . allowed some concessions*: Schram, 2, pp. 420–2 (Dec. 20 1926).

171   *Colossal event . . . make the choice quickly*: Ibid., p. 430 (February

1927). *Reality of the peasant movement*: Ibid., p. 425 (Feb. 16 1927).
I called together fact-finding conferences: Ibid., p. 429.

172 *The associations' membership*: Ibid., p. 430. See also McDonald, pp. 270–9.

The main targets . . . having seemed to leap: Schram, 2, pp. 431–55. There were recent precedents in Hunan for the kind of peasant behaviour Mao was describing, albeit on a far smaller scale. After the 1910 rice riots, Governor Chen Chunming reported: 'In Xiangtan, Hengshan, Liling and Ningxiang there have been incidents of poor people occupying rich households and eating the grain, and destroying the rice-mills' (quoted in Esherick, *Reform and Revolution in China*, p. 139).

174 *In January 1926* Schram, 2, p. 309. *Brutal methods*: *Nianpu*, 1, p. 165.

175 *Sharp disagreement . . . summarily executed*: Mao submitted his report on or about February 18. The Hunan Party journal, *Zhanshi*, began serialising the full text on March 5. *Xiangdao* started publishing extracts a week later, on March 12 (*Nianpu*, 1, p. 184). The pamphlet version of the full text, with a preface by Qu Qiubai, appeared in April. Qu and Peng Shuzhi were by this stage openly at war with each other (Li Yuning, p. 183–7 and 194–8); Chen's overriding concern was to appease the GMD-Left so as to keep the united front together. See also Schram, 2, p. 426 (anarchy); and Zhang Guotao (1, pp. 596–613 [blind Red terror]).

New instructions: The theses of the Comintern's Seventh Plenum were adopted in Moscow on December 16 1926 and published in its weekly newspaper, *Inprecorr* (International Press Correspondence), on February 3 1927 (Eudin, Xenia, J., and North, Robert C., *Soviet Russia and the East 1920–27: A Documentary Survey*, Stanford University Press, 1957, pp. 356–64). It is not clear exactly when a copy reached Shanghai. Cai Hesen says it was 'approximately January' ('Istoria Opportunizma v Kommunisticheskoi Partii Kitaia', in *Problemy Kitaia*, Moscow, 1929, no. 1, p. 16), but it may in fact not have been until mid-February, when M. N. Roy and Tan Pingshan, who both attended the plenum, arrived in Canton from Moscow (Zhang Guotao, 1, p. 712, n.17).

Until then the Comintern line: In October 1926, Moscow sent a telegram to the CCP leaders, urging them to restrain the peasant movement at least until Shanghai fell to the Northern Expedition, for fear of antagonising the GMD commanders. On November 30, 1926, Stalin attributed this 'mistaken view' to 'certain people' in the GMD and the CCP. In August 1927, he conceded that it was in fact Moscow's error (Eudin and North, *Soviet Russia and the East*, pp. 293 and 353).

Chinese leaders were unsure how to respond: According to Cai
Hesen, the theses triggered (yet another) angry debate between
himself and Qu Qiubai, on the one hand, and Chen Duxiu, Peng
Shuzhi and the Shanghai CCP Committee Secretary, Luo Yinong,
on the other (*Problemy Kitaia*, 1, pp. 16–18).

176   *If the peasant movement*: Snow, p. 188. *On February 17 ... to hunt
down activists*: Isaacs, pp. 132–3. *The executioners, bearing
broadswords*: *New York Herald Tribune*, Feb. 21 1927. The *North China
Herald* found a silver lining: 'Revolting though the executions have
been,' it noted, 'they have at least had a quieting effect. Agitators ...
have [become] conspicuous by their absence'. *By this time ... to stop
it*: Wilbur and How, pp. 385–8 and 392–6.

177   *The balance tipped ... a genuine coalition*: Ibid., pp. 396–8. *Borodin
(and Moscow)*: Zhang Guotao, 1, p. 576; Eudin and North, *Soviet
Russia and the East*, p. 361. *Mao spoke at length*: *Nianpu*, 1, pp. 187–9;
Schram, *Mao Tse-tung*, p. 98. See also Schram, *Mao's Road*, 2, pp.
467–75 (March 16 1927). *Threw himself into preparations*: *Nianpu*, 1,
pp. 190–6; Schram, 2, pp. 485–503. *Yang Kaihui*: *Nianpu*, 1, p. 181.

178   *Anlong*: Ibid., p. 192. *Wang Jingwei ... CCP–GMD amity*: Isaacs,
p. 165, and Zhang Guotao, 1, p. 587. *The air was thick*: Isaacs,
pp. 128 and 163; Chen Duxiu, in Evans and Block, p. 603; North,
Robert C., and Eudin, Xenia J, *M. N. Roy's Mission to China*,
University of California, Berkeley, 1963, p. 54.
      Fabrications: On Wang's part, this was disingenuous to the extent
that Chiang had already made clear to him, in private talks earlier
that week, that he wanted Borodin removed and the communists
expelled. On the other hand, Chiang appeared to accept Wang's
counter-proposal that these issues be dealt with by a full CEC
plenum, and on April 3 had issued a public statement explicitly
pledging obedience to Wang's leadership (CHOC, 12, pp. 623–4).
      Bukharin wrote ... Stalin said laconically: North, Robert, *Moscow
and Chinese Communists*, Stanford University Press, 1963, p. 96; North
and Eudin, *Roy's Mission to China*, pp. 54–8.

CHAPTER SIX: EVENTS LEADING TO THE HORSE DAY INCIDENT AND ITS BLOODY AFTERMATH

179   *Shortly after 4 a.m.*: *The Times*, London, April 13 1927; Isaacs,
Tragedy of the Chinese Revolution, pp. 175–85. See also Clifford,
Nicholas R., *Spoilt Children of Empire: Westerners in Shanghai and the
Chinese Revolution of the 1920s*, Middlebury College Press, Hanover,
1991, pp. 242–75; and Martin, Brian G., *The Shanghai Green Gang:*

Politics and Organized Crime, 1919–37, University of California Press, Berkeley, 1996, ch. 4, especially pp. 100–7.

180 *Horrible Fight in Zhabei*: NCH, April 16 1927, p. 103.

For an entire month: Or perhaps longer: Harold Isaacs viewed Bai Zhongxi's failure to send troops to aid the Shanghai workers during the first insurrection on February 19 as a deliberate ploy by Chiang to weaken the workers' movement in the city (p. 135). The Indian communist M. N. Roy, then in Canton, took a similar view (North and Eudin, *Roy's Mission to China*, p. 157).

Starting in mid-March: If not earlier: the communist head of the General Labour Union in Ganzhou (Jiangxi), Chen Zanxian, was executed on March 6 on the orders of one of Chiang's subordinates (*Nianpu*, 1, p. 189). See Isaacs, pp. 143–4 and 152–3; Martin, pp. 93–5; Wilbur, CHOC, 12, pp. 625–34; Wilbur and How *Missionaries of Revolution*, pp. 398 and 404–5.

181 *Economic disaster*: Sokolsky, George E., 'The Guomindang', in *China Yearbook*, 1928, Tianjin Press, Tianjin, p. 1349. *Black-gowned gunmen*: *The Times*, London, March 25, 1927. *'Naked body procession' . . . our own beloved America*: Strother, Rev. Edgar E., 'A Bolshevized China – The World's Greatest Peril', North China Daily News and Herald Press, Shanghai, 1927 (11th edn), pp. 4 and 14–15. *A fear psychology*: Sokolsky, p. 1349. *On March 24*: *The Times*, London, March 25 and 29, 1927; Wilbur and How, pp. 400–1. *Question on every foreigner's lips*: NCH, March 12 1927, p. 402. *Chiang Kai-shek stands*: *North China Daily News*, March 28 1927.

182 *In stages*: This is not to suggest an orchestrated campaign. The evidence suggests rather that the Chinese loan, the Powers' authorisation of the Beijing raid, the restrictions on the Soviet consulate; and the Shanghai Municipal Council's decision to allow passage to Du Yuesheng's 'armed labourers' to reach their staging points, were all *separate* consequences of the situation that had been created by early April 1927 (see Clifford, pp. 255–9).

First instalment of a loan: Sokolsky, p. 1360; Isaacs, pp. 151–2. *On April 6 . . . Russian officials*: Wilbur and How, pp. 403–4; *The Times*, London, April 7, 8 and 9, 1927. *Du Yuesheng*: Martin, pp. 101–4.

Taken unaware: Vishnyakova-Akimova, *Dva goda v Kitae*, p. 345. In Shanghai, the CCP District Committee, meeting on April 1, knew that Chiang Kai-shek had paid the Green Gang 600,000 Mexican dollars to make trouble for the labour movement in Jiangxi, and that similar moves were afoot in the city itself. But while its Secretary, Luo Yinong, spoke of an ever more serious conflict 'between revolution and counter-revolution' with Chiang at its centre, he appeared to believe that, for the time being, it could be contained at the political level without developing into armed confrontation (Xu Yufang and Bian Xianying, *Shanghai gongren sanci wuzhuang qiyi yanjiu,* Zhishi chubanshe Shanghai, 1987, pp. 227–8). Subsequently the General Labour Union received warnings that gangsters were planning an attack on the pickets, but clashes with gangs were not unusual, and the GLU apparently did not believe they would be part of a broader clamp-down (*Diyici guonei geming zhanzheng shiqi di gongren yundong,* Renmin chubanshe, Beijing, 1954, pp. 492–3); see also Chesneaux, *Chinese Labour Movement,* pp. 367–71. In Hankou, Borodin's main concern was not Chiang's intentions towards the communists, but the news that he planned to transfer his headquarters to Nanjing. On April 7, the GMD Political Council met in emergency session and resolved (too late for any action to be taken) that the Hankou government should move there first to forestall him. Events in Shanghai were not discussed (Wilbur, CHOC, 12, pp. 632–3). It seems to have been a case of everybody looking the wrong way.

Wang Shouhua: Martin, pp. 104–5; Clifford, p. 253. *As early as January*: Wilbur and How, pp. 806–9. See also Borodin's anxieties in late March (ibid., p. 400).

183 *'Frankly anti-communist' stand*: *North China Daily News,* April 8 1927. *Piecemeal efforts*: In Nanjing, for instance, Zhang Shushi, a communist member of the Jiangsu provincial GMD committee, did not realise that Chiang Kai-shek himself was behind the repression until he was arrested on April 9 and held overnight by GMD security officials (Wilbur, CHOC, 12, p. 633). According to Zhou Enlai, the Shanghai Party leaders first learned that Chiang was responsible for the killings at Jiujiang and Anqing (which occurred on March 17 and 23) only on April 14 (Zhou Enlai, SW1, pp. 18 and 411, n.7), although how this can be reconciled with the Shanghai CCP committee meeting of April 1 (which Zhou himself attended), where they discussed Chiang's financing of Green Gang violence against the Left in Jiangxi, is unclear. Similarly, Roy spoke in mid-April of having 'just received reports that Chiang Kai-shek has sent his agents to Sichuan' (North and Eudin, p. 169), where fierce repression had begun at the end of March (Wilbur, pp. 626–7).

Wedded to the alliance: Pavel Mif, who became Comintern representative in China in 1930, wrote later: 'The Shanghai comrades were hypnotised by the old line, and could not imagine a revolutionary government without the participation of the bourgeoisie' (*Kitaiskiya Revolutsiya,* Moscow, 1932, p. 98). As Harold Isaacs noted, Mif tactfully omitted to mention that the 'old line' had been laid down by Stalin (p. 170).

In Hankou, on April 12: *Nianpu,* 1, p. 193. *He and Qu Qiubai*: Ibid., p. 192. *Chen Duxiu was on his way*: Kuo, Thomas C., *Ch'en Tu-hsiu (1879–1942) and the Chinese Communist Movement,* Seton Hall

University Press, South Orange, 1975, p. 161. *For the next six days*:
See North and Eudin, M. N. Roy's Mission to China, pp. 160–82.
According to this source, Roy, Borodin, Chen Duxiu and 'others'
spoke between April 13 and 15, and on April 16, the CC passed a
resolution based on Roy's speech. It was annulled, however, on April
18, and a new resolution passed on April 20.

Borodin, supported by Chen Duxiu: No text of Borodin's speech is
available, but its tenor is evident from Roy's rejoinder (North and
Eudin, esp. pp. 160, 163 and 172). A few days later, Borodin told
Guomindang leaders there was 'no choice but to make a temporary,
strategic retreat' by damping down the revolutionary movement
both among the peasants in Hubei and Hunan and among the
workers in Wuhan (Li, Dun J., *The Road to Communism: China since
1912*, Van Norstrand, New York, 1969, pp. 89–91). For a retrospec-
tive account, see Fischer, Louis, *The Soviets in World Affairs: A History
of the Relations between the Soviet Union and the Rest of the World*,
Jonathan Cape, London, 1930, vol. 2, pp. 673–7.

Roy held that this: North and Eudin, pp. 163–72.

184 *A telegram arrived*: History of the CCP, Chronology, p. 46; Zhou Enlai,
SW1, pp. 18–19. *Qu Qiubai . . . old base in Guangdong*: North and
Eudin, pp. 63 and 170. *The Bureau eventually endorsed*: Ibid.,
pp. 176–7.

Next day Wang Jingwei: Wilbur, CHOC, 12, p. 639. The Wuhan
government had decided on April 12 (before the news of Chiang's
coup arrived) to press for a resumption of the Northern Expedition.
This decision was publicly reiterated with much fanfare on April 19.
If Roy's dating of the CPC CC resolutions is correct, it must have
been confirmed by the Left-GMD leadership on April 17 (North and
Eudin, p. 75).

Mao did not attend: The *Nianpu* (1, p. 193) states that Mao took part
in a three-day meeting of the CPC Peasant Committee 'in the second
10 days of April', but otherwise lists no activities by him from April
13–17.

He spent that month . . . landowning families: Accounts of these
important but ultimately irrelevant negotiations may be found in
Schram, *Mao Tse-tung*, pp. 99–102, Wilbur, CHOC, 12, pp. 648–9;
and *Nianpu*, 1, pp. 191–9. See also Schram, *Mao's Road*, 2, pp. 487–91
and 494–503. Three regular meetings, six enlarged meetings and four
sub-committee meetings were held between April 2 and May 9 1927.

185 *Mao's efforts in his own Party*: Snow, *Red Star over China*, p. 188;
Nianpu, 1, pp. 197–8. In his report to the Fifth Congress, Chen criticised Mao and Li Lisan by name (Saich, *Rise to Power*, p. 241). For
the background to Mao's draft resolution, see Carr, Edward Hallett,

A History of Soviet Russia: Foundations of a Planned Economy, 1926–1929, vol. 3 pt 3, Cambridge University Press, 1978, p. 788.

Lip service: Saich, pp. 243–51. **Very dissatisfied**: Snow, p. 188. **Mao scraped in**: *History of the CCP, Chronology. Zhongguo gongchandang huiyi gaiyao* (Shenyang chubanshe, Shenyang, 1991, pp. 54–60) gives slightly different figures.

A week later: *Nianpu*, 1, p. 199. Conrad Brandt (*Stalin's Failure in China*, Harvard University Press, 1958, p. 128) identifies Qu Qiubai as Mao's successor. Peng Pai, who had joined Mao at the Fifth Congress in opposing Chen Duxiu's agrarian policy, also left the committee at this time (*Nianpu*, ibid., and Galbiati, *Peng Pai and the Hailufeng Soviet*, p. 258).

All-China Peasants' Association: Schram, 2, pp. 504–17. For Mao's role in the association, see ibid., pp. 485–6. **In Canton . . . Zhang Zuolin**: Wilbur, CHOC, 12, pp. 630 and 636–8. **Even more serious . . . hold down prices**: Ibid., pp. 637 and 640–1; *The Times*, London, March 30 1927; and Kuo, p. 161.

186 **At Borodin's insistence**: Wilbur, CHOC, 12, pp. 641–3.

Tang Shengzhi's forces . . . Wuhan's defences: Ibid., pp. 651–2. Chiang's forces, under Li Zongren and Bai Zhongxi, separately resumed their Northern Expedition at about the same time. Each side announced that it would not attack the other while the conflict against the northerners was under way.

General Xia Douyin . . . men were routed: Ibid., pp. 652–3; Zhang Guotao, *Rise of the Chinese Communist Party*, 1, pp. 627–32. **In Changsha, wild rumours . . . communist demonstrators**: McDonald, *Urban Origins*, pp. 314–15 (also pp. 290–9 and 304); Wilbur, CHOC, 12, pp. 638 and 653–4; Li Rui, *Early Revolutionary Activities*, pp. 313–17.

187 **Xu Kexiang decided**: Xu Kexiang, 'The Ma-jih [Horse Day] Incident', in Dun Li, *Road to Communism*, pp. 91–5. **Got wind of**: Liu Zhixun, 'Ma ri shibian di huiyi' [Recollections of the Horse Day Incident], in *Diyici guonei geming zhanzheng shiqi di nongmin yundong*, Renmin chubanshe, Beijing, 1952, pp. 81–4 (partial translation in Li Rui, pp. 315–16). **3,000 workers' pickets**: Xu Kexiang, pp. 93–4. Xu himself, according to Zhang Guotao, had only about 1,000 rifles (1, p. 615).

No contingency plans . . . places of safety: Liu Zhixun claimed that there was 'a plan for a counter-attack', but it was too vague to be of any practical use. 'We knew the coup was coming . . . [but] the Communist Party of that time . . . had no experience in struggle . . . Thus when the coup broke, we were disorganised and confused, and all our plans failed' ('Ma ri shibian di huiyi', p. 383; see also Zhonggong Hunan shengwei xuanchuanbu, *Hunan geming lieshi zhuan*, Tongsu duwu chubanshe, Changsha, 1952, p. 96).

Shooting began at 11 p.m.: Xu Kexiang, p. 94. **Flames lighted the**

heavens: *Hunan geming lieshi zhuan*, p. 96 (translated in McDonald, p. 315). ***Xu Kexiang boasted later***: Xu Kexiang, p. 94.

10,000 people: McDonald, p. 316. Isaacs reports 20,000 dead 'in the course of the next few months' (p. 236). Both figures are consistent with available primary accounts. Mao reports 'well over 10,000' deaths in Hubei, Hunan and Jiangxi by June 13, with some supporting figures for individual counties (Schram, 2, p. 516). See also *Minguo ribao*, Hankou, June 12 1927 (quoted in Isaacs, pp. 225–6). ***Groups of suspected communists***: Isaacs, pp. 235–6.

Others died: Liu Zhixun, 'Ma ri shibian di huiyi'; Wilbur, pp. 656–7. The order to call off the attack was given by Li Weihan, who had succeeded Mao as Hunan Party Secretary in April 1923, and held the post until the end of May 1927 (Brandt, Conrad, Schwartz, Benjamin and Fairbank, J. K., *A Documentary History of Chinese Communism*, Harvard University Press, 1952, pp. 112–13). See also Zhang Guotao, 1, p. 636. ***Repression spread into Hubei***: Wilbur quotes a report in GMD archives as estimating that 'four to five thousand persons were killed and many villages devastated' by Xia's troops in Hubei (p. 654, n.220). See also Isaacs, pp. 225–7. In Jiangxi, the death-toll was lower (Wilbur, pp. 660–1; see also Schram, 2, pp. 514–17).

188 ***In Hunan they beheaded***: Schram, 2, pp. 514–17 (June 13 1927). ***80,000 people . . . nearly 300,000 perished***: McDonald, p. 316. ***From this bloody lesson***: Zhang Guotao, 1, p. 615. Wang Jingwei's adviser, T'ang Leang-li [Tang Liangli], also saw the Horse Day Incident as the moment of realisation 'that the time had arrived for the Guomindang and the Communist Party to separate' (*The Inner History of the Chinese Revolution*, E. P. Dutton, New York, 1930, p. 279). ***Concluding for the umpteenth time***: Wilbur, CHOC, 12, p. 655; North and Eudin, *Roy's Mission to China*, pp. 100–6 and 293–304; ZZWX, 3, pp. 138–41. See also Roy, M. N., *Revolution and Counter-Revolution in China*, Renaissance Publishers, Calcutta, 1946, p. 615. ***May 25***: ZZWX, 3, pp. 136–7. ***Borodin set out for Changsha***: North and Eudin, p. 104; Wilbur, p. 655. ***Mao, on behalf of***: North and Eudin, p. 103. Mao was then responsible for drafting most of the association's directives. How, and to whom, he sent it is unclear, since both the provincial peasants association and the provincial labour union had been suppressed.

189 ***It was turned back***: Ibid., p. 104. ***Central Committee appeal***: Ibid., pp. 314–17 (June 3 1927). ***Mao asked the Politburo . . . rescinded almost at once***: *Nianpu*, 1, p. 201. Mao's appointment was announced on June 7. ***From early June***: Ibid., pp. 201–5. ***Attempted with some success***: Schram, 2, pp. 504–8 (May 30) and pp. 510–13 (June 7 1927). ***Stalin had been locked***: Isaacs, pp. 190–6. Eudin and North, *Soviet Russia and the East*, pp. 301–2. For Trotsky's side of the argument, see Evans and Block, *Trotsky on China*, pp. 443–61. ***On June 1***: *History of*

the CCP, Chronology, p. 49. **Comintern plenum**: North, *Moscow and Chinese Communists*, pp. 100 and 104–5. The resolution it approved on May 30 is translated in Eudin and North, pp. 369–76. **Stalin instructed ... drive them out altogether**: North, pp. 105–6; Eudin and North, pp. 379–80.

190   **Cry or laugh**: Zhang Guotao, 1, pp. 637–8. **Bath in shit**: Evans and Block, p. 606. See also 'Gao chuandang tongzhi shu', Shanghai, 1929. **Borodin and Voitinsky**: Zhang Guotao, 1, p. 638. **Begged for 5,000 rifles**: Evans and Block, p. 601. **Mao and Cai Hesen**: Schram, 2, p. 426; Cai Hesen, *Problemy Kitaia*, 1, p. 39.
   At this juncture ... in Nanjing: Wilbur, CHOC, 12 pp. 661–2; North and Eudin, pp. 110–18; T'ang Leang-li, pp. 280–3; Zhang Guotao, 1, pp. 638–46. Roy's attitude may be inferred from his speech to the Politburo on June 15 1927: 'We must place the Guomindang in a position where it must of necessity give a direct answer. We must force it to give an explicit declaration before the masses as to whether it is prepared to lead the revolution forward or wants to betray it.' (North and Eudin, p. 355).

191   **On June 15**: North and Eudin, pp. 338–40. **As late as May 26**: The Central Committee stated: 'There is a risk of immediate armed conflict with the enemy. This is not desirable for our Party' (ZZWX, 3, p. 138). **Enduring significance**: After Mao's death, it was acknowledged that 'although the Comintern had made a series of errors in its advice to the Chinese revolutionaries, this particular directive correctly addressed the crucial question of the time: how to save the revolution' (Hu Sheng [editor], *A Concise History of the Communist Party of China*, Foreign Languages Press, Beijing, 1994, p. 103).
   Secret Central Committee commission: From June 7, when Mao was first appointed Secretary of the Hunan Committee, to June 24, when the appointment was made for a second time, the CC's policy on 'the Hunan problem' was in flux (*Nianpu*, 1, pp. 203–4). Cai Hesen wrote later that the CC and the Comintern delegates (Borodin and Roy) set up a special commission to plan armed peasant uprisings in Hunan, and that 'a large group of army comrades was sent to Hunan' for this purpose (*Problemy Kitaia*, 1, p. 44). Mao addressed this group in Wuhan in the second ten days of June (*Nianpu*, 1, pp. 203–4). Zhou Enlai, as director of the CC Military Committee, submitted to the Politburo Standing Committee on June 17 'a plan for dealing with the [consequences of] the massacre in Hunan', and Qu Qiubai later confirmed that the CC that month took a 'final decision' for an offensive in Hunan (Qu, 'The Past and Future of the Chinese Communist Party', in *Chinese Studies in History*, 1971, 5, 1, pp. 37–8). When Mao travelled to Hunan a week later, he briefed Party cadres there on the commission's plan (*Nianpu*, ibid.). But the Party Centre then suddenly ordered him to abandon the mission and return

to Wuhan (Snow, p. 189). What had apparently happened was that Tang Shengzhi had issued a statement on June 29, supporting Xu Kexiang (North and Eudin, pp. 120–1), which meant that the planned uprising would be opposed by the GMD-Left's military forces. Borodin had therefore ordered the plan aborted (*Nianpu*, 1, p. 203).

192 ***Began quietly packing to leave***: Wilbur, CHOC, 12, p. 668; Vishnyakova-Akimova, p. 362. ***Feng Yuxiang***: Wilbur, CHOC, 12, pp. 664–5. ***Mood of black pessimism***: Cai Hesen, *Problemy Kitaia*, pp. 56–7. See also Qu Qiubai, pp. 41–2. ***On June 23***: North and Eudin, pp. 361–5; Wilbur, CHOC, 12, pp. 665–6.
The idea of collaboration with the Guomindang: North and Eudin, pp. 366–9. Chen Duxiu claimed later that he twice proposed (apparently in June) that the CCP leave the united front, but that the rest of the Politburo, with the exception of the Youth League leader, Ren Bishi, were against it (Evans and Block, p. 604). Zhang Guotao also claimed to have proposed a break in mid-June, but found the rest of the leadership cautious (1, p. 647).
On June 30: Wilbur, CHOC, 12, p. 667. ***Mao received an urgent summons . . . any possible gains***: *Nianpu*, 1, pp. 203–4; Snow, p. 189. ***On Monday July 4***: *Nianpu*, 1, p. 204; Schram, 3, pp. 5–12.

193 ***General He Jian . . . rapidly to the right***: Wilbur, CHOC, 12, p. 667. ***In Mao's words . . . no decision was taken***: Schram, 3, pp. 8–11. ***In Mao's mind***: According to the *Nianpu*, Mao and Cai discussed these issues at length in the first ten days of July; afterwards Cai wrote to the Politburo, accusing it of paying insufficient attention to military planning (1, p. 205). ***Stalin had not been pleased . . . continued to exist***: *Pravda*, July 10 1927, p. 2; *History of the CCP, Chronology*, p. 50; Wilbur, CHOC, 12, pp. 669–71.

194 ***General He Jian's troops***: Wilbur, pp. 669–70; Isaacs, p. 270. ***Mao and the rest of the Party leadership***: *Nianpu*, 1, p. 206; Zhang Guotao, 1, pp. 656–9. ***Borodin***: Wilbur, pp. 671–2.
Yang Kaihui: It is not known exactly when Yang Kaihui left Wuhan, but it was probably at the end of July. Given Anlong's birth in April and the chaos in Hunan after May 21, it is unlikely that she departed before then. According to the *Nianpu* (1, p. 209), Mao was briefly reunited with her in Changsha in August, when he was organising the Autumn Harvest Uprising, but the months in Wuhan would be the last time they lived together as a family.

CHAPTER SEVEN: OUT OF THE BARREL OF A GUN

195 ***Zhang Guotao remembered . . . imperial edict***: Zhang Guotao, *Rise of the Chinese Communist Party*, 1, pp. 669–72. I have substituted the

word 'spiv' for the anachronistic 'teddy boy' which Zhang's English translator has employed.

Arrogant and insecure young men: They included Meyer, who acted as Soviet consul and Comintern representative in Changsha, and Heinz Neumann, 26, a German who worked for the Youth International (Ristaino, Marcia R., *China's Art of Revolution: The Mobilization of Discontent*, 1927 and 1928, Duke University Press, Durham, NC, 1987, pp. 41 and 103–4). Both shared Lominadze's strongly leftist views.

196   ***Just starting to pull themselves together***: Zhang Guotao, 1, pp. 657–60. ***On July 20***: Schram, *Mao's Road*, 3, pp. 13–19. ***Central Standing Committee***: *Nianpu*, 1, p. 206. This was evidently a follow-on from the aborted Hunan uprising project in which Mao had been involved. ***Nanchang***: See Zhang Guotao, 1, pp. 660–76 and 2, pp. 3–16; Hsiao Tso-liang, *Chinese Communism in 1927, City vs Countryside*, Chinese University of Hong Kong, 1970, pp. 81–90; Ristaino, pp. 21–38; Guillermaz, Jacques, 'The Nanchang Uprising', CQ, 11 (1962), pp. 161–8; and Wilbur, C. Martin, 'The Ashes of Defeat', CQ,18 (1964), pp. 3–54. Initial discussion of the Nanchang Uprising, involving Li Lisan in Jiujiang and Zhou Enlai in Wuhan, was under way by July 20 (if not earlier). ***Delphic double negative***: Quoted by Zhang Guotao in Wilbur, CQ, 18, p. 46.

197   ***New base area***: Schram, 3, p. 25 (Aug. 1 1927). The *Nianpu* says the decision to make Guangdong the final destination was taken by the Standing Committee on July 24 or 25 (1, p. 206). ***Deng Xixian***: Goodman, David S. G., *Deng Xiaoping and the Chinese Revolution*, Routledge, 1994, p. x; and Evans, Richard, *Deng Xiaoping and the Making of Modern China,* Penguin, Harmondsworth, 1995, p. 44. ***Reorganise the Party's forces***: Saich, *Rise to Power*, p. 308.

198   ***Twenty-two CCP members . . . shareholders' meeting***: Ristaino, p. 41. Two foreigners were present: Lominadze, and a 'representative of the Youth International', whom Li Yuning suggests was Chitarov (*Biography of Ch'u Ch'iu-p'ai*, p. 227, n.4). ***Qu was dressed incongruously***: Li Ang, *Hongse wutai*, Chongqing, 1942 [no page number]. 'Li Ang' (a pseudonym for Zhu Xinfan) was a communist renegade. He did not attend the conference. ***Lominadze insisted***: Saich, p. 309. ***Congress . . . within the next six months***: ZZWX, 3, p. 302. ***Centre of gravity . . . had been abandoned***: Saich, pp. 296–313. ***Criminal act***: Ibid, pp. 306–7. ***Solid combative secret organs***: ZZWX, 3, p. 303. ***Circular Letter***: Saich, pp. 296–308.

199   ***Mao was implicitly***: The resolution censured, for example, a directive (ibid., p. 303) which had been drafted by Mao on May 30 1927 for the All-China Peasants' Association (Schram, 2, p. 506). ***The connection***

which Lominadze drew: Brandt et al., *Documentary History*, p. 119. *Capable comrade*: Schram, 3, p. 33 (Aug. 9 1927). *He was rewarded ... CCP Northern Bureau*: *History of the CCP, Chronology*, pp. 52–3.

200 *Sichuan*: That Zhou Enlai was responsible may be inferred from Zhang Guotao's account (1, p. 659) and is consistent with Mao's later blame of Chen Duxiu (Snow, *Red Star over China*, p. 189). In 1936, after all, he could hardly have named Zhou as the culprit. Mao was not a native of Sichuan and had had no experience in that province (see also *Nianpu*, 1, p. 206). Why Zhou should have wished to see him marginalised is unclear.

Good man to have as an ally: See Qu's comment on 28 September 1927: 'We must have Zedong ... If you're looking for someone who is independent-minded in our Party, it's Zedong' (*Nianpu*, 1, p. 221). *Shortly before Lominadze's arrival*: Ibid., p. 206. *His first proposal ... launched to overthrow him*: Schram, 3, pp. 27–8. *On August 3*: Saich, pp. 317–19 (Aug. 3 1927).

Two days later a revised plan was sought ... needed to be reorganised: See ibid., pp. 319–21; *Nianpu*, 1, pp. 207–9; and Schram, 3, pp. 33–4 (Aug. 9 1927). From the fragmentary evidence available, it seems that on August 3, only hours after the Standing Committee issued the new 'Outline ... of the Autumn Harvest Uprising', Mao was told he would not be returning to Hunan after all but should stay in Wuhan (possibly in connection with Qu's subsequent suggestion that he should be assigned to Shanghai). He apparently had no input into the revised proposal drafted by the Hunan committee.

200n *After the August 7 Conference*: Saich, p. 209.

201 *To Mao's credit*: Mao's outspokenness was all the more striking because, as Lominadze hinted (Schram, 3, p. 33) and Peng Gongda later confirmed (Saich, p. 322), Yi Lirong was really being punished for demanding that the Comintern take part of the blame for the 'opportunist errors' of the past. *Trying ... to pick up the pieces*: Schram, 3, pp. 33–4. *Peng Gongda*: Saich, p. 321. *On August 12*: *Nianpu*, 1, p. 209. *A week later, the new reorganised Hunan*: Saich, pp. 322–3. *Nianpu*, 1, pp. 209–10. *On hearing this ... raise the Red flag*: Schram, 3, pp. 39–40 (Aug. 20 1927).

202 *The peasantry associated*: Ibid., and *Nianpu*, 1, p. 210. See also Li Lisan's vitriolic comments on the Nanchang rebels' continued use of 'the flag of the White Terror' (Wilbur, CQ, 18, p. 23). Qu Qiubai later admitted that the initial decision in August to keep the flag had been wrong (*Chinese Studies in History*, 5, 1, p. 53). *Finally approved a month later*: ZZWX, pp. 369–71. See also Stalin's speech to the Comintern of Sept. 27 (Eudin and North, *Soviet Russia and the East*, p. 307). *August 7 Conference had skirted round*: ZZWX, 3, pp. 294–7; and Schram, 3, p. 32 (Aug. 7 1927). *He now put forward*

... minds be set at ease: Schram, 3, p. 35 (Aug. 18) and p. 40 (Aug. 20 1927). *On August 23*: Pak, Hyobom (ed.), *Documents of the Chinese Communist Party*, Union Research Institute, Hong Kong, 1971, pp. 91–5.

203 *We used to censure Sun Yat-sen*: Schram, 3, pp. 30–1 (Aug. 7 1927). *Lominadze himself*: Saich, p. 310. A week earlier, the Standing Committee had approved Mao's proposal that a regiment of regular troops be the core force in the southern Hunan uprising (Schram, 3, p. 28). *Putting the cart before the horse*: Saich, pp. 319–21. For a similar debate over the use of military forces in the Hubei uprisings, see Roy Hofheinz, 'The Autumn Harvest Insurrection', in CQ, 32, 1967, p. 47. *Gun-barrel-ism*: See Qu Qiubai, pp. 21 and 70. *It 'did not quite accord'*: *Nianpu*, 1, p. 212.

204 *'Light the fuse'*: Saich, p. 315. *Local Party officials*: Hofheinz, CQ, 32, p. 48. *In Hunan*: Saich, p. 324. *One or two regiments*: Ibid. and Schram, 3, p. 36 (Aug. 18 1927). *August 22*: *Nianpu*, 1, p. 212. *In his written proposals*: Schram, 3, pp. 37–8 (Aug. 19 1927). *The Standing Committee acknowledged*: *Zhongyang tongxin*, 3, pp. 38–41 (Aug. 30 1927). Differing translations appear in Pak, pp. 91–2, and Hofheinz, p. 65.

205 *He had indeed abandoned*: *Nianpu*, 1, p. 213. See also Saich, p. 504, n.90. *Reluctantly to the Centre's will*: Hofheinz, pp. 49–57. *Bolstering the courage*: *Nianpu*, 1, p. 213. *With regard to the two mistakes*: Schram, 3, pp. 41–2 (Aug. 30 1927).

207 *Angry counterblast ... a few days earlier*: Pak, pp. 99–101.
Even more elaborate programme: Ibid., pp. 60–6; Hofheinz, pp. 37–87. An almost complete Chinese text is in *Zhongyang tongxin*, 11 (December 1927). In Hunan, four centres were specified: Changsha, Hengyang, Changde in the west and Baoqing in the south-west. Hofheinz mistakenly dates Qu Qiubai's plan to the beginning of August, which invalidates much of his chronology. See also Hsiao Tso-liang, pp. 44–80, and Ristaino, pp. 56–74.
He simply ignored it: *Nianpu*, 1, p. 213; Saich, p. 504, n.90. *He left for Anyuan*: *Nianpu*, 1, p. 214. *These comprised ... Peasants' Revolutionary Army*: Ibid., p. 215; Hofheinz, pp. 67–70. *By September 8 ... fifty miles north-east of the capital*: *Nianpu*, 1, p. 216; Hofheinz, pp. 71–2.

208 *The Guomindang terror ... in my pocket*: Snow, p. 193. *The 1st regiment marched ... remotely threatened*: *Nianpu*, 1, pp. 217–18; Hsiao Tso-liang, pp. 67–77; and Hofheinz, pp. 72–9.

209 *For three days, they argued*: *Nianpu*, 1, pp. 218–9. *Early in August*: Schram, 3, p. 34 (Aug. 9 1927). *On September 19 ... heading south*: *Nianpu*, 1, pp. 219–20. See also He Changgong, 'The deeds of Jinggangshan will be remembered for thousands of years', BBC Summary of World Broadcasts, June 18 1981, FE/6752/BII/1. *In*

Hubei: Hofheinz, pp. 51–60. **13,000 of its 21,000 men . . . very juvenile**: Wilbur, CQ, 18, pp. 33–4; Ristaino, p. 35.

210   **Two small military units**: Ristaino, pp. 127–9. **Politburo met in Shanghai . . . motley troops**: Saich, pp. 331–41; ZZWX, 3, pp. 478–84.
At Lominadze's insistence: See Zhou Enlai, SW1, p. 194. **Mao was dismissed . . . expelled from the Party**: ZZWX, 3, pp. 482–4.
Another round of . . . ordered to close: Ristaino, pp. 97–108; Hsiao Tso-Liang, pp. 135–48; Wilbur, 'The Nationalist Revolution', CHOC, 12, pp. 692–5; Isaacs, *Tragedy of the Chinese Revolution*, pp. 282–91; and North, *Moscow and Chinese Communists*, p. 120. *History of the CCP, Chronology*, lists some twenty-five uprisings, almost all of them short-lived, between November 1927 and June 1928 (pp. 56–9).

211   **10,000 by December**: *History of the CCP, Chronology*, p. 56. **Isolated communist hold-outs**: Ibid., pp. 56–9, and Ristaino, pp. 126–39.

211   **For the next three years . . . the Congress proceedings**: No texts of Mao's
 /   speeches or writings between September 1927 and April 1928 have
224   survived. This section is therefore drawn largely from the *Nianpu* (1, pp. 220–44) – which itself is based on oral accounts given to a CCP CC Commission which visited the Jiangxi base areas in 1951 (Grigoriev, A. M., *Revolyutsionnoe Dvizhenie, v Kitae v 1927–1931/gg*, Izdatelstvo Nauka, Moscow, 1980, p. 62), on later researches by Party historians, and on memoir material; from my own visits to the area in 1979/80 and 1997; and from four major monographs on the period: Gui Yulin, *Jinggangshan geming douzheng shi* (History of the Revolutionary Struggles on Jinggangshan), Jiefangjun chubanshe, Beijing, 1986; *Jinggangshande wuzhuang geju* (The Armed Independent Regime on Jinggangshan), Jiangxi renmin chubanshe, Nanchang, 1979; *Jinggangshan geming genjudi shiliao xuanbian* (Selected Historical Materials on the Jinggangshan Revolutionary Base Area), Jiangxi renmin chubanshe, Nanchang, 1986; and *Jinggangshan geming genjudi* (The Jinggangshan Revolutionary Base Area), vols 1 and 2, Zhonggong dangshi ziliao chubanshe, Beijing, 1987. One of the few recent accounts in English is contained in the introduction to Stuart Schram's *Mao's Road to Power* (3, pp. xxiv–xxix).

211   **Political commissars**: Schram, 3, p. 59. Mao's letter referring to political commissars was probably written early in June, not in August 1928.

213   **Just under 2,000**: Ibid., p. 102 (Nov. 25 1928).

215   **The technique proved so effective**: Schram, 3, p. 119 (Nov. 25 1928).
Qu Qiubai, who recognised and admired: Qu told a Jiangxi Party official on February 17 1928 that the development of the revolution in south-western Jiangxi would have a 'very important' knock-on effect in Hunan, so 'should Mao, then, be [Party] secretary in south-

western Jiangxi?' (*Nianpu*, 1, p. 234). In the end, nothing came of this proposal, but it showed the way Qu was thinking.

216   ***Bandit character***: Carr, *Foundations of a Planned Economy*, 3, pt 3, p. 867 (quoting *Stenograficheskii Otchet VI Siezda KPK*, vol. V, Moscow, 1930, pp. 12–13.) ***Such leaders do not trust***: Schram, 3, p. xxvi; ZZWX, 4, pp. 56–66. ***Another CC directive***: *Nianpu*, 1, p. 229 (31 Dec. 1927).

216n   ***In January 1928 . . . operated sporadically***: Ibid., ZZWX, 4, pp. 71–5; and Grigoriev, *Revolyutsionnoe Dvizhenie*, p. 71. ***Injustice of the rebuke***: Schram, 3, p. 52 (May 2 1928).

217   ***Front Committee was abolished***: Ibid., p. 84.

       In December . . . Leiyang, further north: History of the CCP, *Chronology*, p. 58. Agnes Smedley's account (*The Great Road*, Monthly Review Press, New York, 1956, pp. 212–25) conveys vividly the reality of the struggle but makes the Party's efforts seem far better organised than they actually were. Contemporary documents show that most of the time the Party leaders in Shanghai did not know even in which province Zhu's forces were operating (Pak, pp. 183–94).

219   ***Strange, brooding mind . . . military organiser***: Smedley, p. 226. ***In height he was***: Ibid., p. 2. ***Yet Zhu's life . . . 'Ironsides'***: Ibid., pp. 9–186. See also Jin Chongji, *Zhu De zhuan*, Zhongyang wenxian chubanshe, Beijing, 1993.

       He learned from Zhu . . . himself as Secretary: Zhu brought with him a copy of the November plenum's resolution (Schram, 3, pp. 83–4). See also ibid., pp. 52 and 54, and *Nianpu*, 1, pp. 236, 238 and 240.

220   ***Clan Hall of the Xie***: He Changgong, FE/6752/BII/1.

       The prolonged existence . . . in a single area: The text of Mao's speech at the 1st Border Area Party Congress has never been published (and may have been lost). He dealt with the same theme twice later in the year, on both occasions in very similar terms. This extract is from the resolution he drafted for the Second Congress on October 5 1928 (Schram, 3, p. 65).

221   ***Old Deaf Ju***: *Nianpu*, 1, p. 229. See also Smedley, pp. 232–3.

222   ***When the enemy advances***: According to the *Nianpu*, Mao put forward a twelve-character formula – 'When the enemy advances, we withdraw; enemy rests, we harass; enemy withdraws, we attack' – in mid-January 1928 (1, p. 232). The full sixteen-character version appeared in May that year. See also Schram, 3, p. 155.

       Concentrate the Red Army . . . rash advance: Schram, 3, p. 85 (Nov. 25 1928).

       Six Main Points: Mao began to formulate these rules in October 1927 (*Nianpu*, 1, pp. 222 and 226). The first formal version of the 'Six Points' appeared on January 25 1928 (ibid., p. 233). It was modified on April 3 (ibid., p. 238), to avoid overlap with the 'Three Rules'. The orthodox rendering of the 'Eight Points' is given in SW4, pp. 155–6.

Even on Jinggangshan: Schram, 3, p. 93 (Nov. 25 1928).

223 *For the same reason*: *Nianpu*, 1, p. 231. See also Schram, 3, pp. 104 and 115 (Nov. 25 1928). *In order to kill people*: Schram, 3, p. 173 (June 1 1929). *Too right-wing*: *Nianpu*, 1, p. 236; see also Schram, 3, p. 115 (Nov. 25 1928). *Qu Qiubai wrote in April*: *Chinese Studies in History*, 5, 1, pp. 69–70. Although Qu's speech was delivered in June, it was evidently prepared two months earlier (see p. 53).

224 *Mao to reply... this mistake again*: *Nianpu*, 1, p. 243; Schram, 3, p. 59. *Preparing for the Sixth Party Congress*: Useful accounts of the congress in English include Grigoriev, A. M., 'An Important Landmark in the History of the Chinese Communist Party', in *Chinese Studies in History*, 8, 3 (1975), pp. 18–44; Carr, 853–75; and Ristaino, pp. 199–214. *Li Weihan*: At the time Mao's letter arrived, Li was the most senior CCP leader in Shanghai. See ZZWX, 4, pp. 71–5 and 239–57; Pak, pp. 371–2; and *Nianpu*, 1, p. 244. *118 delegates*: Grigoriev, *Revolyutsionnoe Dvizheniye*, p. 81; *Zhongguo gongchangdang huiyi gaiyao*, p. 79; Zhang Guotao, 2, pp. 68–9. *No 'revolutionary high tide'... could come later*: Saich, pp. 341–58. See also pp. 358–86; and *Chinese Studies in History*, 4, nos 1 (1970), 2–3 and 4 (1971).

Comintern resolution : Thornton, Richard, *The Comintern and the Chinese Communists*, 1928–31, University of Washington, Seattle, 1969, pp. 32–8. Although approved in Moscow on February 25 1928, the Qu Qiubai leadership began publicising it only on April 30, and the Party journal, *Buersheweike* (which had replaced *Xiangdao* in October 1927) did not publish it until July (Grigoriev, *Revolyutsionnoe Dvizhenie*, p. 78).

We may maintain: Nikolai Bukharin, speech to the Sixth Congress, in *Chinese Studies in History*, 4, 1 (1970), pp. 19–22.

225 *In one county . . . in the countryside*: Saich, pp. 374 and 355–7. *If uprisings*: Bukharin, speech, p. 21. *The peasantry*: Ibid., p. 13: 'It is the peasants themselves who are just now rising up, and it is the workers who are oppressed and blocked, who still cannot straighten their backs.' The theme of proletarian leadership, with the peasants as the main revolutionary force, runs through all the resolutions.

Correct theoretical basis: Mao Zedong, SW1, 1, p. 196 (December 1936). *She was eighteen years old*: The following account is drawn from Wang Xingjuan, *He Zizhende lu*, Zuojia chubanshe, 1988, pp. 1–23, 44–5, 60, 67–9, 78–9 and 87–8; and from Liu Xianong 'Mao Zedong dierci hunyin neiqing' ('Inside Information on Mao Zedong's Second Marriage'), *Jizhe xie tianxia*, no. 21, May 1992, pp. 4–11.

226 *Nuptial supper*: Wang Xingjuan, p. 90. ***Wang Zuo***: Ibid., p. 45. ***Zhu De . . . much younger woman***: Smedley, pp. 137, 223–4 and 272–3.

226n ***In 1972, a cache***: Oral sources.

227 *Attack the city of Jian*: Schram, 3, pp. 50 and 52.

A succession of envoys: The welter of conflicting messages to Jinggangshan at this time reflected the efforts of a new, very young and very inexperienced provincial leadership to assert its authority. The first envoy, Du Xiujing, arrived in Jinggangshan on May 29 with one directive; the second, Yuan Desheng, in late June, bearing another. Du then returned with a third, conflicting, directive, dated June 19, and a letter, dated June 26, at variance with all three. The one common theme was the need for Mao's forces to advance into Hunan, but whereas the first directives from the provincial committee also stressed the need to retain the Ninggang base, the later ones did not (see *Jinggangshan geming genjudi*, 1, pp. 133–44; Schram, 3, pp. 55 and 117; *Nianpu*, 1, pp. 243 and 247–8; and Pak, pp. 369–77).

The Hunan Party committee . . . the Hengyang plan: *Nianpu*, 1, pp. 247–8; *Jinggangshan geming genjudi*, 1, p. 511. Yang Kaiming, who had left Changsha with Du, did not join Mao until some days after the June 30 meeting (*Jinggangshan geming genjudi*, 1, p. 425). *In a letter to Changsha*: Schram, 3, pp. 55–8 (July 4 1928). *Word then came . . . battle-plan went well enough*: *Nianpu*, 1, pp. 248–9. *As Zhu was about to . . . set off for Hengyang*: Ibid., p. 250. See also Schram, 3, pp. 68 and 117.

228 *His own troops . . . the discussion ended*: *Nianpu*, 1, pp. 250–1; Schram, 3, pp. 86 and 117. *The Fourth Army's troubles . . . morale had been broken*: *Nianpu*, 1, pp. 252–3; Schram, 3, pp. 87–8. *Commemorate the event*: *Mao Zedong shici duilian jizhu*, Hunan wenyi chubanshe, 1991, pp. 23–5; see also Schram, 3, p. 61. *Mao's position . . . himself as Secretary*: *Nianpu*, 1, pp. 249–50 and 252; Schram, 3, pp. 85–6 and 113; and *Jinggangshan geming genjudi*, 1, pp. 471–2.

229 *Tensions between himself and Zhu De*: See Schram, 3, p. 178. Zhu had at first been reluctant to join up with Mao's forces (proposed by the CC in December 1927, but not carried out until April 1928); and Mao was careful not to exacerbate tensions ahead of the Guidong meeting in August 1928 (*Nianpu*, 1, p. 252).

Some of Zhu's followers: Mao afterwards referred to 'a bizarre view' held by 'a minority of comrades' that it had been 'wrong to stay in the border area' (Schram, 3, p. 183). *Formal division of powers*: *Jinggangshan geming genjudi*, 1, pp. 471–2. *Tan Zhenlin*: *Nianpu*, 1, pp. 228 and 254; *Jinggangshan geming genjudi*, 1, pp. 472 and 523. *Near the bottom of the list*: *Jinggangshan geming genjudi*, 1, p. 472. *The explanation . . . the main offenders*: Schram, 3, p. 71 (Oct. 5 1928). *His policies were still respected*: *Nianpu*, 1, p. 254. *At the beginning of*

November: Ibid., p. 256. *Excellent letter*: Schram, 3, pp. 80–1 (Nov. 25 1928). *New Front Committee*: Ibid., pp. 113–14.

230 *In a report to*: Ibid., pp. 80–121. The text contradicts itself at several points. Thus, on pp. 96–7, Mao refers to acute shortages of food and clothing, but then declares on p. 118 that 'food and clothing are no longer a problem'; on p. 115, he says there are 'hardly any cases of mutiny or desertion' among the enemy troops, but on p. 119 asserts that 'more and more of them will defect to our side'. It is possible that he wrote the first part before the battles in Ninggang and Yongxin on November 9 and 10, and the remainder later.
One key problem: Ibid., pp. 108–9 and 114 (see also pp. 70–1 and 75). *Proletarian consciousness*: Ibid., p. 114. *The purge*: Ibid., pp. 111–12; *Nianpu*, 1, p. 256. *The core activity ... without complaint*: Schram, 3, pp. 92–7.

231 *Exhaustion and defeat*: Ibid., p. 151 (March 20 1929). *Troops began to starve*: Smedley, p. 235. *An ounce of salt*: Schram, 3, pp. 104–5; Peng Dehuai, *Memoirs of a Chinese Marshal*, Foreign Languages Press, Beijing, 1984, p. 231. *Other daily necessities*: Schram 3, pp. 92–7. *Wages were abolished*: Ibid., pp. 96–7; see also He Changgong, FE/6752/BII/1. *Official fund-raising letter*: Ibid., p. 139 (Feb. 13 1929). *Opium*: Mao acknowledged the Red Army's dealing in opium in 1928 and 1929 (Schram, 3, pp. 57 and 173–4). See also Peng Dehuai, p. 248. *Base might have to be abandoned*: Schram, 3, pp. 105 and 119. *Contingency plan*: Ibid., p. 119.

232 *Two events ... five different routes*: Peng Dehuai, pp. 193–229 and 233–4; *Nianpu*, 1, pp. 259–61. *Enlarged meeting of the Front Committee*: *Nianpu*, 1, pp. 261–2. *At dawn ... field kitchens*: Smedley, p. 236. *Dayu*: Ibid.; *Nianpu*, 1, p 263.

233 *Still rankled*: In the mid-1960s, Peng complained: 'If the Fourth Army [had] manoeuvred well, it could have destroyed or routed the enemy brigade. [But instead] it pushed on to Dayu ... [and] lost contact with the Jinggang Mountains completely' (Peng Dehuai, p. 233). *Peng held out ... 283 remained*: Ibid., p. 234–7. *Mao's army ... the Red Army's creation*: Schram, 3, pp. 159 (April 5 1929) and 150. *For He Zizhen*: Wang Xingjuan, pp. 118 and 135–6. He Zizhen remembered that the baby was born in Longyan, in Fujian. Mao's forces stopped there briefly in late May 1929 (*Nianpu*, 1, p. 276; Schram, 3, p. 166). *To Zhu De*: Smedley, p. 237. *They soon abandoned ... flexible guerrilla war*: *Nianpu*, 1, pp. 265–6 and 270; Schram, 3, p. 150.

234 *Four ounces of gold*: Schram, 3, p. 119. *5,000 dollars' worth of opium*: Ibid., pp. 173–4. *Mao's letters*: Ibid., pp. 151 (March 20), 161 (April 5), 172 (June 1 1929). *Indeed, one of the lessons ... insubordination [and] defeat*: Ibid., pp. 117 and 120 (Nov. 25 1928). *Even newspapers*: Ibid.,

p.161 (April 5 1929). *The resolutions*: Ibid., p. 151 (March 20 1929). *Listed twelfth... the end of the year*: It may reasonably be assumed, although it cannot be proved, that Mao received a list of the new Central Committee and Politburo members at the same time as the (incomplete) set of Sixth Congress documents that reached Jinggangshan. He may first have got a sense of the real shape of the new leadership when a CC envoy, Liu Angong, reached the Fourth Army in May 1929. However, Mao's first (known) written comment on the leadership changes came in late November 1929, when he told Li Lisan: 'Only with Comrade Chen Yi's arrival [two days earlier] did I learn of your situation' (ibid., pp. 151–2 and 192; and *Nianpu*, 1, pp. 274 and 289–90).

235   *First reports reached Shanghai*: *Nianpu*, 1, pp. 264–5. *In these circumstances . . . climate to emerge*: Saich, pp. 472–4. ZZWX, 5, pp. 29–38. *Mao disliked this approach*: Schram, 3, p. 100.

235n *Rank order*: *Zhongguo gongchangdang huiyi gaiyao*, p. 84.

236   *The two comrades*: Saich, pp. 473–4. *After the disorderly retreat . . . southern Jiangxi*: Ibid., pp. 147–52; *Nianpu*, 1, pp. 264–70; Smedley, pp. 237–9 and 248–51.

237   *Two weeks later*: The CC messenger arrived in Ruijin on April 3 (Schram, 3, p. 153). *Mao's response . . . time-limit of one year*: Ibid., pp. 153–61 (April 5 1929), 168 and 172; Peng Dehuai, p. 250. *This proposal . . . a mistake*: Schram, 3, pp. 244–5 (Jan. 5 1930). *Zhou had written*: ZZWX, 5, p. 30.

238   *The struggle in the countryside*: Schram, 3, p. 154. *As reports of the Red Army's . . . also rescinded*: Ibid., p. xli; Jin Chongji, *Zhou Enlai zhuan, 1898–1949*, Zhongyang wenxian yanjiushi chubanshe, Beijing, 1989, p. 193; *Nianpu*, 1, p. 272. *In June*: Saich, p. 395. *Nianpu*, 1, pp. 278–9. *Many shared the Centre's*: Schram, 3, pp. 243–4 (Jan. 5 1930). *At Yudu*: Ibid., p. 244; *Nianpu*, 1, p. 272.

239   *Over the course of*: *Nianpu*, 1, pp. 275–8. See also Mao's letters to Lin Biao of June 14 1929 and January 5 1930 (Schram, 3, pp. 177–89 and 234–46); and the CC's 'Directive to the Front Committee of the Fourth Red Army', Section 8, 'The Zhu-Mao Problem', in ZZWX, 5, pp. 488–9. *Different histories*: See Schram, 3, pp. 178–9, 184 and 187. *Even He Zizhen*: Wang Xingjuan, p. 139. *Complaints were heard*: *Nianpu*, 1, p. 277; Schram, 3, p. 181 and 185–7. *Running too many things*: Schram, 3, p. 181. *Cannot keep track*: Ibid., p. 171. *At the beginning of February*: Ibid., pp. 156, 159 and 171; *Nianpu*, 1, pp. 264 and 268–9.

240   *Liu Angong*: *Nianpu*, 1, p. 274. *Military Committee*: Ibid., pp. 276–7; and Schram, 3, pp. 180–5. *Long-suppressed ambitions*: Schram, 3, p. 184. *Liu's first act*: *Nianpu*, 1, pp. 274 and 276–7; Schram, 3, p. xliv; Jin Chongji, *Zhu De zhuan*, pp. 175–80. *At Baisha . . . intended to*

resign: *Nianpu*, 1, p. 278. ***Thirty-six votes to five***: Schram, 3, p. 182
(June 14 1929).
When this body met . . . the post of Secretary: *Nianpu*, 1, pp. 280–1;
Zhongguo gongchangdang huiyi gaiyao, pp. 88–90; Xiao Ke, *ZhuMao
hongjun ceji*, Zhonggong zhongyang dangxiao chubanshe, Beijing,
1993, pp. 88–102.

241 ***He Zizhen . . . gave birth***: Wang Xingjuan, pp. 135–7. ***The pretext
was ill-health . . . made him sicker***: Ibid., pp. 140–2. He was almost
certainly suffering from neurasthenia. ***The West Fujian Special
Committee***: *Nianpu*, 1, pp. 281–3. ***But he refused . . . screaming at each
other***: Wang Xingjuan, p. 143. ***Front Committee decided***: Ibid.; the
Nianpu (1, pp. 283–4) gives a slightly different sequence of events.
Malaria: Mao wrote in late November that he had been 'very ill for
three months' (Schram, 3, p. 192). According to the *Nianpu*, his
malaria was cured by the end of October (1, p. 288). Both are consis-
tent with his having contracted the disease around the beginning of
August (see also *Nianpu* 1, p. 284). ***Remote hamlet . . . over the door***:
Nianpu, 1, p. 285.
Even before Chen Yi . . . political responsibilities: Ibid., pp. 284–5.
It is not clear how the letter setting out Mao's views (which he had
sent privately to Lin Biao on June 14) came to reach Shanghai.
Presumably Lin or Mao himself arranged for it to be included with
the Congress resolutions.

242 ***Liu Angong***: Ibid., p. 285. Smedley reported that Zhu De remembered Liu with affection (*Great Road*, p. 266). ***When Zhu received . . .
no state to work***: *Nianpu*, 1, p. 286. ***Three weeks later . . . within a
year***: Ibid., p. 289; ZZWX, 5, pp. 473–90. ***On the crucial question . . .
work together sensibly***: ZZWX, 5, pp. 488–9. ***He ignored it . . . learn
English***: *Nianpu*, 1, pp. 288–90.

243 ***Disastrous campaign***: Ibid., p. 295. ***'Absolutely no problem'***: Schram,
3, p. 194. ***For ten days***: *Nianpu*, 1, pp. 291–2; see also *Zhongguo
gongchangdang huiyi gaiyao*, pp. 98–102. ***Mao's political
report***: Schram, 3, pp. 195–210 (December 28 1929). ***The Party
commands***: SW2, p. 224 (Nov. 6 1938). ***Mao flayed . . . violation of
Party principles***: Schram, 3, pp. 207–30.

244 ***Marxists are not fortune-tellers***: Ibid., pp. 234–46 (Jan. 5 1930). ***No new
revolutionary upsurge***: See Zhou, SW1, p. 44, and Saich, pp. 388–9.
All through 1929 . . . teach the Chinese a lesson: Thornton, pp. 93–6;
Carr, 3, pt 3, pp. 895–910.

245 ***In October, the Comintern***: Saich, pp. 400–7, esp. p. 406; Thornton's
analysis (pp. 96–101) is marred, as throughout his otherwise very
useful book, by the false assumption that communications between
Moscow and Shanghai were virtually instantaneous. ***Moscow had
proclaimed . . . surely arrive***: Saich, pp. 400 and 406.

It convinced Li Lisan: For a contrary (but partisan) view, see Grigoriev, *Revolyutsionnoe Dvizheniye*, pp. 170–4. Much sinological ink has been spilt, in China, the West and Russia, in trying to determine the degree of Moscow's responsibility in promoting the policies that became known as 'the Li Lisan line'. The most plausible explanation is that a summary (though probably not the full text) of the Comintern letter was received in Shanghai in November, and quickly led to the writing of the CC Circular which proclaimed the coming of the new 'revolutionary high tide'. In any event, there is little doubt that Li Lisan was longing to pursue a more aggressive, urban-based strategy, and that the ambiguities of the Comintern's stance that winter gave him the opportunity he was looking for. *Central Committee directive*: ZZWX, 5, pp. 561–75 (esp. Section 8, pp. 570–1).

246   *End of January 1930*: Mao's 'Letter . . . to the Soldiers of the Guomindang Army', issued in January, was plainly written after he had received the December 8 Circular (Schram, 3, pp. 247 and 249). *Pitou*: *Nianpu*, 1, pp. 297–8; *Zhongguo gongchandang huiyi gaiyao*, pp. 102–4; and Peng Dehuai, p. 265. *Final statement*: Schram, 3, pp. 268–9 (Feb. 16 1930). *This call to action . . . next stage*: Ibid., p. 263 (Feb. 14 1930).

247   *In the event . . . called off altogether*: *Nianpu*, 1, pp. 299–300. *Ganzhou . . . serious opportunism*: Ibid., p. 301; Schram, 3, pp. 273–9 (March 18) and 280–2 (March 19 1930). *Lip service*: Schram, 3, p. 269. *At Gutian*: Ibid., pp. 204 and 206.

248   *Rather awkward note*: Ibid., pp. 192–3 (Nov. 28 1929). *Circular no. 70*: ZZWX, 6, pp. 25–35, esp. Section 3. *March 10*: *Nianpu*, 1, p. 300. *Another Central directive*: ZZWX, 6, pp. 57–60. *Zhou then departed*: Jin Chongji, *Zhou Enlai zhuan*, pp. 210–13; Grigoriev, p. 186. *Refused to budge . . . their military strength*: *Nianpu*, 1, pp. 303–8. *Mao himself ignored*: See ZZWX, 6, pp. 15–20; *Nianpu*, 1, p. 305; Hsiao Tso-liang, *Power Relations within the Chinese Communist Movement, 1930–34*, University of Washington Press, Seattle, 1961–67, vol. 1, pp. 16–18, and vol. 2, pp. 28–9. *'A form of sabotage'*: Schram, 3, pp. 420–1 (May 1930). *Like Qu, Li declared*: See Grigoriev, pp. 181–7; and Thornton, pp. 123–54. The points which follow are taken from *Buersheweike*, April 1930; ZZWX, 6, pp. 57–60 and 98–110; *Nianpu*, 1, pp. 304–6; and Saich, pp. 428–39.

249   *Blistering criticisms*: *Nianpu*, 1, pp. 308–9 (June 9); Saich pp. 428–39 (June 11); and ZZWX, 6, pp. 137–41. *China is the weakest link*: Saich, pp. 429–32. *The plan*: Smedley, p. 276; Peng Dehuai, pp. 286–99. *Political and military reorganisation*: Grigoriev, pp. 201–2; Thornton, pp. 165–6.

250   *Tu Zhennong*: Jin Chongji, *Zhu De zhuan*, p. 205; *Nianpu*, 1,

pp. 310–11. *Sweeten the pill*: The Politburo had decided on Zhu's promotion in April, but he did not learn of the decision until Tu Zhennong's arrival (*Nianpu*, 1, p. 305).

Poem: *Mao Zedong shici duilian jizhu*, pp. 35–7 (translation adapted from Schram, 3, p. 460). The poem was apparently written on the march, between Mao's leaving Tingzhou and the army's arrival near Nanchang. The Chinese editors describe it as 'obscurely conveying [Mao's] complicated feelings at the time'.

Extremely slowly: *Nianpu*, 1, pp. 311–12. *Nanchang was too well-defended... and so on*: Ibid., pp. 312–13; Schram, 3, pp. 482–4 (Aug. 19 1930). *In May the Comintern . . . major provinces*: Saich pp. 439–45. For timing, see Grigoriev, p. 190.

251 *'Extremely erroneous'*: Saich, p. 431. *On July 23 . . . the rest of the Politburo*: Grigoriev, p. 202; Saich, pp. 439–45; ZZWX, 6, p. 595. *Two days later... compelled to withdraw*: Peng Dehuai, pp. 294–7. *Mao was evidently persuaded*: Mao's letter to the South-West Jiangxi Special Committee on August 19 indicated that he began moving towards Hunan *after* learning of the capture of Changsha. Even so, he again demanded urgent reinforcements in order to be able to take advantage of the 'increasingly intense revolutionary situation' (Schram, 3, pp. 482–4; Peng Dehuai, p. 299).

August 23: *Nianpu*, 1, p. 314; Peng Dehuai, pp. 300–1. *Revolutionary Committee*: *Nianpu*, 1, p. 314; ZZWX, 6, pp. 178–80 and 248–9. *His misgivings were reflected*: Schram, 3, pp. 488–9 (Aug. 24 1930).

252 *Stubborn resistance*: Ibid., pp. 500 and 501 (Aug. 30 and 31 1930). *Bogged down*: *Nianpu*, 1, p. 315. See also Schram, 3, pp. 490–502 and 508–21. *On September 12*: Schram, 3, pp. 524–5. *Twenty-four hours later . . . on Jian*: Ibid., pp. 526–8 (Sept. 13 1930).

Eight times: Documentation at Jian Revolutionary Museum, which now occupies the former landlord's house where Mao and Zhu De made their headquarters in the city. *October 4*: *Nianpu*, 1, p. 318; Schram, 3, pp. 552–3 (Oct. 14 1930). *First seizure*: Schram, 3, p. 574 (Oct. 26 1930). *Six weeks*: *Nianpu*, 1, p. 326. *Hyperbolic proclamations*: Ibid., p. 318; Schram, 3, pp. 553–4; *Shihua*, 2, Dec. 9 1930, pp. 3–4 (extracts quoted in Grigoriev, p. 215, and Schram, 3, p. lx). *Secret radio transmitter*: See Grigoriev, pp. 202–3 and 208.

253 *On July 28*: Ibid., pp. 202–3. *But a month later*: This message, sent on August 26, marked a key turning-point in Moscow's assessment of Li's policies. The full text has not been published, either in China or Russia, but extracts are given by Grigoriev (pp. 206–7). *Zhou Enlai and Qu Qiubai*: Ibid., p. 206; Jin Chongji, *Zhou Enlai zhuan*, pp. 218–20. *He refused to cancel*: *Nianpu*, 1, p. 317. See also Grigoriev, 'The Comintern and the Revolutionary Movement in China', in Ulyanovsky, *Comintern and the East*, p. 372.

When, in September: Saich, pp. 445–57. See also Thornton, pp. 187–200; and Grigoriev, pp. 208–214. During the plenum none of those present – not even the local Comintern representative – regarded Li's errors as a problem of line (see Saich, p. 470, quoting a letter from the Comintern's Shanghai bureau). Qu, writing from prison in 1935, just before his execution, remembered seeing no 'fundamental difference' at that time between Li's position and that of the Comintern (Dun Li, *Road to Communism*, p. 169). The paradoxical result was that Li and his supporters, despite the criticisms aimed against them, emerged from the meeting with a stronger presence in the Politburo (and the Central Committee) than when it began.

Some of Li's wilder statements: Li discussed Manchuria in Politburo meetings on August 1 and 3 (Grigoriev, *Revolyutsionnoe Dvizheniye*, pp. 203–4 and 216), but his statements may not have reached Stalin's ears until October. That month the Comintern began drafting its 'November 16 letter' (so-called because that was the date when it reached Shanghai) which ended 'the Li Lisan line' (Mif, *Kitaiskiya Revolutsiya*, pp. 283–90). Li almost certainly left Shanghai in mid- to late October since, according to Grigoriev (p. 218), he was interrogated by the Comintern in Moscow in the last ten days of November. Pavel Mif probably also set out in late October (ibid., p. 216), for he arrived in Shanghai shortly after the Comintern letter.

Public insistence: Schram, 3, p. 667 (Nov. 11 1930); see also pp. 574 and 579–82 (Oct. 26). Even after 'the Li Lisan line' was publicly repudiated at the end of 1930, Mao continued to use this phrase, though it became increasingly a ritual incantation: thus on April 19 1931, he prefaced an order for the troops to assemble before a battle with the words, 'The tide of the Chinese revolution rises higher every day' (Schram, 4, p. 67).

After the capture of Jian: *Nianpu*, 1, p. 319. See also Schram, 3, pp. 558 and 577. *Mao countered*: After abandoning the attack on Changsha, Mao constantly sought to refocus his colleagues' attention on the provincial, rather than the national, struggle (see Schram, 3, pp. 552–3, Oct. 14; p. 558, Oct. 19; p. 572, Oct. 24; p. 574, Oct. 26, and so on).

254   *He planned to use 100,000 men . . . modern rifles*: *Selected Military Writings of Mao Zedong*, Foreign Languages Press, Beijing, 1966, p. 117. *Orders had to be posted*: Schram, 3, p. 539 (Sept. 25 1930). *Literacy campaigns . . . officer corps*: Ibid., p. 588 (Oct. 26); pp. 283–4 (March 21); pp. 285–90 (March 29 1930). *Recruits had to be . . . diseases to others*: Ibid., pp. 289–90 (March 29) and p. 291 (April 1930). *On the battlefield . . . communication before*: Schram, 3, passim.

255   *Mao issued standing instructions*: Ibid., p. 555 (Oct. 14 1930). See also Schram, 4, pp. 88–9 (May 31 1931) and *Nianpu*, 1, p. 332. *'Poorly armed'*: Mif, p. 287. *On October 30*: *Nianpu*, 1, p. 322. *In its new form*:

Schram, 3, p. 656 (Nov. 1 1930). *'The tactic of protracted war'* ... ***mighty blow***: Ibid., p. 718 (Dec. 22 1930). *The new strategy ... military commanders next day*: *Zhongguo gongchangdang huiyi gaiyao*, pp. 120–22; Peng Dehuai, p. 308; *Nianpu*, 1, pp. 321–2. See also Yu Boliu and Chen Gang, *Mao Zedong zai zhongyang suqu*, Zhongguo Shudian, Beijing, 1993.

256 ***For six weeks ... 30 machine-guns***: *Nianpu*, 1, pp. 323–30; Schram, 3, pp. 699–703 (Nov. 27 and Dec. 14 1930) and pp. 722–32 (Dec. 25, 26, 28, 29 and 30 1930). ***January 3***: *Nianpu*, 1, pp. 330–1; Schram, 4, pp. 5–8 (Jan. 1 and 2 1931). ***Radio section***: *Nianpu*, 1, pp. 332–3; see also Schram, 4, pp. 88–9 (May 31 1931).

257 ***Zhang Huizan***: In 1997, Zhang's fate was still commented on approvingly by elderly people in Donggu. ***Alternate membership***: *Zhongguo gongchangdang huiyi gaiyao*, p. 119. The Front Committee discussed the decisions of the Third Plenum at an enlarged meeting at Huangpi in the first ten days of December (*Nianpu*, 1, p. 327); see also Schram, 4, p. 59. ***Xiang Ying***: *Nianpu*, 1, p. 332. The Politburo had decided to establish the Central Bureau on October 17 1930 and had named Mao acting Secretary eight days later, pending Xiang Ying's arrival (ibid., pp. 319 and 321). ***January 15***: *Nianpu*, 1, p. 332. ***Developments in Shanghai***: *Zhongguo gongchangdang huiyi gaiyao*, pp. 123–7; Grigoriev, *Revolyutsionnoe Dvizheniye*, pp. 227–9; *History of the CCP, Chronology*, pp. 72–3. See also Thornton, pp. 213–17.

258 ***March 1931***: *Nianpu*, 1, p. 337. On March 20, Mao wrote of unnamed emissaries having arrived from Shanghai 'in the last few days' (Schram, 4, p. 36), presumably bringing the documents discussed at the enlarged Central Bureau meeting at Huangpi from March 18 to 21. These included the Comintern's 'November 16 letter', denouncing Li Lisan, but no materials from the Fourth Plenum (see Hsiao Tso-liang, *Power Relations*, vols 1, pp. 152–3, and 2, pp. 352–60). ***Ren Bishi***: *Nianpu*, 1, p. 339. ***Directive from the new Party Centre ... Red base areas***: ZZWX, 7, pp. 139–42; *Nianpu*, 1, p. 337. Even earlier, Mao had persuaded Xiang to set up a General Political Department of the Military Commission, with himself as its director (Schram, 4, pp. 12–13, Feb. 17 1931). ***Distrusted Xiang Ying***: The Fourth Plenum sharply criticised the 'reconciliationist line' which the Third Plenum leadership, of which Xiang Ying had been part, adopted towards Li Lisan (see Saich, pp. 459–61). ***Second encirclement***: Hu Sheng, *Concise History of the Communist Party of China*, p. 158; Schram, 4, pp. xxxiv–v.

259 ***Mao and Zhu De had been observing***: *Nianpu*, 1, p. 334; Schram, 4, p. 14 (Feb. 21 1930). ***Disagreement***: There was a hint of this in Mao's order of March 20, when he wrote: 'Victory in the second campaign will certainly be

ours, provided only that we are all resolute' (Schram, 4, p. 38). See also Yu and Chen, *Mao Zedong zai zhongyang suqu*, pp. 246–50; and Ma Qibin et al., *Zhongyang geming genjudi shi*, pp. 285–8.

Abandon the base area altogether: Yu and Chen, pp. 246–50; Ma Qibin et al., pp. 285–8. **Pulled back its main forces**: Schram, 4, pp. 42–3 (March 23 1931); *Nianpu*, 1, p. 337. **April 17**: Saich, pp. 530–5; and Schram, 4, pp. 56–66. **Next day, Mao got his way**: *Nianpu*, 1, pp. 339–42; Schram, 4, pp. 67–8. **Almost exactly . . . their flanks**: *Nianpu*, 1, pp. 344–5; Schram, 4, pp. 74–5 (May 14 1931). See also Peng Dehuai, pp. 316–18.

260   **300,000 men**: *Nianpu*, 1, pp. 349–50; Schram, 4, p. xli. **End of May**: Schram, 4, p. 92 (June 2), pp. 98–103 (June 22 1931); *Nianpu*, 1, pp. 347–9. **In late June**: Schram, 4, p. 102. **On the 28th . . . cut to ten days**: Ibid., pp. 107–9 (June 28) and pp. 110–12 (June 30 1931). **'Emergency circular'**: Ibid., pp. 115–17 (July 4 1931).

260   **In the next two months . . . heading north**: This account of the third
/   encirclement is taken from the military orders issued by Mao
262   himself, in Schram, 4, pp. 118–37 (July 12 to Aug. 17) and pp. 142–53 (Aug. 22 to Sept. 23 1931); from ibid., pp. xli–ii; *Nianpu*, 1, pp. 350–5; and Peng Dehuai, pp. 322–4.

262   **Parting gesture**: *China Weekly Review*, Aug. 29 1931, p. 525.

263   **Seventeen nationalist regiments . . . two million people**: *Nianpu*, 1, p. 355. **Communist losses**: Peng Dehuai wrote that his 3rd Army Group lost about a third of its 15,000 men during the three encirclement campaigns (p. 325). Accounts of the individual engagements suggest most of the losses occurred in the third campaign (see, for instance, *Nianpu*, 1, p. 355). **Letter from a Guomindang prison**: Dun Li, pp. 159–76.

264   **Totally overlooked the necessity**: Saich, p. 458.
       The Comintern decided . . . Guomindang-ruled white areas: Mif, p. 296. The Comintern's August 26 1931 resolution stated explicitly that the 'immediate goal' to which the Party must devote 'all its strength' in the White areas was the promotion of 'a powerful mass movement in defence of the soviet areas' (ibid., pp. 300–2). This, of course, was the exact reverse of its (and the Party's) opening position four years earlier, which had been that the struggle in the urban areas was primary, and that the rural revolution was merely an adjunct.
       'Far outstripped': See the Comintern's 'November 16 letter', in Mif, pp. 284–5. The terms used recall Mao's warning to the Party Centre, eighteen months earlier, not to be concerned if the peasant movement 'outstripped' the movement in the cities.

CHAPTER EIGHT: FUTIAN
LOSS OF INNOCENCE

266 *Such coercive tactics*: Qu Qiubai, in *Chinese Studies in History*, vol. 5, 1, pp. 58–9 and 69. *When Mao's forces*: Schram, *Mao's Road*, 3, pp. 172–3. *Red execution squads*: Ibid., p. 74. *There is a severe crisis*: Ibid., p. 269 (Feb. 16 1930). *The local leaders ... families and clans*: Averill, Stephen C., 'The Origins of the Futian Incident', in Saich, Tony, and Van de Ven, Hans, *New Perspectives on the Chinese Communist Revolution*, M. E. Sharpe, Armonk, New York, 1995, pp. 80–3 and 95–9.

267 *Dissolution*: *Nianpu*, 1, p. 298; Schram, 3, pp. 270–1. *Brother-in-law*: See Ch'en, Yung-fa [Chen Yongfa], 'The Futian Incident and the Anti-Bolshevik League: The "Terror" in the CCP Revolution', in *Republican China*, vol. 19, 2, April 1994, p. 37, n.30. *Second, secret directive*: Dai Xiangqing and Luo Huilan, *AB tuan yu Futian shibian shimuo*, Henan renmin chubanshe, 1994, pp. 81–2. *'Four Great Party officials'*: Averill, pp. 98–9. *Individualistic aversion*: Schram, 3, pp. 198–9.
Contradictions: 'On Contradiction', in SW1, pp. 343–5; 'On the Correct Handling of Contradictions among the People', February 27 1957, in MacFarquhar, Roderick, Cheek, Timothy and Wu, Eugene (eds), *The Secret Speeches of Chairman Mao*, Harvard University Press, Cambridge, MA 1989, pp. 131–89.
Openly tried: Schram, *Mao's Road*, 4, p. 105 (June 1931).

268 *Having been given a mandate ... executed as AB-tuan members*: See Dai and Luo, pp. 83–9, and Chen Yongfa, pp. 2–6. Stephen Averill argues, to my mind convincingly, that the AB-*tuan* was still very much alive in Jiangxi in 1930 (pp. 88–92 and 109–10). Whether it made any serious attempt to subvert the CCP, let alone on the scale claimed by the communists, is a totally different matter.
Mao's personal involvement: See Dai and Luo, p. 167; and *Zhongyang geming genjudi shiliao xuanbian*, Jiangxi renmin chubanshe, Nanchang, 1982, vol. 1, pp. 222–63, esp. p. 248.

269 *Li Wenlin*: Averill, pp. 85, 104 and 111, n.12. In February 1929, Mao assigned his youngest brother, Zetan, to work with Li in Donggu, and a year later went out of his way to praise Li's policies (*Nianpu*, 1, pp. 265–6; Schram, 3, p. 236). See also Dai and Luo, p. 172.
In August: The plenum was held from August 5 to 11, overlapping with a longer work conference which took place in late July and August (*Zhongyang geming genjudi shiliao xuanbian*, 1, pp. 264–322). With hindsight, Mao saw this meeting as a crucial step in the Southwest Jiangxi Party's transition to openly opposing his authority (see Schram, 3, pp. 710–12; Dai and Luo, p. 172).

Head of the Provincial Action Committee: Schram, 3, pp. 553–4.
There is no evidence that Mao tried to prevent Li's appointment,
and at this stage he may well have thought they would be able
to work together. *Most merciless torture*: Dai and Luo, pp. 89 and 92.
See also *Zhongyang geming genjudi shiliao xuanbian*, pp. 639–51. *Filled
with AB-tuan members . . .*: Schram, 3, p. 554 (Oct. 14) and p. 560
(Oct. 19 1930). *Joint statement*: Schram, 3, pp. 574–89 (Oct. 26
1930).

270   *Appearance of unity*: *Nianpu*, 1, p. 322; Chen Yongfa, p. 13; Dai and
Luo, p. 94.
Consolidation campaign . . . summarily shot: This account is drawn
primarily from Dai and Luo, pp. 94–6, and Chen Yongfa, pp. 13–14
and 16–17. Most of the Red Army main forces reached the area
around Huangpi on November 30 or December 1 (Schram, 3,
p. 700). Although a letter from the General Front Committee
(drafted, or at least approved, by Mao) stated on December 3 1930
that 'in the Red Army, the crisis has already been remedied' (Dai and
Luo, p. 98), the 'Huangpi sufan' (Huangpi Elimination of Counter-
revolutionaries), as this part of the purge was afterwards called,
actually continued for much longer. The figure of 4,400 arrests was
given by the Front Committee itself towards the end of December
(Schram, 3, p. 705). The total number killed in the military purge that
winter was probably of the order of 3–5,000, or roughly 10 per cent
of the army's total strength.

271   *Inextricably confused*: See, for example, section 8 of the Front
Committee's joint statement of October 26 (Schram, 3, pp. 586–7),
where the three terms are used interchangeably. *Coloured by
national disputes*: The SW Jiangxi leaders' supposed allegiance to Li
Lisan became a key part of the indictment against them *after* the
event but it was not the main factor at the time.

271   *On Sunday afternoon . . . neither living nor dead*: This account of
/   the 'Futian events' relies heavily on Dai Xiangqing and Luo Huilan
273   (pp. 98–9 and 103–6), who have evidently had access to unpublished
documents in Party archives, notably the two letters from Mao's
General Front Committee. These letters, written on December 3 and
5, constitute the 'smoking gun' linking Mao directly to the Futian
arrests. The December 5 letter, which supplemented the original
instructions, was sent to Li Shaojiu by military courier while he was
en route; I have assumed that it reached him before his arrival at
Futian. Li's heavy-handedness undoubtedly made matters worse, but
his actions were fully in accord with the Front Committee's orders,
which, given their importance, Mao would certainly have drafted
himself, or, at the very least, personally approved. I am indebted to

the Futian Party Committee for allowing me to visit the buildings where these events took place.

273 *Instructions of the Front Committee*: Letter of December 5 1930, quoted in Dai and Luo, p. 99. *All the AB-tuan cases*: Chen Yongfa, p. 48; see also *Zhongyang geming genjudi shiliao xuanbian*, 1, pp. 476–89.

274 *Like all the others … from all his posts*: Dai and Luo, pp. 104–8 and 117–21; Chen Yongfa, pp. 15–16. According to Dai and Luo, of the 120 who had been arrested at Futian, Li Shaojiu ordered about 25 to be killed before he left for Donggu. Liu Di's relief column freed 'more then 70' on the night of December 12.

275 *The three army commanders*: Hsiao Tso-liang, *Power Relations*, 2, pp. 259–62. *Incriminating letter*: For the text, and a covering letter from the Action Committee dated December 20, see Ibid., 1, pp. 102–5, and 2, pp. 262–4. See also Peng Dehuai, *Memoirs* (pp. 308–16), for his own account, fortified by hindsight, of how the forged letter arrived. *Long rambling rebuttal*: Schram, 3, pp. 704–13. *Bonded by the fury*: For a discussion of the effects of terror, see Benton, Gregor, *Mountain Fires: The Red Army's Three-Year War in South China, 1934–1938*, University of California, Berkeley, 1992, pp. 478 and 506–7. *By now, Mao, too*: Chen Yongfa, p. 17. Despite his ruthlessness towards the Futian rebels, and in purging opponents within the Red Army, Mao did not favour indiscriminate killing (see, for example, Schram, 3, p. 693). *Li Wenlin*: Chen Yongfa, p. 18. *Li Shaojiu*: Ibid.; 'Resolution on the Futian Incident, April 16 1931' in Saich, *Rise to Power*, p. 534. *January 16*: 'Circular No. 2', in Hsiao Tso-liang, 1, pp. 108–9 and 2, pp. 269–73. *Cautious hints*: See the Central Bureau's letter to the rebels on February 4, and its 'Circular No. 11' of February 19 1931, in ibid., 1, pp. 109–13, and 2, pp. 274–83. *Factional struggle*: 'Circular No. 2'; see also Saich, pp. 534–5. *On the essential question, however*: Circulars nos. 2 and 11.

276 *Throughout January and February*: Chen Yongfa, p. 42, n.63; see also Mao's reference (in March 1931) to ferreting out AB-*tuan* members 'right now' (Schram, 4, p. 48). *Even the rebels*: Hsiao Tso-liang, 1, p. 104, and 2, pp. 262–4. *In March 1931 … were also executed*: Chen Yongfa, p. 18; Dai and Luo, pp. 149 and 188; Yu Boliu and Chen Gang, *Mao Zedong zai zhongyang suqu*, pp. 201–2. See also Hsiao Tso-liang, 1, p. 113, and 2, p. 358. *The new approach … struggle against the AB-tuan*: 'Resolution on the Futian Incident'; and Schram, 4, pp. 56–66.

277 *Its conclusion*: 'Resolution on the Futian Incident', p. 532. *The purge resumed*: Chen Yongfa, pp. 21–5; Yu Boliu and Chen Gang, pp. 202–11; Dai and Luo, pp. 189–200. *Repeated efforts to centralise*: 'Resolution on the Futian Incident', s. 4b, p. 535; Chen Yongfa, p. 23. *Uneducated, often illiterate*: For a contemporary description of a

typical district soviet government, see Mao's 'Xingguo Report', in Schram, 3, pp. 646–9 (October 1930). Of the eighteen members, six lived by gambling, one was a Daoist priest; fewer than half were able to read. ***Those who complained . . . were killed***: Chen Yongfa, pp. 48–51.

278   ***In July . . . communist army again***: Chen Yongfa, pp. 24 and 44, n.87; Schram, 4, p. xliii; Averill, p. 106.

  A month later: Agnes Smedley described the trial (in *China's Red Army Marches*, Lawrence & Wishart, London, 1936, pp. 274–9) on the basis of information from a Chinese communist who had returned from the base area to Shanghai (see Braun, *Comintern Agent*, p. 6). Assuming that her account is correct, it took place at Baisha in the second half of August 1931 (see *Nianpu*, 1, pp. 353–4).

  Overall death-toll: Smedley, p. 279; Chen Yongfa, pp. 25 and 44, n.87; Dai and Luo, pp. 192 and 206.

279   ***Provisional Procedure***: Schram, 4, pp. 171–4 (Dec. 13 1931).

  Zhou Enlai: Zhou is often credited with having intervened to stop the purge. In fact, he did not reach the West Fujian base area, on his way to the communist headquarters in Ruijin, until December 15, two days after Mao had approved the new procedures for dealing with counter-revolutionaries.. It is true, however, that Mao acted only after being prodded by the Party Centre; and Zhou's concerns about the way the purge was being conducted, expressed forcefully in a letter written from West Fujian on December 18, did help to ensure that the new regulations were (to some extent) implemented. See *Nianpu*, 1, pp. 362–3; Dai and Luo, p. 205.

  Killing people was regarded as a trifle: ZZWX, 8, pp. 18–28, esp. pp. 21–2.

280   ***'Completely correct'***: Ibid; and Schram, 4, p. 171. ***In May 1932 . . . being shot***: Chen Yongfa, pp. 29–30; Dai and Luo, pp. 217–18. ***Part of a wider pattern***: Benton, *Mountain Fires*. ***In west Fujian***: Kong Yongsong, Lin Tianyi and Dai Jinsheng, *Zhongyang geming genjudi shiyao*, Jiangxi renmin chubanshe, Nanchang, 1985, pp. 211–17. ***Peng Dehuai's old base***: Benton, p. 354. ***In E-Yu-Wan . . . the enemy is***: Saich, pp. 541–50. ***Zeng Hongyi***: Benton, pp. 198 and 239.

281   ***You force him to confess***: Ibid., p. 283. ***Early in 1931 . . . the search halted***: Wakeman, Frederic, Jnr, *Policing Shanghai: 1927–1937*, University of California Press, Berkeley, 1995, pp. 138–9 and 151–60.

282   ***In Hubei . . . hunted down and killed***: Snow, *Red Star over China*, pp. 342–3. ***In November 1930***: *Nianpu*, 1, p. 325. ***Their children . . . of Mao's parents***: Zhong Wenxian, *Mao Zedong: Biography, Assessment, Reminiscences*, pp. 222–4 and 236–7; *Nianpu*, 1, p. 192. ***In   Xu***

Haidong's base area ... through the mountains: Benton, pp. 314–22, 327–30 and 357–60; Snow, pp. 341–7.

283 *Worst butchery*: Benton, pp. 67–8 and passim. *Quotas for purge victims*: McCord, *Power of the Gun*, pp. 196–7. *Gao Jingtang*: Benton, pp. 316–17 and 337–9.

284 *Chen Yi*: Ibid., pp. 506–7. *All-volunteer force*: See, for instance, Schram, 3, pp. 668–70 (Nov. 11 1930). *Mistake in terminology*: 'Resolution on the Futian Incident', p. 533.

CHAPTER NINE: CHAIRMAN OF THE REPUBLIC

285 *Acting Party leader*: An emergency conference of the Centre could change the membership of the Politburo, pending ratification by the next CC plenum, and the membership of the CC, pending ratification by the next Party Congress, but it could not appoint a new General Secretary.

286 *At the end of August*: Nianpu, 1, p. 354; ZZWX, 7, pp. 355–75. *In mid-October ... to be kicked upstairs*: Nianpu, 1, pp. 357–8. Wireless contact between Ruijin and Shanghai had been established in the first half of October.
Base area Party Congress: Ibid., pp. 359–60; *Zhongguo gongchangdang huiyi gaiyao*, pp. 127–9. Some Western scholars claim that the Congress removed Mao as acting Bureau Secretary and appointed Xiang Ying in his place (see, for instance, p. xlvii of Stephen Averill's introduction to Schram, *Mao's Road*, 4). The *Nianpu* specifically states that Mao was still acting Secretary in the second half of December (1, p. 363; see also p. 361).
On November 7 ... Red Army parade: Hsiao Tso-liang, *Power Relations*, vol. 1; Agnes Smedley gives a highly-coloured account in *China's Red Army Marches*, pp. 287–311.

287 *From now on, Mao declared*: Schram, 4, pp. 820–1 (Dec. 1 1931). *Appointed Mao state chairman*: Nianpu, 1, p. 359. *Occupy a major city*: Ibid., p. 364. *Mao was able to convince ... of proving Mao wrong*: Ibid; Peng Dehuai, *Memoirs*, pp. 326–9.

288 *Ten days later ... General Political Department*: Nianpu, 1, pp. 365–6; see also Jin Chongji, *Mao Zedong zhuan. Abandoned temple ... sent up from Ruijin*: Wang Xingjuan, *He Zizhende lu*, pp. 167–8; Nianpu, 1, p. 366.

289 *Comintern's China operation*: Wakeman, *Policing Shanghai*, pp. 147–51; Braun, *Comintern Agent*, pp. 2–3; Litten, Frederick S., 'The Noulens Affair', in CQ, 138, pp. 492–512. *Infiltrate the highest levels*: Wakeman, p. 222.

290 *We used to avoid attacking ... policy needed to change, too*: CC

Resolution of January 9 1932, in Saich, *Rise to Power*, pp. 558–9 and 563. *'Forward, offensive line'*: Ibid., pp. 563–4. *One afternoon . . . his sickness had gone*: Wang Xingjuan, pp. 168–9; *Nianpu*, 1, p. 367; Peng Dehuai, pp. 328–9.

291   *By the time Mao . . . the Central Bureau*: *Nianpu*, 1, p. 368; Peng Dehuai, pp. 329–31. *This time Mao prevailed*: *Nianpu*, 1, p. 369.

292   *One fait accompli after another*: Throughout this period, Mao acted first and sought approval afterwards. There is no evidence, however, that he consciously manoeuvred to stay one step ahead of Zhou. Stephen Averill writes that 'Zhou Enlai went . . . to Changting [Tingzhou] . . . only to find that Mao . . . had already moved on' (Schram, 4, pp. lii–iii). But Mao had sent a wireless message to Zhou on April 2, in which he said that he would leave Changting on the 7th. Although the town was only a day's journey from Ruijin, Zhou did not arrive there until the 10th. See ibid., p. 203; *Nianpu*, 1, p. 370. *Their first goal was Longyan . . . five-pointed red star*: Schram, 4, pp. 204–5; *Nianpu*, 1, pp. 370–2. *Telegram to Zhou Enlai*: Schram, 4, pp. 215–16 (April 22 1932). *Zhangzhou was a rich prize*: Ibid.; *Nianpu*, 1, p. 372.

293   *Drumbeat of criticism*: *Nianpu*, 1, pp. 371–5, quoting a Central directive of April 14, amplified by subsequent articles by Bo Gu and Zhang Wentian in *Hongqi zhoubao* (Red Flag Weekly) later that month, and by a Central telegram of May 20. *Bureau was contrite*: Ibid., p. 375. *Mao's reaction*: Schram, 4, pp. 217–18 (May 3 1932). *Shanghai had been complaining*: See, for example, Saich, pp. 558–66.

294   *He was bombarded . . . across the border*: *Nianpu*, 1, pp. 376–9. *Old position as General Political Commissar*: Ibid., p. 379; Schram, 4, p. 244 (July 25 1932).

295   *By the time Zhou*: *Nianpu*, 1, pp. 379–80. *Mao proposed that*: Ibid., pp. 380–1; Schram, 4, pp. 247–8 (Aug. 15 1932). *The first stage . . . on the base area itself*: *Nianpu*, 1, pp. 381–4. See also Schram, 4, pp. 249–53 (Aug. 28 and 31), and the order of September 5 (p. 254), stressing the need for mobility and 'swift operations'. *Increasingly acrimonious exchanges*: Schram, 4, pp. 275–7 (Sept. 23) and pp. 280–9 (Sept. 25 and 26 1932); *Nianpu*, pp. 386–8. *At the beginning of October*: A near contemporary account of this crucial meeting is given in ZZWX, 8, pp. 528–31. See also Jin Chongji, *Mao Zedong zhuan*, pp. 296–8; *Nianpu*, 1, pp. 389–90; and Schram, 4, pp. lix–lx.

297   *He Zizhen about to give birth*: Wang Xingjuan, pp. 163–6; *Nianpu*, 1, p. 391. *Bo Gu and Zhang Wentian . . . the Centre's decisions*: *Nianpu*, 1, p. 389; Jin Chongji, pp. 297–8; Schram, 4, p. lx. *Judgement in absentia*: Jin Chongji, p. 298.
Zhou had been appointed: *Nianpu*, 1, p. 390. There was apparently

a continuing groundswell of support for Mao among military cadres at the front, for an order dated October 14, two days after Zhou's appointment, was issued over the names of 'Commander-in-Chief Zhu De, Chief Political Commissar Mao Zedong and Acting Chief Political Commissar Zhou Enlai' – designations in flagrant violation of the Ningdu conference decisions, both before and after the Centre's intervention (Schram, 4, pp. 303–7).

298   ***Small sanatorium***: Wang Xingjuan, p. 170; Fu Lianzhang, *Zai Mao zhuxi jiaodaoxia*, Zuojia chubanshe, Beijing, 1959, pp. 6–9. ***Those, like Zhou Enlai***: Zhou was harshly criticised by the rear echelon leaders for his support of Mao (see Ma Qibin et al., *Zhongyang geming genjudi shi*, pp. 367–8). This caused concern in Shanghai lest the Central Bureau become irremediably split (*Nianpu*, 1, p. 391). ***He grew very thin ... punish me to death***: Wang Xingjuan, pp. 167 and 172. ***Luo Ming ... a judgement of this kind***: Ibid., p. 171; *Nianpu*, 1, pp. 391 and 393–4.

299   ***Luo's words were ... of Mao's supporters***: See Saich, pp. 596–602; *Nianpu*, pp. 393–4 and 398–400; Schram, 4, pp. lxi–iii; Deng Maomao, *Deng Xiaoping, My Father*, Basic Books, New York, 1995, pp. 211–15. ***By then Mao was back in Yeping***: *Nianpu*, 1, p. 394. ***Support from the Comintern***: Ibid., p. 398.

300   ***Fine old stone-built mansion***: The 'CC building', as it was called, has been preserved as part of the Yeping historical site. This description of the living arrangements in 1933 is based on the recollections and memoirs of those who lived and worked there. ***Sometimes days passed***: Wang Xingjuan, pp. 172–3. ***Regular air raids***: *Nianpu*, 1, p. 400. Otto Braun recalled that when he arrived in Ruijin, in October 1933, the Central Bureau and Military Commission were still based in Yeping (*Comintern Agent*, p. 33). See also Wang Xingjuan, p. 177. ***There, his only social contact***: Wang Xingjuan, pp. 172–3. ***He used to discuss poetry ... literature was mentioned***: Ibid., pp. 114–15. ***Large pockets***: Ibid.; Chen Changfeng, *On the Long March with Chairman Mao*, Foreign Languages Press, Beijing, 1972, p. 5.

301   ***Sat up arguing***: Wang Xingjuan, p. 115. ***Immense numbers of laws***: See Schram, 4, pp. 783–960. ***Patriotic appeals***: Ibid., for instance, pp. 328–9 (Nov. 25 1932). pp. 348–9 (Dec. 28 1932) and pp. 382–3 (April 22 1933).
His job was to ensure ... 'revolutionary war bonds': Ibid, passim. An overview of the economic policies of the Soviet Republic is given in Mao's 'Report to the Conference on Economic Construction of the 17 Southern Counties' (pp. 479–90) and his 'Report ... to the Second National Congress' (pp. 656–713, especially pp. 688–94 and 705–7). See also Lotveit, Trygve, *Chinese Communism, 1931–1934*, Scandinavian Institute of Asian Studies, London, 1979, pp. 185–209; and Hsu,

King-yi, *Political Mobilization and Economic Extraction: Chinese Communist Agrarian Policies during the Kiangsi Period*, Garland Publishing, New York, 1980, pp. 279–305.

302 *On the Jinggangshan*: Schram, 3, pp. 128–130 (December 1928). *Merit of simplicity*: Ibid., p. 128. *Li Lisan and Bo Gu . . . more exploitative position*: For a discussion of the different communist land policies in the early 1930s, see Hsiao, Tso-liang, *The Land Revolution in China, 1930–34: A Study of Documents*, University of Washington, Seattle, 1969, pp. 3–77; and Schram, 3, pp. xli–iii and 4, pp. xlv–vii. *'Intermediate class'*: Schram, 3, pp. 102–6 (Nov. 25 1928).

303 *Method of assessment*: Mao spent much time from 1930 to 1933 studying these issues, in the process producing a series of rural investigation reports of which the most important were: The Xunwu Investigation, May 1930 (Schram, 3, pp. 296–418); The Xingguo Investigation, October 1930 (pp. 594–655); Investigations in Dongtang and Mukou, November 1930 (pp. 658–66 and 691–3); The Changgang and Caixi Investigations, November 1933 (Schram, 4, pp. 584–640); and the protracted investigation around Ruijin in the spring and summer of 1933 which culminated in the 'Decision Regarding Certain Questions in the Agrarian Struggle' of October 10 1933 (4, pp. 550–67).
       In a village consisting of 37 households: Thompson, Roger R. (trans.), *Mao Zedong: Report from Xunwu*, Stanford University Press, 1990, pp. 178–81.

304 *If one rides a horse*: Ibid., pp. 64–5. *The most detailed of these . . . hired hands the remainder*: Thompson, pp. 45–217.

305 *Mao obtained similar figures*: Schram, 3, p. 610 (October 1930). *Extremely isolated minority*: Ibid., p. 436 (June 1930).

306 *Drawing on the fat*: This formula first appeared in June 1930 (ibid., p. 445, s. 17), and was included in the new land law promulgated that August (pp. 503–7). *The Returned Students decreed*: ZZWX, 7, pp. 355–75 and pp. 500–11; and Hsiao, *Land Revolution*, pp. 47–77. *Land Investigation Movement*: The initial decision was announced on February 8 1932 (Schram, 4, p. lxvi) not acted on until a year later.

307 *Encyclopaedic set of regulations*: Ibid., 4, pp. 546–9 and 550–67 (Oct. 10 1933). *'Extreme caution'*: Ibid., p. 437 (June 1933). *Violent and ruthless . . . by the masses and killed*: Ibid., pp. 425–6, 434 and 507.

308 *Terror-stricken middle peasants*: Ibid., p. 511. *Feudal and superstitious*: Ibid., p. 368 (March 15 1933). *Large numbers of*: Ibid., pp. 394–5 (June 1 1933). *Swashbuckling character*: Braun, p. 31; Benton, *Mountain Fires* p. 132.

309 *Lists of doubtful class elements*: 'Instruction No. 7 of the State Political Security Bureau', Summer 1933, in Hsiao, *Land Revolution*, pp. 231–2. *'Denunciation boxes'*: Schram, 4, pp. 427–8 and 471.

'Obviously guilty': Ibid., pp. 369–70; see also Hsiao, *Land Revolution*, pp. 233–4. *'Single-minded Society'* . . . *'Secret Watch Brigade'*: Schram, 4, pp. 368 (March 15) and 378 (April 15 1933). *Regulations for the Punishment of*: Ibid., 4, pp. 954–7. *Legacy of the Chinese Empire*: Bodde, Derk, *Law in Imperial China*, Harvard University Press, Cambridge, MA, pp. 11, 517–33 and 541–2

Guomindang law of 1931: 'Emergency Law for the Suppression of Crimes against the Safety of the Republic', January 31 1931, in Tang, Leang-li, *Suppressing Communist-Banditry in China*, China United Press, Shanghai, 1934, pp. 111–13. Where the communist law refers to 'counter-revolutionary intent', the nationalists employ the equally vague formula, 'with a view to subverting the Republic'.

Election procedures: Schram, 4, pp. 794–9 (Nov. 1931). *Candidates were nominated*: The extremely detailed regulations on the formation of election committees, issued in December 1931, said nothing about how, or by whom, the lists of candidates should be drawn up (ibid., pp. 827–9). In January 1934, Mao stated that, in practice, the work was done by CCP branch committee staff members. The list, which was promulgated a few days before the vote was taken, might contain the same number of names as there were deputies to be elected, or a larger number (pp. 591–4 and 626–7).

'The right kind of thinking': Ibid., p. 533 (Sept. 6 1933).

310   *If 90 per cent*: Ibid., pp. 469–78 (Aug. 9 1933). *A quarter of those elected*: Ibid., p. 533. *In Hunan*: Ibid., 2, p. 454 (February 1927). *First law to be enacted*: Ibid., 4, pp. 791–4 (Nov. 28 and Dec. 1 1931). *Peasant husbands complained . . . in as many years*: Thompson, pp. 216–17; Schram, 4, p. 616. *To preserve military morale*: Schram, 4, p. 715 (Jan. 27 1934). See also 'Regulations on Preferential Treatment for the Chinese Workers' and Peasants' Red Army', Nov. 1931, Article 18 (p. 785); and the revised Marriage Law enacted on April 8 1934 (pp. 958–60). *This democratic marriage system*: Ibid., p. 698.

310n *Couples made free*: Professor Thompson translates this phrase as: 'couples had dates freely in the hills' (pp. 216–17). The sense of the Chinese is of couples 'sporting together', rather than merely meeting (*Mao Zedong wenji*, Renmin chubanshe, Beijing, 1994, 1, p. 241).

311   *Encouraged, Mao attempted in March*: Schram, 4, p. 367 (March 5 1933). *Mao asked the Bureau*: *Nianpu*, 1, p. 403.

Negotiations with the Fujian-based . . . the encirclement campaign: Schram, 4, pp. lxxv–xxxiv. If Mao did favour military co-operation with the 19th Route Army, as He Zizhen claimed in her memoirs (see Wang Xingjuan, pp. 176–7), and as he himself told Edgar Snow two-and-a-half years later (*Red Star over China*, pp. 411–12), it would be consistent with his record, both before and after the Fujian Incident, in seeking pragmatically to exploit differences between Chiang Kai-shek and other warlords (*Nianpu*, 1, p. 426). But Mao's views carried no weight in Party councils. Bo Gu opposed giving the Fujian rebels military support (Saich, pp. 612–13), and was criticised for it when he lost power a year later (ibid., p. 642). The rest of the leadership was divided. Otto Braun confirms that 'rather than acting vigorously, [they] discussed for almost a month' (*Comintern Agent*, pp. 61–6). See also Litten, Frederick S, 'The CCP and the Fujian Rebellion', *Republican China*, 14, 1 (Nov. 1988).

312   *Fifth plenum*: *Zhongguo gongchangdang huiyi gaiyao*, pp. 134–7; *Nianpu*, 1, p. 420.

313   *'Diplomatic disorders'*: Braun, p. 49. *Later Mao would argue*: Saich, p. 1168. *Bo's report*: Ibid., pp. 609–22. *'Blockhouse tactics'*: Wei, William, *Counter-revolution in China*, University of Michigan Press, Ann Arbor, 1985, pp. 104–25. *Otto Braun*: Braun, pp. vii–ix. *'Short, sharp thrusts'*: Ibid., pp. 266–9; and Saich, pp. 627–35.

314   *The alternative, which Mao suggested*: Towards Zhejiang, in January 1934 (Wang Xingjuan, p. 177; and SW1, pp. 247–8); and towards Hunan in July 1934 (*Nianpu*, 1, p. 432; SW1, p. 248).
All similar proposals: Manfred Stern, the Comintern's senior adviser in Shanghai, proposed a break-out towards north-west Jiangxi (Braun, pp. 63–4); Peng Dehuai wanted to head for Zhejiang (*Memoirs*, pp. 344–5). *Geng Biao*: Geng Biao, *Reminiscences*, China Today Press, Beijing, 1994, pp. 205–7. *Red pogrom*: See Zhang Wentian's directives of March 20 and June 28 1934, in Hsiao, *Land Revolution*, pp. 282–90. *Guangchang*: Benjamin Yang, *From Revolution to Politics*, pp. 81–2; Peng Dehuai, pp. 352–8.
Soon after the Guangchang defeat ... through the summer: The decision to evacuate the base area was taken in May by the 'Central Secretariat' (*Nianpu*, 1, p. 428). This consisted of Bo Gu (Party affairs), Zhang Wentian (government) and Zhou Enlai (military). It appears, however, that Zhang was not party to the initial discussions (see Benton, pp. 13–14 and p. 524, n.51).

315   *He stopped attending*: Braun, pp. 49 and 70–1; see also Yang, pp. 93–99. *Whole of May and June*: *Nianpu*, 1, pp. 426–30. *Yunshishan*: Ibid., p. 432; Wang Xingjuan, pp. 183–4. *Another village nearby*: *Nianpu*, 1, p. 432 see also Chen Changfeng, pp. 19–20. *Nelson Fu ... caffeine and quinine*: Chen Changfeng, pp. 20–1; Fu Lianzhang, pp. 29–37. *The man who ordered ... dogmatism and inexperience*: Fu Lianzhang, p. 31; Braun, p. 71; *Nianpu*, 1, p. 434; oral sources.

316   *Bo Gu at first gave instructions*: *Nianpu*, 1, p. 434. *The man Mao really needed*: See Wang Xingjuan, pp. 194–5. *Zhou had been pushed*

aside: Yang, p. 81. *He sent Zhou a careful briefing*: *Nianpu*, 1, p. 429.
Handbook on guerrilla warfare: Ibid., p. 435; Chen Changfeng,
p. 20. *Mao's request to go to Yudu*: *Nianpu*, 1, p. 433. *Security report*:
Tan Nianqing (ed.), *Changzheng diyidu:Yudu, Neibu chuban*, Yudu,
1996, pp. 31–2. *Thus when Mao, accompanied . . . safely on the other
side*: Chen Changfeng, pp. 22–3; Salisbury, *Long March*, p. 15. *He
Zizhen . . . Xiao Mao was never found*: Wang Xingjuan, pp. 185–9.

CHAPTER TEN: IN SEARCH OF THE GREY DRAGON
THE LONG MARCH NORTH

318 *From the murderous seeds*: Fest, Joachim C., *Hitler*, New York, 1974,
p. 470.
320 *The Guomindang, Mao wrote . . . 'shameless non-
resistance'*: Schram, 4, pp. 361–3 (March 3 1933). *Formal
declaration of war*: Ibid., pp. 206–8 (April 15 1932). *Truce*: Ibid.,
pp. 355–6 (Jan. 17 1933). *'Anti-Japanese vanguard'*: *Nianpu*, 1,
p. 431. *Communism in China*: Tang Leang-li, *Suppressing Communist-
Banditry*, p. v. *If the government*: *China Weekly Review*, Feb. 16 1935,
p. 381. *Only the Japanese correspondents*: Ibid., p. 381 and May 4
1935, pp. 307–8.
321 *30,000 men*: Salisbury, *Long March*, pp. 109, 127 and 150. See also
Braun, *Comintern Agent*, p. 92. *Instinct for self-preservation*: See
Yang, *From Revolution to Politics*, p. 104; Salisbury, pp. 93–4. *The
Zunyi meeting*: Yang, pp. 111–12.
322 *An attempt to cross*: Salisbury, pp. 147–50; *Nianpu*, 1, p. 445.
He Zizhen: In her own account, He Zizhen confuses Mao's whereabouts at the time of the baby's birth and at the time she was
wounded, two months later. In 1950, she returned to the area in a
fruitless search for the child (Wang Xingjuan, *He Zizhende lu*,
pp. 199–200 and 206; Salisbury, pp. 151–3).
Battle of Loushan Pass: Salisbury, pp. 154–6; Yang, p. 126. *One of
his loveliest poems*: *Mao Zedong shici duilian jizhu*; this translation is
adapted from Mao Tse-tung, *Nineteen Poems*, Foreign Languages
Press, Beijing, 1958, p. 16. *That spring . . . providing strategic guidance*: *Nianpu*, 1, pp. 450–2. *First Front Army*: In January 1934, it had
been renamed the Central Red Army. The First Front Army designation was in official use again by June 1935 (*Nianpu*, 1, pp. 423 and
459–61). *Pyrotechnic display*: Salisbury, pp. 160–72 and 178–87. See
also Braun, pp. 112–16.
323 *Proudest moment*: *Nie Rongzhen huiyi lu*, Beijing, 1983, 1, p. 256.
The Red forces have brainy men: *China Weekly Review*, April 13 1935,
p. 220. After this admission, the *Review* went on to predict that Mao,

having made a feint to the west, would now head east. Chiang Kai-
shek had reached the same conclusion. Mao, of course, did just the
opposite. *Guomindang garrison commander*: Wang Tianxi, quoted
in Salisbury, p. 165. *Chiang's spokesmen scrambled*: *China Weekly
Review*, April 13, pp. 214–15; April 20, p. 247; April 27, pp. 283–4;
May 4, p. 318, and May 18 1935, p. 385.

Enlarged Politburo meeting: *Nianpu*, 1, p. 455; Yang, pp. 127–8;
Salisbury, pp. 192–5; Peng Dehuai, *Memoirs*, pp. 366–71; *Nie
Rongzhen huiyi lu*, 1, p. 13. According to Braun (pp. 116–18), Mao's
critics included Zhang Wentian.

324 *20,000 men*: Braun, p. 116. *At Huili, at long last*: *Nianpu*, 1, p. 455;
Braun, p. 118. *Land of the Yi*: Salisbury, pp. 196–200; Braun,
pp. 116–17; Snow, *Red Star Over China*, pp. 225–6.

325 *Anshunchang*: *Nianpu*, 1, p. 457; Braun , p. 119; Yang Dezhi [Yang
Teh-chih], 'Forced Crossing of the Tatu River', in *Recalling the Long
March*, Foreign Languages Press, Beijing, 1978, pp. 79–88. *Yang
Chengwu*: Salisbury, pp. 224–9; for Yang's own account, entitled
'Lightning Attack on Luting Bridge', see *Recalling the Long March*,
pp. 88–100. *Most critical single incident*: Snow, p. 224. *Tenuous
cobweb*: Grace Service, quoted in Salisbury, p. 222.

326 *At the eastern end … for the assault*: Yang Chengwu, pp. 95–8. *Hand
grenades and Mausers*: Snow, pp. 229–30. *Only slightly more
prosaic*: Both Snow and Otto Braun, who also wrote of men
swinging from the chains, 'hand over hand' (p. 119), relied on
second-hand accounts. Yang Chengwu, who was there, said the men
'crept along the chains' (*Recalling the Long March*, p. 98). *The leadership then met*: *Nianpu*, 1, p. 457; Salisbury, p. 231.

327 *One of Mao's bodyguards*: *Nianpu*, 1, p. 457. *Otto Braun remembered*:
Braun, p. 120. *Two-thirds of its baggage animals*: Snow, p. 231.
Dong Biwu: Quoted in Smedley, *Great Road*, pp. 325–6.

328 *He Zizhen*: Wang Xingjuan, pp. 204–8; Salisbury, pp. 172–3. She
had been wounded at Panxian, on the Yunnan–Guizhou border, at
the beginning of April 1935.
On June 12 … position of the other: *Nianpu*, 1, p. 458; Yang,
p. 140. According to Otto Braun (p. 120), Mao first heard uncon-
firmed reports of the Fourth Army's whereabouts when he reached
Tianquan, at the southern foot of the Jinjiashan. Zhang Guotao
knew even less about the First Army's movements (*Rise of
Chinese Communist Party*, 2, pp. 372–3; Salisbury, pp. 232–3 and
239–40).

328 *Mao, Zhu De and the headquarters … there was no response*: The
/   account that follows of the reunion and subsequent separation of
334   the First and Fourth Armies, covering the period from June to
September, 1935, is drawn principally from the *Nianpu*, 1,

pp. 458–74; Zhang Guotao, 2, pp. 374–428; Braun, pp. 129–39; *Nie Rongzhen huiyi lu*, passim; Yang, pp. 129–61; Jin Chongji, *Mao Zedong zhuan*; and Salisbury, pp. 240–82. Where specific references are called for, they are given below.

329 *Fewer than 15,000*: The official Chinese estimate today is that Mao had 20,000 men at Dawei; Zhang had 80,000 (see, for instance, *Zhongguo gongchandang huiyi gaiyao*, p. 156). Both figures appear inflated. Zhang himself put the strength of the Fourth Army at only 45,000 men, and the strength of the First Army at 10,000 (2, pp. 379 and 382–3). If Braun is correct in saying that the First Army had about 20,000 men at Huili, the number must have been much smaller two months later. The likeliest figure, taking into account all the information currently available, is that the two armies' total strength at Dawei was about 60,000 men.
Police in the French concession: *China Weekly Review*, Oct. 20 1934, p. 256. *Summer of 1936*: Zheng Yuyan, 'Liu Changsheng tongzhi huiyilu', Shanghai wenshi ziliao, 10, pp. 68–9; Yang Yunruo and Yang Guisong, *Gongchanguoji he Zhongguo geming*, Shanghai renmin chubanshe, Shanghai, 1988, p. 367.

330 *Played up the role of Otto Braun*: Yang, p. 141, and Braun, p. 121; see also Zhang Guotao, 2, p. 383. *Exchange of probing telegrams*: *Nianpu*, 1, pp. 458–60; Yang, p. 142. *A compromise was patched together*: *Nianpu*, 1, pp. 460–1; *Zhongguo gongchandang huiyi gaiyao*, pp. 156–9.

331 *To prevent an open split*: The changes were proposed at a Military Commission meeting at Shawo on August 3, and ratified by the Politburo at its meeting there from August 4 to 6 (*Nianpu*, 1, pp. 464–5; Saich, *Rise to Power*, pp. 677–85; *Zhongguo gongchandang huiyi gaiyao*, pp. 164–7). The left column probably contained 45,000 men, the right column about 15,000.
Ten days later: *Nianpu*, 1, p. 467. *Central Committee resolution*: Ibid., p. 468; *Zhongguo gongchandang huiyi gaiyao*, pp. 167–70. *Darkest moment of my life*: Mao interviewed by Edgar Snow in Beijing in 1960 (*Red Star over China* [rev. edn], Grove Press, New York, 1969, p. 432). *'Inland Sargasso sea'*: Salisbury, p. 263.

332 *Deceptive green cover*: Braun, p. 136. *Undigested kernels ... into the bog, dead*: Salisbury, pp. 269–70. Chinese prisoners ate grains recovered from horse manure during the famine years in the early 1960s (Bao Ruo-wang [Jean Pasqualini] and Rudolph Chelminski, *Prisoner of Mao*, Penguin, Harmondsworth, 1976, pp. 241–2).
Several thousand casualties: Zheng Shicai, 'Battle for Pao-tso [Baozuo]', in *Recalling the Long March*, pp. 156–62; see also Yang, p. 156. *Oddly childish wireless signal*: Yu Jinan, *Zhang Guotao he*

'*Wode huiyi*', Sichuan renmin chubanshe, Chengdu, 1982, p. 218.

333   **We, your brothers**: *Nianpu*, 1, pp. 470–1. **He appeared to back down**: Ibid., pp. 471–2; Peng Dehuai, pp. 372–8.

    Between the lines: The text of the second telegram has never been made public, prompting some historians to suggest that Mao may simply have invented it in order to persuade the rest of the leadership to press on towards the north regardless (Yang, pp. 158–61 and p. 294, n.88; Salisbury, pp. 279–80; see also Braun, pp. 137–8). However, Peng Dehuai's account makes clear that the leadership was concerned about a *coup de force* by Zhang even before the second telegram arrived, and that Zhang himself, by withdrawing the First Army's codebooks, had given grounds for such suspicions (pp. 374–6). Moreover, at least one near-contemporary Party document explicitly accused him of having 'gone as far as to use his armies to threaten the Party Centre' ('Politburo Decision Concerning Zhang Guotao's Mistakes', March 31 1937, in Saich, p. 755).

    Hung by a thread: Snow, *Red Star over China* (rev. edn), p. 432, and *The Other Side of the River*, Random House, New York, 1962, p. 141.

334   **Mao punctured the tension**: Yang, p. 294, n.92. **One last message**: Yang, p. 159. Although exchanges continued between the two armies after Mao's forces left Baxi, this signal, sent on September 10, marked the Politburo's final attempt to dissuade Zhang from going south.

    Unhappy Zhu De: Even Zhang Guotao, in his memoirs, acknowledged that Zhu was 'depressed' at the situation in which he found himself (2, p. 427). But short of slipping away on his own and trying to rejoin Mao (which would have been suicidal), or inciting the small First Army units in the left column to break out under his leadership (which would have been equally foolhardy), Zhu and his Chief of Staff, the 'One-eyed Dragon', Liu Bocheng, had no choice but to accept the fait accompli. Mao evidently recognised this. In July 1936, the Politburo told the Comintern: 'Zhu is under constraint by Guotao and has no freedom to show his opinion independently' (*Nianpu*, 1, p. 470).

    Nationalist troops were advancing: Yang, p. 163. **Peng took Zhu's place**: *Nianpu*, 1, p. 473. **Mao revived an idea**: Ibid., p. 458; Braun, p. 121. **Lazikou Pass**: Salisbury, pp. 282–4; see also Hu Bingyun, 'How we captured Latzukou [Lazikou] Pass', in *Recalling the Long March*, pp. 111–17.

335   **From a GMD newspaper**: *Nianpu*, 1, p. 476; Peng Dehuai, p. 381. **Plan to make for the Soviet Union**: *Nianpu*, 1, p. 477; Yang, pp. 167–9. **Skirmishes with Moslem cavalry**: Salisbury, pp. 288–9. **Liu Zhidan . . . order their release**: *Nianpu*, 1, p. 484; see also Salisbury, pp. 289–93, and Yang, pp. 176–81.

    October 22: *Nianpu*, 1, p. 482. Although the Politburo's declaration that the march was at an end was not made until the 22nd, they actually arrived at Wuqi three days earlier. *Fewer than five thousand*: According to Peng Dehuai (p. 383), the First Army had 7,200 men when it reached Wuqi, but about a third of these had been recruited along the way. *In the south-west*: Slogans illustrated in photographs at Zunyi Museum; see also Mao's speech at Zunyi on 12 Jan. 1935 (*Nianpu*, 1, p. 443).

336 *Mao had learned*: Ibid., pp. 458 and 461; Braun, p. 122. *That summer*: Coble, Parks M., *Facing Japan: Chinese Politics and Japanese Imperialism, 1931–1937*, Harvard University Press, Cambridge, MA, 1991, pp. 182–225. *Zhang Guotao calls us*: Yang, p. 167. *New anti-Japanese base*: *Zhongguo gongchandang huiyi gaiyao*, pp. 173–5. *High on the crest of Liupan Mountain*: *Mao Zedong shici duilian jizhu*; this translation is adapted from Mao, *Nineteen Poems*, p. 19.

337 *On August 1, Wang Ming*: Saich, pp. 692–8. *News of these developments reached Shensi in November*: *Nianpu*, 1, p. 489. *Red Army had moved south*: Ibid., pp. 483–9; Peng Dehuai, pp. 384–7. *On Christmas Day, 1935*: Saich, p. 709; see also *Nianpu*, 1, pp. 497–9. *In its place came*: Saich, pp. 709–23.

338 *Zhang Wentian*: Oral sources. *The advocates of closed-door tactics*: SW1, pp. 164–8 (Dec. 27 1935).

339 *Even before the Wayaobu conference*: See Mao's instructions to Lin Biao on November 26, urging 'positive and honest methods to win over [the NE Army]'; his overtures to Zhang Xueliang's ally, Yang Hucheng, in early December, and his repeated orders to release captured officers (*Nianpu*, 1, pp. 490–1 and 493; Yang, p. 187). *From late November 1935*: See, for instance, Mao's letters to GMD commanders in *Nianpu*, 1, pp. 490 (26 Nov.), 494–5 (Dec. 5 1935), and 506 (Jan. 1936). *We are Chinese*: Ibid., p. 490.

340 *Gao Fuyuan*: Ibid., pp. 483, 502 and 505; Peng Dehuai, pp. 387–9. *On January 19 ... against his own Commander-in-chief*: *Nianpu*, 1, pp. 506–8, 512 and 514. *At the beginning of March*: Ibid., pp. 516–17 and 519. *Five weeks later*: Ibid., p. 534. See also pp. 522, 527–8 and 532–3; and Saich, pp. 741–2. Formal guidelines on dealings between the Red Army and the North-East Army were issued on June 20 (Saich, pp. 742–8).

341 *Free to pursue the other main task*: Saich, p. 705; *Nianpu*, 1, p. 493; Peng Dehuai, pp. 385–6 and 389. *The only realistic way ... watch over the Shensi base*: *Nianpu*, 1, pp. 499, 504 and 506; Peng Dehuai, pp. 390–3. *Eastern expedition*: *Nianpu*, pp. 508–39; Yang, pp. 187–9; Peng Dehuai, pp. 394–7. *Zhang had orchestrated ... CCP Northern Bureau*: Yang, pp. 191–3, 195 and 299, n.10; *Nianpu*, 1, p. 495. See also Salisbury, pp. 311–12, and Zhang Guotao, 2, pp. 424–8.

342 *At Ejie*: *Nianpu*, 1, pp. 472–3; Saich, pp. 685–6; Yang, pp. 160 and 164–5. *Chairman of the North-West Bureau*: *Nianpu*, 1, pp. 484–5.

Only in January, 1936: Saich, p. 741. *Zhang's star... isolated regions bordering Tibet*: Yang, pp. 193–8. *In May, when Mao returned*: *Nianpu*, 1, pp. 541–2. *Second Front Army . . . four hundred men*: Yang, pp. 211–18; Salisbury, pp. 319–21; Peng Dehuai, pp. 401–5; *History of the CCP, Chronology*, pp. 108–9.

343   *A month after Zhang's fateful order*: *Nianpu*, 1, p. 619. *Fifteen months earlier*: Ibid., p. 467 (Aug. 19 1935). *Peace feelers*: Ibid., p. 519. *'Chief traitor and collaborator'*: Saich, p. 711 (Dec. 25 1935). The CCP continued to describe Chiang as a traitor well into the summer of 1936 (ibid., p. 742, June 20 1936; *Nianpu*, 1, pp. 527–8). *One inner-Party directive*: Saich, p. 699 (October 1935).

344   *An artful mixture of substance and spin*: *Nianpu*, 1, p. 519. *They would be made public*: Ibid., pp. 527–8. *Hatred of Japan*: See Coble, Ch. 8.

Discreet meetings with Wang Ming: These occurred independently of Mao's initiatives. Several meetings were held in Moscow in January 1936, but Stalin, despite his interest in an alliance with Nanjing, was unconvinced of Chiang's sincerity and the talks fizzled out (*Chinese Law and Government*, vol. 30, 1, pp. 13–15 and 79–100; *Nianpu*, 1, p. 568).

Contact with Chen Lifu . . . in Hong Kong or Canton: *Nianpu*, 1, pp. 516, 519, 594, 596 and 607.

Our stand is to oppose Japan: Ibid., p. 533. Mao's attitude evidently evolved faster than Moscow's. The Soviet Union began to take seriously the possibility of a united front between the CCP and the GMD only in July 1936 (*Kommunisticheskii Internatsional i Kitaiskaya Revolutsiya, Dokumenty i Materialy*, Moscow, Izdatelstvo Nauka, 1986, pp. 263–6). *A month later he was wondering aloud*: *Nianpu*, 1, pp. 541 (15 May) and 551 (June 12 1936).

345   *The Politburo moved its headquarters*: Ibid., pp. 552–6. Unknown to Snow, Mao reached Bao'an on July 12, only a day before he did. *Those who imagine*: Snow, pp. 126–32.

Public and private appeals: *Nianpu*, 1, pp. 544 and 553. In telegrams to the CCP on July 23 and August 15, the Comintern urged that these efforts be intensified (Garver, John W, 'The Soviet Union and the Xian Incident', *Australian Journal of Chinese Affairs* [AJCA], no. 26, pp. 158–9). See also *Nianpu*, 1, pp. 568–618 passim; and Saich, pp. 764–8.

All-China United Democratic Republic: Saich, p. 572 (Aug. 25 1936). *For a people being deprived*: Snow, p. 439. *Change the designation . . . concession was possible*: *Nianpu*, 1, pp. 589 (September) and 608–9 (Nov. 12–13 1936).

346   *Chen Lifu*: Ibid., pp. 607 and 619–20. *On December 4*: Bertram, James, *First Act in China*, Viking Press, New York, 1938, pp. 110–12.

Ultimatum: Snow, p. 430; Wu, Tien-wei, *The Sian Incident: A Pivotal Point in Modern Chinese History*, University of Michigan Press, Ann Arbor, 1976, pp. 66–71; Coble, p. 343. *Marched in protest to Lintong*: Bertram, pp. 114–15; Wu, pp. 72–3; Snow, Helen Foster (Nym Wales) *The Chinese Communists: Red Dust*, Greenwood Publishing, Westport, CT, 1972, pp. 194–6. *On Thursday, the 10th*: *Nianpu*, 1, pp. 619–20. *Ye Zilong*: Wang Fan, *Yu lishi guanjianrenwude duihuao* (*Zhe qing zhe shuo*, vol. 2), Zhongguo qingnian chubanshe, Beijing, 1997, pp. 212–13. *Otto Braun*: Braun, pp. 182–3.

347 *The story . . . and resist Japan*: Bertram, pp. 115–23; Wu, pp. 75–80. *At a mass rally . . . drop of a hat*: Ibid.; Kuo, Warren, *Analytical History of the Chinese Communist Party*, vol 3, Institute of International Relations, Taibei, 1970, pp. 228–9; Zhang Guotao, 2, pp. 480–1. *Politburo meeting*: Ye Yonglie, *Mao Zedong yu Jiang Jieshi*, Fengyun shidai chubanshe, Taibei, 1993, vol. 1, pp. 168–77; *Nianpu*, 1, p. 621. See also Zhang Guotao, pp. 480 and 482–3. The main difference in these accounts is over the position of Zhang Wentian, whom Zhang Guotao says wanted Chiang killed and Ye says wanted him spared. All agree that Mao wanted Chiang brought to trial. *Judgement of the people*: *Nianpu*, 1, p. 621. The same wording was used in a telegram from the Red Army high command to the GMD national government on December 15 1936 (ZZWX, 11, pp. 123–5). On January 24 1937, Mao told a meeting of the Politburo Standing Committee that the use of this phrase had been 'incorrect' (*Nianpu*, 1, pp. 645–6). *Series of telegrams*: The *Nianpu* records five telegrams from Mao to Zhang Xueliang from December 12–15 (1, pp. 621–3).

348 *Zhang made clear*: Quoted in Bertram, pp. 126 7. *By the time Zhou Enlai*: *Nianpu*, 1, p. 624; see also Warren Kuo, 3, p. 228.

349 *The idea of putting Chiang on trial*: From December 13 onwards Mao stressed that the CCP's quarrel with Chiang was not 'on the same level' as its opposition to Japan (*Nianpu*, 1, p. 621). The last communist reference to putting Chiang on trial appeared on December 15. *Speechless with rage*: Snow, Edgar, *Random Notes on Red China*, Harvard University Press, Cambridge, MA, 1957, pp. x, 21. See also Zhang Guotao, 2, p. 484. *Far from being a revolutionary event . . . leading socialist power*: Yang, pp. 224–5; Garver, AJCA, 26, pp. 153–4, 157–8 and 164–73. Mao used the term 'revolutionary event' at the Politburo meeting of December 13 (*Nianpu*, 1, p. 621). Dimitrov's telegram was written in Moscow on the 16th, but given transmission difficulties and the time needed for coding and decoding, it is unlikely to have reached Mao in Bao'an before the morning of the 17th at the earliest

and very possibly not until the 18th. That day the CCP requested that it be retransmitted because part of the text was garbled. A complete version was received on the 20th (Yang Yunruo and Yang Guisong, *Gongchanguoji*, p. 392), when it was passed on to Zhou Enlai in Xian (*Nianpu*, 1, p. 626).

The CCP had already accepted: The editorial which appeared in *Jiefang bao* on December 17 (and which must therefore have been written on the 16th, before Dimitrov's telegram arrived) already pointed towards a peaceful resolution (see Yang, p. 303, n.25).

350   *The Generalissimo himself*: See Zhou Enlai's telegram to Mao on December 18 1936 (*Nianpu*, 1, p. 624). *Soong Mei-ling . . . went with him*: Bertram, pp. 143–52; Wu, pp. 135–53. *Chiang maintained*: Chiang Kai-shek, *General Chiang Kai-shek: The Account of the Fortnight in Sian when the Fate of China Hung in the Balance*, Doubleday, Garden City, 1937, pp. 149–50. *Zhou Enlai told Mao*: Zhou, SW1, pp. 88–90 (Dec. 25 1936). *'Ambiguous and evasive'*: Mao, SW1, p. 255 (Dec. 28 1936). *The first signs . . . 'firmly prepare for war'*: Wu, pp. 155–65; Bertram, pp. 205–6 and 219–20; *Nianpu*, 1, p. 639. *Two months later*: Wu, pp. 170–72; Coble, pp. 356–8.

All through the spring: *Nianpu*, 1, pp. 651 (Feb. 9); 657 (March 1); 657–9 (March 5 and 7); 674 (May 9); 676–7 (May 25); *Nianpu*, 2, pp. 9 (Aug. 4), 13 (Aug. 18) and 23 (Sept. 22 1937). See also Mao's interview with Nym Wales, Aug. 13 1936 (Wales, *My Yenan Notebooks*, privately published, 1961, pp. 151–3).

Mao was closer: *Nianpu*, 1, p. 633 (Dec. 28 1936).

351   *They were not the chief factor*: Mao told a Party conference on August 9 1937 that Chiang's change of policy had been 'forced on him by the Japanese' (*Nianpu*, 2, p. 12). *Lugouqiao*: Sun, Youli, *China and the Origins of the Pacific War, 1931–1941*, St Martin's Press, New York, 1993, pp. 87–90. *Even then the Generalissimo*: Ibid.; *Nianpu*, 2, p. 4. *Mao urged caution*: *Nianpu*, 2, p. 3. *Zhou Enlai went to Lushan*: Zhou, SW1, pp. 93–5; Yang, p. 241. *Ultimatum*: *Nianpu*, 2, p. 6. *Next day, Japanese troops occupied Beijing . . . National Revolutionary Army*: Ibid., pp. 6 and 16; Youli Sun, pp. 91–2; Yang, pp. 242–4; Wales, *Yenan Notebooks*, pp. 151–3.

352   *September 22*: *Nianpu*, 2, p. 23.

CHAPTER ELEVEN: YAN'AN INTERLUDE
THE PHILOSOPHER IS KING

353   *Red Army moved its headquarters*: The decision to move to Yan'an was taken in late December 1936. Mao himself arrived there on January 13 (*Nianpu*, 1, pp. 633 and 641).

Walled town of Yan'an: See Band, Claire and William, *Two Years with the Chinese Communists*, Yale University Press, New Haven, 1948, pp. 258–9; Cressy-Marcks, Violet, *Journey into China*, Dutton, New York, 1942, pp. 157–9; Forman, Harrison, *Report from Red China*, Henry Holt, New York, 1945, pp. 46–7; Hanson, Haldore, *Humane Endeavour*, Farrar & Rinehart, New York, 1939, pp. 292–5; Snow, Helen Foster, *The Chinese Communists*, p. xiv, and *My China Years*, William Morrow, New York, 1984, pp. 231–3 and 257–86; Payne, Robert, *Journey to Red China*, Heinemann, London, 1947, pp. 7–11.

354 *Standard Oil drums*: Wales, *My Yenan Notebooks*, p. 135. *Rather ordinary Chinese town*: Bisson, T. A., *Yenan in June 1937: Talks with the Communist Leaders*, University of California, Berkeley, 1973, p. 71. *Gallant youth*: Helen Snow, *Chinese Communists*, p. 251. *Heroic age*: Lindsay, Michael, *The Unknown War: North China 1937–1945*, Bergstrom & Boyle, London, 1975, n.p. *Steady fighting enthusiasm*: Stein, Gunther, *The Challenge of Red China*, McGraw-Hill, New York, 1945, pp. 88–9. *Special quality of life*: Bisson, pp. 70–1.
Darker side: Helen Snow and William Band both noted the proliferation of armed guards. See also Fitch, George, *My Eighty Years in China*, privately printed, Taibei, 1967, p. 150. For a hostile Russian eyewitness account, see Vladimirov, Pyotr Y., *China's Special Area, 1942–1945*, Allied Publishers, Bombay, 1974.

355 *Chinese Party should run things by itself*: *Nianpu*, 1, p. 525. *Soviet and Chinese policies*: Snow, *Red Star over China*, pp. 504–5. *Daoist temple*: Ibid., p. 547. *The 'university' was re-established*: Interviews in Bao'an, June 1997. *Problems of Strategy*: The revised text is in SW1, pp. 179–249. Extracts of the original version appear in Schram, Stuart R., *Political Thought of Mao Tse-tung*, pp. 202–5.

356 *Leftist adventurism*: Liu Shaoqi *nianpu*, 1, Zhongyang wenxian chubanshe, Beijing, 1996, pp. 173–7; Saich, *Rise to Power*, pp. 773–90. *Mao came out openly . . . to be overcome*: *Nianpu*, 1, pp. 677–9.

357 *Mao resumed his study*: Ibid., 1, pp. 615–17. *He annotated*: *Mao Zedong zhexue pizhuji*, Zhongyang wenxian chubanshe, Beijing, 1988; Shi Zhongquan, 'A New Document for the Study of Mao Zedong's Philosophical Thought', in *Chinese Studies in Philosophy*, vol. 23, 3–4, pp. 126–43. *Mitin*: For a detailed discussion of Mao's use of the Mitin group's texts, see Knight, Nick (ed.), *Mao Zedong on Dialectical Materialism: Writings on Philosophy, 1937*, M. E. Sharpe, Armonk, 1990. *Twice-weekly lecture course*: *Nianpu*, 1, p. 671; Knight, p. 78, n.154.
His opening talks: Mao's talks were based on written notes, first circulated in 1937 as a mimeographed study text under the title 'Dialectical Materialism, Lecture Outlines' (Gong Yuzhi, 'On Practice: Three

Historical Problems', in *Chinese Studies in Philosophy*, vol. 23, 3–4, p. 145).
The opening section deals with 'Dialectical Materialism', and in the
West – though not in China– it is usually referred to by that title. The
second text, 'On Practice', comes towards the end of this section, which
is followed by Mao's essay on 'The Law of the Unity of Contradictions',
hereafter referred to by its more familiar title, 'On Contradiction'.
Mao himself warned his audience: Knight, p. 126. ***Sought to deny
authorship***: Mao told Edgar Snow in 1965 'he had never written an
essay entitled "Dialectical Materialism". He thought he would
remember if he had' (*The Long Revolution*, Hutchinson, London,
1971, p. 207). ***He did break new ground***: Wylie, Raymond, F., *The
Emergence of Maoism: Mao Tse-tung, Ch'en Po-ta and the Search for Chinese
Theory, 1935–1945*, Stanford University Press, 1980, pp. 55–8.
'Oppose Book-worship': Schram, *Mao's Road*, 3, pp. 419–21.

358   ***'On Practice'***: Knight, pp. 132–48; rev. version, SW1, pp. 295–308.
'On Contradiction': Ibid., pp. 154–203; rev. version, SW1,
pp. 311–46. ***Life is death and death is life***: Schram, 1, p. 306. ***Later
commentators***: For example, Zhang Wenru, in 'Mao Zedong's
Critical Continuation of China's Fine Philosophical Inheritance',
Chinese Studies in Philosophy, vol. 23, 3–4, pp. 122–3. ***When the superstructure***: Knight, p. 186.

359   ***In August 1937***: *Nianpu*, 2, p. 10; Knight, p. 78, n.154. ***That
autumn***: Fogel, Joshua A., *Ai Ssu-ch'i's Contribution to the Development
of Chinese Marxism*, Harvard University Press, Cambridge, MA, 1987,
p. 30. ***Chen Boda***: Wylie, p. 13. ***Reading diary***: Gong Yuzhi,
pp. 161–2. ***He plainly found them***: Even the revision of 'On
Contradiction' for publication in 1951 took Mao far longer than he
expected (Schram, *Thought of Mao Tse-tung*, p. 64).
November 29 1937: *Nianpu*, 2, p. 40. See also Braun, *Comintern Agent*,
pp. 217–18. John Byron and Robert Pack give a colourful account of
Wang's return in *The Claws of the Dragon* (Simon & Schuster, New
York, 1992, pp. 135–6).

360   ***'Blessing from the sky'***: Shum Kui-Kwong, *The Chinese Communists'
Road to Power: The Anti-Japanese National United Front, 1935–45*,
Oxford University Press, 1988, p. 114.
Wang was too astute: Teiwes, Frederick C., *The Formation of the Maoist
Leadership: From the Return of Wang Ming to the Seventh Party Congress*,
Contemporary China Institute, London, 1994, pp. 5–7. Many early
accounts of Wang's return, apparently based on Taiwanese sources,
allege that he brought with him a directive from Stalin, endorsing
Mao's claims to be Party leader while at the same time sharply criti-
cising his ignorance of Marxism. No such directive ever existed.
Luochuan: The Politburo held an enlarged session at Luochuan,
attended by the principal military commanders, from August 22–25,

1937. This was followed by a Standing Committee meeting, at which Mao also spoke, on August 27. He was reappointed Chairman of the Military Commission, with Zhu De (replacing the disgraced Zhang Guotao) and Zhou Enlai as his deputies. The same meeting named Zhu Commander-in-Chief of the Eighth Route Army. The full texts of Mao's speeches are not available, but a summary is given in the *Nianpu* (2, pp. 14–17).

Chiang Kai-shek, he believed: On September 12, Mao warned Peng Dehuai, then Zhu De's deputy, 'they [the GMD] want to force our Red Army to fight the tough battles' (ibid., p. 20). *Campaign was launched*: Ibid., pp. 17 (Aug. 27), 21 (Sept. 14), 26–7 (Sept. 30), 31–2 (Oct. 13 and 22). *Telegrams to the Red Army commanders*: Saich, pp. 792–4 (Sept. 21 and 25).

361 *Pingxingguan*: Ibid., p. 668; *History of the CCP, Chronology*, pp. 116–17. *Fresh unease*: *Nianpu*, 2, pp. 26–7. See also Benton, *Mountain Fires*. *Separate peace*: *Nianpu*, 2, p. 33 (Oct. 19). *Keep its own counsel*: Ibid., p. 37 (Nov. 11). *Reject, criticise and struggle*: Ibid., p. 31 (Oct. 13). *Wang Ming, fresh from Moscow*: Saich, pp. 795–802; *Nianpu*, 2, p. 40; Peng Dehuai, *Memoirs*, pp. 415–19; Shum Kui-Kwong, pp. 115–16. *Mao retorted*: *Nianpu*, 2, pp. 40–1. *To Zhou Enlai*: Peng Dehuai, p. 418; Teiwes, pp. 7 and 44–5; *History of the CCP, Chronology*, pp. 120–1. See also Saich, p. 667.

362 *My authority did not*: Teiwes, p. 8. *Wang's efforts*: Ibid., pp. 5–8; Saich, pp. 668–70; Fei Yundong and Yu Guihua, 'A Brief History of the Work of Secretaries in the Chinese Communist Party (1921–1949)', *Chinese Law and Government*, vol. 30, 3 [May–June 1997], pp. 13–14. *Initially, Wang's policies*: Shum Kui-Kwong, pp. 122–5.

363 *The defence of that city*: *Nianpu*, 2, p. 51. See also Saich, pp. 802–12. *His own, bleak analysis*: *Nianpu*, 2, p. 51; Saich, p. 670. The Politburo met from February 27 to March 1. *'Luring the enemy in deep'*: In 'On Protracted War', three months later, Mao revived this formula explicitly, arguing that it was 'the most effective military policy for a weak army strategically on the defensive to use against a strong army' (SW2, p. 172). *Problems of Strategy*: Ibid., pp. 79–112.

364 *'On Protracted War'*: Ibid., pp. 113–94. See also Schram, *Thought of Mao Tse-tung*, pp. 206–9.

365 *Once again, the Politburo split*: Saich, p. 670. *Ren Bishi*: *Nianpu*, 2, p. 51. *Communist leaders' unanimous support*: Wang's actual words were: 'The comrades attending the Politburo meeting had the same views concerning the current situation.' (Saich, p. 802). See also Shum Kui-Kwong, p. 126.

Where Mao denounced: Shum Kui-kwong, p. 126. See also Mao's criticisms of 'unhealthy phenomena' under the GMD (SW2, p. 131), and his insistence at the February Politburo meeting (and on other occasions) that the communists 'should mainly depend on ourselves' (*Nianpu*, 2, pp. 48 and 51).

When Mao instructed them: *Nianpu*, 2, p. 66; ZZWX, 11, pp. 514–15 and 518–19; Shum Kui-kwong, p. 134. **Emulate Madrid**: *Liuda yilai – dangnei mimi wenjian*, Renmin chubanshe, Beijing, 1981, vol. 1, pp. 946–64. See also Garver, John W. *Chinese Soviet Relations, 1937–1945*, Oxford University Press, 1988, pp. 74–5. **In August, Chiang Kai-shek's police**: Saich, p. 671; Shum Kui-kwong, pp. 134–8. **When Ren Bishi**: Garver (pp. 76–7) gives the best account, but compresses the chronology. See also Teiwes, pp. 28 and 30, n.90.

366 **By July**: Teiwes (pp. 29–30) regards a Comintern resolution of June 11, criticising 'the capitulationist tendency of right opportunism' (in other words, the policies of Wang Ming) as marking the crucial shift. In July, *Pravda* for the first time published Mao's photograph, together with that of Zhu De.

Dimitrov had warned him: Ibid., p. 29. **One morning in the second week**: *Nianpu*, 2, p. 90.

He knew, as Wang did not: Mao had evidently received word of Moscow's decision by August 3, for on that date the Standing Committee proposed that the full Politburo should meet in enlarged session (the first gathering of the entire leadership since December 1937). When more details arrived, it was decided to hold a CC plenum instead (ibid., p. 84; Saich, p. 671). Wang Ming was told that a new directive had come from Moscow, but not what it contained (Garver, p. 78; *Renmin ribao*, Dec. 27 1979).

Wang Jiaxiang read out . . . growing struggle: *Nianpu*, 2, p. 90.

367 **Sixth Plenum**: Ibid., p. 91. **If a Chinese communist**: Schram, *Political Thought*, pp. 113–14; SW2, pp. 209–10. **Wuhan fell . . . in his absence**: Saich p. 672; *Nianpu*, 2, p. 92.

368 **Ridiculed Wang's slogan . . . when they held power**: SW2, pp. 213–17 and 219–35.

369 **Party Secretariat**: Teiwes, pp. 8–9; *Nianpu*, 2, p. 98. **Acting General Secretary**: Teiwes, p. 10. **Japanese bombers**: *Nianpu*, 2, p. 96. **That November Mao married**: Ibid., p. 97. See also Ye Yonglie, *Jiang Qing zhuan*, Shidai wenyi chubanshe, Changchun, 1993, pp. 164–5; Wang Fan, *Zhe qing zhe shuo*, 2, pp. 217–18.

370 **Edgar Snow remembered**: Snow, pp. 107, 124 and 132–3. **We are like iron and steel . . . felt herself excluded**: Wang Xingjuan, *He Zizhende lu*, pp. 224–6. **A real crisis in Yan'an . . . to wear lipstick**: Snow, Helen Foster, *Chinese Communists*, pp. 250–61; Wales, *Yenan Notebooks*, pp. 62–4.

371 **Bottled up her feelings**: Wang Xingjuan, p. 226. **She was pregnant . . .**

decided to leave him: Ibid., p. 227; see also Ye Yonglie, *Jiang Qing zhuan*, p. 157.

Only then, it seems: By then two months had elapsed since the fateful evening in Smedley's cave. Mao presumably thought He Zizhen would get over it, unaware of her deeper frustration at the way their relationship had changed.

He Zizhen recalled . . . return to China in 1947: Wang Xingjuan, pp. 227–45. For the expulsion of Smedley and Lily Wu, see Snow, *Red Star Over China*, p. 532. The exact date of He's departure is uncertain, but Zhang Guotao's wife, Ye Ziliao, met her in Xian in September (Zhang Guotao, *Rise of the Chinese Communist Party*, 2, p. 562); Ye Ziliao's own account of the meeting (*Zhang Guotao furen huiyilu*, Hong Kong, 1970, pp. 333–4) is suspect. Jiang Qing's claim to Roxane Witke that He Zizhen beat her children – like much else in her account of those years – was untrue (Witke, *Comrade Chiang Ch'ing* [Jiang Qing], Weidenfeld & Nicolson, London, 1977, pp. 160–1).

371n *This begs the question*: See Wales, *Yenan Notebooks*, p. 63; Snow, *Red Star over China*, p. 532; Smedley, *Battle Hymn of China*, p. 123.

372 *Jiang Qing made her entrance*: Mao's secretary, Ye Zilong, has confirmed Jiang Qing's claim to have arrived in Luochuan during the Politburo conference of late August, 1937, though her description of the entire leadership turning out to greet her is pure fantasy. She was presented to Mao in Yan'an a few days later by the wife of the veteran Jinggangshan commander, Xiao Jingguang (Wang Fan, pp. 213–15; Witke, p. 146).

Like the Party's Security chief . . . she, not he, took the initiative: Much of Jiang Qing's early life, especially the years she spent in Shanghai, has been deliberately obscured. The following account is drawn mainly from Ye Yonglie, *Jiang Qing zhuan*; Byron and Pack, *Claws of the Dragon*: Witke, *Comrade Chiang Ch'ing*, and Terrill, Ross, *Madame Mao: The White-Boned Demon*, New York, 1992.

373n *Kang Sheng*: Byron and Pack, pp. 405–7.

374 *Nothing he could do would bring her back*: It was actually not quite so clear-cut. In the spring or early summer of 1938, Mao sent a telegram to He Zizhen in Moscow, asking her, yet again, to return to Yan'an. In her reply, she indicated for the first time that she might be prepared to do so – but not until she had completed her studies in two years' time. Mao was not prepared to wait (Wang Xingjuan, p. 234).

Mao was the type of man: Snow, Helen Foster, *Chinese Communists*, p. 251. *In August . . . officiated as hostess*: Ye Yonglie, pp. 161–5; Wang Fan, pp. 217–18. *Three conditions*: Ye Yonglie, pp. 162–3. *Where there was real concern . . . similar doubts*: Wang Fan, pp. 217–18.

Officially, he maintained . . . Mao's pillow companion: Ibid.; Ye Yonglie, pp. 148, 162 and 173. Byron and Pack (pp. 147–9) give a highly-coloured and often exaggerated account of Kang's role, but their thesis that Kang promoted Jiang Qing's cause to serve his own interests is undoubtedly correct. There is no evidence that Jiang Qing knew Kang before her arrival in Yan'an, and still less that they had an affair.

His new wife should stay: This is implicit in Jiang Qing's own account of her life to Roxane Witke. See also Ye Yonglie, p. 166.

375 *Jiang Qing knitted*: Ibid., p. 167. *Li Yinqiao*: Ibid., pp. 159–61. *In August 1940 . . . sterilised*: Ibid., pp. 168–9. *At Yangjialing . . . separate quarters*: Ibid., pp. 165 and 171–3.

376 *Her importunities . . . I've just got to put up with her*: Ibid., pp. 175–7. *Anying and Li Min*: Li Min had joined He Zizhen in the Soviet Union in 1941. She was sent back to Yan'an after her mother was committed to an asylum in 1945 (Wang Xingjuan, p. 239).

377 *Secret decision*: Shum Kui-kwong, pp. 149 and 154.

Mao's counter-order: Mao first used this phrase, which became the Party guideline for communist forces in their dealings with GMD military units, at a Secretariat meeting on January 12 1939 (*Nianpu*, 2, p. 103). It was not made public, however, until eight months later (*History of the CCP, Chronology*, p. 132).

'Frictions': *Nianpu*, 2, passim; Shum Kui-kwong, pp. 153–4. *These tensions reached their peak*: See Shum Kui-kwong, pp. 184–8; Saich, pp. 860–3; and *History of the CCP, Chronology*, pp. 140–2. *'Hundred Regiments Campaign'*: *History of the CCP, Chronology*, p. 139; Saich, pp. 859–60; Peng Dehuai, pp. 434–47. *The legitimacy it conferred . . . halt new admissions*: Yang, *From Revolution to Politics*, p. 307, n.3; Saich, pp. 888–90. *'Magic weapon'*: Saich, pp. 906–12.

378 *The entry of the Soviet Union*: Ibid., pp. 863–4.

Mao himself had written . . . 'soundly on the Bolshevik road': Saich, pp. 910–12 (Oct. 4 1939). By then, a campaign to collect historical texts had been under way for more than a year in preparation for the Seventh Congress, which was to make a 'basic summation' of Party history from 1928 onward (Wylie, pp. 74–5).

To try to head off this challenge: Shum Kui-kwong, pp. 214–5. See also Teiwes, p. 10, n.31. *In December 1940*: SW2, pp. 441–2.

379 *When Liu Shaoqi urged him*: Teiwes, p. 10. *'Melons ripen'*: Dai Qing, *Wang Shiwei and 'Wild Lilies'*, M. E. Sharpe, Armonk, 1994, p. 155.

He opened his attack . . . movement he was about to unleash: *Nianpu*, 2, pp. 326–7; *Zhongguo Gongchandang huiyi gaiyao*, pp. 216–17; Saich, *Rise to Power*, pp. 1008–1011. See also Saich, Tony, 'Writing or Rewriting History? The Construction of the Maoist Resolution on Party History', in Saich and Van de Ven, *New Perspectives on the*

Chinese Communist Revolution, pp. 312–18; Teiwes, pp. 11–16; SW3, pp. 17–25 (subjectivism) and 165–6 ('one of the half-dozen crucial steps'). A week before the meeting opened, the Yan'an Party newspaper, *Jiefang ribao*, published an editorial lamenting the fact that Mao's calls over the last three years for the 'sinification of Marxism' had still not been put into effect (Wylie, p. 167).

380 **Uppermost echelons**: Shum Kui-kwong, p. 218; Saich, *Rise to Power*, p. 972. **Even Peng Dehuai**: *Memoirs*, pp. 424–5. **Two major speeches**: 'Rectify the Party's style of work', Feb. 1 1942, and 'Oppose stereotyped Party writing', Feb. 8 1942, in Compton, Boyd, *Mao's China: Party Reform Documents, 1942–44*, University of Washington Press, Seattle, 1952, pp. 9–53, and SW3, pp. 35–68. **We are communists**: SW3, p. 35. **As an arrow**: Ibid., p. 42, and Compton, p. 21.

381 **In future . . . every sentence from memory**: Compton, pp. 13–14. **Book-learning**: Ibid., pp. 16–17 (translation amended). **We must plant our backsides**: 'How should we study the history of the Chinese Communist Party?', March 30 1942, *Dangshi yanjiu*, 1, 1980, pp. 2–7, translated in Schram, Stuart R., *Foundations and Limits of State Power in China*, University of London, 1987, p. 212.

382 **The Party's ruling organs**: Teiwes, pp. 17–18.

383 **Regardless of their class origin**: Saich, p. 722.
The open-door approach . . . patriotism more than communist conviction: These issues are discussed in Shum Kui-kwong, pp. 164–73, 189–211 and 224; Wylie, pp. 162–5; and Saich, 855–9 and 974–7. Excerpts from the original text of 'On New Democracy' are translated in Saich, pp. 912–29; see also SW2, pp. 339–84, esp. pp. 353–4 and 358. **By the end of the Long March**: *Nianpu*, 1, p. 489. See also SW2, p. 441.

384 **Stemmed from the Classical teachings**: See Schram, *Political Thought*, p. 113. **If our Party's style**: Compton, p. 11. **As Confucius had written**: Schram, Stuart R., Mao Zedong: *A Preliminary Reassessment*, Chinese University Press, Hong Kong, 1983, pp. 39–40. **'The masses are the real heroes'**: SW3, p. 12 (March 17 1941). **All correct leadership**: Ibid., p. 119 (June 1 1943). **'Movement of enlightenment' . . . encourage slavishness**: Compton, p. 31. **Uniformity of thought**: Ibid., p. 24. **Submission to Central leadership**: Saich, p. 1007 (July 1 1941).

385 **'The first step'**: Compton, p. 37 (Feb. 8 1942).

385 **Wang Shiwei**: The following account of Wang's persecution is
/ based mainly on Dai Qing's splendid book, *Wang Shiwei and 'Wild*
389 *Lilies'*. See also Apter, David E., and Saich, Tony, *Revolutionary Discourse in Mao's Republic*, Harvard University Press, Cambridge, MA, 1994, pp. 59–67; Benton, Gregor, and Hunter, Alan, *Wild Lily, Prairie Fire*, Princeton University Press, 1995, pp. 7–13; Byron and Pack, *Claws of the Dragon*, pp. 176–83; Fu Zhengyuan, *Autocratic Tradition and Chinese Politics*, Cambridge University Press, 1993, pp. 269–74;

Goldman, Merle, *Literary Dissent in Communist China*, Harvard University Press, 1967, pp. 23–50; Saich, *Rise to Power*, pp. 982–5; Teiwes, Frederick C., *Politics and Purges in China: Rectification and the Decline of Party Norms, 1950–1965*, M. E. Sharpe, New York, 1979, pp. 74–5; and Wylie, *Emergence of Maoism*, pp. 178–90.

386 *Typically, he encouraged both interpretations*: Dai Qing, pp. 37 and 39. *Forum on literature and art*: SW3, pp. 69–98, esp. pp. 90–93. For a translation of the unrevised text, see McDougall, Bonnie S., *Mao Zedong's 'Talks at the Yan'an Conference on Literature and Art'*, University of Michigan, Ann Arbor, 1980, esp. pp. 79–83.

387 *A 'cadre screening movement' . . . in some cases posthumously*: Byron and Pack, pp. 176–82; Teiwes, *Formation of the Maoist Leadership*, pp. 54–7.

389 *A hundred leagues*: Mao, *Nineteen Poems*, p. 22. Many Chinese regard this as the best of Mao's poems.

390 *In June 1937 . . . printed in Shanghai*: Wylie, pp. 41 and 62. *'Genius in leadership'*: Ibid., p. 75. *What might almost be called*: Braun, p. 249. *'No rhythm in his being'*: Smedley, *Battle Hymn of China*, p. 123. *I could hear a string bass*: Rittenberg, Sidney, *The Man Who Stayed Behind*, Simon & Schuster, New York, 1993, p. 72.

391 *The biggest naked sword*: Cressy-Marcks, pp. 162–7. *Mao no longer visited*: Ibid. See also Band, pp. 251–2. *Chevrolet*: Terrill, Ross, *Mao*, Simon & Schuster, New York, 1993, p. 184. *Plethora of superlatives . . . guiding doctrine in the Red areas*: Wylie, pp. 110–13, 155–7 and 190–203'; SW3, pp. 103–7 ('Red Verdun').

392 *Hagiographic article*: Saich, pp. 1145–52 (July 6 1943). *That was the signal . . . 'Selected Works' were compiled*: Wylie, pp. 207–18; White, Theodore H., and Jacoby, Annalee, *Thunder out of China*, William Sloan, New York, 1946, pp. 229–34. *Mao's portrait*: Deane, Hugh (ed.), *Remembering Koji Ariyoshi: An American GI in Yenan*, US-China People's Friendship Association, Los Angeles, 1978, p. 22.

Zedong Youth School: Schram, *Foundations and Limits of State Power in China*, p. 213. *Toddlers*: I have not been able to establish exactly when this began, but by the early 1950s it was standard practice in Chinese kindergartens (Liang Heng and Shapiro, Judith, *Son of the Revolution*, Random House, New York, 1983, pp. 6–8).

393 *Labour heroes . . . first furrow*: Schram, p. 213. *All through Chinese history*: Saich, 'Writing or Rewriting History?', pp. 302–4 and 317; Wylie, pp. 226–8.

393 *The crux of the problem . . . and Ren Bishi, fifth*: This account of
/   Mao's campaign to win acceptance of his new version of Party
395 history draws on Saich, 'Writing or Rewriting History', pp. 299–338; Saich, *Rise to Power*, pp. 985–91; Teiwes, *Formation of the Maoist*

Leadership, esp. pp. 19–23 and 34–59; and Wylie, pp. 228–33, 237–8 and 272–4.

395   *Sage-like serenity*: Snow, *Random Notes on Red China*, p. 69. *Abstraction*: Carlson, Evans Fordyce, *Twin Stars of China*, Dodd, Mead & Co. New York, 1940, p. 167.

396   *Sitting next to history*: Rittenberg, p. 77. *On July 22*: Barrett, David D., *Dixie Mission: The United States Army Observer Group in Yenan, 1944*, University of California Press, Berkeley, 1970, pp. 13–14, 29–30. *Mao set the tone*: Carter, Carolle J., *Mission to Yanan*, University Press of Kentucky, Lexington, 1997, p. 35. See also 'Directive of the CC on Diplomatic Work', Aug. 18 1944, in Saich, *Rise to Power*, pp. 1211–15. *The decision to send . . . mediation effort*: Barrett, pp. 19–28; Westad, Odd Arne, *Cold War and Revolution*, Columbia University Press, New York, 1993, pp. 7–30; Carter, pp. 106–16.

397   *Unfortunately . . . astonished disbelief*: Barrett, pp. 56–7; Deane, pp. 21–3.

398   *He offered Mao . . . strength of their position*: Barrett, pp. 57–76.

399   *At the end of 1944 . . . at its peril*: Saich, p. 1234. See also van Slyke, Lyman, *The Chinese Communist Movement during the Sino-Japanese War, 1937–45*, in CHOC, 13, p. 709. *'Margarine communists'*: Westad, p. 14. See also Molotov's conversation with Hurley, quoted in Carter, pp. 107–8. *'Campaign of moderation'*: Shum Kui-kwong, pp. 227–9; Garver, pp. 254–5; Roderick, John, *Covering China*, Imprint Publications, Chicago, 1993, p. 34. *Secret overtures*: Garver, pp. 257–8.

400   *A month later the Yalta summit . . . they had to acquiesce*: From
/   February 1945 to mid-1946, US and Soviet policy towards China
403   was in flux. Mao's views during this complex and confusing period are a matter of intense controversy, with scholars disagreeing over even such basic questions as whether he was seeking a military or a diplomatic solution to CCP–GMD rivalry. John Garver (esp. pp. 209–30 and 249–65), Odd Arne Westad, and Michael M. Sheng (*Battling Western Imperialism: Mao, Stalin and the United States*, Princeton University Press, 1997) provide carefully researched factual accounts of the period (but divergent interpretations). My own view is that Mao was quite simply out of his depth. For further discussion, see Goldstein, Steven M., 'The CCP's Foreign Policy in Opposition, 1937–1945', in Hsiung, James C., and Levine, Steven I. (eds), *China's Bitter Victory*, M. E. Sharpe, Armonk, 1992, pp. 122–9; Hunt, Michael H., *The Genesis of Communist Chinese Foreign Policy*, Columbia University Press, New York, 1996, pp. 159–71; Niu Jun, 'The Origins of Mao Zedong's Thinking on International Affairs', in Hunt, Michael H., and Niu Jun (eds), *Towards a History of Chinese Communist Foreign Relations, 1920s–1960s*, Woodrow Wilson Center,

Washington, 1997, pp. 10–16; and the pioneering though now somewhat dated account by James Reardon-Anderson (*Yenan and the Great Powers*, Columbia University Press, New York, 1980).

400   **Comprehensive strategy**: 'On Coalition Government', and 'Speech to the Seventh Congress', 24 April, 1945, Saich, pp. 1216–43. See also van Slyke, CHOC, 13, p. 717.
    In coded cables: On June 15, 1945, Mao wrote that a renewed civil war was 'possible'; on July 22, that the danger of civil war was 'unprecedently serious'; and on August 4 that it was 'inevitable'. See Zhang, Shu Guang and Chen, Jian (eds), *Chinese Communist Foreign Policy and the Cold War in Asia*, Imprint Publications, Chicago, 1996, pp. 22–3 and 25–6. On August 13, he told a meeting of cadres in Yan'an that Chiang Kai-shek's 'policy is set'; the most that would be possible would be to keep the civil war 'for a time . . . restricted in size and localised' (SW4, p. 22).

401   *Own crucifixion*: Vladimirov, p. 491. *Mao in a baggy blue suit*: Jin Chongji, *Mao Zedong zhuan*, pp. 727–35. *Mao, Chiang fumed*: Westad, p. 109. *Memorandum of understanding*: China White Paper, US Department of State, Washington, 1949, pp. 577–81. See also SW4, pp. 53–63.

403   *His neurasthenia*: *Nianpu*, 3, p. 49; Jin Chongii, p. 749. See also Rittenberg, pp. 106–10. *Visitors were told*: Roderick, p. 32. *All through November*: Shi Zhe, *Zai lishi juren shenbian*, Zhongyang wenxian chubanshe, Beijing, 1991, p. 313. *In the end it was President Truman*: Westad, pp. 118–39.

404   *A glimmer of hope*: *Nianpu*, 3, p. 50. *Marshall*: Westad, pp. 143–7. *Mao was ecstatic*: Zhang and Chen pp. 58–62 (Feb. 1 1946). *That night, he gave a banquet . . . Napoleon and Lenin*: Roderick, pp. 32–4.

405   *For a few weeks more . . . possibility of warfare resuming*: Westad, pp. 150–8; Sheng, pp. 123–33. *A week later*: *Nianpu*, 3, pp. 62–3; Sheng, p. 133. See also Reardon-Anderson, p. 151. *Changchun . . . ten days later*: Westad, pp. 159–61. *Mao continued to urge*: Ibid.; Zhang and Chen, pp. 67–8 (May 15 1946). This period is well discussed in Sheng, pp. 134–44. *Marshall's mediation effort . . . central and northern China*: Zhang and Chen, pp. 68–70 (May 28 1946). See also Reardon-Anderson, pp. 157–9.

406   *Irreplaceable guide and symbol*: During his illness, his colleagues sent a panic-stricken appeal to Stalin to send a Russian doctor (the Soviet leader obliged, and Dr Andrei Orlov came to Yan'an by special plane). Shi Zhe, p. 313. *Still rankled 20 years later*: Westad, p. 155 and p. 216, n. 59. *Not only unavoidable*: SW4, p. 89 (July 20 1946).

407   *Mao burst out laughing*: Shi Zhe, pp. 337–8. *At dusk on March 18*: *Nianpu*, 3, p. 176.

CHAPTER TWELVE: PAPER TIGERS

408   *For the first nine months . . . regain control of the villages*: Pepper, Suzanne, 'The KMT-CCP conflict, 1945–1949', in CHOC, 13, pp. 758–64.

409   *Mao ordered his forces*: SW4, pp. 103–7 (Sept. 16 1946). *By February 1947*: Ibid., pp. 119–27 (Feb. 1 1947). *The Party leaders divided*: *History of the CCP, Chronology*, p. 183. *A sardonic cat-and-mouse game*: Rittenberg, pp. 118–9.

410   *'Tactics of wear and tear'*: SW4, pp. 133–4 (April 15 1947). *Mao (and quite separately the Americans)*: SW4, p. 114 (Oct, 1 1946); Pepper, CHOC, 13, pp. 758 and 764. *Generalissimo later acknowledged*: Pepper, CHOC, 13, p. 728; Eastman, Lloyd E., *Seeds of Destruction: Nationalist China in War and Revolution, 1937–1949*, Stanford University Press, 1984, p. 210. *Matters were not helped by*: Pepper, CHOC, 13, pp. 766–7. *Communist retreat ended . . . Beijing to Wuhan*: Ibid., pp. 764–6 and 770–4; Hu Sheng, *Concise History of the CCP*, pp. 346–51. *Mao was able to announce . . . wail about a crisis*: SW4, pp. 160 and 162–3 (Dec. 25 1947).

411   *All through the spring and summer*: Pepper, CHOC, 13, pp. 772–4; *History of the CCP, Chronology*, pp. 192 and 194–5. *Mao began to calculate . . . by mid-1951*: SW4, pp. 223–5 (March 20 1948). See also Saich, *Rise to Power*, pp. 1319–20 (Oct. 10 1948). *Eight months later*: SW4, p. 288 (Nov. 14 1948).
       Astonished even him: On October 10, 1948, Mao still expected it would take until mid-1951 to overthrow GMD rule. Only three weeks later, on October 31, he revised that estimate to the autumn of 1949 (*Nianpu*, 3, p. 378). See also his remarks to Anastas Mikoyan in February 1949 (Shi Zhe, *Zai lishi juren shenbian*, p. 375).

411   *One factor . . . was more than enough*: The following is based
  /   largely on Lloyd Eastman's classic account in his book, *Seeds of*
413   *Destruction* (especially chs 6, 7 and 9). See also Pepper CHOC, 13, pp. 763 (communists' inability to protect the population) and 737–51 (in the cities, the regime fared no better).

412   *Topple over*: For Barrett's bleak appraisal of the nationalist armies, see *Dixie Mission*, pp. 60 and 85–7. *Another American officer reported*: Deane, *Remembering Koji Ariyoshi*, p. 29.

413   *Mao responded by*: The shift to a more radical land policy was signalled in a CC Directive, drafted by Liu Shaoqi and issued on May 4, 1946. In December 1947, Mao called it 'the most fundamental condition for the defeat of all our enemies' (SW4, p. 165). The following year, however, it was recognised that it had become excessively leftist and efforts were made to rein it in (Saich, pp. 1197–1201 and 1280–1317).

Two years earlier: SW3, pp. 271–3 (June 11 1945).

414 *It was not the atom bomb*: *Nianpu*, 2, pp. 616–17; SW4, pp. 21–2 (Aug. 13 1945). *The atom bomb is a paper tiger*: SW4, pp. 100–1 (August 1946). *Three climactic battles*: Pepper, CHOC, 13, pp. 774–83; Winnington, Alan, *Breakfast with Mao*, Lawrence & Wishart, London, 1984, pp. 82–106. For a recent official CCP account (placing appropriate emphasis on the role of Deng Xiaoping!), see Hu Sheng, pp. 370–81. *Overall plan of campaign*: SW4, pp. 261–4 (Sept. 7 1948).

415 *Again, Mao drew up a plan*: Ibid., pp. 289–93 (Dec. 11 1948).

416 *Chiang Kai-shek resigned*: Pepper, CHOC, 13, p. 784; Barnett, A. Doak, *China on the Eve of the Communist Takeover*, Praeger, New York, 1963, pp. 304–7. *Country bumpkin*: For Mao's defence of 'bumpkins', see Saich, p. 1069 (Feb. 1 1942). *Apart from one moment*: Sheng, *Battling Western Imperialism*, pp. 100 and 102–4.

417 *Take medium and small cities*: SW4, p. 144 (Sept. 1 1947). *Shifting the centre of gravity*: Saich, p. 1321 (Oct. 10 1947). *That month Mao embarked*: See SW4, pp. 361–75 (March 5 1949) and Saich, pp. 1338–46 (March 13 1949). *Small progressive parties*: Barnett, pp. 83–95. *[The reactionaries say]*: 'On the People's Democratic Dictatorship', June 30 1949, in Saich, pp. 1364–74. A revised text is included in SW4, pp. 411–23.
     For all those who happened: In January 1948, when Mao was trying to maximise the Party's support in the countryside, he offered yet another view of this question, stating: 'Our task . . . is to wipe out the landlords as a class, not as individuals' (SW4, p. 186). Individual landlords and rich peasants, he argued, should be 'saved and remoulded'.

418 *Streets lined by a mass*: Winnington, p. 103. *Feeling of relief*: Bodde, Derk, *Peking Diary: A Year of Revolution*, Henry Schuman, New York, 1950, p. 99. *Foreign captain*: Winnington, p. 106. *Uncharted territory*: Saich, p. 1374 (June 30 1949). *With victory*: SW4, p. 374 (March 5 1949) [translation amended]. See also Saich, p. 1346.

419 *On the afternoon*: Quan Yanchi, *Mao Zedong: Man not God*, pp. 119–23; for a conflicting version, see Li Zhisui, *Private Life*, pp. 51–2. *The Chinese people*: SW5, pp. 16–17 (Sept. 21 1949). *Enormous red silk lanterns . . . the old imperial city*: Kidd, David, *Peking Story*, Aurum Press, 1988, pp. 64–73. *We, the 475 million*: SW5, p. 19 (Sept. 30 1949).

420 *Next day the Soviet Union*: JYMZW, Zhongyang wenxian chubanshe, Beijing, 1993, 1, pp. 17–18. *Motley group*: Kau, Michael Y. M. and Leung, John K. (eds), *The Writings of Mao Zedong*, M. E. Sharpe, Armonk, 1986, 1, pp. 16 and 31. *Most of south-west China . . . temporary capital*: Pepper, CHOC, 13, pp. 783–4; Zhang, Shu Guang, *Deterrence and Strategic Culture*, Cornell University Press, Ithaca, NY, 1992, pp. 70–1. *On December 6*: Shi Zhe, p. 432.

Foreign policy priorities: Mao's 'lean to one side' policy, his evolving attitude to the United States and his decision to delay diplomatic relations with the West, are discussed at length in Chen Jian, *China's Road to the Korean War*, Columbia University Press, New York, 1994, pp. 15–23, 33–57 and 64–78; Hunt, *Genesis of Communist Chinese Foreign Policy*, pp. 171–80; Sheng, pp. 158–86; and Zhang, pp. 13–45. For relevant documents, see also Zhang and Chen (eds) *Chinese Communist Foreign Policy*, pp. 85–126. The crucial period was the first half of November 1948, when the capture of Shenyang forced Mao for the first time to confront the practicalities of dealing with US diplomats. At that point his emphasis shifted abruptly from an overriding desire to avoid provoking the West to an aggressive assertion of New China's sovereign rights.

Anastas Mikoyan: Shi Zhe, p. 379.

421 *In a speech*: Saich, pp. 1368–9.

Not to send his forces across the Yangtse: This remains contentious. Michael Sheng, among others, argues that having erred in 1945, Stalin would have not tried, four years later, to hold Mao back a second time (p. 169). Chinese Party historians, however, insist that the Russians had strong reservations about the PLA advancing into southern China lest it provoke American intervention (Salisbury, *New Emperors*, p. 15). Mao himself, in 1956, told the Soviet Ambassador: 'When the armed struggle against the forces of Chiang Kai-shek was at its height, when our forces were on the brink of victory, Stalin insisted that peace be made with Chiang Kai-shek, since he doubted the forces of the Chinese Revolution' (*Cold War International History Project Bulletin* [CWIHP], nos 6–7, Winter 1995, p. 165). See also Chen Jian, pp. 67 and 245–6, n. 13, for later comments by Mao and Zhou Enlai. Russia's decision to maintain its ambassador to the national government through the summer of 1949, often cited as evidence of Stalin's reluctance to abandon his ties with Chiang Kai-shek, is not directly relevant. It reflected, above all, Moscow's desire for continuity regarding the Sino-Soviet Friendship Treaty, which enshrined Chinese recognition of the independence of Outer Mongolia and gave the USSR special privileges in Manchuria.

Real friends and false friends: Shi Zhe, p. 385. *Winners are always right*: Ibid., pp. 414 and 426; for a slightly different version, see Chen Jian, pp. 72–3. *Mao's train . . . an attack of neurasthenia*: Shi Zhe, p. 433.

422 *That night at 6 p.m. . . . the road to socialism*: Detailed and
/   conflicting accounts of Mao's stay in Moscow, may be found in:
425 Chen Jian, pp. 78–85; Goncharov, Sergei N., Lewis, John W., and Xue Litai, *Uncertain Partners: Stalin, Mao and the Korean War*, Stanford University Press, 1993, pp. 76–129; Shi Zhe, pp. 433 et seq.; Zhang,

pp. 29–33. Mao's own recollection of the visit, in his conversation with Pavel Yudin in March 1956, is published in CWIHP, pp. 165–6, as are the Russian minutes of Mao's meetings with Stalin on December 16, 1949, and January 22, 1950 (ibid., pp. 5–9).

422   *The Soviet leader ... cut in*: Shi Zhe, pp. 434–5.

422n *Kennan*: Zhang, *Deterrence and Strategic Culture*, p. 36; CWIHP, 6–7, pp. 148–9 and 165. *Mao had started telling*: Shizhe, p. 435

425   *He thought our revolution was a fake*: 'Speech to the Chengdu Conference', March 10 1958, *Mao Zedong sixiang wansui*, Beijing, 1969, pp. 159–72. *4.40 a.m.*: Shtykov to Zakharov, June 26 1950, in CWIHP, 6–7, pp. 38–9. *Kim Il Sung*: Shtykov to Vyshinsky, May 12 1950, ibid. *Stalin, wily as ever ... part of the conversation*: Goncharov, Lewis and Xue, pp. 145–6.

   Deeply unwelcome: Ibid., p. 146. At a meeting with the North Korean Ambassador, Li Zhouyuan, in late March, Mao had treated the question of American intervention in characteristically elliptical fashion, stating that, on the one hand, the US 'would not get into a Third World War for such a small territory [as Korea]', but, on the other hand, if a world war did break out, North Korea would not escape it and should therefore begin to prepare itself (CWIHP, 6–7, pp. 38–9).

   Mao had been suspicious ... decision should be postponed: Roshchin to Stalin, May 13, and Stalin to Mao, May 14 1950, in CWIHP, 4, p. 61.

426   *A hundred thousand Koreans*: Chen Jian, pp. 106–9; Zhang, Shu Guang, *Mao's Military Romanticism*, University Press of Kansas, 1995, pp. 44–5. *Kim decreed*: Goncharov, Lewis and Xue, pp. 152–4.

   To Chiang Kai-shek ... the following year: Zhang, *Deterrence and Strategic Culture*, pp. 51–73. Mao wanted to invade Taiwan in the summer of 1950, but preparations took longer than expected and, at the beginning of June, the attack was postponed until mid-1951 (Goncharov, Lewis and Xue, pp. 148–9 and 152). On August 11 the CCP CC Military Commission directed that the invasion be delayed further, until 1952 or later, as a result of developments in Korea (Zhang and Chen, *Chinese Communist Foreign Policy*, pp. 155–8; Chen Jian, p. 132).

   Korea changed all that: US policy on Taiwan was in any case hardening in the spring and early summer of 1950 (Chen Jian, pp. 116–21). Even so, military action to support the Chinese nationalists would have been far more difficult for America to justify than the defence of South Korea.

426 *Mao's initial response ... had a proper night's sleep*: A wealth of new
 /   evidence, including documents from the Chinese Central Archives,
431   memoirs by Chinese participants and recently declassified Soviet materials, made public since 1990, has cast fresh light on the arcane manoeuvring between Stalin, Mao and Kim Il Sung in the summer

and autumn of 1950 which led to China's decision to intervene in Korea. See, in particular Chen Jian, pp. 131–209; Goncharov, Lewis and Xue, pp. 130–99; Hunt, *Genesis of Communist Chinese Foreign Policy*, pp. 183–90; Zhang, *Mao's Military Romanticism*, pp. 55–94, and *Deterrence and Strategic Culture*, pp. 90–100.

429 ***A crisis had erupted over Soviet military support ... Mao's bluff had been called***: On the morning of October 2, Mao drafted a telegram to Stalin, informing him of China's decision to intervene (oral sources; and Chen and Zhang, pp. 162–3). When, later that day, he received Stalin's message, he scrapped his original draft (a hand-written copy of which is held in the Chinese Central Archives), and sent a new version via the Soviet Embassy in Beijing (which was received by Stalin on October 3, and a copy of which is held in the Russian Presidential Archive). Zhou later confirmed that he presented Stalin with 'two options, and asked him to decide', while in later years Mao remembered only that China had threatened not to send troops (discussion with Kim Il Sung, 1970, quoted in Chen Jian, p. 199). For Stalin's cables to Mao on October 1; to Kim on October 8; and the second version of Mao's October 2 cable to Stalin, see CWIHP, 6–7, pp. 114–17 and 106–7, n. 30.

431 ***After initial defensive skirmishing ... armistice to be signed***: The best, and fullest, account of Chinese military strategy and tactics in Korea, and of Mao's pre-eminent role in defining them, is given by Shu Guang Zhang in *Mao's Military Romanticism*, pp. 95–244.

432 ***Peng and the other Chinese commanders***: See Domes, Jurgen, *Peng Dehuai: The Man and the Image*, Hurst, London, 1985, pp. 65–70. ***He exulted that autumn***: SW5, pp. 115–20 (Sept. 12 1953). ***Mao's impatience ... back into the Chinese fold***: Chen Jian, p. 104; Zhang, *Military Romanticism*, pp. 253–4.

433 ***China's attitude to the Soviet Union***: Mao claimed in later years that Stalin came to trust the Chinese communists only after the Korean War (CWIHP, 6–7, pp. 148–9 and 156). On the other hand, Xu Xiangqian, in Moscow in 1951 to negotiate arms supplies for the war, concluded that the Russians were holding back military aid because they did not want China to become too strong (Zhang, *Military Romanticism*, p. 222). The two are not mutually exclusive. See also Goncharov, Lewis and Xue, pp. 217–25 and 348, n. 9.
400,000 casualties: Zhang, *Military Romanticism*, p. 247.
Anying: Ibid., pp. 193–4; Liu Jiecheng, *Mao Zedong yu Sidalin*, Zhonggong zhongyang dangxiao chubanshe, Beijing, 1996, pp. 645–7. Quan Yanchi, quoting Mao's bodyguard, Li Yinqiao, says that Jiang Qing and Ye Zilong broke the news to Mao (*Mao Zedong: Man not God*, pp. 43 and 172). See also Kau and Leung, 1, pp. 147–8

434 ***Anying's relationship with his father***: Quan Yanchi, pp. 168–72.

In the spring of 1950 . . . might be shown leniency: Kau and Leung, 1, pp. 97–103 (June 6 1950). Mao's stress on leniency towards counter-revolutionaries in mid-1950 was not quite as marked as it is usually painted. His statement that '[we must not] execute a single secret agent and not arrest the majority of them', usually dated September 27 1950, was actually made seven years earlier. None the less, he wanted the campaign kept within bounds.

435 *3,000 officials*: Teiwes, Frederick C., 'Establishment and Consolidation of the New Regime', CHOC, 14, p. 84. *The Korean War changed all that*: Chen Jian, pp. 139–40 and 193–4; and Teiwes, Frederick C., *Elite Discipline in China: Coercive and Persuasive Approaches to Rectification, 1950–1953*, Australian National University, Canberra, p. 54. *Anti-American demonstrations*: Chen, Theodore, H. E., *Thought Reform of the Chinese Intellectuals*, Hong Kong University Press, 1960, pp. 24–7. *Huge hoarding*: Lum, Peter, *Peking*, Robert Hale, 1958, p. 60. *People were encouraged . . . donors' names*: Zhang, *Military Romanticism*, pp. 201–2. *An Italian . . . harsher social controls*: Lum, pp. 33–9, 67–74 and 83–92. *Germ warfare*: Zhang, *Military Romanticism*, pp. 181–6; Lum, pp. 177–84.

436 *Campaign to suppress counter-revolutionaries*: Chen Jian, p. 194. See also Teiwes, *Elite Discipline*, p. 55, and CHOC, 14, pp. 88–92. *Mao himself fine-tuned*: Kau and Leung, 1, pp. 162–3 (Jan. 17); SW5, pp. 54–6 (March 30, May 8 and June 15 1951) *Land reform lurched violently*: Teiwes, CHOC, 14, pp. 83–8.

437 *To cleanse our society*: SW5, p. 72 (Jan, 1 1952) *Mao launched*: For the 'Three Antis' and the 'Five Antis', see ibid., pp. 88–92; Teiwes, *Elite Discipline*, pp. 17–48 and 115–48; and Chen, *Thought Reform*, pp. 51–3. *The bourgeoisie, Mao explained*: SW5, p. 77 (June 6 1952). *Intellectuals were treated*: Chen, *Thought Reform*, pp. 54–71.

438 *Silver lining*: Chen Jian, pp. 215 and 220–23.
Two million deaths: This is a conservative figure. Nearly 150,000 died in Korea; 710,000 counter-revolutionaries had been executed by May 1951 (in a campaign which continued until 1953); at least a million landlords and family members died; and 'several hundred thousand' citizens perished in the 'Antis' campaigns.
Like students in the old days: Bo Yibo, *Ruogan zhongda juece yu shijiande huigu*, Zhonggong zhongyang dangxiao chubanshe, Beijing, 1993, 1, p. 155.

CHAPTER THIRTEEN: THE SORCERER'S APPRENTICE

439 *Not Mao's strong point*: 'I am an outsider in the field of economics,' he told businessmen in December 1956 (Kau and Leung, *Writings of*

Mao, 2, p. 200). ***Avowed aim***: Thompson, *Mao Zedong: Report from Xunwu*, p. 64. ***Two substantial innovations***: Saich, *Rise to Power*, pp. 976–7. ***When the PLA occupied Tibet***: SW5, pp. 73–6 (April 6 1952).

440   ***Five-year credit***: Chen Jian, *China's Road to the Korean War*, pp. 77 and 84; Goncharov, Lewis and Xue, *Stalin, Mao and the Korean War*, p. 95. ***Mao spoke publicly***: Saich, p. 1374 (June 30 1949); SW4, p. 423. ***Five-Year Plan***: Teiwes, CHOC, 14, pp. 92 and 96–7. ***Dogmatism***: Talk at the Chengdu conference, March 10 1958, in Schram, Stuart R., *Mao Tse-tung Unrehearsed*, Penguin, Harmondsworth, 1974, p. 98. ***Whip up a high tide***: Kau and Leung, 1, p. 318 (Feb. 7 1953).

     Voluntary, step-by-step approach: Friedman, Edward, Pickowicz, Paul G. and Selden, Mark, *Chinese Village; Socialist State*, Yale University Press, New Haven, 1991, pp. 112–84; Teiwes, CHOC, 14, pp. 110–11. For Mao's subsequent acknowledgement that in agriculture, China did not follow the Soviet lead, see Schram, *Unrehearsed*, p. 98.

441   ***'General line for the transition to socialism'***: SW5, pp. 93–4 (June 15) and 102 (August 1953). ***Fifteen years or a little longer***: Ibid., pp. 93, 101 (July 9) and 110 (Aug. 12 1953). ***Eighteen years***: Teiwes, Frederick C., and Sun, Warren (eds), *The Politics of Agricultural Cooperativization in China*, M. E. Sharpe, Armonk, 1993, p. 49. ***Already in 1951 . . . must be clarified***: Ibid., pp. 28–32 and 53–4; Teiwes, Frederick C., *Politics at Mao's Court: Gao Gang and Party Factionalism in the Early 1950*, M. E. Sharpe, Armonk, 1990, pp. 42–3, 62–71 and 187–212; Teiwes, CHOC, 14, pp. 99–101. Mao's criticisms of Bo may be found in SW5, pp. 103–11 (Aug 12 1953).

442   ***The dispute between Bo and Gao . . . he merely went too far***:
/   The definitive account of the Gao Gang affair is Frederick Teiwes's
444   study, *Politics at Mao's Court*, which concludes that Mao had no intention of replacing Liu and Zhou but leaves open the key question of how far the Chairman may have gone in encouraging Gao's ambitions. Oral sources, knowledgeable about the history of the period, insist that Mao did lead Gao on and that the latter's suicide was a mute protest against his betrayal.

442   ***In May 1953 . . . they are invalid***: SW5, p. 92 (May 19 1953). Liu Shaoqi was criticised implicity, because he was in charge of the day-to-day running of the Secretariat.

444   ***'Sinister wind'***: Ibid., p. 162 (March 21 1955).

444n ***In the mid-1980s***: Oral sources.

445   ***Reduced to tools***: Quan Yanchi, *Mao Zedong: Man not God*, pp. 152–5. ***Ended with no clear consensus . . . he was mistaken***: This section is

based on documents contained in Teiwes and Sun, especially pp. 82–154; and Teiwes, CHOC, 14, pp. 110–19.

446 *The peasants want freedom*: Teiwes and Sun, p. 42 (May 9 1955). *Deng told his subordinates*: Ibid., p. 107 (July 11 1955). *Shelled with artillery*: Ibid., p. 136 (July 11 1955). *A high tide . . . by whatever means*: SW5, p. 184 [translation amended] (July 31 1955). *Targets were raised . . . victory over Chiang Kai-shek*: Teiwes and Sun, pp. 47–8 and 107–18.

447 *In the first half of 1955 . . . largely assured*: SW5, pp. 249–50 (December 1955). *Only 3 percent*: Teiwes, CHOC, 14, p. 113. *Bourgeoisie was now isolated . . . a thing of the past*: SW5, p. 214 (Oct. 11 1955).

448 *'How to make a cat eat pepper'*: Roderick MacFarquhar deserves the credit for spotting this revealing little fable, which is recounted in Karl Eskelund's *The Red Mandarins* (Alvin Redman, London, 1959, pp. 150–1). See MacFarquhar, *Origins of the Cultural Revolution*, vol. 1, Oxford University Press, 1974, p. 327, n. 51.
Mao asked his private-sector interlocutors: Loh, Robert, and Evans, Humphrey, *Escape from Red China*, Michael Joseph, London, 1963, p. 136; Teiwes, CHOC, 14, p. 120. *Even so, the speed*: MacFarquhar, 1, pp. 22–5, *History of the CCP, Chronology*, p. 254. *Rightist conservatism*: MacFarquhar, 1, p. 27; SW5, p. 240 (Dec. 27 1955). *Number-one country*: Kau and Leung, 2, p. 13 (Jan. 20 1956).

449 *As a first step*: MacFarquhar, 1, pp. 27–9. *More, faster, better*: Teiwes and Sun, p. 49. *More, faster, better and more economically*: MacFarquhar, 1, pp. 30–1. *Saltationist socialism*: Ph.D. thesis by Michael Schoenhals (University of Stockholm, 1987). *On February 25, 1956*: Short, Philip, *The Dragon and the Bear*, Hodder & Stoughton, London, 1982, pp. 265–76. A text of the Secret Speech was issued by the US State Department on June 4, 1956. *A week later, Deng Xiaoping*: MacFarquhar, 1, pp. 43. *Such criticisms, he said*: Conversation with Yugoslav Communist Delegation, September 1956, CWIHP, 6–7, p. 151. *Meeting with the Soviet Ambassador*: Conversation with Pavel Yudin, March 31 1956, in ibid., pp. 164–7.

450 *On the Historical Experience*: Bowie, Robert and Fairbank, J. K. (eds), *Communist China 1955–1959: Policy Documents with Analysis*, Harvard University Press, 1962, pp. 144–51 (April 5 1956). *Mikoyan and Peng Dehuai*: MacFarquhar, *Origins*, 2, p. 194.
The efforts of Khrushchev: Mao described Sino-Soviet relations in September 1956 as 'more or less . . . brotherly, but the shadow of the father-and-son relationship is not completely removed' (CWIHP, 6–7, p 151). Two years later the shadow was omnipresent as Mao raged at the Soviet Ambassador about Moscow's paternalism and contempt for Chinese abilities (ibid., pp. 155–9).

451 **Communist baby**: Zagoria, Donald, S., *The Sino-Soviet Conflict, 1956–1961*, Princeton University Press, 1962, p. 44. **After riots**: CWIHP, 10, pp. 152–5; MacFarquhar, *Origins*, 1, pp. 169–71. **Great power chauvinism**: 'More on the Historical Experience of the Dictatorship of the Proletariat', in Bowie and Fairbank, pp. 261 and 270 (Dec. 29 1956). See also 'Zhou Enlai to Mao Zedong', CWIHP, 10, p. 153. **I think there are two 'swords'**: SW5, pp. 341–2 (Nov. 15 1956). Mao had earlier used the 'sword' analogy at a meeting with the Soviet Ambassador, Pavel Yudin, on October 23 (CWIHP, 10, p. 154).

452 **Second People's Daily editorial**: Bowie and Fairbank, pp. 257–72 (Dec. 29 1956). **Displeased**: CWIHP, 10, p. 154. **Three parts bad**: Kau and Leung, 2, p. 114 (Aug. 30 1956). The same formula appears in the version of Mao's speech, 'On the 10 Great Relationships' (April 25 1956), published in SW5 (p. 304), but this appears to be a later addition, not in the original version. **Imperialism, in Mao's view**: Bowie and Fairbank, pp. 257–9 (Dec. 29 1956).

453 **Existence of contradictions**: Ibid., p. 258 (Dec. 29 1956). **'Communiqué'**: MacFarquhar, 1, p. 176. **While Zhou complained**: CWIHP, 10, pp. 153–4. **Not all Soviet farts**: Kau and Leung, 2, p. 71 (April 1956); see also p. 114 (Aug. 30 1956). **Personalised attacks**: Chen, *Thought Reform*, pp. 37–50 and 80–5; see also Kau and Leung, 1, pp. 481–4 (Oct. 16 1954), on Yu Pingbo, and 506–8 (Dec. 1954), on Hu Shi.

454 **Secret History**: Kau and Leung, 1, pp. 72 (March 1950) and 496 (Oct. 1954). **Wu Xun**: Ibid., pp. 196–201 (May 20 1951). **Liang Shuming**: SW5, pp. 121–30 (Sept. 16–18 1953). See also Zhou Jingwen, *Fengbao shinian*, Shidai piping chubanshe, 1962, pp. 434–7. **Hu Feng**: Goldman, Merle, *Literary Dissent*, pp. 129–57; Chen, *Thought Reform*, pp. 85–90.

April 1956: Mao's first known use of the full 'Hundred Flowers' slogan was at an enlarged Politburo meeting in April (Kau and Leung, 2, p. 70). He repeated it on May 2, in a speech to the Supreme State Conference, and it was diffused to a wider audience by the Propaganda Department chief, Lu Dingyi, on May 26 (MacFarquhar, 1, pp. 51–6; Bowie and Fairbank, pp. 151–63).

455 **Stony ground**: MacFarquhar, 1, p. 84. **Discipline that stifles ... won't work**: Kau and Leung, 2 pp. 66–75 (April 1956). **If war is not brewed**: Ibid. p. 255 (Jan. 27 1957). **Shortage of skilled manpower**: MacFarquhar, 1, pp. 33–5; Chen, *Thought Reform*, pp. 104–16; Goldman, pp. 158–60. **Party bureaucrats**: *Guangming Ribao*, May 7 1986; MacFarquhar, Cheek and Wu, (eds), *Secret Speeches of Chairman Mao*, p. 43. **The most visible effect . . . stories less boring**: MacFarquhar, *Origins*, 1, pp. 37–8 and 75–7.

456 **Personality cult**: Ibid., p. 47. The *People's Daily* specifically affirmed

that 'leaders play a big role in history' and said it was 'utterly wrong' to deny this (Bowie and Fairbank, p. 147). See also CWIPH, 6–7, p. 149. *The only significant change . . . would assume his mantle*: MacFarquhar, 1, pp. 99–109 and 149–51; see also Terrill, *Mao*, pp. 272–3. *Beginning to feel his age*: Kau and Leung, 2, p. 19 (Jan. 26 1956). *China was no exception*: See ibid., pp. 203 and 233 (Dec. 8 1956 and Jan. 18 1957). *Part of the answer . . . full of contradictions*: Ibid., pp. 158–95 (Nov. 15 1956). Like most of Mao's speeches in his later years, this is a discursive, rambling text, made the more so because it is available only in two (significantly different, but overlapping) Red Guard versions.

456n *Sleeping pill*: Oral sources, Beijing, 1997. It may seem hard to believe that, in a Party as centralised and disciplined as the CCP in 1956, such an important issue could be decided in so haphazard a fashion. However, that is apparently what happened. In China, as elsewhere, muddle is more often an explanation than conspiracy in politics.

457 *If there is a pustule*: Kau and Leung, 2, p. 205, Dec. 8 1956. *Some of the younger writers*: MacFarquhar, 1, pp. 178–9; Goldman, pp. 165–82; Teiwes, *Politics and Purges*, pp. 232–4.

458 *Selection of his poems*: Kau and Leung, 2, pp. 223–4 (Jan. 12 1957). *Critics had got it wrong*: Ibid., p. 243 (Jan. 18 1957); see also MacFarquhar, Cheek and Wu, pp. 168–9.
Writings hostile to Marxism . . . bourgeois thinking: Kau and Leung, 2, p. 279 (Chiang Kai-shek); pp. 255 and 280–1 (Cankao Xiaoxi) [Jan. 27 1957]. He later backtracked on Chiang's works, saying that they should be published only in a restricted edition (ibid. p. 356, March 1 1957).
Let them fart: Ibid., pp. 260–1 and 290 (Jan. 27 1957). *Quarantine*: Ibid., p. 256 (Jan. 27) *Truth stands in contrast*: Ibid., p. 253 (Jan. 27)

459 *Wouldn't it be a little strange*: Ibid., pp. 258–9 and 289 (Jan. 27). *A few weeks later*: MacFarquhar, Cheek and Wu, p. 121 (50 to 60 per cent) [Feb. 16] and p. 241 (90 per cent) [Mar. 8 1957]. *Normal*: Kau and Leung, 2, p. 303 (Feb. 16 1957). *We'd just go back to Yan'an*: Ibid., p. 258 (Jan. 27 1957). *He paraphrased*: Ibid., pp. 253 and 292 (Jan. 27). See also the revised version of Mao's February 27 speech (ibid., p 317).

460 *Proletariat of 12 million . . . the petty bourgeoisie*: This message is spelt out, in somewhat disjointed fashion, in Mao's two speeches on February 16 (MacFarquhar, Cheek and Wu, p. 117; Kau and Leung, 2, pp. 302–5). See also ibid, p. 260: 'We must allow the democratic personages to stage their play opposite ours, and let them go ahead and criticise' (Jan. 27 1957); and SW5, pp. 313–14 (Aug. 30 1956). *Nearly two thousand*: MacFarquhar, *Origins* 1, p. 184. *Mao began by*

speaking ... Guomindang methods: MacFarquhar, Cheek and Wu, pp. 113–89 (Feb. 27 1957).

461 *So stimulated*: MacFarquhar, Roderick, *The Hundred Flowers Campaign and the Chinese Intellectuals*, Praeger, New York, 1960, p. 19. *I was in a daze*: Loh and Evans p. 222. *Fei Xiaotong*: MacFarquhar, *Hundred Flowers*, pp. 24–5. *Jian Bozan*: Ibid., pp. 27–8.

Their prudence ... isolate themselves: MacFarquhar, Cheek and Wu, p. 156 (great progress) [Feb. 27]; Kau and Leung, 2, pp. 229–30 (untrustworthy) [Jan. 18]; MacFarquhar, Cheek and Wu, p. 144 (loving their country) [Feb. 27]; p. 257 (nothing strange) [Jan. 27]; MacFarquhar, Cheek and Wu, p. 173 (allowing poisonous weeds to grow) [Feb. 27]; Kau and Leung, 2, p. 234 (fertiliser) [Jan. 18]; MacFarquhar, Cheek and Wu, p. 144 (only very, very few) [Feb. 27]; Kau and Leung, 2, p. 243 (resolutely suppressed) [Jan. 18]; MacFarquhar, Cheek and Wu, pp. 175–6 (disturbances) [Feb. 27]; Kau and Leung, 2, p. 233 (expose and isolate) [Jan. 18].

462 *Unity of opposites*: Ibid., p. 256 (Jan. 27 1957). *Alone with the people*: Malraux, André, *Anti-mémoires*, Paris, 1968.

So long as his colleagues: Roderick MacFarquhar discusses at length purported leadership differences over the Hundred Flowers campaign (*Origins*, 1, chs. 13–16), and many later writers have followed his lead. More recent information casts doubt on his conclusions: not only was there no high-level leadership split in 1957, but Mao was never under significant pressure from his colleagues. Although it is plausible (and I personally believe) that Liu and Peng Zhen were somewhat less enthusiastic about the 'Hundred Flowers' than Deng and Zhou, it is certainly not proven. Most of the evidence adduced from Kremlinological analysis of Chinese public statements (which, in 1974, when MacFarquhar's book was published, were virtually the only sources available) has since proved erroneous, a salutary warning of the limitations of the method!

Wandering lobbyist: MacFarquhar, Cheek and Wu, p. 321 (March 19). *Half his time ... scolded for a while*: Ibid., p. 359 (calm and unhurried) [March 20]; pp. 300 and 329–30 ('In the past ... who can they argue with?') [March 18 and 19]; pp. 292–4 (think for themselves) [March 17]; p. 305 (vitality) [March 18]; p. 303 (sarcastic) [March 18]; Kau and Leung, 2, p. 517 (scolded) [early April].

463 *Up till now ... chief is in charge*: MacFarquhar, Cheek and Wu, pp. 366–7 (April 30). See also p. 229 (March 8) and Kau and Leung, 2, p. 522 (early April). *He had found it necessary*: MacFarquhar, Cheek and Wu, pp. 351–62 (March 20). *Intellectuals' fears*: Ibid., pp. 201 and 210 (March 6); Kau and Leung, 2, p. 517 (early April). *Stopped dragging its feet*: MacFarquhar, Cheek and Wu, pp. 210, 240, 336 and 357 (March 6, 8, 19 and 20). *Even the People's Daily*:

Ibid., pp. 50–2; Kau and Leung, 2, p. 515; and interviews with Wang Ruoshui, Beijing, June 1997.

464 **Politburo met**: *Liu Shaoqi nianpu*, 2, p. 398; JYMZW, 6, pp. 423–3. **In practice, he said**: MacFarquhar, Cheek and Wu, p. 366 (April 30). **May day holiday**: Wu Ningkun, *A Single Tear*, Hodder & Stoughton, London, 1993, pp. 50–51. **Let's try it**: Kau and Leung, 2, p. 519 (early April). **Participation by non-communists**: JYMZW, 6, pp. 417–18 (April 27). **Wu Ningkun**: Wu, p. 54. **Woman cadre**: Liang and Shapiro, *Son of the Revolution*, pp. 8–9. **One of the leaders**: This was my father-in-law, Gu Zhen.

465 **The main thrust . . . one thinks is another**: MacFarquhar, *Hundred Flowers*, pp. 44–109, esp. pp 51–3 (Chu Anping); 87–9 (economics lecturer); 65 (dog-shit) and 68 (no one dares).

466 **On May 4**: JYMZW, 6, pp. 455–6. **On May 15**: Ibid., pp. 469–76; see also SW5, pp. 440–6.

467 **This is not setting an ambush**: Kau and Leung, 2, p. 524. **The movement next spread**: MacFarquhar, *Hundred Flowers*, pp. 130–73. **Any word or deed**: SW5, p. 447 (May 25). **'Arbitrary and reckless'**: MacFarquhar, *Hundred Flowers*, pp. 108–9. **'Malevolent tyranny'**: Ibid., pp. 94–5. **In Wuhan . . . Shandong**: Ibid., pp. 145–61. **Certain people**: Kau and Leung, 2, pp. 566–7. **Central Committee directive**: Ibid., pp. 562–4.

468 **Six criteria**: SW5, p. 412. **On July 1**: Kau and Leung, 2, pp. 592–6. **A mouthpiece**: Ibid., p. 596. **The people themselves . . . to discriminate**: MacFarquhar, Cheek and Wu, pp. 203 and 247 (March 6 and 8). **There is no simple answer**: Mao's statements for the next six months were riddled with contradictions. In the editorial of July 1, for instance, he accused the Rightists of trying 'to unseat the Communist Party and take its place themselves', but then insisted: 'We can be lenient and not mete out punishment . . . We should allow them to retain their own views [They] will still be allowed freedom of speech' (Kau and Leung, 2, pp. 593 and 595). A few days later, he wrote of an 'irreconcilable, life-and-death contradiction' with the Rightists, but then stated that 'some of them', perhaps a majority, would be able to reform (pp. 654 and 659). In October, he was still ambivalent, declaring that 'there are bothersome problems. This business of revolution is troublesome' (p. 742).

469 **Slip of the tongue**: MacFarquhar, Cheek and Wu, p. 204 (March 6). Mao said: 'Now it's an ideological struggle, it's different . . . We should not over-estimate the enemy and under-estimate ourselves.' **Hair and skin**: Kau and Leung, 2, pp. 510 (April 30), 524 (April) and 631 (July 9). **What had started . . . on its head**: Mao's claim in July that 'we had anticipated these things' was fictive (ibid., p. 602).

Some reluctance: The clearest indication of this came in Mao's editorial of July 1, where he wrote that a new round of struggle between the proletariat and the bourgeoisie had been 'independent of people's will. That is to say, it [was] unavoidable. Even if people wanted to avoid it, it couldn't be done. The only thing to do then was to follow the dictates of the situation and obtain victory' (Ibid., pp. 594–5). See also his insistence, later the same month, that 'blooming and contending' should not be completely abandoned (p. 640).
'Confused by false appearances': Kau and Leung, 2, p. 639 (July 17). ***Panicking about the risk***: MacFarquhar, *Hundred Flowers*, p. 167–70 (June 6 and 7). ***In speeches . . . more far-sighted***: Kau and Leung, 2, pp. 654–5 and 662 (July).

470 ***Leniency***: In October, Mao drew an explicit comparison with earlier campaigns, declaring: 'We are not going to handle them the way we did the landlords and counter-revolutionaries in the past' (ibid., p. 732). ***The 'Rightists' were not shot . . . chosen first***: Teiwes, *Politics and Purges*, pp. 300–20. ***Wu Ningkun***: Wu, pp. 72–173. ***Woman police cadre***: Liang and Shapiro, pp. 9–15. ***These people not only talk***: Kau and Leung, 2, p. 596 (July 1). ***Goal***: Ibid., p. 655 (July).

471 ***Zhongnanhai***: Li Zhisui, *Private Life*, pp. 76–80. Dr Li, who had not yet become Mao's physician, says he moved into Zhongnanhai on his return from Moscow in February 1950 (p. 52). A well-informed oral source dates the move to November 1949.

472 ***For Mao . . . for not doing so***: Ibid.; see also p. 60; Quan Yanchi, pp. 84–9.

473 ***Anqing***: Li Zhisui, pp. 56–8. ***Bedridden***: Ibid., pp. 140–5, 187–8 and 190; Witke, *Comrade Chiang Ch'ing*, pp. 254–62. ***Separate lives***: Li Zhisui, p. 85. ***Even Li Yinqiao***: Quan Yanchi, pp. 107 and 134–41. ***He Zizhen***: Ye Yonglie, *Jiang Qing zhuan*, pp. 239–42. ***Immortals***: Mao, *Nineteen Poems*, p. 30 [translation amended]. See also the version in Terrill, *Mao*, pp. 276–7.

474 ***Into the gap . . . good communist husbands***: Oral sources; see
/ also Li Zhisui, pp. 355–64, and Salisbury, *New Emperors*, pp. 134,
475 217–19, 221. Some of those who worked with Mao in the 1950s and '60s, including Wang Dongxing and Lin Ke, have sought publicly to cast doubt on Dr Li's account, alleging that it is exaggerated and sometimes inaccurate. Minor details apart, however, his version has been confirmed, under conditions of anonymity, by several of the Chairman's former partners. Its essential veracity is not in doubt.

474 ***Union of man and woman***: Van Gulik, Robert, *Erotic Colour Prints of the Ming Period*, privately published, Tokyo, 1951 [Taiwan Reprint], p. 39.

474n ***A few weeks***: *Peking Review*, Oct. 14 1977.

475   ***Obsessed with old age***: Li Zhisui, p. 363. ***Li Yinqiao***: Quan Yanchi, p. 137. ***Surrogate family***: Ibid., p. 12. ***Friendship was ruled out***: Ibid., pp. 153–5. ***Relationship between man***: Ibid., p. 88.

476   ***Khrushchev had disapproved***: MacFarquhar, *Hundred Flowers*, p. 306. ***Petrified***: Kau and Leung, 2, pp. 255 and 262 (Jan. 27 1957). ***Attempted to apply... 'Not read'***: MacFarquhar, *Origins*, 1, pp. 59–61, 86–91 and 126–9. ***At the time***: Kau and Leung, 2, pp. 159 and 179–80 (Nov. 15 1956). ***Agricultural surpluses***: MacFarquhar, 1, pp. 293–4; and 2, pp. 2–4.
    Intellectuals needed to run it: Kau and Leung, 2, pp. 660 (July) and 702 (Oct. 9 1957). Although Mao began emphasising the need for a corps of proletarian intellectuals from the summer of 1957 onward, he did not entirely abandon the possibility of utilising the skills of the bourgeoisie, and this idea resurfaced at intervals throughout the late 1950s (MacFarquhar, *Origins*, 2, pp. 40 and 179–80).
    Soviet financial aid: MacFarquhar, 2, p. 19.

477   ***'Basically over'***: MacFarquhar, Cheek and Wu, pp. 280, 285, 288, 301, 308, 352, and especially 371. Liu Shaoqi would later be accused of having fabricated this notion in his report to the Eighth Congress (MacFarquhar, *Origins*, 1, pp. 119–21 and 160–4). However, Mao did not object *at the time* either to Liu's report or to the Congress resolution. On November 15 1956, he told the Second Plenum of the Eighth CC: 'In today's China, the class contradiction has already been basically resolved, and the primary domestic contradiction is the contradiction between an advanced social system and backward forces of production' (Kau and Leung, 2, p. 184). This corresponds precisely to the incriminated section of the resolution Liu drafted. Mao emphasised from the start that 'basically' meant 'not yet entirely' (ibid., p. 197, Dec. 4 1956), but this was also made clear in Liu's report, which stated that class struggle would continue until socialist transformation was completed (see text in Bowie and Fairbank, p. 188). It was only after the spring of 1957, when Mao began to revise his ideas about the struggle between the proletariat and the bourgeoisie, that the position taken at the Eighth Congress was put in question.
    Large-scale turbulent: SW5, p. 395 (June 19). For intermediate formulations as the new line was emerging, see Kau and Leung, 2, pp. 566–7 (June 8) and p. 578 (June 11 1957). ***Elemental fault-line***: Kau and Leung, 2, pp. 809–12 (undated, but probably September 1957). ***Plenum***: Ibid., pp. 696–713. Mao's vision of future plenty led him to imagine a future in which a peasant could feed himself from 'several fen of land' (p. 700); a fen is one sixtieth of an acre, or an area roughly eight yards square. ***Visiting Russian***: Klochko, Mikhail A., *Soviet Scientist in Red China*, International Publishers, Montreal, 1964, p. 68. ***Hecatombs***: MacFarquhar,

Origins, 2, p. 23. **Sparrowcide**: I cannot, alas, pretend to have invented this magnificent neologism: the term is Roderick MacFarquhar's, but it deserves wider currency, which is my excuse for borrowing it here.

478 **On October 4**: Ibid., p. 10; Kau and Leung, 2, p. 720 (Oct. 9 1957). **Not an arithmetical matter**: MacFarquhar, 2, p. 16. **Politics is primary**: Kau and Leung, 2, p. 702 (Oct. 9 1957). **Overtake the United States**: MacFarquhar, 2, p. 16. **Overtake Britain**: Kau and Leung, p. 787 (Nov. 18 1957). **Either the East Wind**: Ibid., pp. 783 and 786. **Mao had committed China**: MacFarquhar, 2, pp. 17–19.

479 **At Hangzhou**: MacFarquhar, Cheek and Wu, pp. 377–91 (Jan. 3–4 1958). **Ten days later**: *Miscellany of Mao Zedong Thought*, 1, pp. 80–84 (Jan. 13 1958). **Zhou Enlai**: Bo Yibo, *Ruogan zhongda juece yu shijiande huigu*, 2, p. 639. **In Chengdu**: MacFarquhar, 2, pp. 36–41. **A month later**: *Miscellany*, 1, p. 89 (Apr. 6 1958).

480 **Nationwide irrigation movement**: MacFarquhar, 2, p. 34. The original target had been to irrigate 7 million acres in twelve months. **Lift the lid . . . not insane**: *Miscellany*, 1, pp. 95–6 (May 8 1958). **Revolutionary romanticism**: MacFarquhar, 2, p. 43. **By May . . . 350 million**: Ibid., pp. 33, 82, 85 and 90; *Miscellany*, 1, p. 123 (May 18 1958). Before the Leap, Mao had predicted it would take fifty years for China to reach US production levels. **China might get there**: Miscellany, 1, p. 105 (May 17 1958).

481 **A large population**: Ibid., p. 115 (May 23 1958). See also MacFarquhar, Cheek and Wu, p. 409 (Aug. 19 1958). **The French**: MacFarquhar, Cheek and Wu, p. 432 (Aug. 30 1958). **After all**: MacFarquhar, *Origins*, 2, p. 84. **Asphalt highways**: MacFarquhar, Cheek and Wu, p. 430 (Aug. 21 1958). **Mahjong**: Kau and Leung, 2, p. 740 (Oct. 13 1957). **Deng Xiaoping**: MacFarquhar, *Origins*, 2, p. 85.

482 **Sputnik**: Kau and Leung, 2, p. 720 (Oct. 9 1957). **Scientific analogies**: See, for instance, *Miscellany*, 1, p. 113 (May 20 1958). **Mao freely admitted**: Ibid., p. 96 (May 8 1958); Kau and Leung, 2, p. 720 (Oct. 9 1957).

483 **Step down as Head of State**: JYMZW, 6, pp. 457–8; MacFarquhar, 2, pp. 173–80. **Still asking plaintively**: *Miscellany*, 1, pp. 120–1 (May 18 1958). **Irrigation movement**: MacFarquhar, 2, p. 77.

484 **A form of 'large commune'**: Ibid., pp. 78–80. **Article in 1926**: Schram, *Mao's Road*, 2, pp. 365–8 (March 18 1926). **People's communes**: MacFarquhar, 2, p. 81; *History of the CCP, Chronology*, p. 273. **Best organisational form**: *History of the CCP, Chronology*, p. 274. **Communism is Paradise**: MacFarquhar, 2, p. 103. **The communist spirit . . . utopian socialism**: MacFarquhar, Cheek and Wu, p. 414 (Aug. 21 1958). **The way forward . . . communism**: Ibid., p. 419. See also MacFarquhar, *Origins*, 2, p. 104. **Money itself might be abolished**:

Kau and Leung, 2, p. 812 (September 1957). See also MacFarquhar, 2, pp. 130–1.

485 *Everything will be called*: MacFarquhar, Cheek and Wu, p. 419 (Aug. 21 1958). *For many . . . money for weddings*: MacFarquhar, *Origins*, 2, pp. 103–8, 115–16, 119–20, 137–8 and 148–9. *Nostalgia*: See Mao's Beidaihe speeches (MacFarquhar, Cheek and Wu, especially pp. 434–5). *Party cadres . . . near Beijing*: MacFarquhar, *Origins*, 2, pp. 75–6. *PLA officers*: Ibid., pp. 67–8.

486 *Militia drive*: Ibid., pp. 100–2. *Every hill, every field*: Rittenberg, *Man Who Stayed Behind*, p. 231. *Albert Belhomme*: Karnow, Stanley, *Mao and China: A Legacy of Turmoil*, Penguin, Harmondsworth, 1990 (3rd rev. edn), p. 93. *English visitor*: MacFarquhar, 2, p. 115. *The same scenes . . . to take part*: Ibid., p. 114.

487 *The result, inevitably . . . lie fallow*: Ibid., pp. 86 and 119–27. *Fateful decision*: MacFarquhar, Cheek and Wu, p. 403 (Aug. 17 1958). *When the Central Committee . . . in 1962*: Ibid., pp. 484–6 (Nov. 21) and 502–5 (Nov. 23 1958); MacFarquhar, *Origins*, 2, pp. 121–2 and 128–30; *Miscellany*, pp. 141, 144–5 and 147 (Dec. 19 1958).

488 *During this [past] year*: MacFarquhar, Cheek and Wu, pp. 449–50 (Nov. 6 1958). *Russians*: Ibid., pp. 474–5 (Nov. 10 1958). *Poor and blank*: Kau and Leung, 2, p. 13 (Jan. 20 1956). *China's 600 million*: Schram, *Political Thought*, p. 253 (April 15 1958).

489 *Offer too good to refuse*: MacFarquhar, 2, pp. 7–15. *Let us speculate*: Kau and Leung, 2, pp. 788–9 (Nov. 18 1957). *If the US*: SW5, p. 152 (Jan. 28 1955).

490 *You never trust the Chinese . . . the same way*: CWIHP, 6–7, pp. 155–9 (July 22 1958).

491 *Like a thunderbolt*: Talbott, Strobe (ed). *Khrushchev Remembers*, Little, Brown, Boston, 1974, p. 290. *Seals*: Ibid., p. 259. *In January 1958 . . . even-numbered days*: This account is taken mainly from Zhang, Shu Guang, *Deterrence and Strategic Culture*, pp. 235–7 and 250–65; and from MacFarquhar, 2, pp. 92–100.

492 *China cooled its rhetoric . . . socialist solidarity*: MacFarquhar, 2, pp. 132–5; Zagoria, pp. 99, 126. *Throughout the spring of 1959 . . . grossly exaggerated*: MacFarquhar, 2, pp. 136–80 and 201. *Just as a child*: *Miscellany*, p. 157 (Feb. 2 1959). *Mao warned chillingly*: MacFarquhar, 2, p. 153.

493 *Achievable in fifteen*: See *Miscellany*, 1. pp. 130–1 and 138 (Nov. 1958). *Shaoshan*: MacFarquhar, 2, pp. 187–92.

493 *Mao, however . . . can be cured now*: The following account of the
/ Lushan conference draws on: Li Rui, *Lushan huiyi shilu*, Henan
497 renmin chubanshe, 1995; Domes, *Peng Dehuai; The Case of Peng Dehuai, 1959–1968*, Union Research Institute, Hong Kong, 1968; Teiwes, *Politics and Purges*, pp. 384–440; MacFarquhar, 2, pp. 187–251.

494 **Only 200 million tons**: MacFarquhar, 2, pp. 328–9.

495 **An individual sometimes**: *Miscellany*, 1, p. 176 (April 1959). Mao had first used this formulation a year earlier at the Second Session of the Eighth Party Congress, when he criticised a speech by one of his more sycophantic followers (the Shanghai First Secretary, Ke Qingshi) who had urged the Party to follow him unconditionally. 'We follow whoever has the truth in his hands,' Mao told him. 'Even if he should be a manure carrier or a street sweeper, as long as he has the truth he should be followed . . . Wherever truth is, we follow. Do not follow any particular individual . . . One must have independent thinking' (Ibid., p. 107, May 17 1958).

496 **In the view of some comrades**: *Case of Peng Dehuai*, p. 12.

497 **Enlarged meeting of the Politburo Standing Committee**: Li Rui, p. 177. **Khrushchev had simplified**: MacFarquhar, 2, pp. 225–8. **Against this background**: Ibid., pp. 222 and 228–33.

498 **Verbatim record**: Li Rui, pp. 192–207.

499 **Speech of self-abasement**: *Case of Peng Dehuai*, pp. 31–8. **The CC**: Ibid., pp. 39–44.

500 **This was presented**: Ibid., p. 30. **Zhang Wentian had complained**: *Chinese Law and Government*, vol. 29, no. 4, p. 58.

501 **Where Peng Dehuai**: Li Rui, pp. 73 and 181. **The struggle at Lushan**: *Chinese Law and Government*, vol. 29, no. 4, p. 58.

502 **Campaign against 'Right opportunism' . . . speak to each other**: Teiwes, *Politics and Purges*, pp. 428–36. **Six million people**: MacFarquhar, *Origins*, 3, p. 61. **Cornucopian production figures**: Ibid., 2, p. 298. **Floods in the south . . . 170 million**: Ibid., 2, pp. 328–9. **Pockets of starvation**: In Guangxi, in 1955, the provincial First Secretary was dismissed for failing to prevent widespread starvation. In Anhui, 500 people starved to death in one county even during the bumper harvest of 1958 (Ibid., 3, p. 210).

503 **Relations with the Soviet Union . . . a foreign power**: Ibid., 2, pp. 255–92.

504 **By July, it was already clear**: Ibid., 2, pp. 322–5 and 329. For a detailed account of the horrors of the famine that followed the Great Leap, see Becker, Jasper, *Hungry Ghosts*, John Murray, London, 1996.

505 **In 1959 and 1960**: MacFarquhar, *Origins*, 3, pp. 1–8.

CHAPTER FOURTEEN   MUSINGS ON IMMORTALITY

506 **Adjustment, consolidation**: MacFarquhar, *Origins of the Cultural Revolution*, 3, p. 11. **Armed rebellions**: Teiwes, *Politics and Purges*, pp. 443 and 678, n.4. **In Henan . . . disintegrated altogether**: Ibid., pp. 455–7; MacFarquhar, 3, pp. 60–1. **Liu Shaoqi warned**: Cong Jin,

Quzhe fazhande suiye (1949–1989 niande Zhongguo, vol. 2), Henan renmin chubanshe, Zhengzhou, 1989, p. 382. *To reduce the pressure ... laundered through Europe*: MacFarquhar, 3, pp. 23–9 and 32–6.

507 *Which emperor*: Ibid., pp. 43–4. *Central Committee strongly reaffirmed*: Ibid., pp. 45–8. *Impediment*: JYMZW, 9, pp. 467–70. *Within days*: MacFarquhar, 3, pp. 49–55 and 66. *Aluminium kitchen utensils*: Bao and Chelminski, *Prisoner of Mao*, p. 269. *In June*: MacFarquhar, 3, pp. 63–5 and 74–5.

508 *Finally, in September*: Ibid., pp. 69–71; Dong Bian, *Mao Zedong he tade mishu Tian Jiaying*, Zhongyang wenxian chubanshe, 1996, pp. 59–60 and 68–9; JYMZW, 9, pp. 565–73 and 580–3.

509 *Zhou Enlai summed up*: Zhou Enlai, SW2, p. 345. *Deng, Liu and the Foreign Minister*: MacFarquhar, 3, pp. 62–3; *Liu Shaoqi xuanji*, 2, Renmin chubanshe, Beijing, 1985, p. 337. *Household responsibility systems*: MacFarquhar, 3, pp. 209–26. *Zhu De*: Ibid., p. 65.

510 *Liu set the tone*: *Liu Shaoqi xuanji*, 2, p. 355. *Peng Zhen*: MacFarquhar, 3, pp. 156–8. *Any mistakes ... they damn well will*: Schram, *Unrehearsed*, pp. 167 and 186.

511 *Tiger after tiger*: MacFarquhar, 3, pp. 172–8. *They complain all day long*: Li Zhisui, *Private Life*, pp,. 386–7. *The meeting had produced ... Party leadership*: MacFarquhar, 3, pp. 163–4.

512 *Successes are primary*: *Liu Shaoqi xuanji*, 2, p. 420. *Like Yugoslavia*: Schram, *Unrehearsed*, p. 167; see also Li Zhisui, p. 386. *Hangzhou*: Dong Bian, p. 62. *In March ... 'responsibility system' into effect*: Ibid., pp. 63–8; MacFarquhar, 3, pp. 226–33 and 263–8.

513 *20 per cent of China's fields*: Bo Yibo, *Ruogan zhongda juece yu shijiande huigu*, 2, p. 1078. Tian Jiaying estimated it at 30 per cent, a figure which Mao also cited [MacFarquhar, 3, pp. 226–7 and 275]. *He told Tian*: Dong Bian, pp. 65–6. *Summer harvest*: MacFarquhar, 3, pp. 281–3. *He ordered Chen Boda*: Ibid., p. 267. *We've been discussing*: Ibid., p. 276. *He was also unhappy ... happen in China*: Ibid., pp. 269–81.

514 *In our country*: Schram, pp. 189–90.

515 *No repetition*: Ibid., p. 194. *Chinese revisionism*: Ibid., pp. 192–3. *Fan xiu, fang xiu*: Cong Jin, p. 519. *The first outward sign ... affronted the Americans*: MacFarquhar, 3, pp. 298–318.

516 *Within days, Sino-Soviet polemics*: Ibid., pp. 318–23. *Open letters*: Ibid., pp. 349–62. *Socialist Education Movement*: Ibid., pp. 334–48 and 399–415; Teiwes, *Politics and Purges*, pp. 493–600. See also Baum, Richard, and Teiwes, Frederick C., *Ssu-Ch'ing: The Socialist Education Movement of 1962–1966*, University of California Press, Berkeley, 1968.

517 *I felt particularly happy*: Quoted in Sheridan, Mary, 'The Emulation of Heroes', CQ, 33, 1969, pp. 52–3. *If things were allowed*: Baum and Teiwes, p. 70.

518   *'All hell broke loose'*: Siu, Helen F., *Agents and Victims in South China: Accomplices in Rural Revolution*, Yale University Press, New Haven, 1989, pp. 201–2.

519   *Malenkov ... before I died*: *Current Background*, no. 891, US Consulate General, Hong Kong, pp. 71 and 75. *Mao told Field Marshal Montgomery*: *Sunday Times*, Oct. 15 1961. *Each May Day . . . 18 million copies*: MacFarquhar, 3, pp. 262–3.

520   *So many deeds*: *Chinese Literature*, no. 5, 1966.

521   *That year his wife*: MacFarquhar, 3, ch. 17. *'I was Chairman Mao's dog'*: From Jiang Qing's evidence at her trial, November 1980–January 1981. *Kang Sheng*: MacFarquhar, 3, pp. 289–96; Byron and Pack, *Claws of the Dragon*.

522   *Lin Biao*: MacFarquhar, 3, pp. 435–7. *Supreme commander*: Ibid., 2, p. 320. *Highest peak*: Ibid., 3, p. 436. *He continued to bracket*: Huang Zheng, *Liu Shaoqi yi sheng*, Zhongyang wenxian chubanshe, Beijing, 1995, p. 374. *Deng Xiaoping*: Evans, *Deng Xiaoping*, p. x.

523   *As Mao took stock*: There can, of course, be no certainty as to Mao's innermost thoughts in the spring and early summer of 1964. What follows is an attempt to point to some of the factors that may have influenced him in reaching the conclusions set out in the CCP's letter to the Russians in July. *We will continue*: Quoted in Wang Ruoshui, *Mao Zedong wei shenme yao fadong wenge*, privately circulated, Beijing, October 1996, pp. 12–14. *Kang Sheng*: Ibid., p. 10. *In the final analysis*: *The Polemic on the General Line of the International Communist Movement*, Foreign Languages Press, Beijing, 1965, pp. 477–8.

524   *Asia is more progressive*: MacFarquhar, Cheek and Wu, *Secret Speeches*, pp. 270–1 (March 10 1957).

525   *You [Liu]*: Cong Jin, p. 602. *Two weeks later ... for the first time*: JYMZW, 11, pp. 265–9. *On December 20 . . . handled later*: *Miscellany*, 2, pp. 408–26. *Unusually, Liu . . . Central Committee departments*: Ibid., pp. 429–32; MacFarquhar, *Origins*, 3, pp. 419–28.

526   *Liu's fate*: Snow, *Long Revolution*, p. 17.

CHAPTER FIFTEEN: CATACLYSM

527   *In February 1965*: MacFarquhar, *Origins of the Cultural Revolution*, 3, p. 440. *Hai Rui*: Ibid., 2, pp. 207–12 and 3, pp. 252–3. *Some of Mao's inner circle*: Barnouin, Barbara, and Yu Changgen, *Ten Years of Turbulence: The Chinese Cultural Revolution*, Kegan Paul, London, 1993, p. 52.

528   *Extraordinary secrecy*: MacFarquhar, 3, p. 645, n.67. *Ten drafts*:

Ibid., p. 441; Yan Jiaqi and Gao Gao, *Turbulent Decade: A History of the Cultural Revolution*, University of Hawaii, Honolulu, 1996, p. 27. *Not even a needle*: *Miscellany of the Mao Tse-tung Thought*, 2, p. 383 (April 28 1966). See also Cong Jin, *Quzhe fazhande suiye*, p. 611; and Milton, David and Nancy, and Schurmann, Franz (eds), *People's China*, Random House, New York, 1974, p. 262.

529   *On November 28*: Shuai Dongbing, 'Peng Zhen zai baofengyu qianye', in *Mingren zhuanyi*, nos. 11–12, 1988, p. 11. See also Zheng Derong (ed.), *Xin Zhongguo lishi (1949–1984)*, Changchun, 1986, p. 381. **Yang Shangkun**: Liao Gailong (ed.), *Xin Zhongguo biannianshi (1949–1989)*, Renmin chubanshe, Beijing, 1989, p. 267; Ma Qibin (ed.), *Zhongguo gongchandang zhizheng sishinian*, Zhonggong dangshi ziliao chubanshe, Beijing, 1989, p. 264.
Luo Ruiqing: Cong Jin, pp. 631–4; Ma Qibin, p. 265; Teiwes, Frederick C., and Sun, Warren, *The Tragedy of Lin Biao*, University of Hawaii Press, Honolulu, 1996, pp. 24–32; Li Zhisui, *Private Life*, pp. 435–6.

530   **Liu Shaoqi**: Ye Yonglie, *Chen Boda qiren*, Shidai wenyi chubanshe, Changchun, 1990, pp. 222–3. *Just before Christmas . . . indeed Hai Rui*: Cong Jin, p. 613; Hao Mengbi and Duan Haoran (eds), *Zhongguo gongchandang liushi nian*, Jiefangjun chubanshe, Beijing, 1984, p. 561. See also Ye Yonglie, pp. 228–30. *More bad news*: MacFarquhar, 3, pp. 451 and 453. *Cultural revolution group*: Ibid., p. 388. *'February Outline'*: Kuo, Warren (ed.), *Classified Chinese Communist Documents*, National Chengchi University, Taibei, 1978, pp. 225–9.

531   *On February 8 . . . deputy mayor*: Cong Jin, p. 616; Wu Lengxi, *Yi Mao zhuxi: Wo qinshen jinglide ruogan zhongda lishi shijian pianduan*, Xinhua chubanshe, Beijing, 1995, pp. 150–1. *Semi-Marxist*: MacFarquhar, 3, p. 456. *Independent kingdom*: Li Ping, *Kaiguo zongli Zhou Enlai*, Zhonggong zhongyang dangxiao chubanshe, 1994, p. 436. *Black anti-Party*: *Peking Review*, June 2 1967. *He then let it be known*: Cong Jin, p. 625; *History of the CCP, Chronology*, pp. 320–1. *Meeting of the Secretariat*: Cong Jin, pp. 623–5.

532   *On May 4*: Wang Nianyi, *Da dongluande niandai*, Henan renmin chubanshe, Zhengzhou, 1988, pp. 9–11. *Zhou Enlai accused*: MacFarquhar, 3, pp. 459–60. *'Smell of gunpowder'*: Kuo, *Classified Chinese Documents*, pp. 646–61. *On May 16*: Ibid., pp. 230–6; *Renmin ribao*, May 17 1966.

533   *The circular announced . . . 'anti-Party conduct'*: Kuo, *Classified Chinese Documents*, p. 230; Yan and Gao, p. 38; Schoenhals, Michael, *The CCP Central Case Examination Group (1966–1979)*, Centre for Pacific Asia Studies, Stockholm University, 1995.

534   *Claiming that she was not a virgin*: Wang Nianyi, pp. 18–19.

535   *Yao Wenyuan*: *Renmin ribao*, May 11 1966. Yao's charges against Deng Tuo are discussed at length by MacFarquhar (3, pp. 249–58).

My own exchanges with prominent Chinese intellectuals, including some of Deng's colleagues, confirm that no one saw them at the time as being aimed at Mao (not least because his prestige was such that it was unthinkable he should be the target). For a contrary view, see Goldman, Merle, *China's Intellectuals: Advise and Dissent*, Harvard University Press, 1981, pp. 27–38.

On May 14: Yan and Gao, p. 40; Wang Nianyi, p. 28; MacFarquhar, 3, p. 652, n.1.

536 *It urged students*: *Renmin ribao*, June 2 1966. *Mao in person endorsed*: Jin Chunming, *Wenge shiqi guaishi guaiyu*, Qiushi chubanshe, Beijing, 1989, p. 155. *Forever nameless pupil*: *Zhongguo Qingnian*, 10, 1986. *Chairman Mao is a genius*: Kuo, *Classified Chinese Documents*, pp. 658 and 661. *Chairman Mao is the red sun ... utterance a truth*: Yan and Gao, pp. 60–1.

537 *Luo Ruiqing*: Cong Jin, pp. 633–4. *Deng Tuo*: Lin Zhijian (ed.), *Xin Zhongguo yaoshi shuping*, Zhonggong dangshi chubanshe, 1994, p. 307. *Tian Jiaying*: Ibid. *Liu telephoned*: Ma Qibin, pp. 272–3. *None the less, on that basis*: *History of the CCP, Chronology*, p. 326.

538 *Within days*: Jin Chunming, p. 135; Liu Guokai, *A Brief Analysis of the Cultural Revolution*, M. E. Sharpe, Armonk, 1987, p. 18. *When radicals at ... severely punished*: Yan and Gao, pp. 46–7.

539 *On July 16*: *Renmin ribao*, July 25 1966. *Two days later ... thorough-going revolution*: Yan and Gao, pp. 49–52; *History of the CCP, Chronology*, pp. 327–8. *You ask us ... you have*: Dittmer, Lowell, *Liu Shao'chi and the Chinese Cultural Revolution: The Politics of Mass Criticism*, University of California, Berkeley, 1974, pp. 89–90.

540 *On August 1*: *History of the CCP, Chronology*, pp. 328–9; Barnouin and Yu, pp. 78–81. *Mao sneered*: Barnouin and Yu, p. 80. *Bombard the Headquarters*: *Peking Review*, Aug. 11 1967 (translation amended).

541 *That afternoon*: Teiwes and Sun, pp. 63–4. *'Sixteen Points'*: Milton et al., pp. 272–83.

542 *'Warm support' for the Red Guards*: Yan and Gao, p. 59. *Two weeks later*: Ibid., pp. 62–3; Rittenberg, *Man Who Stayed Behind*, pp. 317–19.

543 *Let me tell you*: Schoenhals, Michael, *China's Cultural Revolution, 1966–1969: Not a Dinner Party*, M. E. Sharpe, Armonk, 1996, pp. 148–9. *A few independent spirits*: Ibid., p. 150. *Lao She*: Yan and Gao, pp. 68–9. *Thousands of lesser victims*: Ibid., pp. 76–7.

544 *Chinese people's fighting spirit*: See Milton et al., p. 265, where Mao is quoted as telling an Albanian delegation in [May] 1967: 'Some people say that the Chinese people deeply love peace. I don't think they love peace so much. I think the Chinese people are warlike.' *Personally pointed the way*: The 'Sixteen Points' quoted Mao's 1927 'Report on the Peasant Movement in Hunan' to the effect that

revolution cannot be 'refined, leisurely and gentle, "benign, upright, courteous, temperate and complaisant"'. Although it did not cite the next sentence, which defines revolution as 'an act of violence' the Red Guards – as Mao certainly intended – seized on the reference as legitimising violence (see, for example, Ling, Ken, *The Revenge of Heaven*, G. P. Putnam, New York, 1972, p. 19). *Lin Biao*: *Peking Review*, no. 35, 1966. *Xie Fuzhi*: Yan and Gao, p. 76. *Mao's own words*: SW4, p. 418 (June 30 1949).

545 *Teacher Chen*: Ling, pp. 20–2. *On the athletic field*: Jing Lin, *The Red Guards' Path to Violence*, Praeger, New York, 1991, p. 23.

546 *It is right*: Milton et al., p. 239 (Dec. 21 1939). It was quoted in the *People's Daily* on Aug. 24 1966. *People-beating meetings*: Yan and Gao, p. 77. *Some lay on the floor . . . the stove*: Gao Yuan, *Born Red: A Chronicle of the Cultural Revolution*, Stanford University Press, 1987, pp. 289–90 and 307–10. *Among the many*: Schoenhals, pp. 166–9.

547 *Nationwide 'networking movement'*: Yan and Gao, ch. 5. *'Four Olds'*: Ibid., ch. 4; Ling, pp. 42–59; Gao Yuan, pp. 85–94; Bennett, Gordon A., and Montaperto, Ronald N., *Red Guard: The Political Biography of Dai Hsiao-Ai*, Doubleday, New York, 1971, pp. 77–83.

548 *Mao himself had opposed*: In his 'Report on the Peasant Movement in Hunan', he wrote: 'It is the peasants who made the idols, and when the time comes they will cast the idols aside with their own hands; there is no need for anyone else to do it for them prematurely' (Schram, *Mao's Road*, 2, p. 455). Qu Qiubai, at the Sixth Congress in 1928, likewise excoriated 'those romantic petty-bourgeois revolutionaries who, instead of concentrating on how to seize political power . . . resorted to forcible means to destroy the ancestral tablets of peasant families, to cut off the pigtails of old women, and to undo the foot-bindings of women – what thorough and brave cultural revolutionaries they were! . . . Marx said that in a revolution there is no lack of foolish things done' (*Chinese Studies in History*, 5, 1, p. 21 [Fall 1971]). Unfortunately, by 1966, such strictures had been forgotten. *Between a quarter*: Oral sources; see also Yan and Gao, pp. 76–81.

549 *All the anthologies*: Schram, *Mao's Road*, 1, p. 139 (Sept. 23 1917). *The piles contained*: Ling, pp. 52–3. *'Four News'*: Yan and Gao, p. 74.

550 *At workplaces*: Ibid, pp. 248–51; Short, *Dragon and Bear*, pp. 148–9; Urban, George [ed.], *The Miracles of Chairman Mao*, Nash Publishing, Los Angeles, 1971, passim; oral sources.

551 *He proposed a toast*: Schoenhals, p. 3, n.1. A different version is given by Wang Li in 'An Insider's Account of the Cultural Revolution', *Chinese Law and Government*, vol. 27 no. 6 (November–December 1994), p. 32. *Zhou Enlai*: Schoenhals, p. 27. *When you are told*: Milton et al., p. 270. *Liu and Deng Xiaoping*:

Dittmer, pp. 97–9; Kuo, *Classified Chinese Documents*, pp. 237–44. *'Beady with fear'*: Rittenberg, *Man Who Stayed Behind*, p. 329. *'A few months of disorder'*: Schram, *Preliminary Reassessment*, p. 67.

552 *No wonder*: Schram, *Unrehearsed*, pp. 270–4. *Not in the same category*: Ibid., pp. 264–9. *If the father*: *Renmin ribao*, Jan, 1, 1967; Yan and Gao, pp. 101–11. See also Barnouin and Yu, pp. 97–106. *Several leaders*: Yan and Gao, ch. 8.

553 *Zhang Chunqiao explained*: Ibid., p. 218. *As the pressure . . . his isolation was complete*: Ibid., pp. 100 and 133–6.

555 *That winter . . . the rest of the country*: Ibid., pp. 379–84; Barnouin and Yu, pp 106–12.

556 *He cited an old proverb*: Schram, *Unrehearsed*, pp. 275–6. *Local PLA units*: Milton et al., pp. 298–9; *History of the CCP, Chronology*, p. 335. *Chen Boda*: Wang Li, pp. 38–9. *System of general elections*: Milton et al., p. 279.

557 *Mao himself*: MacFarquhar, Cheek and Wu, *Secret Speeches*, p. 419. *A series of problems*: Schram, *Unrehearsed*, pp. 277–9. *There must be a Party*: *Miscellany*, 2, pp. 451–5. *Truly free elections*: Ibid., p. 460.

558 *Confused by false appearances*: Kau and Leung, *Writings of Mao Zedong*, 2, p. 639. *'The great disorder'*: Kuo, *Classified Chinese Documents*, pp. 54–7. *'Capitalist restoration'*: See, for instance, the long essay entitled, 'Whither China?', in ibid., pp. 274–99.

559 *First secretaries*: Wang Nianyi, p. 187. *Crowds gathered . . . beaten to death*: Ibid., pp. 150–1; Yan and Gao, p. 202. *At the same time . . . thoroughly disgruntled*: Yan and Gao, pp. 123–4; Barnouin and Yu, pp. 131–7.

560 *Trouble flared up . . . seven other provinces*: Liu Guokai, p. 61; Wang Nianyi, pp. 202–4; Peng Cheng (ed.), *Zhongguo zhengju beiwanglu*, Jiefangjun chubanshe, Beijing, 1989, pp. 3–4; Barnouin and Yu, pp. 138–41. *'February Adverse Current'*: Yan and Gao, pp. 125–6; Barnouin and Yu, pp. 116–19. *Mao himself inadvertently*: Wang Li, pp. 41–2.

561 *Masses this and masses that*: Zhou Ming, *Lishi zai zheli chensi*, Huaxia chubanshe, Beijing, vol. 2, pp. 66–7; Yan and Gao, p. 127. *They are completely ruthless*: Quoted in Yan and Gao, p. 129. *Mao's first impulse*: Wang Nianyi, 'Guanyu eryue niliude yixie ziliao' in *Dangshi yanjiu ziliao*, 1, 1990, p. 4. *What kind of Party leadership . . . guerrilla war*: Ibid.

562 *Suspecting everyone*: *History of the CCP, Chronology*, p. 336. *Over the next month . . . ruffled feelings*: Ibid.; Wang Li, pp. 52–4; Barnouin and Yu, pp. 119–20. *Politburo ceased to function*: Wang Nianyi, 'Guanyu eryue niliude yixie ziliao', p. 6.

563 *Armed Liu-Deng line*: Wang Li, p. 54. *Arbitrary stigmatising*: Wang

Nianyi, *Da dongluande niandai*, p. 218. **I went out . . . burned to the ground**: Liang and Shapiro, *Son of the Revolution*, pp. 133–7.

564 **At this juncture**: The following account is drawn from Wang Nianyi, *Da dongluande niandai*; Peng Cheng, *Zhongguo zhengju beiwanglu*; Barnouin and Yu, esp. pp. 144–6; and Yan and Gao, pp. 235–7.

565 **Storm Zhongnanhai**: Wang Li, pp. 65–6. **Wang Li . . . had dispersed**: Yan and Gao, pp. 237–9.

566 **Lin Liguo**: *Renmin ribao*, July 22 1967. **In mid-July**: Wang Li, p. 75. **Attack by reasoning**: *History of the CCP, Chronology*, p. 338. **On August 4**: Wang Li, p. 75. **Red Flag**: *Hongqi*, no. 12, 1967.

567 **On August 11 . . . scrawled on it**: Wang Li, p. 76; Yan and Gao, p. 239. **All three were arrested . . . international obligations**: Wang Li, p. 81; Dong Baocun, *Yang Yu Fu shijian zhenxiang*, Jiefangjun chubanshe, Beijing, 1988, pp. 74–5. **'May 16 group'**: Wang Li, p. 82; Barnouin and Yu, pp. 192–8; Yan and Gao, pp. 252–6.

568 **Conspiratorial**: *Renmin ribao*, Sept. 8 1967; Barnouin and Yu, pp. 194–5. **Weapons seizures**: Domes, Jurgen, Myers, James T., and von Groeling, Erik, *Cultural Revolution in China: Documents and Analysis*, n.p., n.d., p. 307. **Jiang Qing**: Ibid., pp. 308–15. **Topic was extremely obscure**: See Goldman, *China's Intellectuals*, pp. 146–7. **On April 6**: Barnouin and Yu, p. 91; Yan and Gao, p. 138. **Wang Guangmei**: Schoenhals, pp. 101–16.

569 **Liu's book**: Yan and Gao, p. 139. **Climax came in July**: Zhou Ming, 1, pp. 27–30; Yan and Gao, pp. 153–7; Li Zhisui, *Private Life*, pp. 489–90.

570 **Mao demurred**: Barnouin and Yu, p. 185. **By February 1967**: Kuo, *Classified Chinese Documents*, pp. 20–4. **'Clique of traitors'**: Jin Chunming, p. 78.

571 **Bo Yibo**: Schoenhals, pp. 122–35. **Peng was beaten**: Yan and Gao, p. 211. **Other investigations**: Ibid., pp. 223, 252 and 266; Barnouin and Yu, pp. 187–9.

572 **In September 1967**: *Renmin ribao*, Dec. 22 1967; see also Milton et al., pp. 356–60. **'Good' faction**: Wang Nianyi, *Da dongluande niandai*, p. 271.

573 **More than three million people**: Wang Li, p. 82. **At the Foreign Ministry**: Barnouin and Yu, p. 198. **'Cleansing of class ranks'**: Ibid., pp. 181–4. **Ninety-one Chinese ambassadors**: Ibid., pp. 164–5.

574 **Bizarre sequence**: Zhang Yunsheng, *Maojiawan jishi*, Chunqiu chubanshe, Beijing, 1988, pp. 113–23; oral sources. **At the beginning of 1968 . . . reversing correct verdicts**: Barnouin and Yu, pp. 165–71. For a more detailed account, see Dong Baocun, *Yang Yu Fu shijian zhenxiang*.

575 **Standing Committee**: Jin Chunming, pp. 243–4. **Mao moved decisively**: Liu Guokai, p. 118; Yan and Gao, p. 393. **In Guangxi**: Zheng Yi, *Scarlet Memorial: Tales of Cannibalism in Modern China*, Westview Press, Boulder, CO, 1996. **'Banquets of human flesh'**: Galbiati,

Fernando, 'Peng Pai: The Leader of the First Soviet' (D. Phil. thesis), Oxford, June 1981, pp. 829–31.

576 **Mangoes**: Hinton, William, *Hundred Day War: The Cultural Revolution at Tsinghua University*, Monthly Review Press, New York, 1972, pp. 226–7; Li Zhisui, pp. 502–3. **Voluntary rustication programme**: Unger, Jonathan, *Education under Mao*, Columbia University Press, New York, 1982, pp. 38–45 and 134. **Industrial output**: Yan and Gao, pp. 393–4. **Five million**: CHOC, 15, p. 189, n.120; see also Unger, p. 162. **'May 7 Cadre Schools'**: Yan and Gao, pp. 270–6.

577 **Softness of urban life**: See Mao's speech to the First Plenum of the Ninth CC, in Schram, *Unrehearsed*, p. 288. **98 per cent**: Teiwes and Sun, p. 128, n.47. **The entire country is Red**: Barnouin and Yu, p. 160 **Zhou Enlai declared**: *Peking Review*, no. 37, Sept. 13 1968.

577 **On October 13 . . . might need his talents again**: Wang Nianyi,
/ *Da dongluande niandai*, pp. 311–15; Yan and Gao, pp. 159–60; Barnouin
579 and Yu, pp. 171–5; *History of the CCP, Chronology*, pp. 344–5.

578 **Three large volumes of evidence**: Yan and Gao, pp. 356–62. **Slim pickings**: Kuo, *Classified Chinese Documents*, p. 40.

579 **Mao was unimpressed**: CHOC, 15, p. 195. **Ninth Congress**: Barnouin and Yu, pp. 175–8.

581 **About half-a-million**: For a discussion of the figures, see CHOC, 15, pp. 213–14. Hu Yaobang, in 1980, put the total death-toll during the Cultural Revolution and related movements at one million. **In Liu's place**: The following account is drawn principally from Zhang Yunsheng, *Maojiawan jishi*.

582 **Two-thirds of the 1,500 delegates**: CHOC, 15, p. 198. **'Proletarian revolution of the mind'**: Milton et al., p. 264. **In 1966**: Kuo, *Classified Chinese Documents*, p. 54. **Now, in April 1969**: Schram, *Unrehearsed*, p. 283.

583 **Cultureless Revolution**: Teiwes and Sun, p. 18. **On the night of August 20**: Clubb, O. Edmund, *China and Russia: The Great Game*, Columbia University Press, New York, 1971, p. 488.
On March 2: CHOC, 15, pp. 257–61; Garver, John W., *China's Decision for Rapprochement with the United States, 1968–1971*, Westview Press, Boulder, CO, 1982, pp. 54–6; Kissinger, Henry, *The White House Years*, Little, Brown & Co., New York, 1979, pp. 171–2. Chinese accounts still maintain that the Russians launched an unprovoked attack (see, for example, *History of the CCP, Chronology*, pp. 345–6).
Mao's plan: See CHOC, 15, pp. 261–75, and Clubb, ch. 36. The centrality of the US dimension – which is now acknowledged (privately) by foreign policy scholars in Beijing – was so glaringly obvious that it was overlooked by both the Americans and the Russians, not only at the time but since.

584   *In mid-October*: *History of the CCP, Chronology*, p. 348; Yan and Gao, p. 162.

585   *Deng was sent*: Goodman, *Deng Xiaoping*, pp. 78–9. *Liu had been*: Yan and Gao, pp. 162–4.

CHAPTER SIXTEEN: THINGS FALL APART

586   *His doctor*: Li Zhisui, *Private Life*, p. 517. *In his later years*: Ji Dengkui, quoted in Teiwes and Sun, *Tragedy of Lin Biao*, p. 21.

587   *Zhou Enlai*: Ibid., pp. 13 and 109. *Zhou survived . . . veteran cadres*: Oral sources. *Even his chief bodyguard*: Li Zhisui, p. 510.

587n *In the 1980s*: Oral sources. See also Deng's interview with Oriana Fallaci, *Selected Works of Deng Xiaoping, 1975–1982*, Foreign Languages Press, Beijing, 1990, pp. 329–30.

588   *Many of those*: Yan and Gao, *Turbulent Decade*, ch. 23. *She laughed in his face*: Wang Li, 'Insider's Account of the Cultural Revolution', p. 44. *Lin Biao*: Wang Nianyi, *Da dongluande niandai*, pp. 384–8; Zhang Yunsheng, *Maojiawan jishi*, pp. 163–5 and 222–4.

589   *In March 1970 . . . did not interest him*: MacFarquhar, Roderick (ed.), *The Politics of China: The Eras of Mao and Deng* (2nd edn), Cambridge University Press, 1997, pp. 256–7; Barnouin and Yu, *Ten Years of Turbulence*, pp. 215–16; Lin Qingshan, *Lin Biao zhuan*, Beijing, 1988, pp. 686–8.

      Mao was intrigued: This is one of the least understood episodes in the whole of Mao's long career. There are two main scholarly interpretations: that summarised by MacFarquhar in *The Politics of China* (pp. 256–62), which holds that Lin was a victim of his own ambition; and the 'revisionist' view, set out by Teiwes and Sun in *The Tragedy of Lin Biao* (pp. 134–51), and by Wu Faxian's daughter, Jin Qiu, in an unpublished Ph.D. thesis, which argues that Lin was a victim of Mao's paranoia. Neither version is satisfactory. The facts fall into place better if it is assumed that Mao became involved at a much earlier stage than has been thought hitherto. Moreover this would be in character: we now know that Mao manoeuvred Gao Gang, Peng Dehuai and Peng Zhen into the actions which caused their respective downfalls. He had already tested Lin once at the Ninth Congress (just as he had tested Liu Shaoqi at the CC work conference in December 1964), by proposing that the Defence Minister, rather than himself, should chair the Congress Presidium – a bait which Lin had wisely refused. Mao's handling of the state chairmanship issue eventually turned it into a similar test, but this time Lin's instincts let him down. *Lin's fetish*: Teiwes and Sun, pp. 1 and 11. *When they fart*: Li Zhisui, p. 518.

590 **Chen had fallen out**: Ye Yonglie, *Chen Boda zhuan*, p. 493. **Mao instinctively mistrusted**: See Li Zhisui, p. 511 for a description of Zhou Enlai's anxiety during this period lest Mao suspect him of forming an alliance with Wang Dongxing.
Blurred his signals: Normally when Mao spoke, that was the end of the matter. His disavowal of the campaign to root our 'capitalist-roaders' in the PLA in August 1967 is a typical example; the moment he hinted at a change of heart, his subordinates scattered in panic. This time he expressed his disagreement on four separate occasions without his words being heeded. The only logical explanation is that he hedged the issue. That ties in with the fact that the CC's General Office, which took its orders from Mao, circulated two versions of the draft constitution – one with, and one without, a state chairman (Teiwes and Sun, p. 139).
Lin persisted: Ibid., p. 140; Wang Nianyi, pp. 392–6. **By then, it had become enmeshed**: Teiwes and Sun, p. 141.

591 **Mao had approved**: Ibid., p. 241; Hao and Duan, *Zhongguo gongchandang liushi nian*, p. 614. **Text was distributed**: Teiwes and Sun, p. 144. **Next day ... state chairmanship**: Ibid., pp. 145–7; Barnouin and Yu, pp. 217–19.

592 **Literati quarrel**: Teiwes and Sun, p. 151. **On the afternoon of August 25**: Ibid., p. 148. **Launching a surprise attack**: Kuo, *Classified Chinese Documents*, pp. 162–3. **Two months later**: Wang Nianyi, pp. 406–9. **Lin's wife ... Central Committee**: MacFarquhar, p. 266. **'Shielding' Lin**: Schram, *Unrehearsed*, p. 294.

593 **When Mao read**: Teiwes and Sun, p. 153; Lin Qingshan, p. 716; Barnouin and Yu, p. 222: Yan and Gao, p. 313. **Whittling down**: Barnouin and Yu, p. 223; Hao and Duan, p. 618. **Second self-criticism**: Wang Nianyi, p. 415. **'Mixing in sand'**: Hao and Duan, p. 618; Schram, *Unrehearsed*, p. 295. **He dismissed**: Li Zhisui, p. 530. **Even those closest**: Teiwes and Sun, p. 155.

594 **Today he uses**: Kuo, *Classified Chinese Documents*, p. 180. **Lin Liguo**: Ibid., pp. 181–5. **At the end of April 1971**: Wang Nianyi, pp. 411 and 415. **New power base**: Barnouin and Yu, p. 225. **On May Day**: Teiwes and Sun, p. 157.

595 **In July**: Barnouin and Yu, p. 226. **His message was the same**: Schram, *Unrehearsed*, pp. 290–9. **Not until the night**: Yan and Gao, pp. 321–2; Barnouin and Yu, p. 235.

595n **Confession by Wu Faxian**: For a fuller discussion of this issue, see Barnouin and Yu, pp. 216–17.

596 / 599 **The following six days ... buried nearby**: This account is drawn from Yan and Gao, pp. 322–33; Barnouin and Yu, pp. 235–42; MacFarquhar, pp. 271–5; Li Zhisui, pp. 534–41; Teiwes and Sun, p. 160; and oral sources. Additional details may be found in Wang Nianyi; and in Zhang Yunsheng, *Maojiawan jishi*.

598   ***Heading north, to Russia***: Although the possibility of making for the
      Russian border had evidently been discussed by Lin Liguo and Ye
      Qun several days earlier, it appears that a decision was taken only at
      the last moment. Lin Biao himself may not even have been aware of
      the Russian option until the last evening. According to his secretary,
      he asked in the car on the way to the airport how long it would take
      to reach Irkutsk, which implies, at the very least, that he had no part
      in the planning (Yan and Gao, p. 331; oral sources).

598n ***This enabled Mao***: Lin's views on the rapprochement with the US
      are discussed in Barnouin and Yu, pp. 228–9.

599   ***KGB forensic experts***: Oral sources. ***His face collapsed***: Li Zhisui,
      p. 536. ***Mao took to his bed . . . refusing medical treatment***: Ibid.,
      pp. 542–51.

600   ***He had not decided***: Oral sources; see also Schram, *Unrehearsed*,
      p. 294. ***Briefings***: *History of the CCP, Chronology*, p. 354; Kuo, *Classified
      Chinese Documents*, pp. 165–85; Wang Nianyi, p. 437. ***He told an
      appalled Zhou Enlai***: Li Zhisui, pp. 551–2.

601   ***The clashes on Zhenbao . . . had already been set***: This account is
/   drawn from Kissinger, *White House Years*, pp. 163–94, 220–2,
605   684–787 and 1029–87; Li Zhisui, pp. 514–6; Garver, *China's Decision*,
      passim; Holdridge, John H., *Crossing the Divide*, Rowman &
      Littlefield, Lanham, MD, 1997; Foot, Rosemary, *The Practice of Power:
      US Relations with China since 1949*, Clarendon Press, Oxford, 1995.
      US accounts give the credit to Nixon, rather than Mao, for initiating
      the U-turn in policy. In fact, both men had decided independently
      that a change was desirable, but it was Mao, by triggering the border
      clashes, who made the process possible.

602   ***Mao's assumption was that Snow***: Kissinger, *White House Years*,
      pp. 702–3. Nixon, in his memoirs, claims that he was aware of Snow's
      interview 'within a few days', but it appears that on this occasion his
      memory played him false (*The Memoirs of Richard Nixon*, Grosset &
      Dunlap, New York, 1978, p. 547). ***This was reported back . . . the
      American players at once***: Li Zhisui, p. 558.

603   ***Mao was preoccupied***: Barnouin and Yu, p. 226. ***The central
      personage***: Li Zhisui, pp. 557–63; Salisbury, *New Emperors*,
      pp. 306–10; Zhang Yufeng, 'Mao Zedong yu Zhou Enlaide yixie
      wannian qushi', in *Guangming Ribao*, Dec. 26 1988 to January 6 1989.

605   ***Nixon had put his finger***: Kissinger, *White House Years*, p. 164.

606   ***Mao acknowledged this***: Ibid., pp. 1062–3; Nixon, p. 563. ***In the
      autumn of 1971***: Schram, *Unrehearsed*, p. 299. ***The following
      November***: *History of the CCP, Chronology*, p. 354; Yan and Gao, p. 407.
      Zhou's discovery: Li Zhisui, p. 572–3; Yan and Gao, p. 412.

607   ***In April***: *Renmin ribao*, April 24 1972. ***Chen Yun***: *History of the CCP,
      Chronology*, p. 356. ***Expertise was emphasised***: Yan and Gao,

pp. 410–11. *Zhou criticised*: Ibid., p. 410; Barnouin and Yu, p. 253. *The trigger was . . . to the wolves*: *Renmin ribao*, Oct. 14 1972; Yan and Gao, pp. 412–16; Barnouin and Yu, pp. 253–5.

608 *New line was spelt out*: *Renmin ribao*, Jan. 1 1973. *Instead, in September 1972 . . . excruciatingly boring*: Ye Yonglie, *Wang Hongwen xingshuailu*, Changchun, 1989, passim.

609 *A young man the Chairman has noticed*: Barnouin and Yu, p. 249. *In March 1973*: Ibid. *On April 12*: Gardner, John, *Chinese Politics and the Succession to Mao*, Macmillan, 1982, p. 62; Short, *Dragon and Bear*, p. 196; Evans, *Deng Xiaoping*, pp. 189–90; *History of the CCP, Chronology*, p. 359.

610 *Shrewdly worded appeal*: MacFarquhar, p. 279, n.114; Jia Sinan (ed.), *Mao Zedong renji jiaowang shilu*, Jiangsu, 1989, p. 319; Yan and Gao, p. 454. *Starring role*: Barnouin and Yu, pp. 249–51.

611 *That autumn*: Evans, p. 197. *Mao had reached . . . General Staff*: Ibid., p. 198; *History of the CCP, Chronology*, pp. 361–2; Hao and Duan, p. 632; Yan and Gao, p. 455. *A man of rare talent*: Peng Cheng, *Zhongguo zhengju beiwanglu*, p. 47. *'Three Worlds'*: *History of the CCP, Chronology*, p. 363; Evans, pp. 199–200.

612 *Campaign to criticise Confucius . . . Cultural Revolution's achievements*: Yan and Gao, p. 422; Barnouin and Yu, pp. 255–6. *'Uncharacteristically tentative'*: Kissinger, Henry, *Years of Upheaval*, Little, Brown, Boston, 1982, pp. 687–8 and 692–3.

613 *Chinese transcripts*: Oral sources. *'Unauthorised statements'*: Barnouin and Yu, pp. 263–4; Wang Nianyi, p. 471. *At that point*: Wang Nianyi, p. 471. *Relinquished responsibility*: Evans, p. 198. *Full-fledged national*: Yan and Gao, pp. 430–2; Barnouin and Yu, p. 258. *To Jiang Qing . . . seven years before*: Yan and Gao, pp. 416–20 and 432–42; Barnouin and Yu, pp. 264–5 and 267–8. *Armed clashes*: Hao and Duan, pp. 636–7.

614 *Wrote reproachfully*: Li Zhisui, pp. 578–9. *He had lost . . . knew him well*: Ibid., 569–70, 573–4 and 576–7. *Kissinger remembered*: Kissinger, *White House Years*, p. 1059. *Mao's eyes*: Li Zhisui, pp. 580 and 604–5. *Zhang Yufeng*: Ibid.; interview with Zhang Yufeng, June 1997; oral sources.

615 *On July 17, 1974*: Peng Cheng, pp. 42–3; *History of the CCP, Chronology*, p. 364. *Immediately afterwards . . . two years to live*: Li Zhisui, pp. 580–6. *On October 4*: *History of the CCP, Chronology*, p. 364. *Jiang Qing was outraged . . . ideological standpoint*: Ibid., p. 365; Yan and Gao, pp. 445–8 and 455–9; *Guangming Ribao*, Nov. 12 1976; Ye Yonglie, pp. 413–15; Hao and Duan, p. 638.

616 *At the beginning of January*: *History of the CCP, Chronology*, p. 366. *From then on*: There were two exceptions: a Politburo meeting on February 15 1975, called to discuss Mao's health, which Zhou chaired (Li Zhisui, pp. 597–9); and a meeting on May 3, 1975, which was the last that Mao chaired (Barnouin and Yu, pp. 282–3 and 286).

Li Zhisui (p. 600 disputes Mao's presence on the latter occasion, but his information is second hand and appears to be incorrect. *I am muddle-headed*: Yan and Gao, p. 458. *What we have in excess*: Kissinger, *Years of Upheaval*, p. 68. *Kiss of death*: Yan and Gao quote Mao as saying of his wife in early 1975: 'Sooner or later she will break with everyone . . . After I die, she will create disturbances' (p. 460). *Zhang Chunqiao*: MacFarquhar, p. 291.

617 *Lenin's dictum*: *History of the CCP, Chronology*, p. 365. *Programme for modernising*: Ibid., p. 366. *'Empiricism'*: Barnouin and Yu, p. 281. *Poor understanding*: Ibid., p. 282; Gardner, p. 106. *On May 3, 1975*: Barnouin and Yu, pp. 282–3; Peng Cheng, pp. 50–1 and 56.

618 *Roxane Witke*: Yan and Gao, p. 471. See also the wall poster illustrated in Witke, *Comrade Chiang Ch'ing* (opposite p. 335). *Kang Sheng*: Byron and Pack, *Claws of the Dragon*, pp. 405–7. Kang was evidently aware that the message had not got through, for in October 1975, only weeks before his death, when his illness allowed him a brief remission, he had a final meeting with Mao but did not mention his 'discovery': by then, Jiang's political situation had improved. In April 1976, Foreign Minister Qiao Guanhua reportedly told Mao that Kang had 'slandered' Jiang Qing and Zhang Chunqiao, but without giving details. *Water Margin*: Barnouin and Yu, pp. 283–5. *Song Jiang made Chao Gai*: Peng Cheng, p. 57. *Shit*: Ibid. *Deng was going too far*: Barnouin and Yu, pp. 279–80; Evans, pp. 206–7. *Mao Yuanxin*: Jia Sinan, pp. 376–8; Hao and Duan, pp. 648–9; MacFarquhar, p. 296.

619 *Deng himself sensed*: Barnouin and Yu, p. 280. *Restless and irritable*: Li Zhisui, p. 605. *Mao asked Deng*: Yan and Gao, p. 480. *Afterwards he told his nephew*: Ibid., p. 479. See also Wang Nianyi, p. 560. *Still on the capitalist road*: Hao and Duan, p. 560. *Seemingly unrelated dispute*: Yan and Gao, pp. 471–2; Barnouin and Yu, pp. 285–6. *In late November*: Barnouin and Yu, p. 286. *Hints of the new line*: *Renmin ribao*, Dec. 4 1975. *Deng had been stripped*: Barnouin and Yu, p. 286.

620 *Zhou Enlai died*: Yan and Gao, pp. 482–5; Li Zhisui, pp. 609–10. *He intended to appoint Hua Guofeng*: Yan and Gao, pp. 485–6.

621 *Non-antagonistic*: Evans, p. 210. *Nixon, who visited him*: Nixon, Richard, *In the Arena: A Memoir of Victory, Defeat and Renewal*, Simon & Schuster, New York, 1990, p. 362. *Lip-read*: Zhang Yufeng, 'Mao Zedong Zhou Enlai wannian ersanshi', *Yanhuang zisun*, no. 1, 1989. *Moving description*: Ibid.

622 *Hearing aid*: Evans, pp. 207–8.

622–
/
624

At a time of mind-numbing . . . held responsible: Oral sources; Garside, Roger, *Coming Alive: China after Mao*, New York, 1981, pp. 115–36; Yan and Gao, pp. 489–503; and MacFarquhar, pp. 301–5.

624 **Mao handed down his decision**: Yan and Gao, p. 502. **Deng himself**: Evans, pp. 212–13. **With you in charge**: MacFarquhar, p. 305. **Death-watch**: Li Zhisui, pp. 614–23: Yan and Gao, pp. 510–15. **Last testament**: Wang Nianyi, p. 601.

625 **Jiang saw herself**: Yan and Gao, pp. 487 and 516. **Nice gentleman**: MacFarquhar, p. 300. **In July . . . Mao was alive**: Ibid., pp. 306–7; Li Zhisui, p. 621; Evans, pp. 214–15; Wang Nianyi, p. 591. **On September 2**: Li Zhisui, pp. 624–5; Yan and Gao, pp. 516–19. **Ye Jianying**: Xiu Ru, *1976 nian dashi neimu*, Beijing, 1989, pp., 403–4.

EPILOGUE

627 **On the night of Wednesday**: Liu Wusheng (ed.), *Zhonggong dangshi fengyunlu*, Renmin chubanshe, Beijing, pp. 439–40.

628 **If our children's generation**: Schram, *Unrehearsed*, p. 190. **Four years later**: Kuo, *Classified Chinese Documents*, p. 57.

629 **'Gross mistakes'**: *Resolution on CPC History (1949–81)*, Pergamon Press, Oxford, 1981. **Had Mao died in 1956**: Oral sources; Chen made his comment at a CC work conference in November 1978. See also *Ming bao*, Hong Kong, Jan. 15, 1979.

630 **In a memorable put-down . . . 'essentially inarticulate'**: Barme, Geremie R., *Shades of Mao*, M. E. Sharpe, Armonk, 1996, p. 34. **The King of Qin**: Chavannes, Edouard, *Les Mémoires Historiques de Se-ma Ts'ien*, Adrien-Maisonneuve, Paris, 1967, vol. 2 pp. 144–5.

631 **You accuse us**: *Miscellany of Mao Tse-tung Thought*, 1, p. 98.
Deaths of more of his: If the death-toll from the Great Leap Forward is taken as 20 million (the official figure given by Hu Yaobang), and it is estimated that a further one million died in the land reform; one million in the political movements of the early 1950s; and one million in the Cultural Revolution – all of which are minimum figures – the number of people who died in China as a direct result of Mao's policies was at least 23 million (and may well have been, in reality, between 30 and 35 million). By comparison, the total death-toll in the Second World War is estimated at 55 million; in the Taiping Rebellion, 20 million; and in the First World War, eight million. None of those events, however, can be ascribed to the will of a single man.

632 **Heads are not like chives**: Oral sources. I have been unable to track down a documentary reference, but Mao expressed the same thought less colourfully at a CC meeting on Dec. 20 1964 (*Miscellany*, 2, p. 426).

633 **Private soirée**: Oral sources: Barme, p. 52.

634 **For others, Mao became an icon**: Barme, passim.

Index